D1598784

The American Synagogue

The American Synagogue

A HISTORICAL DICTIONARY AND SOURCEBOOK

Kerry M. Olitzky

Marc Lee Raphael
ADVISORY EDITOR

Greenwood Press
Westport, Connecticut • London

Library of Congress Cataloging-in-Publication Data

Olitzky, Kerry M.
   The American synagogue : a historical dictionary and sourcebook /
Kerry M. Olitzky.
     p.   cm.
   Includes bibliographical references and index.
   ISBN 0–313–28856–9 (alk. paper)
   1. Synagogues—United States—Dictionaries. 2. Synagogues—
Canada—Dictionaries. 3. Judaism—United States—History.
4. Judaism—Canada—History. I. Title.
BM205.045   1996
296.6'5'0973—dc20   95–49681

British Library Cataloguing in Publication Data is available.

Library of Congress Catalog Card Number: 95–49681
ISBN: 0–313–28856–9

First published in 1996

Greenwood Press, 88 Post Road West, Westport, CT 06881
An imprint of Greenwood Publishing Group, Inc.

Printed in the United States of America

The paper used in this book complies with the
Permanent Paper Standard issued by the National
Information Standards Organization (Z39.48–1984).

10 9 8 7 6 5 4 3 2 1

For Rabbi Sheldon Zimmerman, President
Hebrew Union College–Jewish Institute of Religion

CONTENTS

PREFACE

The core institution of the Jewish community is the synagogue. Though it is true that the synagogue has changed throughout its development, it remains the focal point for communal Jewish life in the modern world, irrespective of the overarching influence of the communal structure known as the Jewish federation. It is also true, however, that, as new communities developed in North America, newcomers were more likely to establish mutual benefit societies and purchase cemetery land before attending to the worship and educational needs of the community. In addition, while the synagogue in North America generally fulfills the same function regardless of the religious (movement) affiliation of its members, the focus of its priorities and activities is often determined by its ideology.

This volume is unique in that it is the first source book for synagogue histories in North America that includes synagogues from the four major movements: Orthodox, Conservative, Reconstructionist, and Reform Judaism. A large number of these synagogues changed their affiliation during their development. In addition, some synagogues are affiliated with more than one movement, are independent, or are part of a small group like Humanistic Judaism that requires further elucidation. Though the goal of preparing a comprehensive volume that includes all synagogues (including those that no longer exist) remains, this book does not document the development of every synagogue because of the vast number of synagogues in North America and the research required to assemble such a book. Instead, it reflects the diversity of synagogues by including a representative sample of all four movements. In order to develop the original list of synagogues from which this current volume emanates, I consulted historians of all four movements. These individuals are included in the acknowledgments.

Ideally, the preparation of such a volume requires travel to each community in order to evaluate fully the individual synagogue archives. Because I was unable to do this in many cases, I depended greatly on library and manuscript collections such as those housed at the American Jewish Archives (Cincinnati) and the Ratner Center for the Study of Conservative Judaism (New York). In addition, I depended on the willingness of individuals to share their printed histories and documents with me through the mail, personal telephone interviews, and the like. In many cases, I found individuals willing to help tell the story of their synagogue. However, in some cases I was unable to secure the data necessary to prepare a complete essay and was therefore forced to leave those synagogues out of this collection. Thus, some synagogue histories that should be included in this volume will have to be left for subsequent volumes. As the North American synagogue continues to evolve, any history of the North American synagogue is a work in progress.

Criteria for including synagogues in this volume are listed here in order of importance:

1. Historical impact (includes congregations that have been merged)
2. Age of congregation/synagogue (especially pioneer status)
3. Contemporary impact
4. Highlighted historical event (that is associated with the synagogue)
5. Impact on local community
6. Movement representation
7. Geographical distribution

Please note that different synagogues count membership units in different ways, not always accounting for singles or alternative family structures. Therefore, I have chosen to designate membership units according to the way individual synagogues have designated them. In the entries, to avoid confusion, the words "temple, congregation, and synagogue" are not taken into consideration in the alphabetical ordering of entries. In a few cases, synagogues may use these words as integral parts of their name or identification. Thus, they are used in the listing.

ACKNOWLEDGMENTS

Like so many other things in life, this volume represents the collected efforts of many individuals, all committed in one way or another to tell the story of the North American synagogue. To these many individuals go my profound thanks. The risk of attempting to list all of these individuals by name includes the possibility that I might unintentionally exclude people who have helped me along the way. To them, I apologize. However, these people I must thank.

Throughout this project, Marc Lee Raphael served as advisory editor and constant guide. Without his keen insight and acumen, the volume would be incomplete. I must also thank Malcolm Stern, *zichron livracha,* historian and genealogist, whose untimely death robbed us of his continued wise counsel.

By representing their individual movements, these historians helped me to identify key synagogues in their representative religious organizations, also often assisting in the clarification of details and developments: Lester Bronstein, David Dalin, Steven Dworkin, Robert Firestein, Jeffrey S. Gurock, Pamela S. Nadell, Moshe Sherman, Alan Silverstein, and Jacob Staub.

Throughout the development of this project, these editors at Greenwood Press stood by me, offering patience, guidance, and encouragement: George Butler and Alicia Merritt.

These students at Hebrew Union College–Jewish Institute of Religion, New York, helped to track down elusive details and confirm various facts and figures: Melissa Adleman, Sarah Reines, Francine Schwartz, and Adam Stock Spilker.

Without the constant guidance of my teacher Jacob Rader Marcus, whose recent death at ninety-nine shocked us all, none of my work in American Jewish history would be possible. My colleague and friend Abraham J. Peck, director of the American Jewish Archives, also provided me with support along the way. These staff members at the American Jewish Archives helped me gather the documents across the miles: Kevin Proffitt and Kathy Spray. I must also thank

Julie Miller at the Ratner Center for the Study of Conservative Judaism for her help.

Members of the staff at Hebrew Union College–Jewish Institute of Religion, New York, gave me invaluable assistance. I must particularly acknowledge the help of my own administrative assistant, Harriet Lewis. In addition, I thank Eve Maslin Goldberg and Arlene Rudykoff.

There are many people who gave of their time all across North America to help gather resources and answer my unrelenting questions. They all deserve my profound gratitude for their willingness to participate in this project: Julia D. Aaronson, B. Elka Abrahamson, Ron Aigen, Morris J. Allen, Marc D. Angel, Phillip Applebaum, Adele Avruch, Herbert Baumgard, Leonard Beerman, Martin P. Beifield, Jr., Arnold Mark Belzer, James Bennett, Alvin K. Berkun, Donald R. Berlin, Harold J. Berman, Howard Berman, Charlotte Viner Bernstein, Miriam Biatch, Jeffrey Bienenfeld, Albert Bilgray, Bradley N. Bleefeld, Abraham P. Bloch, Irving J. Block, P. Irving Bloom, Jan Brahms, Ely Braun, Solomon Breibart, Herbert N. Brockman, Lillian Brodkey, Herbert Bronstein, Samuel Broude, Jonathan M. Brown, Reuven P. Bulka, Hannah Cahn, Morris N. Capouya, Paul Citrin, Joni Cohen, Edward Paul Cohn, Jerold B. Coburn, Suzanne S. Connell, Mark H. Cousens, Gerry Cristol, Eric Cytryn, Jerry Danzig, Jerome Davidson, Edward Davis, Sanford M. Davis, Gerald Debruin, Myer Dorn, A. Stanley Dreyfus, LaDonn Eckberg, Joseph Edelheit, Lisa Edwards, Dan Ehrenkrantz, Joseph H. Ehrenkranz, Robert J. Eisen, Sidney Eisenshtat, Jeffrey Eisenstat, Charles H. Elias, Sheldon Ezring, Claudia Z. Fechter, Sylvan Feit, Edward Feld, Ilan D. Feldman, Harvey Fields, Arnold Fink, Reuven Fink, Steven Fink, Ruth S. Frank, Stephen D. Franklin, Wayne M. Franklin, John Freedman, Allen H. Freehling, Harvey Freeman, Barry Freundel, Lilian Friedman, Sarah Friedman, Alan D. Fuchs, Stephen Fuchs, Albert Gabbai, Nancy Gad-Harf, Barbara Gallas, David Gelfand, Jonathan H. Ginsburg, Roland Gittlesohn, Steven M. Glazer, Susan Scharf Glick, Moe Goldberger, Gideon M. Goldenholz, Shmuel Goldin, Hilton Goldman, Jeannette Goldman, Mark N. Goldman, David Goldstein, Paul Golumb, Arnold M. Goodman, Joel S. Goor, Helen Gordon, Julie K. Gordon, Eilein Gorlyn, Murray Grauer, Barry H. Greene, Kenneth Greene, Howard Greenstein, Judith Greenwald, Oscar Groner, Peter Grumbacher, Lee Haas, E. David Hart, Maurice "Bob" I. Hattem, Carl Hayslett, Floyd L. Herman, Eli Herscher, John Hirsch, Eric Hoffman, Anthony D. Holz, Reva Homnick, David Horowitz, Thomas Jablonski, Richard J. Jacobs, Tevie Jacobs, Harriet Janover, Jeani Johnson, Michael Joseph, Martin Judovits, Yoel H. Kahn, Frances Kallison, Lewis H. Kamrass, Samuel Karff, Abraham J. Karp, William B. Katz, Lyn Kelsey, Jimmy Kessler, Jenny Klein, Stephen A. Klein, Walter J. Klein, Jerry Klibanoff, Selma F. Klingenstein, Peter Knobel, Jonathan Kohn, Benjamin Kreitman, Donald M. Kunstadt, Lawrence Kushner, Bernard Kusinitz, Eliezer Langer, Robert L. Lehman, Robert Liefert, Leigh Lerner, Joseph Levenson, Robert Levine, Joy Levitt, Mel Levy, Alan Lew, Judith Lewis, Theodore Lewis, Samuel Lieberman, David Lincoln, Dan Lincove, Myra

Lipper, Stephen Listfield, Robert Loewy, Haskel Lookstein, Charles F. Ludwig, Jerome Malino, Eliot Isaac Malomet, Vanessa Mandel, David Mann, Sanford Marcus, Ralph D. Mecklenberger, Michael Menitoff, Bennett F. Miller, Judea Miller, Stanley I. Minch, Anne Mininberg, Herbert Morris, Jackie Morrison, Elazar R. Muskin, Soraya Nazarian, Bill Nerenberg, Etta Fay Orkin, Jack Paskoff, David Passman, Ruth Marcus Patt, Sylvia Pearlman, Marc Penner, Rex Perlmeter, Midge Pines, Richard Polirer, David Polish, Ervin Preis, Estelle Presner, Sally Priesand, Brandy Primak, Steven Pruzansky, David Radinsky, Sanford Ragins, Joe Rooks Rapport, Fred N. Reiner, Joseph Resnick, Steven Carr Reuben, Jack Riemer, Sheila Riger, Leslie Rivlin, Leonard Rogoff, Emanuel Rose, Rochelle Rosenberg, Ronnie Rosenberg, Seymour Rosenbloom, Harry Rosenfeld, Robert F. Rosin, Sol Roth, Moshe Rothblum, Samuel Rubenstein, Peter Rubinstein, Solomon Ryback, Marjorie Sachs, Richard Safran, Murray Saltzman, Sanford E. Saperstein, Dennis C. Sasso, Jacob J. Schacter, Susan Scharf-Glick, David Schechner, Harold Schulweis, Allen Schwartz, Douglas Schwartz, Fred Schwartz, Norman D. Schwartz, Ronald Z. Schwartz, Wendy Robinson Schwartz, Jack Segal, Kenneth Segel, Florence Seglin, Muriel Selling, Chaim Shapiro, Charles Sherman, James Sherman, Amy Hill Shevitz, Mark L. Shook, Marvin Shore, Scott Shpeen, Howard Siegel, Francis Barry Silberg, James L. Simon, Merle Singer, Ronald B. Sobel, Susan Sokalsky, David Sofian, Jack Spiro, John Spitzer, Samuel M. Stahl, Arthur Starr, Jeffrey Stiffman, Marcie Y. Storch, Michael Strassfeld, Alvin M. Sugarman, Harvey Tattlebaum, Elazar Teitz, Reuven Tradburks, Lawrence Troster, Mara Vasslides, Helen Vigderhous, Stanley M. Wagner, Hershel Walfish, Roy Walter, Amy E. Waterman, Gerald Weider, Herbert Weinberg, Joseph P. Weinberg, Arthur D. Weiner, Martin Weiner, Samuel R. Weinstein, Ruth Weintraub, David M. Weis, Kenneth J. Weiss, Joseph Weizenbaum, Frederick L. Wenger, Bernice Wiener, Irvin M. Wise, Frances Wolf, Jeffrey A. Wohlberg, Mitchell Wohlberg, Gerald I. Wolpe, David Young, Jessica Young, Michael Zedek, Isaiah Zeldin, Gerald B. Zelermyer, Daniel G. Zemel, Robert J. Zietz, Sidney Zimelman, and Sheldon Zimmerman.

The American Synagogue

INTRODUCTION: "NO PERSON SHALL BE CALLED TO SEIPHER IN BOOTS," THE HISTORY OF THE SYNAGOGUE IN AMERICA

Frances Weinman Schwartz

The synagogue is the core institution in the Jewish community—the heart of Jewish religion and the Jewish people.[1] As a two-thousand-year-old institution, the synagogue actually traces its roots prior to the destruction of the ancient Temple in Jerusalem. In a variety of ways, these ancient synagogues mirrored the cultic rituals that took place in Jerusalem for those who could not make pilgrimages to the holy city. However, after the destruction of the Second Temple (70 C.E.), the synagogue—as a portable institution—quickly became the central Jewish institution that joined the Jewish people throughout the diaspora. As an American institution, the synagogue dates back three hundred years to the early development of the North American Jewish community. While the synagogue served as a locus for a prayer community, Jewish immigrants initially founded synagogues to take care of the basic ritual needs (like circumcision and the ritual slaughter of meat) and social needs of community members (like sick care for the indigent), usually beginning with a cemetery society. Unlike its European predecessor, the American synagogue developed as a voluntary religious association in accord with the democratic environment established by North American pioneers. In most cases, synagogues emerged as institutions that reflected the growth and development of neighboring churches, particularly Protestant ones, albeit refracted through a Jewish prism. Throughout its history, the synagogue—in whatever community Jews found themselves—adapted to the challenges its members faced in adjusting to a new community.[2]

To understand the nature of the American synagogue, one must gain an un-

---

This chapter title is a direct quote from the 1791 constitution of Congregation Mikve Israel, Savannah, Georgia; this document illustrates both the uniquely secular and the religious dimensions of the synagogue. Because many members of Mikve Israel spent time tramping through the marshy Georgia terrain, they inevitably collected mud on their boots. The requirement that a man change his boots before accepting a Torah honor treated the synagogue and its most ancient sacred rituals with respect, even in eighteenth-century rural America.

derstanding of American Judaism. From the outset, Jews in America controlled their own religious life, with maximum individual freedom to choose their own level of observance and behavior.[3] As a product of a free, generally open environment, thriving in a continuously evolving Jewish community, the synagogue changed.[4] Thus, the synagogue is the premier example of the development of a "*minhag* America (American ritual)" that emerged within the context of an indigenous pattern of American Jewish religious life.

As the institution of the American synagogue changed to meet the varying needs of its congregants, distinctive forms developed as immigrants from diverse geographic areas sought to make this country their home. So, too, the traditional role of the religious leader evolved to meet the demands of a dynamic American environment. Similarly, the only constant in synagogue architecture is the consistency with which it changed, reflecting the current architectural styles—particularly of churches—in both America and Europe, the burgeoning growth of the U.S. Jewish population, and population shifts from city to suburb to exurb.

THE TRANSFORMATION OF THE SYNAGOGUE

Twenty-three refugees from the Dutch colony in Recife, Brazil, founded the American Jewish community upon their arrival in New Amsterdam in 1654. They fled Brazil and its recent conquerors, the Portuguese, who had brought their religiously oppressive Inquisition with them. Two weeks before the group of twenty-three arrived, a single Jew, Jacob Barsimson, came to New Amsterdam directly from Holland. The following winter, six Jewish merchants from Amsterdam joined the group already in the New World. They began meeting for worship in a private home, holding the first Jewish services in North America.[5] While New Amsterdam accepted, with some trepidation, these first Jews as potential citizens, the Dutch authorities did not permit them to establish a synagogue building. A letter from the directors of the Dutch West India Company in Amsterdam to the colony's governor, Peter Stuyvesant, dated March 13, 1656, stated as much, but also allowed the Jews to "quietly and peacefully carry on their business as before said and exercise in all quietness their religion within their houses."[6]

Following its establishment as the first synagogue in North America, Shearith Israel requested a small plot of land to consecrate as a cemetery.[7] The local government granted the community's request on July 14, 1656. The community built ritual baths, supervised the slaughtering of animals, arranged for Passover matzah baking, and monitored the education of their youth in a congregational school.[8] As a result, the young traditional community developed to meet the needs of the expanding community.[9] Shearith Israel and the handful of other synagogues founded in colonial America replicated in form and function the Jewish houses of worship in Europe, adopting the same general models for leadership and organization they had left behind. Synagogue and community were synonymous; the congregation served all communal needs, providing worship, socialization, marriage, and burial, as well as opportunities to give or receive charity.[10] However, these communities unsuccessfully threatened excommunication to those who did not follow accepted standards of Jewish practice, as stated in the constitutions of the individual synagogues. Within the rapidly developing American framework of social laissez-faire, the synagogue conformed to the American reality of compromise to retain its membership and its standing in the wider, secular community.[11]

In 1695 an English clergyperson speculated that twenty Jewish families lived among the approximately 850 families who had settled in New York, although he indicated on a map of the city a site identified as "Jewish Synagogue."[12] There are no extant records to document his claims. However, written records do indicate that, by 1728, Shearith Israel felt prosperous enough to erect its first synagogue building. Shearith Israel followed the worship ritual of its Sephardic, Spanish-Portuguese founders, even though most American Jews by this time came from Central Europe and considered themselves of Ashkenazic descent.[13] To raise money for their new edifice, American Jewish leaders wrote to wealthy Sephardic congregations in Amsterdam, London, and various places in the Caribbean asking for funds. A reply from the congregation in Curacao states, "We understand that your congregation is full of Germans. Our gift is predicated on your using the Sephardic ritual." This posture, replicated elsewhere in Colonial America, helped pave the way for the Sephardic mode of worship to serve as the American Jewish mode for subsequent American synagogues established before the end of the eighteenth century.[14]

The synagogue slowly became part of the religious landscape of Colonial America. In an effort to gain acceptance, Jews copied Protestant culture and built synagogues (to mimic the church) as the primary religious institution that anchored their community. Not always an expression of piety, the founding of a synagogue reflected an expression of Jewish identity, a response to what many perceived as an American demand to practice some form of organized religion. The synagogue evolved as the community and its religious needs changed—as did the culture in which it found itself. Thus, it developed as it became Americanized, reflecting American social customs and (Protestant) patterns.[15]

By the onset of the American Revolution, six congregations served the approximately two thousand Jews scattered throughout the colonies.[16] The six small synagogues—located in New York, Philadelphia, Richmond, Charleston, Newport, and Savannah—were geographically isolated from each other. Without exception, they observed the Sephardic ritual of worship.[17] In 1784, Congregation Shearith Israel formally incorporated under New York State law. According to its charter, every Jew residing in the city who attended services for one year, contributed an unspecified amount of money, and signed the synagogue's constitution had to be at least twenty-one years old to be eligible for membership.[18] In 1788, the Jews of Philadelphia solicited contributions for building a synagogue from citizens of every religious denomination: Benjamin Franklin contributed a generous five pounds, the first to respond to this solicitation, indicating the high level of acceptance of Jews by the wider community. Philadelphia also became the first multisynagogue city when, in 1795, a group left the Sephardic Mikveh Israel to pray according to German and Dutch customs and formed the first Ashkenazi congregation in America, Rodeph Shalom.[19]

The institution of the synagogue in the young country quickly became thoroughly American. Religious freedom, church-state separation, and volunteerism won acceptance as the religious norms of the new country, with the result that the synagogue gradually shed its status as a community institution and evolved into a private, voluntary association. A Jewish spokesperson at the 1818 dedication of Shearith Israel's newest building described American Judaism as the "religion of nature, reason and philosophy."[20] The American Judaism that developed in the early decades of the nineteenth century was highly acculturated. People spoke, read, and wrote English and prided themselves on their friendship with Christian neighbors. These rapidly acculturated Jews punctuated their distinctively American style of thought, action, and outlook by only occasional excursions to the synagogue, for the performance of increasingly brief ceremonial functions.[21]

In America, Jewish reform emerged from the desire to join the established social and political order, rather than to change it.[22] The first congregational split, because of "decorum," rather than "ritual," came about in 1824 in Charleston, South Carolina, the American city with the largest Jewish population at the time.[23] A group who belonged to Congregation K. K. Beth Elohim petitioned the temple board to include prayers and hymns in English and Torah explanations in the worship service, a somewhat shortened service, and the replacement of public solicitation with annual subscriptions.[24] When the synagogue board denied these requests, the group formed a new congregation called the Reformed Society of Israelites, for the purpose of "perpetuating pure Judaism, and enlightening the rising generation on the subject of their Holy Religion."[25] While the new synagogue fell victim to a general economic depression and disbanded in 1833, other Jewish groups successfully duplicated this effort to "Americanize" their congregations.[26] Thus, the year of 1825 represented a sea change in the development of the American Jewish community from one of relative uniformity to significant diversity. Prior to that year, Jews who lived in cities with a synagogue seemed content to practice their religion in the Sephardic ritual. Beginning in 1825, however, disgruntled synagogue members moved to modify the manner in which they worshipped and established new congregations in which like-minded Jews could join in prayer.

As a matter of policy, American Sephardic leadership did not encourage the establishment of more than one synagogue per city. But, in 1825, New York's Shearith Israel realized that if it admitted all who wanted to join, Ashkenazi immigrants would soon overwhelm the original Sephardic core of families. Therefore, while denying the right of a small group of its members to hold services in the German-Polish ritual, it did submit graciously to the formation of B'nai Jeshurun, the first Ashkenazi synagogue in New York.[27] The breakaway synagogue in Charleston previously argued for a relaxation of certain Old World traditions. In contrast, the "new" New York congregation defended its right to form a separate institution by stressing the importance of personal piety. This move indicated dissatisfaction with the ritual laxness the congregation had observed at the affluent, already-Americanized Shearith Israel.[28] These two patterns, to adhere to European traditions and to "Americanize" various rituals, operated simultaneously as successive waves of immigrants came to America. The new arrivals claimed that their predecessors failed to maintain Jewish traditions because they attempted to "purify," to Americanize Judaism by making "decorum" changes. To illustrate the "back to tradition" response, in 1828 a group of German, Dutch, and Polish Jews left B'nai Jeshurun to form the third New York synagogue, Anshe Chesed. Eleven years later, Polish dissidents from both B'nai Jeshurun and Anshe Chesed started Shaarey Zedek. In turn, a group of Shaarey Zedek congregants founded Beth Israel in 1843.[29] In these cases, men and women established new synagogues to worship as they formerly worshipped in their recently abandoned European surroundings.

The American Jewish community, consisting of some three thousand persons in 1818, doubled in number by 1826, and rose to fifteen thousand by 1840.[30] Whereas the first Jews had concentrated along the Atlantic seaboard (as did their Christian counterparts), the 1830 census also identified Jews in New Orleans, St. Louis, and Fort Wayne, Indiana. In 1824 Jews established the first synagogue west of the Alleghenies in Cincinnati. Adath Israel, founded in Louisville in 1836, included in its charter a proviso that called for the expulsion of members who married contrary to Jewish law. In 1838, the first congregation established west of the Mississippi River, United Hebrew Congregation of St. Louis, stated in its constitution that prayers shall never be performed otherwise than among Polish Jews in the Minhag Polin (Polish ritual). The United Hebrew Congregation's constitution further stated, "This section shall never be altered or amended under any pretense whatsoever."[31] These documents illustrate that new immigrants, as they pushed West, insisted on taking their traditional observances with them.

Meanwhile, back East, two congregations founded by upwardly mobile individuals, well along the road to acculturation and economic stability, determined that their synagogues would include certain reforms at the time of their founding.[32] In 1842, in Baltimore, a group of German immigrants, influenced by the Hamburg (Germany) Reform Temple, protested the traditionalism of the lone Baltimore synagogue and formed the Har Sinai Verein (Association).[33] The men wore hats and sat apart from the women in the traditional manner; yet, the introduction of an organ—more than anything else—marked the congregation off from its predecessors. Har Sinai became decidedly Reform in 1855, when Rabbi David Einhorn, considered a radical reformer in Europe, left Germany to become Har Sinai's religious leader.[34]

In 1845, a group of economically and socially successful New York Jews established another "Reform" synagogue, Emanu-El. Unlike their counterparts in Baltimore, these German-Jewish immigrants did not import their Reform ideas from Germany. The founders of Emanu-El approached reforms gradually, as they became more comfortable as Americans. They identified their Judaism by religion, similar to the way their neighbors approached their Protestant Christianity. Initially, a hazzan (cantor) conducted worship; however, unlike other synagogues, the service also included a discourse by a lecturer. Quite soon after founders established Emanu-El, according to synagogue minutes, its members began referring to the institution as a "temple." Historian Leon Jick claims that this nondenominational English word has the attraction of being closely related to the German "tempel." Thus, American Jews responded to an appropriately dignified and elegant reference to the new congregation. As Emanu-El grew prosperous and respectable, it sought an increasingly "decorous" service. When Emanu-El purchased its first building in the late 1840s, the congregation installed an organ. By 1853, the temple eliminated the practice of honors such as calling individuals to the reading of the Torah. By the end of 1855, Emanu-El discontinued separate seating, the use of the tallit (prayer shawls) and the celebration of the second days of festivals.[35] Though approaching Reform for different reasons, both Har Sinai and Emanu-El reached similar stages in their search for Americanizing decorum at approximately the same time.

By 1850, the Jewish population in America reached fifty thousand.[36] The propensity of new immigrants to follow their own traditional liturgy, based on their country of origin, led to the proliferation of synagogues. By the middle of the nineteenth century, fifteen types of worship customs, including Sephardic, Polish, Bohemian, Dutch, and English, existed in New York alone.[37] Jews throughout the country founded ninety synagogues.[38] Followers of each ritual preferred establishing their own congregations; when members of different groups joined, a split often followed. Then, from 1850 to 1860, immigration from Germany trebled the Jewish population in America to 150,000.[39] These newcomers rarely found themselves total strangers. Wherever they went, they usually discovered landsman (people from the same geographic area) who preceded them. They found a synagogue, or at least a *minyan* (prayer quorum), already in existence. Wherever even a handful of Jews settled, they attempted to establish the rudiments of a religious community.[40]

Only a small number of Reform congregations existed prior to the Civil War. The vast majority of synagogues, close to two hundred by 1860, still adhered to most of the same rituals followed by Europe's traditional congregations.[41] However, already in the 1850s, some synagogues initiated mixed, or "family" seating, as well as other modifications (reforms) in the liturgy of the worship service itself. Rabbi Isaac Mayer Wise, the leading organizer of American Reform, claimed to introduce Jewish mixed seating in America in his temple in Albany, New York, in 1851.[42] His synagogue, Anshe Emeth, purchased a former church building already equipped with family pews. Anshe Emeth voted unanimously to retain the furniture when the congregation dedicated its new edifice.

Perhaps pragmatism more than principle brought mixed seating into American

Judaism. Anshe Emeth members voted to use the building as they found it and did not want to spend additional money to convert the church's pews into a more traditional, separate seating arrangement. The introduction of mixed seating in New York's Temple Emanu-El in 1854 occurred for similar reasons. Emanu-El also moved into a building formerly used as a church and saw no reason to change the pews already in place for the separate seating of its earlier place of worship. When ideological discussions over mixed seating did develop, issues concentrated on the elevation of the women's role in the synagogue rather than on the merits of family worship. By physically changing the location of women in the synagogue (usually from an isolated balcony gallery), Jews sought to "modernize," to worship in a style much like that of their Christian neighbors. By abolishing the women's section, synagogue leaders sought to raise not only the status of Jewish women, but also the status of Judaism itself.[43] After the 1870s, the once-controversial mixed seating became part of the status quo as virtually every new Reform temple building included family pews in its architectural design.

The removal of men's hats during worship became the last step in the creation of a truly acculturated Judaism. While not really a concern of Jewish law (and more of a custom), the practice of men covering their heads during prayer served as a visible distinction between Jewish and Christian worship and therefore took on a symbolic character.[44] In 1859 Emanu-El in New York adopted a compromise that hats might be removed if members desired, but only during the sermon. By 1864 the Board of Trustees recommended a binding law that required all attending the service at Temple Emanu-El to uncover their heads; it passed with only a single dissenting vote.[45] In 1871, Rabbi Isaac Mayer Wise, by this time well-entrenched as the religious leader of K. K. Bene Yeshurun in Cincinnati, refused to follow a resolution allowing worshipers in his congregation to bare their heads, an order recently passed by his congregation. Four years later, the synagogue's Committee on Order and Decorum was instructed to enforce the rule. Committee members asked any male visitor who wore a hat for worship to remove it.[46]

By 1870 many congregations in America had still not introduced substantial reforms, although the number of immigrants subsided in the decade following the Civil War. Without new immigrants insisting on familiar forms of worship and thus separating themselves from their more acclimated neighbors, American Judaism attained the greatest degree of homogeneity since the 1820s.[47] Reformers thus felt that the time was ripe for the formation of a loosely conceived federation of American synagogues, although several unsuccessful attempts had been made. In 1873, at the instigation of Isaac Mayer Wise—with the indispensable support of B'nai Yeshurun's leaders—thirty-four congregations met in Cincinnati to form the Union of American Hebrew Congregations (UAHC). Yet, the UAHC included only a handful of America's well-established congregations.[48] Because of its isolation from the more traditional synagogues in the East, the Reform movement developed its greatest strength in the South and

Middle West. Reform synagogues in the East usually found themselves as single congregations among many traditional ones; in the South and Middle West, they tended to be the only congregation in their communities.[49] In 1875, Isaac Mayer Wise founded Hebrew Union College to train rabbis to serve the American Jewish community (read the Reform movement). This assured the predominance of Reform—rather than Orthodox—rabbis as religious leaders of American Jewry in the latter part of the nineteenth century.[50]

By the mid-1880s, the American Jewish Reform community generally accepted synagogue changes such as the introduction of an organ, revision of the liturgy, and mixed seating as standard American Jewish practice. The subsequent convening of a conference of rabbis in Pittsburgh in 1885 to draw up a written platform served to confirm rather than to create already-established ritual change. The Pittsburgh Platform addressed a growing concern among Reform rabbis that an indifference to all things religious among the acculturated elements of American Jewry was gaining strength at an alarming rate. A series of statements of generalized beliefs and intellectual justifications, the platform gave Reform Judaism a rational dimension which its writers found to be more modern and therefore American. It negated the idea of a national religion and accepted only those rituals that could serve as aids to bring about a universal Age of Good Feeling.[51] In 1886, traditional leaders representing the more-recently arrived Eastern European Jews established the Jewish Theological Seminary of America (JTS) in New York, to ordain rabbis trained in (Conservative) "historical Judaism."[52] Some argue incorrectly that founders established JTS in reaction to the Pittsburgh Platform and what it represented. Instead, JTS grew out of the desire by leaders to train rabbis in the Historical School. Nevertheless, JTS provided an institutional counter to change, to represent synagogues where more traditional worship would be conducted.[53]

The first group of immigrants from Russia founded Beth Hamidrash in New York (1852) as the model of the distinctively Eastern European synagogue in America.[54] Struck by the marginality of religion in the lives of the more established, acculturated American Jews, its founders wanted a synagogue that followed traditional ritual. Beth Hamidrash (later Beth Hamedrash Hagadol) developed a reputation for orthodoxy and learning; congregations from New York and elsewhere addressed questions regarding ritual to its rabbis and even required *shochtim* (ritual slaughterers providing kosher meat) to be certified by its leadership.[55] Before 1870, relatively few Russian Jews came to America. After 1870, this increased to a steady trickle; after 1881, the trickle became a flood. The first generation of Russian Jews founded their synagogues on a stronger ethnic base than any previous or subsequent group. Reasons for this stemmed from both the inclusionary factors of the Russians' distinctive language and outlook and the social exclusion that these immigrants experienced from their more Americanized, "German" brethren. Between 1855 and 1880, the period immediately preceding the mass migration of Russian Jews, immigrants founded more than twenty traditional Eastern European synagogues in New York and at least six other American cities, from Boston westward to Chicago.[56]

The mass immigration of Eastern European Jews changed the size and character of the American Jewish community. Estimates put the Jewish population of the United States at 230,000 in 1880, 400,000 in 1888, and 937,800 in 1897. Then, in less than twenty years, the Jewish population more than trebled—to 2,933,374 by 1914.[57] These immigrants swamped the more established Jewish community in America. The Reform congregations, which for a brief time considered themselves to represent the totality of American Jewry and the future of American Judaism, suddenly found themselves on the margins of communal life. Almost every congregation established committees to provide basic assistance to the immigrants, while at the same time distancing themselves from them.[58] By 1887, Eastern European immigrants established 130 Orthodox congregations on the Lower East Side of Manhattan, for the primary purpose of gathering for daily worship, on Sabbath and holidays; to visit the sick; to help a member in time of need; and, when necessary, to provide a ritually correct burial.[59] Acculturated and immigrant Jews viewed their place of worship very differently. The "temple" of the German Jewish immigrant served as a gateway to a more secularized America. While it too made changes, the synagogue of the Eastern European immigrant served members as a sanctuary, a haven in an America. It soon became clear that the small, autonomous traditional synagogue needed to gain national, institutional underpinnings to provide for the spiritual safekeeping of the burgeoning Eastern European American community. In 1896 Eastern European Jews founded the Rabbi Isaac Elchanan Theological Seminary to train traditional rabbis; the Seminary merged with the Yeshiva Etz Chaim in 1915, becoming Yeshiva College in 1928, and is presently part of Yeshiva University.[60] Lay and rabbinic leadership founded the Orthodox Union in 1897 to help immigrants with their practical, everyday needs.[61] In 1898, fifty congregations established the Union of Orthodox Jewish Congregations of America as an Orthodox alternative to the Union of American Hebrew Congregations, with the mandate of "protesting against the declarations of Reform rabbis not in accordance with the teachers of our Torah."[62]

By the end of the nineteenth century, descendants of the first German and Central European Jews crystallized their concept of the synagogue as a place of worship using a maximum amount of English, where members listened to a "minister" or even a "reverend" spread the messages of moral enlightenment and progress on a once-a-week basis with a minimum of additional activities.[63] By way of contrast, the Eastern European worshipers developed a very different establishment whose chief characteristics included the use of Yiddish in prayer, the *landsmanshaft* (coming from the same town) composition of its membership, and the centrality of the hazzan (cantor) as the prayer leader.[64] In 1913 a group of young men studying at the Jewish Theological Seminary founded the Young Israel movement, whose programs consisted of classes, lectures, and Americanized Orthodox religious services.[65] But members of the more traditional Orthodox synagogue, who viewed many changes as potential threats to Jewish survival, maintained its worship as closely as possible to that of the Old World synagogues of their parents and grandparents. In 1901, they established the Jewish Endeavor Society, holding services on Sabbath and festival afternoons, which instituted English-language prayers, weekly English sermons on topics related to American Jewish life, and congregational singing in English and Hebrew.[66] In contrast to Reform and Orthodox practices, moderates founded the Conservative movement to provide for innovation in a more "controlled" manner. The Jewish Theological Seminary assumed a direct leadership role in Conservative synagogue affairs when it organized the United Synagogue of America (now United Synagogue of Conservative Judaism) in 1913 as a national organization of Conservative synagogues.[67]

In 1918, Mordecai M. Kaplan, one of the young rabbis from the Jewish Theological Seminary, proposed a new type of synagogue to supply all who used it with "pleasures of a social and intellectual, as well as spiritual character."[68] With the creation of the Jewish Center on Manhattan's West Side, Kaplan founded an institution to serve as a prototype for hundreds of Jewish synagogue-centers over the next decades. When fully equipped, Kaplan envisioned the Center to contain "Jewish elementary school facilities; recreational facilities such as a gymnasia, showers, bowling alleys, pool tables and game rooms; adult study and art groups; communal activities; religious services, festival pageants and plays; and informal meetings of friends and associates."[69] This synagogue model evolved from a worship-centered institution, like the Reform and the Orthodox synagogue, into a multifaceted entity, usually belonging to the Conservative movement, that fulfilled social, cultural, and religious objectives. Its successful development can be attributed to both the changing needs of the rapidly Americanized Jewish community and similar changes at work in the contemporary American church.[70] At its peak, in the years following World War II, at least one hundred "Jewish centers" existed in the New York area alone.[71] Some might argue that the synagogues added centers to keep members attending the synagogue and to attract nonmembers to join in its spiritual activities also. One prominent rabbi, Abraham J. Feldman, writing in 1949, observed that "the recreational and social attractions are primary, while the religious functions are little more than concessions to propriety."[72]

During the 1920s and 1930s, the Jewish population increased by approximately 40 percent, while the number of synagogues almost doubled: from 1,901 in 1916, to 3,118 in 1926, to 3,738 in 1937.[73] During this period of tremendous synagogue growth, significant changes took place in the three major branches of American Judaism. Conservative congregations, with their emphasis on youth-oriented programs, shifted educational priorities from a once-a-week Sunday format to a three-day-per-week Hebrew school schedule.[74] By the mid-1930s, many Reform temples reinstated Bar Mitzvah. Earlier, these congregations nearly eliminated this ceremony in favor of the more secular, egalitarian ceremony of Confirmation (for children a few years older). In Reform synagogues, leaders increased the Hebrew content in prayer and no longer prohibited worshipers from covering their heads.[75] In the Orthodox community, university-trained, English-speaking rabbis attempted to make congregational life more inclusionary, with the primary objective of maintaining traditional ritual practices in the sanctuary, while tacitly allowing fewer traditional observances to be practiced in the home.[76] Beginning in 1933 and lasting until after World War II, groups of Orthodox Jews fleeing Hitler and Stalin settled in America. Far more than any previous wave of migration, these various Hasidic groups maintained their separateness from the rest of the American Jewish community, having no desire to assimilate or to accommodate themselves to the American milieu.[77]

In the postwar years, Americans came to accept the image of themselves as living in the land of three great faiths: Protestant, Catholic, and Jew. Non-Jewish Americans no longer considered Jews as one of many "fringe" groups in their midst. A critical factor in boosting Judaism to this level was the preeminent position of the synagogue, still the central institution in American Jewish life. The move by the middle class to the suburbs after 1945 greatly affected the country's Jewish population. For the first time in the history of the American Jewish community, synagogue affiliation became de rigueur.[78] In 1950, Will Herberg noted that the Jews of suburbia engaged in a building frenzy as they built or expanded hundreds of synagogues: "Synagogue membership is probably at a record level. Many synagogues have been compelled to close their books and establish waiting lists."[79] The upsurge of Jewish community life in suburbia made the synagogue its most important Jewish institution. Young couples newly arrived from the cities' urban cores joined a congregation for a variety of reasons beyond their personal religious needs; these included a desire to provide for their children's religious education and the wish for a context for their own social and fellowship interests.

A fourth branch of Judaism gradually evolved, following the separation of Reconstructionism from the Conservative movement. Conceived by Mordecai Kaplan as a conscious rebuilding of Jewish life to reflect the changes in the American Jewish environment, Reconstructionist synagogues dedicated to the concept of Judaism as a "people" came into their own in the decade after World War II. Kaplan proposed a Judaism without a supernatural Deity, without divine commandments, miracles, or the concept of "chosenness." Thus conceived, Classical Judaism could harmonize with modernity; it served Jews as a group, stressing participation in the richness of the Jewish tradition, with its abundance of customs, rituals, holidays, and festivals.[80] Kaplan established the Society for the Advancement of Judaism in New York, a Reconstructionist synagogue, in 1922. Other synagogues followed. By the end of the 1950s these synagogues united under the banner of the Federation of Reconstructionist Congregations and Fellowships. In 1968 the movement began training its own rabbis at the Reconstructionist Rabbinical College in Philadelphia.[81]

By the late 1960s, the "return to religion" movement in America waned; synagogues lost some of the preeminence previously assumed within the Jewish community. In their place, local Jewish federations (umbrella community organizations) and fund-raising, particularly focused around support for the state of Israel, became increasingly important.[82] However, additional changes confirmed the institution of the synagogue as a reflection of the shifting patterns in American social mores. Following nationwide trends, the synagogue became attuned to demands for female equality. While the Reform movement, on a theoretical level, always stood for equality of the sexes, the participation of women on synagogue boards increased in the 1960s and became commonplace in the 1970s. In 1972 Hebrew Union College–Jewish Institute of Religion ordained a woman as rabbi, the first in North America.[83] The Conservative Jewish Theological Seminary soon followed suit, admitting women into its rabbinic program in the 1980s.[84] The Reconstructionist Rabbinical College admitted women into its establishment in 1968, yet did not ordain women until 1974, after Hebrew Union College had done so. While members of Orthodox synagogues still exclude women from the opportunity to participate equally in the worship service, an increasing number of congregations seat women on their lay boards of trustees and permit the formation of separate women's prayer groups within the synagogue.[85]

From the mid-1970s through the mid-1990s, a significant number of non-Orthodox Jews rejected both the national secular search for self-fulfillment and the particularist American Jewish trend of serving individual rather than collective needs.[86] Many synagogue leaders recognized this desire for communal spiritual intimacy and, beginning in the early 1970s, responded by organizing the *havurah,* a small group within the congregation that meets together frequently in worship, celebration of Jewish holiday and life-cycle events, and adult study.[87] One of the early organizers of the synagogue havurah, Rabbi Harold M. Schulweis, describes a major function of the synagogue as a "*shadchan* (matchmaker) to bring together separate, lonely parties into the fellowship of authentic community."[88] Leadership of the havurah comes from within the group, with minimal dependence on a synagogue professional. Members of the havurah understand that they make a commitment to actively participate in the running of the havurah, that their Judaism is no longer something that may be passively delegated to the rabbi.[89] Total member involvement in the planning and implementation of all havurah programming is one of the hallmarks, and success stories, of this recent addition to the American synagogue.

THE ROLE OF THE RABBI

With the introduction of the lay-led havurah, the synagogue in America comes full circle. In addition to the creation of a totally transformed institution with its own version of the synagogue, American Judaism gave birth to a professional leader quite different from the European model. In the traditional Jewish com-

munity a rabbi functioned primarily as a judge of religious practice, an inter-
preter of Jewish law, and an arbitrator in disputes of all kinds. As his most
important duty, he led the Bet Din (religious court); he also supervised Jewish
schools and kashrut and performed a few Jewish life-cycle events, among them
circumcision, Bar Mitzvah, and marriage. The synagogue did not employ the
rabbi; instead, the entire Jewish community engaged him as the religious head
of the community. Thus, the rabbi oversaw the conformity of all individuals to
the traditional standards of Jewish life.[90]

In contrast, laypersons governed the earliest American synagogues, often
functioning without concern for consistent standards or religious knowledge.
The congregation gave the *parnass* (president) and his board of trustees both
the power and the authority to run the congregation. The parnass fixed the time
of worship, distributed Torah honors, approved the performance of weddings
and burials, regulated the *mikvah* (ritual bath), supervised the preparation and
distribution of meat under the laws of kashrut, and even oversaw the baking of
Passover matzah.[91] Hazzanim (cantors), the religious leaders of the first American synagogues, conducted worship and handled other congregational religious
and educational programs. The title *hazzan,* rather than rabbi, reflected the lay
founders' idea of the modest nature of the rabbinical role in America.[92] Gershom
Mendes Seixas, the prototypical hazzan, served as "minister" of Shearith Israel
from 1768 to 1776 and from 1784 to 1816. The congregation limited his duties
to conducting public worship under the strict supervision of the adjunta (board
of trustees), tutoring the young people of the congregation, and performing circumcisions. Lacking formal ordination or even a comprehensive Jewish education, he nevertheless became an early model of the American rabbi. While a
traditional rabbi seldom conducted services and infrequently delivered sermons,
Seixas began giving sermons early in his career; such Protestant-like preaching—new to the community—became an important aspect of his job as hazzan.[93]

Isaac Leeser is another early example of the early American Jewish spiritual
leader. Leeser served as hazzan of Congregation Mikveh Israel in Philadelphia
beginning in 1829. The next year he started to preach regular sermons in English. In 1843 he began publishing *The Occident,* the first Jewish newspaper in
America. Leeser also edited his own prayer book and participated in early,
unsuccessful attempts at forming a national association of synagogues.[94] Lesser's
noteworthy accomplishments, indispensable to the early American Jewish community, probably would not have been undertaken by a traditional European
rabbi.

Isaac Mayer Wise, the organizer of American Reform Judaism, came to the
United States in 1846. Unlike his colleague Leeser, he claimed to lack only the
credentials confirming his ordination. In his first pulpit, in Albany, New York,
a fist fight between Wise and the president of the congregation led to a major
brawl that required the intervention of the local police.[95] At the time of this
altercation, in 1850, Wise described his adversary as the "Mighty Parnass":

"the law and the revelation, the lord and the glory, the majesty and the spiritual guardian of the congregation."[96] As a result, Wise left this synagogue and, with a sizable group from the old congregation, shortly thereafter founded a second synagogue in Albany. Four years later he left New York State for Cincinnati, to become rabbi of Bene Yeshurun, later rising to national prominence. Wise published a revised prayer book in 1857 to which he gave the all-inclusive title, *Minhag America.* While he omitted prayers for the return to Palestine and for the restoration of the Davidic dynasty and sacrificial cult, the prayer book maintained the traditional framework for Jewish worship.[97]

Max Lilienthal, a native of Bavaria and the first man to arrive in America with a rabbinic as well as a university degree, served as rabbi of three German congregations in New York from 1846 to 1848. The dominance of the lay leaders of the synagogues that he served was a source of continuous friction. These lay persons prohibited him from lecturing in synagogues outside of those that hired him, from visiting other schools, or from answering questions regarding ritual without the approval of his lay "bosses."[98]

David Einhorn, a leader in Germany's Reform movement prior to his arrival in America, became the rabbi at Congregation Har Sinai in Baltimore in 1855. However, Einhorn could not adjust to what he perceived as the lay domination of the synagogue, nor could he change what he saw as the emergent American pattern in which the rabbi does not appear to make final decisions in matters of religious reform.[99] Einhorn also prepared a prayer book, *Olath Tamid,* written primarily in German, that radically changed the traditional liturgy. Synagogues rarely used the German version. However, more congregations adopted *Olath Tamid* once it became available in English in the 1880s, as English replaced German as the vernacular of the rapidly Americanized Jews.

In 1849, New York's B'nai Jeshurun invited Morris Raphall of Birmingham, England, to be its rabbi. Synagogue leaders awarded him the princely salary of $2,000 a year, in contrast to Isaac Mayer Wise's salary of $250 a year plus $9 for every pupil he tutored. As Raphall lectured in English, he often represented the Jewish community to the non-Jewish world, a qualification held in the highest regard by his congregation.[100] The contrast between the acceptance of Raphall and the harassment of his contemporaries demonstrated the importance of image over learning for the acculturated American Jew.

The role of the American rabbi in the twentieth century expanded to encompass pastoral duties as well as representing the congregation in the community. Synagogue leaders expected the rabbi to comfort the sick and guide the perplexed and offer advice on questions regarding law or ritual matters. Nevertheless, the rabbi of an American synagogue essentially assumed the functions of a Protestant minister, to become what Daniel Elazar refers to as a "professional leader."[101] Control of the synagogue today often rests in the hands of its lay leadership. It might be said that contemporary American rabbis remain the servants of their congregation, rather than their masters.[102]

THE AMERICAN SYNAGOGUE BUILDING:
FORM FOLLOWING FUNCTION

Concurrent with the evolution of the American synagogue as an institution and of the rabbi as religious leader of that institution, the physical plant that houses the American synagogue also developed as a hybrid. At different times, ancient Near East and Mid-East Jewish houses of worship, churches, and European government buildings, from palaces to houses of Parliament, influenced American synagogue architecture. All of these factors, plus the "look" of other churches and synagogues in the same city, neighborhood, or block, with the constant reminder of economics, combined to produce synagogues that usually resembled the current fashion.

In a review of a 1977 exhibit at Brandeis University entitled "Two Hundred Years of Synagogue Architecture," J. H. Kay wrote, "Jews, like other Americans, were no orphans. Visually, as in all other ways, they came carrying the cultural parentage of Europe."[103] So it should come as no surprise that the first synagogue building designed as such, built in 1730 for New York's Shearith Israel, reproduces on a more modest scale the Sephardic synagogues of Amsterdam and London.[104] The architect of the oldest surviving synagogue building in the United States, the Touro Synagogue, built in 1763 in Newport, Rhode Island, used a chapel at Whitehall Palace in London as a model.[105] Both the Touro Synagogue and the first building to house Mickve Israel (Philadelphia), built in 1782, follow the Colonial architectural style. It is interesting to note that Mickve Israel's facade of plain brick made the building appear similar to others in the community. Its founders had served as major financiers of the just-completed Revolutionary War.[106] Mickve Israel's second building, dedicated in 1825, had no such modesty. This edifice demonstrated features of the Egyptian Revival period and came complete with an interior dome, supported by columns copied from an ancient Egyptian temple.[107]

All three of the just-described synagogues were established in the Sephardic manner by early Spanish and Portuguese immigrants who could afford to buy land and build from scratch. On the other hand, members of early Ashkenazi congregations generally refurbished former churches for their first buildings. This use of church buildings as synagogues is unique to the United States. A mission for an African Presbyterian Church became the first building used by New York's B'nai Jeshurun in 1826. Protestant denominations built the first and second buildings that housed Philadelphia's Rodeph Shalom before their conversion as synagogues.[108]

Because of the popularity of the Greek Revival architectural style in America in the 1830s and 1840s, buildings in New York, Cincinnati, Charleston, and Baltimore all looked as though they were really ancient Greek temples instead of nineteenth-century synagogues. In 1841 Congregation K. K. Beth Elohim sported a six-column Theseum portico as an exterior embellishment.[109] Baltimore's Lloyd Street Synagogue, built in 1845 in the Greek Revival style, featured the Star of David as an exterior decoration, the first synagogue in the United States to do so.[110] Other congregations followed suit in using the Star of David, including Baltimore's Har Sinai synagogue (1849).[111]

Many German-Jewish congregations used the Moorish or Byzantine design. Leading Jewish communities in Germany were building in this Oriental Revival style; their prosperous American cousins could not wait to copy them. Bene Yeshurun in Cincinnati became the first "Byzantine" synagogue to be built in the United States; its sanctuary seated two thousand persons. Two steeples and several minor towers topped the exterior. The building, in the "Alhambra" mode, still stands and is in use. New York's Emanu-El built a similarly spectacular synagogue in the Byzantine style, with seating for eighteen hundred on the main floor of the sanctuary and room for five hundred more in the overflow gallery (1868). Interior illumination required the use of more than five hundred gas jets. The effect of arches of various shapes and decorations executed in red, blue, yellow, white, and gold overwhelmed visitors.[112] As late as 1925, critic Lewis Mumford said this about the signature piece of architecture of the Moorish school: "If it were possible for the dome to be used consistently in synagogue architecture in America, a very definite step would be taken toward a coherent architectural style, which would give the stamp of Judaism to a synagogue."[113]

By the beginning of the twentieth century, synagogue architecture returned to the secular American mainstream, with its emphasis on Classical Revival designs. This change may be attributed to the interest generated by the classical models displayed at the 1893 Colombian Exposition. Archaeological discoveries of Palestinian synagogues built in Roman times also influenced synagogue architecture.[114]

A study conducted by Rabbi Daniel Freelander categorizes synagogue architecture into three stages by function, rather than building style. All of the preceding synagogues qualify for Freelander's Stage One designation, erected by Central European immigrants between 1840 and 1930. Synagogue leaders hoped to win the respect of their Christian neighbors by combining then-current architectural styles with traditional Jewish decorative motifs. Thus, these prosperous new Americans constructed huge sanctuaries with awe-inspiring spaces, hiding the organ and choir behind a rear balcony. Stage One builders concerned themselves with the look of their sanctuary and devoted little thought, or space, to possible social functions or administrative needs.[115] New York's Temple Emanu-El built the last great Stage One synagogue in 1929 for $4,000,000. Its Italian Romanesque sanctuary seats nearly two thousand worshipers, all in individual, permanent seats.[116]

American Jews built few synagogues between 1930 and 1945; with the Depression that began in late 1929 and the onset of World War II in 1941, synagogue leaders struggled to pay mortgages on their existing structures. However, when the war ended, families left the cities for the open spaces of suburbia. There the Jewish community needed a completely different synagogue design.

Stage Two buildings called for considerably smaller, less-soaring sanctuaries. Often synagogue leaders approved the use of cinder blocks rather than the fine mahogany wood of their predecessors. The retractable wall that separated the sanctuary from the much larger social hall identified these buildings as Stage Two facilities.[117] When opened, the combination sanctuary–social hall could seat the entire congregation for High Holiday worship. When closed, the often-used social hall, together with the greatly expanded educational and administrative wings, constituted the spaces predominantly used by the Stage Two synagogues.

Two architects, Eric Mendelsohn and Percival Goodman, strongly influenced post–World War II synagogue design and style. Mendelsohn's new building for Congregation B'nai Amoona (St. Louis) in the late 1940s featured a sanctuary that seated six hundred, but could be expanded by adding both the foyer and assembly hall spaces to accommodate fifteen hundred.[118] Percival Goodman, who designed or built more than fifty synagogues during his long career, wrote that he sought to create an atmosphere of "sober joy, as befits a celebration of the Creator, the air pure, the color gay rather than somber."[119] Synagogue buildings consciously integrated their external surroundings through the maximum use of glass, which brought natural elements into the sanctuary.[120] In 1953, architect Frank Lloyd Wright designed a new sanctuary building for Beth Shalom Congregation (Elkins Park, Pennsylvania) with a forty-foot-high ark sheathed in glass, which he described as a "traveling Mt. Sinai, a mountain of light."[121]

By the late 1960s, in reaction to the shifting social and political climate in America, the style of worship once again changed. Women demanded full participation in worship; both men and women engaged in personal quests for meaning and intimacy. Stage Three congregations of the 1970s, 1980s, and 1990s are modest, designed with small sanctuaries with flexible seating, which allows for multiple uses of the space. The *bimah* (raised platform in front of the sanctuary) is built low and open; no space separates the congregation and its rabbi. Seating is often in the round to enable worshipers to see each other; organs and choir lofts rarely exist, even in Reform synagogues.[122]

THE SYNAGOGUE OF THE FUTURE: BET SHALOM

Two opposing forces are at work in the contemporary synagogue, making confident predictions about its future rather risky. On the one hand, the desire for participation, involvement, and the search for spiritual meaning by segments of American Jewry show no sign of abating. Perhaps as a reflection of this trend, the American synagogue is experiencing renewed interest in worship, with an articulated demand for added ritual and a resurrection of classic liturgy, brushed with an egalitarian veneer. The marginalized, rather than being barred at the synagogue door, which often occurred in the past, are now embraced with a welcoming hug through programs of outreach.

No clear pattern emerges that might offer insight regarding future developments in the American synagogue. While regular attendance at synagogue worship services is down in some locations, it is experiencing a resurgence in others. Using data from the 1990 National Jewish Population Survey, sociologists Gary Tobin and Gabriel Berger learned that while 40 percent of all adult Jews belonged to a synagogue at the beginning of the 1990s, 60 percent actually had been members at some point in their adult lives.[123] Among other conclusions, Tobin and Berger's analysis revealed that synagogue affiliation rates increased with age and is higher among midwesterners than among those living elsewhere in the United States. Rates also increased with the number of years of formal Jewish education received and the number of religious practices observed. The single strongest predictor of adult synagogue membership remained the desire for enrollment of children in synagogue religious schools.[124]

In an article written in 1980, Rabbi Lawrence Hoffman called the contemporary synagogue "a community of limited liability—a community to which we belong for certain clearly defined discrete goals. Jews join it and expect certain specific things in return. When they no longer feel they need the items on the list, they quit."[125] In a recent article, however, Hoffman sounds more hopeful, calling the synagogue "the sacred center of Jewish community."[126] In the ultimate synagogue sanctuary, artist Yaacov Agam suggests the use of revolving chairs to enable worshipers to face different people at different times in the service, creating constantly changing worship groupings. He advocates painting the walls with rainbow colors, thereby expressing the Jews' direct, personal relationship with God.[127]

To the three functions of a synagogue ascribed by Jewish tradition, Bet Knesset (house of assembly), Bet Tefillah (house of prayer), and Bet Midrash (house of study), there are indications that the American synagogue is developing into a Bet Shalom, a space whose purpose is to bring spiritual wholeness to all those who enter.[128] Rabbi Harold Schulweis said it best when he wrote, "My grandfather came to the synagogue because he was a Jew. His grandchildren come to become Jewish. The synagogue is no longer the consequence, but the cause of one's Jewishness."[129] The function of the American synagogue thus shifts again, from an institution that helped to Americanize its worshipers to an institution that shut out the secular world to keep separate its worshipers and finally, in the waning years of the twentieth century, to an institution that gives worshipers the spiritual tools and vision needed to change the secular world into a better place.

NOTES

1. Martin A. Cohen, "The Synagogue, Yesterday, Today and Tomorrow," Paper delivered to the Assembly of Delegates of the New York Federation of Reform Synagogues (April 9, 1978), p. 3.

2. Daniel J. Elazar, "The Development of the American Synagogue." *Modern Judaism* 4 (October 1984): 255.

3. Daniel J. Elazar, *Community and Polity: The Organizational Dynamics of American Jewry* (Philadelphia: 1976), p. 99.

4. Moshe Davis, "The Synagogue in American Judaism," in *Two Generations in Perspective: Notable Events and Trends 1896–1956: A Study of Congregation B'nai Jeshurun, New York City,* ed. Harry Schneiderman (New York: 1957), p. 210.

5. Jacob Rader Marcus, *Early American Jewry,* vol. 1 (New York: 1975), pp. 24–33. See also Eli Farber, *A Time for Planting: The First Migration 1654–1820* (Baltimore: 1992), p. 32.

6. Peter Wiernik, *History of the Jews in America* (New York: 1912), p. 65.

7. Joseph L. Blau, "The Spiritual Life of American Jewry, 1654–1954," *American Jewish Yearbook* (hereafter referred to as *AJYB*) 56 (1955): 112.

8. Ibid., p. 113.

9. Martin A. Cohen, "Synagogue: History and Tradition," in *The Encyclopedia of Religion,* ed. Mireca Eliade (New York: 1987), p. 213.

10. Abraham J. Karp, "Overview: The Synagogue in America—A Historical Typology," in *The American Synagogue, A Sanctuary Transformed,* ed. Jack Wertheimer (Cambridge: 1987), pp. 2, 4.

11. Elazar, "Development of the American Synagogue," p. 256.

12. Leon A. Jick, *The Americanization of the Synagogue, 1820–1870* (Hanover, NH: 1976), p. 4.

13. Jonathan D. Sarna, introduction to *American Synagogue History: A Bibliography and State-of-the-Field Survey,* by Alexandra Shecket Korros and Jonathan D. Sarna (New York: 1988), p. 6.

14. Marcus, *Early American Jewry,* vol. 2, p. 438.

15. Karp, "Synagogue in America," pp. 2–3.

16. Jick, *Americanization of the Synagogue,* p. 4.

17. Karp, "Synagogue in America," p. 3.

18. Jick, *Americanization of the Synagogue,* p. 15.

19. Edwin Wolf II and Maxwell Whiteman, *The History of the Jews of Philadelphia* (Philadelphia: 1957), pp. 143–144, 225.

20. Joseph L. Blau and Salo W. Baron, *The Jews of the United States, 1790–1840: A Documentary History,* vol. 1 (New York: 1963), p. 85.

21. Jick, *Americanization of the Synagogue,* pp. 7–8.

22. Ibid., p. 81.

23. Charles Reznikoff and Uriah Z. Engelman, *The Jews of Charleston* (Philadelphia: 1950), p. 67. See also Jick, *Americanization of the Synagogue,* p. 12.

24. Blau and Baron, *Jews of the United States,* vol. 2, pp. 554, 559.

25. Article I, Constitution of the Reformed Society of Israelites, 1825, in Elazar, *Double Bond,* p. 131.

26. Jick, *Americanization of the Synagogue,* p. 12.

27. Davis, "Synagogue in American Judaism," p. 213.

28. Jick, *Americanization of the Synagogue,* p. 22.

29. Karp, "Synagogue in America," p. 7.

30. Davis, "Synagogue in American Judaism," p. 212.

31. Jick, *Americanization of the Synagogue,* pp. 49–50.

32. Leon A. Jick, "The Reform Synagogue," in Wertheimer, *American Synagogue,* p. 86.

33. W. Gunther Plaut, *The Growth of Reform Judaism* (New York: 1965), p. 9.

34. Jick, *Americanization of the Synagogue,* p. 88.

35. Ibid., pp. 91–94.

36. Karp, "Synagogue in America," p. 5.

37. Jeffrey S. Gurock, "The Orthodox Synagogue," in Wertheimer, *American Synagogue,* p. 42.

38. Karp, "The Synagogue in America," p. 5.

39. Ibid., p. 9.

40. Jick, *Americanization of the Synagogue,* pp. 137, 42.

41. Gurock, "Orthodox Synagogue," p. 43.

42. Jonathan D. Sarna, "The Debate over Mixed Seating in the American Synagogue," in Wertheimer, *American Synagogue,* p. 364.

43. Ibid., pp. 367–70.

44. Jick, *Americanization of the Synagogue,* p. 182.

45. Minutes, Temple Emanu-El, May 22 and 29, 1859; April 3, May 1, 1864.

46. Minutes, Congregation B'nai Yeshurun, September 23, 1871; November 3, 1875.

47. Jick, *Americanization of the Synagogue,* p. 175.

48. Ibid., p. 190; Jick, "Reform Synagogue," p. 88.

49. Elazar, *Community and Polity,* p. 101.

50. Blau, "Spiritual Life," p. 132.

51. Jick, *Americanization of the Synagogue,* pp. 191, 193.

52. Henry Pereira Mendes, "The Beginning of the Seminary," in *The Jewish Theological Seminary of America: Semi-Centennial Volume,* ed. Cyrus Adler (New York: 1939), pp. 35–41. For a full discussion on the origins of JTS, see Moshe Davis, *The Emergence of Conservative Judaism: The Historical School in 19th Century America* (Philadelphia: 1963), pp. 231–41. See also Robert Gordis, *Conservative Judaism: An American Philosophy* (New York: 1945); Jacob Neusner, *Understanding American Judaism* (New York: 1975); Marshall Sklare, *Conservative Judaism: An American Movement* (New York: 1972); and Mordecai Waxman, *Tradition and Change: The Development of Conservative Judaism* (New York: 1978).

53. Gerald Sorin, *A Time for Building: The Third Migration, 1880–1920* (Baltimore: 1992), p. 183.

54. Gurock, "Orthodox Synagogue," p. 57.

55. Alfred A. Greenbaum, "The Early Russian Congregation in America in Its Ethnic and Religious Setting," *American Jewish History* 62 (December 1972): p. 166.

56. Gurock, "Orthodox Synagogue," p. 48.

57. *AJYB* 5 (1904): 306; *AJYB* 17 (1916): 349.

58. Jick, "Reform Synagogue," p. 93.

59. Karp, "Synagogue in America," p. 15.

60. Blau, "Spiritual Life," p. 142.

61. Gurock, "Orthodox Synagogue," p. 52.

62. *American Hebrew,* June 10, 1889, p. 172; January 4, 1901, pp. 231–34.

63. Elazar, "Development of the American Synagogue," p. 259.

64. Karp, "Synagogue in America," p. 19.

65. Gurock, "Orthodox Synagogue," p. 56.

66. Jeffrey S. Gurock, "Resistors and Accommodators: Varieties of Orthodox Rabbis in America, 1886–1983," in *The American Rabbinate,* ed. Jacob Rader Marcus and Abraham J. Peck (Hoboken, NJ: 1983), pp. 24–25.

67. Jack Wertheimer, "The Conservative Synagogue," in Wertheimer, *American Synagogue,* p. 115.

68. *The American Hebrew,* March 22, 1918.

69. Mordecai M. Kaplan, *Judaism As a Civilization* (New York: 1934), p. 428.

70. Karp, "Synagogue in America," pp. 19–20.

71. Abraham Cronbach, "American Synagogues: The Lessons of the Names," *American Jewish Archives* 16 (1964): 126.

72. Abraham J. Feldman, "The Changing Functions of the Synagogue and the Rabbi," *Reform Judaism: Essays by Hebrew Union College Alumni* (Cincinnati: 1949), p. 211.

73. *AJYB* 39 (1938): 61; *AJYB* 41 (1940): 217.

74. Wertheimer, "Conservative Synagogue," p. 118.

75. Jick, "Reform Synagogue," p. 100.

76. Gurock, "Orthodox Synagogue," p. 61.

77. Ibid., p. 64; Elazar, *Community and Polity,* p. 111.

78. Karp, "Synagogue in America," pp. 27, 24; Lance Sussman, "The Suburbanization of American Judaism as Reflected in Synagogue Building and Architecture," *American Jewish History* 75 (September 1985): 31.

79. Will Herberg, "The Postwar Revival of the Synagogue," *Commentary* 9 (April 1950): 315.

80. Mordecai Kaplan, *Society for Advancement of Judaism Review* 5, no. 4 (October 9, 1925), cited in Marc Lee Raphael, *Profiles in American Judaism* (San Francisco: 1984), pp. 180–182.

81. Elazar, *Community and Polity,* pp. 107–8.

82. Jick, "Reform Synagogue," pp. 104–5.

83. Jick, "Reform Synagogue," pp. 106.

84. Wertheimer, "Conservative Synagogue," p. 137.

85. Gurock, "Orthodox Synagogue," p. 68. Before World War II, Regina Jonas completed her studies in Berlin, received private ordination, and served as a rabbi for a few years in Germany before she perished in the Holocaust. Thus, Jonas was the first woman ordained as a rabbi who was not first married to a rabbi. Simon Schwarzfuchs, *A Concise History of the Rabbinate* (Oxford and Cambridge, MA: 1993), p. 127.

86. Sarna, introduction to *American Synagogue History,* p. 10; Sussman, "Suburbanization of American Judaism," p. 43.

87. Jick, "Reform Synagogue," p. 105.

88. Harold M. Schulweis, "Restructuring the Synagogue," *Conservative Judaism* 27 (Summer 1973): 19.

89. Daniel J. Elazar and Rela G. Monson, "The Synagogue Havurah: An Experiment in Restoring Adult Fellowship to the Jewish Community," *Jewish Journal of Sociology* 21 (June 1979): 67–68.

90. Feldman, "Changing Functions of the Synagogue," pp. 208–9.

91. Israel Goldstein, *A Century of Judaism in New York: B'nai Jeshurun, 1825–1925* (New York: 1930), p. 48.

92. Elazar, "Development of the Modern Synagogue," p. 267.

93. Jick, *Americanization of the Synagogue,* pp. 9–10.

94. Blau, "Spiritual Life," p. 118; Jick, *Americanization of the Synagogue,* pp. 59, 68–69.

95. Elazar, *Community and Polity,* p. 101; Jick, *Americanization of the Synagogue,* p. 128.

96. Isaac Mayer Wise, *Reminiscences* (Cincinnati: 1901), pp. 45, 51.

97. Jick, *Americanization of the Synagogue,* p. 155.

98. Ibid., pp. 116, 119.

99. Hyman B. Grinstein, *The Rise of the Jewish Community of New York 1654–1860* (Philadelphia: 1945), p. 365.

100. Grinstein, *Rise of the Jewish Community,* pp. 130–32.

101. Elazar, *Community and Polity,* p. 120.

102. Blau, "Spiritual Life," p. 150.

103. J. H. Kay, "Synagogue Architecture," *Midstream* 24 (October 1978): 44.

104. Rachel Wischnitzer, *Synagogue Architecture in the United States: History and Interpretation* (Philadelphia: 1955), pp. 5, 11.

105. Wischnitzer, *Synagogue Architecture,* pp. 13, 16.

106. Evelyn Alloy, "Three Paths toward Synagogue Buildings," *Jewish Digest* 26 (February 1981): 66.

107. Wischnitzer, *Synagogue Architecture,* pp. 27–32.

108. Ibid., pp. 5, 25; Alloy, "Three Paths," pp. 68–69.

109. Wischnitzer, *Synagogue Architecture,* p. 37.

110. Mark W. Gordon, "Rediscovering Jewish Infrastructure: The Legacy of United States Nineteenth Century Synagogues," *American Jewish History* 75, no. 3 (March 1986): 303.

111. Wischnitzer, *Synagogue Architecture,* pp. 41–42.

112. Gordon, "Rediscovering Jewish Infrastructure," p. 297; Wischnitzer, *Synagogue Architecture,* pp. 7, 70–75; Jick, *Americanization of the Synagogue,* p. 180.

113. Lewis H. Mumford, "Toward a Modern Synagogue Architecture," *Menorah Journal* 11, no. 3 (June 1925), p. 232.

114. Gordon, "Rediscovering Jewish Infrastructure," p. 297.

115. Daniel H. Freelander, "Why Temples Look the Way They Do," *Reform Judaism* 23, no. 1 (Fall 1994): 35.

116. Sussman, "Suburbanization of American Judaism," p. 33.

117. Freelander, "Why Temples Look," p. 36.

118. Wischnitzer, *Synagogue Architecture,* p. 137.

119. Percival Goodman, "On Designing a Synagogue," *Jewish Digest* 13 (June 1968): 20.

120. Joseph Guttmann, "Architectural Aspects of the Synagogue," *Encyclopedia of Religion,* p. 218.

121. Alloy, "Three Paths," p. 70.

122. Freelander, "Why Temples Look," pp. 36–37.

123. Gary A. Tobin and Gabriel Berger, *Synagogue Affiliation: Implications for the 1990s* (Waltham, MA: 1993), p. 2. Tobin and Berger agree that the National Jewish Population Survey served as a landmark study for the sociological analysis of American Jewry.

124. Tobin and Berger, *Synagogue Affiliation,* pp. 2, 26–27.

125. Lawrence A. Hoffman, "The Synagogue, the Havurah and Liable Communities," *Response* 38 (1980): 37–38.

126. Lawrence A. Hoffman, "In Search of a Spiritual Home," *Reform Judaism* 23, no. 1 (Fall 1994): 78.

127. Yaacov Agam, "My Ideal Synagogue," *Reform Judaism* 23, no. 1 (Fall 1994): 45.

128. Kerry M. Olitzky, "Synagogue: A New Concept for a New Age," *Journal of Jewish Communal Service* 62 (Fall 1985): 10.

129. Schulweis, "Restructuring the Synagogue," p. 23.

PART I
UNITED STATES

A

ALABAMA

TEMPLE BETH EL, CONSERVATIVE. *Birmingham, Alabama.* Forty people—dissatisfied with the strict synagogue doctrine at K'nesseth Israel—organized Temple Beth El in 1907, feeling a need to establish an Americanized congregation that maintained an Orthodox approach to Judaism. In Beth El's first constitution, its founders asserted their desire to affiliate with the Union of Orthodox Hebrew Congregations, the national organization of Orthodox synagogues. For several years, the incipient congregation held its services in various leased quarters on the north side of town, with Rabbi A. Rapport serving as spiritual leader. The congregation secured its first permanent building in 1914 on the corner of Seventeenth Street and Sixth Avenue North, only blocks away from K'nesseth Israel. Perhaps because there seemed to be no need for two traditional congregations in the same area, Beth El's membership dwindled. Furthermore, while Rabbi F. Mogitz led the congregation from 1914 to 1918, the congregation was without rabbinical leadership from 1918 to 1923. Thus, in 1922, the leaders of Beth El turned over the assets to a group of people with the understanding that the name of Beth El would be perpetuated.

This new group purchased land on the south side (at Highland Avenue and Beech Street) to show others that the Orthodox Jews in that part of town supported the new undertaking. Although members did not dedicate a new synagogue there until 1927, the congregation grew under the leadership of its rabbi Solomon Katz (1923–1929). After a year without a rabbi, the congregation was served by Rabbi Abraham Bengis (1930–1933), until his ill health forced him to retire. Rabbi E. A. Levi succeeded him. As Levi's liberal views quickly conflicted with the congregation, he left in 1935. That summer members elected Rabbi Abraham J. Mesch to the pulpit. He held the position until his death in 1962. An ardent Zionist, Mesch encouraged interest in building the land of

Israel. Nevertheless, Mesch succeeded in "unifying the various elements of the congregation to work in harmony for the common needs." Under his leadership, the congregation grew in size; he instituted numerous programs, including a Junior Congregation and a Young People's League (youth group). Somewhat radical for his day, Mesch also introduced the Beth El Forum, a discussion group that replaced the sermon following an abbreviated Friday evening service. The women of Beth El founded a sisterhood (also referred to as its Ladies Auxiliary) in 1922. And in 1939, the congregation's Hebrew School grew rapidly when it began to utilize a school-owned vehicle to transport its students from home to synagogue. Because of Beth El's approach to Jewish tradition, K'nesseth Israel continued to maintain a close affiliation with its neighboring synagogue. Mesch led services regularly at K'nesseth Israel. (In 1927, the congregations formed a joint cemetery association to service the members of both congregations.)

In 1944, following a debate over the eligibility of women to become members of the synagogue in their own right, the congregation moved from its former traditional stance and affiliated with the United Synagogue of America (now the United Synagogue of Conservative Judaism), the national organization of Conservative synagogues. This move, however, did not sever the relationship between K'nesseth Israel and Beth El until 1960, when disagreement over the sponsorship of the cemetery association ended in an out-of-court settlement. Throughout these years of tension, the membership of K'nesseth Israel shrank; its members blamed Beth El, as the latter continued to grow in numbers to become the largest congregation in Alabama by 1960.

In 1958, police found a bomb (which misfired) in Beth El's basement, only eight years after it built its new structure, primarily designed to accommodate its program of religious education. Following Rabbi Mesch's death in 1962, these men served the congregation: Rabbis Morton A. Wallach (1965–1967), Philip Silverstein (1967–1968), Mark A. Elovitz (1969–1976), Steven Glazer (1976–1993), and Michael Wasserman (1993–   ). During Elovitz's tenure, the congregation gave women Torah honors; during Glazer's tenure, Beth El counted women in its minyan. In 1995, the congregation of seven hundred family units dedicated a classroom wing and cultural center.

Reference

Elovitz, Mark H. *A Century of Jewish Life in Dixie: The Birmingham Experience* (University, AL: 1974).

TEMPLE EMANU-EL, REFORM. *Birmingham, Alabama.* Although congregations often grew out of cemetery associations or benevolent societies, a group of men organized this congregation to provide religious services to a small Jewish community amid the two thousand residents who made up this southern mining town. Incorporated in 1882 as the first synagogue in Jefferson County, charter members organized this congregation on a liberal basis. They did not opt for any class division or selling of pews. Joseph Stolz, then a student rabbi, led the first services. Alexander Rosenspitz served as the congregation's first full-time rabbi, elected in 1886 and serving only four months. In 1887, Dr. Maurice Eisenberg began serving the congregation. The presence of a spiritual leader undoubtedly caused a growth spurt; only four years after incorporation the congregation built its first building in 1889 at Fifth Avenue and Seventeenth Street North. Yet, in 1890, over serious dissension with the rabbi, a small group left the congregation to form B'nai Israel (which disbanded following the resignation of Eisenberg).

Throughout its early history, the congregation saw itself as an ambassador of Judaism to the general community. Its early years, particularly during 1890–1894, were difficult ones. During this period, congregational president Samuel Ullman led the congregation. The absence of a trained rabbi and the financial panic of 1893 ill-affected the congregation's growth. After a nine-month tenure as rabbi in 1894, David Marx left to serve Hebrew Benevolent Congregation in Atlanta; members then elected Rabbi Morris Newfield as spiritual leader of the congregation. It was his first and only congregation. Using the Pittsburgh Platform of 1885 as guidance, he instituted the principles of Reform Judaism of the time. Under his direction, the synagogue prospered and grew significantly. In 1902 the congregation organized the city's first free kindergarten. During Newfield's tenure, numerous Christian congregations used the Temple for Sunday services. In 1884 women of Temple Emanu-El organized the Ladies Aid Society (later called the Sisterhood) for the purpose of keeping the cemetery and physical plant of the synagogue in good condition. That same year, congregational women organized the Ladies Benevolent Society among other activities "to buy cows for poor families with little children unable to get pure milk."

With land purchased in 1908, the congregation moved to Twenty-first and Highland Avenue in 1914. This building was later expanded. In 1900, Temple Emanu-El housed the first public kindergarten in Birmingham.

On the death of Morris Newfield, members promoted Rabbi Myron Silverman (who had been serving as assistant rabbi) to the position of senior rabbi. He served for only one year, until members named Rabbi Milton Grafman (who served from 1941 to 1975) as senior rabbi. Membership totaled 325 family units on Grafman's arrival. Through Grafman's efforts, the congregation was heavily involved in financial support of the state of Israel, as well as social action and specifically civil rights activities. In addition, he initiated a long-standing Institute on Judaism for Christian Clergy in 1944. In 1955, those who were unhappy with Grafman's leadership, led by Milton Fies, formed a breakaway congregation to be known as The congregation of Reform Judaism, which lasted until 1959. By 1962, membership grew to 630 family units. Grafman's emphasis on interfaith activities continued when rabbis Henry Bamberger (1975 to 1979) and David Jeremy Zucker (1979 to 1983) served as leaders of the congregation. Dr. Steven L. Jacobs led the congregation from 1983 to 1990, and in 1991, Rabbi Jonathan A. Miller became Emanu-El's rabbi.

References

A Century of Reverence 1882–1992 (Birmingham: 1982).
Cowett, Mark. Birmingham's Rabbi Morris Newfield and Alabama 1895–1940 (University, AL: 1986).
Elovitz, Mark H. A Century of Jewish Life in Dixie: The Birmingham Experience (University, AL: 1974).
Synagogue Histories File, American Jewish Archives.

K'NESSETH ISRAEL SYNAGOGUE, ORTHODOX. Birmingham, Alabama. In 1888, a small group of men met to address the needs of the growing number of Eastern European Jewish immigrants in Birmingham. By 1889, the presence of a sufficient number of Eastern European immigrants arrived in Birmingham challenged Temple Emanu-El, which had been the only synagogue. Where previously a need for the requirements of a traditional community had not existed, a demand had developed. Thus, K'nesseth Israel (the Assembly of Israel) was born (1891). The members of this fledgling congregation established their own cemetery, but in the early years the congregation worshipped in private homes and rented halls—sometimes even in the classrooms of Temple Emanu-El. From 1891 to 1899, services were held at 521 North Twenty-Second Street and then at 401 Third Avenue until 1903, when the congregation erected its own building on the corner of Seventh Avenue and Seventeenth Street North. (This site served the congregation for fifty-two years.) In 1955, the congregation built a new building in the Mountain Brook section of Birmingham. From 1891 to 1896, M. Herman served the congregation as a religious leader and much of this area of Alabama as *mohel* (ritual circumciser). The congregation grew rapidly even without the direction and guidance provided by a trained rabbi. Eastern European immigrants continued to pour into Birmingham. Thus, the congregation's membership fostered the development and growth of two benevolent-aid societies: the Daughters of Israel and the Hebrew Men's Aid Association. In addition, a group associated with the congregation founded the Birmingham Hebrew School in 1912. Four years later, the congregation purchased a home on the corner of Seventh Street and Seventh Avenue, which it remodeled into a Hebrew school.

In 1956, the congregation moved to its present location on Montevallo Road in Mountain Brook, a suburb of Birmingham. With the founding of the Birmingham Jewish Day School in 1973, the Knesseth Israel Hebrew School became unnecessary and thus was discontinued. In 1993, membership stood at 125 family units.

Though numerous rabbis have served the congregation over the years for short tenures, these rabbis led the congregation over the past generation: Moshe Stern (1968–1979), Harry Rosen (1979–1986), and Reuven Tradburks (1986–   ).

Reference

Elovitz, Mark H. A Century of Jewish Life in Dixie: The Birmingham Experience (University, AL: 1974).

CONGREGATION SHA'ARAI SHOMAYIM (LATER, SPRING HILL AVENUE TEMPLE), REFORM. *Mobile, Alabama.*

David Salomon, a new-comer to Mobile in 1839, called together the Mobile Jewish community in 1841 for the purpose of founding Congregation Sha'arai Shomayim for worship and the study of sacred text. However, it appears that Israel I. Jones (ca., 1831–1832), who became the new congregation's first president, had been soliciting support since he had arrived in Mobile. The young synagogue organization purchased land in 1841. However, members waited until 1844 before gaining a charter for the congregation under the full name *Sha'arai Shomayim u-Maskil el Dol* (Gates of Heaven and Society of Friends of the Needy). Subsequently, the synagogue community occupied its first building on St. Emanuel Street. Its first religious leader, Mendes da Silva, a Sephardic scholar, began his service to the congregation in December 1846 (serving to 1848). Though the congregation's constitution (as revised, 1869) indicates that the "mode of worship should be according to the German custom," it is not clear whether the Ashkenazic (German) or the Sephardic ritual was used during those first few years.

Baruch M. Emanuel succeeded da Silva as religious leader in 1848. In 1853, the congregation moved to a building on Jackson Street in Spring Hill—primarily to escape the yellow fever epidemic striking Mobile—about the same time that Julius Eckman succeeded Emanuel in the pulpit. Eckman remained in the pulpit less than a year. In his stead, members elected Dr. Isaac Schatz (1854–1855). When he arrived, he found that some members left the congregation to form Dorshey Zedek, the split caused by a disagreement over the introduction of Sephardic ritual. Isaac Epstein succeeded Schatz (1855–1865). In 1857, fire destroyed Sha'arai Shomayim's building. The following year, members dedicated a new structure on Jackson Street. Dorshey Zedek members rejoined Sha'arai Shomayim in 1859.

In 1865, the congregation instituted a school, at just about the same time that Dr. Leopold Winter (1865–1868) came to serve the congregation as its religious leader. Its curriculum included religious and secular studies until 1878, at which time secular studies were dropped from the curriculum. While little is known about another split in the history of the congregation, it appears that in 1869 a short-lived group separated from Sha'arai Shomayim to form another congregation. During Adolph Moses' tenure (1871–1881), the congregation joined the Union of American Hebrew Congregations (1878), becoming one of the early members of the Reform movement in North America. Ten years later, the congregation joined the Hebrew Sabbath School Union of America.

Many rabbis served the congregation over its history: Emanuel Schreiber (1881–1883), Henry Berkowitz (1883–1888), Oscar Cohen (1888–1898), and Tobias Schanfarber (1898–1901). Rabbi Alfred G. Moses served for the longest period of time (1901–1940). Moses focused his rabbinate on the education of young people, in particular. He also supported congregational efforts in community work.

Early in Moses's tenure, members built a new synagogue on Government

Street (1907). In 1914, the board reintroduced Bar Mitzvah, a ceremony that had been rejected in place of Confirmation early in the history of the synagogue. In 1940, Dr. Sidney Berkowitz succeeded Moses as rabbi of the congregation. When Berkowitz enlisted in the Army Chaplain Corps in 1942, Rabbi Bertram Korn came to serve instead (1943–1944). Through worship, Rabbi Korn reached out to military personnel stationed in the area. When Korn himself left for army duty, Rabbi Joshua O. Haberman led the congregation (1944–1946). During Rabbi Haberman's tenure, the congregation initiated its Institute on Judaism for Christian Ministers.

Rabbi Samuel Gup joined Sha'arai Shomayim in 1946. Gup did much to foster intergroup relations in Mobile. In 1947, the congregation formed the Temple Guild and a Men's Club to "assist with the spiritual and social life of the congregation." Rabbi Solomon Cherniak succeeded Gup (1949–1960). During his rabbinate, congregants dedicated the present synagogue structure on Spring Hill Avenue (1955).

When Cherniak left the pulpit due to ill health, Rabbi P. Irving Bloom came to Mobile (1960–1973). Prior to his tenure, Mobile's population grew, but temple membership remained constant at 215. During Bloom's rabbinate in Mobile, membership declined. In 1971, the temple considered merging with the local Congregation Ahavas Chesed. The merger did not take place.

Rabbis Richard Messing (1973–1976), Steven Jacobs (1976–1984), and Gordon Geller (1984–1987) served Sha'arai Shomayim before Rabbi Donald M. Kunstadt joined the temple in 1987. In 1994, membership stood at 240.

References

Korn, Bertram. *1844–1944, Congregation Sha'arai Shomayim* (Mobile: 1944).
———. "The Jews of Mobile, Alabama, Prior to the Organization of the First Congregation in 1841." *Hebrew Union College Annual* 40–41 (1969–1970): 469–502.
Moses, Alfred G. "A History of the Jews of Mobile." *Publications of the American Jewish Historical Society,* no. 12 (1904): 113–25.
125th Anniversary, Springhill Avenue Temple, 1844–1969 (Mobile: 1969).
Shpall, Leo. "The First Synagogue in Alabama." *Jewish Forum* (February 1950/March 1950): 31–32, 47–48.
Synagogue Histories File, American Jewish Archives.
Zietz, Robert. *The Gates of Heaven: Congregation Sha'arai Shomayim, The First 150 Years, Mobile, Alabama 1884–1994* (Mobile: 1994).

ETZ AHAYEM SEPHARDIC CONGREGATION, ORTHODOX. *Montgomery, Alabama.* By 1908, a small colony of Sephardic Jews held their first High Holiday services in Montgomery. The immigrants came primarily from the Isle of Rhodes, Turkey, and Asia Minor. With the growth of their community, they needed to care for their ill and impoverished and later to arrange for burials. Thus, a benevolent society was created. By 1912, they created a permanent organization: an Orthodox congregation for Spanish-speaking (or Sephardic) Jews, and they secured a charter (in Ladino) from the state of Alabama.

(However, it wasn't until 1916 that the congregation was incorporated.) The congregation's first president, Solomon Rousso, the owner of the local delicatessen, played an important role in the congregation during its first twenty-five years. In its early years, the congregation's financial stability seemed a bit precarious. But as early as 1918, they raised funds to purchase their first building (a converted old house on Sayre Street). After 1919, the children attended Sunday School at the neighboring Temple Beth-Or.

In 1927, the congregation rebuilt its house of worship, having filed new papers of incorporation that same year. A Hebrew School was organized, to be followed several years later, in 1930, by the creation of the Judean Club, a youth group.

The first ordained rabbi to serve the congregation was Rabbi Raphael Abagli (from Rhodes), between the years 1938–1940 and 1952–1953, with Rabbi Elias Levy serving as spiritual leader in the intervening years. In 1951, in a radical departure, the congregation replaced its traditional Hebrew-Ladino service with a Hebrew-English liturgy. The temple issued its first bulletin in 1955, the same year the congregation rejuvenated its own religious school. After a long time without a rabbi, Rabbi Israel Shemoni was elected rabbi in 1959, but he served for only one year. He was followed by Rabbi Solomon Acrish (1959–1966). In 1962, the congregation built a new home at Augusta and Lebron Streets. During the 1950s and 1960s, anti-Semitic incidents increased as more Jews moved into the area. These incidents also came as a result of the position of Jews in the North on civil rights issues, a position generally not shared by southern Jews.

In 1966, Rabbi Raphael Wizman joined the congregation as its religious leader. When he left in 1967, the congregation entered the service of military rabbis, all graduates of Hebrew Union College–Jewish Institute of Religion, the Reform seminary, including Rabbi Colonel Howard Zyskind, who began his service to the congregation in 1992. The congregation has diminished greatly in membership, with only thirty regular members and fifty associate members in 1994.

References

Hanan, Rubin Morris. *The History of the Etz Ahayem Congregation* (Montgomery: 1962).
Synagogue Histories File, American Jewish Archives.

KAHL MONTGOMERY/BETH-OR, REFORM. *Montgomery, Alabama.* Jacob Sacerdote was probably the first Jew to arrive in Montgomery City. In 1846, at his home, where worship services were held, he, along with twelve other men, formed a society called *Chevra Mevaker Cholim* (the Society for Relieving the Sick). One of its first acts was to purchase land for a cemetery. In 1852, this society of thirty German and Polish Jews was augmented to form Kahl Montgomery. (Although the decision to form a congregation was made in 1849, the congregation was not actually incorporated until 1852.) Josiah Weil served as the first president. The new congregation sought the services of a lay reader. Initially, the congregation met in members' homes, before holding services in public buildings. Receiving a bequest from Judah Touro, the congregation was able to set aside funds to build a synagogue. Once a building was constructed in 1860 (dedicated 1862) at Church and Catoma Streets, the congregation began its first reforms when a choir and organ were used, and a partial English liturgy as well. While other reforms were slowly introduced, heads remained covered and dietary laws were observed. That same year, a school for secular and religious subjects was instituted. In 1863, James K. Gutheim was engaged as the congregation's first rabbi. However, he and the president resigned a year later. The following year, M. H. Meyers was elected to the pulpit, but his tenure lasted only a year, as well. In the early years, there was a great deal of turnover in the religious leadership of the congregation: G. L. Rosenberger (1866–1869), E. B. M. Browne (1869–1870), Adolph Moses (1870–1872), B. E. Jacobs (1872–1876), Sigmund Hecht (1876–1888), E. K. Fischer (1888–1892), David Davidson (1892–1895), Israel Joseph (1895–1896), Aron J. Messing, Jr. (1897–1906), B. C. Ehrenreich (1906–1921), William Schwartz (1921–1928), Benjamin Goldstein (1928–1933), Eugene Blachschleger (1933–1964), David A. Baylinson (1965–1994), and Glenn M. Jacob (1994–   ).

Following the Civil War, more Jews arrived in Montgomery. By 1870, plans to enlarge the building were made, and the placement of family pews seems to indicate that women were no longer seated separately from the men. In 1874, the Reform ritual used by Congregation Emanu-El of New York City was formally adopted by the congregation. When these changes were adopted, the congregation officially named its house of worship Beth-Or (House of Light). In 1879, the congregation became members of the Union of American Hebrew Congregations, the national organization of Reform synagogues. In 1893, the congregation was legally incorporated and received a new charter. In 1896, the *Union Prayer Book,* the Reform movement's prayer book, was officially adopted.

In 1902, a new building was erected at Sayre and Clayton Streets. This new building had no trace of the orthodoxy of its founders. During World War I, the membership of the congregation was enlarged as a result of the personnel stationed at local Camp Sheridan. A Men's Club was formed in 1926 and a sisterhood in 1949. (A committee from the Council of Jewish Women had previously filled this role.) In 1934, a Young People's League was formed, representing all of the Montgomery congregations and affiliated with the North American Federation of Temple Youth. During World War II, the temple was used by the Jewish Welfare Board (JWB) as a social center. The congregation's religious leader, Rabbi Eugene Blachschleger, served as chaplain at Maxwell and Gunter Fields. In his rabbinate he emphasized interfaith activities. During his tenure, the congregation moved to its new facility on Narrow Lane Road (1961). Anti-Semitic incidents increased as more Jews moved into the area during the 1950s and 1960s. While members of the congregation generally did not support the position of desegregation and civil rights, tension between Jews and non-Jews increased because of the activist posture taken in the community by Jews from the North.

After Blachschlager's long tenure, Rabbi David A. Baylinson succeeded him. With an emphasis on family and education, he instituted family services in the congregation, with a biweekly early Shabbat service as well. During Baylinson's tenure as president of the Montgomery Ministerial Association (white ministers), he orchestrated its merger with the Montgomery Ministerial Alliance (black ministers) to form the Montgomery Ministerial Union. The Beth-Or Sunday School serves children from the neighboring congregations of Etz Ahayem and Agudath Israel. Beth-Or reinstituted Bar Mitzvah and introduced Bat Mitzvah in 1968. Two years later, a Yizkor Memorial service was added to the seventh-day observance of Passover. In 1994, membership reached 255.

References

The First Hundred Years of Kahl Montgomery (Montgomery: 1952).

Moses, Alfred G. *Publications of the American Jewish Historical Society,* no. 13 (1905): 83–88.

Synagogue Histories File, American Jewish Archives.

ALASKA

CONGREGATION BETH SHOLOM, REFORM. *Anchorage, Alaska.* Formally organized on October 3, 1958, as the first Jewish congregation in the state (with an estimated total of only forty-five Jewish families in Anchorage), holding services in homes and various buildings in the early years, and enlisting the services of a lay leader, visiting rabbis, and local military chaplains, the congregation served a small permanent Jewish community substantially made up of service personnel from Elmendorf Air Force Base and Fort Richardson and the civil service. While the Jewish Welfare Board had established a committee in Anchorage during World War II to help with military personnel, the impetus for a congregation came from Leonard Bazell, formerly a student at Hebrew Union College–Jewish Institute of Religion. A Sunday School was established in September 1959. In 1960, the congregation voted to become a member of the Union of American Hebrew Congregations, the national organization of Reform synagogues. While the congregation was ready to build a synagogue structure in 1964 (dedicated in 1965), with a loan from the Union of American Hebrew Congregations, the earthquake of that year nearly devastated the congregation's ability to raise funds. Thus, it solicited funds from around the country. Rabbi Lester Polonsky served as the first full-time rabbi between the years 1978 and 1983. Rabbi Harry Rosenfeld joined the congregation in 1984.

Reference

Synagogue Histories File, American Jewish Archives.

ARIZONA

TEMPLE BETH EL, CONSERVATIVE. *Phoenix, Arizona.* A small group founded Beth El in 1926 and purchased a building at Fourth Street and Fillmore (1931), which served the synagogue as its first permanent home. This group elected Sol Kartus its first president. Y. Dow led the congregation in its early years, and Nathan Barack (1939–1945; 1946–1949) became the congregation's first ordained rabbi. At the time of Barack's election to the pulpit, membership numbered only twelve.

During Rabbi Harry Schectman's tenure (1949–1956), the congregation moved to Third Avenue and McDowell (1951). In the new location, membership grew to 416. Other rabbis who served Beth El include Carol Klein (1956–1962), Moshe Tutnauer (1962–1970, 1971–1972), David Goldstein (1970–1971), Baruch Gold (1972–1977), and Herbert Silverman (1977–1992).

In 1968, the congregation moved to its present site at Glendale and Eleventh Avenue. Beth El began a day camp, Camp Shemesh, in 1975 and established the Solomon Schechter Day School in the early 1980s. In 1993, membership stood at 950 family units when Beth El elected Rabbi Richard Sherwin to its pulpit.

Reference

Synagogue Histories File, American Jewish Archives.

TEMPLE BETH ISRAEL, REFORM. *Phoenix, Arizona.* As early as 1906, the few Jewish settlers in the area gathered together for worship, especially during the High Holidays. However, the beginning of a formal congregation can be traced to Barnett Marks, an attorney from Chicago with two young sons for whom he wanted to provide a Jewish education. As a result, he organized the first Sunday School. During services, he read from rabbis' sermons that he gathered. Through various means, he sought to demystify Jewish ritual.

In 1917, Jewish women established the Phoenix section of the National Council of Jewish Women. This organization joined with B'nai B'rith (which had been formed in Phoenix only two years earlier) to build the city's first synagogue. Originally, it was operated under the auspices of the Phoenix Hebrew Center Association; eventually, it became Temple Israel.

Founders formally incorporated the congregation in 1920. Rabbi David L. Liknaitz (1920–1924) served the congregation during its early years. Following his retirement, the diversity of opinion (as reflected in the minute books) regarding the religious direction the synagogue should take made for difficulties in maintaining consistent rabbinic leadership during its formative history. Various people serviced the congregation throughout its early stages, and these individuals led Beth Israel as religious leaders of the congregation: A. I. Goldberg (1924–1925), Adolph Rosenberg (1926–1929), S. D. Hurwitz (1930–1935),

Philip W. Jaffa (1935–1938), Abraham Lincoln Krohn (1938–1953), Albert Plotkin (1955–1992), and Kenneth I. Segel (1992–   ).

The same year the congregation was founded, it took over the building from the inactive Phoenix Hebrew Center Association. The following year, Beth Israel built its new home at Second and Culver. The argument over whether to hire a Reform or a Conservative rabbi became resolved when Beth Israel's desire for Reform forced a group to break away and form Temple Beth El.

The congregation adopted the *Union Prayer Book* in 1935, when Rabbi Jaffa came to the congregation. He introduced choir music into the liturgy and implemented the religious school curriculum of the Union of American Hebrew Congregations. During Jaffa's first year, a fire destroyed a large part of the building. Beth Israel restored the building and added a religious school building.

When Rabbi Krohn joined the congregation in 1938, membership of Beth Israel totaled nearly a hundred families, with sixty-four children in the religious school. Krohn introduced a choir into worship. The congregation moved to Eleventh and Flower in 1949 to serve its three hundred families (dedicated 1950, expanded 1959). That same year, Beth Israel joined the Union of American Hebrew Congregations, the national organization of Reform synagogues.

Under the direction of Krohn's successor, Rabbi Albert Plotkin, the congregation continued to grow. Plotkin expanded the educational offerings of the synagogue and introduced special worship services for children and families. Beth Israel expanded the physical plant once again in 1966, the same year it established a nursery school. When Plotkin retired in 1992, Rabbi Kenneth Segel succeeded him. In 1994, membership stood at nearly 950.

References

Stocker, Joseph. *Jewish Roots in Arizona* (Phoenix: 1954).
Synagogue Histories File, American Jewish Archives.
Yovel, Temple Beth Israel 1920–1970 (Phoenix: 1970).

TEMPLE EMANU-EL, REFORM. *Tucson, Arizona.* In 1910, under the influence of Terese Marx Ferrin, a small group founded the Hebrew Benevolent Society in Tucson. This congregation of twenty-five families immediately dedicated a building on South Stone Avenue and readied it for use for the High Holidays that same year. This building became the first edifice for Jewish worship in the territory of Arizona (two years before it became a state). The congregation served the entire community.

The women of the congregation had in 1904 founded the Ladies Aid Society, the first organized sisterhood in the state. This organization became affiliated with the National Federation of Temple Sisterhoods (now called the Women of Reform Judaism) in 1917.

The congregation acquired a building two doors down from the synagogue for use as a community center. A small group of congregational members who sought a more traditional expression for their Judaism met in this building regularly for worship. Eventually, with Emanu-El's positive encouragement, this group left the congregation to found Congregation Anshe Israel (Conservative) in 1935.

The men of Emanu-El formed a Men's Club in 1943. At the same time, the membership of the congregation stood at one hundred. This dwindled to sixty following the resignation of Rabbi Joseph Gumbiner (1947) and the election of Rabbi Albert Bilgray (who simultaneously served the Hillel Foundation at the University of Arizona until 1968). During the first year of Bilgray's tenure, membership returned to one hundred.

Although the congregation did not fully vacate its original building on Stone Avenue until 1955, the Jewish community moved out of the downtown area many years prior to the move of the synagogue itself. Therefore, under Bilgray's direction, Emanu-El sponsored activities in various locations in the community. The dedication of the new synagogue building on North Country Club Road took place in stages, beginning in 1949. The congregation dedicated the religious school in 1951 and the convocation building in 1956, before dedicating the entire facility in 1962. In 1966, the temple established a religious school branch in Nogales, Arizona, sixty-five miles away. By 1971, Emanu-El's membership exceeded five hundred families. In 1995, membership exceeded nine hundred families.

Rabbi Moise Bergman (1930–1933) served the congregation as its first full-time religious leader. These men followed: William Rosenblatt (1935–1937), Hyman Iola (1937–1941), Joseph Gumbiner (1941–1947), Albert T. Bilgray (1947–1972), Joseph S. Weizenbaum (1972–1993), and Arnold Levine (1994–   ).

References

Herzberg, Nat. "Cornerstone Laying of the First Synagogue in Arizona—1910." *Western States Jewish Historical Quarterly* 19, no. 3 (April 1987): 255–56.
Stocker, Joseph. *Jewish Roots in Arizona* (Phoenix: 1954).
Synagogue Histories File, American Jewish Archives.

ARKANSAS

CONGREGATION B'NAI ISRAEL, REFORM. *Little Rock, Arkansas.* The history of the Congregation B'nai Israel can be traced to a cemetery plot purchased by Morris Navra to bury his child Jonas in 1860. Five years later, a self-constituted committee collected funds for the purchase of a Torah and a shofar in anticipation of the High Holidays that same year. Led by Morris Navra, founders made an effort toward the formal organization of the synagogue in 1866. The new congregation received a charter the following year (as Congregation Children of Israel of Pulaski County). The new synagogue community met in a small rented room on East Markham Street, and in 1869 it purchased land for a synagogue building on Center Street. B'nai Israel engaged Samuel Peck as its first religious leader (1867–1868).

Members established the ritual direction of the synagogue when they adopted Isaac Mayer Wise's *Minhag America* for use in worship services. The congregation celebrated its first Confirmation on Shavuot (Pentecost) in 1873. In addition, in 1873, Congregation B'nai Israel joined the Union of American Hebrew Congregations, the national organization of Reform synagogues, making it one of the first to do so. That same year B'nai Israel purchased an organ for use in the worship services. A short time later B'nai Israel adopted the *Union Prayer Book,* the uniform prayer book of the Reform movement, for worship. Jacob Block served the congregation as its religious leader from 1872 to 1880; he established a school during the first year of his tenure. In 1875, B'nai Israel purchased what is now known as Oakland Cemetery. J. B. Benson served B'nai Israel (1881–1884) before members elected Rabbi Joseph Stolz (a graduate of Hebrew Union College) to the pulpit (1884–1887). Between the years 1887 and 1889, the congregation functioned without the services of a rabbi, although it did engage interim rabbis for the High Holidays and life-cycle events. From 1889 to 1891, Emanuel Schreiber served the congregation, succeeded by Charles A. Rubenstein (1891–1897). In 1897, B'nai Israel erected a second synagogue on Broadway. Next on its roll of rabbis came Harry H. Mayer (1897–1899), to serve in this new location.

In 1908, the temple elected its first woman to the board of trustees. While the Ladies Benevolent Society had been organized in 1867, the congregation's sisterhood affiliated with the National Federation of Temple Sisterhoods in 1928.

B'nai Israel abolished its policy of assigned pews in 1925. Four years later, the congregation organized its Temple Youth Group. In 1930 the men of B'nai Israel formed a Men's Club. That same year, B'nai Israel purchased property to erect a new temple. Yet, the effects of the Depression prevented the immediate erection of a building, even though the congregation's previous home had been sold. In 1934, B'nai Israel revoked its sale agreement and returned to its original building, which it remodeled (rededicated 1937). In 1949, members expanded the facility to include a Temple House.

During the Little Rock racial incidents of the late 1950s B'nai Israel women participated in the "Panel of American Women" designed to promote understanding between Little Rock's ethnic and religious groups. In 1971, the temple at Capitol and Broadway was demolished. Four years later, B'nai Israel dedicated a new temple on Rodney Parham Road.

These rabbis served B'nai Israel in the twentieth century: Louis Wolsey (1899–1907), Louis Witt (1907–1919), James G. Heller (1919–1920), Emanuel Jack (1921–1925), Ira E. Sanders (1926–1963), Elijah E. Palnick (1963–1986), and Eugene Levy (1987–   ). Under Rabbi Levy's leadership, the congregation participated in R.A.I.N. (Regional Aids Interfaith Network) and the Shepherd's Center (an interfaith discussion program). In 1994, membership exceeded 380 family units.

References

One Hundred Twenty-Five Years: Congregation B'nai Israel (Little Rock: 1991).

Sanders, Ira, and Elijah Palnick. *The Centennial History of Congregation B'nai Israel* (Little Rock: 1966).

Synagogue Histories File, American Jewish Archives.

C

CALIFORNIA

TEMPLE BETH SOLOMON OF THE DEAF, REFORM. *Arleta, California.* The Hollywood Hebrew Society for the Deaf (later called the Hebrew Association of the Deaf of Los Angeles) was founded in 1947. However, it was not until 1960, following the search of one Rose Zucker for a way to provide a Jewish education for her deaf daughter, that the first synagogue of deaf Jews in the world was founded. Temple Beth Solomon was incorporated with the help of the Union of American Hebrew Congregations (UAHC) and the advice of Rabbi Solomon Kleinman (for whom the synagogue is named). Beth Solomon remains a pioneer in the exploration of Jewish identity on the part of deaf people. In 1968, the temple affiliated with the National Congress of the Jewish Deaf.

During its first five years, the congregation, known as "the mobile congregation," traveled to various host congregations. However, it spent most of its time at Wilshire Boulevard Temple in Los Angeles. Rabbinical students from Hebrew Union College–Jewish Institute of Religion served the congregation throughout the 1960s and 1970s. In 1965, the congregation purchased facilities in Arleta from Temple Beth Torah, which was relocating. A religious school was established, as was a regular schedule for Shabbat and holiday worship. And in 1981, as a result of a grant from the local Jewish Federation Council's Council on Jewish Life (and UAHC support), various projects of the congregation such as its Visual Media Project and Prayer Book Video Tape Project were launched.

Beginning in 1980, the congregation engaged full-time rabbis: Alan Henkin (1980–1989), Aliza Berk (1989–1991), and Miriam Biatch (1991–   ).

References

Henkin, Alan. "A Brief History of Temple Beth Solomon of the Deaf" (American Jewish Archives, Synagogue Histories File, n.d.).
Synagogue Histories File, American Jewish Archives.

CONGREGATION BETH JACOB, ORTHODOX. *Beverly Hills, California.*
Following an initial discussion in 1925 between Morris Weinstein, E. M. Karas,
and William Weinstein, a group of thirty-three people decided that Jews who
lived in the West Adams area needed a synagogue with a Talmud Torah and
social center close to their homes. This small group chose the name "West
Adams Hebrew Congregation." Historians Max Vorspan and Lloyd P. Gartner
call the congregation "semi-orthodox." The new congregation purchased a lot
at West Adams Street and Hillcrest Drive. By the following year, the women
of the congregation organized a sisterhood. In 1928, the congregation dedicated
its first building.

Rabbi Nathan Addelson joined the congregation in 1933 and remained until
1938. Rabbi Simon Dolgin followed in 1939 and led the congregation from
West Adams to Beverly Hills (1955), gradually moving the congregation to a
more meticulous Orthodox practice. In 1949, Beth Jacob established its own
day school. Changing its name to Hillel Hebrew Academy in 1955, it moved
in 1964 into a new building located one block from the congregation. In 1959,
separate seating was reintroduced to the congregation for the High Holidays.
Up to that time, the congregation maintained separate seating for all services
except for the High Holidays. This decision could have caused a schism in the
congregation. However, the majority of congregants supported the decision, and
membership in the congregation increased.

In 1964, Beth Jacob merged with local congregation B'nai Israel. When Dolgin left the congregation to open a branch of Beth Jacob in Ramot Eshcol
(Jerusalem) in 1971, Rabbi Maurice Lamm succeeded him. Lamm remained with
the congregation until 1984, when Rabbi Abner Weiss was elected to the pulpit.

In 1993, Hillel Hebrew Academy's enrollment stood at nearly seven hundred
students in grades K-8. Membership in Beth Jacob reached about 750 families
the same year. On Sabbath morning, up to seven simultaneous services are in
the congregation. In addition to regular services held in the main sanctuary, a
"no-frills *minyan*" is held, led completely by congregants. There is an additional service led by congregants (with a lesson offered by the rabbi), a Sefardic
minyan led in the style of Jerusalem Sefardim, and a teen *minyan.* Every morning, there are three concurrent services, as well.

References

Synagogue Histories File, American Jewish Archives.
Vorspan, Max, and Lloyd P. Gartner. *History of the Jews of Los Angeles* (Philadelphia:
        1970).

TEMPLE VALLEY BETH SHALOM, CONSERVATIVE. *Encino, California.* In 1950, a group organized High Holiday services in the San Fernando
Valley under the name Encino Jewish Center. The following year a second group

was organized in Sherman Oaks under the title of Valley Institute. This second group split into two groups. One became the Valley Synagogue. The second became the Sherman Oaks Temple. Both splinter groups competed for membership from the earlier Encino Jewish Center. Shortly thereafter, the Sherman Oaks Temple merged with the families of the Encino Jewish Center to form Valley Beth Sholom (*sic*).

Rabbi Henry Radlin joined the congregation as religious leader the following year. After acquiring a lot on Sepulveda Boulevard, the congregation purchased a building from the City of Long Beach and moved it to the new location as a synagogue. At this point, Valley Synagogue joined forces with Valley Beth Sholom. The combined membership of one hundred families established a men's club and a sisterhood.

Rabbi Kalman Friedman joined the temple in 1953. The following year, members acquired an adjacent parcel of land for the expansion of the synagogue. Members initiated daily services. In 1955, Rabbi Sam Sherman succeeded Friedman as an interim rabbi. Under his leadership, the congregation grew to two hundred families through a series of parlor meetings. The synagogue established a school and an extensive program for its youth.

In 1956, Valley Beth Sholom sold its property and purchased a former motel at Densmore and Ventura, converting it for use as classrooms, kitchen, and chapel. In the new location, Rabbi Sydney Guthman joined the temple. Members formed an adult choir to enhance worship.

The following year, members officially changed the name of the synagogue to Valley Beth Shalom. The women of the congregation introduced sisterhood catering and a party shop. Two years later, with a membership of three hundred families, Rabbi Ben Zion Bergman succeeded Guthman. The temple dedicated a new school building in 1961.

A growing membership elected Rabbi Moshe Babin to the pulpit in 1963. Under his leadership, members dedicated a new sanctuary (1964) and a new school building and social hall (1965). Rabbi Matthew Simon came to Encino in 1967, remaining for two years. By 1969, Valley Beth Shalom's membership exceeded five hundred families.

Rabbi Harold Schulweis—whose name is best associated with this innovative congregation—came to Valley Beth Shalom in 1970. Under his progressive leadership, members formed *havurot* (fellowships), establishing a model for other congregations to follow. He also instituted paraprofessional training for members, established a food bank, a counseling center, a community lecture series, and a major choral program. In 1978, Valley Beth Shalom opened its own day school.

Valley Beth Shalom established a program for pararabbinic training in 1979 and a special outreach program for the physically challenged. Other creative programs like Tot Shabbat were started as well. In 1991, the temple dedicated new additions and a complete educational center on Moorpark. In 1994, membership reached 1,760.

References

Schulweis, Harold. *In God's Mirror: Reflections and Essays* (Hoboken, NJ: 1990).
Synagogue Histories File, American Jewish Archives.

CONGREGATION BETH CHAYIM CHADASHIM, REFORM. *Los Angeles, California.* The roots of this congregation can be traced to the development of a gay and lesbian movement in the early 1970s, when groups of Jewish homosexuals began gathering together for religious, educational, and social purposes. Inspired by the existence of the Metropolitan Community Church, the national gay and lesbian Protestant denomination, gay and lesbian Jews founded Beth Chayim Chadashim in Los Angeles in 1972. As the first synagogue of its kind in history, Beth Chayim Chadashim became a place where Jewish lesbians and gay men could shape their own ritual life and social environment. Borrowing prayer books from the Wilshire Boulevard Temple and with the support of the Pacific Southwest Council (regional office) of the Union of American Hebrew Congregations, the congregation began its program of worship and outreach to homosexual Jews. While the existence of the synagogue engendered much discussion and debate, it successfully became a member of the Union of American Hebrew Congregations, the national organization of Reform synagogues, in 1973.

In 1979, the congregation engaged Allen B. Bennett, a member of the congregation, as its first rabbi. In 1983, the congregation joined the movement's formal system for a rabbinic search and engaged Rabbi Janet Ross Marder. Two years later, Beth Chayim Chadashim dedicated its Cele Bernstein Library. In 1986, the congregation established Nechama: A Jewish Response to AIDS (which later became an independent organization known as the Los Angeles Response to AIDS).

In 1989, the congregation engaged Rabbi Denise L. Eger as its religious leader. The following year, the congregation established a children's programming effort and sisterhood. In 1992, Rabbi Marc S. Blumenthal succeeded Rabbi Eger. Following his resignation in 1994, the congregation engaged Rabbi Lisa Edwards to serve its over 325 membership units.

References

Cooper, Aaron. "No Longer Invisible: Gay and Lesbian Jews Build a Movement." In *Homosexuality and Religion,* ed. Richard Hasbany (Binghamton, NY: 1989), pp. 83–94.
Synagogue Histories File, American Jewish Archives.

LEO BAECK TEMPLE, REFORM. *Los Angeles, California.* During an appeal at a meeting of the Wilshire Boulevard Temple Brotherhood, William Rosichan, DeWald Baum, Bertram Harris, and their families joined with other families in order to form Temple Beth Aaron in 1947. Holy Day services that first year were held in a Presbyterian church, and Shabbat evening services were often held in the Rosichan garden. The sisterhood of Wilshire Boulevard Temple helped the young congregation organize a religious school, which met above a market.

In 1948, Rabbi Leo Baeck spoke in Los Angeles. Impressed by his message, several members of Beth Aaron sought to change the congregation's name to Leo Baeck Temple. Through the efforts of Rabbi Alfred Wolf, director of the western region of the Union of American Hebrew Congregations and a former student of Baeck, Baeck gave the congregation permission to use his name. The following year, the congregation secured the services of Rabbi Leonard Beerman, who had just been ordained at the Hebrew Union College–Jewish Institute of Religion. The congregation moved into rented church quarters before it converted a former Canadian Legion Hall. Cantor William Sharlin joined the congregation in 1954. In 1956, land was purchased on North Sepulveda, and a new facility was dedicated and occupied in 1963. Rabbi Sanford Ragins joined the congregation as assistant rabbi in 1964 during Beerman's sabbatical and then left upon his return, only to be invited back as the associate rabbi in 1972. When Beerman retired in 1986, Ragins was named senior rabbi. Arguing that large synagogues become impersonal, the founders of Leo Baeck decided to close its membership and limit it to three hundred. As there are other Reform synagogues in the area, early members were comfortable with the moral impact of this decision. As financial demands made this small membership difficult, the limitation was expanded to the current 750. Leo Baeck generally does not participate with other synagogues in the community, perhaps because it has historically taken bold stands—like promoting the nuclear freeze and advocating pacifism—which is often contrary to the mainstream approach of the Jewish community. Other congregations and rabbis made no secret of their disagreements with the Leo Baeck Temple and, in particular, with Leonard Beerman, its rabbi.

Known for its liberalism, bolstered by the Hebrew prophets and expressed primarily through its extensive program of social action, the congregation is nonetheless somewhat eclectic in its expression of the prophetic principles of Reform Judaism. For example, there is no brotherhood or sisterhood in the congregation. The congregation generally uses its own prayer book, which is noticeably limited in its Hebrew. English renderings of prayers focus on themes of universalism. Participation is encouraged during worship where the sermon is central and the clergy and congregants seldom wear any ritual garb.

References

Furman, Frida Kerner. *Beyond Yiddishkeit: The Struggle for Jewish Identity in a Reform Synagogue* (Albany: 1987).

Synagogue Histories File, American Jewish Archives.

Vorspan, Max, and Lloyd P. Gartner. *History of the Jews of Los Angeles* (Philadelphia: 1970).

BETH ISRAEL/OLIVE ST., ORTHODOX. *Los Angeles, California.* In 1892, an orthodox congregation began to hold services in Forresters Hall in Los Angeles under the name "Bnai Israel." Founders incorporated this congregation two years later as Kehal Yisrael, the name adopted by the group the previous year. The new synagogue held services in McDowell Hall. Shortly after the founding of the Conservative People's Congregation Beth-El (1899), Kehal Yisrael merged with this newly formed synagogue and the Moses Montefiore Hebrew Congregation to form Kehal Adath [Congregation] Beth Israel (Assembled Community of the House of Israel). During 1901, the congregation worshipped in Lincoln Hall on Spring Street. In the new location on Olive Street (dedicated 1902), the congregation came to be known as the Olive Street Shul. Following the move into the new building, the women of Beth Israel formed a ladies auxiliary and organized the Beth Israel Hebrew School (Talmud Torah). In 1906, members purchased cemetery land on Downey Road. In 1907, the congregation merged with Nusach Sefard on Custer Street.

In 1914, Rabbi Isaac Werne became the first religious leader of the congregation. He remained until 1920, but he returned in 1930 and led the congregation until his death in 1942. The Hebrew School moved from the Olive Street location in 1927 to Centennial Street. In 1932, members remodelled the Olive Street synagogue; later they sold it (1940). They sold the Nusach Sefard synagogue building in 1945, when Beth Israel moved to Temple Street. The congregation remained in this Temple Street facility until 1953, when it moved to Beverly Boulevard.

The congregation, which is not affiliated with any national organization, calls itself "traditional." While there has never been a *mechitza* (partition separating men and women during prayer), women are not permitted on the *bima* (raised platform in the front of the synagogue). Since a fire destroyed most temple records, it is difficult to precisely date the temple's activities in the latter part of the twentieth century.

These religious leaders led Beth Israel: Rudolph Lupo (1959–1962), Jacob Levine (1962–1963), and Samuel Lieberman (1964–   ). In 1995, membership of Beth Israel exceeds three hundred family units.

References

Personal interview, Walfish, Hershel. June 7, 1995.
Synagogue Histories File, American Jewish Archives.
Vorspan, Max, and Lloyd P. Gartner. *History of the Jews of Los Angeles* (Philadelphia: 1970).

SEPHARDIC TEMPLE TIFERETH ISRAEL, ORTHODOX. *Los Angeles, California.* Jews from all over the Levant organized Congregation Ahavat Shalom in 1912. Rabbi Alexander Carasso led the fledgling group, which lasted only two years. The group broke up when differences between the Turkish Jews and those from Rhodes could not be resolved. In 1917, the Rhodes group formed the Peace and Progress Society, which later evolved into the Sephardic Hebrew Center, now Sephardic Beth Shalom. Thirty-nine men founded the Sephardic community of Los Angeles (La Comunidad Sefardi) in 1920. Six years later, a third group emerged: the Sephardic Brotherhood, also called Haim Vahessed.

In 1932, members of the Sephardic Community dedicated their new synagogue on the corner of Santa Barbara and La Salle Avenues. While the sanctuary reflected a traditional Sephardic layout (with rows facing one another on the opposite sides of the sanctuary), men and women sat together for worship. In 1959, the Sephardic Brotherhood and the Sephardic Community of Los Angeles merged to become the Sephardic Community and Brotherhood, known today as Sephardic Temple Tifereth Israel. As the congregation grew and the community moved west in Los Angeles, synagogue leadership saw the need for a new synagogue in a new location. In 1963, Rabbi Jacob M. Ott joined the congregation as its spiritual leader. In 1981, the congregation dedicated a new sanctuary on Wilshire Boulevard at Warner Avenue, a gift of the Maurice Amado Foundation. In 1994, the congregation listed membership at over six hundred family units, the largest Sephardic congregation west of New York City.

References

Synagogue Histories File, American Jewish Archives.
Vorspan, Max, and Lloyd P. Gartner. *History of the Jews of Los Angeles* (Philadelphia: 1970).

CONGREGATION SINAI, CONSERVATIVE. *Los Angeles, California.* Early in 1904, less than four years after local residents founded Reform Beth Israel, another group of people joined together to organize a Conservative synagogue. This new Congregation Sinai held its first services at the end of 1906 in B'nai B'rith Hall on Figueroa Street. Arguing that they did not found the congregation in opposition to others, members believed that its interpretation of Conservative Judaism meant that moderate changes should take place in worship. An organ played. The rabbi preached at late Friday evening and Saturday morning services, as well as conducting the liturgy. Sinai also introduced new ceremonies such as confirmation. Members saw Sinai as an attempt to accommodate traditional Judaism to the general environment for acculturated Jews and their children. The intellectual basis for such change, however, was barely visible. The congregation developed rapidly, meeting in rented facilities until it dedicated its own building on Twelfth and Valencia Streets in 1909.

Rabbi Isidore Myers served the congregation for six years; Rabbi Rudolph Farber succeeded him. Yet poor health limited Farber's tenure to three years, when Rabbi David Liknaitz joined the congregation. Liknaitz left after three years, in 1918, citing a lack of religious clarity. He felt Sinai had a "conglomerate ritual," using various prayer books and mixing Hebrew and English prayers. Despite Liknaitz's criticism, the congregation continued to grow rapidly. Rabbi Moses Rosenthal came to the congregation for four years, as the first rabbi ordained by the Conservative Jewish Theological Seminary to serve the congregation, directly linking the congregation with Conservative Judaism with his more traditional tendencies. During his tenure, the congregation contemplated its move to Fourth and Hampshire Avenue.

Rabbi Mayer Winkler left Sinai in 1929 in order to found his own Community Temple. In his place, members installed Rabbi Jacob Kohn in 1931. Rabbi Israel Chodos, a powerful orator, who led the congregation in its move from its Moorish edifice at Fourth and Hampshire to a modern facility on Wilshire Boulevard, succeeded Kohn. Once again, change in Jewish demography prompted a congregational move. In 1956, Sinai purchased land further west on Wilshire Boulevard at Beverly Glen (dedicated 1960). Throughout its tenure in this new location, additional building took place. In 1968, members built a religious school building, especially suited to house Sinai Akiba Academy, a day school founded the same year. In 1981, Sinai built the Kraus Pavilion and Don Rickles Gymnasium. Yet, space remained a commodity. Thus, the congregation intends to build a multipurpose facility adjacent to its current structures. Camp Maoz, Sinai's summer day camp, shares the space, as well. Sinai also claims the twenty-thousand-volume Blumenthal Library. Under the guidance of Rabbi Allan Schranz, it is not unusual for one thousand people to be in attendance for Sabbath morning services.

References

The Burning of the Mortgage, An Historic Record of Congregation Sinai, Los Angeles, California, 1908–1945 (Los Angeles: 1945).
Synagogue Histories File, American Jewish Archives.
Vorspan, Max, and Lloyd P. Gartner. History of the Jews of Los Angeles (Philadelphia: 1970).

STEPHEN S. WISE TEMPLE, REFORM. Los Angeles, California. In 1964, a group of thirty-five families met with Rabbi Isaiah (Shai) Zeldin in order to explore the possibility of forming a new (second) Reform congregation in the Westwood section of Los Angeles. These families were members of Emanu-El of Beverly Hills, where Zeldin served as rabbi. The birth of the congregation included prominent lawsuits and bitter debates at meetings of the Union of American Hebrew Congregations (UAHC), the national organization of Reform synagogues. Representatives of the UAHC were disturbed because members of Emanu-El who joined with Zeldin refused to redeem building-fund pledges to the former institution. As a result, the UAHC refused to admit the new congregation as a member for the first five years of the synagogue's existence. Impressed as a child by Stephen S. Wise, Rabbi Zeldin sought to mold this congregation (and his rabbinate) in Wise's spirit. In the spirit of Wise's democratic Free Synagogue, each member had a voice in decisions and policies affecting the congregation. As the congregation focused on families, the original vision included no sisterhood or brotherhood. Only when the flow of operations required the development of committees would they be formed. Instead, congregational leadership emphasized education and social justice. Originally, Stephen S. Wise Temple members wanted to limit the number of membership families (units) in order to achieve a high level of intimacy among the member families and their rabbi. (Members officially broadened this policy of limiting the size of the congregation in 1969, as the congregation quickly grew in size.) The congregation first started meeting in St. Alban's Episcopal Church. The synagogue used other sites for High Holiday services and the religious school. As attendance at services increased, the congregation sought out permanent quarters and acquired its current property in the San Fernando Valley after only a year of existence.

Though the building project was modest at first, it quickly evolved into a staged plan of buildings on ten acres at Mulholland and Sepulveda. Members dedicated the first building in 1968. In 1970, the Stephen S. Wise Temple merged with the Westwood Temple (whose membership had dwindled, primarily as a result of an impending freeway building project). This merger pushed the ambitious building project further more quickly. Following the merger, which included an active women's group from the Westwood Temple, the women at Stephen S. Wise formed the sisterhood "Wise Woman" in 1970. By 1975 and with the addition of a swimming pool, the Temple had adopted a Religious Jewish Center model for its program (which had been discussed as early as 1970).

This congregation made its mark on the community in various ways. To support its programs, it developed a large rabbinic staff, a fleet of school buses, a major library, a parenting center, and a day school. It continues to build and to grow. Zeldin retired in 1994; Eli Herscher, who had been serving as associate rabbi, became the congregation's religious leader. In 1994, Stephen S. Wise Temple served eighteen thousand people with a membership of over twenty-seven hundred family units and fifteen hundred students in its day-school programs.

References

Plotkin, Fred, et al. *Once upon a Mountaintop* (Los Angeles: 1989).
Synagogue Histories File, American Jewish Archives.
Vorspan, Max, and Lloyd P. Gartner. *History of the Jews of Los Angeles* (Philadelphia: 1970).

UNIVERSITY SYNAGOGUE, REFORM. *Los Angeles, California.* In 1943, five families left a Santa Monica synagogue and joined together for prayer. As more families joined this infant group, they could no longer meet in homes. Even the chapel at the YMCA, which the group used in 1944, soon became too small. By 1945, under the leadership of Rabbi Samuel Chomsky (1943–1946), the congregation moved to the First Congregational Church of Westwood. In 1948, the congregation, named University Synagogue probably because of its proximity to UCLA, moved into a converted church building on Gorham Avenue in Brentwood. There Rabbi Julian Feingold joined as University Synagogue's first full-time rabbi.

By 1950, the membership roster listed three hundred families. A nursery school was started in 1949 and a day camp in 1952. As a result of continued growth, University Synagogue needed larger quarters. The congregation built a new facility on Sunset Boulevard in 1955, much to the chagrin of the planning board, whose rejection of the synagogue's building plan was overturned by the city council. By 1957, the membership roster swelled to nearly 625 families.

Following Feingold's retirement in 1963, Harry Essrig became the University Synagogue's rabbi in 1964. When he left in 1971, membership had dwindled to fewer than 250 families. Following the stabilizing of a financial crisis, which threatened the survival of the synagogue, Allen I. Freehling was named rabbi of the congregation. Under his leadership, the congregation in 1973 became one of the earliest congregations to open its doors to A.A. meetings. University Synagogue continues to host some twelve hundred Jewish people in recovery each week. By 1975, membership was back up to five hundred family units; in 1993, membership reached over eight hundred family units.

References

Synagogue Histories File, American Jewish Archives.
University Synagogue 50th Anniversary (Los Angeles: 1993).
Vorspan, Max, and Lloyd P. Gartner. *History of the Jews of Los Angeles* (Philadelphia: 1970).

WILSHIRE BOULEVARD TEMPLE/B'NAI B'RITH, REFORM. *Los Angeles, California.* German Jews organized Congregation B'nai B'rith in 1862. Members of an earlier congregation, Beth El, which was established in 1861 by Polish Jews (and not heard from following its establishment), joined them in their efforts. The new congregation secured the services of a rabbi shortly after its founding: Rabbi Abraham Wolf Edelman stayed with B'nai B'rith for twenty-five years.

The congregation established *minhag Polen* (Polish ritual practice) as its standard for worship. By 1872, after using public places for worship, the congregation laid a cornerstone on South Fort Street (now Broadway) for its new building, which members dedicated for use the following year. By the end of the 1880s, while B'nai B'rith remained the focal point for religious affairs in Los Angeles and the primary concern of the organized Jewish community, its members infrequently attended the Orthodox worship services. Following the death in 1881 of Joseph Newmark, one of the congregational patriarchs who had led worship prior to the arrival of Rabbi Edelman, members vocalized their demands for change. As a result, B'nai B'rith introduced a mixed choir for the holidays in 1883. The congregation also agitated for shorter services and a Friday evening service with a "lecture."

When the congregation moved from an Orthodox model of worship, Rabbi Edelman resigned. However, he had allowed congregants to remove their hats during sermons (removed fully in 1888), had never opposed family pews, and had even eventually introduced an organ. In 1885, members invited Rabbi Ephraim Schreiber to lead their congregation. During his first services for the high holidays, a group of Orthodox worshippers hotly opposed him. (This group eventually formed Moses Montefiore Congregation with Rabbi Edelman as its leader.) But Schreiber took the congregation forward by introducing Saturday morning children's services and other liturgical reforms. Yet interest in these new innovations waned, and Rabbi Schreiber left the congregation (by mutual consent).

In 1889, Rabbi Abraham Blum took over the reins of the congregation. Curiosity about the new rabbi renewed interest in the congregation, and the trend toward reform continued. Yet economic depression forced the sale of the building on Fort Street. The congregation worshipped in the Unitarian Church (Third and Hill Streets). In 1895, criticism of Rabbi Blum mounted. The temple's board dismissed him amid scandalous speculation. Rabbi Moses G. Solomon replaced Rabbi Blum. That same year, the congregation began to use the *Union Prayer Book*. In 1896, the congregation dedicated a new building.

In 1899, B'nai B'rith elected Dr. Sigmund Hecht as its rabbi. In 1903, the congregation joined the Union of American Hebrew Congregations, the national organization of Reform synagogues, thereby fully adopting a variety of practices consistent with Reform Judaism of the time: the organ, a mixed choir of professional non-Jewish singers with instrumental music, bare heads, one day of holiday observance, English as the basic language of the liturgy, the centrality of the sermon, the rabbi as the leader in worship, and a solemn atmosphere.

Known for his leadership during most of the twentieth century, Rabbi Edgar Magnin was elected as the congregation's assistant (later associate) rabbi in 1915 and assumed full leadership in 1919, when Hecht retired. Magnin remained in that position until his death in 1984. He championed the Americanizing of Reform Judaism, focusing his efforts during worship on creating an atmosphere of dignity, decorum, and solemnity.

In 1922, B'nai B'rith members acquired part of the Wilshire Boulevard property, where the congregation remains. In 1926, Maxwell Dubin was appointed to the position of Director of Religious Education and Social Activities, and the Wilshire Boulevard Temple was dedicated for use. (The congregation adopted the Wilshire Boulevard Temple name in 1933.) Rabbi Alfred Wolf joined the temple staff in 1949 and became the senior rabbi of the congregation following Magnin's death. Wolf led the congregation in the area of interfaith activities and was responsible for the congregational development of both Camp Hess Kramer and Grindling Hilltop Camp.

Wolf retired in 1985, when the congregation named Rabbi Harvey Fields as its senior rabbi. As a result of his personal leadership and interest, Fields led the congregation in the area of adult Jewish studies. At his urging, the congregation adopted the *Gates of Prayer* and a full schedule of family holiday programming. Fields also introduced a new constitution, which limited the length of time a person could serve in office and provided more opportunity for the empowerment of the laity in the congregation. With Fields as the senior rabbi, membership stood at over twenty-five hundred family units in 1994.

References

Breuer, Stephen E. "Cowtown Congregation: The Early Jewish Settlement of Los Angeles—From 1850 through 1885." Synagogue Histories File, American Jewish Archives.

"Congregational Politics in Los Angeles, 1897." *Western States Jewish Historical Quarterly* 6, no. 2 (January 1974): 120–24.

Goldmark, Lawrence. "The History of the Wilshire Blvd. Temple, 1900–1920." Synagogue Histories File, American Jewish Archives.

Kramer, William M., and Reva Clar. "Emanuel Schreiber: Los Angeles' First Reform Rabbi, 1885–1889." *Western States Jewish Historical Quarterly* 9, no. 4 (July 1977): 354–70; 10, no. 1 (October 1977): 38–55.

———. "Rabbi Edgar F. Magnin and the Modernization of Los Angeles Jewry." *Western States Jewish Historical Quarterly* 19, no. 3 (April 1987): 233–51; no. 4 (July 1987): 346–62.

Newmark, Marco. "Wilshire Boulevard Temple/Congregation B'nai B'rith, 1862–1947." Synagogue Histories File, American Jewish Archives.

Owen, Tom. "The First Synagogue in Los Angeles." *Western States Jewish Historical Quarterly* 1, no. 1 (October 1968): 9–13.

"Rabbi Edgar F. Magnin, Leader and Personality." Oral History Interview by Maka Chall, University of California and Judah L. Magnes Memorial Museum, 1975. Synagogue Histories File, American Jewish Archives.

Vorspan, Max, and Lloyd P. Gartner. *History of the Jews of Los Angeles* (Philadelphia: 1970).

YOUNG ISRAEL CENTURY CITY, ORTHODOX. *Los Angeles, California.* Five individuals gathered together in January 1976 to plan a new Orthodox minyan that would serve the Beverly Hills–Beverlywood sections of Los Angeles. By March of the same year, the new synagogue was underway. Initially called Ohavei Israel, the congregation met for Sabbath services in a local hotel and became known as "the Ramada Minyan." By 1978, the congregation outgrew its temporary facilities and rented a local storefront. At that time, members engaged Rabbi Kenneth Cohen to lead them. By 1979, over one hundred people were attending services regularly.

The synagogue affiliated with the National Council of Young Israel in 1982 and officially changed its name to Young Israel of Century City. That same year, the congregation purchased a Pico Boulevard building that its eighty member families converted into a synagogue and began to use in 1983. This Young Israel group engaged its first full-time rabbi, Elazar R. Muskin, in 1986. The congregation doubled its membership within two years of his arrival. By 1993, membership exceeded 215 family units.

Reference

Synagogue Histories File, American Jewish Archives.

ADAT ARI EL CONGREGATION, CONSERVATIVE. *North Hollywood, California.* Although Jews can be traced to the area as far back as 1869, it was not until 1938 that fifteen families led by Dr. Maurice Young joined to create the (San Fernando) Valley Jewish Community Center, the first organized Jewish institution in the San Fernando Valley. A desire to provide a Jewish education for Young's children fueled the effort. In 1939, the wives of the founders formed a sisterhood, which was to provide the nucleus for the Jewish educational program. In 1940, the financial structure of membership changed, as did the group's by-laws, in order to transform the organization from one designed for social purposes and the education of the children (with some religious services) to form a "temple center." At the same time, a small building was purchased on Chandler Boulevard and a rabbi was engaged (Eugene N. Rosenberg), but the building wasn't ready for use until the High Holidays in 1941. The rabbi resigned when it was learned that he had married a Christian woman. Rabbi Sidney Goldstein was then engaged to lead the congregation. Rabbi Goldstein (a Reform rabbi) clashed with the board over various issues, and his call to serve as a chaplain in the U.S. Army provided him with a two-year leave of absence. Rabbis Joseph Levine and Joseph Jasin served in his stead. When Cantor Paul Discount joined the congregation in 1941, a number of figures in the entertainment industry also affiliated, as Discount worked in the Warner Brothers Studio music department. A drive to build larger facilities (to be located on Laurel Canyon Boulevard) began in 1944. The congregation grew rapidly. As the congregation was originally founded as a community center, it had attracted members from all of the major movements. Slowly, these divergent views brought the congregation into crisis. A small group broke away to form the Burbank Jewish Community Center (now Temple Emanuel), and in 1946 fifteen families broke away to found nearby Temple Beth Hillel. The following year, the congregation affiliated with the United Synagogue of America, soliciting its help in the selection of a replacement for Rabbi Goldstein, whose contract was not renewed following his return from military duty.

Rabbi Aaron M. Wise was elected to the pulpit in 1947. Influenced by Mordecai Kaplan, Wise moved quickly to include women in the religious activity of the congregation, calling on girls to read from the Torah on Saturday morning for their Bat Mitzvahs beginning in 1950. In 1949, the David Familian chapel was built. That same year, the congregation organized Camp Emek as a summer day camp. And in 1952, Allen Michaelson was named cantor of the congregation.

The congregation grew steadily, reaching a membership of nine hundred families by 1960, serving over fourteen hundred children in its programs of religious education. Combining this growth with the closing of the synagogue's second-floor classrooms by the city for lacking safety standards, the congregation initiated a new capital building campaign. A new facility was dedicated in 1968. The congregation was heavily involved with politics during the era of the Vietnam War, focusing on the war, civil rights, and fair housing.

In 1972, there was a move to adopt a Hebrew name for the congregation. While other names were suggested, Adat Ari El was chosen. In 1978, Aaron Wise became rabbi emeritus; Moshe Rothblum, who had served the congregation as associate rabbi, was elected to fill the position. Under his guidance, a day school was started at the synagogue. In 1981, a Holocaust memorial was dedicated. By the end of 1985, the educational programs had developed to the point that the congregation became a laboratory school for the University of Judaism. That same year, Allen Michaelson retired as cantor and was replaced by David Silverstein. In 1986, the congregation elected Leslie Alexander as assistant rabbi, the first woman elected to serve as a rabbi in a major Conservative congregation.

References

Rawitch, Cynthia and Robert. *The First 50 Years: Adat Ari El* (North Hollywood: 1988). Synagogue Histories File, American Jewish Archives.

TEMPLE SINAI, REFORM. *Oakland, California.* The first Jewish settlers in Oakland were part of the group of gold seekers who descended on California between 1849 and 1850. Growing out of the Hebrew Benevolent Society organized in 1862, the First Hebrew Congregation of Oakland was incorporated in 1875 by these early settlers. By January of the following year, this small group raised enough funds to purchase land for the building of a synagogue. This growth spurt was followed by two years of relative inactivity, given that the congregation was founded at the onset of one of California's most serious depressions. By 1878, amid signs of economic recovery, members built the first temple on the south side of Fourteenth Street and Webster. Early services were traditional and the Sabbath was "strictly observed," yet the *mechitza,* a partition separating men and women during worship, was quickly abandoned. In 1879, leaders planned the merger of the congregation with the Hebrew Benevolent Society, led by David Hirschberg. Later that year, the Society transferred its cemetery to the congregation; two years later, the remainder of the Society's property followed.

Sinai's first rabbi, Meyer Solomon Levy, came to Oakland in 1881 and remained with the congregation until 1891. In 1881, amidst a heated discussion, David Hirschberg, elected to the presidency of the congregation the following year, convinced a narrow majority to introduce reforms such as a mixed choir, organ music, and the abrogation of the requirement of a minyan (prayer quorum). Following the 1885 Pittsburgh Platform, in which rabbinic leaders stated the working principles of American Reform Judaism, leaders attempted additional reforms, including the adoption of Isaac Mayer Wise's moderate prayer book *Minhag America,* but failed. In the meantime, fire destroyed the synagogue building in 1885. Members erected a new structure on the southeast corner of Thirteenth and Clay Streets and dedicated it the following year. Rabbi Morris Sessler (whose ideas did not harmonize with those of the congregation) succeeded Levy for six months. Rabbi Marcus Friedlander followed, beginning his service to the congregation in 1893. At this time, a financial panic, like the one twenty years earlier though more short-lived, took its toll on the congregation. And so, in 1895, the congregation sold its land, which was by then in the heart of the business district, and moved the synagogue building to a less expensive site at the northwest corner of Twelfth and Castro Streets. Members renovated and rededicated the building in 1896. In this location, under Friedlander's influence and utilizing the strength of past president Abraham Jonas, a gradual shift from traditional practices toward Reform took place. The congregation adopted the Jastrow prayer book, which, though still considered a traditional prayer book, does contain some innovations. By 1908, the congregation began to celebrate the festivals for one day only, with the exception of Rosh Hashanah. The congregation discontinued the practice of auctioning Torah honors, a common practice in orthodox synagogues of the time. Although the congregation had not yet taken an official position on the wearing of head covering, few men chose to cover their heads during worship in the early years of the century. Shortly thereafter, the congregation adopted the *Union Prayer Book*. Friedlander and Jonas published it in an edition revised for the congregation, feeling the earlier edition was too radical.

Members purchased a lot in 1910 on Telegraph near Twenty-sixth (which it did not sell until 1921); however, two years later, a better location was available. In 1914, they dedicated a new building, named Temple Sinai, on Twenty-eighth and Webster Streets. Friedlander left Sinai in 1915, because of the financial strain the new building placed on the congregation; Sinai waited until 1917 to elect Rabbi Harvey B. Franklin to the pulpit, where he led until 1919. Rabbi Rudolph I. Coffee guided the congregation from 1921 to 1933. His liberal politics led the congregation to speak out for disarmament and birth control. He opposed Prohibition and Tammany Hall. Amid growing anti-Semitism, he spoke out against the critics of Jews and Judaism and as an advocate of the separation of church and state. He also favored disarmament. Coffee was forced to leave, as his predecessors, as a result of the congregation's financial instability and for the political stance he had taken for higher salaries for government employees while congregational members were stricken in the midst of the Depression. In 1934 the congregation elected Rabbi William M. Stern (originally Sternseher) to occupy its pulpit. Even more than Coffee, Stern was preoccupied with stopping the spread of anti-Semitism and led congregants by example to join patriotic clubs and service societies. Originally an anti-Zionist, Stern changed his position in the early 1940s, leading the congregation toward a more neutral position. By the time the modern state of Israel was established in 1948, he spoke about "the new Maccabees" and the congregation became decidedly supportive of the Zionist movement. In 1948, Sinai erected and dedicated a Religious School building, followed in 1950 by the construction of the Temple House, Covenant Hall, as it was called.

Stern died in 1965; Sinai leaders brought Rabbi Samuel Broude to lead the congregation the following year. Broude led the congregation toward a reintroduction of ritual. But by the time he came to the congregation, it was already heavily embroiled in the debate over Vietnam and the issue of civil rights in America. The issue of mixed marriage ultimately tested the relationship between Broude and the congregation. Stern had officiated at mixed marriages (under certain conditions), but Broude chose not to do so. A compromise was attempted with the suggestion that a rabbi willing to officiate at mixed marriages be invited to officiate at such ceremonies, but Broude refused. A congregational vote supported the rabbi in 1972, but the debate over rabbinic officiation continued throughout his tenure.

There were other challenges, as well. The post–World War II surburbanization baby boom placed demands on urban synagogues. At one point in 1965, the congregation purchased land as it contemplated another move; but in 1975 the congregation decided to remain in its current location. Instead of building a new building, it would concentrate on serving its membership. Temple Sinai survived the earthquake of 1989 and the Oakland/Berkeley Hills fire of 1991 with minimal damage. However, that great fire displaced nearly forty member families. When Rabbi Broude retired in 1989, the congregation elected Rabbi Steven Chester to the pulpit. In 1993, membership stood at over 640.

References

Rosenbaum, Fred. *Free to Choose: The Making of a Jewish Community in the American West; The Jews of Oakland, California, from the Gold Rush to the Present Day* (Berkeley: 1976).
Synagogue Histories File, American Jewish Archives.
Temple Sinai, 1875–1975 (Oakland: 1975).

KEHILLATH ISRAEL, RECONSTRUCTIONIST. *Pacific Palisades, California.* Led by Maury Leibovitz, who had moved to the area in 1947 (and guided by Dr. Max Vorspan at the University of Judaism), a group of families met in 1948 to begin a discussion concerning the needs of the Jewish community. Under Vorspan's influence, they did not initially seek to establish a congregation. Rather, the early members sought to create an organic Jewish community in which everyone would feel comfortable. Worship services were scheduled on Friday evening at the homes of various members of the original planning committee. Later, the group met at St. Matthew's Episcopal Church and in a variety of other temporary locations. Some discussion arose over which movement this small group would affiliate with; the group borrowed prayer books from the University of Judaism, made a moderate affiliation with the Conservative movement, and adopted the Reconstructionist prayer book. In 1950, the group formally incorporated, taking its name as the Jewish Community of Pacific Palisades and adopting Reconstructionism as its guiding philosophy. Beginning in 1952, Rabbi Abraham Winokur served this fledging group on a part-time basis until the position grew into a full-time position in 1954.

The congregation's first building project became a community effort by its sixty-five member families. A small group of craftspeople donated their talents, and a significant portion of the labor was donated by the members themselves— building first a social hall, office, and kitchen. They built the classroom building and sanctuary in 1960, when membership stood at 147, and added a sanctuary two years later.

When Rabbi Winokur retired in 1980, Rabbi Abner L. Bergman succeeded him. Congregational affiliation stood at 254 households. Bergman left in 1984 and was succeeded by Rabbi Jack Bemporad. Kehillath Israel elected Rabbi Steven Carr Reuben to the pulpit in 1986. At the beginning of his tenure, membership in the congregation numbered 329 family units. Under Rabbi Reuben's guidance, the congregation formed Ethical Action Task Forces. These task forces focus on building literacy, helping homeless people move into permanent housing, feeding the homeless at local shelters, rebuilding race relations (especially after the 1992 Los Angeles riots), looking after the elderly in nursing homes, helping newly arrived Russian families adjust to American life, and reading to children at orphanages and shelters.

In 1994, membership had grown to over 440. As a result, Kehillath Israel is the largest Reconstructionist congregation in the West. The congregation is considering a new building project to meet the needs of its growing membership.

References

The Founding Years 1950–1960: The Creation of Kehillath Israel, the Jewish Congregation of Pacific Palisades (Pacific Palisades, CA: 1960).
Synagogue Histories File, American Jewish Archives.

TEMPLE ISAIAH/JEWISH COMMUNITY CENTER. *Palm Springs, California.* The Palm Springs Jewish Women's Group and the Thursday Night Men's Club, both formed in 1946, joined together to organize the Jewish Community Center (JCC) of Palm Springs in 1947. The JCC sponsored a variety of programs and activities, including a religious school, all of which met in members' homes. In 1949, this small group built a synagogue, adding the name Temple Isaiah. This synagogue community center quickly became the focal point of all Jewish activities in the Palm Springs area. Jews from various movements made their religious home there, including a Hasidic Chabad school for children. The early institutional life of the congregation focused on the education of its youth and adult members. Between 1949 and 1950, the congregation added classrooms to its building. Rabbi Leon Rosenberg joined the JCC in 1954. Under his direction, the congregation developed educational programs such as the Speakers Forum and Educational Series and the Community Forum.

Rabbi Joseph Hurwitz, a graduate of the Conservative Jewish Theological Seminary and active in the field of family counseling, joined the congregation in 1958. Under his direction, the JCC added a religious school building (dedicated 1962). The congregation is not affiliated with any particular movement and serves Reform, Conservative, and Orthodox Jews. In 1995, membership fluctuated at around one thousand family units.

References

Footsteps in the Sand (Palm Springs, CA: 1988).
Synagogue Histories File, American Jewish Archives.

B'NAI ISRAEL, REFORM. *Sacramento, California.* In 1850, the Jewish community of Sacramento formed a Hebrew Benevolent Society to care for the sick within its midst and began gathering for religious services shortly thereafter, meeting in a Methodist Church on Seventh between L and M Streets. In 1852, the congregation, incorporated as Congregation Children of Israel, purchased the lot and building from the church. The building was transported around Cape Horn from Baltimore, where it had been prefabricated in 1849, and became the first synagogue building owned by a congregation in the West. However, the congregation worshiped in the building for only two months before it was destroyed by fire.

Between 1853 and 1858, the congregation occupied three different locations on Fifth Street. In 1858, the congregation purchased a building on Seventh Street from the same Methodist Church from which it had purchased the 1850 property and in the exact same location. At this time, there seems to have been some tension between the Polish and German segments of the synagogue membership; there is evidence of a second congregation meeting separately during the early years of B'nai Israel's history.

During the same year, a Ladies' Benevolent Society was formed; this group would evolve into one of the earliest groups—if not the first—to use the term *Sisterhood.* Samuel Peck served the congregation in 1859, followed by Simon Rosenthal in 1860 and R. M. Cohen from 1861 to 1862. After only two years' residence in this new building, the congregational home was once again destroyed by fire. Members met in Graham's Hall from 1861 to 1863. During this time, Louis Elkus began his thirty-year term as congregational president. M. Silberstein occupied the pulpit from 1862 to 1865.

In 1864, the congregation purchased a building from the First Presbyterian Church on Sixth Street between J and K, consecrating it that same year after extensive remodeling. Soon after the congregation moved into its new home, M. Stamper came to officiate as its religious leader (1865–1868). He was followed by H. P. Loewenthal, who served the congregation for eleven years.

The congregation maintained an orthodox order of worship until 1879, when the beginnings of reform are evident. Under the leadership of M. Gerstman, the reforms included the congregational adoption of *Minhag America* as its official prayerbook, the substitution of three men (for seven) called up to the Torah, the reading (rather than chanting) of the Haftarah, and the dispensing of the services of a *shochet* (ritual slaughterer).

At the same time, an organ was installed in the Temple. Though Gerstman stayed at B'nai Israel for only one year, it seems that not all of the congregants agreed with his reforms. Jacob Bloch came to replace him in 1881 and remained with the congregation until 1884. He was soon followed in 1885 by G. Tau-benhaus, who remained with the congregation until 1888. The congregation was without professional leadership from 1888 to 1889, when Rabbi Joseph Leonard Levy came from England to lead the congregation. He stayed for three years. During his tenure, a heated debate occurred regarding the covering of one's head during worship. As a compromise, members were given the option to cover their heads or not. During the tenure of Rabbi Barnett Elzas, who succeeded Levy in 1893 (serving until 1894), the congregation adopted the *Union Prayer Book,* the uniform prayer book of the Reform movement. In 1895, Rabbi Abram Simon accepted the B'nai Israel pulpit.

During this time in its history, the congregation remained divided regarding the observances of certain practices. Half sat on one side of the sanctuary with covered heads while the other half sat on the other side with bare heads. Some demanded a second day of holiday services, and services were held for those desiring them. In 1895, the congregation affiliated with the Union of American Hebrew Congregations, the national organization of Reform synagogues. Simon left the congregation in 1899.

Rabbi William H. Greenberg occupied the pulpit from 1900 to 1901 and was succeeded by Rabbi Bernard Kaplan (1902–1904), who was followed by Rabbi Montague N. A. Cohen (1904–1907). Cohen arrived in Sacramento shortly before the Sixth Street location was sold; for some months, the congregation met in the IOOF Hall. Members finally occupied the new building on Fifteenth Street in 1904.

Rabbi Michael Fried led the congregation from 1908 to 1924. During his tenure, in 1912, the synagogue building was practically destroyed by fire. The synagogue was rebuilt, and the congregation met in the interim at Westminster Presbyterian Church. Rabbi Harold F. Reinhart led the congregation from 1924 to 1930 and was succeeded by Rabbi Norman Goldburg, from 1930 to 1941. Next came Rabbi Alexander Feinsilver (1941–1946), who was followed by Rabbi Irving Hausman, who served from 1947 to 1964. Hausman ushered in a new era for B'nai Israel, leading the congregation of 250 families to a new site on the corner of Riverside Boulevard and Eleventh Avenue in 1954.

Rabbi Cyrus Afra, an ardent spokesman for the state of Israel, occupied the pulpit from 1965 to 1967. During his tenure, serious discussions took place regarding a possible merger between B'nai Israel and the Mosaic Law Congregation. In 1968, Amiel Wohl became B'nai Israel's new rabbi. He worked to foster better relations between Jews and non-Jews in the community. Congregational membership neared five hundred by the end of his tenure in Sacramento in 1973. When Rabbi Wohl left, about 125 families also left to form another congregation, Beth Shalom. In 1974, the remaining members elected Rabbi Lester Frazin to the pulpit. He concentrated his efforts on rebuilding the congregation, which reached 725 families in 1994. Frazin believed that by making worship services informal, he could attract people to the congregation.

References

Kaplan, Bernard M. "An Historical Outline of the Jews of Sacramento in the Nineteenth Century." *Western States Jewish Historical Quarterly* 23, no. 3 (April 1991): 256–67.

The Seventy-fifth Anniversary of the Consecration of the First Synagogue Building in the West, 1852–1927 (Sacramento, CA: 1927).

Sidewalk History, Pioneer Sites of Old Sacramento (Sacramento, CA: n.d.).

Synagogue Histories File, American Jewish Archives.

BETH ISRAEL, REFORM. *San Diego, California.* In 1851, Jacob Marks and Charles A. Fletcher joined together with Lewis A. Franklin to observe Yom Kippur in his home. Over the next six years, a handful of worshipers gathered annually for the High Holidays. In 1859, the group reached the minimum of ten to make up a minyan. Two years later, the small Jewish community, led by Marcus Schiller, organized its first congregation, Adath Yeshurun, purchasing land for a cemetery. But the drought of 1863, which stifled business, forced most of the Jewish families to leave the area, and apparently Adath Yeshurun dissolved.

Encouraged by the railroad, Schiller tried again in the early 1870s, organizing the First Hebrew Benevolent Society, otherwise referred to simply as the "Hebrew Congregation." But the boom collapsed with the railroad in 1873, and once again few Jewish families remained. According to at least one recollection, an early attempt at organizing B'nai Israel took place in 1876, when a group of local Jewish people rented a hall at Sixth and F Streets. In 1886, the railroad company completed its connection to the East; this began a frenzied building boom in the area. Schiller organized the new Jewish community into Beth Israel, informally established in 1886 and formally incorporated the following year. Riding the boom, the congregation sought to erect a building, only to run into the slump of 1888. Even amid the problems, congregational members decided to build. Swelling the ranks of Congregation Beth Israel to sixty male members, many with families, the congregation sought the services of its first full-time religious leader, Samuel Freuder (1888–1889). In 1889, this community met at Second and Beech Street for worship and celebration of the New Year. Three hundred worshipers gathered for the High Holidays.

As the congregation had previously allied itself with Reform Judaism, this new building reflected certain reforms like mixed seating for worship, an organ, and a choir loft. The zeal of a new era continued when Marx Moses led the congregation (1890–1893). But the collapse of 1886–1888 led to the Panic of 1893, and the congregation cut back considerably. Thus Moses left the congregation. The congregation discontinued Friday evening services, further demoralizing the eighteen to twenty families who remained. As the synagogue building had fallen into relative disuse, the remaining members rented it out to various groups, including the First Universalists and the Christian Scientists.

By 1905, the prosperity of the congregation reflected a revived economy. Jews again came to San Diego. But this time the immigrants (from Eastern Europe) sought Orthodox Judaism and held separate services at the synagogue. In 1909, the congregation engaged Emil Ellinger as its religious leader (1909–1912). He did much to revitalize congregational life, rededicating the temple during the first year of his arrival. By exchanging pulpits with a Unitarian minister, he established a pattern for interfaith relations that remained throughout the history of Beth Israel. Montague N. A. Cohen (1912–1916) succeeded Ellinger. He organized a Beth Israel Young Peoples Club in 1914. Rabbi Julius Halperin succeeded Cohen (1916–1918).

In 1916 the congregation became embroiled with the city over the ownership of the Home of Peace Cemetery, jointly administered by Beth Israel and Tifereth Israel, whose ownership remained. Rabbi Alex Siegel succeeded Halperin, but this rabbi remained with the congregation for only eight months. The congregation remained without the services of a full-time religious leader for an entire year, engaging different individuals to lead High Holiday services. The congregation engaged Rabbi Ernest R. Trattner in 1920 and later, after his resignation in 1922, engaged Maxwell H. Dubin (1922–1925) as religious leader.

The congregation continued to grow and expanded the facilities to meet its needs. In 1920, the congregation moved a recreation center—originally built by the Jewish Welfare Board—to an adjacent lot, serving as a Jewish community center with classes, meetings, and social events. The following year, the synagogue expanded its loft into a full balcony. In order to anticipate future growth, Beth Israel members built a new temple on the corner of Third and Laurel Streets (dedicated 1926). In 1973, the congregation successfully arranged to have the old synagogue building designated as a historic landmark; it later moved the building to Heritage Park near San Diego's Old Town and opened it as a community center and museum in 1989.

These men succeeded Dubin: Jacob K. Levin (1926–1930), H. Cerf Strauss (1930–1934), and Moise Bergman (1934–1946). Fiscal problems during the 1930s threatened to close Beth Israel. During post–Pearl Harbor blackouts, the congregation, which had discussed suspending services entirely, held services in the Council Room of the Temple Center.

Following Rabbi Bergman's retirement, due to ill health, Rabbi Morton J. Cohn joined the congregation (1946). His service began with the reorganization of the Religious School, as well as the establishment of a Men's Club and Youth League. In 1947, he formed two additional groups at the Temple: the Parent-Teachers Association and the Temple Senior League (for young adults in their twenties and early thirties). The synagogue also enlarged its interfaith program during this period of time and instituted an annual Institute on Judaism for local Christian clergy. These rabbis succeeded Cohn: Michael Sternfield (1973–1993), Robert Shapiro (1993–1994), and Jonathan Stein (1994–   ). In 1995, the membership of Beth Israel stood at 1250.

References

Lustig, Myron. *The Anniversary Story* (San Diego, CA: 1951).

Schwartz, Henry. "The First Temple Beth Israel: San Diego." *Western States Historical Quarterly* 11, no. 2 (January 1979): 153–61.

———. "Temple Beth Israel." *Journal of San Diego History* 27, no. 4 (Fall 1981): 227–37.

Synagogue Histories File, American Jewish Archives.

BETH JACOB, ORTHODOX. *San Diego, California.* Following an organizational meeting, founders established Beth Jacob Center and Synagogue in 1939. Shortly after this initial meeting, members converted a house on Thirty-second Street and Myrtle Avenue for use by the congregation. Rabbi Abraham Rosenblum became the first religious leader of the new congregation. Rabbi Baruch Stern joined the congregation in 1950. Three years later, Beth Jacob built its own structure on Thirtieth Street. The congregation affiliated with the Union of Orthodox Jewish Congregations of America.

By 1964, membership reached two hundred families, with 180 children attending the Sunday School. Ten years later, Beth Jacob dedicated its Perlmutter Judaica Library. In 1977, Beth Jacob moved to College Avenue. In order to accommodate members who wanted to live close to the synagogue, Beth Jacob built an apartment building next to the synagogue (1977).

Rabbi Eliezer Langer succeeded Stern in 1977, when the latter retired. Under his guidance the congregation launched a major program in adult Jewish education. In the early 1980s, Beth Jacob dedicated a second set of apartments, Casa Ma'arav. The San Diego Kollel and Esther Soille Mesivta High School are also housed in the apartment building. In 1994, membership at Beth Jacob stood at 220 family units.

Reference

Synagogue Histories File, American Jewish Archives.

CONGREGATION BETH ISRAEL-JUDEA, CONSERVATIVE, REFORM. *San Francisco, California.*

Beth Israel

In 1860, a group of pioneer Jews banded together in order to form the "Congregation Beth Israel." The synagogue, in its incipient stage, leased a small building on the south side of Sutter Street, between Dupont and Stockton Streets. Members held services in that location until 1874. When it outgrew these accommodations, the congregation moved to another leased building on Mission Street, between Fifth and Sixth Streets. It remained there four years.

The group grew so rapidly that it needed larger quarters as early as 1878, when it purchased property on Turk Street between Jones and Taylor Streets. Here Beth Israel erected a synagogue (dedicated 1879). This facility met the needs of the congregation until 1890. When again membership growth forced the congregation to seek larger quarters, Beth Israel built a new structure on Geary Street near Octavia, which became known as the "Geary Street Temple" (1891). In 1905, requiring more space, the congregation began building at another location on Geary, between Fillmore and Steiner Streets. In April 1906, an earthquake completely destroyed the nearly completed building.

Led by Max Goldberg, a synagogue trustee, the distraught congregation (with little funds and occupying rented facilities) sought to rebuild on the site of the demolished structure.

These religious leaders served Beth Israel: M. Wolf (1860–1874), A. Streisand (1874–1878), Rabbi Aron J. Messing, Jr. (1878–1890), M. S. Levy (1901–1916), H. Lissauer (1916–1926), and Rabbi Elliot Burstein (1927–1969).

Temple Judea

Founders established Temple Judea in 1953 in San Francisco, where a new Reform synagogue had not been built in nearly 125 years. Rabbi Robert W. Shapiro served the congregation as its first spiritual leader. Temple Judea purchased land in 1957 (and persuaded the city to change the name of the street from Stanley Drive to Brotherhood Way). It did not build until 1963, following the sale of part of the land to the Jewish Community Center the previous year, the same year Judea engaged Rabbi Herbert Morris (1962).

Beth Israel-Judea

In 1969 Beth Israel merged with Judea: The oldest Conservative congregation in the city merged with San Francisco's youngest Reform synagogue. Rabbi Elliot Burstein of Beth Israel became rabbi emeritus as a result of the merger. During merger discussions, three major issues focused the discussion. As a result, members resolved the following: The new congregation established a restricted kosher kitchen; Rabbi Morris continued to officiate at interfaith marriages; and Judea's custom of reading the Torah on Friday evening continued. According to Rabbi Herbert Morris, the merger led to "a unique and exciting combination of traditional and modern Judaism." As a merged congregation, Beth Israel-Judea expanded its facilities and built a religious school in 1976. In 1995, the congregation listed 486 membership units.

References

Diamond Jubilee Souvenir Volume, Congregation Beth Israel 1860–1935 (San Francisco: 1935).
Messing, Aron J. "A Rabbi's Survey of his Nineteenth Century Career in the West." *Western States Jewish Historical Quarterly* 22, no. 2 (January 1990): 150–51.
Morris, Herbert. *Congregation Beth Israel-Judea* (San Francisco: 1987).
Synagogue Histories File, American Jewish Archives.
Weiner, Carolyn. "The Merger of Synagogues in San Francisco." *Jewish Journal of Sociology* 14, no. 2 (December 1972): 167–96.

BETH SHOLOM, CONSERVATIVE. *San Francisco, California.* A small group of individuals who met in privates homes for worship founded Congregation Beth Sholom in 1906, the year of the great San Francisco earthquake and fire. The congregation moved into its first permanent facility on Fourth Avenue, a former Baptist Church, in 1921, when it took the name Beth Sholom.

The congregation outgrew this building and moved to its current location at Fourteenth and Clement Street in 1934. This facility was expanded in 1960 and in 1965. In 1935, Rabbi Saul White, a graduate of the Jewish Institute of Religion in New York, joined the congregation. White served the congregation until 1976. It was not until 1946 that Beth Sholom joined the United Synagogue of America, the umbrella organization of Conservative synagogues in North America. At about the same time, the congregation eliminated separate seating for men and women.

In 1970, Beth Sholom became one of the first Conservative congregations to allow the Bat Mitzvah to have an *aliyah* to the Torah, although it had celebrated Bnot Mitzvah on Friday evenings for many years. More recently, Beth Sholom began the practice of counting women in its minyan (prayer quorum).

Following Rabbi White's retirement, due to a serious illness, several rabbis were elected to lead the congregation: Allan Schranz, Alexander Graubart, and Jacob Milgrom. In 1991, Rabbi Alan Lew became Beth Sholom's rabbi.

Under Rabbi Lew's guidance, the synagogue discontinued the gender-specific groups of sisterhood and brotherhood, replacing them by activity-specific groups like Vaad Zedek (social action), Bikur Cholim (visiting the sick), and a *chevra kadisha* (which prepares the body for burial and assists those in mourning). In 1993, membership stood at 450 family units.

Reference

Synagogue Histories File, American Jewish Archives.

CONGREGATION EMANU-EL, REFORM. *San Francisco, California.* Among the gold-rush pioneers of 1849 were Jews of German ancestry who sought to develop a Jewish community with those few who had preceded them by only a few years. And so, some thirty Jews worshipped together for the first time, in a makeshift tent, in San Francisco during the High Holidays of 1849. Because of what appears to have been a calendar miscalculation, a second Yom Kippur service was also held in a room on the west side of Montgomery between Washington and Jackson Streets (where the Metropolitan Theater was later built). This second service appears to have attracted fifty people.

Congregation Emanu-El was incorporated in 1851 with forty members, less than two years after these services, with Emanuel Berg as its president. It appears that the group that eventually formed Emanu-El was part of the original Sherith Israel venture, but it went its own way when the two groups could not reach a compromise between their religious traditions. While the congregation initially followed an orthodox pattern of worship and ritual, such practice met with great difficulty.

In 1854, Julius Eckman assumed his duties as Emanu-El's first rabbi. Some changes, like a mixed choir, were made before Eckman's arrival; and he established a daily religious school and continued the orthodox ritual in the congregation. By this time, the membership had already grown to nearly 175. However, such success was short lived. In 1855, the congregation was beset by financial problems. Membership dropped by one-half, and Rabbi Eckman resigned, probably more because of personality conflict than because of the congregation's financial instability. Hoping to attract new members and making a marked change from orthodoxy, the congregation purchased a melodeon for use during worship services.

The congregation was struggling with religious reform and moving toward Reform Judaism during this period of time. By 1860, the congregation began to grow once again and the search for a new synagogue site was initiated; in the same year, Dr. Elkan Cohn joined the congregation as its rabbi. (He served until his death in 1889.) He immediately proceeded to reorganize the congregation, concentrating both on religious education and on ritual. The building campaign resulted in the purchase of a lot on Sutter Street the following year; the building was dedicated in 1866. Among other reforms, Cohn instituted late Friday evening services (one of the first rabbis in the country to do so), gave up the wearing of prayer shawl and head covering, eliminated the observance of Hoshanah Rabbah, and permitted men and women to sit together during worship. A short time later, girls were invited to join the religious school. For some, these reforms were intolerable. In 1864, after a heated debate over the introduction of *Seder Tefillah* (a moderate prayer book prepared by Rabbi Leo Merzbacher), a group resigned to form Congregation Ohabai Sholome. This placed great financial strain on the congregation but allowed more rapid reform to take place. Although the new building on Sutter Street survived the earthquakes of 1866 and 1906, the interior was destroyed by a fire during 1906; it was rebuilt and rededicated the following year.

In 1877, the congregation voted to give its support to Hebrew Union College and formally ally itself with the Reform movement, the first western congregation to do so. While debate continued over issues like the wearing of a hat, the congregation passed a resolution in 1881 to require worshipers to sit with their heads uncovered. In 1886, Dr. Jacob Voorsanger was named assistant rabbi. That same year, copying other congregations, Emanu-El unsuccessfully experimented with moving Friday evening services to Sunday morning. In 1889, Voorsanger succeeded Cohn, and he remained rabbi until his own death in 1908, at a young age. With Voorsanger, the congregation made numerous additional reforms including the introduction of modern music and hymns for worship and the reading (rather than chanting) of the Torah. Voorsanger added dignity and decorum to the service, and women were given equality in religious obligation and practice. While many of the reforms that would identify Emanu-El were established by Cohn, it was left to Voorsanger to articulate for the community the philosophy of Reform Judaism that fueled the congregation.

After Voorsanger's death, Rabbi Martin Abraham Meyer, a Zionist, served the congregation, from 1910 until his sudden death in 1923. During his tenure, the congregation grew. He opened religious school branches in suburban communities, leading worship services there as well. In 1911, a building for religious education was erected on Sutter Street between Van Ness Avenue and Franklin Street. Meyer also sought to restore certain traditional rituals to the service, such as public prayers for the sick and the naming of babies in the synagogue. In addition, he worked on behalf of women, establishing a Women's Guild in the congregation in 1917. Following Meyer's death, Louis I. Newman was elected to the pulpit to succeed him (1924). During his tenure the congregation moved into a new building at Arguello Boulevard and Lake Street in 1926. Newman left the congregation in 1930 in order to lead New York's Congregation Rodeph Sholom. Rabbi Irving F. Reichert took his place and remained in the pulpit until 1947 when he was named rabbi emeritus, leaving the pulpit rabbinate at a relatively young age. Like Voorsanger, Reichert was a defender of classical Reform Judaism and an anti-Zionist. It was his liberal leadership that led the congregation to open its gymnasium as a dormitory for the homeless and unemployed. Later, in 1941, the facilities of the Temple were offered to the commanding general of the Presidio. But the congregation did not grow under Reichert's leadership.

Rabbi Alvin I. Fine was elected to the pulpit in 1948. Fine challenged the congregation to reintroduce certain traditional rituals and garments, such as the wearing of the prayer shawl by rabbi and cantor and the introduction of Hebrew (and a positive approach to Israel) into the religious-school curriculum. Fine was a Labor Zionist, a foe of McCarthyism, and a fighter against racial discrimination. While he led the congregation in this direction (and it grew under his leadership), the heat of controversy was constantly felt during his tenure. As a result of concern over his health, Fine resigned in 1964 and was succeeded by Irving Hausman. Rabbi Hausman served less than a year, stricken by a rare disease that left him paralyzed. He was forced to resign in 1967.

In 1968, Rabbi Joseph Asher (originally Ansbacher) was invited to lead the congregation. Opposing the Vietnam War and supporting busing, he was particularly interested in the centrality in Judaism of the struggle for social justice. While he engaged the congregation in fierce debate over these issues, membership continued to decline at Emanu-El. Following its historical pattern of activity, Emanu-El continued to offer its congregants a rich menu of Judaic offerings, including educational programs for all ages. The 1970s proved to be as financially difficult as were the times of the Great Depression. When Asher retired in 1985, he was succeeded by Robert Kirschner, who was forced to resign in 1993 and was succeeded by Rabbi Stephen Pearce. Membership in 1994 reached nearly 1450.

References

Kahn, Edgar M. "The Saga of the Congregation Emanu-El." Synagogue Histories File, American Jewish Archives.

————. "The Saga of the First Fifty Years of Congregation Emanu-El." *Western States Jewish Historical Quarterly* 3, no. 3 (April 1971): 129–47.

Kramer, William M., and Norton B. Stern. "A Search for the First Synagogue in the Golden West." *Western States Jewish Historical Quarterly* 7, no. 1 (October 1974): 3–21.

Rinder, Rueben. *The Story of Congregation Emanu-El* (San Francisco: 1958).

Rosenbaum, Fred. *Architects of Reform: Congregational and Community Leadership, Emanu-El of San Francisco, 1849–1980* (Berkeley, CA: 1980).

Silverstein, Alan. *Alternatives to Assimilation: The Responses of Reform Judaism to American Culture 1840–1930.* (Hanover, NH: 1994).

Synagogue Histories File, American Jewish Archives.

Temko, Allen. "A Glory of the West," *Commentary* 26, no. 2 (August 1958): 107–18.

Zucker, Jeffrey S. "Cantor Edward J. Stark at Congregation Emanu-El." *Western States Jewish Historical Quarterly* 17, no. 3 (April 1985): 231–49; 17, no. 4 (July 1985): 315–24.

CONGREGATION SHA'AR ZAHAV, REFORM. *San Francisco, California.* Congregation Sha'ar Zahav, the Congregation of the Golden Gate, was established in 1977 by three men who had a desire for spiritual growth and for the companionship of other Jewish gay men and lesbians. It identifies itself as a "progressive reform Jewish congregation with a special outreach to lesbians and gay men." What identified this congregation in its early years was its emphasis on volunteerism and the participation of congregants in all of the affairs of the congregation, including the leading of worship services and the administrative functions of the synagogue office, with a balance of "gender parity and equality" throughout the institution, devising "a homegrown system of co-leaders," as they are called. This system was changed in 1980, when these leadership positions were replaced by the normative president and vice-president structure more common to synagogues, with one exception: the roles alternate between men and women in alternating years.

In the early years, Sha'ar Zahav met at various locations, including a Buddhist monastery, often struggling for public recognition. In 1978, the congregation met at the Jewish Community Center; only two years earlier the *Northern California Jewish Bulletin* refused to allow the congregation to advertise for services. In 1982, the congregation prepared its own liturgy, *Machzor U'v'charta Bachayim.* In 1983, the congregation purchased a building, the former church of Latter-day Saints at Caselli and Danvers, the same year it affiliated with the Union of American Hebrew Congregations, the synagogue organizational arm of the Reform movement. It is also a member of the World Congress of Gay and Lesbian Jews. In 1988, the congregation opened Kadimah, its religious school for children.

Following a major discussion concerning the direction of the congregation with regard to rabbinic leadership, Rabbi Yoel Kahn became Sha'ar Zahav's first full-time rabbi in 1983, but members continue to lead services. When Rabbi

Kahn joined the congregation, Sha'ar Zahav estimated its membership at two hundred people. In 1993, it numbered approximately 525 individuals.

Reference

Synagogue Histories File, American Jewish Archives.

CONGREGATION SHERITH ISRAEL, REFORM. *San Francisco, California.* The congregation can be traced back to 1849, when a group of pioneers met for the High Holidays. As Passover approached, this *minyan* (prayer quorum) grew to one hundred pioneers at a Passover seder meal. This gathering formed a temporary congregation under the name "Sherith Israel," taking a phrase from the book of Isaiah meaning "loyal remnant of Israel." Later, in 1850, the group met again and formed a permanent congregation with the requisite constitution and by-laws. It appears that the group that eventually formed Emanu-El was part of this original venture, but went its own way when it and the congregation could not reach a compromise about the preferred approach to Jewish ritual. They rented rooms in the Merchants Court on Washington Street, between Montgomery and Sansome. These temporary quarters were destroyed by fire in 1851, when the congregation moved to a new site on Kearny Street between Washington and Jackson. This site too was later destroyed by fire.

Julius Eckman resigned from Emanu-El and became Sherith Israel's rabbi, but here too, where members interpreted Jewish law more strictly than at Emanu-El, he was considered "old-fashioned." After a few months, he resigned. It was two years after Eckman's resignation before Dr. Henry A. Henry arrived from London to serve Sherith Israel. Henry retired in 1869; Rabbi Aron J. Messing, Jr. succeeded him the following year. Thinking that the congregation was Orthodox and not understanding that congregants—not rabbis—determined synagogue policy in North America, his tenure was only three years. Even the modest reform of mixed seating was too much for him.

On August 6, 1854, the cornerstone for a permanent synagogue was laid on Stockton Street, between Broadway and Vallejo. The congregation called this location home until August 26, 1870, when it dedicated a new synagogue at Post and Taylor. Rabbi Falk Vidaver led the congregation from 1883 to 1892. He had replaced his brother Henry, who had died the previous year. In 1893, Rabbi Jacob Nieto came to the congregation. He served until 1930.

On February 22, 1904, the congregation moved again—to California Street. Although much of the surrounding area was destroyed by the great earthquake and fire of 1906, Sherith Israel survived the smoking ruins in that part of the city. As a result, the city used the building for its Superior Court for two years.

Rabbi Jacob J. Weinstein became Sherith Israel's rabbi in 1930. His constant advocacy of social justice led to disharmony in the congregation that forced his resignation in 1932. Rabbi Morris Goldstein succeeded him in 1932, serving until 1972. It was not until 1949 that the entire lower floor of the synagogue building was reconstructed, with new offices, classrooms, and a chapel. That same year, a new Temple House was also built adjacent to the Temple itself. It contained classrooms, kitchen facilities, and a large all-purpose auditorium.

In 1972, Sherith Israel's six hundred member families elected Rabbi Martin Weiner to its pulpit. By reaching out to the Jewish community in Marin county, the congregation increased its membership considerably. The synagogue also received national recognition for its work in absorbing immigrants from the former Soviet Union. In addition, Rabbi Weiner emphasized youth and social action during his tenure with the congregation. In 1994, membership in Sherith Israel stood at fifteen hundred.

References

Congregation Sherith Israel Collection, Western Jewish History Center, Judah L. Magnes Museum.

Feldstein, Janice J. *Jacob J. Weinstein, Advocate of the People.* (New York: 1980).

Henry, Marcus H. "Henry Abraham Henry, San Francisco Rabbi, 1857–1869." *Western States Jewish Historical Quarterly* 10, no. 1 (October 1977): 31–37.

Kramer, William M., and Norton B. Stern. "A Search for the First Synagogue in the Golden West." *Western States Jewish Historical Quarterly* 7, no. 1 (October 1974): 3–21.

Stern, Norton B. "A San Francisco Synagogue Scandal of 1893," *Western States Jewish Historical Quarterly* 6, no. 3 (April 1974): 196–203.

———. "An Orthodox Rabbi and a Reforming Congregation in Nineteenth Century San Francisco." *Western States Jewish Historical Quarterly* 15, no. 3 (April 1983): 275–81.

Synagogue Histories File, American Jewish Archives.

Temko, Allen. "A Glory of the West." *Commentary* 26, no. 2 (August 1958): 107–18.

Zwerin, Kenneth C. "Rabbi Jacob Nieto of Congregation Sherith Israel." *Western States Jewish Historical Quarterly* 18, no. 1 (October 1985): 30–42; 18, no. 2 (January 1986): 159–70; 18, no. 3 (April 1986): 243–55.

EMANU-EL, REFORM. *San Jose, California.* Like many communities, the San Jose Jewish community did not see the need to organize until it experienced its first death in 1857. In 1861, three men advertised a meeting "for the purpose of organizing a Hebrew society." The group would conduct its first holiday services that year. It incorporated the following year and immediately initiated a building fund. In 1863, founders purchased a lot on the northeast corner of Third and San Antonio Streets. Yet, the city waited until 1869 before deeding three acres of its Oak Hill Cemetery to the "San Jose Bickur Cholim Society," upon petition of its "Hebrew citizens." That same year, local women organized a Hebrew Young Ladies Benevolent Society. Men formed a similar but short-lived association in 1872.

In 1870, the congregation's membership of only thirty-nine families dedicated the Bickur Cholim synagogue. Meyer Solomon Levy arrived from London in 1873 to lead the congregation as its first ordained rabbi. The following year, Rabbi Levy officiated at the city's first (all-girl) confirmation ceremony; he left to serve Temple Sinai in Oakland in 1881. These men succeeded him as religious leaders: Henry Philip Loewenthal (1881–1893), Gustave Adolph Danziger (1894–1896), Aaron B. J. Brown (1897–1899), and Julius David Nathanson (1903–1916). At times, the temple went without rabbinic leadership. Emanu-El affiliated with the Reform movement by joining the Union of American Hebrew Congregations, the national organization of Reform synagogues, in 1917, although there remained in the congregation a significant and vocal traditional element. Rabbi Harvey B. Franklin, engaged in 1921, tried to meet the diverse needs of the congregation by holding traditional services followed by Reform services during the High Holidays. Under his direction, the congregation built a community house adjacent to the synagogue (1923).

In 1940, fire destroyed the seventy-year-old synagogue building. As a result, members sold the property in 1948. Delayed by World War II, the congregation built a new synagogue, Temple Emanu-El, at University and Myrtle Street. In 1950, the congregation engaged a new spiritual leader, Rabbi Joseph Gitin. Following his arrival, the community grew rapidly. The synagogue expanded in three phases during the 1950s (a social hall in 1955, a chapel in 1956, and a school building in 1959). As the congregation grew, it helped to establish additional synagogues in the Santa Clara Valley, an area of rapidly expanding Jewish communities. Under Gitin's direction, the congregation became a catalyst for community interfaith activities. In addition, members of Emanu-El helped to establish other synagogues in the Santa Clara Valley, such as Congregation Sinai in 1952.

David Robins succeeded Joseph Gitin when he retired in 1976, becoming rabbi emeritus. Under the guidance of Fred W. Marcus, who served as the synagogue's educator from 1964 to 1981, the religious school became the first to be accredited by the UAHC in 1970. During the tenure of Rabbi Robins, members remodeled the *bimah* (raised platform in the front of the sanctuary). In 1985, members named Dr. Jonathan V. Plaut as senior rabbi. Under his guidance, Emanu-El remodeled its community house and transformed the social hall into a multipurpose room known as the Temple House (1986). Plaut left the congregation in 1993; Rabbi Alan Berg succeeded him the following year. In 1995, membership stood at over five hundred family units.

References

Synagogue Histories File, American Jewish Archives.
Temple Emanu-El of San Jose, 125th Anniversary Commemorative Yearbook (San Jose, CA: 1987).

COLORADO

BETH HAMEDROSH HAGODOL, ORTHODOX. *Denver, Colorado.* Henry Plonsky founded the Beth Hamedrosh Hagodol (BMH) as an Orthodox congregation in 1897, and he remained president until 1927. That first year, Hyman

Saft led worship services for the congregation in Plonsky's shoe store on Larimer Street. The congregation then moved to a location on Nineteenth and Curtis Streets for a short time before purchasing a large synagogue building on Twenty-fourth and Curtis Streets from Congregation Emanuel in 1898. That same year, Rabbi R. Farber joined the congregation; he served until 1901. Rabbi Charles Eliezer Hillel Kauvar succeeded Farber and served the congregation until 1952. As an active leader in community affairs, Kauvar helped to found the Jewish Consumptive Relief Society in Denver (1904) and the Denver Hebrew School (1905). Other rabbis included Gershon Winer (1954–1956), Samuel Adelman (1957–1967), and Elihu J. Steinhorn (1967–1971).

In 1921, BMH moved to a facility at Sixteenth and Gaylord. In 1956, the congregation left the United Synagogue of America, the national organization of Conservative Synagogues, which it had joined in founding. In 1967, BMH moved to South Monaco; in 1972, Rabbi Stanley Wagner came to the congregation. That same year, BMH joined the Union of Orthodox Jewish Congregations of America, a national organization of Orthodox synagogues. Under Wagner's leadership, the congregation embarked on a strong educational program, including many adult education courses. During his tenure, the congregation grew to over eight hundred families and built the Mizel Museum of Judaica. Its religious school, called the Community Talmud Torah, is a cooperative venture among BMH, Congregation Beth Joseph (Orthodox), and Congregation Rodef Shalom (Conservative). At the risk of being expelled from the Union of Orthodox Jewish Congregations, BMH remains as one of the few Orthodox congregations with mixed seating. As a compromise, it holds a secondary service with separate seating for men and women. It refrains from the use of a microphone on Sabbath and holidays—except for Rosh Hashanah and Yom Kippur, when more than sixteen hundred worshipers are in attendance. The synagogue also established a regional office for the National Conference of Synagogue Youth, the Orthodox Union's youth movement. In addition, the synagogue brings many speakers to the community from the Orthodox Union in order to maintain connections with this organization. In an effort to include women in ritual, BMH permits women to introduce the Torah and Haftarah readings, as well as to deliver sermons and addresses to the congregation.

Reference

Synagogue Histories File, American Jewish Archives.

CONGREGATION EMANUEL, REFORM. *Denver, Colorado.* The development of several organizations, prior to the formal founding of Congregation Emanuel in 1874, contributed to the synagogue's growth. Established in 1866, the Hebrew Cemetery Association, also referred to as the Hebrew Burial and Prayer Society, held services on various holidays and festivals. The community formed the Hebrew Benevolent Society in 1871; the following year, women created the Hebrew Ladies' Benevolent Society. Denver's small community of

Jewish men established the Denver lodge of B'nai B'rith the same year. And in 1872, A. H. Fleischer led services at Congregation Emanuel, which met "every Friday evening and Saturday at their hall" on Holiday Street (now called Market Street), according to the *City Directory*. Two years later, this group of Jews decided to prepare a constitution and to incorporate their congregation.

As part of its constitution, the congregation adopted Reform Judaism and chose Isaac Mayer Wise's *Minhag America* as its official prayer book. Early discussions took place concerning locating a place of worship, and a temple was constructed in 1875 at Nineteenth and Curtis Streets. Shortly thereafter, an organ was purchased and installed, and professional singers were engaged to augment a volunteer choir. Such ritual decisions were not easily made. In 1876, a dispute developed over the use of the *shofar*. A compromise was eventually reached: "the *shofar* would be blown only once, and that at the morning service." The debate over hats, which was never officially resolved, went on for several years. Eventually, the decision was made de facto by the majority of men, who chose not to cover their heads during worship.

By 1875, the congregation decided it was ready to engage a rabbi. Yet finances continued to be a problem threatening the viability of the synagogue. The congregation survived its financial difficulties, establishing a religious school in 1876. That same year, Emanuel joined the Union of American Hebrew Congregations. However, because of a variety of problems generally unrelated to the finances of Emanuel, religious leaders quickly came and went: Samuel Weil (1877), Marx Moses (1878), Henry Bloch (1878), M. Elkin (1881–1883), Rabbi Emanuel Schreiber (1883–1885), and Rabbi J. Mendes de Sola (1885–1889).

During Elkin's tenure, there was talk about building a new synagogue. The eventual sale in 1881 of the temple to Ahawu Emuno, Denver's first Orthodox synagogue, spurred this activity. Congregation Emanuel constructed a new synagogue building in 1882 at Twenty-Fourth and Curtis Streets. With this new building came nagging financial problems. It seems unbelievable, but an innovative and rather aggressive fair raised the necessary money and the congregation paid off its entire debt. In 1897, the synagogue suffered a serious fire. The congregation met temporarily in the Unity Church until a new building was built at Sixteenth and Pearl Streets, selling its former holdings to the Beth Hamedrosh Hagodol congregation. This building at Pearl Street is now known as the Pearl Street Temple Center and has become a multipurpose community performance and conference center.

Temple Emanuel engaged Rabbi William S. Friedman, a graduate of Hebrew Union College, in 1889, and he led the congregation until 1938. Friedman led the congregation to create a Temple Emanuel Alumni Association for post-confirmands, the Temple Emanuel Literary Society, and a kindergarten at Fourteen and Blake Streets. When the congregation became fearful that he would take a position at Temple (Adath) Israel in Boston—a position to which he was unanimously elected—Friedman was given a life contract at Emanuel. Yet,

Friedman administered the synagogue with his own friends as part of a self-perpetuating board. Following a sermon in 1910 in which Friedman verbally attacked several men in the congregation—and threatened the stability of the temple—Friedman's hegemony over the congregation was questioned, but quickly restored.

In 1909 the congregation took over the Hebrew Burial Society, which had been founded independently in 1860. Though the congregation considered moving as early as 1912 to a site between York and Columbia Streets and between Ninth and Eleventh Streets that had been the Old Capitol Hill Cemetery, the plan was suddenly abandoned in 1922 because of what were considered exorbitant architectural fees. A more modest plan of action was taken when the congregation purchased four lots south of the current location and enlarged the facility, which it dedicated in 1924. By this time, the congregation had grown to a membership of 486 families.

After Rabbi Friedman was disabled by a stroke in 1938, Congregation Emanuel engaged an interim rabbi, Ernest Trattner, until Friedman initiated the process to become emeritus. In 1939, Rabbi Abraham Feinberg was engaged by the congregation. Feinberg immediately changed practices that Friedman had put into place, introducing Hebrew in the program of religious education and encouraging the Bar Mitzvah, at which Friedman had officated with great reluctance on several occasions.

Feinberg was active in working with armed-services personnel and developed many programs at the congregation for them. His introduction of Sunday services in 1942 was said to be for their benefit. Eventually Feinberg decided to become a chaplain, and he resigned from the congregation in 1943. In fact, physical requirements prevented Feinberg from entering the chaplaincy, and instead he went to Holy Blossom Temple in Toronto. Rabbi Herbert Friedman was elected to the pulpit in 1943, having been brought to the congregation as assistant only several months earlier. A disciple of Stephen S. Wise, Friedman did not hesitate to use the pulpit in the espousal of Zionism and democratized the congregation, allowing congregants, for the first time since the congregation's early days, to participate in congregational affairs.

Freidman worked hard to build up the educational programs of the temple, later bringing Rabbi Joel Zion as assistant to focus on the educational needs of the congregation. Both rabbis, Friedman and Zion, advocated for changes in ritual, including the introduction of more Hebrew into the liturgy. The congregation received as a donation in 1952 what eventually became Shwayder Camp, and Rabbi Zion transformed it into a successful experiment in informal Jewish education. When Friedman left the congregation in 1952, Zion became the rabbi of the congregation and Rabbi Richard Hirsch was engaged as assistant. When problems of divided responsibility and authority between Zion and Hirsch arose in 1956, both submitted their resignations. That same year, the congregation installed Rabbi Earl Stone as its rabbi.

In 1957, the congregation moved to the Hilltop area in the eastern part of the city, between Grape and Glencoe Streets and between Ellsworth and First Avenues. Emanuel built a new sanctuary the following year.

Rabbi Stephen Foster joined the congregation as assistant rabbi in 1970 and succeeded Stone when he retired in 1981. In 1994 the congregation served over sixteen hundred membership units.

References

Breck, Allen Dupont. *The Centennial History of the Jews of Colorado, 1859–1959* (Denver: 1960).
Hornbein, Marjorie. "Denver's Rabbi William S. Friedman: His Ideas and Influence." *Western States Jewish Historical Quarterly* 13, no. 2 (June 1981): 142–54.
———. *Temple Emanuel of Denver: A Centennial History* (Denver: 1974).
Synagogue Histories File, American Jewish Archives.
Uchill, Ida Libert. *Pioneers, Peddlers, and Tsadikim* (Denver: 1957).

CONNECTICUT

B'NAI ISRAEL, REFORM. *Bridgeport, Connecticut.* When the Connecticut General Assembly passed legislation in 1843 that permitted Jews freedom of religious expression, Jews began to immigrate to the Bridgeport area. In 1852, several immigrant families from Germany gathered for worship. Though they initially gathered for the purpose of acquiring land for use as a cemetery, they organized Congregation B'nai Israel for the purpose of worshipping in 1859. However, it did not receive a state charter until 1895. A. Jacobs served the congregation as its first "rabbi" and the congregation followed an orthodox ritual, with women sitting separate from men during worship. A Hebrew School was established in 1863.

During its early years, as the congregation did not have a permanent meeting place, it met in lofts, storefronts, and in people's homes. In 1875, a Ladies Hebrew Charitable Society was formed to help alleviate the needs and suffering of immigrants who were coming into the city.

In 1885, as the ritual of the congregation became more liberal, a small group broke away in order to form the orthodox congregation Adath Israel. During that same year, B'nai Israel began its planning for a permanent building. As plans for the building were being formulated, a second group broke away in 1909 to form Rodeph Sholom, a congregation that later became Conservative.

In 1911, the membership of B'nai Israel built its first synagogue structure, which came to be known as the Park Avenue Temple at the corner of Park Avenue and Washington Avenue. In this new building, evidence of Reform Judaism was obvious in its family pews, the absence of Hebrew in worship, and a decorous Sabbath service. This trend evolved into a study of Reform Judaism by the congregation and the eventual adoption of the Reform *Union Prayer*

Book in 1916. B'nai Israel later affiliated with the national Reform organization, the Union of American Hebrew Congregations.

Through the efforts of its women's auxiliary (later called sisterhood), formally established in 1911 and merged in 1917 with the Ladies Aid Society, the congregation offered free religious education to the community without regard to synagogue affiliation. It wasn't until 1934 that women of the congregation were permitted to attend congregational meetings and shortly thereafter given the right to vote. The first Bar Mitzvah took place at B'nai Israel in 1951, but the first Bat Mitzvah had to wait until 1973.

The suburbanization of the community after World War II placed demands on the Temple building, and it became obvious that a new structure was needed. In 1958, the second Park Avenue Temple was completed for use.

Rabbi Albert Martin was elected to the pulpit of B'nai Israel in 1928. Martin retired in 1958, and his former assistant Alton M. Winters became the rabbi of the congregation. A year later, Rabbi Sanford Shapero was elected to the pulpit, followed six years later by Charles Davidson and in 1968 by Rabbi Arnold Sher. When Sher left the congregation in 1990, James Prosnit became B'nai Israel's rabbi.

References

Synagogue Histories File, American Jewish Archives.
Weindling, Myrna, and Robert Gillette. *A Short History of Congregation B'nai Israel 1859–1984* (Bridgeport, CT: 1984).

UNITED JEWISH CENTER, REFORM. *Danbury, Connecticut.* The United Jewish Center was founded in 1926 as an attempt to establish a compromise between the traditional forms of prayer practiced by Congregation Children of Israel and those who desired near-total rejection of the traditional Jewish rituals practiced in its Reform worship services. The idea did not gain initial favor among large numbers of Danbury's Jewish residents and attracted only thirty-one names to its original roster.

The new group begin to worship at the Heim Homestead on West Street, to which a sanctuary was added. The United Jewish Center engaged its first permanent rabbi in 1929, Rabbi Ben Ezra, but he lasted only six months, after which he was replaced by Rabbi Alter Abelson. Beginning in 1930, Rabbi Maurice A. Lazowick led the congregation for four years. The synagogue found permanent rabbinic leadership in 1935, when the United Jewish Center engaged Rabbi Jerome Malino. He remained until 1981, when Robert Levine was elected to the position of senior rabbi, having come to the congregation as assistant rabbi in 1977. In 1991, Rabbi Paul Golomb succeeded Levine.

By the 1940s, with a membership of 150 families, the need for a larger facility was apparent, but because of financial constraints the congregation did not move to its current location on Deer Hill Avenue until 1954.

Malino led this congregation with great innovation, including two worship services on Saturday morning, one following a traditional format and the second using first the newly revised *Union Prayer Book* (introduced to the congregation in 1943) and more recently the *Gates of Prayer,* the Reform movement's official prayer book. Malino introduced the Bat Mitzvah in 1955 during the Reform service, but the congregation waited until 1984 before allowing girls to celebrate B'not Mitzvah along with boys marking their B'nai Mitzvah in the traditional service. In 1975, the United Jewish Center joined the Union of American Hebrew Congregations, the national organization of Reform synagogues. In 1994, membership stood at nearly five hundred family units.

Reference

Synagogue Histories File, American Jewish Archives.

BETH ISRAEL SYNAGOGUE CENTER, CONSERVATIVE. *Derby, Connecticut.* Jews began to arrive in the Lower Naugatuck Valley in the late 1800s, first from Germany and later from Eastern Europe. By 1891, people gathered for worship services. A year later, the newly founded Sons of Israel (B'nai Israel) leased premises on Water Street in Ansonia. In 1893, the organization received its formal charter, and three years later, the congregation built its first synagogue building on Colbern Street.

By 1915, the Jews of Derby and Shelton (numbering perhaps thirty-four families) established their own congregation, Congregation Sons of Israel. This new congregation met in a building on Main Street with Rabbi Solomon Siegel as its religious leader. At about the same time, arguments over ritual resulted in the splitting of the original congregation and the founding of Sons of Jacob Congregation. In 1932, the community founded a Jewish community center, which helped in the merger of B'nai Israel and B'nai Jacob into Beth El, which met in the B'nai Jacob building. The Jewish Community Center sponsored a Sunday School, primarily for girls, which merged with the Sons of Israel Sunday School in 1948.

In 1958, Beth El and the Sons of Israel merged into Beth Israel. The following year, the amalgamated institution built the Beth Israel Synagogue Center in Derby. These rabbis served Beth Israel: Theodore Gluck (1958–1966), Alan Lovins (1966–1971), Robert Marcus (1971–1976), Michael Laxmeter (1976–1979), Aryeh Wineman (1979–1984), Dov Rubin (1984–1986), Gershon Friedlin (1986–1988), Jonathan Kohn (1989–1994), and Sanford Davis (1994–   ). In 1995, Beth Israel Synagogue Center's membership included two hundred family units.

Reference

Synagogue Histories File, American Jewish Archives.

CONGREGATION MISHKAN ISRAEL, REFORM. *Hamden, Connecticut.* Located in the New Haven suburb of Hamden, Connecticut, since 1965, Congregation Mishkan Israel began in 1840, when a small group of Jews gathered together for worship. It was not until 1843 that the fifteen to twenty Jewish families living in New Haven gathered informally in order to purchase a plot of land for cemetery purposes under the registered name "society of Mishgan [*sic*] Israel." Up until that time, Connecticut law had prohibited the incorporation of non-Christian groups. In 1843 this congregation, which had been worshiping in a variety of locations, formally dedicated a one-room synagogue on the corner of Grand and State Streets.

While the local community seemed to accept this foundling congregation, internal strife over ritual practices and synagogue governance threatened to tear it asunder. In 1846, a majority of members withdrew and formed Mishkan Sholom, which was considered by its members to be liberal, leaving the more traditional Jews behind at Mishkan Israel. The clash was really more over the German and Polish rites of synagogue practice (*Minhag Ashkenaz* vs. *Minhag Polin*) than the attitude toward ritual itself. Three years later, the breach was apparently repaired, and the two groups reunited under the original name of Mishkan Israel at a new location on the corner of State and Chapel Streets. Even before the merger, however, there was little evidence of an inclination toward reform. Members had engaged a *shochet* (ritual slaughterer), elected a regular Torah reader, and considered the construction of a *mikveh* (ritual bath). Men and women sat separately during worship, and all members were expected to maintain the laws of traditional Sabbath observance. Yet, in an effort to Americanize its worship, decorum was emphasized. For example, worshipers were asked to pray quietly and at the same pace as the cantor.

A nascent sisterhood, under the name *Ahavas Achos* (sisterly love) formed in 1853 in order to assume traditional obligations of visiting the sick and attending to the dead. (It would take until 1922, however, before women were given the right to hold membership in Mishkan Israel.) By 1855, while still financially unstable, the congregation again felt the strains of discord that had divided it once before. This time, members who preferred the Polish rite of worship withdrew to form B'nai Sholom synagogue, which functioned until the 1930s.

Like other synagogues of this period, Mishkan Israel acquired its first permanent building with funds bequeathed by philanthropist Judah Touro. After it purchased the Third Congregational Church on Court Street in 1856 with these funds—a location it called home until 1897—the congregation introduced modest reforms, such as an English sermon.

Active in local and national concerns, Congregation Mishkan Israel was one of the early members of the Board of American Israelites, which had been formed as an attempt to unify American Jewry following the Mortara Affair in Bologna, Italy.

More reforms were introduced in the 1850s and 1860s, including the introduction of a choir and the requirement that the clergy leading services wear robes. An organ was installed in 1863, and separate seating was eliminated in 1864 when Mishkan Israel introduced the notion of a family pew. Amidst outside criticism from such national leaders as Isaac Leeser, reforms continued.

Between the years 1856 and 1873, Mishkan Israel was led by three individuals, who served in different capacities as cantor, teacher, *mohel,* and often secretary. It was not until 1873, when Judah Wechsler was elected to the pulpit, that Mishkan Israel had its first ordained rabbi as leader. Though Wechsler was originally an Orthodox rabbi, he abandoned his orthodoxy in favor of Reform Judaism. Contending that orthodoxy could not be sustained in America, he endeavored to make significant reforms in the congregation. He resigned in 1878, to be succeeded by Rabbi Leopold Kleeberg. Like Wechsler, Kleeberg was an orthodox rabbi who had abandoned his orthodoxy but was much more moderate in his advocacy of reforms. He attempted no drastic changes during his fifteen years with the congregation. The sanctuary was enlarged and a new organ was installed, but little significant change was made in ritual.

Members of the congregation assisted the wave of Eastern European Jews entering the community, but it was not until the early 1890s, during Kleeberg's last few years with Mishkan Israel, that the synagogue felt the impact of this Eastern European immigration. The debate over Sunday services in place of Saturday worship, which had been discussed periodically as a way to improve attendance at worship services, surfaced once again. Though the issue threatened to divide the congregation once again, no secession took place. In 1892, Mishkan Israel did indeed institute alternative Sabbath services on Sunday for a short period of time before they were discontinued.

When Kleeberg retired in 1893 and Rabbi David Levy became his successor, the congregation rapidly instituted a series of reforms. With the full support of temple membership, Levy removed all elements of German from the worship service. He preached in English and replaced German readings with English prayers. Under his leadership the congregation reinstituted Sunday services and modernized the religious school. In 1897, the members of Mishkan Israel decided that it was time for a new synagogue building. Stressing the need for a larger facility in a more centrally located area, Levy led the campaign to build a new synagogue at the corner of Orange and Audubon Streets.

In its new building, the congregation continued to make reforms. Mishkan Israel joined other congregations that had dispensed with head coverings and the wearing of prayer shawls during services. Confirmation had been introduced in the 1860s, and members now discussed the possibility of replacing Bar Mitzvah entirely with confirmation. Conversion was also a topic of concern. In 1907, the congregation resolved to accept non-Jews as members, providing that "the applicant voluntarily renounces the Christian faith and professes a knowledge and acceptance of the Jewish faith and is willing to appear before the Board of Trustees and acknowledge his act as his own free will." Several years later, the congregation became a member of the national organization of Reform congregations, the Union of American Hebrew Congregations, affirming its commitment to Reform Judaism.

When Rabbi Levy requested permission from the congregation to officiate at a mixed marriage, after studying the issue by soliciting the advice of four leading

Reform rabbis, the congregation denounced the practice. This revealed the cleavage between congregational members and the rabbi that had already been visible. Apparently, Levy had also established other practices without the support of members, such as the elimination of the reading of the Torah. In 1913, Levy took "voluntary retirement."

Rabbi Louis Mann came to Congregation Mishkan Israel in 1913 and served until 1923. During his tenure, issues such as seating assignments and financial allocations replaced the heated debates over reforms that had marked his predecessor's tenure. During the 1910s and 1920s, the program of activity at Mishkan Israel expanded to include social, cultural, and philanthropic organizations. Mann also sought to improve the program of religious education at the temple, adding a four-year high school course to its curriculum in 1917, claiming to be the first to do so in the country. A Young People's Society was organized at the synagogue in 1920. Three years later, the men of the congregation organized its first Brotherhood. Rabbi Mann, an anti-Zionist, urged the congregation to continue its anti-Zionist stance by generally refusing to send funds for the upbuilding of Palestine.

When Mann left in 1923, he was replaced by Sidney S. Tedesche, who remained for six years before Rabbi Edgar Siskin was elected to the pulpit. With the exception of a leave for military service from 1943 to 1946, Siskin served the congregation between 1929 and 1948. The early years of his tenure presented the congregation with difficult financial times. As the financial crisis in the country continued, leaders at Mishkan Israel were worried about its future. It debated seriously whether to continue the policy of allowing nonmember children to attend its religious school, a policy in which it had taken pride for many years. Even a discussion over Sunday services took place. However, this time it was discussed solely as a means of getting people into the synagogue rather than as an ideological debate over modernization, which had formed the core of the discussion during a prior generation. Somehow, amid these financial concerns, Mishkan Israel maintained its program of activity in various arenas. It remained a steadfast proponent of Reform Judaism and moderated its position on Zionism (following the Columbus Platform of 1937) only slightly.

While Rabbi Siskin was on military duty, two interim rabbis led the congregation: Abraham Klausner, who after a year entered the military, and Robert Goldburg, who returned to succeed Siskin in 1948. Goldburg, committed to progressive Judaism and social justice, was unabashedly pro-Zionist and politically outspoken. His leadership until 1982, when he retired, roused congregants to a flurry of activity inside the congregation and outside it in the community. The practices of assigned seating and public collections were abolished in 1952 and 1955 respectively. In 1958, women were given full voting rights in the congregation.

By 1955, it was clear that Mishkan Israel had outgrown its building, and land was purchased on Ridge Road in Hamden. Originally, the building plan called only for a religious school, to be followed some years later with a sanctuary in order to allow worship to continue at the Orange Street site. However, the board managed to evolve the construction plan into a full-scale facility, which was completed in 1960. The Orange Street location was not sold until 1965, which caused significant financial distress for the synagogue. As a result of what was considered mismanagement, a group withdrew from Mishkan Israel and founded a new congregation in nearby Orange, Connecticut. It would take fifteen years before the financial problems were resolved and an accord was achieved between the two congregations.

Like other Reform congregations, members of Mishkan Israel reconsidered certain traditional practices in the 1970s. *Mezuzot* were placed on all Temple doors, and the sisterhood pressed that people be prohibited from bringing shellfish and pork products into the temple.

Rabbi Mark Panoff, who had served as assistant rabbi in the congregation from 1976 to 1982, succeeded Robert Goldburg in 1982 and led the Mishkan Israel as its rabbi from 1982 to 1986, when Rabbi Herbert Brockman was elected to the pulpit.

References

Sarna, Jonathan, ed. *Jews in New Haven* (New Haven: 1978).
Siskin, Edgar, and Rollin G. Osterweis, eds. *Centennial Volume: Congregation Mishkan Israel, New Haven, Connecticut, 1840–1940* (New Haven: 1940).
Synagogue Histories File, American Jewish Archives.
Wenger, Beth. *Congregation and Community: The Evolution of Jewish Life at Congregation Mishkan Israel, 1840–1990* (Hamden, CT: n.d.).

CONGREGATION AGUDATH SHOLOM, ORTHODOX. *Stamford, Connecticut.* Having emigrated from Eastern Europe, with a stopover in New York City's Lower East Side, a group of twenty-two individuals established Agudath Sholom Synagogue in 1889. This date marked the time when the group finished its payments for a previously acquired Torah scroll. Members conducted worship in various places like an empty attic, a boarding house, a room in a tailor's shop, and then a rented store. This new synagogue community immediately purchased land for a cemetery, but members did not purchase land for a synagogue until 1902. After the congregation laid a cornerstone in 1904, it quickly built a basement, where it held activities. Eventually Agudath Sholom built a fully functional structure, the Greyrock Synagogue, in 1908.

The formation of organizations quickly followed: the Hachnasat Orchim, to welcome newcomers to the community; the Gemilut Chassadim, to help people in need; and the Hebrew Society, to raise funds for the establishment of a Hebrew School. Tragedy struck in 1932, when fire completely destroyed the synagogue building. It took six years before the community mobilized to build again. In the interim, the congregation held worship services at the Jewish Center on Prospect Street. Then members erected a new structure for Agudath Sholom on Grove Street (dedicated 1938).

Agudath Sholom engaged Joseph Ehrenkranz as its rabbi in 1948, shortly before he received his rabbinical ordination. At the time, congregational membership numbered 150 families. Funded by Agudath Sholom, the community established the Bi-Cultural Day School (1956). In 1965, the congregation dedicated a new synagogue building at Strawberry Hill Avenue and Colonial Road, built with a ritual bath and a separation between men and women in worship. By this time, membership had reached five hundred families. When Rabbi Ehrenkranz retired in 1993, the congregation elected Rabbi Ely J. Rosenveig to its pulpit. In 1994, membership exceeded eight hundred family units.

References

Bauman, Lorraine. *Agudath Sholom Centennial Manual* (Stamford, CT: 1990).
Koenig, Samuel. *An American Jewish Community, 50 Years, 1889–1939: The Sociology of the Jewish Community in Stamford, CT* (Stamford, CT: 1991).
Synagogue Histories File, American Jewish Archives.

THE CONGREGATION BETH ISRAEL, REFORM. *West Hartford (originally Hartford), Connecticut.* Organized in 1843 as an orthodox congregation by a small group who came mainly from Germany, this congregation was the first in Hartford and, for nineteen years, the only one. (Originally named Congregation Beth Israel, the article "The" was later added to distinguish it from a small traditional congregation in the city.) It was founded in this particular year because of a change in Connecticut law that permitted Jewish congregations to exist. Moses L. Strauss was engaged as the synagogue's *shochet* (ritual slaughterer) and cantor (later identified as reader and minister of the congregation). The congregation did not occupy its first building until 1855, when a bequest from Judah Touro provided the necessary funds to purchase a former Baptist church building, renamed Touro Hall. The following year the congregation engaged its first rabbi, Isaac Mayer. When fire destroyed Touro Hall, Beth Israel moved to what eventually became known as the Charter Oak Temple and remained there from 1876 to 1935. Its current building, actually located in West Hartford, was built in 1936.

The founding of the synagogue roughly coincided with the development of the Reform movement in Europe and in North America. The synagogue slowly made changes and evolved into a Reform congregation, beginning with the introduction of a mixed choir and family pews as early as 1856. An organ was introduced in 1869, and *aliyot* (Torah honors) were abolished in 1872. The adoption of reforms accelerated in 1874, when Solomon Deutsch became the congregation's rabbi and *Olath Tamid,* edited by David Einhorn, a radical reformer, was adopted as the prayer book. The *Union Prayer Book* was adopted in 1902 and has been continually in use, with revisions, since that time, until the adoption of *Gates of Prayer.* In 1872 the triennial cycle for reading the weekly Torah portion was introduced. A disagreement over reform in ritual led a group of liberals to leave the congregation and form Ohaba Shalom. (This congregation lasted only from 1876 to 1880, when its members rejoined Beth

Israel.) In 1877 the congregation affiliated with the Union of American Hebrew Congregations, with which it has remained since that time. While identified with classical Reform Judaism, especially in regard to ritual, it has slowly moved toward mainstream reform under its current leadership. However, the congregation has always been pro-Zionist and maintained daily services for many years, positions contrary to congregations of its vintage.

The Ladies Deborah Society (originally called the Frauen Verein), an affiliate of the congregation, was organized in 1854. Women were given the right to participate in synagogue meetings in 1907, but a women's auxiliary (whose name was later changed to Sisterhood) was not established until 1915.

Abraham Feldman served the congregation as rabbi from 1925 to 1968 and is most closely identified with the congregation. Rabbi Harold Silver served the congregation from 1968 to 1993, when Rabbi Simeon Glaser was elected to the pulpit to succeed him.

References

Feldman, Abraham J. *Remember the Days of Old* (Hartford: 1943).
————. *A Modern Synagogue* (Hartford: 1967).
Lenn, Theodore I., ed. *Binding the Generations Each to Each* (West Hartford, CT: 1968).
Silverman, Morris. *Hartford Jews* (Hartford: 1970).
Synagogue Histories File, American Jewish Archives.

EMANUEL SYNAGOGUE, CONSERVATIVE. *West Hartford (originally Hartford), Connecticut.* A group of ten men met in Hartford in 1919 in order to discuss the formation of a new synagogue, Connecticut's first Conservative congregation. Initially, these founders held services in an Orthodox synagogue on Winthrop Street. Later they worshipped in Talmud Torah Hall on Pleasant Street. Rabbi Leon Spitz, a U.S. Army chaplain, provided them with organizational leadership.

Emanuel members dedicated their first synagogue in 1920, converting the North Methodist Church on North Main Street for use as a synagogue. The synagogue invited its first full-time rabbi, Abraham Nowak, to join the congregation the same year. He quickly established a sisterhood and a brotherhood in the congregation. By 1922, Emanuel's membership grew to 220 families, with the city's largest religious school of 320 children. Needing more space to accommodate a growing membership, the synagogue purchased a working farm on Woodland Street to build a new synagogue (dedicated 1927).

Following Rabbi Nowak's resignation in 1922, Rabbi Morris Silverman joined the congregation. Rabbi Silverman introduced organ music and formed a Junior Congregation, a Bar Mitzvah Club, a Young Peoples League, athletic programs, and a Boy Scout Troop. By 1957, religious school enrollment exceeded eight hundred. Toward the end of Rabbi Silverman's tenure, Emanuel members contemplated moving from Hartford to West Hartford, where many of its members had already moved. Emanuel purchased land on Mohegan Drive, building a social hall and religious school in 1959. However, they held services on Woodland Street until 1970, when the present sanctuary on Mohegan Drive was completed.

When Rabbi Silverman retired in 1960, Emanuel engaged Rabbi Simon Novick, who emphasized adult education in his rabbinate at Emanuel. He remained until 1969, when Rabbi Howard Singer succeeded him. During Singer's tenure, the congregation became fully egalatarian, granting full ritual rights to women. Singer used the pulpit as a primary means of educating the congregation.

Rabbi Gerald Zelermyer succeeded Rabbi Singer in 1983. During his first few months with the congregation, arson fire destroyed the chapel. The congregation rebuilt the chapel shortly thereafter. In 1994, membership stood at 750 family units.

Reference

Synagogue Histories File, American Jewish Archives.

B'NAI JACOB, CONSERVATIVE. *Woodbridge (originally New Haven), Connecticut.* Before the formal organization of B'nai Jacob in 1882, its founders met for worship in several temporary places. When these charter members prepared a constitution, they sought to establish an Orthodox congregation whose members would worship ''according to the Polish-Jewish Ritual.'' They incorporated B'nai Jacob for ''the advancement of the interests of the Jewish people.'' Shortly after its organization, the congregation purchased land for a cemetery. It acquired its first building in 1885, a former Congregational church located on Temple Street. The synagogue grew steadily through the 1890s and into the early years of the twentieth century. B'nai Jacob became known in the community as the *Risishe Shiel* (Russian Synagogue), a result of its distinctive membership.

In 1913, B'nai Jacob built the George Street Synagogue, which it occupied until 1961. As a bold move of optimism, members built the sanctuary to accommodate 750 people, although the synagogue's membership numbered only ninety at the time of its construction. During that time, the congregation evolved from a small group of Orthodox Jews into a Conservative congregation. Significant change began when separate pews gave way to family pews beginning in 1917, although members had campaigned for such a change since the opening of George Street Synagogue. In 1921, B'nai Jacob joined the United Synagogue of America (now the United Synagogue of Conservative Judaism), the national organization of Conservative synagogues. The same year, the congregation instituted late Friday evening services and established a men's choir. B'nai Jacob added women to the choir the following year, and in 1931, it installed an organ for daily worship, to be used for Sabbaths and holidays beginning in 1937. The congregation discontinued the practice of selling Torah honors and the offering of the traditional priestly benedictions in 1934. By 1944, membership in B'nai Jacob neared four hundred families.

In 1945, B'nai Jacob purchased the property next to the synagogue, but it never expanded the facility in that location. That same year the congregation adopted the new Conservative prayer book prepared by the Rabbinical Assembly. In 1950, B'nai Jacob acquired additional land for building purposes at Boulevard and Dyer Street. The congregation never built there either. In the interim, members converted a house on High Street for use as a school. When congregational membership grew to six hundred families in 1951, B'nai Jacob instituted double services for High Holidays. Ten years later the congregation moved to Rimmon Road in Woodbridge and built a synagogue center there.

While Cantor Charles Sudock (1924–1972) was more closely identified with B'nai Jacob than any other person, the rabbis who served the congregation included Abraham Burstein (1920–1921), Reuben Rubins (1921–1922), Leon Spitz (1922–1927), Louis Greenberg (1928–1946), Stanley Rabinowitz (1947–1953), Joseph Tabachnik (1953–1961), Arthur Chiel (1962–1984), Michael Menitoff (1984–1992), Herbert Weinberg (1992–1994), and Richard Eisenberg (1994–   ).

Reference

Ladin, Harvey N. *The George Street Synagogue of Congregation B'nai Jacob* (New Haven: 1961).

D

DELAWARE

ADAS KODESCH SHEL EMETH, ORTHODOX. *Wilmington, Delaware.*
As early as 1873, Orthodox Jews in the community unsuccessfully attempted to
hold regularly scheduled worship services. In 1883, Jewish residents of Wilmington formed the Moses Montefiore Mutual Beneficial Society. In 1885,
members of the society joined together to form Orthodox Adas Kodesch Congregation (incorporated 1889). In 1887, the congregation engaged Hyman Rezits
(1887–1919) to serve as its religious leader. The early congregation met for
worship in the Morrow Building on Market Street. In 1890, Adas Kodesch
merged with local Ahavath Achim congregation (founded 1889). As a result,
the congregation took on the name Orthodox Adas Kodesch K'nesseth Israel
Congregation and moved to Third and Shipley Streets. The following year, the
enlarged congregation built a ritual bath elsewhere on Shipley Street, where the
entire congregation moved. Then, twelve months later, it established a Sunday
School. In 1895, a break in the congregation became manifest in a failed attempt
to form a Reform congregation. A short time later, these disaffected members
returned to Adas Kodesch.

In 1898, Adas Kodesch moved into a former church at Sixth and French
Streets to become the first permanent synagogue in Delaware and changed its
name to Adas Kodesch Baron DeHirsch Congregation, with a membership of
eighty-four and with 123 children in its school. In the new building, the women
of the congregation formed a Bichor Cholem Society (to visit the sick). Synagogue members established a daily Hebrew School in 1904.

In 1908, members of Adas Kodesch built a new synagogue on the same site
on Sixth and French Streets, dropping Baron DeHirsch from its name. Rabbi
David Swiren (1917–1921) led the congregation in this new building. After his
tenure, the women of Adas Kodesch formed a sisterhood (1924). In 1928, mem-

bers of the synagogue built a community center adjacent to the existing building. Synagogue members closed the center two years later. In 1934, this center reopened as the YM/YWHA (later to become a Jewish community center). During this period, Samuel Berliant (1929–1931) led the congregation. These men succeeded Berliant: Solomon Schulson (1936–1944) and Joseph Singer (1945–1947). Singer introduced mixed seating to the congregation. He delivered sermons in English and initiated occasional late services on Friday evening.

In 1943, Adas Kodesch and Chesed Shel Emeth merged schools to form the Associated Hebrew Schools. Four years later, Leonard Gewirtz (1947–1989) succeeded Joseph Singer in the pulpit at Adas Kodesch. Under Gewirtz's direction, after a debate as to whether the Adas Kodesch was Orthodox or Conservative, Adas Kodesch members began calling their congregation Traditional rather than Orthodox. Nevertheless, it affiliated with the Union of Orthodox Jewish Congregations of America. Gewirtz developed study groups and established a new level of decorum during worship. Under his direction, Adas Kodesch reestablished its own religious school.

Local congregation Chesed Shel Emeth merged with Adas Kodesch in 1957. Residents who preferred a Sephardic ritual had founded Chesed Shel Emeth in 1900, initially meeting for worship at Third and Shipley Streets. Members built a permanent home on Shipley Street just below Third Street in 1916, adding a school building in 1926. It occupied this building until the 1957 merger. In 1928, Rabbi Philip First (1928–1948) joined the congregation as its religious leader, followed by Rabbi Eliezer Ebner (1949–1952). These men followed: Moses Ruttner (1952–1955) and Israel Turner (1955–1957).

The merged synagogue Adas Kodesch Shel Emeth gave over its facilities to the Jewish Community Center, while maintaining its right to use the premises for religious and social purposes. It built its own new facility on North Washington Boulevard (1963). The board gave women the right to celebrate Simchat Torah in their own service in 1981, and it began sponsoring separate women's Sabbath morning services in 1994. In 1995, the congregation listed four hundred family units as members under the religious leadership of Rabbi Sanford Dresin.

References

Frank, William. *Adas Kodesch Shel Emeth Dedication Book* (Wilmington, DE: 1963).
Synagogue Histories File, American Jewish Archives.
Young, Toni. *Delaware and the Jews* (Wilmington, DE: 1979).

CONGREGATION BETH EMETH, REFORM. *Wilmington, Delaware.* Eighteen members of the Orthodox congregation Adas Kodesch formed Congregation Oheb Shalom, the forerunner of Congregation Beth Emeth, in 1895 as the first attempt in the Wilmington area to organize a Reform synagogue. With Rabbi Jacob Korn as its leader, this group quickly grew to forty-five members, meeting in rented quarters. However, the congregation survived only three years. In 1906 this original group of German-Hungarian merchants—joined by a few professionals and manufacturers—grew sufficiently prosperous to successfully establish a second Reform institution. They named the congregation Temple of Truth, Beth Emeth.

Beth Emeth members invited Rabbi Jacob Korn to lead them in their new venture, but he served only one year. Rabbi Isaac Aaron Rubenstein succeeded Korn in 1907. Rubenstein successfully campaigned for a permanent structure for Beth Emeth. This thirty-eight-member congregation built a permanent home for itself on Washington Street in 1908. Rubenstein left the following year, and Rabbi Moses Abels occupied the pulpit. Conflict with the president forced Abels to leave in 1912, but a breakaway Conservative synagogue, Beth Shalom, called him back to Wilmington in 1923. Rabbi Emanuel Schreiber succeeded Abels and remained until 1915, when Beth Emeth elected Dr. Samuel Rabinowitz to its pulpit.

In 1921 Beth Emeth engaged Rabbi Moses Baroway, ordained at the (Conservative) Jewish Theological Seminary, but he stayed for only one year. It was during his tenure that a group within the congregation left to form Temple Beth Shalom. Talk of introducing the Reconstructionist philosophy, as a means of holding the congregation together and later as a philosophy for merger, held sway over neither congregation.

Following the split, Rabbi Lee Levinger, ordained at Hebrew Union College, joined the congregation and introduced the *Union Prayer Book,* the prayer book of the Reform movement. Shortly thereafter, Levinger led the congregation to join the Union of American Hebrew Congregations, the national organization of Reform synagogues. When Levinger left in 1925, Rabbi Louis A. Mischkind came to the congregation. He remained four years before Rabbi Henry Tavel succeeded him. Tavel led the congregation until 1946, when he entered Army chaplaincy. During his absence, the congregation instituted a midweek Hebrew school.

Rabbi Herbert Drooz permanently joined the congregation in 1948, having served as interim rabbi during Tavel's days in the military. In 1951, the congregation instituted regular Saturday morning services and conducted daily services beginning in 1956. Beth Emeth built a new facility in 1953, and in 1976 the congregation adopted *Gates of Prayer,* the prayer book of the Reform movement. In 1972, Beth Emeth restored the practice of wearing prayer shawls. Two years later, the congregation reintroduced the custom of covering the head during worship. In 1978, as a step toward equality, the congregation introduced the ceremony of *B'not Torah* (literally, Daughters of Torah) for girls.

Drooz remained at Beth Emeth until 1982 when the congregation named Rabbi Peter Grumbacher as senior rabbi. Shortly thereafter, Grumbacher replaced the *B'not Torah* ceremony with Bat Mitzvah. The congregation built a new wing on the building (dedicated 1991). In 1994, membership at Beth Emeth exceeded 725 family units.

Reference

Synagogue Histories File, American Jewish Archives.

TEMPLE BETH SHALOM, CONSERVATIVE. *Wilmington, Delaware.* A group of six families from Temple Beth Emeth founded Temple Beth Shalom in 1922. They had previously joined Beth Emeth hoping to steer the congregation away from Reform Judaism and toward a more centrist position. They also felt that the Jewish community growing in the area known as Washington Heights or the Boulevard Section called for the establishment of a Conservative congregation. This small group secured a building at the corner of Eighteenth and Washington Streets, which it refurbished for use as a synagogue building. The congregation affiliated with the United Synagogue of America (now the United Synagogue of Conservative Judaism), the national organization of Conservative synagogues, after the High Holidays and next established its Hebrew School.

In 1923, Moses J. S. Abels became Temple Beth Shalom's first rabbi, but he stayed for only one year. Members elected Rabbi Ralph D. Hershon (1924–1927) to the pulpit. Rabbi Abraham E. Milgram succeeded Hershon in 1927. By this time, the congregation reached a membership of over one hundred families. In 1930, Rabbi Jacob Kraft accepted the pulpit that had Milgram vacated. Kraft remained with the congregation until 1970, when he became emeritus.

Because of financial difficulties experienced by Beth Shalom in the 1930s, members of the board discussed the possibility of merging with Beth Emeth. However, they determined that ideological differences prevented a merger. Yet, serious discussions took place once again in 1944.

In 1939 the board succeeded in persuading congregants to wear skullcaps rather than hats during worship. In 1946, the congregation acquired property at Eighteenth Street and Baynard Boulevard, but it waited until 1954 to build a new facility on the site. In 1948, the congregation adopted the new prayer book prepared for the Conservative movement. This meant the abandonment of the Jastrow-Szold prayer book and of what congregants considered to be the last vestige of its liberal religious outlook. When Rabbi Kraft retired in 1970, members chose Rabbi David Geffen to succeed him. Under his guidance the congregation grew to over seven hundred families. This growth prompted the purchase in the early 1970s of property adjacent to Beth Shalom. In 1977, Rabbi Kenneth Cohen became the religious leader of Beth Shalom.

References

Jacob Kraft: The Man, The Rabbi, The Community Leader (Wilmington, DE: 1980).
Synagogue Histories Collection, the Joseph and Miriam Ratner Center for the Study of Conservative Judaism.
Synagogue Histories File, American Jewish Archives.
Temple Beth Sholom Fifty-Year Historical Record, 1922–1972 (Wilmington: 1972).

DISTRICT OF COLUMBIA

ADAS ISRAEL, CONSERVATIVE. *Washington, District of Columbia.* In 1869, thirty-eight members, led by Bendiza Behrend, withdrew from Washington Hebrew, when that synagogue began its liturgical reform, to form the Adas Israel Hebrew Congregation. The newly formed institution conducted its Orthodox worship in the homes of congregants and rented rooms in a variety of locations before building its first synagogue at Sixth and G Streets NW in 1876. Stanley Rabinowitz characterizes these early years of Adas Israel as "a series of financial crises, delinquencies in collection of dues and payments of loans, bitter disputes, innumerable resignations, and incidents of shocking pettiness" as well as "a portrait of a handful of dedicated people determined to establish a synagogue despite overwhelming problems, willing to give sacrificially of self and means in the face of nationwide economic recessions, and firmly resolved to preserve their religious traditions in spite of competition from a less demanding and more successful alternative movement."

Members used German as the language of discourse in worship until the dedication of the new synagogue in 1876, when members introduced English prayers. The congregation engaged a variety of personnel in its early years, charging them with a multiplicity of responsibilities including ritual slaughter, Torah reading, teaching, and leading worship. Most notably, Jacob Voorsanger, who went on to a distinguished career as the rabbi of San Francisco's Emanu-El, served from 1876 to 1877. Because of itinerant personnel, the religious school in particular suffered from a considerable lack of attention in its early years. Following a bitter dispute involving one of Adas Israel's early religious leaders, Joseph A. Cohen, a number of his friends resigned from the congregation in 1874 in order to form a new congregation (referred to as Neveh Israel or Bet Israel). This secession threatened the very survival of Adas Israel. After the board resolved the dispute, the secessionists rejoined Adas Israel.

After the assassination of President James Garfield in 1881, Adas Israel led a movement to establish a local hospital in memory of the slain president, at the urging of congregational leader Adolphus Solomons. (This hospital later merged into the Washington Hospital Center.)

In 1898, Adas Israel participated in a meeting of congregations to form what eventually became the Union of Orthodox Jewish Congregations of America. Though Adas Israel did not fully support the efforts of this new body, it did not want to support the Union of American Hebrew Congregations, the national body of Reform synagogues. That same year, the congregation elected to its pulpit Rabbi Morris Mandel, the first rabbi ordained at the Jewish Theological Seminary of America, to serve Adas Israel. At this point, the congregation and its school improved considerably, reflecting faith in its new leadership and the improved economic conditions in the District of Columbia, bolstered by the federal payroll. In 1901, membership stood at 141, an increase of 81 since 1899.

Members invited Rabbi Julius (a.k.a. Judah) Loeb to lead the congregation in 1901. He reorganized the curriculum of the school. Six years later, Adas Israel sold its building and moved to a larger facility at Sixth and I Streets NW. With this move came a growth in membership. Rabbi Louis Egelson served the congregation beginning in 1908. Under his leadership, Adas Israel joined with local congregations Ohev Shalom and Talmud Torah in the formation of a short-lived citywide Talmud Torah in 1910. Egelson's attempts to introduce English into worship met strong opposition. He encountered the same difficult relations with the board as had his predecessors, particularly with the president Simon Oppenheimer, who governed with a heavy hand for thirty-six years.

Rabbi Benjamin Grossman came in 1914. He successfully introduced English without an initial backlash, but relations eventually deteriorated between Grossman and the board of trustees. Rabbis Nathan Colish (1920–1921) and Theodore Shabshelowitz (1921–1922) succeeded Grossman.

Rabbi Louis Schwefel (1923–1929) attempted a variety of changes that met with bitter opposition. These included confirmation for girls, a reduction in the number of times congregants were asked to rise for the recital of certain prayers, and a cessation of the practice of auctioning off Torah honors. By 1924, the impact of Russian immigration could be felt at Adas Israel, with a great many members leaving the congregation and affiliating with Washington Hebrew Congregation because of the relative social class of other German Jews. Ironically, this process helped move Adas Israel from Orthodoxy fully into the sphere of Conservative Judaism. By 1925, membership grew to 341, and to 420 one year later.

During the initial years of Rabbi Solomon Metz's tenure (1930–1951), activity declined at Adas Israel, most probably because of the severe Depression that ill-affected the entire nation. Under his guidance, the congregation opened Hebrew programs in three different locations in 1939. In the area of ritual, he followed a less innovative path than had his predecessors. This probably contributed to his ability to remain longer at the helm of the congregation.

Just prior to World War II, Adas Israel joined the effort to rescue German Jewish scholars and invited Rabbi Gerhard Frank of Ichenhausen, Germany, to join the congregation as associate rabbi. While he was unable to leave Germany, the congregation joined local congregations in bringing Rabbi and Mrs. Hugo Schiff from Karlsruhe to the community.

Adas Israel joined the United Synagogue of America, the organization of congregations of the Conservative movement, in 1948, at the same time as it adopted the practice of a triennial Torah reading in an effort to shorten the Sabbath morning service. Rabbi David Panitz served the congregation from 1951 to 1959. He gave priority to daily and Sabbath services. School enrollment increased, as did extracurricular programming. As a result of these activities, members built an annex specifically for youth activities and named it for Joseph Wilner (1959).

In 1951, Adas Israel built a new synagogue at Connecticut Avenue and Porter Street. Members unsuccessfully asked the United Synagogue to designate it the national synagogue. In the new facility, planners installed an organ, ostensibly not to be used on Shabbat, which eventually did happen. They also planned for mixed seating.

Rabbi Stanley Rabinowitz led the congregation from 1960 to 1986. At his initiative, Adas Israel conducted a survey of its membership in 1962. As a result, the congregation implemented a variety of changes including the discontinuation of nonmember Bar/Bat Mitzvahs, limiting the number of Torah honors on the Sabbath, the celebration of a Bat Mitzvah on Saturday mornings, and the use of the sanctuary for funerals. Rabinowitz went further. The year following the survey, Rabbi Rabinowitz introduced dramas like *J.B.* to the Friday night service.

Membership increased in the 1960s, as did school enrollment. But with the migration to the suburbs that followed the civil unrest of the decade, enrollment dropped precipitously. In order to cope with the challenge of a declining school enrollment, the board of trustees allowed nonmembers to enroll their children in the religious school. As a Washington congregation, Adas Israel actively participated in the arena of social action and the struggle for civil rights for African Americans, particularly in the area of fair housing.

The Jewish Historical Society of Greater Washington restored the original Adas Israel Synagogue in 1975 as the Lillian and Albert Small Jewish Museum of Washington (it having been moved to Third and G Streets in 1969).

Following the retirement of Rabbi Rabinowitz in 1986, members elected Rabbi Jeffrey Wohlberg to the pulpit of Adas Israel. Under his direction, Adas Israel led the community in reaching out to the area's young single population. In 1992, membership in the congregation stood at 1504 families, with 669 children in the religious school.

References

Rabinowitz, Stanley. *The Assembly: A Century in the Life of the Adas Israel Hebrew Congregation of Washington, DC* (Hoboken, NJ: 1993).
Synagogue Histories File, American Jewish Archives.

KESHER ISRAEL/THE GEORGETOWN SYNAGOGUE, ORTHODOX. *Washington, District of Columbia.* In 1910, Jewish residents of Georgetown organized a benevolent society, Gemilut Hesed, which met for worship services in a rented facility on M Street NW. This group purchased a small house on N Street NW, which it remodeled as a synagogue (1915). In 1935, the congregation built a new synagogue on the same site. Throughout most of its history, membership in the congregation remained small. The congregation purchased a private home adjacent to the synagogue in 1991 and used it for offices, additional worship services, children's programs, and social activities.

During its early years of operation, lay leaders led worship. These rabbis served Kesher Israel: Jacob Ozer Dubrow (1924–1945), I. Meckler (1945–1946), Sidney Shulman (1946–1949), Philip Rabinowitz (1949–1984), Rod Glowgower (1985–1987), and Barry Freundel (1989–   ). Rabbi Dubrow concentrated his efforts on education and the building of a community ritual bath. Rabinowitz formed the local *Bet Din* (rabbinical court) and a *vaad hakashrut* (community organization of rabbis to supervise kosher dietary laws). During the first year of Rabbi Freundel's tenure, he established an *eruv* in order to encourage younger, observant families to move into the neighborhood around the synagogue. The *eruv* is a wire that encompasses a public space and turns it into private space in order to permit the carrying of objects on the Sabbath. He has also encouraged the participation of women (and girls celebrating Bat Mitzvah) in the congregation by permitting them to speak from the pulpit following the formal conclusion of worship. Under his direction, Kesher Israel instituted a *Rosh Chodesh* (celebration of the new month) study group for women, as well as a broad series of adult education offerings. In 1995, membership exceeded three hundred family units.

Reference

Epstein, David. *Kesher Israel—The Georgetown Synagogue* (Washington, DC: 1988).

OHEV SHOLOM–TALMUD TORAH CONGREGATION, ORTHODOX.
Washington, District of Columbia.

Talmud Torah Congregation

In 1889, several families joined together for worship at the home of Isaac Levy on 4½ Street in order to found Talmud Torah Congregation. After meeting in private homes for several years, the group purchased land on E Street SW. With eighty-five families, the congregation dedicated its first permanent home in that location (1905). From that time, Moshe Rubin Yoelson, father of singer Al Jolson, led the congregation in worship. In 1912, members elected Moses Aaron Horwitz as their first rabbi.

The Talmud Torah Congregation established the first community Hebrew School in Washington, under the name Talmud Torah Tifereth Zion (1915). By 1917, enrollment reached 120 children. Two years later, congregants established the Free Loan Society of Talmud Torah.

When Rabbi Horwitz died in 1935, Talmud Torah Congregation invited Rabbi Joshua Klavan to serve in its pulpit. Because of demographic change in the area surrounding the synagogue, the congregation sold its building in 1951, moving to a new location at Fourteenth and Emerson Street NW the following year. During his tenure, Klavan established a successful Hebrew day school. One year later, Rabbi Klavan died; his son, Rabbi Hillel Klavan, became the religious leader of the congregation.

Demographic change affected the congregation once again. Thus, the congregation sold its building and moved to the Hebrew Academy building until 1960.

Ohev Sholom

In 1886, a group of Russian immigrants founded Chai Adom Congregation. This group of ten men worshipped above a clothing store on Seventh Street between L and M Streets NW before moving to Louisiana Avenue, then H Street NW. In 1906, increased membership necessitated a move to a larger facility at Fifth and I Streets NW. The congregation remained in this location until 1956.

In 1897, Ohev Sholom started a Hebrew School. In 1906, Rabbi Gedaliah Silverstone came to serve the congregation. He concurrently served Kesher Israel in Georgetown after its 1910 founding. He organized a day school, which lasted only two years (1910–1911). When Silverstone immigrated to Palestine, Rabbi Julius T. Loeb joined the congregation. He served until 1930. Rabbi Zemach Green (Yarkoni) succeeded him and led Ohev Sholom for twenty years. Green directed much of his energy to the education of children in the community. In addition, he emphasized Zionism in the congregation. During the 1960s, amid drastic demographic changes in the neighborhood surrounding the synagogue, these rabbis served the congregation: Nahum Eliezer Rabinowitz, Benzion Kaganoff, and Albert J. Davis.

Ohev Sholom–Talmud Torah Congregation

In 1958, Talmud Torah Congregation merged with Ohev Sholom to become Ohev Sholom–Talmud Torah. Together, the merged congregation of 610 family units dedicated a new synagogue at Sixteenth and Jonquil Streets (1960). By 1994, membership had declined to two hundred family units.

Reference

Synagogue Histories File, American Jewish Archives.

TEMPLE MICAH, REFORM. *Washington, District of Columbia.* A group of nineteen residents of the River Park cooperative community in Southwest Washington met at the home of Bert and Theodor Schuchat in 1963 in order to "form a nucleus for initiating a program and plan of activities for Jewish residents of the Southwest"—especially High Holiday services and a program of religious education for children. Using the working name of the Southwest Hebrew Congregation, the congregation attracted city dwellers, particularly singles who moved to the Southwest as part of the District's plan for urban renewal. Thus, the congregation became the first urban congregation to be developed after World War II.

As Jews from a variety of backgrounds joined the congregation, members used Reform, Conservative, and Orthodox prayer books. Known from the beginning as "a teaching congregation," the synagogue formed a variety of on-going discussion groups, with topics determined by the membership. In 1964, congregants invited Rabbi Richard G. Hirsch, director of the Reform movement's Religious Action Center in Washington, to lead them. After meeting in a variety of private homes, the congregation met for monthly worship in the local Pentecostal Church.

In 1966, the congregation affiliated with the Union of American Hebrew Congregations, the national organization of Reform synagogues, and engaged Rabbi Bernard Mehlman as its first full-time religious leader the following year. Under his direction, the congregation experienced a ten-year period of intellectual growth and social activism. Amid a great deal of opposition, Mehlman insisted on using the *Union Prayer Book,* the prayer book of the Reform movement, shortly after his arrival. Among other programs of adult education, he developed a series of Downtown Study Groups.

When Mehlman arrived, the synagogue rented office space in a building occupied by Southeastern University. In 1968, the congregation's two hundred members moved into the church building of St. Augustine in order to share its facilities, the same year the Southwest Hebrew Congregation changed its name to Temple Micah. This name change reflected the phase of political (antiwar) activism Rabbi Mehlman initiated. At the same time, Temple Micah members worked to resolve the social problems of their local community. The relationship with St. Augustine evolved over time to a nearly equal partnership.

Between the years 1971 and 1977, Temple Micah participated in a unique internship program called Intermet for the purpose of practical training in the congregational setting. In 1977, with nearly four hundred members, Temple Micah decided to limit membership.

Rabbi Robert Baruch succeeded Mehlman in 1978. During his tenure, membership declined. He initiated a series entitled Joint Colloquia, a program of dialogues between Jews and non-Jews. In 1979, the congregation instituted a program called Qiyum Habrit, a program of affirmation and commitment for those high school students who did not celebrate a Bar/Bat Mitzvah at age thirteen.

Rabbi Daniel Zemel succeeded Baruch in 1983. Shortly after his arrival, Zemel changed the music in order to encourage congregational participation. He also focused his attention on the education of children in the congregation. In 1990, Temple Micah opened Micah House, a group home for the homeless. Temple Micah anticipates moving to a new facility on Wisconsin Avenue in Northwest Washington in 1995. In 1994, Temple Micah listed its membership at 220. It remains an informal congregation with an emphasis on teaching and education.

References

Levenson, Brenda. "Temple Micah" (unpublished manuscript).
Synagogue Histories File, American Jewish Archives.

TEMPLE SINAI, REFORM. *Washington, District of Columbia.* Looking for a new interpretation of Reform Judaism "that would offer Reform worship in a warm and friendly atmosphere to unaffiliated Jewish families of Washington," a small group of Jews founded Temple Sinai in 1950 (chartered 1951). Initiated by only seven families, Sinai met in a variety of temporary locations including the Dupont Plaza Hotel, the Wardman Park Hotel, and the Jewish War Veterans Building. Upon its founding, Temple Sinai joined the Union of American Hebrew Congregations, the national organization of Reform synagogues. The women of the congregation formed a Ladies Auxiliary shortly after the congregation's founding (1951); that same year, members organized a religious school. When the school and its seventy-five children outgrew its temporary home in the basement of an office building on Massachusetts Avenue, it moved to the Jewish Community Center. The founding of a Men's Club followed one year later.

Rabbi Balfour Brickner served as the congregation's first religious leader, beginning in 1952. That same year, Sinai found a semipermanent home in the Bethlehem Chapel of the National Cathedral and met there until it built its own facility on Military Road in 1961. By 1955, religious school enrollment surpassed 470; temple membership exceeded five hundred families. In 1957, the congregation initiated a College of Jewish Studies for adults. By the time members dedicated their new building, membership had reached over 750 families.

Following Brickner's resignation, Rabbi Eugene Lipman came to Temple Sinai in 1961, the same year the congregation moved into its present home on Military Road. During his tenure, Temple Sinai helped found Temple Beth Ami in Rockville, Maryland. As a civil rights and civil liberties activist, Lipman encouraged the congregation's involvement with other faith communities. Lipman retired in 1985, when Rabbi Fred Reiner succeeded him. Reiner continued the congregational emphasis on adult education and social action. In 1993, the congregation fully renovated its building and added a chapel and all purpose room to its physical plant. Temple Sinai's membership stood at over 975 family units in 1994.

References

Cohen, Stanley. *Temple Sinai 1950–1961* (Washington, DC: 1961).
Synagogue Histories File, American Jewish Archives.
Temple Sinai Ritual Policy Compendium (Washington, DC: 1991).

WASHINGTON HEBREW CONGREGATION, REFORM. *Washington, District of Columbia.* Charter members founded Washington Hebrew Congregation in 1855 as the first synagogue in the nation's capital. These founding members incorporated the congregation under a congressional charter signed by the president of the United States, perhaps the only synagogue to hold this distinction. Meeting in rented facilities and private homes until 1863, the synagogue acquired a former church at Eighth and I Streets to serve as its first permanent home.

In 1869, members installed an organ and, less than two weeks later, introduced a choir to enhance worship. The president "ordered" that prayers be conducted in English and the Kiddush eliminated (perhaps because of its reference to the "chosen people"). A protest erupted, and more than thirty-five members, including some of the Washington Hebrew founders, left to form Adas Israel in 1869. Following this separation, members introduced more reforms to congregational ritual, including the abolition of the practice of distinguishing between descendants of the priestly class, their Levitical assistants, and the rest of the people.

Louis Stern served Washington Hebrew Congregation as "hazan and teacher" beginning in 1872. In 1897, congregants built a new facility on its Eighth and I site, worshiping there until 1954, when the congregation built a structure on Macomb and Massachusetts Avenue.

Rabbi Abram Simon, one of the first nativeborn leaders of American Judaism ordained at Hebrew Union College in Cincinnati, succeeded Stern in 1904. Simon introduced the notion of lighting candles and saying blessings over wine in the synagogue, a practice previously reserved for home observance (1934), and served as president of the District of Columbia Board of Education.

In 1935, Rabbi Norman Gerstenfeld came to Washington Hebrew Congregation and in 1938 succeeded Rabbi Simon, at his death. Gerstenfeld's long rabbinate was marked by much controversy, especially over his vigorous opposition to Zionism, as well as by tremendous growth in the membership. Noted rabbis who served through the years include Hugo B. Schiff, William S. Rosenblum, William A. Rosenthal, Alexander B. Goode, and E. William Seaman. Washington Hebrew Congregation engaged Rabbi Joshua Haberman as its religious leader in 1969. Haberman emphasized adult education in his rabbinate. He remained until the congregation elected Rabbi Joseph Weinberg to succeed him. Weinberg previously served as assistant and then associate, beginning in 1968. Under Weinberg's guidance, the congregation continued to expand its offerings in education. Washington Hebrew Congregation has an extensive program of activity, with a full complement of auxiliaries serving a variety of constituencies. Recognizing the demographic change in the population it serves, it built a social and educational facility in neighboring Potomac, Maryland (1976), where it intends to establish a day school. In 1995, membership neared 2,750 family units.

References

Altschuler, David, ed. *The Jews of Washington, DC: A Communal History Anthology* (Chappaqua, NY: 1985).

Nordlinger, Bernard I. "A History of Washington Hebrew Congregation." *The Record* 4, no. 2 (November 1969): 1–82.

Rabinowitz, Stanley. *The Assembly: A Century in the Life of the Adas Israel Hebrew Congregation of Washington, DC* (Hoboken, NJ: 1993).

Synagogue Histories File, American Jewish Archives.

F

FLORIDA

BOCA RATON SYNAGOGUE, ORTHODOX. *Boca Raton, Florida.* A small group joined together in 1983 to establish an Orthodox synagogue in Boca Raton. Subsequently, these founders incorporated the Boca Raton Synagogue. This group immediately established scheduled regular worship services and formed a *chevra kadisha* (burial society). Rabbi Mark Dratch joined the synagogue as its first religious leader (1984–1987), and he nurtured the early religious education program for adults and children. The congregation met in a variety of locations in its early years, and in 1987 members dedicated their first synagogue home on Montoya Circle. That same year, Rabbi Mordecai Winyarz assumed the pulpit (1987–1989). During his rabbinate, the congregation affiliated with the Union of Orthodox Jewish Congregations of America (1988). At the end of his tenure, the synagogue completed its *eruv* (a way of enclosing public space through the erection of a perimeter wire and thereby making it private space so that things can be carried on the Sabbath).

Rabbi Mordecai Neuman (1989–1990) succeeded Winyarz before Rabbi Kenneth Brander (1991–   ) led the congregation. Under Brander's guidance, the congregation expanded its educational and outreach programs. In its Montoya Circle location, members built a mikveh (dedicated 1993), the first in Palm Beach County, Florida. They expanded their facility to include a new sanctuary and social hall in 1994. The congregation serves the needs of four hundred children in its youth department with educational and social programs. In 1995, membership of the synagogue stood at nearly 280 family units.

References

Boca Raton Synagogue First Annual Journal (Boca Raton, FL: 1989).
Boca Raton Synagogue Dedication Ceremony (Boca Raton, FL: 1994).
Boca Raton Synagogue Fifth Annual Journal (Boca Raton, FL: 1995).

TEMPLE BETH EL, REFORM. *Boca Raton, Florida.* Following a series of organizational meetings, local Jewish residents held the first regular Sabbath service in the Boca Raton area at Marymount College (now the College of Boca Raton) in 1967. Using the name the Hebrew Congregation of Boca Raton, the group elected officers and established a religious school; it formed a sisterhood a year later. In the early years, the congregation found temporary housing in a variety of locations, including the clubhouse of the Lions International and the local Moravian Church.

In 1970, the congregation joined the Union of American Hebrew Congregations, the national organization of Reform synagogues, and changed the name of the synagogue to Temple Beth El of Boca Raton the following year. Beth El grew from a dozen initial families to over 350 by 1977. As a result of its growth, the congregation moved into its own newly constructed building on Southwest Fourth Avenue after seven years in the Moravian Church. It underwent major expansion in 1986. In 1989, Beth El opened its first satellite midweek Hebrew School location. In 1993, the congregation opened a second satellite location. It is currently anticipating the installation of an on-site mausoleum.

When members founded the congregation, men did not wear head coverings during worship. Thus, the congregation made yarmulkes available only on request. In 1979, Beth El made head coverings available upon entering the synagogue. The following year the congregation also made prayer shawls available at the entrance to the synagogue. The congregation permitted congregants to ask the rabbi to cover his head during a Bar/Bat Mitzvah service. In 1989, the rabbis began wearing head coverings on the pulpit at all times.

Leonard Harris guided the congregation in its early years (1967–1972). The congregation then elected Rabbi Benjamin Roisan to the pulpit (1972–1975). Rabbi Norman Mendel succeeded Roisan (1975–1977). Serving since 1977, Rabbi Merle Singer now oversees a congregation of nearly seventeen hundred family units with a full range of activities and an expanded religious education program.

References

Synagogue Histories File, American Jewish Archives.
Temple Beth El of Boca Raton, Dedication of New Building (Boca Raton, FL: 1977).
Temple Beth El of Boca Raton, Celebration of Rededication (Boca Raton, FL: 1986).

YOUNG ISRAEL HOLLYWOOD–FT. LAUDERDALE, ORTHODOX. *Ft. Lauderdale, Florida.* In 1972, a small group founded Young Israel of Hollywood–Ft. Lauderdale out of a minyan that met only for Sabbath worship. Upon its founding the synagogue joined the National Council of Young Israel and the Union of Jewish Orthodox Congregations of America. Rabbi Moshe Bomzer (1979–1980) served the synagogue as its first religious leader. Rabbi Edward Davis succeeded him in 1981. This Young Israel congregation built on Stirling Road in Ft. Lauderdale, at the thoroughfare that divides Ft. Lauderdale and

Hollywood, in 1987. In addition to a sanctuary and chapel, the congregation built a *mikvah* (ritual bath) as well as a ritual bath for "koshering" vessels and a ballroom, a youth lounge, a playroom, and classrooms. The congregation of 250 families holds worship services (morning and evening) each day with concurrent Junior Congregation services on Saturday morning. Sabbath afternoon groups for elementary and middle school students are also held.

Reference

Synagogue Histories File, American Jewish Archives.

CONGREGATION AHAVATH CHESED, REFORM. *Jacksonville, Florida.* Although there was a nearly successful attempt to establish a congregation in Jacksonville as early as 1867, it was not until 1882 that Ahavath Chesed was chartered. Morris A. Dzialynski led twenty-three other charter members to form the congregation and served as its first president, a year after he was elected mayor of Jacksonville. Its early building campaign was fostered by non-Jewish merchants of the city. Apparently there was some tension between members of Ahavath Chesed and those of the Hebrew Benevolent Society, which was a well-formed group by the time the synagogue was organized. In 1882, these tensions were ameliorated by the purchase of Benevolent Society property by the congregation. That same year, Ahavath Chesed engaged Rabbi Marx Moses and its membership dedicated the congregation's first building. Moses remained until 1885. Rabbis who succeeded him are A. Rosenspitz (1885–1886), Ignatz Kaiser (1886–1887), J. Kahn (1888–1890), J. Rosenberg (1890–1893), B. Babbino (1893–1900), and David H. Wittenberg (1900–1906).

When Jacob D. Bucky consented to take the presidency of Ahavath Chesed, it was on condition that certain reforms be implemented, including organ music in the liturgy. By 1892, clergy led worship without head covering or prayer shawl, and the male members of the congregation followed their example.

During Wittenberg's tenure, in 1901, fire devastated Jacksonville, taking the synagogue building and its records with it. Members rebuilt the Temple in 1902 on the same site. Two years later, Ahavath Chesed joined the Union of American Hebrew Congregations, the national organization of Reform congregations. Congregational facilities soon proved inadequate, and in 1910 the congregation and its seventy-five members moved to a new building on Laura and Ashley, where it would remain for the next forty years.

Rabbi Pizer Jacobs (1906–1912) succeeded Rabbi Wittenberg. Jacobs left the congregation when fiscal restraints forced him to take a major cut in salary. Rabbi Samuel Schwartz led the congregation for the next four years (1912–1916). Rabbi Israel Kaplan joined the congregation in 1916 and remained until 1946. In 1922, Ahavath Chesed voted to discontinue the practice of assigned seats on a permanent basis. By 1924, the congregation claimed 152 members. Another fire destroyed what was called the Temple Home, a religious community center adjacent to the sanctuary in 1940. Like the fire of 1901, this fire destroyed all temple records.

Elected to congregational leadership in 1946, Rabbi Sidney Lefkowitz led the congregation until his retirement in 1973. During his tenure, he faced considerable opposition during the civil rights movement. In 1950, the congregation dedicated its new building on St. Johns and Mallory. Membership stood at 550 families in 1962. The following year, the congregation purchased land on San Jose Boulevard in order to relocate to the Southside. But ten years passed before the congregation constructed its first building on the new site.

Ahavath Chesed elected Rabbi Howard Greenstein to its pulpit in 1973 after Rabbi Lefkowitz's retirement. In 1974, Ahavath Chesed joined with local Orthodox Congregation Etz Chaim and Conservative Congregation Beth Shalom to form a kindergarten in its own quarters on Sunbeam Road. In 1978, the congregation moved into its new sanctuary at the San Jose location. Membership stood at nearly 750 in 1994.

References

Glickstein, Natalie H. *That Ye May Remember: Congregation Ahavath Chesed, 1882–1982* (Jacksonville, FL: 1982).
Synagogue Histories File, American Jewish Archives.

TEMPLE BETH ISRAEL, REFORM. *Longboat Key, Florida.* The rapid development of Longboat Key brought with it an increase in the Jewish population and a need to build a house of worship to serve this unique population of exclusively older adults. In 1979, a group of thirty founding families, led by Sydney Flanzbaum, decided to organize a Reform congregation. Thus, Temple Beth Israel became formally incorporated the following year. Originally, some residents thought about a collaborative effort in building an ecumenical house of worship on land set aside by the Arvida Corporation for that purpose.

Since its inception, retired rabbis have served Beth Israel. In its early years, the congregation met for services at the Coast Federal Bank under the religious leadership of Rabbi Albert Shulman (1979–1985). When membership grew, Beth Israel moved its services to a local church. In 1982, the synagogue's women formed Beth Israel Women. Two years later, the congregation dedicated its Temple building on Bay Isles Boulevard.

Since there are no young member families of the congregation, Beth Israel never established a religious school. However, congregants developed courses for adults and an active volunteer choir. Rabbi Philip Frankel (1985–1987) succeeded Rabbi Shulman.

Rabbi Sanford Saperstein joined Beth Israel as its religious leader in 1988, the same year that Beth Israel added a social hall, expanded its kitchen, and added offices to its building. In 1994, membership neared 450 family units.

Reference

Synagogue Histories File, American Jewish Archives.

TEMPLE BETH AM, REFORM. *Miami, Florida.* New residents who migrated to the Coral Gables, South Miami, and Kendall areas of Miami in the early 1950s felt the need to build a local Jewish facility. These new families founded the South Dade Jewish Community Center in 1955. This organization quickly became more than just a social club or even a vehicle to provide Jewish education for the children of member families. However, the congregation affirmed the establishment of a Hebrew School as its first organizational priority. One hundred fifty-five children joined the first religious school, which met in churches before meeting at the University of Miami.

The following year, with membership at one hundred families, the desire to evolve into a synagogue was evident when, in a close vote, the membership chose to affiliate with the Union of American Hebrew Congregations. At the same time, the UAHC established a new regional office in Miami. Thus, synagogue leadership and UAHC leadership determined that its regional director, Rabbi Herbert Baumgard, might serve both institutions. By this time, membership reached 170 families. When the congregation moved to its new facility on North Kendall drive in 1958, it adopted a new name: Temple Beth Am. The following year, Rabbi Baumgard joined the temple full time. Members constantly expanded the physical plant. In 1962, the congregation dedicated a new sanctuary. In 1994, Beth Am encompassed six large buildings.

Influenced by Rabbis Stephen Wise and Mordecai Kaplan, Baumgard sought to transform Beth Am into a synagogue-center. His rabbinate emphasized education. In the first summer, Beth Am instituted a camp program. Given the diversity of congregants, the congregation gave individual members the right to choose whether or not to cover the head during worship. Five years after the founding of the congregation, a debate over prayer shawls resulted in the same option, but although skullcaps were provided, prayer shawls were not provided. In addition, although pork and shellfish were prohibited from the kitchen, it was not kosher. Rabbi Leonard Schoolman (1986–1989) succeeded Rabbi Baumgard when the latter retired. Rabbi Jonathan Kendall (1989–1994) successfully argued to have prayer shawls available to members. Rabbi Terry Bookman succeeded Kendall in 1995.

The congregation continued its religious school program, opening a day school in 1970, evolving out of its nursery school. In addition, it provides a wide range of activities for its membership of 1350, including a variety of auxiliaries and affiliates, such as a basketball league with over 325 members.

Reference

Synagogue Histories File, American Jewish Archives.

BETH DAVID, CONSERVATIVE. *Miami, Florida.* In 1913, a small group of men met at the home of Mendel Rippa to form a new congregation. The group elected Morris Zion its president and named the congregation B'nai Zion. When this congregation of seventy grew ready to build its own structure, David Afremow donated a large portion of the funds to purchase the land for building on Northeast Eighth Street and Second Avenue. As a result, the congregation changed its name to Beth David (incorporated 1917). M. Samuelson came to serve the congregation as its first religious leader, and he organized a mixed choir.

In 1920 members exchanged the land they owned for the building of the First Christian Church on Northwest Third Avenue and Second Street. The following year, Rabbi Salo Stein came to serve Beth David. In 1922, a contingent of liberal members broke away to form Temple Israel of Greater Miami. When Stein resigned to lead Temple Israel, Rabbi Julian Schapo came to Miami (1922). At the same time, the congregation affiliated with the Conservative movement. The remaining Orthodox Jews attempted to maintain their Orthodox ritual within the context of a Conservative synagogue, holding separate services. Two years later, members who preferred this Orthodox approach to Judaism broke away and formed the Miami Orthodox Congregation, later called Beth El. Rabbi Shapo joined them.

Rabbi Murray Alstet succeeded Schapo before Rabbi Max Shapiro succeeded Alstet in 1932. In 1948, the congregation moved to Coral Way (Southwest Third Avenue and Twenty-sixth Road). In 1955, Rabbi Yaakov Rosenberg joined the congregation, serving until 1960. Rabbi Rosenberg pioneered a new form of adult education by sponsoring weekly "Businessmen's Torah Luncheons" in downtown Miami (1960). Beth David invited Rabbi Norman Shapiro to become its religious leader after Rosenberg left the congregation. When Shapiro resigned in 1964, Rabbi Sol Landau came to Beth David. During Landau's tenure, Beth Solomon: Flagler Granada merged into Beth David (1968). Landau retired in 1980, and Rabbi David Auerbach came to Beth David.

During Rabbi Auerbach's tenure, Beth David established a suburban center in South Dade County at Southwest 120th Street and Seventy-seventh Avenue, to which it moved its religious school and offices in 1983. However, when a group left to form a new Conservative congregation, Bet Shira (founded 1985), out of Beth David's suburban branch and took Rabbi Auerbach along, Rabbi Landau returned to serve Beth David. During this second brief tenure of Landau, Beth David extended full ritual privileges to women in the congregation. In addition, he initiated the practice of members presenting lessons from the Torah each week from the pulpit.

In 1986, Rabbi Jack Reimer joined Beth David as its religious leader. Under his direction, the congregation reestablished its education program on Southwest Third Avenue and started a preschool which quickly evolved into a Solomon Schechter Day School. In 1988, Beth Kodesh merged into Beth David. After the devastation caused by Hurricane Andrew in 1993, Beth David introduced Mitzvah Day, an annual event at which members devote an entire day to helping the community. In 1994, membership at Beth David exceeded seven hundred family units.

References

Lehrman, Irving, and Joseph Rappaport. *The Jewish Community of Miami Beach* (New York: 1959?).

Synagogue Histories File, American Jewish Archives.

TEMPLE BETH OR, RECONSTRUCTIONIST. *Miami, Florida.* Several individuals joined together in 1980 to establish a "liberal, liturgically creative, and philosophically challenging synagogue" and invited Rabbi Rami Shapiro to lead the congregation. This group affiliated with the Federation of Reconstructionist Synagogues and Havurot, the national organization of Reconstructionist synagogues (1982). After three years of existence, the congregation succeeded in developing services, activities, and a program of education, but it failed in developing an infrastructure to support such a venture. Thus, in 1983, twenty households met to dissolve the original community and found a new one, Beth Or. Its unique approach to synagogue life is evidenced in its purpose statement: "Our primary goal is the creation of a loving environment for Jewish learning and spirituality that is not just the best, but legendary." Services remained informal, and Beth Or established few policies in an effort to maintain a democratic culture. It met from 1984 to 1986 at the Jewish Community Center at 124th and 102nd in Miami. From 1984 to 1986, Beth Or met at a local church at Seventy-seventh Avenue and Seventy-sixth Street.

Beth Or purchased a private home on Southwest Eighty-seventh Avenue in 1987 and converted it for use as a synagogue. It uses a prayer book prepared by Rabbi Shapiro. As active members of Shomrei Adamah (guardians of the earth), the congregation established a community organic vegetable garden, where congregants maintain individual 4 × 4 parcels (1991). In 1995, Beth Or built a meditation garden. In order to maintain a level of intimacy, the congregation capped its membership at two hundred. In 1995, membership slightly exceeded that number.

Reference

Shapiro, Rami M. "We Hold These Truths to Be Self-Evident: Beth Or's Corporate Culture." *Reconstructionist* (May–June 1987): 21–25.

TEMPLE ISRAEL, REFORM. *Miami, Florida.* Twenty-two people, formerly members of Beth David, the local Conservative synagogue, met in the home of Harry V. Simons in 1922 and founded Temple Israel Reform Jewish Congregation of Miami (incorporated 1923), which is now known as Temple Israel of Greater Miami (adopted 1957). Simons served as its first president. The membership invited Rabbi Joseph Jasin (1923–1925) to serve as the temple's first religious leader. Initially meeting at the Young Men's Hebrew Association on Flagler Street, the congregation built its first home on Northeast Fourteenth Street in 1924. That same year, the congregation sold the building as a right of way for Biscayne Boulevard. The tropical storm of 1926 and the depression which followed severely strained the financial stability of the congregation. Before securing a new home, Temple Israel members worshiped at a variety of temporary facilities. Rabbi Jacob H. Kaplan (1926–1941) saw the congregation through this difficult period. Kaplan emphasized interfaith activities in his rabbinate.

In 1928, with a membership of 216 families, the temple moved to Northeast Nineteenth Street. Rabbi Colman E. Zwitman (1941–1949) succeeded Kaplan. Zwitman previously served as assistant and then associate to Kaplan before becoming senior rabbi. He attempted to return the place of ritual to Reform Judaism at Temple Israel. He spent most of his tenure at Temple Israel in chaplaincy service in the U.S. Army. His illness, contracted during service, prevented his return to an active rabbinate at Temple Israel.

In 1947, after twenty-five years, the temple finally began to recover from two depressions and a world war. As membership grew, the congregation required additional facilities. Membership exceeded 650 families in 1949. The following year, Rabbi Joseph R. Narot joined the congregation as its religious leader. The synagogue added a religious school (named in memory of Rabbi Colman Zwitman) and social hall in 1954 and a community house with office space, as well as classroom and recreational space, in 1960. Narot built the congregation in the context of post–World War II expansion. He concentrated on religious education during his tenure at Temple Israel, which was cut short by his death in 1980. In 1969, the temple transformed the street in front of its facility into a mall with a new chapel. In 1972, Temple Israel built a new sanctuary for its membership of eighteen hundred families. Shortly thereafter, congregants quickly began to leave the neighborhoods around the synagogue. Membership dwindled rapidly.

Following Narot's death, Temple Israel elected Rabbi Haskel Bernat to become its religious leader (1981–1987). During his tenure, Temple Israel affirmed it commitment to urban Jewry by remaining in the urban area rather than following the movement of the Jewish community to the suburbs. However, he recognized that Temple Israel needed to serve those congregants who chose to leave the city for the suburbs. Thus, Bernat also sought to develop a presence for Temple Israel there. As a result, the congregation developed a religious education center in the suburban Kendall area (which it subsequently closed in 1987) and purchased a lot on Southwest 167th Avenue for retreats (which it also sold in the later 1980s). In 1989, Rabbi Rex Perlmeter became senior rabbi of Temple Israel, having served as assistant and then interim rabbi since 1985. Perlmeter focused his rabbinate at Temple Israel on its redevelopment as an urban center for Jewish culture and learning. In 1994, membership at Temple Israel exceeded 615 family units.

References

Synagogue Histories File, American Jewish Archives.
Tebeau, Charlton W. *Synagogue in the Central City: Temple Israel of Greater Miami* (Coral Gables, FL: 1972).

BETH JACOB, ORTHODOX. *Miami Beach, Florida.* While residents of Miami Beach rebuilt the community following the havoc created by a hurricane in 1927, a small group of people who had joined together originally in 1924 received a charter to form Beth Jacob. Founders initially held services in the basement of David Court, with Zvi Hirsch Masliansky and Cantor Yosselle Rosenblatt participating. In 1929, the congregation moved into its quarters at Washington Avenue and Third Street, which housed a Hebrew School and Vaad Hakashrut (committee for the supervision of Jewish dietary laws). In 1934, members built a large center adjacent to this original building that included an office, a kitchen, and a Hebrew school.

In 1936, the congregation built a larger building on the same location (placed on the National Registry of Historic Places in 1980) to serve the growing Miami Beach Jewish community of the 1940s and 1950s. In 1994, despite the dwindling membership of 250, they built a chapel. That same year, the congregation, which is not affiliated with any national organization, adopted a more liberal ("Conservative") stance on ritual in order to attract new members to join. Several rabbis served the congregation during its history, including Rabbi Moses Mescheloff (1933–ca. 1955), Tebor Stern (ca. 1955–1965), and Shmaryahu T. Swirsky (1965–1992).

References

Lehrman, Irving, and Joseph Rappaport. *The Jewish Community of Miami Beach* (New York: 1959?).
Synagogue Histories File, American Jewish Archives.

TEMPLE EMANU-EL, CONSERVATIVE. *Miami Beach, Florida.* Organized in 1938 by former members of Beth Jacob Synagogue under the religious guidance of Rabbi Joseph Rackovsky, the congregation called itself Congregation Joseph Jacob. With two hundred members, the synagogue—which later changed its name to the Miami Beach Jewish Community Center—claimed its first home, a converted residence on Euclid Avenue. Following a dispute over whether or not to become a Conservative congregation, Rabbi Rackovsky departed to form an Orthodox synagogue elsewhere in Miami Beach (1941).

Rabbi Samuel Bension succeeded Rackovsky, in the same year as the Jewish Center added a sanctuary to its building. Rabbi Irving Lehrman came to the congregation in 1943. During World War II, the congregation joined with the local USO to provide services to armed forces personnel in a building on Lincoln Road. After World War II, Emanu-El grew into the largest congregation in Miami Beach at the time and built a facility at Washington Avenue and Seventeenth Street in 1948. The following year this seven-hundred-family congregation built a school building adjacent to its sanctuary. In 1950, Lehrman arranged for a branch of the Jewish Museum in New York to open in the synagogue. By 1953, the congregation religious school reached a population of over 510 students. In 1954, the congregation officially adopted the name Temple Emanu-El. It continued its building project, dedicating a social hall in 1957.

Lehrman worked on behalf of Israel and the struggle for civil rights. In 1958, Emanu-El purchased land at Dickens and Seventy-seventh Street to build a school to serve children living north of Forty-first Street (dedicating a branch school there in 1959). This developed into a Solomon Schechter Day School.

By 1960, Emanu-El's membership exceeded one thousand families. Its activities met the interests of all age groups. In 1962, the congregation established the Dr. Irving Lehrman Chair in Modern Jewish History at the Jewish Theological Seminary in America. The following year, Emanu-El remodeled its synagogue and added a social hall and classroom building in 1966. In 1968, Emanu-El renamed its day school Lehrman Day School.

By 1970, Emanu-El's membership exceeded thirteen hundred families. Its summer day camp served 150 campers. But by the early 1980s, day-school registration and attendance at late Friday evening services dwindled, because of demographic changes in Miami Beach. As a result, the day school transferred its classes to the main building in 1984–1985. In 1985, the school returned to its facilities, newly refurbished during its absence. In addition, the congregation purchased land adjacent to the school. In 1994, membership stood at 850 family units.

References

Event of the Decade, Temple Emanu-El of Greater Miami (Miami Beach: 1988).
Lehrman, Irving, and Joseph Rappaport. *The Jewish Community of Miami Beach* (New York: 1959?).
Synagogue Histories File, American Jewish Archives.

RAMAT SHALOM, RECONSTRUCTIONIST. *Plantation, Florida.* Ramat Shalom began as a small discussion group in 1975 for those interested in the philosophy of Reconstructionist Judaism. Under the guidance of Rabbi Lavy Becker, the group joined with others who wanted to start a synagogue in the area. The founders of this multidenominational synagogue, using the name Plantation Jewish Center, intended to create an institution that encouraged a variety of worship styles within one organization. The two groups split, however, when it became clear that one group wanted to affiliate with the Reform movement. The second group, with the help of the Federation of Reconstructionist Congregations and Havurot, with which it affiliated, rented space in a local building as it developed from a study group into a synagogue.

The congregation quickly outgrew its facilities, about the same time as it chose the name Ramat Shalom (Height of Peace) in order to maintain the initial "RS" for Reconstructionist Synagogue. In 1982, this young congregation of fifty member families dedicated a new building on West Broward Boulevard. While the congregation engaged student rabbis and interim rabbis in its early years, the congregation engaged Rabbi Elliot Skiddell in 1982. In 1993, with 150 families (and a membership limit of 250), the congregation initiated an expansion program. That same year, Ramat Shalom invited Rabbi Jeffrey Eisenstat to serve the congregation.

Reference

Synagogue Histories File, American Jewish Archives.

CONGREGATION SCHAARAI ZEDEK, REFORM. *Tampa, Florida.* A charter was granted to form Congregation Schaarai Zedek following a meeting of a group of thirty-one men and women led by M. Henry Cohen, Sr., in 1894. This group rented quarters for the new congregation on Florida Avenue. That same year the members opened a religious school. Rabbi D. Jacobson was elected Schaarai Zedek's first rabbi as it made plans to build its first building, which it dedicated in 1899.

By 1902, there was considerable friction, which developed into a lawsuit, over control of the congregation between those who opted for Reform Judaism and those who preferred orthodoxy. In 1902, the synagogue's constitution was amended to read "The form of worship shall be in accordance with Reform services." The following year, Schaarai Zedek joined the Union of American Hebrew Congregations, the national organization of Reform congregations. The Orthodox faction regrouped to form Rodeph Sholom, a Conservative congregation.

Between the years 1902 to 1904, the temple was without rabbinic leadership. Rabbi Henry S. Stolinitz served the congregation in 1905–1906, but from 1907 to 1920, Schaarai Zedek was without a rabbi once again. By 1923, the building on Florida Avenue was too small, and the board purchased property on DeLeon and Delaware. Rabbi L. Elliott Grafman was elected to the pulpit the following year, with membership at forty. Under Grafman's leadership, in 1924, the congregation moved to a new structure on Delaware and DeLeon Streets.

In 1930, following several years of desperate finances, Rabbi David L. Zielonka joined the congregation. With 150 members in 1947, there was talk about looking for another site to house the growing congregation. Although a new Sunday School building was built in 1949, Schaarai Zedek broke ground for its current building in 1957 on Swann and Lincoln Avenues. Additional religious school classrooms were built in 1962, as was an all-purpose space called Zielonka Hall. Additional expansion later took place.

Rabbi Frank Sundheim succeeded David Zielonka in 1970, after four years as his associate. Sundheim left the congregation under difficult circumstances in 1985 and was succeeded the following year by Rabbi Richard Birnholz. In 1993, membership stood at over 750 family units.

Reference

Synagogue Histories File, American Jewish Archives.

G

GEORGIA

AHAVATH ACHIM, CONSERVATIVE. *Atlanta, Georgia.* The majority of the founders of the Ahavath Achim Congregation were among the wave of immigrants who came to America in the 1880s. These newly arrived Jews immediately clashed with the German Jewish founders of the Hebrew Benevolent Congregation. Ahavath Achim received a charter in 1887, although its originators filed a petition for charter in 1877. Nevertheless, little is known about the incipient stages of congregational development because the records of Ahavath Achim only date back to 1890. Ahawas Achim, as the petition listed the congregational name, was started by eighteen men who met in a room on Gilner Street, later meeting in a rented hall on the same street and meeting for the High Holidays in larger facilities such as Concordia Hall and the Lyceum Theater. The congregation eventually moved to a newly constructed facility on Piedmont and Gilmer Street in 1895.

By 1892, the congregation employed an individual whose responsibility as *shohet* was to slaughter the meat according to ritual specifications and a sexton or shammes. Between 1886 and 1902, lay readers Abraham Jaffe and Jacob J. Simonoff led services. It took longer for this congregation, which was used to rabbis in Europe who served solely in the context of adjudication, to get used to the notion of an American rabbi and eventually engage one. The congregation has been served by Rabbis Berachya Mayerowitz (1901–1907), Julius Levin (1907–1915), Dr. Hyman Yood (1915–1919), Abraham Hirmes (1919–1928), Harry H. Epstein (1928–1982), and Arnold Goodman (1982–   ).

The climate of early meetings of Ahavath Achim was tense. While the meetings also served as social gatherings, the lack of established authority and the novelty of democratic principles led to many heated disagreements among members. As a result of a consolidation in 1893 with the membership of B'nai

Abraham Congregation, an Orthodox synagogue established in 1890, membership doubled at Ahavath Achim. As the consolidation between B'nai Abraham and Ahavath Achim was unstable, the former congregation reappeared in 1897, only to be absorbed by Ahavath Achim several months later. By 1901, larger quarters were necessary. Thus, the congregation moved to Piedmont Avenue and Gilmer Street. At about the same time, Joel Dorfan began his term as president, which did not end until 1928. Services continued to be Orthodox, with a *bima* (raised platform for leading worship) in the middle of the sanctuary. Women sat in a balcony. For some, ritual practices at Ahavath Achim were not "religious enough." Those who had lived in Atlanta the longest—and tended to be beardless—were given Torah honors, yet the more newly arrived were not given such honors. This kind of practice was taken as an affront by those who left the congregation and formed Shearith Israel in 1902. A second group, including four former Ahavath Achim presidents, who left Ahavath Achim only to be coolly received by the Hebrew Benevolent Congregation, went on to form Beth Israel in 1905 (eventually disbanding in 1920).

There were over four hundred synagogue members when it moved to Washington Street. Members built this new structure with a center-aisle reading desk and a women's balcony. The United Hebrew School, a community institution that Ahavath Achim had founded in 1913, met downstairs. When Rabbi Epstein arrived in 1928, he immediately made changes that directed the future of the congregation. In addition to improving the educational program and a variety of administrative procedures, Rabbi Epstein integrated English into the worship service, as well as emphasizing punctuality and decorum. In addition, he instituted late Friday evening services. Epstein had the spittoons removed from the sanctuary and transformed the chaotic Simchat Torah celebration into an orderly commemoration.

As the size of Ahavath Achim's membership increased, more families lived beyond the synagogue neighborhood. Thus, a minyan was arranged on the north side for the Sabbath and holidays. As this proved to be inadequate, that group formed Adas Yeshurun. Although this group eventually rejoined Ahavath Achim, the Beth Jacob Congregation, as result of Ahavath Achim's dispersion, was formed in the north side in the 1940s. Around the same time, a new facility for education was built on Tenth Street, just east of Piedmont Avenue.

In the 1950s, Rabbi Epstein introduced additional innovations to the congregation. Women sat with men during worship. He inserted English responsive readings and explanations of the weekly Torah reading into the service. The introduction of Confirmation and Bat Mitzvah made the 1952 affiliation with the United Synagogue of America, the synagogue organizational arm of the Conservative movement, acceptable to Ahavath Achim's fourteen hundred member families.

Ahavath Achim moved to the area of Peachtree Battle in 1958 after an original plan to move to Monroe Drive in the present vicinity of the Northeast Expressway was abandoned. By 1969, membership reached nearly 1750. The continual increase in student enrollment at Ahavath Achim led the congregation to open the Rabbi Harry H. Epstein Solomon Schechter School in 1973. By 1986, membership numbered over two thousand family units. Congregational activity, which includes full participation of women—something finally reached in 1983—reflects the diversity of interests of its membership.

References

Goldstein, Doris. *From Generation to Generation: A Centennial History of Congregation Ahavath Achim, 1887–1987* (Atlanta: 1987).

Hertzberg, Steven. *Strangers within the Gate City: Jews of Atlanta 1845–1915* (Philadelphia: 1978), pp. 86–97.

Stein, Kenneth W. *A History of the Ahavath Achim Congregation, 1887–1977.* (Atlanta: 1977).

———. "A History of Ahavath Achim Congregation, 1887–1927." *Atlanta Historical Journal* 23, no. 3 (Fall 1979): 106–18.

Synagogue Histories File, American Jewish Archives.

BETH JACOB, ORTHODOX. *Atlanta, Georgia.* Eight founders established Beth Jacob as an Orthodox synagogue in 1943, as a result of what these individuals perceived as a move away from orthodoxy at local Ahavath Achim. The group purchased a residence on Boulevard, which it converted for use as a synagogue. Rabbi Yosef Saffra became the first religious leader of Beth Jacob's forty members (1951). Under his guidance, the congregation established a religious school and a program of adult education. Rabbi Emanuel Feldman joined the congregation as its religious leader in 1952. Shortly before his arrival, members argued over whether the synagogue should maintain a *mechitza* (partition separating men from women in worship). Throughout its history, the congregation raised the height of the *mechitza* three times. Feldman's efforts concentrated on maintaining an Orthodox presence in the community. In 1956, Beth Jacob moved to a former church, also on Boulevard. It also led the effort to establish the Hebrew Academy, the city's first permanent full-day Jewish day school.

Under a great deal of protest from residents in the area, Beth Jacob's 190 families moved to LaVista Road (1962). There it also built a ritual bath and established a Hebrew School. Despite a surge in membership, Beth Jacob experienced difficult financial times in the early 1960s. Membership at Beth Jacob reached five hundred in 1978, with two hundred people attending Saturday morning worship services. Feldman led the congregation on behalf of Israel and Soviet Jewry. In 1977, Beth Jacob added an educational wing to its building. Feldman also led the congregation's efforts in establishing the Torah Day School (1984).

Rabbi Ilan D. Feldman, having joined as assistant in 1980, succeeded his father upon his retirement in 1991. During the tenure of Rabbi Ilan Feldman, the congregation extended its efforts in the area of outreach to unaffiliated and nonobservant Jews in the community. Feldman helped to establish a *Kollel,* an intensive learning environment, in the community. Beth Jacob helped form an independent Orthodox synagogue, Congregation Ariel, in the Dunwoody section of Atlanta. In 1994, membership exceeded 560 family units.

Reference

Rogoff, Leigh H. *Congregation Beth Jacob's First Fifty Years, 1943–1993* (Atlanta: 1993).

HEBREW BENEVOLENT CONGREGATION, REFORM. *Atlanta, Georgia.* In 1867, having set up the Hebrew Benevolent Society to bury its dead in 1860, sixty-six men determined to establish a synagogue under the inspiration of Isaac Leeser, who had come to Atlanta from Philadelphia in order to officiate at a wedding ceremony. Thus, this group founded the Hebrew Benevolent Congregation, Kehilah Kodesh Gemilath Chesed. Several years later, in 1870, the women of the congregation formed the Ladies' Hebrew Benevolent Society.

In the beginning of its development, the new congregation occupied several locations. At Rabbi Isaac Mayer Wise's suggestion, the new synagogue community called David Burgheim to serve as the first religious leader of the new synagogue community in 1869. He quickly introduced four reforms in the congregation, including the melodeon, mixed choir, weekly sermons in German, and the *Minhag America* prayer book. Perhaps he pushed the congregation further than it was willing to go toward Reform or perhaps his progressive civil rights attitudes in a city undergoing Reconstruction contributed to his short tenure in Atlanta. His successor, Benjamin Aaron Bonnheim, served from 1870 to 1873; the difficult finances that affected Atlanta and the temple during that time contributed to the ending of his tenure. During the rabbinate of Bonnheim's successor, Henry Gersoni (1874–1876), who was unrelenting in his criticism of Orthodox Judaism and its adherents, the synagogue's members laid plans for a permanent structure. The sanctuary structure itself was an ornate Moorish-style red brick building featuring a domed tower with a number of smaller domes adorning the remainder of the roof (dedicated 1877). The congregation built this structure at the corner of Garnett and Forsyth streets. Dr. Edward Benjamin Morris Browne served the congregation in this new building, with only fifty-seven members. Nicknamed "Alphabet" Browne, he served only four years (1877–1881).

In the early years of the congregation, its members followed Orthodox ritual practices, which included separate seating for men and women and the traditional chanting of the liturgy. This changed after the death of Isaac Leeser. As was noted above, the congregation soon adopted Isaac Mayer Wise's prayer book, *Minhag America,* for use in worship. Confirmation in the congregation dates back to the 1870s. In 1877, the congregational board of directors tabled a motion to permit worship with uncovered heads. A year later, the congregation joined the Union of American Hebrew Congregations, the national organization of Reform synagogues. An attempt to establish an "open temple" in 1881, to be maintained only by voluntary contributions, failed. It may be that the congregation at this time wanted to reconsider its Reform posture when it consulted Marcus Jastrow, a leader of the Conservative movement. As a result, the congregation withdrew from the Union of American Hebrew Congregations.

During the tenure of Jacob S. Jacobson (1881–1887), membership increased considerably. When his successor, Leo Reich (1888–1894), joined the congregation, it adopted the *Minhag Jastrow* prayer book. Throughout its early years, the congregation seemed to flip-flop between orthodoxy and Reform. By the end of the century, in 1895, a slight majority of Temple members decided to affiliate once again with Reform Judaism. They voted to instruct the rabbi to abandon his ritual garb and the requirement of a covered head for the worshiper. In addition, the congregation observed holidays for one day and finally adopted the *Union Prayer Book*. As Reich could not abide these changes, he left the congregation. The Hebrew Benevolent Congregation engaged Rabbi David Marx (1895–1946), who led the way to Reform. During Marx's first year, Temple membership grew from 169 to 214.

In 1902, the congregation built its second sanctuary: a classic-style structure with one central dome, still standing at the corner of South Pryor and Richardson Streets. In 1904, the congregation instituted Sunday morning services. These services eventually evolved to Sunday morning addresses, because of the difficulty of securing a choir on Sunday morning. In 1909, fire damaged the building and disrupted activities in the temple. Services were held at the Hebrew Orphans' Home. While congregational membership continued to grow, it did not grow in proportion to the growth of Atlanta's Jewish community. Perhaps its slow growth can be attributed to the temple's vote to disavow its stand on political Zionism even after other national Reform bodies had changed their positions. The establishment of a sisterhood in 1912 helped the congregation to grow as it became a center of religious, social, and educational activities for its members. By 1919, membership increased to nearly four hundred members, with an equal number of children in the religious school. In 1927, the synagogue established a program to train all the religious-school teachers in Atlanta.

In 1928, amidst difficult financial times, congregational leaders decided to build again, at the present Peachtree site (dedicated 1931). However, the members optimistically built this structure far beyond neighborhoods where the congregants lived. The decades of the 1930s and 1940s proved to be among the most difficult for the congregation, spiritually and financially. The congregation and its members felt the impact of the Great Depression. In addition, Marx continued to preach against Zionism, to the growing consternation of many members.

Under the leadership of Marx's successor, Rabbi Jacob M. Rothschild (1946–1973), the congregation grew considerably, beginning with five hundred members in 1940. In 1958, a bomb, believed to have been set by a group of neo-Nazis, perhaps in reaction to the pro–civil rights stance of Rothschild, destroyed temple classrooms and the assembly hall. In 1960 the temple dedicated a new educational building and auditorium, which it named "Friendship Hall" in honor of all those who extended their support in the days and weeks following the bomb blast.

Rabbi Alvin M. Sugarman succeeded Rothschild in 1972, having joined the congregation as assistant rabbi in 1971. Considered by some as the "mother congregation" of the Reform movement in Atlanta, with a current membership of fourteen hundred families, it has spun off at least four local congregations. Under Sugarman's guidance, the congregation developed a wide variety of programs, with the ultimate goal of service to all of its congregants.

References

Hertzberg, Steven. *Strangers within the Gate City: Jews of Atlanta 1845–1915* (Philadelphia: 1978), pp. 55–72.

Marx, David. *A History of the Hebrew Benevolent Congregation of Atlanta, Georgia* (Atlanta: 1917).

Miesels, Stanley. "The Hebrew Benevolent Congregation of Atlanta, Georgia: A History" (Term paper, Hebrew Union College–Jewish Institute of Religion, Cincinnati, 1968).

Rothschild, Janice O. *As But a Day: The First Hundred Years, 1867–1967* (Atlanta: 1967).

Shankman, Arnold. "A Temple Is Bombed—Atlanta, 1958." *American Jewish Archives* 23, no. 2 (November 1971): 125–53.

Synagogue Histories File, American Jewish Archives.

CONGREGATION MICKVE ISRAEL, REFORM. *Savannah, Georgia.* In the very first month of their landing in 1733, the Spanish-Portuguese Jews who arrived in Savannah only five months after Oglethorpe established the Colony of Georgia founded K. K. (Kehillah Kadosha/Holy Congregation) Mickve Israel. This group met regularly in a rented house in Market Square from 1733 to 1740 or 1741, when its fortunes faded along with those of other members of the colony, and the dissension that developed from social and cultural issues, rather than religious ones, created a schism. The group had constructed, in 1738, a ritual bath. The few remaining Jews met in Mordecai Sheftall's home until he established a perpetual trust that led to the purchase of land for a synagogue building. By 1786, the group reorganized to form K. K. Mickve Israel and met at rented quarters at Broughton Street Lane. In 1790, a perpetual charter was granted for Parnas and Adjuntas (president and board) of Mickve Israel at Savannah. Finances again proved difficult for the fledgling congregation, which was forced in 1797 to give up its quarters and meet in private homes once again. In 1789, the congregation received a now well-known letter from President George Washington, a response to a letter of congratulations that the congregation had sent the new president on his election.

By 1818, the congregation, led by Dr. Jacob De la Motta, again sought its own facilities. This building at Liberty Street and Perry Lane, dedicated in 1820, became the first synagogue to be erected in the state of Georgia. The small wooden structure was destroyed by fire in 1829; because of Savannah's economy and the heat and drought that brought sickness with them, nearly ten years had passed before a new brick building was built in 1839.

Throughout its early history, the congregation attempted to persuade rabbis to come to Savannah to serve the congregation, but its resources were too limited to allow it to make any acceptable offers. Jacob Rosenfield served the congregation from 1852 until he was forced to resign in 1862 over differences with the board and his assertion of authority in the congregation. Immediately upon his arrival, he inspired the creation of the congregation's first religious school. When Rosenfield resigned, a group of his followers joined with members of the local chapter of B'nai B'rith to form a new synagogue, K. K. B'nai Berith Jacob. Discussions regarding a merger in 1872 did not come to fruition. There were too many ideological differences that divided the congregation by that time. Yet, Rosenfield returned to Mickve Israel to serve two interim years, 1870–1872. Except for the years 1867–1869, when Raphael de Castro Lewin read services, a variety of congregants led services until the arrival of Abraham Harris in 1873.

The early congregation followed the Portuguese ritual until 1868, during Lewin's brief tenure, when it took the first major steps toward reform by eliminating the observance of the second day of holidays and introducing a mixed choir with music during worship. Lewin also altered the manner in which children were named on the pulpit. Previously, the congregation had used the choir on the Sabbath, and women were permitted to come down from the balcony and sit in the sanctuary. But it was Lewin's sermon "Orthodoxy vs. Reform" that really laid the groundwork for reform in the temple. When Isaac P. Mendes was elected to the pulpit in 1877, following Harris' hasty departure in the midst of a yellow-fever epidemic that afflicted members of the temple, he advised against the hasty abandonment of ritual. In 1880, he instituted confirmation. That same year, the marital canopy became optional. He fought against these reforms and succeeded for a short time. But ultimately, these reforms and others were introduced in the congregation. Moreover, in 1894, members were permitted to attend services without head coverings. Though Mendes was Orthodox, during his tenure the music program flourished at the temple, without his encouragement. He strove to restore orthodoxy to the congregation, urging the restoration of the traditional observance of the Sabbath, but to no avail. In 1902, the *Union Prayer Book* was adopted. Little of the congregation's heritage remained until the Sephardic pronunciation of Hebrew was restored in 1948.

With the growth of Savannah's Jewish community, temple membership expanded. This growth necessitated larger facilities, and a new building was consecrated on Monterey Square in 1878. This building was built without a balcony. Fire damaged the interior of the synagogue building in 1899 and severely damaged the entire building in 1927. The second fire required substantial rebuilding efforts.

In 1903, with the retirement of Mendes because of ill health, Rabbi George Solomon was elected to the pulpit. Mendes died shortly thereafter. Solomon led the congregation in efforts to officially link itself to Reform Judaism. In 1904, the congregation joined the Union of American Hebrew Congregations, the umbrella organization for Reform congregations. Among other reforms that Solomon instituted was the late Friday evening service. As the Portuguese tradition of the congregation gave way, the spelling of the congregation's name changed as well. In 1913, the spelling changed from Mickva to Mickve Israel.

Spurred by the Hebrew Benevolent Congregation of Atlanta, Mickve Israel joined efforts in 1924 to form the Union of Georgia Hebrew Congregations, which eventually merged into the Southeast Federation of the Union of American Hebrew Congregations.

Solomon was followed by Rabbi Louis Youngerman, who occupied the pulpit from 1946 to 1948. His short tenure was a result of his outspoken support of a federal antilynching law and the synagogue's board's attempt to censure the rabbi. Rabbi Solomon Starrels served from 1948 to 1965. During the 1960s, Reform Jewish leaders, particularly rabbis, came from the North to support the struggle over civil rights in the South. As a congregation, Mickve Israel did not support their efforts, reacting strongly against the UAHC's support of these "freedom riders."

References

Blumenthal, Walter. "Congregation Mickve Israel, Savannah, Georgia, 1840–1860" (Term paper, Hebrew Union College–Jewish Institute of Religion, Cincinnati, 1957).

Hershman, Morris. "Culture, Practices, and Ideals of Congregation Mikveh Israel Savannah, Georgia" (Term paper, Hebrew Union College–Jewish Institute of Religion, Cincinnati, 1956).

Levy, B. H. *A Short History of Temple Mickve Israel* (Savannah, GA: 1957).

Morgan, David T. "Judaism in Eighteenth-Century Georgia." *Georgia Historical Society Quarterly* 58, no. 1 (Spring 1974): 41–54.

Rubin, Saul Jacob. *Third to None, The Saga of Savannah Jewry* (Savannah, GA: 1983).

Synagogue Histories File, American Jewish Archives.

H

HAWAII

TEMPLE EMANU-EL, REFORM. *Honolulu, Hawaii.* The Honolulu Jewish community, where the majority of Hawaii's Jews live, was formally organized in 1938 by the Jewish Welfare Board (JWB) to serve thirty-five member families. The JWB built a chapel on Young Street, which was staffed by military chaplains and later converted into a Jewish Community Center. In 1947, the JWB sent Rabbi Emanuel Kumin to Hawaii to serve the center as its director and lead the congregation. Incorporated in 1948, it relocated the following year to the new Berentania Street JWB–USO Club in downtown Honolulu. This center was closed in 1949, when Kumin returned to the mainland and the JWB closed down its Hawaiian operations.

The Congregation of the Honolulu Jewish Community was established in 1949. Justice Bernard Levinson served as temple president for ten years, beginning in 1950. Under his leadership, the congregation evolved. Initially, services were held at a military chapel and then in a home on Oahu Avenue, converted for use as a synagogue. At this new location, the congregation began to refer to itself as Temple Emanu-El.

In 1951 Dr. Francis Hevesi was engaged to serve the community as its rabbi. Although he died ten months later, he had been able to institute weekly Sabbath services on Friday evening and Saturday morning. Rabbi Alexander Segal, the congregation's first Reform rabbi, was elected to the pulpit in 1952. Membership grew to one hundred families, and the congregation sponsored a joint Sunday School with the recently formed Armed Forces Aloha Jewish Chapel. Though its services had been essentially Conservative, the congregation joined the Union of American Hebrew Congregations the same year and officially adopted the name Temple Emanu-El. Rabbi Roy Rosenberg succeeded Segal in 1958.

A new Temple Emanu-El was built in 1960 on Pali Highway, with a learning center in 1969. When Rosenberg left in 1966, the congregation had grown to 160 families. Rabbi Robert Schenkerman succeeded Rosenberg and served the congregation until 1971. Upon his departure, Rabbi Julius Nodel was asked to assume the pulpit. With Nodel's encouragement and direction, in 1975, a group of members instituted traditional services on Saturday mornings and the festivals in addition to services that follow a Reform liturgy. Rabbi Arnold (Avi) Magid followed Nodel when the latter retired in 1980. By 1985, membership had grown to over four hundred. When Magid left in 1989, he was succeeded by Rabbi Stephen Barack. In 1993, membership stood at nearly 375.

Reference

Synagogue Histories File, American Jewish Archives.

I

ILLINOIS

ANSHE EMET, CONSERVATIVE. *Chicago, Illinois.* A group of about twenty Bohemian, English, German, and Russian North Side Jews who found it difficult to travel to the South Side synagogues gathered together for worship in 1873 in the home of Louis Sax. Calling themselves Anshe Emes (later changing to Anshe Emet), the assembly stayed in this location for six months before moving to the home of another member on Sedgwick Street. In 1876, the group felt ready to rent a permanent meeting place on Division Street and engage the services of A. A. Lowenheim as religious leader. Two years later, Anshe Emet moved to another Division Street location.

In 1893, the congregation decided to construct its own building on Sedgwick Street. In this new location, members invited Rabbi Solomon Bauer to serve as their religious leader. When the women of Anshe Emet established a Ladies Auxiliary, the congregation became one of the few Eastern European congregations to do so at the time. When Bauer left in 1916, Rabbi Joseph Hevesh (1913–1916) succeeded him.

Little is known about the congregation during the years 1916–1922, as a fire destroyed all of the records from this period. Yet, growth took place in the membership. Rabbi Phillip Langh served the congregation (1920–1928). During his association, the congregation moved into a new building on Gary Place (later Patterson Place) near Broadway in 1922. Langh started a religious school in the new location during its first year of operation. The following year, he introduced Confirmation to the congregation. By 1924, membership reached two hundred families. When Temple Sholom moved to its new temple on Lake Shore Drive in 1928, Anshe Emet purchased Sholom's Grace and Pine Grove facility. However, the facility proved to be too big a financial burden to the congregation, which dwindled to ninety families in 1929.

Rabbi Solomon Goldman joined the congregation in 1928. A well-known scholar and ardent Zionist, Goldman energized this failing congregation. Each week, increasing numbers of people came to hear him deliver sermons from the pulpit. He also initiated a variety of academic programs, which attracted large groups of young people and adults. Goldman established daily morning and afternoon worship services and a wide variety of cultural programs, including a full-day kindergarten and dance and drama groups. The Anshe Emet Forum attracted people from all walks of life with speakers like Eleanor Roosevelt and Clarence Darrow. By 1930, membership exceeded three hundred families. In 1934, the synagogue officially adopted the name Anshe Emet Congregation of Chicago. The following year, membership reached eleven hundred families.

In 1946, Anshe Emet opened a day school, the first in the Conservative movement. In 1950, the congregation called women to the honor of the Torah for the first time in the congregation's history. The following year, the congregation acquired the Sheridan Theater building on Sheridan Road. In 1953, Rabbi Solomon Goldman died suddenly. Anshe Emet honored his memory by publishing his works and establishing an annual creativity award in his name (1967).

In 1954, Anshe Emet elected Rabbi Ira Eisenstein, a Reconstructionist leader, to its pulpit. He remained with the congregation until 1959, when he left to work for the Reconstructionist movement. The following year, Anshe Emet elected Rabbi Seymour J. Cohen to lead the congregation. Concerned with social welfare, Cohen worked with a variety of local and national organizations. Cohen also concentrated his efforts in the area of adult education and increasing the role of women in worship. He introduced the prayer book prepared by the Conservative Rabbinical Assembly to the congregation and restored the traditional Jewish calendar of holiday worship, adding a second day of holiday observance. In 1965, the congregation expanded the synagogue building. Two years later, Anshe Emet dedicated the Cummings Gallery, dedicated to philanthropist Nathan Cummings.

In 1970, Anshe Emet initiated the formation of the Friendship Circle, a joint project of the synagogue and the Jewish Community Centers of Chicago, designed to serve older adults in the community. In the 1980s, the congregation became a center for young Jewish adults in the city. When Rabbi Cohen retired in 1990, Rabbi Michael Siegel succeeded him, having joined as an assistant rabbi in 1982. During his early tenure, the congregation refurbished nearly the entire facility. He concentrated his efforts on single adults and special programs for children. In 1994, membership stood at one thousand.

References

Goldman, Solomon. *A Rabbi Takes Stock* (New York: 1931).

Gutstein, Morris A. *A Priceless Heritage: The Epic Growth of Nineteenth Century Chicago Jewry* (New York: 1953).

The Sentinel's History of Chicago Jewry (Chicago: 1961).

EMANUEL, REFORM. *Chicago, Illinois.* In 1880, German-speaking Jews organized Emanuel Congregation at Blackhawk and Sedgwick Streets in a rented building, Schlotthauer Hall. Striving to retain a German Jewish culture, the only compromise made at the time was a slightly modern approach to its Orthodox Judaism. Emanuel's first religious leader was Adolph Dushner, who served only one year, from 1880 to 1881. He was succeeded by Mr. Austrian, who in turn was succeeded by Rabbi Darmstadter, who led the congregation from 1881. Emanuel's second home was located at Phoenix Hall on Division Street and was replaced in 1886 by a Swedish Church on Franklin Street. By 1893, members of Emanuel were swept by the tide of Reform Judaism and adopted David Einhorn's *Olath Tamid* as their prayer book. In addition, the congregation passed a resolution to worship with uncovered heads. Other gradual changes took place during this early period. English slowly was replacing German as the language of the congregation. (A complete shift was made in 1901.) In 1894, Congregation Or Chadosh united with Emanuel, completing the congregation's transition to Reform Judaism.

Other rabbis who served the congregation were E.B.M. Browne (1892–1894), Julius Newman (1894–1899), Dr. Emanuel Schreiber (1899–1907), and Leo Mannheimer (1907). While Mannheimer's illness forced him to retire after only a few months, he did institute Friday night services and also introduced the *Union Prayer Book,* the uniform prayer book of the Reform movement. When the converted Swedish Church was sold in 1893, a Baptist Church on Belden Avenue and Halstead Street was rented to house congregational activities temporarily. By 1896, Emanuel was losing members. A building would solve the problem. The congregation purchased a lot on Burling Street and Belden Avenue. Before building commenced, members realized that the membership had moved further north. The Burling lot was sold, and a second lot was purchased on Buckingham Place near Halsted Street. The new building was dedicated in 1908 by the newly installed Rabbi Felix A. Levy, who remained as rabbi of the congregation for forty-seven years.

During Levy's tenure, the congregation grew considerably. Under his direction, affiliates emerged. A fire destroyed the organ and choir loft in 1916. The congregation subsequently rebuilt facilities for the choir. Emanuel added Sunday morning services, but this innovation, designed to resolve the problem of poor attendance at Saturday worship services, was short lived.

By 1943, it was evident that the membership had outgrown its building and a new lot on Surf Street and Sheridan Road was purchased for building in 1944. Again, the population had moved farther out, and the lot was sold and replaced in 1949 by a lot farther out on Sheridan Road at Thorndale Avenue. This new temple was dedicated in the early days of 1955, the same year that Rabbi Herman E. Schaalman succeeded Felix Levy in the pulpit.

Schaalman retired in 1986 and was succeeded by Rabbi Joseph Edelheit, who had served the congregation previously as assistant rabbi. When he left in 1993, members elected Rabbi David Sofian to the pulpit. Emanuel's membership reached nearly 650 family units in 1994.

References

Bregstone, Philip P. *Chicago and Its Jews* (Chicago: 1933).
Gutstein, Morris A. *A Priceless Heritage: The Epic Growth of Nineteenth Century Chicago Jewry* (New York: 1953).
Synagogue Histories File, American Jewish Archives.

KAM ISAIAH ISRAEL, REFORM. *Chicago, Illinois.*

Kehilath Anshe Mayriv (KAM)

Dilah Kohn arrived in Chicago in 1846 from Moenichsroth, Bavaria. She was amazed that the community did not employ ritual slaughterers so that she might observe Jewish dietary laws. As a result of her urging, the tiny community engaged Ignatz Kunreuther as both a *shochet* and a religious community leader. Months later, in 1847, following Yom Kippur services, fourteen men assembled in the Rosenberg and Rosenfeld Emporium in order to sign papers of incorporation for Kehilath Anshe Mayriv (KAM—Congregation of the Men of the West), the first congregation in the Midwest and the mother synagogue of the Chicago area. At the same time, the Jewish Burial Ground Society, which had been formed the previous year, ceded its property to the new congregation and discontinued its independent existence. Three years later, in 1851, on a leased lot between Adams and Quincy Streets (where the U.S. Court House now stands), KAM built its first house of worship and established the first Jewish day school in the city (maintained until 1875).

By 1853, intragroup differences threatened congregational viability, and a group of German-Polish Jews established the B'nai Sholom Congregation. In the midst of this controversy, Kunreuther resigned. Rabbi M. Mensor succeeded him. Amid accusations of fraud and plagiarism, he left rather quickly. Dr. Solomon Friedlander succeeded him but died shortly thereafter from a fatal bite from a black widow spider. Arguing over radical or moderate reform, another group of KAM dissidents founded the Israelite Reform Society five years later, in 1857. This group initially floundered but eventually evolved into the Juedischer Reformverein (later to join with another dissident group, "the Lovers of Light," to become Sinai Congregation).

In 1855, the congregation moved to Adams and Wells. Rabbi Liebman Adler joined the congregation in 1861. As he spoke only German, others gave the weekly sermon in his place. As a founding member of the Union of American Hebrew Congregations, it joined in 1873. In 1874, KAM purchased the Plymouth Church building on Indiana and Twenty-sixth Street and dedicated it the following year. In 1883, Dr. Samuel Sale was called to the pulpit and remained for four years when Rabbi Isaac Moses succeeded him. In 1891, KAM moved to Indiana and Thirty-third Street. Moses left in 1896 to found Temple Israel, succeeded by Rabbi Moses Perez Jacobson. Membership reached 186.

Rabbi Tobias Schanfarber (a.k.a. "Uncle Toby") came to the congregation in 1901. His rabbinate focused on pastoral visits at home and at work. Finally

KAM moved in 1923 to Drexel Boulevard and Fiftieth Street, where it remained until 1971. Rabbi Solomon B. Freehof succeeded Schanfarber in 1924. When he left in 1934, KAM engaged Rabbi Joshua Liebman, who remained five years. Liebman insisted that the congregation return to Friday evening services and that Hebrew be taught in the religious school. The congregation invited composer Max Janowski to the congregation in 1937 to serve as music director and enrich the liturgical life of the congregation.

KAM next turned to Rabbi Jacob J. Weinstein for leadership. With congregational president Max Robert Schrayer, Weinstein empowered the congregation through the development of a framework for committee structures and total membership participation. He initiated a forum following his sermon in which congregants might respond to his controversial sermons. Under his guidance, KAM took the lead as a major force in congregational social action in the Reform movement. As the neighborhood around the synagogue changed in its ethnic makeup, Weinstein insisted the congregation remain at its site and help stabilize the neighborhood. A few hundred congregants fled the area—and the synagogue—nonetheless. During 1946–1947, a schism developed over the speed at which lay participation was to be encouraged in the congregation. As a result, Schrayer and assistant Rabbi Eric Friedland withdrew from KAM to form another congregation. Seven hundred families remained. Ten years later, they built a new community house for the congregation in 1952. By 1957, the congregation established a north shore branch, in Highland Park, eventually developing into Solel Congregation. Rabbi Simeon Maslin succeeded Weinstein in 1967.

Zion Congregation

When Rabbi Bernhard Felsenthal requested a contract of longer than a year at a time at Sinai Congregation, his request was denied. Felsenthal resigned in 1864 and, joined by a group of loyal followers, founded (B'nai) Zion congregation, the first synagogue on Chicago's west side. He served until 1887. As Zion's membership scattered, some formed what later was Washington Boulevard Temple, Temple Mizpah when it was founded, and finally the congregation disbanded. Zion's last rabbi, Dr. Samuel Cohon, became Mizpah's first.

Isaiah Temple

Organized in 1895, Isaiah Temple was formed by those families of Zion Congregation who had moved out of the area of Washington Boulevard and Ogden Avenue, from the west to the south side. Zion's preamble was adopted word for word. Joseph Stolz, who had been rabbi at Zion, was elected to the pulpit of this new congregation and served from 1896 to 1927. Women were given full voting rights as members. The fledgling group met in Oakland Club Hall and used David Einhorn's *Olath Tamid* as its prayer book. Services were held on Saturday and Sunday. It dedicated its first house of worship in 1899 at Forty-fifth Street and Vincennes Avenue.

The congregation grew to 270 members by 1908 with an enrollment of nearly

450 children in the religious school. By 1919, the congregation considered moving again, given the changing demography of the neighborhood. This same year, Friday evening services were introduced to the congregation. While negotiations between KAM and Isaiah for a merger (and move to one new building) were initiated at this time, nothing came of these discussions. Instead, Isaiah moved to Hyde Park Boulevard and Greenwood Avenue in 1921 and refurbished one of the buildings already located on the property. In the new location, Sunday services were temporarily dropped.

In 1923, negotiations for merger with KAM began again, with the provision that Isaiah would join KAM in KAM's new building, a provision that Isaiah members were not willing to accept. That same year, Isaiah dedicated its own new structure for worship. Less than two months after the dedication of this new building, B'nai Sholom and Isaiah merged, incorporating Temple Israel, which had already merged with B'nai Sholom. The full merger took place in 1924; the new congregation was called the Temple Isaiah Israel.

B'nai Sholom

In 1852, eleven Jews met in the home of Solomon Harris to form this new congregation, holding services in a loft above Harris's store on Lake Street. While KAM had been founded only five years earlier, these Prussian Polish Jews from Posen did not feel welcome in the German KAM Temple and also preferred their own order of worship. Edward Meirs served the congregation as its first religious leader, followed by several readers who shared a variety of responsibilities in the congregation: Samuel (Lowenthal?) Rosenthal (1855), Alexis Alexander (1856–1863), and Israel R. Warrensky. The congregation grew rapidly as did the Jewish population of Chicago. By 1855, its membership had doubled to forty members, and the congregation moved to larger quarters above Kendall's Bakery at the corner of Washington and Dearborn Streets. Three years later, it moved to rented rooms on South Clark Street.

Some members of B'nai Sholom founded a separate relief and burial society in 1861, the Chebra Kaddisha Ubikkur Cholim. This organization also held worship services. Two new groups of immigrants provided membership to B'nai Sholom during the Civil War period: German-speaking Jews from Holland who came by way of England, and Polish Jews from Lithuanian communities near the Prussian borders. In 1864, B'nai Sholom dedicated a new building at Harrison Street and Fourth Avenue (now Federal Street).

Rabbi Aron J. Messing, Jr. came to B'nai Sholom in 1868, as the congregation's first ordained rabbi. While the congregation had advertised for a rabbi fluent both in German and English, he was really not yet equipped to preach in English. Messing was not comfortable with even the moderate attempts at reform and left after a few years. In the absence of any religious leader, the congregation succeeded in introducing family pews. Messing was succeeded by Moritz Spitz, but he did not remain long after the Great Fire of 1871, which destroyed B'nai

Sholom's edifice. Thus, the congregation was forced to worship in rented quarters as it had in its early stages of development. Following several moves, the congregation built again in 1877.

Aron J. Messing, Jr. returned to the congregation in 1874. While still not prepared for radical reform, he was more comfortable with some change and, for example, confirmed his first class of boys and girls that same year. The congregation affiliated with the Union of American Hebrew Congregations in 1875. Dr. Henry Gersoni was called to the pulpit of B'nai Sholom in 1877. The choice of Gersoni confirmed the congregation's interest in Reform. Shortly after his arrival in Chicago, Gersoni introduced the three-year cycle of Torah reading and revised the worship service. As a result of accusations that Gersoni had converted to Christianity and then returned to Judaism, Gersoni remained only a year. He was succeeded by Samuel Marks. He introduced a mixed choir with a melodeon, but he maintained religious practices of a highly traditional nature. Marx was succeeded briefly by Marcus Bonheim, Max Heller (still a student at Hebrew Union College), and Solomon Kauffmann. This constant turnover of rabbinic leadership was reflective of a lack of ritual direction among the congregation as much as it was the cause of a lack of ritual direction. And the turnover continued.

Matters worsened, and the congregation was forced to sell its building on Michigan Avenue, where it had relocated to the Beth Hamedresh Hagadol Ub'nai Jacob. In 1890, B'nai Sholom purchased the KAM building at Indiana and Twenty-sixth Streets. And after the short-term engagement of a series of rabbis, Messing was called back to the congregation for his third ministry with B'nai Sholom. While ten years of growth accompanied Messing's return, eventually B'nai Sholom entered decline once again. As a result, B'nai Sholom merged with Temple Israel in 1906 to form Congregation B'nai Sholom Temple Israel.

Temple Israel

Following his tenure at KAM, Rabbi Isaac S. Moses founded Temple Israel (which he called the People's Synagogue) in 1896, on the basis of "cheap individual membership and complete freedom of the pulpit." He adopted the *Union Prayer Book* and used an organ with choir for worship. His congregation found its first real home in the rented quarters of the Baptist Memorial Church on Oakland Boulevard. In 1898, congregants dedicated their own structure at Forty-fourth and St. Lawrence Avenue. Against Moses' original vision, dues were increased to support the building. He left in 1900.

A nephew of Rabbi Emil G. Hirsch of Chicago's Sinai Temple, Edward Baker led the congregation as a "lay rabbi" following Moses' departure. Ordained rabbis led services on occasion, but it was not until its merger with B'nai Sholom that the congregation gained rabbinic leadership.

Congregation B'nai Sholom Temple Israel

Rabbi Gerson B. Levi was elected to the united congregation of Congregation B'nai Sholom Temple Israel in 1906. Levi was an ardent reformer who followed Rabbi Emil G. Hirsch's extreme attitude toward ritual and his opposition to political Zionism. The growth of the congregation and the neighborhood encouraged the merged temple to build a new structure in 1914 at Michigan Avenue and Fifty-third Street. But by 1924, the neighborhood had changed once again, and the congregation sought a new home. This time, it was through a merger with Isaiah Temple, which had just built a new facility at Hyde Park Boulevard and Greenwood Avenue. This amalgamation took place in 1924; the new congregation was called Temple Isaiah Israel.

Temple Isaiah Israel

Both Dr. Joseph Stolz of Isaiah and Dr. Gerson B. Levi of B'nai Sholom Temple Israel became rabbis of the new synagogue, which had voted to hold services on Saturday and Sunday. This merger brought the total membership of the new congregation to nearly nine hundred families.

When Stolz retired in 1927, Levi took full charge of the congregation. The following year, the congregation began celebrating Shavuot (and Confirmation) on the nearest Sunday, rather than on the festival itself, following a practice established by Chicago's Sinai Congregation. When Levi retired in 1937, consideration was given to consolidating once again with either KAM or Sinai. Following Levi's retirement, Rabbi Morton M. Berman was elected to the pulpit. He immediately discontinued Sunday morning services and introduced Friday evening worship. He next revised the school's curriculum to reflect a positive approach to Jewish ceremonial ritual and Palestine; under his direction, the congregation actively supported the establishment of the pro-Zionist American Jewish Conference. Throughout his tenure, he reintroduced traditional rituals and ceremonies to the congregation. Within a year of his arrival, temple membership grew to 522, but the congregation continued to face financial trouble, which it eventually resolved. During Berman's Navy service, the congregation was led by Rabbis Asher T. Katz (1943–1944) and Aaron M. Kamerling (1944–1946). In the interim, plans for building a community house took shape, and it was dedicated in 1949. Rabbi Hayim Goren Perelmuter succeeded Berman (1957–1980).

KAM Isaiah Israel

KAM merged with Isaiah Israel in 1971. Rabbis Maslin and Perelmuter served as co-rabbis until Maslin left in 1980. With the merger, KAM gave up its building on East Fiftieth Street, joining Isaiah Israel in its building as the merged congregation (designated as a national landmark in 1977). Rabbi Arnold Jacob Wolf succeeded Perelmuter on his retirement in 1981. In 1994, 550 membership units were listed as members of the congregation.

References

Berman, Morton M. "The History of Temple Isaiah Israel, Chicago 1852–1952: The Story of the United Congregations B'nai Sholom, Temple Israel, and Isaiah Temple" (Term paper, Hebrew Union College–Jewish Institute of Religion, 1952).

————. *Our First Century 1852–1952, Temple Isaiah Israel: The United Congregations of B'nai Sholom, Temple Israel and Isaiah Temple* (Chicago: 1952).

Bregstone, Philip P. *Chicago and Its Jews* (Chicago: 1933).

Feldstein, Janice J. *Jacob J. Weinstein, Advocate of the People* (New York: 1980).

Felsenthal, Emma. *Bernhard Felsenthal, Teacher in Israel* (New York: 1924).

Gutstein, Morris A. *A Priceless Heritage: The Epic Growth of Nineteenth Century Chicago Jewry* (New York: 1953).

Mazur, Edward Herbert. *Minyans for a Prairie City: The Politics of Chicago Jewry, 1850–1940* (New York: 1990).

The Sentinel's History of Chicago Jewry (Chicago: 1961).

Weinstein, Jacob J. *KAM Temple New Century Book* (Chicago: 1951).

RODFEI ZEDEK, CONSERVATIVE. *Chicago, Illinois.* A few families established Rodfei Zedek as an Orthodox congregation in the then independent town of Lake (popularly called Canaryville), southwest of the city limits. While the founding date is generally accepted as 1874, there are no extant records to substantiate this date. By the 1890s, this small group grew to nearly fifty families. Thus, the congregation moved from a storefront location to its own building, a small frame structure at Forty-second and Union Streets.

Rodfei Zedek received its state charter in 1899. The following year a fire destroyed the entire synagogue. Members used rented quarters on South State Street for worship for six years after the disaster. The congregation purchased a former Baptist Church on Forty-eighth between Wabash and Michigan, in the fashionable area of Grand Boulevard (known today as Martin Luther King, Jr., Drive), moving to this new location in 1906.

In this new facility amid several large and influential Reform congregations, Rodfei Zedek continued to follow Jewish tradition but made some striking changes in its East European orthodoxy. For example, while members of the congregation maintained a women's gallery for those who chose to segregate themselves, they permitted men and women to sit together. Second, members of the board also developed a corps of ushers with the responsibility to maintain decorum during worship. Finally, women actively participated in synagogue affairs, organizing a women's auxiliary in 1906.

By 1908, the congregation hired its first rabbi, Noah Zev Bressler. He remained only two years. With growing financial strain, the congregation merged with a small Canaryville synagogue, Rodfei Emunah, in 1911, comprised primarily of former Rodfei Zedek members who had refused to join their congregation in its move to Grand Boulevard. Unlike many congregations that began burial societies, Rodfei Zedek waited until 1911 to purchase land for use as a cemetery.

Though the Women's Auxiliary joined the Women's League for Conservative

Judaism in 1918, it waited several years to become a member of the United Synagogue of America (now the United Synagogue of Conservative Judaism), the national body of Conservative congregations established in 1913. Even before it officially joined the Conservative movement, Rodfei Zedek's board looked to Solomon Schechter, president of the Jewish Theological Seminary of America, to help with its search for an English-speaking rabbi.

While not accepting Schechter's recommendation, the congregation engaged a Rabbi Kotov in 1912. He only remained a year, but his successor, Rabbi Aaron Cohen, did not come to the congregation until 1918. Cohen resigned before completing his one-year contract.

When Rabbi Benjamin Daskal became Rodfei Zedek's rabbi shortly after Cohen's resignation, membership reached 125. He introduced late Friday evening worship conducted mainly in English. He also implemented a Confirmation program in 1920, when he noted that most of the children attended religious schools at local Reform synagogues. Daskal also introduced a uniform prayer book for worship in an effort to bring decorum to the congregation. During the 1920s and 1930s, Rodfei Zedek dispensed with the practice of selling Torah honors.

With the growth of the congregation and with the racial conflict that took place in the Grand Boulevard area, congregants decided to leave the area and move to Hyde Park. Rodfei Zedek moved to a residence on Greenwood Avenue in 1923, with plans to build a synagogue on adjacent land. With two hundred families, the congregation dedicated a new building in 1926.

The Depression severely affected the synagogue, and a considerable number of members resigned. But by 1934, the financial health of the congregation improved, and membership grew to 134. The congregation introduced more English into worship during the 1930s. Skullcaps replaced hats for worship. In addition, the congregation held special Sabbaths in an effort to increase Friday-night attendance.

Rabbi Ralph Simon succeeded Rabbi Daskal when he became rabbi emeritus in 1943. Simon invigorated the educational program and introduced new prayer books to the congregation. He also became a driving force behind the Ramah camp established in Wisconsin, the backbone of the Conservative movement's summer camping program. Attempting to establish decorum in worship, Simon discontinued the Kol Nidre (Yom Kippur) appeal for funds.

By the mid-1940s, Rodfei Zedek readied itself for a new home in East Hyde Park. Though the synagogue initially purchased land on Forty-fourth Street and Hyde Park Boulevard, the congregation later bought land to build on East Hyde Park Boulevard. Its 427 families overflowed the sanctuary, where the congregation had to turn away nearly one hundred potential members until making interim arrangements. Before constructing a new building, the congregation purchased a mansion just south of the new property to be transformed into a social center (as the Hoffman House). While Hyde Park's demography changed, the congregation remained committed to the urban renewal of the area. With a membership of 585 families, Rodfei Zedek dedicated its new synagogue building in 1955. Over the next ten years, members strove to break the cycle of urban decay in its neighborhood.

Members moved to the South Shore, nonetheless. The congregation felt the change in its declining religious school enrollment. Rodfei Zedek responded by introducing bus transportation into its school program, which worked to restore the school's population. In 1965, the congregation built the Harry I. Hoffman Educational Center despite declining enrollment.

The 1960s decline of the South Shore threatened the survival of Rodfei Zedek. The ingredients for renewal that worked in Hyde Park did not work in the South Shore. By 1966, membership dropped 15 percent. In 1969, with a declining religious school enrollment, Rodfei Zedek merged its program with the Mandel Consolidated School of Rodfei Sholom-Oir Chodosh. In 1970, the congregations themselves merged.

In 1966, Rodfei Zedek opened a Solomon Schechter day school. In five years, it grew to 120 children. When an Orthodox Akiba school did not fare as well in the South Shore, the schools merged in 1971 as a joint enterprise between Chicago's Orthodox and Conservative congregations to become the Akiba-Schechter Jewish Day School. Following the retirement of Rabbi Ralph Simon, Rabbi Elliot Gertel became the religious leader of the congregation.

References

Gutstein, Morris A. *A Priceless Heritage: The Epic Growth of Nineteenth Century Chicago Jewry* (New York: 1953).
Krucoff, Carol. *Rodfei Zedek, The First Hundred Years* (Chicago: 1976).
The Sentinel's History of Chicago Jewry (Chicago: 1961).

TEMPLE SHOLOM, REFORM. *Chicago, Illinois.* Founded under Orthodox principles as the North Chicago Hebrew Congregation in 1867, it quickly became the pioneer of Reform Judaism on the north side. Its first meeting took place at Turner Hall on North Clark Street. This German-Jewish group of thirty-two charter members purchased a building on the corner of Wells and Superior Streets. The group secured the services of Rabbi Adolph Ollendorf, who stayed with the young congregation for two years, caught in a dispute between the Reform and Orthodox factions. Rabbi Aaron Norden, an ardent exponent of Reform Judaism, succeeded him in the pulpit in 1870. Under his direction, the congregation made steady progress. He introduced mixed seating, abolished the second days of holidays, abbreviated the Torah readings, stressed the importance of the sermon, discarded the prayer shawl and head covering, and promoted decorum during worship.

Following the great fire of 1871, which destroyed the synagogue building, Rabbi Norden left the city. Thus, the congregation struggled without rabbinic leadership, meeting in a variety of temporary quarters. By 1876, thirty-five families reorganized the congregation, adopting the Reform prayer book of David

Einhorn. Members debated Sunday services but opted for late Friday evening worship instead. Realizing a need for leadership, the group succeeded in persuading Rabbi Norden to return to Chicago and help the congregation rebuild. In 1881, with one hundred member families, the congregation acquired its official document of incorporation.

After twelve years of temporary locations, the members built their own house of worship at Rush Street and Walton Place in 1883. In twelve more years, the congregation outgrew this facility and moved to Goethe Street and La Salle Avenue (to a building still standing as the First St. Paul Evangelical Lutheran Church). Rabbi Norden retired in 1898. The congregation elected Rabbi Abram Hirschberg as Norden's successor. At the turn of the century, under Rabbi Hirschberg's guidance, Temple Sholom's membership roster neared 150 families.

In 1909, the congregation purchased the land at Grace Street and Pine Grove Avenue where it dedicated its new synagogue in 1911. In 1910, members voted to change the name of the congregation to Temple Sholom. The design of the new structure was a refinement by the architect of Sinai Temple, which he had just completed. Early in the new building, Temple Sholom members witnessed the congregation's first Bar Mitzvah in the congregation in 1912.

Temple Sholom grew rapidly and needed a new facility. In the early 1920s, the Sunday School roster listed seven hundred students. By the end of the decade, it exceeded nine hundred. Thus, the congregation sold its building to Anshe Emeth in 1926. At the same time, Sinai Congregation and Temple Sholom considered merging, with the anticipated building of three locations: downtown, on the south side, and on the north side. When the merger did not take place, construction began on a new Temple Sholom on Lake Shore Drive. Even with the disastrous effects of the Depression threatening Temple Sholom's building efforts, it dedicated its new facility in 1930. But by 1932, residual financial problems threatened the seven-hundred-family synagogue.

The board felt that new leadership might be able better to steer the course. After several attempts to engage an assistant or successor to Rabbi Hirschberg, Temple Sholom—with membership down to four hundred families—called Rabbi Louis Binstock to its pulpit in 1936. With new leadership—lay and rabbinic—the congregation rapidly increased its membership. By 1937, Temple Sholom felt somewhat more stable. It engaged a professional choir and introduced the *Union Prayer Book*. In order to meet the needs of its members and attract congregants to worship, it took a bold step by instituting Sunday services at the same time as, in 1945, the congregation instituted daily afternoon services in order to accommodate those members in mourning. Three years later, to accommodate a continually growing membership already over eleven hundred, Temple Sholom instituted double services for the High Holidays, a practice now followed by many congregations throughout North America. In 1949, Temple Sholom invited its first Bat Mitzvah to the pulpit. The synagogue also made interior changes to accommodate a growing religious school population (dedicated 1954). Sisterhood claimed a membership of 1,750 with Brotherhood only slightly behind at fifteen hundred.

In 1961 Temple Sholom purchased a mansion on Lake Shore Drive and Stratford Place to protect itself from the encroachment of high-rise apartment buildings and for possible future expansion, especially for the religious school. By 1967, religious school enrollment exceeded 1020 children, and temple membership approached twenty-three hundred families.

Yet, in the decade that followed, this unprecedented growth came to an end. Membership in the temple and enrollment in the religious school dropped dramatically. Both brotherhood and sisterhood membership fell as well. The board revisited the discussion of a merger with Temple Sinai, an action that could bolster both institutions. After a long debate, both congregations defeated the proposal.

Rabbi Frederick Schwartz succeeded Rabbi Binstock in 1974. According to temple historian Elliot Leftkovitz, under Rabbi Schwartz's leadership, Temple Sholom members recovered Jewish tradition with a renewed sense of ethnic pride and identity. Shortly after his arrival, he moved the central service of the week from Sunday morning to Friday evening. He also insisted that holiday observances take place on their actual dates rather than on the closest Sunday. Schwartz also upgraded the program of Jewish education at the temple, beginning with a move of Confirmation from ninth grade to tenth grade.

One year after the arrival of Rabbi Schwartz, Beth Am Congregation, located on Chicago's South Side, amalgamated with Temple Sholom. Demographic change on the South Side prompted the move. Beth Am dated from 1948, with Rabbi Eric Friedland serving as its first and only rabbi. Friedland joined Sholom's rabbinical staff until retiring in 1977. One hundred and seventy-five Beth Am members joined Sholom as a result of the merger. Temple Sholom underwent a major phase of reconstruction beginning in 1977, adding badly needed space for its expanding activity program. In 1994, membership exceeded two thousand.

References

Gutstein, Morris A. *A Priceless Heritage: The Epic Growth of Nineteenth Century Chicago Jewry* (New York: 1953).
Lefkovitz, Elliot. *Temple Sholom: 125 Years of Living Judaism* (Chicago: 1993).
A Struggle toward Greatness: 100th Anniversary Temple Sholom 1867–1967 (Chicago: 1968).
Synagogue Histories File, American Jewish Archives.

SINAI, REFORM. *Chicago, Illinois.* A group of KAM dissidents founded the Israelite Reform Society in 1858. Radical in its reform, this group initially floundered. It eventually evolved under Dr. Bernhard Felsenthal's leadership into the Juedischer Reformverein (the Jewish Reform Society), "to awaken and cultivate truer conceptions of Judaism and a higher realization of Jewish religious life, first among its members, and if possible, also in wider circles." As part of its rejection of orthodoxy and its commitment to Reform Judaism in its most radical sense, which it retains to this day, the Verein also declared, "all religious truths shall be based on free investigation and demonstration" and "by virtue of reason, which we also consider a divine manifestation, as well as the whole of nature, we distinguish in Holy Scripture the treasures of eternal truth which are deposited in it, from that which is merely the result of primitive conceptions of the time and faulty views of the world and of life, and also from that which was merely meant as law for transitory conditions which have long since become obsolete." In 1861, the members of the society formed Sinai Congregation and, as such, purchased an Episcopal church, which it moved to Monroe between Clark and LaSalle Streets and converted it into Chicago's first "temple." During these Civil War years, Sinai's tradition of social activism was firmly established with passionate preaching of abolitionism.

A new structure was built in 1863 at Van Buren Street and Plymouth Court (then known as Third Avenue). Twelve months later, when Felsenthal requested a contract of longer than a year at a time, his request was denied. Felsenthal resigned and, joined by a group of loyal followers, founded Zion congregation. In his stead, Dr. Isaac Chronic was elected to the pulpit. Unwilling to acquire fluency in English, Chronic returned to Europe in 1869. However, he left his liberal legacy with the congregation. He was the first of the rabbis in America to propose Sunday services (which his successor implemented); and under his direction, Sinai established a cemetery in 1867 at Rosehill, the first instance in America of a Jewish section in an interdenominational cemetery.

Following the 1871 Chicago fire, which destroyed its building, the congregation met in rented facilities. That same year, Dr. Kaufmann Kohler came to Sinai to become its rabbi. Though Kohler (but not the congregation) would later regret his action, he instituted a Sunday service in 1874. Originally intended to supplement Saturday worship, it soon became the central service at Sinai, an example which a number of other congregations sought to follow. While KAM was considering a merger with Sinai at the time, the institution of Sunday services at Sinai created an obstacle for the members of KAM that they felt that they could not overcome.

The congregation relocated in 1876 on Indiana and Twenty-first Street. Kohler resigned in 1879, when he realized that his efforts did not cause an increase in worship-service attendance. Members elected Rabbi Emil G. Hirsch to Sinai's pulpit the following year, and he guided the congregation for forty-three years. Immediately Hirsch established a vision for the congregation of radical religious and social liberalism. Within five years, Sinai became the largest Jewish congregation in Chicago. Under his leadership, a Jewish Training School for immigrants was established in 1890. Hirsch's reforms included the abolishment of all Hebrew readings, the transfer of all holidays to the nearest Sunday, and the elimination of the ark (when the synagogue was remodeled in 1892).

With the continued growth of the congregation, Sinai moved to Forty-sixth and Grand Boulevard (now Martin Luther King, Jr. Drive) in 1912. Emil Hirsch died in 1923 and was succeeded by Rabbi Louis Mann. The Grand Boulevard facility was sold in 1944; but because of postwar building restrictions and financial considerations, Sinai did not build a new home for five years, worshiping temporarily at the University of Chicago and then with KAM. In 1950, the congregation built a facility at Fifty-fourth Street and South Shore Drive.

When Mann retired in 1962, he was succeeded by Samuel Karff. Karff reinstituted Sabbath morning services and established a variety of decentralized programs to attract the members living outside the Hyde Park area. In 1975, Karff left the congregation and was succeeded by Philip Kranz, who had served the congregation as assistant rabbi. Kranz left in 1980; Rabbi Howard Berman was elected in 1982 to the pulpit, where he remains. Under his leadership, the congregation has developed new programs of adult education, with particular emphasis on outreach to intermarried families. Following the trend of its membership, Sinai has decided to sell its facility and move back downtown.

References

Berman, Howard. *Chicago Sinai Congregation: A Pictorial History* (Chicago: 1990).
Bregstone, Philip P. *Chicago and Its Jews* (Chicago: 1933).
Felsenthal, Bernhard. *The Beginnings of the Chicago Sinai Congregation* (Chicago: 1898).
Felsenthal, Emma. *Bernhard Felsenthal, Teacher in Israel* (New York: 1924).
Gutstein, Morris A. *A Priceless Heritage: The Epic Growth of Nineteenth Century Chicago Jewry* (New York: 1953).
Mazur, Edward Herbert. *Minyans for a Prairie City: The Politics of Chicago Jewry, 1850–1940* (New York: 1990).
The Sentinel's History of Chicago Jewry (Chicago: 1961).
By Virtue of Reason: A History of Chicago Sinai Congregation (Chicago: 1981).

BETH EMET THE FREE SYNAGOGUE, REFORM. *Evanston, Illinois.* When local congregation Temple Mizpah denied Rabbi David Polish entrance to the synagogue one Friday evening in 1950, having moved to break his contract earlier that week over freedom of the pulpit, among other things, Beth Emet came into being. A group accompanied the rabbi to an office over the Adelphi Theatre on Clark Street in Chicago and held services there. Shortly thereafter, the group of forty families, joined by an additional forty families, held services at Nichols School in Evanston. Growing to over two hundred families in a few months, the group formally organized Beth Emet The Free Synagogue, "to secure certain basic freedoms, among which are the freedom of the membership, the freedom of the Rabbi, and the freedom of Jewish self-expression."

The new congregation purchased a building on Ridge and Dempster the same year. By 1962, congregants realized that the building required replacement, especially with a sanctuary, to accommodate its growing population. Following a struggle with the local zoning board, Beth Emet dedicated a new facility in 1964.

Among its liturgical innovations, the congregation claims to be the originator of *Selichot* (prayers of contrition prior to Rosh Hashanah) services in the Reform movement. David Polish retired in 1980; Rabbi Peter Knobel, the current rabbi, succeeded him. During his tenure, the congregation introduced regular healing services. Knobel implemented a biennial study trip to Israel. In his rabbinate, he emphasizes educational programs for children and adults. During Knobel's tenure with the congregation, Beth Emet introduced a variety of worship experiences, including a monthly feminist minyan, monthly Torah study on the Sabbath, and early Sabbath services on Friday evenings. In 1994, the congregation listed 810 family units on its roster.

References

Polish, David. *At Home, In Limbo: An Autobiography of Rabbi David Polish* (Typescript, in possession of the author's wife).
Synagogue Histories File, American Jewish Archives.

JEWISH RECONSTRUCTIONIST CONGREGATION, RECONSTRUC-TIONIST. *Evanston, Illinois.* Eleven families founded the Jewish Reconstructionist Congregation (JRC) in Evanston in 1964. Its roots can be traced to a study group at local congregation Anshe Emet led by Rabbi Ira Eisenstein. By 1970, membership reached seventy families, meeting primarily in the Wilmette area. The congregation subsequently moved to larger quarters at Chute Middle School in Evanston, where members formed a social action committee and celebrated the congregation's first Bat Mitzvah. Affiliated with the Federation of Reconstructionist Congregations and Havurot, the national organization of Reconstructionist synagogues, since its founding, the JRC became the first congregation to adopt the Rabbinic Intern Program of the Reconstructionist Rabbinical College.

In 1975, JRC engaged Arnold Rachlis to be its spiritual leader, prior to his ordination as rabbi. Yet, members continued to lead services on Saturday mornings. Following the installation, the JRC moved to temporary residence at the First Baptist Church in Evanston. In 1978, membership neared 160 families, with 120 students in the religious school. Two years later, JRC moved to the Covenant United Methodist Church.

In 1985, the JRC moved into its first permanent home on Dodge Avenue in Evanston. There the congregation instituted a wide-ranging early childhood program. Rachlis left in 1992, and Rabbi Richard Hirsch joined the congregation the following year. Under his direction, JRC introduced a variety of programs, including a Friends and Neighbors Program (FAN) established to help recreate a sense of Jewish neighborhoods. In 1995, membership of the congregation neared five hundred family units.

Reference

A Condensed History of the Jewish Reconstructionist Congregation (Evanston: 1994).

NORTH SHORE CONGREGATION ISRAEL, REFORM. *Glencoe, Illinois.* Fifty-eight members of Sinai Congregation established the congregation as the North Shore Branch of Chicago Sinai Congregation. Thus, North Shore Congregation Israel became the oldest Reform congregation on the North Shore. Charter members organized the new congregation in 1920 primarily for the purpose of providing religious education for the children and for worship services, especially during the High Holidays. An informal Sabbath school predated the formal establishment of the congregation by eight years. The new congregation held services at Hubbard Woods School and systematized the school, which met in the Winnetka public schools.

As its first full-time rabbi, Harvey Wessel served the congregation from 1926 to 1927. Membership grew dramatically. In 1928, with 324 members, the congregation dedicated its first building at Lincoln and Vernon Avenues in Glencoe. Still following the model established by Sinai Congregation, the congregation sponsored a Sunday School and provided worship services on Sunday morning. Bar/Bat Mitzvah was not marked with ceremony, there was no teaching of Hebrew in the school, and little Hebrew was evident in worship either. However, the congregation celebrated Confirmation and observed the major festivals. Slowly, members made changes. Amid a major protest by the board, services moved back to Friday evening.

By the end of World War II, membership grew to nearly five hundred families. At about the same time, Rabbi Edgar Siskin became NSCI's rabbi (1948); and in 1952 the temple expanded its facilities with a school addition and library, extending the building to Dundee Road. But the facilities were still too small to accommodate the incredible growth of over eighteen hundred families, with nearly two thousand children in the religious school.

In 1961, the congregation acquired an estate on Sheridan Road on which it initiated a multiphase building program under the guidance of architect Minori Yamasaki. In the new facility, change was evident. The congregation introduced a Bar/Bat Mitzvah program. The school board introduced Hebrew into the curriculum, and the board undertook a concerted effort to encourage the celebration of holidays. In addition, a group of members supported the election of the assistant rabbi to the position of senior rabbi when Siskin retired. When this did not take place and the congregation elected Rabbi Herbert Bronstein to the pulpit in 1972, dissenters formed Am Shalom. In addition, these changes took their toll on the congregation. Members who preferred the model of Reform Judaism originally in place at North Shore Congregation Israel left the congregation.

Bronstein worked to heal the rift and focused on strengthening the program of worship and youth in the congregation. During his tenure, the congregation completely vacated the facility on Vernon Avenue (eventually turning it over to Am Shalom) and built a chapel and education center on Sheridan Road. Membership in 1994 reached nearly sixteen hundred.

Reference

Synagogue Histories File, American Jewish Archives.

OAK PARK TEMPLE B'NAI ABRAHAM ZION, REFORM. *Oak Park, Illinois.*

B'nai Abraham

German-speaking Bohemian Jews founded B'nai Abraham on the southwest side of Chicago around Halsted and Fourteenth Streets in 1871. The group moved to Marshfield Avenue near Roosevelt Road in 1892. These religious leaders served the congregation in its early years: Isaac Fall (1876?–1878?), Ignaz Grossman (1880–1885), Datner Jacobson (1885–1888), and A. R. Levy (1888).

During Grossman's tenure, the congregation adopted several reforms, including Isaac Mayer Wise's prayer book, *Minhag America* (1881). During the last decades of the century, preachers delivered sermons in both German and English.

Zion Congregation

In 1864, members of Sinai Congregation refused to renew the contract of its rabbi, Bernhard Felsenthal, for more than a year at a time. Thus, Felsenthal resigned and, joined by a group of loyal followers, founded (B'nai) Zion congregation, the first synagogue on Chicago's west side. He served until 1887. As Zion's membership scattered, some formed what later was Washington Boulevard Temple, Temple Mizpah when it was founded, and finally the congregation disbanded.

B'nai Abraham Zion

In 1919, B'nai Abraham joined with a group of former members of Zion Congregation (who took the name with it) and formed B'nai Abraham Zion. The new congregation erected a building on Washington Boulevard and Karlow Avenue (Washington Boulevard Temple). In 1921, members elected Rabbi Samuel Schwartz to its pulpit. He served until 1945, when his assistant, Rabbi W. Gunther Plaut, succeeded him. Plaut served until 1949, when Rabbi Wendell Phillips joined the congregation (1949–1951). Rabbi Leonard Mervis succeeded Phillips (1951–1979). During his tenure, members voted to relocate to Oak Park on North Harlem Avenue (dedicated 1957). Mervis focused his rabbinate on education and social action.

When Mervis retired in 1979, B'nai Abraham Zion invited Rabbi Gary Gerson to lead the congregation. His rabbinate focused on interfaith relations. In 1995, membership of the temple neared 420 membership units.

References

Gutstein, Morris A. *A Priceless Heritage: The Epic Growth of Nineteenth Century Chicago Jewry* (New York: 1953).
The Sentinel's History of Chicago Jewry (Chicago: 1961).

INDIANA

ACHDUTH VESHOLOM CONGREGATION, REFORM. *Ft. Wayne, Indiana.* Though the Chevras Bikkur Cholim Uk'vuras Meisim (Society for Visiting the Sick and Burying the Dead) was formed to serve the community in a variety of functions, its thirty members also joined together to form the first Jewish congregation in the state of Indiana (1848). Led by Frederick Nirdlinger as its first president and initially meeting in his private home, the congregation purchased its first formal house of worship in 1857. Membership had grown to only thirty-two members.

Established as a German Orthodox congregation that conducted its worship, education, and business in the German language, the congregation maintained a private school that taught Hebrew and German. The school was led by Joseph Solomon, the congregation's first rabbi (1848–1859).

By 1859, with an increase in membership, the congregation moved to its first temple, the former German Methodist Episcopal Church on the west side of Harrison Street. Solomon was succeeded by Rabbi Isaac Rosenthal (1859–1861). This temple was called the Synagogue of Unity and Peace. During his tenure, the name of the congregation was officially changed in 1861 to Congregation Achduth Vesholom.

With the election to the pulpit of Rabbi Edward Rubin in 1862, the congregation began its introduction to the Reform movement. It adopted David Einhorn's prayer book, *Olath Tamid.* In 1866, the notion of family pews was introduced, except during the High Holidays, when a traditional holiday prayer book was used. As a result of these reforms, a small group left Achduth Vesholom in order to found its own congregation, Fort Wayne Hebrew Congregation Emunot Avosenu. After a few years, the group returned to the congregation. In 1874, the congregation joined the Board of Delegates of American Israelites and the Union of American Hebrew Congregations. The growth of temple membership required another move in 1876. This time, Achduth Vesholom moved to the corner of Harrison and Wayne.

When Rabbi Solomon died in 1881, the congregation elected Rabbi Adolph Dushner to its pulpit. He left in 1883, and Isaac Mayer Wise sent Rabbi Israel Aaron to lead the congregation. Thus, the congregation was the first to engage a graduate of Hebrew Union College. In 1887, Aaron was succeeded by Rabbi Tobias Shanfarber, who served only one year. Rabbi Samuel Strauss served as interim rabbi until Rabbi Adolph Guttmacher joined the congregation in 1889. He remained until Rabbi Abraham Hirschberg came in 1891, the same year the congregation adopted the *Union Prayer Book* and English as the primary language for sermons and High Holiday services.

Rabbi Frederick Cohen led the congregation from 1896 to 1904; Rabbi Harry Ettleson served from 1904 to 1910. Tired of a lack of attendance, Ettleson convinced the congregation to give Sunday services a try. The experiment failed, and the congregation returned to a Saturday service a short time later. Rabbi William Rice served from 1911 to 1914. Rabbi Mayer Lovitch arrived in 1914 and helped to form the Sisterhood. When Rabbi Aaron Weinstein came in 1915, the facilities for the congregation were too small, and he led the move to a new structure on Wayne and Fairfield in 1917. Membership stood at 144.

Rabbi Samuel Markowitz succeeded Weinstein in 1924 and remained until 1939. He attempted Sunday services once again with no success, and the temple continued its Sabbath services on late Friday evening. Rabbi Frederic Doppelt was elected to the pulpit in 1939 where he remained until his retirement in 1969. During his tenure, the congregation moved in 1961 to its current facility on Old Mill Road, the same year the congregation held its first Bat Mitzvah. When Rabbi Doppelt retired, Rabbi Richard Safran became Achduth Vesholom's seventeenth rabbi.

References

Indiana Jewish Chronicle 27, no. 2 (April 23, 1948): entire issue.
Mather, George Ross. *Frontier Faith: The Story of the Pioneer Congregations of Fort Wayne, Indiana, 1820–1860* (Fort Wayne, IN: 1992).
Safran, Richard B. *Congregation Achduth Vesholom: Our Story* (Fort Wayne, IN: 1993).
Zweig, Ruth G. "The First Hundred and Twenty-Five Years." Publication No. 2 of the Indiana Jewish Historical Society, Fort Wayne, Indiana, 1973.

CONGREGATION BETH EL-ZEDECK, CONSERVATIVE, RECON-STRUCTIONIST. *Indianapolis, Indiana.* In 1915, Alexander Cohen organized a group of people to participate in High Holiday services at Sixteenth and Illinois Streets. This group, many of whom were former members of local congregation Sharah Tefilla, which had moved to the north side of Indianapolis, became the nucleus for Congregation Beth-El. Following more frequent gatherings for worship in a variety of temporary locations, the group purchased a lot at Thirtieth and Talbot for a permanent synagogue. In 1922, this small cluster of men hired Jacob Bienfeld as its first rabbi; he remained with the congregation until 1925. Still nominally Orthodox, the group continued to grow and dedicated a new structure at Thirty-fourth and Ruckle Streets in 1925.

Immediately thereafter, Rabbi Isadore Goodman became the congregation's rabbi and served for two years, until Rabbi Milton Steinberg—while still a student—succeeded him. During Steinberg's first year, Beth El affiliated with the Conservative movement. Until his arrival, the congregation varied little from orthodoxy, except that men and women sat together during worship. Under the influence of Mordecai Kaplan, Steinberg introduced a liberal direction to the synagogue. He introduced Confirmation, Yom Kippur children's services, and High Holiday choirs. Ohev Zedeck, a neighboring synagogue, merged with Beth-El in 1928 to become Beth-El Zedeck.

Rabbi Elias Charry succeeded Rabbi Steinberg in 1933. At the same time, in its egalitarian spirit, the congregation gave women the right to vote. Membership grew to over three hundred families in the late 1930s. Rabbi Israel Chodos joined the congregation in 1942, when Rabbi Charry left. He stayed until 1946, when Rabbi William P. Greenfield succeeded him. He introduced the Bat Mitzvah ceremony to Beth-El Zedeck, as well as the practice of calling women to the Torah. Rabbi Greenfield discontinued the Musaf service (an additional service for Sabbath and holidays) and introduced organ music. He incorporated Confirmation into the first day of Shavuot and consecration (a ceremony that marks the child's entry into formal Jewish education) into Simchat Torah. Congregational membership continued to grow.

When Mordecai Kaplan launched a national Reconstructionist Fellowship (now the Federation of Reconstructionist Congregations and Havurot) in 1955, Beth-El Zedeck became a founding member, while still participating in the activities of the United Synagogue of America. Throughout its history, Beth-El Zedeck pioneered in the synergism of the salient elements of Conservative Judaism and Reconstructionism "to maintain, in the general spirit of Reconstructionist philosophy, a modern yet traditional [Conservative] synagogue for dignified, meaningful Jewish worship." At the same time, the congregation broke ground for a new facility in the Spring Mill Estates. Originally, the local Jewish federation purchased a larger plot of land in the area, with the intention that both Beth-El Zedeck and the Indianapolis Hebrew Congregation would relocate and cooperate in the building of a community center to serve both congregations. The plan did not materialize, and Beth-El Zedeck dedicated a new structure three years later. Rabbi Sidney Steiman was elected to the pulpit in 1961.

In 1977, with over eight hundred family units, Beth-El Zedeck became a pioneer congregation when it elected Rabbi Dennis C. Sasso and Rabbi Sandy Eisenberg Sasso, the first rabbinic couple in history, as its new spiritual leaders. During their tenure (1980), the congregation discontinued the celebration of the second day of festivals.

References

Endelman, Judith E. *The Jewish Community of Indianapolis, 1849 to the Present* (Bloomington, IN: 1984).

Memories and Visions: A Tribute to Our Past Presidents on the 65th Anniversary of Congregation Beth-El Zedeck (Indianapolis, IN: 1992).

Sasso, Dennis. "A Case Study in Congregational Pluralism and Vitality" (Doctor of Ministry dissertation, Christian Theological Seminary, Indianapolis, Indiana, 1985).

CONGREGATION B'NAI TORAH, ORTHODOX. *Indianapolis, Indiana.* When the center of the Jewish population moved north from the south side of Indianapolis, a few traditional Jews established an Orthodox congregation in 1923, under the name Central Hebrew Congregation. As few traditional Jews lived on the north side to support the congregation, this fledgling congregation struggled in its incipient stages. Members led services and conducted all affairs of synagogue business. Reform rabbis from the Indianapolis Hebrew Congregation helped out on the second day of holidays, when their congregation did not hold services. The congregation built its facility at Central and Twenty-first Street.

With a membership of thirty-five in 1942, the congregation engaged its first rabbi, Nandor Fruchter. The congregation expanded its facilities in 1947, celebrating its first Confirmation in 1951. Fruchter initiated monthly late Friday evening services the following year, while still conducting traditional services at sunset. In 1955, members of the United Hebrew Congregation (called the "union shul" because it was on Union Street)—without a rabbi since 1950—initiated a discussion concerning a possible merger. In 1957, the congregations merged to become the United Central Hebrew Congregation with a joint membership of 385 families, making it the largest Orthodox congregation in Indiana at the time.

UNITED HEBREW CONGREGATION

Founded in 1903, with a building during its entire existence at Union Street and Madison Avenue, the United Hebrew Congregation once counted a membership of four hundred. Members also called their synagogue the "Frantesesishe (French) Shul" because, to them, French stood for progressive and the community considered the Union Street Shul (which it was also called) to be more progressive than the other Orthodox synagogues in town. It operated the only Talmud Torah in Indianapolis until 1911, when members transformed it into a community institution.

Rabbi Charles Hoffman served the congregation as its first religious leader. Rabbis Rabinowitz and Lazar succeeded him. Rabbi Aaron E. Miller served the congregation from 1940 to 1941. Rabbi Samuel Fox succeeded him, leading the congregation until 1950.

United Central Hebrew Congregation (B'nai Torah)

Beth El-Zedeck sold its property on Thirty-fourth and Ruckle Street to the newly merged congregation in 1957; it occupied the property the following year. At this time, the new congregation chose a Hebrew name for itself: B'nai Torah. By the 1960s, the congregation realized that it had to follow the move of the Jewish community farther north and relocated in 1966 to Sixty-fifth and Hoover Road. Rabbi Fruchter retired in 1971. Rabbi Ronald Gray succeeded him, having served as associate rabbi since 1970.

References

Endelman, Judith E. *The Jewish Community of Indianapolis 1849 to the Present* (Bloomington, IN: 1984).
Fruchter, Mrs. Nandor. *Congregation B'nai Torah: The First Fifty Years* (Indianapolis, IN: 1973).

INDIANAPOLIS HEBREW CONGREGATION, REFORM. *Indianapolis, Indiana.* Congregational life began officially in 1856, when fourteen men assembled at the home of Julius Glaser to formally establish a congregation. Like other congregations, its first activities included the selection of land to be developed into a cemetery, the renting of a room for worship, on Washington Street, and the securing of services of a spiritual leader, S. Berman. With the growth of Indianapolis, the congregation grew also, to forty members. By 1858, the synagogue readied itself for a new home and a replacement for Berman, who left over a salary disagreement. The congregation engaged Rabbi Judah Wechsler to succeed Berman, and the congregation moved into a new home on East Washington Street.

Nevertheless, the congregation remained in a state of flux and slowly lost its members, dwindling to sixteen in its third year of existence. Wechsler left in 1861, to be replaced by Rabbi Max Moses for six months, since the congregation was not ready for even moderate reforms. It was Moses who introduced *Minhag America* and the choir to the congregation. Rabbi Isidor Kalisch followed, serving only one year. Wechsler returned to the congregation in 1864 and remained until 1867.

By 1864, membership grew to fifty-three members, finances stabilized, and the congregation sought new quarters. Indianapolis Hebrew Congregation purchased a lot on East Market Street, between New Jersey and East Streets. In 1867, the congregation celebrated its first Confirmation, the same year Rabbi Mayer Messing succeeded Wechsler in the pulpit.

Just before the congregation built its new Market Street Temple in 1868, Messing introduced Sabbath (Friday) evening services. And in 1873, Indianapolis Hebrew Congregation joined as charter members of the Union of American Hebrew Congregations. While Messing remained until 1907, his early years were fraught with difficulties. When local congregation Ohev Zedeck offered in 1897 to purchase the Market Street Temple, which the congregation had long since outgrown, the board made plans to construct a new facility on the corner of Delaware and Tenth Streets. (Eventually Ohev Zedeck abandoned the building as well and razed it in 1933.)

Members dedicated the new Tenth Street Temple in 1899. And in 1907, members installed Morris M. Feuerlicht as rabbi of Indianapolis Hebrew Congregation. Throughout the years, members discussed whether a new facility should be built, but the time never seemed right for such a move.

Rabbi Feuerlicht retired in 1946, to be succeeded by Rabbi Maurice Goldblatt, the congregation's assistant and then associate rabbi since 1938. His election did not come easily. The congregation supported Feuerlicht's anti-Zionist stance. Goldblatt, on the other hand, was a Zionist. Additionally, Goldblatt sought to bring more ritual into the congregation, a practice not well received by many. Goldblatt initiated birthday blessings for children during services, consecration, and interfaith institutes on Judaism.

The board passed a resolution in 1944 permitting women to vote in the congregation. Congregational membership stood at 412 the following year, but members were still unwilling to move. The building was deteriorating and in need of repair. By 1948, membership reached 489. In 1956, Goldblatt retired. That same year, sixty-five students who had left the congregation to study at the School for Reform Judaism (affiliated with the American Council for Judaism) returned to the congregation's religious school. Rabbi Maurice Davis succeeded Goldblatt and served until 1967. During Davis' first year, the congregation drew plans for its new synagogue at Sixty-fifth and Meridian and dedicated it the following year, despite Federation plans for a joint land purchase with Beth-El Zedeck. In this new facility, the congregation discontinued its practice of selling pews. Membership stood at six hundred families.

At the same time, the congregation purchased Big Eagle Camp for use in the congregation's youth activities program. Under Davis' direction, the congregation involved itself in civil rights issues of the day. Davis himself marched in the Selma-Montgomery civil rights march in 1965, continuing the fight for equality, particularly with regard to housing, in Indianapolis. In addition, he spoke out against U.S. involvement in Vietnam. Rabbi Murray Saltzman succeeded Rabbi Davis in 1967. During his tenure, he established a variety of programs that reflected his interest in adult education, interfaith relations, and music. In 1968, Saltzman invited the first woman in the congregation to sit on the *bima* (a raised platform in front of the synagogue). By this time, membership reached over 850 family units. In 1971, the congregation engaged its first cantor.

The congregation built an outdoor chapel in 1973, and in 1975, struggling against a long-standing policy that prohibited the wearing of prayer shawls and head coverings, the worship committee moved that "no written or implied rules regarding the wearing of *tallitim* [*sic*] or *yarmulkes* on the *bima* be established." Jonathan Stein became senior rabbi in 1978 and served until 1994. Prior to his appointment, Stein served the congregation as intern and then as assistant rabbi. Among other innovations, he instituted a family Rosh Hashanah retreat service. He also insisted on wearing an *atarah* on his robe; he sees it as a transfer of political power in the congregation to the new generation. In 1995, Robert Shapiro became the religious leader of the congregation. That same year, the congregation's membership numbered over 1350 family units.

References

Endelman, Judith E. *The Jewish Community of Indianapolis, 1849 to the Present* (Bloomington, IN: 1984).

Indianapolis Hebrew Congregation, 125th Anniversary (Indianapolis, IN: 1981).

Rosenberg, Ethel and David. *To 120 Years! A Social History of the Indianapolis Hebrew Congregation (1856–1976)* (Indianapolis, IN: 1979).

IOWA

B'NAI JESHURUN, REFORM. *Des Moines, Iowa.* Des Moines' early Jewish residents formed the Emanuel Cemetery Association in 1870. In addition to the handling of burial issues, its members conducted worship services, beginning in 1869. Following Yom Kippur services held in the home of David Goldman in 1873, this small group of sixteen men gathered to discuss the need to organize a congregation. By the end of the evening, they established Congregation B'nai Jeshurun "for religious and charitable promotion." The Emanuel Cemetery Association merged with B'nai Jeshurun in 1879.

Originally Orthodox, holding services on Friday evening and Saturday only, the congregation joined the Union of American Hebrew Congregations in 1874, the national organization of Reform synagogues, the same year the congregation engaged its first religious leader, who officiated only a few weeks. B'nai Jeshurun's second religious officiant, Florian Schauer, served from 1874 to 1878.

In 1875, B'nai Jeshurun adopted Isaac Mayer Wise's *Minhag America* as its prayer book. Members organized a religious school in 1877. In 1881, members decided to worship with uncovered heads and conducted their first Confirmation service in 1886. The congregation conducted its first services in a rented hall on Court Avenue; it purchased a building in 1878 at Seventh and Mulberry Streets, converting it into use as a synagogue. With thirty-seven members and feeling the need for larger quarters, it erected a new facility in 1887 at Eighth and Pleasant Streets. The congregation moved again in 1932 to Grand Avenue and Country Club Boulevard. Members enlarged this building in 1956 with the dedication of the Eugene Mannheimer Memorial Building. This addition included extra classrooms. Restoration of the temple took place in 1990.

The women of the congregation launched their Ladies Hebrew Benevolent Society in 1874, the first women's organization of its kind in Des Moines. In 1895, these same women initiated an organization that became the Des Moines Section of the National Council of Jewish Women, transformed into the B'nai Jeshurun Sisterhood in 1904. The two women's groups merged into 1914 to become the United Benevolent Society and then in 1920 the Temple Sisterhood.

These other men served B'nai Jeshurun as religious leaders: Pollak (1878–1879), Dushner (1879–1881), David Davidson (1881–1885), L. Freudenthal (1885–1889), Ignatius Mueller (1889–1894), Seymour Bottigheimer (1894–1898), Solomon H. Sonnenschein (1898–1905), Eugene Mannheimer (1905–1943), Louis Cashdan (1943–1945), Martin M. Weitz (1945–1948), Bernard H. Lavine (1948–1954), Edward Zerin (1954–1967), Jay B. Goldburg (1967–1983), and Steven M. Fink (1983–   ). Under Goldburg, the congregation focused its attention on issues of social action. Rabbi Zerin emphasized education in his rabbinate. Since Rabbi Fink joined the congregation, he has focused his efforts on social issues such as reproductive choice, as well as outreach to intermarried couples. In 1983, the congregation began Saturday Sabbath services, a service abandoned many years ago. In 1995, membership at B'nai Jeshurun numbered 350 family units.

References

Rosenthal, Frank. *The Jews of Des Moines* (Des Moines: 1957).
Synagogue Histories File, American Jewish Archives.

CONGREGATION BETH SHALOM, CONSERVATIVE, REFORM. *Sioux City, Iowa.* A group of Jews gathered in 1910 to discuss the possibility of founding a Conservative congregation sensitive to tradition and modernity. In 1914, a second group met—with the support of Rabbi Charles Eliezer Hillel Kauvar of Denver—and affiliated with the United Synagogue of America, the national organization of Conservative synagogues. The new congregation held services for a short period of time at Adas Yeshurun Synagogue, but eventually disbanded. This group eventually reorganized into the founders of Shaare Zion Synagogue in 1925. Two years prior to the founding of the congregation, local women formed a Ladies Auxiliary.

Shaare Zion members engaged Rabbi H. R. Rabinowitz as its first religious leader. Prior to actual founding of the congregation, the founders rented a building on Fourteenth and Jackson Street for use as a Hebrew School. Once they incorporated the congregation, they moved to Seventh and Court Streets. The Ladies Auxiliary, which changed its name to the Women's League in 1939, took upon itself the task of building a modern synagogue at Douglas and Sixteenth Streets (dedicated 1927). In 1944, the men of Shaare Zion formed a Men's Club, and the synagogue's youth formed a United Synagogue Youth chapter in 1951.

Rabbi Philip Silverstein succeeded Rabbi Rabinowitz in 1959. During his tenure, the congregation remodeled the building and built a social hall. Silverstein left in 1968, and Rabbi David Zisenwine became the rabbi of the congregation. These rabbis followed: Ronald Garr (1972–1977), Martin Berman (1977–1981), Shawn Zell (1981–1983), and Daniel Allen (1983–1986). After Rabbi Allen's departure, James Sherman, a layperson, became "Spiritual Leader" of the congregation. During his tenure, Shaare Zion's youth group merged with the youth group from (Reform) Mt. Sinai. Other mergers followed. In 1994, Shaare Zion merged fully with Mt. Sinai's (founded 1898) ninety-six members to form Congregation Beth Shalom, the result of discussions since 1977. As a consequence of this consolidation, the congregation alternates Friday evening prayer books, but maintains a daily service and Saturday morning service using the Conservative prayer book. It also maintained its membership in the United Synagogue of Conservative Judaism and the Union of American Hebrew Congregations. In 1994, the combined congregational membership exceeded 220 family units.

Reference

Synagogue Histories File, American Jewish Archives.

K

KENTUCKY

CONGREGATION ADATH ISRAEL–BRITH SHOLOM, REFORM. *Louisville, Kentucky.*

Adath Israel

Adath Israel was chartered in 1843 "according to the form and mode of worship of the German Jews of Louisville." Although the Jewish population in Louisville consisted of only six or seven families for the years prior and the group met for several years in boarding-house rooms, the group grew large enough to found a congregation. During the first five years, the temple experienced rapid growth. Membership reached seventy-six families by 1847. The group considered building a permanent structure to house the new congregation. Members purchased a lot on Sixth Street between Chestnut and Broadway. But after laying a cornerstone, members grew dissatisfied with the location and purchased an alternative lot on Fourth Street between Green and Walnut Streets. Adath Israel congregants consecrated their new synagogue building in 1849. The early congregation served as the central focus for all Jewish communal and charity work in Louisville.

When this first synagogue building neared completion in 1848, members adopted a series of regulations to "reform" the service. These reforms focused on the maintenance of decorum and warned among other things that "All the shaking, bowing, jumping and all other misbehaviors are strictly forbidden." Slowly, more substantial liturgical reforms were made as well. However, at the same time, congregational regulations prohibited members who kept their businesses open on Saturday from certain ritual honors. Though one can easily see the early trend toward reform, these reforms came at the expense of explosive discussions during synagogue meetings.

B. H. Gotthelf was elected to the position of hazan in 1849 and also had the obligation to lead its newly founded school. Gotthelf traveled to Cincinnati in 1855 to observe and adopt on his return the reforms of Congregation Bene Jeshurun, the congregation of Isaac Mayer Wise (the organizer of Reform Judaism in North America). *Minhag America,* Wise's prayer book, was adopted by the congregation in 1857 following the delivery of a sermon by Wise in Indianapolis, making Indianapolis Hebrew Congregation the first congregation in America to adopt this prayer book, two months before Wise's own congregation did so. The High Holiday edition was adopted in 1867. However, David Einhorn's radical *Olath Tamid* prayer book displaced Wise's volume in 1873 until the original edition of the *Union Prayer Book* was adopted in 1894.

While the congregation had outgrown its building and was preparing to secure a new location, the synagogue was consumed by fire in 1866. This motivated the congregation to move forward in its plans and purchase a lot on the corner of Sixth and Broadway. A new building was erected there in 1868, just after Dr. Leopold Kleeberg was elected the congregation's first rabbi.

With a membership that neared 170 families, new battles over reform developed. In 1869, Kleeberg was asked to preach at least once a month in English, and the following year, the rabbi introduced Friday (Sabbath eve) services to the congregation. Yet, in 1871, it was impossible to pass a resolution that would require men to remove their hats during worship services.

Dr. Emil G. Hirsch succeeded Kleeberg as rabbi in 1878. When he tendered his resignation in 1881, members quickly elected Rabbi Adolph Moses to the pulpit in his stead. During his tenure, in 1891, a proposition to introduce Sunday services was adopted, although similar resolutions had been defeated twice in 1889. Congregants were probably afraid that instituting Sunday services might lead to the abrogation of the Saturday Sabbath. Moses's deteriorating health necessitated the engagement of Dr. Hyman G. Enelow as junior rabbi in 1901. Enelow succeeded Moses after his death the following year. Enelow remained with Adath Israel until 1912, when Dr. Joseph Rauch came to Louisville. He served the congregation for forty-four years. As an early supporter of the American Council for Judaism, an anti-Zionist organization, he led the congregation in an early anti-Zionist stance until he later became a strong supporter of the state of Israel upon its founding. Rauch was also very active in building relationships between the congregation and its non-Jewish neighbors, working especially hard for desegregation and better education.

In 1932, Rauch discontinued the services that had been held on Sunday mornings since 1891 and moved them back to Friday evenings. In 1957, following the death of Dr. Rauch, Dr. Herbert Waller, who had been serving as co-rabbi since 1955, assumed the full burden of rabbinical leadership for the congregation.

Brith Sholom

Brith Sholom was organized in 1880 by a handful of Jews who were dissatisfied with the mode of worship at the local Beth Israel synagogue, which had been founded in 1856 by Polish and West German Jews. They desired certain reforms in ritual and felt that the only way to accomplish their goal was through the establishment of another synagogue. Within a year, the membership had raised sufficient funds to build a house of worship on First Street near Walnut. The congregation elected E. N. Myers as its first rabbi, who served until 1885. He was succeeded by H. Kutner, who served until 1892. When Falk Vidaver became rabbi, the practice of aliyahs, calling members up to the Torah on the Sabbath, was abolished.

In 1895, Dr. Ignatius Mueller was hired, and he served thirty years. Under his leadership, Brith Sholom outgrew its first facility and purchased a church on Second and College Streets. Mueller retired in 1921, and Rabbi Jerome Rosen succeded him. When he resigned in 1926, the congregation engaged Rabbi Solomon N. Bazell. He remained with the congregation until he entered the chaplaincy in 1943, having received a leave of absence from the congregation. When his term in the United States Navy expired, he resigned from the pulpit of Brith Sholom. Following the tenure of interim rabbis Alfred Barnston and David Raab, Martin M. Perley came to the congregation in 1946. In 1951, the congregation moved to Cowling Avenue. In 1969, Rabbi Leonard Devine was elected to the pulpit.

Adath Israel–Brith Sholom

In 1977, Adath Israel and Brith Sholom merged to become one congregation. Rabbi Chester Diamond was named senior rabbi of the merged congregations in 1986, having been elected to the position of co-rabbi of Adath Israel in 1975. In 1979, the merged congregation, now referred to as The Temple, moved from Cowling Avenue (where Brith Sholom had been) to Lime Kiln Lane. Members built a new sanctuary the following year at that location. In 1994, membership stood at over 750.

References

Dembitz, Lewis N. "Jewish Beginnings in Kentucky." *Publications of the American Jewish Historical Society* 1, No. 1 (December 1892): 99–101.

Goldsmith, Charles. *History of Congregation Adath Israel* (Louisville, KY: 1906).

Landau, Herman. *Adath Louisville, The Story of a Jewish Community* (Louisville, KY: 1981).

Rapport, Joe Rooks. *The Roots of Reform in Louisville* (Louisville, KY: 1993).

L

LOUISIANA

GATES OF PRAYER, REFORM. *New Orleans (later Metarie), Louisiana.*
The origins of Congregation Shaarai Tefiloh (Gates of Prayer of the City of
Lafayette), organized in 1850, can be traced to a minyan established for prayer
in about 1840 and to the Jewish Benevolent Society of Lafayette (Der israe-
litschen Wohltaetigkeits Verein), which dates back to 1848. The congregation
took over the activities of the benevolent society. These founders were German
immigrants who had moved to the working-class suburb of Lafayette City, two
miles upriver from New Orleans (which became part of the city in 1853). As
the charter, constitution, and by-laws were available at the organizational meeting, it can be assumed that preparations for the creation of a congregation were
underway for some time. Originally, founders wanted to establish a branch of
Shangarai Chessed, but members of Shangarai Chessed rejected their petition.

Gates of Prayer worshiped in a house rented for that purpose on Washington
Avenue. In 1855, the congregation moved to a house on St. Mary and Fulton
Streets. By 1866, members built a new synagogue on Jackson Street. Gates of
Prayer became Reform by evolution, not revolution, according to its historian,
Nathaniel S. Share. Following the dedication of the new synagogue, the con-
gregation retained the choir and requested the installation of an organ. Other
innovations followed, including the reading of the selection from the prophetic
literature in both German and English.

In 1873, the congregation appointed a special committee to draw up plans for
the modification of the worship service. This committee abbreviated the liturgy
and changed the location of the reading desk from the center of the congregation
to the front facing the congregation. Other resolutions overturned these changes
before the congregation made them permanent. Yet, in 1874, the congregation
permanently instituted family pews. Gates of Prayer eliminated most Torah hon-

ors ten years later, at about the same time that it adopted the prayer book prepared by Marcus Jastrow, a traditional prayer book with some innovations.

In the early years of the congregation, many readers led the congregation in worship. When the congregation neared a membership of one hundred in 1906, members elected Rabbi Moise Bergman to serve the congregation, the first ordained rabbi to do so. His leadership brought an increase in membership. By 1908, membership grew to 150, the same year the congregation affiliated with the Union of American Hebrew Congregations, the national organization of Reform synagogues.

Rabbi Bergman left the congregation in 1914 because of his wife's ill health. Dr. Mendel Silber succeeded him. Silber led the congregation to build a new synagogue, against the opposition of several board members, who resigned in protest. Thus, Gates of Prayer moved to a former church on Napoleon Avenue in 1920. By the following year, membership grew to over 325. Still trying to chart a course for its religious future, the congregation adopted the *Union Prayer Book* in 1928.

About the same time, membership declined and debts—due to the construction of a social center—increased substantially. The Depression hit the congregation hard and threatened its ability to survive. Rabbi Silber's health deteriorated during these same trying years, and he left the congregation. Rabbi Joseph Freedman succeeded him in 1934 for a few months. During this brief tenure, he quickly abolished the practice of covering the head during worship. Rabbi Nathaniel S. Share succeeded him. By 1942, membership neared the three hundred mark once again and reached four hundred by the end of the decade.

In 1949, the congregation abolished the practice of fixed seating. It introduced late Friday evening services in 1951. As congregational members moved out of the area and into Metarie, Congregation Gates of Prayer followed suit. In 1975, the congregation moved to Richland and West Esplande Avenues, the same year Rabbi Kenneth Segel joined Congregation Gates of Prayer. Under his direction, the congregation moved its religious school from Sunday to Saturday (1982). This move caused controversy lasting until the congregation moved its school back to Sunday three years later. Rabbi Robert H. Loewy succeeded Segel in 1984. The congregational program reflects his emphasis on adult education and outreach to all segments of the Jewish population. In 1994, membership stood at nearly 475.

References

Share, Nathaniel S. *Centennial Volume, Congregation Gates of Prayer* (New Orleans: 1950).
Shpall, Leo. *The Jews in Louisiana* (New Orleans: 1936).
Synagogue Histories File, American Jewish Archives.

TEMPLE SINAI, REFORM. *New Orleans, Louisiana.* Thirty-seven founders established Temple Sinai in 1870 as the first Reform congregation of New Orleans. Members dedicated Sinai's first building on Carondelet Street in 1872, the same year they elected James K. Gutheim as their rabbi. Gutheim had previously been rabbi at both the Shangarai Chessed and Nefutzoth Jehudah (prior to the merger of these two synagogues into Touro Synagogue). By 1874, however, even with 174 members, limited finances troubled the congregation. The yellow-fever epidemic of 1878 worsened the young congregation's financial condition, but by 1881 Temple Sinai declared itself free of debt.

From the beginning, Sinai required its worshipers to pray with uncovered heads. In 1877, the congregation joined the Union of American Hebrew Congregations, the national organization of Reform synagogues.

The year following Rabbi Gutheim's death in 1886, Temple Sinai invited Rabbi Maximilian Heller to lead it. The membership grew to nearly five hundred family units under his leadership. Heller introduced the *Union Prayer Book* for adoption by Temple Sinai in 1895. He also initiated the late Friday evening service in 1887. Heller responded to the growth in membership by expanding the activities at the Temple and within the Temple auxiliaries. In order to extend the influence of the congregation, Heller served as a circuit preacher for communities in Louisiana outside of New Orleans. As an early anti-Zionist who later changed his position in support of the settlement of Palestine, he published many articles and sermons.

Temple Sinai elected Rabbi Louis Binstock to its pulpit in 1926. During his tenure, Sinai members dedicated their present building at St. Charles Avenue and Calhoun St.

Rabbi Julian B. Feibelman succeeded Rabbi Binstock in 1936. Under his leadership, meeting opposition from the membership, Temple Sinai became the first house of worship to host a racially integrated meeting in the early 1950s. He worked to bring non-Jews into the temple and to foster positive interfaith relationships in the community through Friday-night book reviews. During Feibelman's tenure, Temple Sinai met the needs of a growing congregation by enlarging its building in the 1950s.

Rabbi Roy A. Rosenberg served Temple Sinai for three years (1967–1970). Rabbi Murray Blackman succeeded him in 1970. During his tenure, the congregation dedicated an addition (1972). Rosenberg focused his attention on building the educational program of the temple, particularly in the area of preschool and outreach to interfaith couples and families.

Upon Rabbi Blackman's retirement in 1987, the synagogue elected Dr. Edward Paul Cohn to serve as religious leader. Cohn emphasizes human relationships in his rabbinate, particularly in the area of intergroup relations in the congregation and in the community. During his time with the congregation, Sinai members embraced many new programs, including midweek Hebrew School, *Selichot* (penitential prayers) services, *havurot* (small group fellowships), outreach to the older adult community, and family education. In 1994, Temple Sinai's membership exceeded 960 family units.

References

Heller, Maximilian H. *Jubilee Souvenir of Temple Sinai* (New Orleans: 1922).
Shpall, Leo. *The Jews in Louisiana* (New Orleans: 1936).

Synagogue Histories File, American Jewish Archives.
Temple Sinai, Our First Hundred Years (New Orleans: 1970).

**TOURO SYNAGOGUE/SHANGARAI CHESSED NEFUTZOTH JEHU-
DAH, REFORM.** *New Orleans, Louisiana.* Founded in 1828 by German settlers
as Shangarai Chessed (Gates of Mercy) and merged with Nefutzoth Jehudah
(Dispersed of Judah), which Sephardic families founded in 1846, Touro Syna-
gogue is the oldest congregation in the United States beyond the coastal cities.
Because of his interest in the Sephardic congregation, Judah Touro presented
Nefutzoth Jehudah with a synagogue building on the corner of Bourbon and
Canal Streets (dedicated in 1850). He donated generously to the German con-
gregation as well, when it built its first building the same year on North Rampart
Street. Two years later, both congregations founded free Hebrew schools.

Rabbi James K. Gutheim became the rabbi of Shangarai Chessed in 1850 and
served until 1853, when he left to serve Nefutzoth Jehudah. He left the city in
1863, when he refused to take the oath of allegiance to the Union during its
army's occupation of New Orleans under the direction of General Benjamin F.
Butler. Rabbi Bernard Illowy succeeded him at Shangarai Chessed, where Gutheim returned after the war, leaving the city once again in 1868 to take a pulpit
at Congregation Emanu-El of the City of New York. During Gutheim's tenure
at Nefutzoth Jehudah, members abolished the auctioning of Torah honors (1860)
and, in 1866, installed an organ for use during worship. Shortly before Gutheim
left the congregation—and perhaps one of the reasons that he did indeed resign—Gutheim suggested the following changes in the synagogue: removal of
the central reading desk and the construction of a platform so that readers might
face the congregation; adoption of the triennial reading of the Torah; reading of
the haftarah in English; adoption of a new prayer book, such as the Reform
Minhag America; introduction of family pews; and abolition of the observance
of the second day of holidays. A great debate ensued; Gutheim resigned. Though
a majority of congregants petitioned for his return to the congregation, he was
already bound by contract to Congregation Emanu-El in New York. However,
he did return to New Orleans two years later to help found Temple Sinai. Reflecting this desire for reform, Shangarai Chessed joined the Union of American
Hebrew Congregations (UAHC), the national organization of Reform synagogues, at its founding in 1873. However, the congregation resigned from the
UAHC for a short period of time after the Central Conference of American
Rabbis issued its radical Pittsburgh Platform in 1885.

Nefutzoth Jehudah readied itself to build a new facility on Carondelet Street
in 1866. However, the Civil War impoverished the community to such an extent
that the congregations decided to merge, under the leadership of Rabbi Isaac L.
Leucht, who had served Shangarai Chessed since 1868. Leucht proposed the
new name Touro Synagogue in order to honor the memory of the benefactor of
both institutions, who died in 1854. The German congregation moved uptown

from the North Rampart location, and the Spanish-Portuguese synagogue became home to the newly merged congregation (1881).

This new congregation made changes clearly in the direction of Reform Judaism. It abbreviated worship on Saturday morning in 1889 so that services might last no longer than one hour. In 1891, the congregation resolved to allow worshipers to pray with uncovered heads. The congregation refused to celebrate the second day of holidays unless requested to do so by at least ten members. The rabbi removed his own head covering in 1893; in 1895, Touro Synagogue adopted the *Union Prayer Book,* the uniform Reform prayer book, for use in worship.

Touro Synagogue moved to St. Charles Avenue in 1907. Membership stood at 250. When Rabbi Isaac Leucht died in 1914, his assistant, Rabbi Emil Leipziger succeeded him. Under Leipziger's leadership, membership increased from three hundred to four hundred. In 1929, members built a social center and religious school building, which allowed for increased activities.

Leipziger retired in 1947, and Leo A. Bergman became rabbi of the congregation the following year. During his tenure, membership grew to over seven hundred. As a Zionist, Bergman guided the congregation to become pro-Zionist. When he retired in 1974, Rabbi Bruce Warshal succeeded him (1974–1976). Warshal actively led the congregation in the area of social action. To succeed Warshal, the congregation elected Rabbi David Goldstein to its pulpit in 1978. Under his guidance, Touro worked toward the release of Soviet Jews. In 1981, Touro nearly merged with local Temple Sinai. The merger failed to come to fruition because of ideological differences between the two congregations. Under Goldstein's guidance, the congregation built a new chapel (1989), which provided a more intimate atmosphere for worship. The following year, Touro members added an adult learning center. In 1991, Rabbi Goldstein began covering his head for worship. In 1995, membership stood at eight hundred family units.

References

Bergman, Leo. *A History of Touro Synagogue* (New Orleans: 1968).
Korn, Bertram W. *The Early Jews of New Orleans* (Waltham, MA: 1969).
Shpall, Leo. *The Jews in Louisiana* (New Orleans: 1936).
Synagogue Histories File, American Jewish Archives.

M

MARYLAND

BALTIMORE HEBREW CONGREGATION/NIDCHE ISRAEL, RE-FORM. *Baltimore, Maryland.* Many historians suggest that, after the first official minyan of the Baltimore Jewish community, thirteen men, led by Zalma Rehine, sought to organize a synagogue. The details regarding the founding of the Baltimore Hebrew Congregation cannot be verified, however. In 1830, the Legislature passed a bill incorporating "Nidche Israel" (The Scattered of Israel), known as Baltimore Hebrew Congregation. It would have been unthinkable to organize a congregation prior to the passage of Thomas Kennedy's bill (commonly known as the "Jew Bill"), which in 1826 extended religious freedom to members of the Jewish community. Even the bill to grant the congregation its charter met stiff opposition from those who had opposed Kennedy's bill.

Beginning on Bond Street, the congregation moved in 1832 to North Exeter (now Lexington) to accommodate its thirty-two members. Another move took place in 1835 to High Street; and in 1837, the congregation moved to Harrison Street, where it worshiped until 1845. In these early years, the Baltimore Hebrew Congregation was referred to as "the first Hebrew congregation" and, up to 1845, as the "Shtadt Shul," to distinguish it from the Fells Point Hebrew Friendship Congregation (later the Eden Street Synagogue). The Fells Point Synagogue was organized by a group who lived near the docks off Broadway and felt that the "Shtadt Shul" was too far to walk on the Sabbath. Organized by German Jews, the Baltimore Hebrew Congregation followed Orthodox Jewish ritual, later installing a ritual bath and a *matzah* baking oven in its facility. Yet, decorum was a priority. Through an elaborate system, fines were levied against members for talking during services, for chewing tobacco, for gathering on the pavement in front of the synagogue, for bringing children under five to services, for putting away prayer shawls before services were over, for leaving the synagogue during services without the permission of an officer, and for singing the final hymn louder than the cantor at the end of the Sabbath.

Baltimore Hebrew Congregation served as the center for Jewish activity in the city. Laypersons led services until the congregation could afford to engage its first service reader, I. Moses, in 1835. He remained until 1840, when Rabbi Abraham Rice came to serve the congregation as the first traditionally ordained rabbi to come to America and the first ordained rabbi of any congregation in the country. As a strict adherent of Orthodox Judaism, his demands on the congregation led to difficulties. He called on the board of the synagogue to censure members who did not observe the Sabbath, which it refused to do. At the funeral of one of the members, he refused to allow the Masons and Odd Fellows, of which the deceased had been a member, to perform their burial rites. This eventually led a group of liberal members of Baltimore Hebrew Congregation to leave and form Har Sinai Verein.

German immigration to the community increased the membership of the congregation. When its list of affiliated families reached sixty, this constituency decided to build a permanent house of worship. Completed in 1845, the Lloyd Street Synagogue was the first synagogue erected in Maryland. As soon as the synagogue changed its venue, Rice established a Hebrew School, which met daily. Frustrated by the increasing trend toward liberalism, Rice resigned his pulpit in 1849. Yet, even Rice's suggestions to eliminate some of the *piyyutim* (liturgical poems) were rejected. Rice organized a small Orthodox synagogue, which eventually became known as Shearith Israel. Rice later returned to Baltimore Hebrew in 1862 when the congregation was without a rabbi, but served only several months before his death. When Rice originally left, in 1845, Dr. Henry Hochheimer succeeded him and immediately introduced German and English instruction into the school and eventually opened a Sunday School, which served as a model for other synagogue schools in Baltimore. While there remained a great deal of tension between the liberal and traditional elements among synagogue membership, the board ruled that officers of the congregation were required to keep their businesses closed on the second day of Jewish holidays. Hochheimer's introduction of Confirmation for girls met with a great deal of protest (1853). Reformers in the congregation who tried to abolish the Bar Mitzvah and introduce the *Minhag America* prayer book were unsuccessful.

By 1854, when membership reached 175, the board determined that membership should be limited to two hundred. Hochheimer left in 1859, frustrated by the bifurcation of the membership regarding ritual and reform. He left to lead the Eden Street Congregation, the old Fells Point Synagogue, where he remained for thirty-two years.

Rabbi Bernard Illoway succeeded Hochheimer in 1859. A staunch advocate of Orthodoxy, in 1861 he led the movement to revise the synagogue's constitution, which included a stipulation that "fixed prayers should always be read in the original Hebrew language, according to the custom of German Orthodox Jews." However, his views that the Bible sanctioned slavery and that the South had the right to secede from the Union were too drastic, and he resigned in 1862.

The Lloyd Street Synagogue was enlarged in 1860; but between 1862 and 1868, a period when the congregation was without a rabbi, Baltimore Hebrew Congregation diminished in size and importance. Moderate liturgical reforms took place during this period, but when Rabbi Abraham Hofmann accepted the pulpit in 1868, important steps toward Reform were taken. A petition to introduce the reforms in accord with the Synod of Leipzig of 1869 was rejected, but a series of proposed innovations by Hofmann were accepted instead. These included shortening prayers characterized by repetition, abolishing prayers making reference to animal sacrifice, eliminating all prayers that were vengeful in spirit, and removing all Talmud quotations from the liturgy because they were not in fact prayers. The resolution to introduce a mixed choir in 1870 engendered fierce debate, which led a minority to take the issue to court, arguing that such changes were contrary to the synagogue's constitution, which, prepared in 1852, stipulated that changes required a two-thirds vote of the membership. In addition, they argued that the intended changes in liturgy were not in accord with German Orthodoxy and that the presence of women in a choir was contrary to ancient synagogue doctrine. The case never made it to court, but the majority of the dissidents resigned to form their own Orthodox Congregation Chizuk Amuno. With their resignation, reforms became easier and more rapid. Family pews and an organ were introduced in 1873. The triennial cycle of the reading of the Torah was adopted—a change from the traditional practice of reading the complete Torah on an annual basis. Wearing prayer shawls became optional. Aliyahs were abolished, as was the recitation of the *Misheberach* public prayers on behalf of the sick. Several years later, the membership discontinued the observance of the second day of holidays, and regular Friday evening services were introduced.

Hofmann resigned in 1873; he was not replaced until 1881, when Rabbi Maurice Fluegel took the post, remaining only three years. Again there was a hiatus in rabbinical leadership, and again membership dwindled. By 1884, only forty-one families belonged to the Baltimore Hebrew Congregation. The Jewish community had also moved uptown by this time. In 1886, the vacant pulpit was filled by Rabbi Aaron Siegfried Bettleheim. His first action was to persuade the remaining membership to move the synagogue. After the building was sold (and eventually restored by the Jewish Historical Society of Maryland in 1960), the congregation worshiped in the First Methodist Church building. Bettleheim died in 1890. That year, Baltimore Hebrew Congregation joined the Jewish Theological Seminary Association of New York. The following year, Dr. Adolf Guttmacher became rabbi just before the congregation moved into its newly built Madison Avenue Temple, with only thirty-eight names on its membership roster. Guttmacher introduced numerous reforms, including the elimination of certain prayers and the shortening of others. The wearing of hats and prayer shawls was also discontinued (1892). In 1894, Baltimore Hebrew Congregation joined the

Union of American Hebrew Congregations, marking its commitment as an institution to Reform Judaism. Guttmacher died in 1915 and was succeeded by Rabbi Morris S. Lazaron. During his tenure, the congregation focused on the education of its youth and introduced the first synagogue bulletin in this country. He also introduced creative worship services for youth. Most significantly, Lazaron worked toward building relationships between members of Baltimore Hebrew and the non-Jewish community. Through his efforts, the board discontinued the policy of assigned seating in 1921. In 1943, the congregation moved its school and Temple Center to Park Heights and Slade Avenues. A sanctuary was not built on this property until 1951. In 1949, Lazaron was named emeritus. Throughout his tenure, Lazaron's anti-Zionist stance was not popular at the Baltimore Hebrew Congregation. His unwillingness to yield to a board request not to preach against Zionism during the High Holidays of 1949 led to his resignation from his emeritus position. He was succeeded by Morris Lieberman, who had been serving the congregation as associate rabbi.

Shortly after the full move to Park Heights took place, membership had grown to twelve hundred family units. By 1954, membership reached fifteen hundred. As a result, Baltimore Hebrew joined other area Reform congregations in helping to establish Temple Emanuel, in 1956. Lieberman died in 1970. Upon his death, Rabbi David Goldstein took over leadership of the congregation, where he had been serving as assistant rabbi. During his tenure, the congregation adopted some of the ritual practices it had previously rejected. Rabbi Murray Saltzman succeeded Rabbi Goldstein in 1978. Under his leadership, the congregation opened a day school in 1990. In 1993, the membership of Baltimore Hebrew Congregation stood in excess of two thousand family units.

References

Greenberg, Rose. *The Chronicle of Baltimore Hebrew Congregation 1830–1975* (Baltimore: 1975).

Guttmacher, Adolf. *A History of the Baltimore Hebrew Congregation, 1830–1905* (Baltimore: 1905).

Lazaron, Morris. *On Common Ground: A Plea for Intelligent Americanism* (New York: 1938).

Rosenwaike, Ira. "The Founding of Baltimore's First Jewish Congregation: Fact vs. Fiction." *American Jewish Archives* 28, no. 2 (November 1976): 119–25.

———. "The Jews of Baltimore: 1810–1820." *American Jewish Archives* 67, no. 1 (September 1977): 101–24.

———. "The Jews of Baltimore: 1820–1830." *American Jewish Archives* 67, no. 3 (March 1978): 246–59.

Shpeen, Scott. "A Man against the Wind: A Biographical Study of Rabbi Morris S. Lazaron" (Rabbinic thesis, Hebrew Union College–Jewish Institute of Religion, 1984).

Synagogue Histories File, American Jewish Archives.

Tabak, Israel. "The Lloyd Street Synagogue of Baltimore: A National Shrine." *American Jewish Archives* 61, no. 4 (June 1972): 342–52.

BETH JACOB, ORTHODOX. *Baltimore, Maryland.* A small group organized

Beth Jacob in 1938 in response to a need it felt for an Orthodox synagogue in the Upper Park Heights community. A rented building on Park Heights and Manhattan Avenues served the congregation as its first home. Dr. Louis L. Kaplan served Beth Jacob as its spiritual leader until members engaged Rabbi Bernard Lander in 1939. David Paritzky succeeded Rabbi Lander in 1944, remaining only one year, after which Rabbi Uri Miller joined the congregation. During Paritzky's tenure, the congregation founded its religious school. It built a structure to house the institution one year later. Under Rabbi Miller's guidance, congregational membership increased from two hundred to six hundred.

In 1952, Beth Jacob initiated the first High Holiday Israel Bond Appeal and shortly thereafter became the first Orthodox congregation to participate in the Red Cross blood program. In 1953, members dedicated the first permanent home for the congregation. In order to accommodate increasing membership, members expanded the synagogue in 1965. Rabbi Nahum Ben-Natan joined the congregation in 1972 to assist Rabbi Miller, whose health had declined. When Rabbi Miller died several months later, Rabbi Ben-Natan succeeded him. Members elected Rabbi Ronald Schwartz to the pulpit in 1984.

Ohr Knesseth Israel–Ansche Sphard

Founded in 1887, Ansche Sphard Congregation met temporarily on Albermarle Street and then on High Street until it occupied its first regular synagogue building elsewhere on High Street in 1891, the former location of Har Sinai Congregation. In 1920, the congregation moved to Aisquith Street, the former home of Machzike Hadath Congregation. It remained there until 1936, when it was forced out of the location by the City of Baltimore as a result of a street widening. After locating elsewhere on Aisquith for a year, Ansche Sphard moved to North Broadway. It remained in this location until 1951, when it merged with Ohr Knesseth Israel Congregation of West Franklin Street. The merged congregation relocated to West Rogers Avenue. Members incorporated the Ohr Knesseth Israel Congregation (Franklin Street Synagogue) in 1894. This synagogue may, in fact, be the congregation recognized as the West End Hebrew Congregation Knesseth Israel located at Green and Lombard Streets, founded in 1885. The Ohr Knesseth Israel Congregation worshipped in China Hall on West Baltimore Street until about 1908, when it moved to Franklin and Abel Streets.

In 1993, Beth Jacob integrated its membership with Rogers Avenue Synagogue, Ohr Knesseth Israel–Ansche Sphard. The commemoration of King David's yahrzeit (anniversary of the date of death) is among the unique rituals that Ohr Knesseth Israel—Ansche Sphard brought to Beth Jacob. Although the congregation maintains separate seating for men and women, this arrangement remains a major topic of controversy within the ranks of congregational leadership. In 1994, membership of the combined institution exceeded 815 family units.

Reference

Synagogue Histories File, American Jewish Archives.

BETH TFILOH, ORTHODOX. *Baltimore, Maryland.* By 1921, the number of Jews in the areas of Forest Park, Walbrook, and Windsor Hills warranted the establishment of a new congregation. Two groups, one from Forest Park and a second from Walbrook, joined together for worship at the home of Max Miller, one of the organizers of the new congregation. At the end of the year, members petitioned for a charter for this new congregation: "The form of prayer shall forever be according to the Orthodox custom of the Hebrews and said customs shall not be changed or any other form of prayer adopted without the consent of the entire congregation."

Meeting in a variety of locations, this small group raised funds to purchase a cottage on Garrison Boulevard and Dalrymple Avenue (later Fairview Avenue), where members prepared their first synagogue home. Conflict quickly developed when members made a decision not to include a women's balcony in the reconstruction of the cottage. The dissidents left the congregation to form Tifereth Israel Congregation. Members raised additional funds the following year to build a community center and school (dedicated 1925), the first to serve children in the area.

Finally ready for religious leadership, members elected Rabbi Samuel Rosenblatt (son of Cantor Yosselle Rosenblatt) to the pulpit in 1927. Membership reached sixty in 1928. While trying to maintain an Orthodox congregation, Rabbi Rosenblatt made certain changes to accommodate his growing congregation, including the installation of a microphone in the sanctuary. Rosenblatt also introduced group Bat Mitzvah (which met with initial opposition) for girls in 1936, held in the spring near the festival of Shavuot. He eventually replaced the selling of aliyahs (Torah honors) on Yom Kippur with the issuance of a memorial book.

The congregation organized a brotherhood in 1929. Beth Tfiloh opened a nursery school (later to evolve into a day school) in 1939. Members dedicated a new school building in 1941 to accommodate the growing population of synagogue youth. Beth Tfiloh started its own day camp in 1943 and purchased a site for this activity in Owings Mills in 1951.

By the middle of the 1940s, the existence of two factions in the congregation became evident. The group that preferred a less Orthodox approach to Judaism left to form Beth El, a local Conservative congregation.

When the sisterhood reached nearly one thousand members in the 1950s, the women argued for the right to participate in services; the congregation granted this privilege but only from a microphone in the separate women's section of the sanctuary. By the end of the decade, as the demography of the Forest Hills area changed, attendance at worship services and membership itself dropped significantly. Thus, in 1960 Beth Tfiloh purchased a tract of land on Old Court Road. As the site was not within walking distance of any established neighborhoods, the congregation argued strongly for zoning changes in the area that would permit the development of apartments and homes in the immediate vicinity of the new synagogue complex. Beth Tfiloh dedicated the new structure with its fifteen-hundred-seat sanctuary in 1966.

When Rabbi Rosenblatt officially retired in 1972, members elected Dr. David Novak as their rabbi. When he left in 1977, Rabbi Mitchell Wohlberg became rabbi to Beth Tfiloh's nine hundred families. In 1978, members decided to add a gymnasium to the building and added a chapel in 1981. During Wohlberg's tenure, many changes took place at Beth Tfiloh. The congregation established a Beth Tfiloh High School and added a chapel, youth center, middle school wing, and gymnasium to its building. Under his direction, Beth Tfiloh affiliated with the Union of Orthodox Jewish Congregations of America. He also orchestrated the establishment of a Hebrew School with Beth Am (unaffiliated) and Adat Chaim (Conservative) congregations. Other activities he initiated include family services, women's Rosh Chodesh (new month) services, and an informal minyan with *mechitzah* (partition separating men and women in prayer). Wohlberg replaced late Friday evening services for Bat Mitzvah with Sunday-morning "creative" services. In 1994, Beth Tfiloh's membership reached nearly thirteen hundred family units, with a day-school enrollment over 730.

References

Fishman, Bess, and Eric Levi, eds. *The Chronicle of Beth Tfiloh Congregation* (Baltimore: 1981).
Memorial History, Beth Tfiloh Congregation (Baltimore: 1936). Synagogue Histories File, American Jewish Archives.

CHIZUK AMUNO, CONSERVATIVE. *Baltimore, Maryland.* A group of twenty-three dissidents from Baltimore Hebrew Congregation formed the Chizuk Amuno in 1871, when the court rejected their civil suit to prevent reforms of the congregation. They were joined by some seceding members from Beth Hamedrosh Hagodol Claus Congregation, then located on Harrison Street. These early members, mainly from southern Bavaria, worshiped in a leased hall on North Exeter Street for five years before moving to Chizuk Amuno's first synagogue building on Lloyd Street.

This Lloyd Street Synagogue—not to be confused with the Lloyd Street Synagogue of Baltimore Hebrew Congregation—became known to many as the "Friedenwald Shul" because of the influence of the Friedenwald family throughout the early years of the life of the congregation. Three members of the Friedenwald family served as president of the congregation: Jonas (1879–1892), Dr. Aaron (1892–1902), and Dr. Harry Friedenwald (1911–1920).

In 1876, Chizuk Amuno established a religious school for the children of its members; ten years later, the women of Chizuk Amuno formed its Sisterhood. Twenty years after the dedication of the Lloyd Street Synagogue, bolstered by an increase in membership of Russian immigrants, Chizuk Amuno members dedicated their McCullough Street Synagogue (1895). Following the movement of its members north and an increase of membership due to those fleeing German anti-Semitism Chizuk Amuno moved to Eutaw Place in 1922. In its new location, members introduced Confirmation (1930) and allowed women to speak from the pulpit. A discussion over family pews took place for several years, until the congregation resolved to institute them in 1948. Chizuk Amuno moved to its current home on Stevenson Road in 1958 when it started construction of a multiphase project, with additions as recent as 1988.

Chizuk Amuno was among the founders of the Jewish Theological Seminary Association, supporting the seminary since 1892. In 1913, the congregation participated in the establishment of the United Synagogue of America, the national organization of Conservative synagogues.

Dr. Henry W. Schneeberger served Chizuk Amuno as its first rabbi (1876–1912). Dr. Eugene Kohn succeeded Dr. Schneeberger and remained until 1918. Rabbi Adolph Coblenz came to the congregation in 1920 and introduced late Friday night services. Following the retirement of Rabbi Coblenz in 1948, Rabbi Israel M. Goldman led the congregation. In 1956, membership exceeded sixteen hundred families. Rabbi Maurice Corson (1976–1979) succeeded Rabbi Goldman, and Rabbi Joel Zaiman joined the congregation in 1980. The following year, Chizuk Amuno formed a Solomon Schechter day school. At that time, sixty-four hundred individuals were affiliated with Chizuk Amuno.

References

Pruce, Earl. *Synagogues, Temples, and Congregations of Maryland, Past and Present, 1830–1990* (Baltimore: 1990).
Synagogue Histories File, American Jewish Archives.

HAR SINAI, REFORM. *Baltimore, Maryland.* Breaking way from the Baltimore Hebrew Congregation when its rabbi, Abraham Rice, refused to allow members of the Masons and Odd Fellows to add their burial rites to those of the Jewish tradition, members of the Har Sinai Verein gathered for their first service of worship in 1842. The following year these same men incorporated Har Sinai. As a result, Har Sinai claims to be the oldest continuously Reform congregation in the United States. Because the Baltimore Hebrew Congregation refused to loan a Torah scroll to the new group—as its first act had been to procure a small organ—the Verein was forced to use a printed Bible. The new congregation began its periodic worship experience in a variety of locations, until it secured a private home on Exeter Street and Eastern Avenue where it could meet regularly.

After its incorporation as a congregation, Har Sinai moved several times, reflecting a need for larger quarters as membership grew. Har Sinai members dedicated their first permanent home on High Street in 1849. While others may have considered worship services at Har Sinai to be radical, men sat separate from women. Male worshipers covered their heads and wore prayer shawls. They observed dietary laws and the Sabbath. Yet, Har Sinai became one of the earliest congregations to introduce Sunday worship services for a limited period in 1845.

Har Sinai's first rabbi, David Einhorn (1855–1861), outlined his approach to Reform Judaism as "by no means to break with the past, but to enlist the old in service of the new and to preserve it in transfigured form." Einhorn led his congregation in its opposition of the forming of the Board of Delegates of American Israelites. They felt that no one group should represent "American Israel." Einhorn had to leave Baltimore in 1861 because of his vociferous opposition to slavery. Dr. Solomon Deutsch succeeded Einhorn in 1862. During his tenure, members dedicated a new synagogue at Lexington and Pine, the same year they changed the name of the congregation, in the context of a new charter, from Har Sinai Verein to Har Sinai Congregation (1873). Later that year, Har Sinai joined the Union of American Hebrew Congregations, the national organization of Reform congregations, shortly after its founding.

In this new building, formerly a church, men and women sat together for worship, much to the consternation of the local Jewish community. In addition, children attended religious school on Saturday afternoons and Sunday mornings, as well as Confirmation classes midweek. Instruction took place in German. English was not introduced to the congregation until 1879.

Dr. Deutsch instituted other changes as well. He did not wear a prayer shawl. Yet, when he encountered a sign in the synagogue's foyer that read, "The men are ordered to remove their hats upon entering the Temple. By order of the President," he fought against the order. Deutsch finally consented to worship without head coverings. When Deutsch left, other rabbis followed in succession: Jacob Meyer (1874–1876), Emil G. Hirsch (1877–1878), and Samuel Sale (1879–1883).

Members elected Rabbi David Philipson, a member of the first graduating class of Hebrew Union College, to the pulpit in 1883. Rabbi Tobias Schanfarber succeeded Philipson in 1888. Membership stood at approximately one hundred families. During Schanfarber's tenure, Har Sinai moved to Bolton and Wilson (1894). When Schanfarber left the congregation in 1898, Rabbi Charles A. Rubenstein succeeded him. During his tenure, Rubenstein introduced late Friday evening worship services, and the congregation adopted the *Union Prayer Book.*

Rabbis Louis Bernstein (1920–1922) and Harvey Wessel (1922–1923) served the congregation until it elected Rabbi Edward L. Israel to fill its pulpit. Active in social justice and labor projects, Israel directed the energies of the congregation in that regard. He also conducted well-attended Sunday morning services. According to historian Abraham Shusterman, Israel "believed the synagogue could be relevant to life by applying the prophetic standards to social affairs." Thus, he led the congregation in his battle for social reform. He also advocated Labor Zionism as an appropriate posture for the congregation.

Israel left the congregation in 1941 (shortly before his death), and the congregation moved to Park Heights Avenue (1959) under the guidance of his successor, Rabbi Abraham Shusterman. Shusterman's initial innovations included wearing a pulpit robe and *atarah* (vestment). During his tenure, Har Sinai operated a nursery school, a summer day camp, and an experimental youth center—later to be displaced by the suburban Jewish Community Center. Har Sinai introduced the first religious school program for the mentally challenged.

In 1971, Har Sinai built a new religious school wing and educational building in order to meet the needs of its growing membership. Rabbi Howard Simon, who had been serving as assistant and then associate rabbi, succeeded Rabbi Shusterman in 1972. Simon introduced the practice of wearing pulpit hats and changed the liturgy to include more Hebrew. Simon resigned in 1973 because of personal problems; Rabbi Herbert Rutman succeeded him.

Members built Har Sinai House, a residence for older adults, in 1971, the first such venture in the United States. Because of the success of this enterprise, members built a second building and named it in memory of a former president of the congregation, Robert B. Balter. In 1975, the congregation adopted *Gates of Prayer* as its standard liturgy.

Rabbi Rutman resigned in 1981 over a conflict with the congregation regarding the position of an invested cantor whom he favored. Members then elected Rabbi Floyd Herman to the pulpit of Har Sinai. He added a second day service for Rosh Hashanah and organized several *havurot,* special fellowship groups designed to enhance worship and study. Since 1989, Har Sinai members participate in a soup-kitchen program based at local Browns Memorial Baptist Church. The same year, the congregation joined other local Reform congregations in the development of a liberal Jewish day school. In 1994, Har Sinai's membership stood at over 650.

References

Aaron, Charles. *History of Har Sinai Congregation of the City of Baltimore* (Baltimore: 1918).
Rayner, William S. *Souvenir Jubilee Year of Har Sinai Congregation* (Baltimore: 1892).
Rubenstein, C. A. *History of Har Sinai Congregation* (Baltimore: 1918).
Shusterman, Abraham. *The Legacy of a Liberal* (Baltimore: rev., 1992).
Synagogue Histories File, American Jewish Archives.

SUBURBAN ORTHODOX CONGREGATION TORAS CHAIM, ORTHO-DOX. *Baltimore, Maryland.* As the first Orthodox synagogue in the Baltimore area outside Baltimore city limits, founders called the congregation the Suburban Orthodox Synagogue (1956). The young congregation began in the basement of a private home on Slade Avenue, northwest of Baltimore. Founders immediately established a brotherhood and sisterhood (1957). Shortly thereafter, members purchased a small cottage on Seven Mile Lane, which they converted for use as a synagogue. There they founded a Hebrew School. On the same location, Suburban Orthodox built a new synagogue building, moving the cottage elsewhere on the property for use as a Hebrew School (1962). Eventually, the school closed, as enrollment dwindled because members sought a day-school education for their children (1970).

Soon after Suburban Orthodox's successful establishment, Shaarei Tfiloh

Congregation, a Baltimore City institution, merged into the new synagogue (1973). Members of both synagogues initially supported the merger, as Jews were moving outside the city limits and needed an Orthodox synagogue in suburbia to serve their needs. However, each group wanted to direct the operation of the synagogue in its own way. As a result, leaders of both synagogues decided to dissolve the merger (1976).

Following the death of Suburban Orthodox's first rabbi, Chaim Gevantman (1957–1976), the congregation honored his memory by changing its name to Suburban Orthodox Congregation Toras Chaim. Rabbi Ervin Preis succeeded Gevantman in 1976. Under Preis' direction the synagogue eliminated the use of microphones on the Sabbath. In 1985, Suburban Orthodox expanded its sanctuary and constructed a small addition to its building. At this time, members moved the *bima* (raised platform from which the prayer leader leads services) from the front of the sanctuary to the middle and raised the women's section of the sanctuary to create a *mechitza* (divider which separates men and women during prayer), which allowed women full view of worship services. In 1995, the membership of Suburban Orthodox stood at 250 family units.

Reference

Helfman, Harold M. *History of the Suburban Orthodox Synagogue* (Baltimore: 1962).

TEMPLE OHEB SHALOM, REFORM. *Baltimore, Maryland.* The first meeting of the group of twenty-one Baltimore Jews who formed Oheb Shalom Congregation took place in 1853. Forty-nine others joined the initial group during the first year and officially incorporated the congregation in 1854. There were already three well-established congregations in this relatively small Jewish community, and it is not entirely clear why this fourth congregation was established—over a store at Gay and Lexington Streets. There is reason to believe that Rabbi Isaac Mayer Wise, the force behind the organization of Reform Judaism in America, exerted a great deal of influence in the development of Oheb Shalom. William Rosenau, later rabbi of the congregation, suggests that when many of the early members applied for seats at the other congregations, they were not well received. As a result, they may have decided to take matters into their own hands by establishing a congregation of their own. About the same time that Baltimore Hebrew Congregation decided to limit its membership, founders organized Oheb Shalom.

From 1858 to 1893, members of Oheb Shalom called the Hanover Street Synagogue home. With a move into this new facility, the membership adopted *Minhag America* as its prayer book and introduced an organ and a choir. This marked a change in ritual. In the early days of the congregation, a number of men, not ordained as rabbis, served the congregation in a variety of capacities including reader and *shochet* (ritual slaughterer). In 1859, Oheb Shalom elected Dr. Benjamin Szold as its rabbi. He served until his retirement in 1892. Szold introduced the weekly sermon (in German) at the synagogue. In 1864, "Lehrer"

Goldsmith moved his school from the Eden Street (Fells Point) Synagogue to Oheb Shalom, where it remained until 1874, when it was disbanded as a result of the expansion of Baltimore's public school system.

The Civil War severely impacted the synagogue's financial stability. However, by the end of the war, the congregation flourished and began to grow once again. Members of Oheb Shalom elected Alois Kaiser as hazan in 1866; he served until his death in 1908. Together with Szold, they sought to establish proper decorum as a priority for worship at Oheb Shalom. Disturbed by the inconsistency between *Minhag America* and *Roedelheim Tefillah,* which the congregation used for the High Holidays, Szold introduced his own High Holiday prayer book, *Abodath Israel* (later called the Szold-Jastrow prayer book), which he prepared specifically for Oheb Shalom. Following adoption of this prayer book, the congregation eliminated the celebration of minor fast days, the observance of the second day of holidays, the practice of *misheberach* (public blessings during the Torah reading), aliyahs, and the wearing of the *tallit* (prayer shawl). Yet men wore hats (or caps for the boys)—not skullcaps—during worship.

The congregation continued to grow and refurbished the synagogue in 1870. Three years later, Oheb Shalom established a religious school. In 1882, Szold began preaching once a month in English, the same year the congregation affiliated with the Union of American Hebrew Congregations (the national organization of Reform congregations). By 1886, Szold delivered English sermons on a biweekly basis. That year, Szold revised his prayer book and added English translations by Rabbi Marcus M. Jastrow. Members quickly adopted this new edition.

Following Szold's retirement in 1892, congregants elected Dr. William Rosenau to the pulpit. He served the congregation until his death in 1943. In 1893, the new synagogue at Eutaw Place and Lanvale Street was completed. This new facility accommodated eleven hundred people in its sanctuary, while its membership rolls listed only 150 members. By 1903, membership increased to 475. German was no longer in use at all during worship. The William Rosenau Memorial Building, adjacent to the Eutaw Place Temple, was built as the Temple Center in 1922 and remodeled and dedicated in Rosenau's memory in 1948. When Rosenau retired in 1940, Rabbi Abraham D. Shaw succeeded him.

In 1960, the congregation moved to upper Park Heights Avenue, south of Slade Avenue. Members celebrated the first Bat Mitzvah at Oheb Shalom in 1973. In 1976, Rabbi Donald Berlin succeeded Rabbi Shaw, the same year the congregation adopted the *Gates of Prayer* as its prayer book. During his tenure, the congregation became one of the first to engage a program coordinator for its extensive activity program. Rabbi Berlin has also led the congregation extensively in the struggle for civil rights. In 1991, the congregation received the Irving Fain award (of the Union of American Hebrew Congregations, for congregation-based social action projects) for sponsoring a homeless shelter, Corner

House, and for its active projects on hunger. In 1994, membership stood at nearly twelve hundred.

References

Cahn, Louis F. *The History of Oheb Shalom, 1853–1953* (Baltimore: 1953).
Synagogue Histories File, American Jewish Archives.

MASSACHUSETTS

TEMPLE ISRAEL, REFORM. *Boston, Massachusetts.* Twenty-five members left Ohabei Shalom to form their own synagogue in 1853. They initially used the name Ohabei Shalom—in order to claim a bequest to that congregation from philanthropist Judah Touro—before eventually adopting the name Adath Israel (1856). This new group dedicated a synagogue on Pleasant Street in 1854. Adath Israel elected Joseph Shoninger as its first religious leader in 1856. Like other traditional Bavarian synagogues, women sat in the balcony of Adath Israel and men wore hats during worship. The hazan chanted the entire service in Hebrew, and rabbis delivered sermons in German. When Rabbi Solomon Schindler came in 1874 to "Americanize" the congregation, he found an organized congregation desiring to be different from the other two congregations in town. He thus initiated a series of radical reforms, but he couldn't achieve them. In fact, it took about twenty years to install an organ, institute a choir, establish family pews, abolish Friday evening services, and discontinue the second day of holidays. Approximately fifteen members eventually left the congregation in response to these changes.

Schindler introduced Sunday evening lectures in 1886. In 1885, with a membership of seventy, the congregation dedicated a new synagogue at Columbus Avenue and Northampton Street. By 1894, the congregational membership reached nearly one hundred families.

Immediately upon the election of Rabbi Charles Fleischer (1894–1911), Adath Israel joined the Union of American Hebrew Congregations, the national organization of Reform synagogues, instituted Sunday services, and adopted the *Union Prayer Book.* During Fleischer's tenure, the congregation dedicated a new temple on Commonwealth Avenue. Much to the consternation of temple members, Fleischer infused his work at Temple Israel with the Transcendentalism of Theodore Parker and Ralph Waldo Emerson. He left in 1911 to found Sunday Commons, a nonsectarian community church.

Rabbi Harry Levi (1911–1939) succeeded Fleischer and halted the universalistic direction of the congregation. He reinstituted Saturday Sabbath services but kept Sundays (broadcast over the radio). As a result, Sunday services became a melting pot for Boston's Jewish community. Levi opened branch schools of the

Religious School for immigrant children. By 1917, membership reached nearly four hundred.

In 1924, the congregation admitted women to full membership and allowed them to hold seats on the board of trustees. Four years later, the congregation built a meeting house in its current location on Longwood Avenue and Fenway to house the expanded activities Levi implemented. The congregation retained its sanctuary on Commonwealth Avenue. Following the eventual sale of the synagogue on Commonwealth (in the 1960s), members expanded the Riverway facility in 1973.

When Levi retired, Rabbi Joshua Loth Liebman came to the pulpit. Liebman eliminated Sunday services and instituted Bar Mitzvah. He also led the congregation in its support of a Jewish homeland. His best-selling *Peace of Mind* and its approach to Judaism's questions of personal meaning colored his rabbinate at Temple Israel. When Liebman died in 1948, Rabbi Abraham Klausner came to serve Temple Israel. Klausner continued the direction for the temple established by Liebman. In the school, Klausner added Hebrew and a two-year post-Confirmation course of study.

Rabbi Roland Gittelsohn succeeded Klausner in 1953. Active in Reconstructionist circles, Gittelsohn reflected the philosophy of Mordecai Kaplan, the founder of Reconstructionism. He also emphasized social action in his rabbinate and fought for desegregation of local schools. An ardent Zionist, who helped to found ARZA (Association of Reform Zionists of America) and serve as its first president, Gittelsohn emphasized Hebrew and an adherence to Zionist thought in his rabbinate at Temple Israel. He opposed the Vietnam War and counseled young men in his congregation who sought to avoid the draft. During his tenure, Temple Israel's membership grew from fourteen hundred to twenty-two hundred, and school enrollment expanded from eight hundred to over fourteen hundred.

Gittelsohn retired in 1977, and Rabbi Bernard Mehlman succeeded him the following year. During Mehlman's tenure the congregation expanded its program of activities, particularly in the area of adult education. In 1994, membership of Temple Israel exceeded fourteen hundred.

References

Ehrenfried, Albert. *A Chronicle of Boston Jewry from the Colonial Settlement to 1900* (Boston: 1963).

Fein, Isaac M. *Boston—Where It All Began: An Historical Perspective of the Boston Jewish Community* (Boston: 1976).

Mann, Arthur. *Growth and Achievement: Temple Israel 1854–1954* (Boston: 1954).

Synagogue Histories File, American Jewish Archives.

CONGREGATION MISHKAN TEFILA, CONSERVATIVE. *Boston (later Chestnut Hill), Massachusetts.* Twelve men seceded from Ohabei Shalom in 1858 to form De Israelitische Gemeinde Mishkan Israel (House of Israel). Alexis Alexander served as its first religious leader. Under the influence of the other congregations, Mishkan Israel instituted reforms such as organ music and family pews. However, it did not change the ritual of worship. This group met for worship on Oswego Street. In 1863, the congregation moved to larger quarters on Harrison Street and established Mishkan Israel's first Hebrew School.

Four years later, in need of larger quarters, the congregation moved to a house on Orange Street, a part of which was sublet to the Congregation of Holland Jews. In 1875, Mishkan Israel dedicated a new house of worship on Ash Street.

In 1895, the congregation joined with Sharei Tefila on Pleasant Street to form Mishkan Tefila. In 1898, the combined group purchased a former church on Shawmut Avenue at Madison Street, and in 1907 the congregation bought the Emmanuel Congregational Church on Moreland Street. Led by H. S. Shoher, members introduced mixed seating and a choir in the new location. Nathan Blechman succeeded Shoher shortly after the dedication. That same year, the women of the congregation formed a women's organization and called it a Frauen Verein. Two years later, the women changed the name of the organization to the Ladies Auxiliary and then later to the Sisterhood Temple Mishkan Tefila. Blechman supported the women of the congregation, who sought recognition for their contribution to the upbuilding of the synagogue; this led to his early dismissal. A Rabbi Brown succeeded Blechman, but illness forced his resignation in 1910.

Rabbi Herman H. Rubenovitz succeeded Rabbi Brown in 1910. Under his direction, Mishkan Tefila built a new building on Seaver Street (dedicated 1925). Rubenovitz retired in 1946, and Rabbi Israel J. Kazis succeeded him. During his tenure, members began to move to Brookline and Newton. By 1952, two-thirds of the membership resided in Newton. In 1954, the board of Mishkan Tefila purchased a tract of land for a synagogue in Chestnut Hill on Hammond Pond Parkway (dedicated 1958). In 1954, a group of members organized themselves into the Mishkan Tefila Forum, a forum for the exchange of ideas, which proved to be the most significant driving force in the congregation as it contemplated moving into a new building. At the same time (1955), the congregation administered a religious education program in a private house on Walnut Street in Newton purchased by the congregation.

Rabbi Richard Yellin (1976–1993) succeeded Kazis. Certain changes were made with regard to the participation of women in ritual during Rabbi Yellin's tenure, and the congregation became fully egalitarian (except with regard to witnessing marriage documents) during the tenure of Rabbi Michael Menitoff (1993–   ). In 1993, the congregation added a nursery school and youth wing to its building. In 1995, Mishkan Tefila listed nine hundred family units on its membership rolls.

References

Ehrenfried, Albert. *A Chronicle of Boston Jewry from the Colonial Settlement to 1900* (Boston: 1963).

Fein, Isaac M. *Boston—Where It All Began: An Historical Perspective of the Boston Jewish Community* (Boston: 1976).

Sieve, Jacob. *L'Dor Vodor, From Generation to Generation: Congregation Mishkan Tefila 1858–1983* (Boston: 1983).
Synagogue Histories File, American Jewish Archives.

CONGREGATION KEHILLATH ISRAEL, CONSERVATIVE. *Brookline, Massachusetts.* Thirty-six founders incorporated Kehillath Israel in 1917 as the (Orthodox) Jewish Congregation of Brookline. The congregation organized in 1915 with a Hebrew School meeting at Oddfellows Hall; however, initial failed efforts can be traced to as early as 1911. Yet shortly after its incorporation, the congregation affiliated with the United Synagogue of America (now United Synagogue of Conservative Judaism). The group met for High Holiday services as Congregation Kehillath Israel. In the early years, the congregation met in a variety of locations for worship before purchasing its first permanent location, a private home on Thorndike Street. The new congregation grew rapidly, primarily by the addition of former members of two Orthodox synagogues (Adath Jeshurun and Beys Midrash Ha-Godel) in Roxbury, who had moved to Brookline. Women formed a sisterhood in 1919; men organized a brotherhood in 1927.

Kehillath Israel members built a new synagogue on Harvard Street (dedicated 1925). Members built an adjacent school building in 1929. In the new sanctuary, women of the congregation joined the men on the same level of the sanctuary. Shortly before the dedication, Kehillath Israel engaged its first religious leader, Louis Epstein (1925–1948). Judah Nadich succeeded him (1948–1958), followed by Manuel Saltzman (1958–1986). Sholom Stern (1986–1992) and Alvin Lieberman (1992–1995) served the congregation before it elected William Hamilton in 1995 as its religious leader.

In 1990, the congregation instituted egalitarian services once a month, granting Torah honors to women. In 1995, membership stood at 435 family units.

Reference

Phillips, Bruce A. *Brookline: The Evolution of an American Jewish Suburb* (New York: 1990).

TEMPLE OHABEI SHALOM, REFORM. *Brookline, Massachusetts.* A group of men gathered together in 1843 in order to give permanence to the temporary religious gatherings previously held in the community. These German Jewish newcomers to the Boston area called their new synagogue Ohabei Shalom (Lovers of Peace). The following year, the group successfully petitioned the Commonwealth of Massachusetts to allow them to establish a Jewish cemetery in East Boston at the corner of Byron and Homer Streets. This dozen or so families founded a school in 1858 to teach German, English, and secular courses, as well as Hebrew and basic Judaism. It operated until 1863, when public schools took over responsibility for basic education.

In its early years, the congregation met for worship in its rabbi's home. In 1845, following formal incorporation as the first legally recognized Jewish congregation in Massachusetts, worship moved to a private home on Albany Street. In 1847, membership reached seventy families. To accommodate institutional growth, Alexander Saroni donated land on which members built the Warren Street (later Warrenton Street) Synagogue (dedicated 1952), the first synagogue building in Massachusetts. Eleven years later, Ohabei Shalom moved across the street to a building purchased from the Church of the First Universalist Society. The synagogue quickly became the focal point for Jewish communal activity. In 1847, members founded the Hebrew Literary Society of Boston and the Ladies' Hebrew Benevolent Society.

While Ohabei Shalom developed into a general center for Jewish life, members argued about the form of worship. The board changed the German form of ritual (from Bavaria) to the Polish (from Posen and northeastern Germany), as newcomers joined the congregation. The change was insufficient. Compromise seemed impossible. When the synagogue engaged a new cantor, the two groups clashed. Eventually, the German faction seceded to form Temple (Adath) Israel. Yet, the secession did not satisfy some of the Polish faction, which went on to form Congregation Mishkan Israel (now Mishkan Tefila) in 1858.

Debates continued over ritual. In 1871, the congregation voted to ''limit reformation to the curtailment of lengthy prayers, establishment of a choir, and strict observance of order.'' Yet, the participation of the congregation's young people in the Civil War—and the American way of life—provided a foundation for a more intense struggle for Reform Judaism in the congregation. In the early 1870s, members introduced a mixed choir. In 1873, they added a boys' choir.

By 1875, the drive for Reform erupted into a full-scale confrontation. Led by president Israel Cohen, younger members argued for family pews. Older members appealed to the court of the Commonwealth of Massachusetts, which decided that ''the respondents might proceed with the alterations, upon giving bond that they would restore the seating arrangement to the former position when appellants produce satisfactory authorities that the acts of their opponents were contrary to Jewish laws.'' Following the court decision, thirty of 138 members and all fifty seatholders withdrew from the congregation. Ohabei Shalom joined the Union of American Hebrew Congregations, the national organization of Reform synagogues, in 1881.

In response to the large number of new immigrants from Eastern Europe to Boston in the years of the late nineteenth and early twentieth centuries, Ohabei Shalom abandoned the *Union Prayer Book,* the uniform prayer book of the Reform movement, in use since 1899, in favor of the more traditional *Abodath Israel* prayer book, prepared by Marcus Jastrow and Benjamin Szold. In 1887, temple members purchased a building on Union Park Street from the Unitarian Society and dedicated it as their new synagogue.

Ohabei Shalom moved into its current structure on Beacon Street between Kent and Marshall Streets in Brookline in 1928, eight years after members elected Rabbi Samuel J. Abrams to the pulpit. He founded the Temple Brotherhood, which claimed to be the largest in the country. Beginning in 1931, members of the Harvard Congregational Church, devastated by fire, worshiped at the Temple until their own place of worship could be reconstructed.

Rabbi Dudley Weinberg succeeded Rabbi Abrams in 1946. Like Abrams, Weinberg developed a series of constructive religious and educational endeavors. He revitalized observance of the three pilgrimage festivals and introduced consecration of children newly enrolled in religious school. He also reinstituted the celebration of Purim and introduced daily services in 1947. Weinberg also expanded the Hebrew School into a three-year daily program of study, required of all pre–Bar Mitzvah students. In 1955, Ohabei Shalom abandoned the Jastrow prayer book for the newly revised edition of the *Union Prayer Book.* In addition, it instituted Bat Mitzvah, at about the same time. In 1965, the congregation opened a childhood center, which it subsequently closed for lack of enrollment. In 1994, a plan to sell off part of the building prompted a revitalization drive in the congregation. Ohabei Shalom merged its religious school with local Temple Sinai, then later brought it back to its own site. These rabbis succeeded Rabbi Weinberg: Albert S. Goldstein (1955–1977), Irwin M. Blank (1974–1977), Dov Taylor (1979–1984), Eric Hoffman (1985–1987), and Emily Lipof (1988–   ). In 1995, membership stood at 650.

References

Broches, Z. "A Chapter in the History of the Jews of Boston." *YIVO Annual of Jewish Social Science* 9 (1954): 205–11.

Ehrenfried, Albert. *A Chronicle of Boston Jewry from the Colonial Settlement to 1900* (Boston: 1963).

Fein, Isaac M. *Boston—Where It All Began: An Historical Perspective of the Boston Jewish Community* (Boston: 1976).

Nizel, Jeannette S. and Abraham E. *Congregation Ohabei Shalom, Pioneers of the Boston Jewish Community* (Brookline, MA: 1982).

Phillips, Bruce A. *Brookline: The Evolution of an American Jewish Suburb* (New York: 1990).

Sarna, Jonathan, and Ellen Smith. *The Jews of Boston* (Boston: 1995).

Synagogue Histories File, American Jewish Archives.

Temple Ohabei Shalom, 110th Anniversary Celebration (Brookline, MA: 1953).

CONGREGATION BETH EL OF THE SUDBURY RIVER VALLEY, RE-FORM. *Sudbury, Massachusetts.* Few Jews lived in the Boston suburbs of Sudbury or Wayland prior to the 1950s. With nearly one hundred Jewish families in these suburbs by the early 1960s, it seemed time to consider building Jewish community institutions. Local residents tired of traveling to Framingham, Natick, or Lexington, where synagoguges already existed. Sixteen families organized Beth El in 1962. In its early years, the congregation used the Sudbury Methodist Church for worship. Rabbi Albert Yanow served the congregation from 1962 to 1963, followed by Rabbi David Neiman (1964–1970). A women's group existed in the congregation between 1967 and 1982. With its emphasis on total family education and participation, the congregation considered such a group anachronistic.

With 120 member families, the congregation dedicated its new facility on Hudson Road in 1970, the same year Rabbi Martin Kessler led Beth El briefly. In that facility, there are no naming plaques anywhere in the building. Rabbi Lawrence Kushner joined the congregation as its rabbi in 1971. At the same time, Beth El's members voted to join the Union of American Hebrew Congregations. As the vote was not unanimous, the board required these conditions: the second day of Rosh Hashanah must be observed, skullcaps and prayer shawls were to be optional, Sabbath morning services were to be held in addition to those on Friday evening, and a kosher kitchen was to be maintained.

Kushner's experimentation in liturgy and his interest in spiritual renewal made its mark on the congregation. In 1975, the congregation published its own prayer book, *Vetaher Libenu (Purify Our Hearts)*. (Members of the liturgy committee revised it in 1980 to exclude gender-specific prayer language.) Beth El maintains a seder-style Shabbat service, held around a table in the middle of its informal sanctuary. With a rising membership—and discussion about limiting it—the congregation expanded its facilities in 1976. In 1978, members published *Beyn Hashmashot (Between the Suns)*, a small prayer book for summer services, the same year Beth El founded its own Hevra Kadisha and Tsedakah Collective. A small group of members of the temple who lived in Wayland left Beth El in 1978 to form their own neighborhood congregation, Temple Shir Tikva.

As part of its educational innovation, the congregation does not celebrate Confirmation. In its stead, for students at the end of high school, Beth El initiated a *siyyum Torah* in 1979. At the same time, the congregation introduced an additional liturgical volume to the congregation, *Limnot Yamaynu (To Number Our Days)*, a prayer book for the house of mourning, and a *Primer of Beth El* that seeks "to define and distill the essence of the Beth El community."

Since 1982, when Beth El founded its interfaith group, members meet regularly with neighbors from the Sudbury United Methodist Church. In 1987, the congregation published *Kanfay Shakhar (Wings of Dawn)*, a weekday prayer book.

In 1992, the congregation began the transformation of its traditional religious school program into one that focuses solely on family education. Membership in the entire congregation in 1993 is at nearly two hundred family units.

Reference

Gossels, Nancy, ed. *Kolenu/Our Voices: The First Twenty-Five Years, 1962–1987* (Sudbury, MA: 1987).

TEMPLE EMANUEL, REFORM. *Worcester, Massachusetts.* There are no complete records of those who attended the formative meeting for Temple Emanuel, but it is estimated that from fifteen to twenty people gathered at the home of Israel Lewis in 1920 in order to found the "Worcester Modern Congregation.'' The group of people who originally gathered to create a religious school for their children met for worship in a hall on Main Street. David B. Isenberg, president of the congregation for fourteen terms, guided the early development of the synagogue. Under the new name West Side Community House, the group rented a home on Suburban Road in 1922 for its twenty-nine Hebrew School and seventy-five Sunday School students.

Because of financial problems, members closed the Hebrew School in 1923. Yet, the synagogue itself seemed to prosper. The board purchased a piano and introduced ''modern conservative ritual'' for services, attracting a growing numbers of attendees at weekly worship services. That same year, board members purchased the Bancroft School on Elm Street and adopted the name Temple Emanuel. With seventy-five members on record, the congregation elected Rabbi Morris M. Mazure as its first full-time spiritual leader. During his three-year tenure, membership grew to 122, and he succeeded in fusing together a variety of factions within the synagogue. He organized a sisterhood and reestablished the Sunday School. He announced High Holiday worship ''in the modern conservative form with traditional music chanted.''

Rabbi Julius Gordon succeeded Mazure in 1926. Gordon combined the Hebrew and Sunday Schools into a Religious School with an enrollment of 110 children. He quickly introduced the *Union Prayer Book,* the uniform prayer book of the Reform movement, to the congregation. This evoked a storm of protest and a discernible cleavage among synagogue members. By the following year, Gordon established a temporary resolution to the matter. He used the *Union Prayer Book* with organ music on Friday evening. Saturday morning services remained the same.

When Rabbi Gordon left Temple Emanuel in 1929, members brought Rabbi Levi A. Olan to lead the congregation. Olan immediately advocated the use of the *Union Prayer Book.* Members defeated a board resolution that supported the rabbi's recommendation and displaced the prayer book's use even for High Holidays. Yet, they supported the use of the organ in worship. By 1937, Olan's position supporting Reform Judaism won over the membership.

The era of financial disaster also proved a difficult time for Olan to lead the synagogue. Yet, he successfully introduced a Young People's League and expanded the Religious School to include weekday and Saturday morning instruction. Eventually, Temple Emanuel overcame its financial problems and purchased a tract of land on May and Chandler Streets.

By 1946, following the delays brought on by the Depression and World War II, Temple Emanuel was ready to build with membership at nearly five hundred and Religious School rolls at over 250. Two years later, Rabbi Olan left the congregation, and Rabbi Joseph Klein succeeded him. Members dedicated the new synagogue in 1949 (enlarged in 1960). The congregation instituted daily worship services in 1953. In 1972, the first girl celebrated her Bat Mitzvah at Emanuel.

Rabbi Klein retired in 1977, and the congregation elected Rabbi Stanley Davids to the pulpit. During his tenure, the congregation sold some land that it owned in order to build a housing project for the elderly. An active Zionist, Davids directed much of the congregation's attention to the support of the Jewish state. Rabbi Davids left in 1986, when Rabbi Norman Mendel succeeded him. Rabbi James Simon joined the congregation in 1991. In 1994, membership exceeded 825 family units.

References

Blumenthal, Lewis. *The First 25 Years of Temple Emanuel* (Worcester, MA: 1946). Synagogue Histories File, American Jewish Archives.

MICHIGAN

TEMPLE BETH EL, REFORM. *Detroit (later Bloomfield Hills), Michigan.* Twelve families gathered in 1850 at the home of Sarah Cozens to form the Beth El Society, which was legally incorporated the following year. These founders organized Beth El as an Orthodox synagogue, Michigan's first congregation. Members elected Samuel Marcus to serve the congregation as its first religious leader. The newly constituted congregation established a Hebrew-German-English Day School (closed in 1869). In 1852, Beth El members rented a room on Jefferson Avenue to be used for worship. Marcus died in the cholera epidemic of 1854; Dr. Liebman Adler succeeded him. Three years later, with twenty-five members, Beth El rented space on Michigan Grand Avenue (now Cadillac Square). It would be 1861, the same year the Beth El membership elected Rabbi Abraham Laser to the pulpit, before the congregation actually built its first synagogue on Rivard Street. Beth El remained there until 1867.

Influenced by the reform that swept across America, the congregation abandoned its traditional ways after the first few years of its birth and introduced mixed choirs, men and women sitting together in family pews, prayers in the vernacular, revised prayer books, abolition of the prayer shawl and covered heads for worship, and Confirmation for boys and girls. Seventeen members left Beth El when it introduced the mixed choir and formed Shaarey Zedek Society (now Congregation Shaarey Zedek) in 1861. Committed to Reform Judaism, delegates from Beth El served as charter representatives when the Union of American Hebrew Congregations was established in 1873.

Beth El members purchased the Tabernacle Baptist Church in 1867 on Washington Boulevard and transformed it into a synagogue that served the congregation until 1903. Here they introduced late Friday evening services the year of the dedication of this new building. By 1870, during the tenure of Rabbi Kaufmann Kohler (noted theologian and later president of Hebrew Union College), the congregation abolished the second day of festivals and the wearing of the prayer shawl by the rabbi. In 1883, Yizkor memorial prayers were also discontinued, except during Yom Kippur.

Nine European-trained rabbis served Beth El before the congregation elected Dr. Louis Grossman to the pulpit in 1884. These religious leaders included Dr. Isidor Kalisch (1864–1866), Rabbi Elias Eppstein (1866–1869), Dr. Kaufmann Kohler (1869–1871), Rabbi Emanuel Gerechter (1871–1873), Dr. Leopold Wintner (1873–1875), and Dr. Heinrich (Henry) Zirndorf (1876–1884).

Grossman ushered in a new era at Beth El with the introduction of *Minhag America* for the High Holidays to replace its prayer book. Grossman introduced Sunday morning lectures to the congregation and organized a variety of internal organizations, including the Emerson Circle (1885) for the promotion of culture and the Woman's Club (1891), which eventually became the Detroit Section of the National Council of Jewish Women. In 1893, the congregation opened a Mission Sunday School, a free afternoon school intended for poor children and for children of members of other congregations that did not have a religious education program for their children. The *Union Prayer Book* was adopted in 1895. The following year, the board passed a resolution prohibiting the wearing of head coverings by men in the synagogue, a practice that had previously remained optional. Rabbi Leo M. Franklin accepted the pulpit of Beth El in 1899. In 1901, Franklin organized the Women's Auxiliary Association, which later became the Sisterhood of Temple Beth El. When Franklin became the editor of *The Jewish American* in 1901, Detroit's first Anglo-Jewish weekly, it became the official organ of Temple Beth El. When Franklin came to the pulpit that year, membership was at 136. As Detroit grew, so did Temple Beth El.

The Beth El community dedicated the Temple on Woodward and Eliot, designed by Albert Kahn, a member of the congregation, in 1903. This facility served the congregation until 1922. In 1904, the Beth El introduced Sunday morning services in the new building and introduced an unassigned seating system the same year. Members added a gym to the new structure in 1905. In 1919, the men of Beth El founded their own Men's Club.

The congregation moved to Woodward and Gladstone in 1922, and in 1925, the synagogue founded the Beth El College of Jewish Studies, one of the first evening schools for adults. When Franklin retired in 1941, the membership of Beth El elected Dr. B. Benedict Glazer to succeed him. As a result, a group of members left Beth El and formed Temple Israel with Rabbi Leon Fram, who had been serving Beth El as assistant rabbi. Glazer died suddenly in 1952; the following year, the congregation elected Dr. Richard C. Hertz to serve the temple as its rabbi. By the time Glazer died in 1952, the congregation listed its membership at 1524 members.

Beth El reintroduced the Bar Mitzvah, which had been discontinued in favor of confirmation, in 1953, with Bat Mitzvah on an optional basis. Once again, the congregation outgrew its facilities and moved in 1973 to Telegraph and Fourteen Mile Road in Bloomfield Hills. Members elected Rabbi Daniel Polish to the pulpit in 1988, succeeding Rabbi Dannel Schwartz. In 1994, membership neared fifteen hundred family units.

References

Edgar, Irving I. "The Early Sites and Beginnings of Congregation Beth El of Detroit, Michigan." *Michigan Jewish History* 10, no. 1 (June 1970): 17–23; 10, no. 3 (November 1970): 5–11; 13, no. 1 (January 1973): 13–20; 20, no. 1 (January 1980): 20–25; 26, no. 1 (January 1986): 13–21.

Franklin, Leo M. *An Outline History of Congregation Beth El, Detroit, Michigan, from Its Founding 1850 to the time of its Ninetieth Anniversary 1940* (Detroit: 1940).

A History of Congregation Beth El, Detroit, Michigan, from its Organization to its Semi-Centennial, 1850–1900, 2 vols. (Detroit: 1900, 1910).

Katz, Irving. *The Beth El Story* (Detroit: 1955).

———. *A History of Temple Beth El, Detroit, 1940–1945* (Detroit: 1945).

———. *110 Years of Temple Beth El, Detroit, 1850–1960: Highlights of Its History* (Detroit: 1960).

Rockaway, Robert. *The Jews of Detroit, from the Beginning, 1762–1914.* (Detroit: 1986).

Warsen, Allen A. "The Detroit Jewish Community from the Founding of Congregation Beth El to the Founding of the Jewish Welfare Federation of Detroit." *Michigan Jewish History* 20, no. 2 (June 1980): 11–23.

TEMPLE ISRAEL, REFORM. *Detroit (later West Bloomfield), Michigan.* In 1941, a group of men and women—members of Temple Beth El—met at a downtown hotel in order to discuss the organization of a new Reform congregation in Detroit. They took with them their assistant rabbi, Rabbi Leon Fram. Beth El had passed over Fram in its election of a new senior rabbi. In the first three months of existence of this new congregation, an unprecedented six hundred members affiliated. The new congregation immediately opened a religious school for the children of these members.

While Temple Israel considered itself a Reform congregation, it took a bold step by engaging a cantor and establishing a music policy that employed traditional Jewish melodies. In addition, it held Sabbath morning services throughout the year, something many Reform congregations reserved for Bar and Bat Mitzvah ceremonies. Temple Israel also introduced a variety of other rituals that the Reform movement had previously discarded. The congregation decided that the individual member should have the option of wearing a head covering or not. Temple Israel instituted daily services in the synagogue. In 1950, Temple Israel's nine hundred members dedicated its home in Palmer Park, bounded by Manderson and Merton Roads and Alwyne Lane, with additional building over the succeeding ten years. Temple Israel determined that membership dues should be determined strictly by one's ability to pay.

Rabbi M. Robert Syme succeeded Rabbi Fram in 1987, having served the congregation since 1953. In 1980, Temple Israel moved to Walnut Lake Road in West Bloomfield. It expanded once in 1989 and again in 1994. The latter expansion included the building of a *mikvah* (ritual bath). In 1994, membership of Temple Israel stood at twenty-seven hundred family households. Because of its size, the congregation offers a diversity of activities and a sizable number of affiliates.

References

Rockaway, Robert. *The Jews of Detroit, from the Beginning, 1762–1914* (Detroit: 1986).
Synagogue Histories File, American Jewish Archives.
Temple Israel, 1941–1991: 50th Anniversary Commemorative Book (Detroit: 1991).
Warsen, Allen A. "The Detroit Jewish Community from the Founding of Congregation
     Beth El to the Founding of the Jewish Welfare Federation of Detroit." *Michigan
     Jewish History* 20, no. 2 (June 1980): 11–23.

SHAAREY ZEDEK, CONSERVATIVE. *Detroit (later West Bloomfield),
Michigan.* In 1861, a group of seventeen men formed Shaarey Zedek Society.
As former members of Beth El, they left the congregation when Beth El introduced a mixed choir upon the move into its Rivard Street synagogue. However,
these men were among a group of traditionalists who previously had challenged
nearly each reform made at Beth El. Within a few months, membership increased to thirty-six. At this time, Shaarey Zedek invited Rabbi M. Sapper to
lead the fledgling congregation.

In 1864, Rabbi Laser Kontrovitch led Shaarey Zedek's sixty-three members.
The women of the congregation organized an auxiliary, and the congregation
organized a Bikkur Cholim (charged with visiting the sick) and a Chevra Kadisha Society (charged with overseeing the preparation and burial of the dead).
That same year, Shaarey Zedek members felt ready to purchase a building of
their own—a frame building on Congress and St. Antoine, formerly belonging
to St. Matthew's Episcopal Church. In the new building, the congregation attempted to run a secular school program. This short-lived school gave way to
public education in 1868. Thereafter, members concentrated their efforts on
providing a religious education for their children.

With sixty-eight members, Shaarey Zedek outgrew its facility but could not
afford to occupy its new building even after constructing it in 1877. Financial
difficulties spilled over to disagreements on ritual, which splintered the congregation into three groups. One group met in a private home on Gratiot (becoming
Beth Jacob in 1878). A second group met at Funke's Hall on Macomb Street
(to form Congregation B'nai Israel in 1881). The third group, the Shaarey Zedek
group of thirty-five remaining members, met at Kittelberger's Hall on Randolph
Street. As a result, the new Shaarey Zedek synagogue remained unoccupied. An
explosion—probably vandalism—rocked the building in 1880, severely dam-
aging it. Financial difficulties eventually forced the sale of the building at auction. As a result, Shaarey Zedek rented the building from its new owners until
1884, when the synagogue purchased the building once again, finally dedicating
it in 1886.

Rabbi Aaron M. Ashinsky became Shaarey Zedek's religious leader in 1889.
While membership reached seventy families, the synagogue still could not afford
a rabbi's salary and therefore shared him with Beth Jacob and B'nai Israel,
where he led services alternately in each congregation. In 1898, Rabbi Judah I.
Levin came to Detroit and replaced Ashinsky, also serving three congregations

simultaneously. Upon his arrival, Shaarey Zedek established a community Talmud Torah.

As the Jewish community moved northward, it became necessary to find a new synagogue site. However, members sold the site at Congress and St. Antoine before building a new structure on Winder Street (dedicated 1903). Detroit grew rapidly, and soon the congregation proved to be too large for its new home. The congregation engaged its first "English-speaking rabbi," Rabbi Rudolph Farber, the following year. He quickly reorganized the Sunday School, introduced a boys' choir under the guidance of Cantor Moses Rogoff, and encouraged congregational singing. When Rabbi Farber resigned in 1907, Shaarey Zedek decided to engage a graduate of the Jewish Theological Seminary, Rabbi Abraham Hershman, an ardent Zionist. Like his predecessor, Hershman reorganized the Sunday School. He also organized a Young People's Society and the Kadimah Society for the study of Jewish history.

Detroit's population continued to grow rapidly, bringing more members into the ranks of Shaarey Zedek, necessitating a move once again to accommodate its two hundred families. Thus, Shaarey Zedek moved to the corner of Willis and Brush (dedicated 1915). When the congregation dedicated its cornerstone in 1913, it marked the occasion by becoming one of the founding members of the United Synagogue of America (now the United Synagogue of Conservative Judaism), the national organization of Conservative synagogues.

By 1917, membership doubled, reaching four hundred family units, most of whom no longer lived in the vicinity of the synagogue, which forced congregational leadership to think about moving once again. Following World War I and a growth in the peacetime economy, Shaarey Zedek prepared to relocate to property on Chicago Boulevard. Neighboring residents protested the erection of a synagogue, to the point of bringing a lawsuit to be heard by the U.S. Supreme Court. As a result of numerous legal battles and the Great Depression, Shaarey Zedek members waited until 1932 to dedicate their new synagogue home. Isaac Shetzer, elected president of the synagogue in 1932, is credited with guiding Shaarey Zedek during the difficult financial times that accompanied the move into the new structure.

In 1946, after serving Shaarey Zedek as assistant rabbi, Morris Adler succeeded Rabbi Hershman. The congregation established the Beth Hayeled nursery school two years later. In 1953, the congregation dedicated a building at West Seven Mile Road and Lesure for use as a branch for school and youth activities. Nine years later, the congregation, with a membership of over fifteen hundred families, dedicated a new synagogue, designed by Percival Goodman, in Southfield Township, on Northwestern Highway and Eleven Mile Road. Following the move, 450 families joined the congregation between 1962 and 1966. The triumph was short lived; a troubled young congregant entered the sanctuary and shot Rabbi Morris Adler (in 1966) in front of the open ark before taking his own life.

After a year of mourning, members invited Rabbi Irwin Groner to lead them.

Under Rabbi Groner's leadership, the congregation instituted late Friday evening services, a practice the congregation experimented with several times during its history. In addition, Rabbi Groner introduced a mixed choir for worship, as well as a modified Torah reading. He slowly attempted to transform the worshiper into a full participant in worship. Of note is the progressive introduction of women into worship. Sensitive to the needs of girls to gain equality, Shaarey Zedek introduced the notion of Bat Torah in 1977. Three years later, the first Bat Mitzvah participated in Friday evening services. In 1992, members dedicated the Shaarey Zedek B'nai Israel Center and the Eugene and Marcia Applebaum Beth Hayeled Jewish Parenting Center on Walnut Lake Road in West Bloomfield.

References

Cantor, Judith Levin. *Congregation Shaarey Zedek 1861–1981/The Supplement 1981– 1982* (Detroit: 1982).
Grad, Eli, and Bette Roth. *Congregation Shaarey Zedek 1861–1981* (Detroit: 1982).
Hershman, Ruth and Eiga. "Rabbi Abraham M. Hershman." *Michigan Jewish History* 21, no. 2 (June 1981): 16–31.
Rockaway, Robert. *The Jews of Detroit, from the Beginning, 1762–1914* (Detroit: 1986).
Synagogue Histories File, American Jewish Archives.
Warsen, Allen A. "The Detroit Jewish Community from the Founding of Congregation Beth El to the Founding of the Jewish Welfare Federation of Detroit." *Michigan Jewish History* 20, no. 2 (June 1980): 11–23.

BIRMINGHAM TEMPLE, HUMANIST. *Farmington Hills, Michigan.* Founders established the Birmingham Temple as an independent Reform institution in 1963. These eight founding families sought to establish a suburban alternative to Detroit's Temple Beth El. Members held initial services—on Sundays, because of founding Rabbi Sherwin Wine's commitment to a congregation in Canada—at Eagle School in Farmington. Because congregants wanted to ask questions about Judaism, the congregation immediately established a series of discussions focusing on topics like, "Why Prayer?" and "Our Concept of Jewish Education." Within six months, its members discarded most Reform practices and began what eventually evolved into a Humanist approach to Judaism. By the end of the first year, the Birmingham Temple included forty members. The temple called its services "meditations" and developed a creative approach to life-cycle events. In 1967, the congregation began publishing *Humanistic Judaism* (later absorbed by the Society for Humanistic Judaism).

The congregation moved to High Meadow School in 1964 to accommodate a membership of seventy-six, with services that often drew five hundred people. Later that year, members moved to the Masonic Temple. When Rabbi Wine came to the congregation full time in 1964, he moved services from Sundays to Friday evenings. When the congregation engendered controversy in the community, the Masons evicted the membership. As a result, the Birmingham Temple moved to the Birmingham Unitarian Church, maintaining an office on

Telegraph Road in Royal Oak. Shortly thereafter, the congregation moved to the Frost Junior High School for services (1965–1971).

The synagogue moved to its present location on Twelve Mile Road in 1971. Rabbi Sherwin Wine and members of the Birmingham Temple founded the national Society for Humanistic Judaism, as well as an international organization and educational institute dedicated to the principles of Humanistic Judaism. Among its various projects, the congregation adopted the John F. Kennedy elementary school in Detroit to provide experiences to the racially mixed enrollment of children from poor and working-class families that the school could not provide. In 1994, the Birmingham Temple exceeded 420 membership units.

References

Cousens, Mark H. *History of the Birmingham Temple* (forthcoming).
Wine, Sherwin. *Judaism without God* (Farmington Hills, MI: 1985).

YOUNG ISRAEL OF OAK-WOODS, ORTHODOX. *Oak Park, Michigan.* Several community meetings took place in 1952 in order to discuss the possibility of a forming a congregation in Oak Park. As a result, participants in these meetings formed the nucleus of two synagogues: (Conservative) Beth Shalom and (Orthodox) Young Israel. Initially calling itself Beth Am and meeting in private homes for Shabbat Services, the Young Israel group formally established a congregation that same year. After a discussion concerning the name, fearing it did not represent their intention to establish a synagogue, founders changed the name to the Oak Park Jewish Center. In order to encourage people to join from a larger geographical area, including Huntington Woods, members enlarged the name to the Oak-Woods Jewish Center, purchasing land at Scotian and Dartmouth.

Recognizing that this congregation would be among the first Orthodox congregations to serve suburban Judaism, members enlisted the support of Rabbi Samuel Belkin, president of Yeshiva University. He supported the endeavor with seed money and the rabbinic guidance of Rabbi Leon Stitskin. Congregational leaders realized that they had not purchased land at the heart of the community. As a result, the congregation sold the land and instead purchased a plot at Allen and Coolidge.

Promising to always remain an Orthodox congregation, the synagogue received a loan from national Young Israel. With these funds, the congregation built the Young Israel Center of Oak-Woods in 1954. Rabbi Yaakov I. Himmick became its rabbi two years later. He remained until 1962. Rabbi James I. Gordon succeeded him in 1963. Among his first tasks, Rabbi Gordon immediately built the Oak-Woods educational program, which eventually became the Akiva Hebrew Day School. In 1967, members expanded the overcrowded building. The Akiva school left the synagogue facilities in 1972.

As a Zionist, Gordon emphasized the state of Israel in his rabbinate. The congregation helped to nurture Young Israel synagogues in Israel: Young Israel of Petach Tikva and Young Israel of Katamon Tet (in Jerusalem). When the Young Israel of Petach Tikva became independent of Young Israel of Oak-Woods, the Oak-Woods congregation adopted Young Israel of Tekoa. Eventually, Young Israel of Katamon Tet became self-sufficient.

In the 1970s, demographic change affected the neighborhoods surrounding the synagogue. In addition, the Kollel Institute attracted newcomers to Orthodoxy who wanted a stricter interpretation of Orthodox Judaism than the liberal orthodoxy of Young Israel of Oak-Woods offered. In the sanctuary, women are in full view of men, although separated by a *mechitza* (partition). Women also have a full view of the service. In addition, decorum is important to worshipers at Oak-Woods. By the 1970s, the Orthodox community moved northward in the city. Young people did not move to the area around the synagogue, and older adults moved out of the area. As a result, the Oak-Woods membership severely declined.

When Rabbi Gordon immigrated to Israel in 1985, the congregation elected Rabbis Eliezer Cohen and Reuven Drucker. Because of other community responsibilities, both rabbis served on a part-time basis. Two years later, Rabbi Cohen became the sole religious leader of the congregation. In 1994, membership at Young Israel of Oak-Woods stood at 103.

Reference

Synagogue Histories File, American Jewish Archives.

MINNESOTA

ADATH JESHURUN, CONSERVATIVE. *Minneapolis, Minnesota.* Two small groups of Rumanian and Russian Jews in 1884 formed Adath Jeshurun. Aaron H. Sinai served the congregation as its first religious leader (1884–1893). Disaster struck this congregation twice in its early years. Following Kol Nidre services in 1888 in rented Turner Hall, a fire destroyed all of Adath Jeshurun's property. The congregation's sixty members held services on Second Street South. Dr. Samuel Marks succeeded Sinai as leader of the congregation. Later, in 1902, a great windstorm destroyed the synagogue completely. The following year, members purchased a former church on Seventh Street South. In this new building, S. Silber served as religious leader (also serving local Kenesseth Israel and Anshei Tarvig).

A windstorm destroyed the Seventh Street synagogue in 1904, forcing the congregation to relocate to another building at Twelfth Avenue South and Ninth Street (dedicated 1906). In this new building, the congregation introduced family pews; and in 1909, the congregation formally changed its name to Adath Jeshurun.

Rabbi C. David Matt came to Adath Jeshurun in 1912 as the synagogue's first American trained rabbi. He preached in English and organized a religious school, introducing a variety of educational programs to the congregation. Under his direction, Adath Jeshurun became a founding member of the United Synagogue of America, the national organization of Conservative synagogues (1913). Five years later, the synagogue's sisterhood helped to found the Women's League for Conservative Judaism. When Matt left the congregation, these rabbis succeeded him: Jesse Schwartz (1927–1929), Albert Gordon (1930–1946), Morris Gordon (1947–1952), Stanley Rabinowitz (1953–1960), Jerome Lipnick (1960–1965), Arnold Goodman (1966–1982), Barry Cytron (1983–1989), and Harold Kravitz (1989–   ).

As congregants moved to the west side, the congregation held classes between 1923 and 1927 in a rented hall on Hennepin Avenue. In 1927, Adath Jeshurun built a new home on Dupont Avenue South. In the new location, the congregation opened a nursery school (1937) and held its first Bat Mitzvah (1943). Membership reached 410 family units by 1946.

In 1953, the congregation dedicated its educational center. Three years later, Adath Jeshurun instituted a policy of open seating. During Arnold Goodman's tenure as rabbi, the congregation began to include women in the minyan. While the congregation decided not to move to the suburbs, it did build a Kallah Center in Minnetonka (dedicated 1974). Besides weekend retreats, the facility houses a nursery school, day care programs, and a summer camp. The congregation intends to dedicate its new sanctuary there in 1995. In 1994, synagogue membership reached eleven hundred family units.

References

Orkin, Etta Fay. *Adath Jeshurun: The First One Hundred Ten Years, 1884–1994* (Minneapolis: 1994).

Plaut, W. Gunther. *The Jews in Minnesota: The First Seventy-Five Years* (New York: 1959).

Synagogue Histories File, American Jewish Archives.

B'NAI EMET, CONSERVATIVE. *Minneapolis, Minnesota.* In 1972, founders established B'nai Emet as a merger of three struggling synagogues: Mikro Kodesh (Orthodox), Tifereth B'nai Jacob (Conservative), and B'nai Abraham (Conservative). Mikro Kodesh (founded 1893), formerly at Oliver Avenue North (dedicated 1926), and Tifereth B'nai Jacob, formerly at Xerxes Avenue, merged into one synagogue in 1969 before joining B'nai Abraham three years later. The name Emet is actually an acronym formed by the Hebrew letters *Alef* from B'nai Abraham, *Mem* from Mikro Kodesh, and *Tov* from Tifereth B'nai Jacob. The merged synagogue affiliated with the United Synagogue of Conservative Judaism, the national organization of Conservative congregations, following the policies established by B'nai Abraham. Upon its founding B'nai Emet established an egalitarian ritual in all aspects of synagogue life.

Rumanian Jews founded B'nai Abraham in the 1880s as an Orthodox congregation (incorporated 1891). It affiliated with the Conservative movement when it moved to St. Louis Park in 1956. In that location, under the leadership

of Rabbi Marc Liebaher and then Rabbi Moses B. Sachs, the congregation grew
from forty family units to 450, building a new structure in 1959.
B'nai Emet's home is built on the site of B'nai Abraham in St. Louis Park.
Rabbi Sylvan Kamens served as B'nai Emet's first religious leader (1972–1983).
Following his resignation, two hundred families left the congregation. Rabbi
Herb Yoskowitz succeeded Kamens (1984–1988). Rabbi Howard Siegel suc-
ceeded Yoskowitz in 1988. With a congregation of seven hundred families,
B'nai Emet under Rabbi Siegel's direction led the way among local Conserva-
tive synagogues in outreach to intermarried couples and the Jewish gay/lesbian
community.

Reference

Plaut, W. Gunther. *The Jews in Minnesota: The First Seventy-Five Years* (New York:
    1959).

TEMPLE ISRAEL, REFORM. *Minneapolis, Minnesota.* In 1878, Edward
Bernstein canvassed the town and encouraged people to join a synagogue known
as Shaarai Tov. This young group held its first services in a rented hall at
Nicollet and Washington. Two years later, members purchased land on Fifth
Street between Marquette and Second Avenues, where they built their first synagogue structure. The congregation invited Henry Friedman to lead them in
worship. Amid a struggle over reform, Rabbi Henry Iliowizi quickly succeeded
him. During Iliowizi's tenure, the congregation permitted worshipers to worship
with their heads uncovered but bylaws required the rabbi to cover his head while
occupying the pulpit. He perceived this as illogical, a posture that drove him
into controversy. As a result, he left Minneapolis in 1888.

Temple membership grew rapidly. Thus, in 1890, the congregation moved its
synagogue building to a new site on Tenth Street and Fifth Avenue South. Rabbi
Samuel Marks succeeded Iliowizi and in turn was succeeded by Rabbi Samuel
Friedman in 1893. Members elected Rabbi Samuel N. Deinard to the pulpit in
1901. Deinard's Zionism helped to keep this decidedly Reform congregation
close to its traditional roots.

Fire completely destroyed the synagogue building in 1902. One year later,
temple members built a new building on the same site. When member needs
increased, the congregation purchased a home in 1910 on Emerson Avenue and
Twenty-fourth Street and converted it into a religious school building. Rabbi
Deinard died in 1921. The following year, Temple Israel invited Rabbi Albert
G. Minda to occupy its pulpit.

Following the war, which suspended any building plans, congregants dedicated a new building in 1928. In 1956, members added a religious-school wing
to the new structure. Rabbi Minda retired in 1963, when members elected Rabbi
Max Shapiro to Temple Israel.

Shapiro served from 1963 to 1985. He focused his rabbinate on improving
relations between Jews and non-Jews in the community. Rabbi Stephen Pinsky

(1985–1990) succeeded Shapiro. During his tenure, the congregation pledged not to leave the Minneapolis city limits and instead expanded its facility. Rabbi Joseph Edelheit came to Temple Israel in 1990. While he has continued the congregation's emphasis on interfaith relations, he also has led the community's effort in reaching out to those with HIV/AIDS. As a matter of policy, Temple Israel's liturgy is gender-neutral; the congregation has made women's spirituality a major priority in its program. In 1994, Temple Israel included nearly twenty-one hundred "households," indicating its desire to include gays and lesbians in its membership.

References

Plaut, W. Gunther. *The Jews in Minnesota: The First Seventy-Five Years* (New York: 1959).
Synagogue Histories File, American Jewish Archives.

KENESSETH ISRAEL, ORTHODOX. *Minneapolis, Minnesota.* Following several attempts by Lithuanian immigrants to establish an ongoing minyan, a group succeeded in 1888, taking the name O'Hel Jacob. This group rented its quarters for worship over a store on Second Street North. When members found their facilities inadequate, they purchased a lot on Fourth Street North in 1891. In doing so, they dissolved O'Hel Jacob and, with forty-six members, incorporated as Chenessis Israel. It took three additional years for this financially unstable congregation to complete construction of its first synagogue.

Rabbi Isaac Jaffa became the new congregation's spiritual leader the following year, amending the spelling of the congregation's name to Kenesseth Israel. During his tenure, Kenesseth Israel founded its Hebrew Free School and joined the Union of Orthodox Congregations of America (1901). Rabbi Jaffa left for Palestine in 1901; Rabbi S. M. Silber succeeded him as chief rabbi for the entire Orthodox community in Minneapolis the following year. Under his guidance, the synagogue enjoyed its greatest period of growth. The Hebrew Free School moved to its own location on Bassett Place in 1910, to be nearer the children it served. When this facility proved inadequate, supporters built a new school at Fremont and Eighth Avenues North (dedicated 1914).

Kenesseth Israel quickly outgrew its building and moved to Lyndale Avenue in 1913. In the new edifice, members temporarily introduced late Friday evening services and engaged an English-speaking rabbi, S. Davidovitz. Though the experiment did not last long, it did give birth to Beth El Synagogue.

Rabbi Silber died in 1925. Rabbi Moses Romm succeeded him (1925–1931), also as chief rabbi of the city. When he resigned in 1931, Rabbi Hirsh Heiman succeeded him. Heiman introduced a variety of traditional educational models to the congregation. Rabbi Milton Kopstein succeeded Heiman in 1941. In the 1940s, members of the congregation moved out of the area surrounding the synagogue, and membership declined. Kenesseth Israel finally moved to Plymouth Avenue North, in the North Side (1948). In the new location, the congregation installed family pews in an effort to attract new members.

In 1948 Rabbi Bernard Walfish succeeded Kopstein, serving until 1952. From 1955 to 1956, Rabbi Louis Ginsberg served the congregation. Faced with the possibility of closing its doors, the congregation reinstituted the separation of sexes during worship through the installation of a *mechitza* (partition designed for this purpose). In addition, the congregation moved its reading table to the center aisle of the sanctuary. At the same time, Kenesseth Israel elected incumbent Rabbi Jerome Herzog to its pulpit (1961). Herzog successfully orchestrated a move to the suburbs of St. Louis Park (1969). There the congregation quickly grew from 120 to 220 members. Herzog worked hard to build bridges between the Orthodox and non-Orthodox congregations (and their rabbis) in the community. In 1985, a group of congregants further to the religious right than the congregation split and formed their own synagogue. In 1994, Kenesseth Israel had 135 member families, representing centrist Orthodox Judaism.

References

Kenesseth Israel, A History of 100 Years (Minneapolis: 1988).
Plaut, W. Gunther. *The Jews in Minnesota: The First Seventy-Five Years* (New York: 1959).
Synagogue Histories File, American Jewish Archives.

TEMPLE OF AARON, CONSERVATIVE. *St. Paul, Minnesota.* A group of men who had moved uptown assembled at Bowlby Hall in 1910 under the leadership of Joseph Levy. The congregation incorporated in 1912 under the name Congregation Aaron, named in memory of Aaron Mark, whose widow contributed generously to the new congregation. When Congregation Aaron purchased land at Ashland and Grotto, there was no national organization of Conservative synagogues to guide its members. Once Rabbi Arthur Ginzler became its rabbi, he introduced innovations such as Friday evening services. Ginzler also organized a Sunday School. About this time (in 1914), people began to refer to Congregation Aaron as a temple. When Rabbi Alfred H. Kahn, a graduate of the Jewish Theological Seminary of America was elected to the pulpit in 1915, the Conservative direction of the synagogue was apparent. Members dedicated a new synagogue in 1916.

Rabbi Philip Kleinman succeeded Rabbi Kahn in 1917. Soon after his arrival, Rabbi Kleinman established a Hebrew School. The following year, he introduced his students to a method of instruction called *Ivrit b'ivrit*, in which Hebrew classes take place exclusively in Hebrew. He came to a congregation whose members attended Aaron on the Sabbath and holidays but went to the local Orthodox synagogue (of which many had previously been members) for daily worship. This characterized the perspective on Judaism held by many Temple of Aaron members. By 1919 Rabbi Kleinman successfully introduced a daily mourner's minyan for its members, in the same year he introduced Confirmation to the congregation, but the congregation still struggled for a consistent religious ideology. This struggle included the role of women in the congregation and their right to sit as members on the synagogue's board of directors.

Though the synagogue membership had planned to build a school building to accommodate a growing school population, Temple of Aaron instead sold its lots on Holly and Grotto—originally set aside for this purpose—to the Jewish Educational Center Association. Temple of Aaron established this association with the Capital City Hebrew School and the West Side Hebrew School to form a citywide Talmud Torah. The new school opened in 1930.

Rabbi Herbert Parzen succeeded Rabbi Kleinman in 1926. He accepted the position on the condition that he had a free hand in directing the future of the congregation toward a full acceptance of Conservative Judaism. He quickly reorganized the Sunday School and introduced women into the choir. He delivered sermons on ethics and morality rather than interpreting the weekly Torah reading. A small group of congregants who were against such changes forced Rabbi Kleinman to resign in 1927. However, the resultant turmoil forced the congregation to take stock of itself. Thus, when Rabbi Herman Cohen came to St. Paul in 1928, he was elected to serve a Conservative congregation.

Rabbi Cohen introduced a variety of changes, including Bat Mitzvah in 1929. During the three years that followed, the synagogue faced difficult financial times. In 1933, the congregation introduced the Oneg Shabbat, a time following services when congregants engaged in singing and discussion. When a balcony was added to the sanctuary in 1935, it was with the hopes of gaining more members at a lower membership fee; these new members would be assigned to the balcony. In 1938, the synagogue increased the program of the religious school to include a weekday afternoon of instruction and an extra year in high school prior to Confirmation.

Following World War II, membership grew dramatically at Temple of Aaron. While plans were made to accommodate this growing population, a fire destroyed the synagogue in 1952. Nevertheless, plans continued for a new building, which included the sharing of space with the St. Paul Talmud Torah. Rabbi Herman Cohen retired in 1953. Rabbi Bernard S. Raskas, who had been serving as assistant rabbi, succeeded him. During his tenure, the congregation grew from six hundred in 1953 to thirteen hundred in 1989. He introduced creative liturgies to the congregation throughout his tenure. Sensitive to the needs of women, he was among the first rabbis in the Conservative movement to count women in the minyan and prepare divorce documents for them by calling a *bet din* (rabbinical court).

In 1956, contractors completed the first stage of the new Temple of Aaron building on Mississippi River Boulevard. The entire building project was completed in 1972. The building, designed by Percival Goodman, received the Guggenheim Recognition Award as an example of outstanding contemporary Jewish architecture.

Rabbi Raskas retired in 1989. Rabbis Jonathan Ginsburg and his spouse Rabbi

Julie Gordon succeeded Raskas, serving as co-rabbis. Together, they expanded young family services, developed a singles program, a young couples club, and an extensive religious school program. In 1994, membership exceeded fourteen hundred family units.

References

Plaut, W. Gunther. *The Jews in Minnesota: The First Seventy-Five Years* (New York: 1959).
Synagogue Histories File, American Jewish Archives.

BETH JACOB CONGREGATION, CONSERVATIVE. *St. Paul, Minnesota.* A group of newcomers from Poland incorporated Hebrah Bene Ya'akob, Congregation Sons of Jacob, in 1875, having held worship services since 1869. The group first met on Payne Street before moving to College Avenue. An increased membership under the leadership of Rabbi Jacob Aronsohn required the building of a larger facility at the same College Avenue location (dedicated 1888). Wanting to make sure that the congregation remained strictly Orthodox, the founders drew up its constitution accordingly. Rabbi Jacob Aronsohn led the congregation for fifteen years.

While Joseph B. Hurvitz ("Der Roiter Rav") was rabbi of Sons of Jacob, beginning in 1908, he guided the entire lower-town Orthodox community. To meet the needs of the Orthodox community in the Midway section of the city, a group founded the Hebrew Seminary Congregation (known as the Beth Gedaliah Congregation) under the leadership of Rabbi Morris C. Katz. The College Avenue Shul, as members knew Sons of Jacob, merged in 1946 with the Hebrew Seminary Congregation's forty member families. Shortly after the merger, this new congregation built a facility on Portland Avenue.

In this new location, Sons of Jacob introduced a mixed choir. In the early 1970s, Sons of Jacob affiliated with the United Synagogue of America (now called the United Synagogue of Conservative Judaism), the national organization of Conservative congregations. In 1982, the congregation sold its Portland Avenue building. Rejecting a proposal to merge with Temple of Aaron, congregants worshiped at the St. Paul Jewish Community Center. At about the same time (1982), a new group emerged to form the "New Conservative Congregation," also meeting at the Jewish Community Center. In 1985, Sons of Jacob and the New Conservative Congregation merged to form Beth Jacob Congregation.

At its founding, Beth Jacob gave men and women equal rights in the ritual of the congregation. In 1986, the synagogue invited Rabbi Morris J. Allen to become its religious leader. He quickly expanded the educational and religious activities of the congregation. Allen enlarged a Saturday morning children's program, experimented with seating arrangements for worship, instituted early evening Friday services, and developed an extensive program of adult Jewish education.

In 1988, Beth Jacob Congregation dedicated its new home in Medota Heights on Hunter Lane. In this new location, the congregation sponsored an active program for all ages, with a large attendance on Shabbat. A building expansion took place in 1994. Membership in 1994 reached 315 households, with 125 children in religious school, a significant increase since 1990 (forty-nine children).

References

Plaut, W. Gunther. *The Jews in Minnesota: The First Seventy-Five Years* (New York: 1959).
Synagogue Histories File, American Jewish Archives.

MT. ZION TEMPLE, REFORM. *St. Paul, Minnesota.* Founded in 1856 by a small group of families and a few single individuals as the Mount Zion Hebrew Association of St. Paul, the group quickly split over the election of officers. The splinter group called itself Congregation Ahabath Achim. This rift left Mt. Zion with eight members. Both institutions considered merging with the other, but neither congregation took action. Eventually the rift was healed. German immigrants—primarily merchants—who lived elsewhere in the United States before coming to Minnesota made up this early congregation.

Beginning in 1862, members of Ahabath Achim started coming back to Mt. Zion until the group totally folded into the original congregation. By 1866, membership reached sixty-four people, including children. The group worshiped in a third-story room on Third Street, but in 1870, Mt. Zion moved into its own building at Tenth and Minnesota Streets. As an Orthodox congregation, the group's early concerns focused on engaging as religious leaders men who were proficient in the ritual slaughtering of animals. Eventually, the congregation expanded this leadership role to include circumcision and the teaching of its children. Mt. Zion brought several people to the position before engaging its first ordained rabbi, Dr. Leopold Wintner, in 1871. He only remained for one year, but he certainly began to steer the path of reform. Wintner introduced Confirmation, permitted the use of the organ, and used Isaac Mayer Wise's prayer book, *Minhag America.* He involved women in the work of the congregation and developed a curriculum for the religious school. The following year, the association officially changed its name to become Mt. Zion Congregation.

Dr. J. Burgheim succeeded Wintner for a year before the congregation brought Dr. Isaac N. Cohen to serve as its rabbi. A controversial figure, Cohen too stayed only a short time. This new rabbi determined to make significant reforms in the congregation, beginning with an appearance at his first worship service without a prayer shawl, for which he ran into significant opposition. He succeeded in omitting the second day of Rosh Hashanah from the calendar and added an afternoon recess during services on Yom Kippur. Cohen also introduced a choir and an organ to Mt. Zion.

As a result of these changes, the more traditional element in the congregation resigned and left room for more reforms to be made by his successor, Rabbi

Judah Wechsler. Wechsler travelled around the state, urging the cause of the Union of American Hebrew Congregations, the national organization of Reform synagogues (which the congregation joined in 1878) and—following the mass migration of refugees from Europe—the development of a Jewish settlement colony near Painted Woods, North Dakota. The failure of this colonization project so disillusioned Wechsler that he left the congregation.

By 1881, members made plans for a new building at the same site at Tenth and Minnesota Streets. Rabbi Samuel Freuder succeeded Wechsler in this new building, but as his innovations were too radical for the congregation, he left after a tenure of less than two years. Solomon Bergman, who served as president for six terms, represented the conservative element in the congregation and, according to W. Gunther Plaut, consistently served as a brake when the congregation turned to more radical reform. Freuder's successor, Rabbi Emanuel Hess, approached ceremonies and rituals more positively. He made Hebrew education obligatory for boys and girls in the temple. Yet, he successfully introduced bare-headed worship and the removal of the prayer shawl.

As a result of failing health, Hess resigned in 1899, and Isaac L. Rypins became rabbi. As a universalist and antitraditionalist, Rypins succeeded for a short time in establishing Sunday services as the main services for the week. During his tenure, Mt. Zion gave women the right to membership in their own name (1900). Following a disagreement over Rypins' desire to speak freely from the pulpit, he resigned in 1921.

In 1904, Mt. Zion members dedicated their new home at Avon and Holly Streets. Although membership reached only 119 in 1902, it neared two hundred by 1921. In these years, ritual changes were few. Members made minor adjustments in the Yom Kippur memorial services; they adopted the custom of full congregational rising during the Kaddish prayer; and they adopted a new edition of the *Union Prayer Book,* the uniform prayer book of the Reform movement. Members rejected Rabbi Rypins's desire to introduce Sunday services at the expense of Friday evening services. Yet, Rypins unsuccessfully attempted to bolster personal observances. As a result, Mt. Zion eliminated summer services entirely in 1912. Even the Sunday School suffered a decline in enrollment.

Rypins left the congregation in 1921, leaving room for the congregation to undergo changes he saw necessary for survival. Rabbi Jacob Meyerowiz followed; his successor, Rabbi Leonard J. Rothstein made significant changes in the congregation, beginning with an open-door policy for the religious school. Allied with Rothstein, congregational president Hiram D. Frankel instituted a variety of changes in the institution in order to secure its future. These included the development of a budget, a brotherhood, and an usher corps. Frankel also led the congregation to purchase additional land for future expansion. Change came too quickly, and Rothstein—after a sermon in which he told his congregants why he would not vote for Coolidge and Dawes—resigned from the pulpit.

Rabbi Harry Sterling Margolis succeeded Rothstein in 1925. The following year, Mt. Zion joined with Temple Israel of Minneapolis in establishing a school for training religious school teachers. During Margolis' tenure, the temple reinstituted Bar Mitzvah (1934) after a lapse of nearly fifty years. Membership grew to 251 in 1930 and to nearly three hundred by 1938. In 1944, president Milton Firestone instituted a program of unassigned pews for the congregation.

In 1946, Rabbi Margolis died. Rabbi Saul Appelbaum succeeded him, but stayed only two years. Membership grew to over 450 members in 1948, when Rabbi W. Gunther Plaut became the new religious leader of the congregation. Plaut's approach to Reform Judaism soon became evident to the congregation. For some, the changes were too few. For others, he made too many changes. He reshaped the focus of the religious school program and developed an active Parent-Teacher Association. He successfully encouraged confirmands to continue their Jewish education in high school. Plaut experimented with a variety of sermon techniques in the pulpit, including what he called a sermon-drama. On Sunday mornings, the new rabbi broadcast weekly messages over the radio. Membership grew to 531 by the end of his first year.

In 1951, Plaut instituted the first adult retreat-type programs in a Reform congregation. Elsewhere congregations replicated these "returns," as he called them. Plaut also initiated daily evening services led by members of the congregation. In 1954, after a long building program, members dedicated a long-awaited facility on Summit Avenue, designed by architect Eric Mendelsohn. These rabbis succeeded Plaut: Bernard Martin (1962–1966), Frederick Schwartz (1966–1974), Leigh Lerner (1972–1989), and Leonard Schoolman (1989–1993). In 1993, Mt. Zion invited Rabbis B. Elka Abrahamsom and Martin Zinkow, a rabbinic spouse team, to lead the congregation. In 1995, temple membership exceeded seven hundred.

References

Plaut, W. Gunther. *The Jews in Minnesota: The First Seventy-Five Years* (New York: 1959).
———. *Mt. Zion, 1856–1956; The First Hundred Years* (St. Paul: 1956).
Synagogue Histories File, American Jewish Archives.

MISSOURI

BETH SHALOM, CONSERVATIVE. *Kansas City, Missouri.* During the late 1870s, Orthodox Jews in Kansas City formed their own burial societies. They separated from the Hebrew Burial Association (founded 1864), which evolved into the Reform Congregation B'nai Jehudah. The cemetery quickly became secondary to the other needs of the religious community. Out of one of these societies grew Keneseth Israel Congregation in 1878. Members of this new congregation conducted services in a variety of locations, such as "above a blacksmith shop" and in a hall over "Joe and Charlie's Saloon."

By 1893, the congregation felt prepared to join with two other Orthodox

congregations, Etz Chaim and Gomlai Chesed, to invite Rabbi Benjamin Bra-
chiah Mayerovitz to serve them as "Rabbi of the Orthodox Jewish Congregations." He remained in Kansas City until 1898. With a membership of ninety
family units, Keneseth Israel built its first house of worship on Locust Street in
1902. In the new building, the synagogue attempted the organization of a Sunday
School, which lasted only a short time. Two years later, Keneseth Israel members invited Rabbi Max Lieberman to lead them. Under his leadership, the congregation grew to 110 families in 1908. By this time, issues surfaced that
eventually divided the congregation: religious instruction for girls, sermons in
English, more dignified worship, and mixed pews.

Rabbi Isidore Koplowitz succeeded Rabbi Lieberman in 1908. When he resigned in 1912, Keneseth Israel turned to the Jewish Theological Seminary of
America, the Conservative rabbinical school, for assistance in selecting his successor. As a result, Rabbi Samuel Cohen led the congregation from 1912 to
1916. He immediately organized a Hebrew School and Sunday School, as well
as a junior congregation, one of the earliest in the country. The congregation
joined the United Synagogue of America (now the United Synagogue of Conservative Judaism), the national body of Conservative congregations, upon its
founding in 1913. Cohen—who later became its head—directed the congregation to formally adopt Conservative Judaism.

Two years later, a small group of Keneseth Israel members gathered together
to form an independent Conservative congregation, Beth Shalom. Rabbi Cohen
became rabbi of this new congregation. Beth Shalom met at Thirty-first and
Linwood before moving in 1916 to Linwood Boulevard. Rabbi Cohen sought
to bring Beth Shalom and Keneseth Israel together before he left the community
in 1917. Rabbi Salo Stein succeeded him, and sentiment to consolidate the
congregations grew. Interest in a merger peaked when Keneseth Israel planned
its move to Thirty-fourth Street and the Paseo. When Rabbi Stein left Beth
Shalom in 1919, the congregations sought to merge. While merger discussions
continued, Beth Shalom invited Rabbi Herman M. Cohen to its pulpit. He established daily worship services and under his leadership, the congregation grew.
As a result of its growth, Beth Shalom rejected the merger proposal.

In the meantime, Keneseth Israel faced serious financial difficulties. Rabbi
Simon Glazer served as rabbi of Keneseth Israel and the "United Orthodox
Jewry of Kansas City." Members of both congregations revived merger talks;
and, in 1924, the congregations merged into Keneseth Israel-Beth Shalom, with
Rabbi Herman M. Cohen at its head. The merged congregation of five hundred
family units, with 325 religious-school children, built a new synagogue in 1927.
Rabbi Cohen found it impossible to remain in the merged congregation as much
still separated the two factions in the congregation. Thus, he resigned in 1928.

While Rabbi Albert Gordon served the congregation for several months, Keneseth Israel–Beth Shalom eventually persuaded Rabbi Gershon Hadas to become its rabbi. Not fully realizing the reduction in membership (to 250) and the
severe financial strain the new building placed on the congregation, he was

unprepared for the task. He battled the crisis in the midst of the Depression. By 1933, membership grew to 395 and, by 1937, to five hundred with a Sunday School enrollment of six hundred. By 1946, membership reached eight hundred, requiring the operation of a branch school (for three years) at Fifty-fifth Street and Brookside. In 1949, the congregation added a new school building to accommodate its growth in student enrollment. One year later, the congregation voted to shorten the name of the congregation to the Beth Shalom Congregation.

With a new name, the synagogue purchased a forty-six-acre site at Wornall Road and Bannister in 1955. The congregation made almost immediate use of the land when it opened Camp Shalom, a day camp, the following year. In 1961, Rabbi Morris Margolies came to the congregation to succeed Rabbi Hadas, just after the congregation moved into its new facilities in 1960. Beth Shalom added several buildings during the succeeding ten years before dedicating a new sanctuary in 1970. A construction workers' strike that delayed the completion of the sanctuary led to the dismantling of the long-standing policy of assigned High Holiday seats. In 1977, the congregation granted ritual equality to women.

Rabbi I. David Oler succeeded Rabbi Margolies in 1986. He served for two years before the congregation elected Rabbi Charles Popky to its pulpit (1988–1989). Rabbi Alan Cohen joined the congregation as religious leader in 1989. During his tenure, the Ohev Shalom Religious School joined Beth Shalom's program of religious education (1991). In 1994, membership neared thirteen hundred family units.

References

Beth Sholom Synagogue Diamond Anniversary Book (Kansas City, MO: 1953).
Shanberg, Arnold. *A Century of Dedication: The Story of Beth Sholom of Kansas City 1878–1978* (Kansas City, MO: 1978).
Synagogue Histories File, American Jewish Archives.

CONGREGATION B'NAI JEHUDAH, REFORM. *Kansas City, Missouri.* Twenty-five men met in a room above a store on Fourth and Walnut in 1870 to found Kansas City's first Jewish congregation: B'nai Jehudah. Led by Louis Hammerslough, the congregation emerged out of the Hebrew Benevolent Society founded in 1866. When this new congregation adopted the Reform *Minhag America* as its prayer book in 1871, a small group withdrew in order to establish Adath Israel. B'nai Jehudah held its Reform worship services in a vacant loft at Eighth and Main Streets, joining as a founding member of the Union of American Congregations, the national organization of Reform synagogues, in 1873. That same year, B'nai Jehudah replaced the more moderate *Minhag America* with the more radical *Olath Tamid,* the prayer book of David Einhorn. This remained in use until 1895.

During its early history, B'nai Jehudah looked to numerous religious leaders to guide its membership, including Marcus R. Cohen (1870–1872), Emanuel L. Hess (1872–1876), David Burgheim (1877–1878), Rabbi Ignaz Grossmann (1879–1880), and Rabbi Elias Eppstein (1880–1884).

In 1874, worship moved to a Unitarian church on New Delaware (now Baltimore) near Tenth before B'nai Jehudah congregants dedicated a modest temple the following year at Sixth and Wyandotte Streets for its forty-member congregation. In 1885, B'nai Jehudah built its second temple, a Moorish-style synagogue at the corner of Oak and Eleventh Street. While the congregation numbered only two hundred families in the latter part of the nineteenth century, it gained national prominence through the reputations of the three rabbis who served B'nai Jehudah between 1883 and 1899, the first two of whom were in the first class of Hebrew Union College graduates: Joseph Krauskopf (1883–1887), Henry Berkowitz (1888–1892), and Samuel Schulman (1893–1899).

Joseph Krauskopf, who preached about "natural religion without supernaturalism," argued for the removal of superstition and worn-out rituals. He strengthened the synagogue's program of religious education and encouraged the study of Hebrew. Berkowitz established the LACE Society (Literary, Lecture, and Library Committee; Aid Committee; Congregational Cooperation Committee; Educational Committee), an auxiliary designed to satisfy the cultural and educational needs of the community. During Rabbi Schulman's tenure, men and women from B'nai Jehudah developed a comprehensive network of services to assist Jewish refugees in their community. At his instigation, the synagogue offered a free Sabbath School for poor children of Orthodox nonmembers.

Rabbi Harry H. Mayer succeeded Rabbi Schulman in 1899. The women of the congregation organized a temple Sisterhood in 1906. During the first decade of Mayer's rabbinic leadership, membership increased from 140 to 300 families. Because most of these families lived in the midtown and uptown areas, the congregation moved to Linwood Boulevard and Flora Avenue in 1908, building an annex in 1927. In 1910, Mayer introduced Sunday services to supplement Friday evening and Saturday morning worship. That same year B'nai Jehudah began the practice of holding Confirmation on the Sunday closest to Shavuot at the board's insistence.

Rabbi Samuel Mayersberg succeeded Rabbi Mayer in 1928. Early in his rabbinate at B'nai Jehudah, Mayersberg led a bitter battle to clean up city hall against the political machine of Tom Pendergast. In the synagogue, he fought successfully for the adoption of a free pew system. He also instituted the practice of blessing the Sabbath candles in the synagogue at the onset of worship. Concentrating on various aspects of the temple's program of religious education, Mayersberg raised the age of Confirmation—which his predecessor had permitted to take place at 13—to ninth grade (about fifteen). He championed the right for women to sit on the board of trustees in 1929.

Following an influx of members in 1936 because of the newly created category of associate member, the men of B'nai Jehudah organized a temple Brotherhood. In 1954, the issue of Bar Mitzvah, which caused controversy for many years in Reform Jewish education, threatened to divide the congregation. At the same time, members petitioned the board for the right of their daughters to enjoy status equal to their male peers. Amid fears that this controversy might ill-effect a building campaign, George Lewis, chairman of that campaign, championed a successful compromise. As the essence of the Bar/Bat Mitzvah ceremony appeared to be the reading of the Torah, the congregation called the ceremony "Reader of the Torah." By 1964, members began calling the ceremony Bar/Bat Mitzvah.

In 1957, B'nai Jehudah's fourteen hundred families began their relocation to the south side at Sixty-Ninth and Holmes. B'nai Jehudah completed the initial phases of the building project in 1967 with the dedication of a new sanctuary. In the new location, the congregation sponsored a variety of social and athletic programs usually found within the confines of a local Jewish community center. In 1958, B'nai Jehudah sponsored the development of Temple Beth El in Overland Park, Kansas, as a compromise between those who wanted to limit membership and those who feared that such limitations would lead to stagnation. Nevertheless, B'nai Jehudah indeed limited its membership to fifteen hundred, beginning in 1959.

Rabbi William B. Silverman became B'nai Jehudah's rabbi in 1960. As soon as he took office, he sought to improve the congregation's program of religious education and add certain traditional rituals to its worship. Though the addition of the Torah processional on Simchat Torah met with only minor opposition, members challenged Silverman on the changes he proposed in the religious school. For example, the rabbi wanted the ninth grade (pre-Confirmation) to meet on Saturday mornings along with the tenth-grade class to create a Confirmation Department and join in Saturday morning worship. Three years later the controversy over Saturday classes arose once again. This time, the dissidents withdrew from B'nai Jehudah in order to establish the community's third Reform congregation, the New Reform Temple. At about the same time, B'nai Jehudah introduced daily services in its chapel (renamed the Mayersberg Chapel to honor the former rabbi on his retirement).

Toward the end of the 1960s, the congregation supported fair housing initiatives in the community, just as previously members had supported equal schooling for blacks. Silverman retired in 1976. Rabbi Michael Zedek succeeded him, having come as assistant in 1974. Under Zedek's direction, the congregation moved into the mainstream of Reform Judaism with a wide-ranging program of activities designed to encourage more participation in ritual and education. In addition, Zedek works to build relationships between the Jewish and Christian communities, as well as with the African American community.

In 1990, Temple Beth El merged into B'nai Jehudah. In 1994, with a combined membership of nearly nineteen hundred member families, the congregation decided to build a learning center on land purchased in the suburbs of Kansas City to complement its ninety-acre retreat site.

References

Adler, Frank J. *Roots in a Moving Stream: The Centennial History of Congregation B'nai Jehudah of Kansas City, Missouri, 1870–1970* (Kansas City: 1972).
Mayer, Harry H. "The Kansas City Experiment with Reform Judaism: The First Eighty Years of Congregation B'nai Jehudah." Small Collections, American Jewish Archives.

Synagogue Histories File, American Jewish Archives.

B'NAI AMOONA, CONSERVATIVE. *St. Louis, Missouri.* Founded in 1884 by a breakaway group from Sheerith Israel (founded in 1868 or 1869) led by Morris Schuchat, seven men met in a room over a millinery shop on Franklin Avenue to form Congregation B'nai Amoona. It is not clear why Sheerith Israel split into two factions, but we do know that Rabbi Aaron Levy from Sheerith Israel joined the new group. The new organization originally took the name "Moses Montefiore Congregation," but it changed to B'nai Amoona in honor of the synagogue Morris Schuchat attended in his native Cracow. The group met in several locations before settling on quarters at Ninth and Washington Avenue, where local citizens eventually built the Statler Hotel (later the Gateway).

Rabbi Levy only remained with his new congregation for three months. Rabbi Adolph Rosentreter became rabbi at B'nai Amoona in 1885, serving until 1911. During this time, membership grew. In 1886, the women of the congregation formed the Frauenverein der Toechter Israels, the Ladies Society of the Daughters of Israel. By 1887, B'nai Amoona moved to a rented hall on Franklin Avenue. Recognizing a need to secure a permanent facility, members moved into a former church at Thirteenth and Carr Streets two years later with a membership of 110 families. During the dedication, the congregation permitted men and women to sit on the same level, a rather modest innovation considered rather radical by some. In 1893, a merger with parent congregation Sheerith Israel boosted membership.

When the congregation of 225 families sold its building to Shirei T'hillim in 1906, it moved to another former church at Garrison and Lucas Avenue, where an apartment building now stands. The congregation joined the United Synagogue of America (now called the United Synagogue of Conservative Judaism), the national organization of Conservative congregations, in 1917. The following year B'nai Amoona built at Academy and Vernon Avenues in 1918. The Eastern European immigrants who arrived in St. Louis between 1900 and 1920 constituted the second wave of immigrants who joined B'nai Amoona.

As a result of a wedding at which Rosentreter officiated between two young people without the consent of their parents, congregants forced him to resign. Although Rosentreter had led the congregation for many years, apparently a gulf developed between him and his congregation as the countries of origin of his constituency changed. Rabbi Moses Hirsch Rabinowitz succeeded Rabbi Rosentreter in 1911. Rabinowitz himself remained as leader of the congregation only until 1913. However, he did occupy the pulpit on several successive occasions until B'nai Amoona selected Rabbi Joseph Glushak in 1914 to be their religious leader. He preached in Yiddish and English in order to meet the needs of his congregants, but he too remained only a short time.

At about the same time, the synagogue anticipated moving once again. Though congregants moved the synagogue westward as the Jewish community

moved, residents skipped over the area surrounding the temple as they moved
west of the city. Thus, membership declined. Discussions about a possible
merger with Shaare Zedek took place on several occasions during this period,
but they did not come to fruition. The congregation's historian suggests that
these discussions may have broken down over the issue of women's seating.
Thus, in 1916, the congregation of seventy-five families purchased a small building at Academy and Vernon Avenues, just before Rabbi Abraham Halpern
joined B'nai Amoona the following year.

Rabbi Abraham Halpern had graduated from the Conservative Jewish Theological Seminary of America. In 1919, B'nai Amoona dedicated its newly built
synagogue at Academy and Vernon. Two years later, the membership built a
Talmud Torah on an adjacent lot. Membership grew so rapidly that by 1924 the
congregation enlarged its synagogue building. In an effort to attract young people, Rabbi Halpern organized numerous groups to bring young people together
in a variety of social contexts. He discontinued Yiddish sermons in 1917 and
introduced late Friday evening services with English responsive readings, as well
as community singing during worship. The novelty of late services wore off;
they were discontinued in 1928, until their reintroduction in 1944.

Rabbi Halpern also reorganized the religious school, adding sessions to its
program until students attended five days a week. He encouraged girls to attend,
as well. In 1922, the congregation discontinued its practice of selling aliyahs to
the highest bidder. At about the same time, the congregation faced severe financial difficulties with a membership that continued to move west. By the end
of the decade, very few families lived in the area surrounding the synagogue.

World War II prevented the congregation from taking a long anticipated
move. In 1942, B'nai Amoona purchased the Xenia United Presbyterian Seminary at Washington and Trinity in University City, using its facilities until a
new building could be erected. As a result of the move to University City,
membership rose to over six hundred families.

B'nai Amoona introduced mixed seating to its congregants in 1948. It held
its first Bat Mitzvah the following year. Several years later, the congregation
created a College of Jewish Studies (as it was called) in order to encourage high
school and college students to continue their Jewish education.

Eric Mendelsohn designed a sanctuary for the new location—his first building
in the United States—which members dedicated in 1950. Additional construction took place throughout the decade. By 1960, membership increased to over
1050 names. When Rabbi Halpern retired in 1963, Rabbi Bernard Lipnick, who
had previously joined the congregation as educational director and then assistant
rabbi, became senior rabbi of B'nai Amoona. While still an assistant, he devoted
his energies to the synagogue's program of religious education.

In the 1960s, B'nai Amoona supported community efforts to rehabilitate deteriorating neighborhoods in University City and worked to improve the quality
of life of poor African Americans in the community. By the 1970s, members
hotly debated the role of women in the synagogue, although women participated

in the board of trustees on a modest level since the 1940s. As a first step, B'nai Amoona moved its celebration of Bat Mitzvah to Saturday morning in 1973. It was 1980 before women became counted in the minyan and welcome to participate fully in the ritual life of the synagogue.

In the early 1970s as well, B'nai Amoona joined in the creation of a community Hebrew School program administered by the newly created Central Agency for Jewish Education. And by 1981, with a membership of over nine hundred families, the congregation initiated the sponsorship of a Solomon Schechter Day School.

Recognizing the move of the Jewish community once again, B'nai Amoona purchased land at Mason and Conway in 1971. Ten years later, members dedicated the first building on the new site. In 1984, B'nai Amoona became fully egalitarian by counting women in the minyan and permitting them to accept all Torah honors. Rabbi Bernard Lipnick retired in 1991, and members elected Rabbi Eric Cytryn to lead them. Under his guidance, women are encouraged to wear *tallitot* (prayer shawls) and *tefillin* (phylacteries). In 1992, the congregation established an extensive program of family education. In 1994, B'nai Amoona listed one thousand membership units.

References

Abrams, Z. *The Book of Memories* (St. Louis: 1932).
Bronsen, Rosalind Mael. *B'nai Amoona for All Generations* (St. Louis: 1982).
Synagogue Histories File, American Jewish Archives.

TEMPLE ISRAEL, REFORM. *St. Louis, Missouri.* In 1886, with the sole objective of "the fostering and promotion of true Judaism," which they interpreted as a radical process of reform, sixty-three original members broke away from Shaare Emeth, taking its rabbi, Solomon H. Sonneschein, with them. Almost immediately, Sonneschein instituted Sunday services. In addition, members formed a Choral Society and a Ladies Aid Society. After only a year in a temporary home in the Pickwick Theatre Hall, just after it joined the Union of American Hebrew Congregations, the national organization of Reform synagogues, the congregation dedicated its first temple at Twenty-eighth and Pine Streets (1887). Shortly thereafter, Temple Israel instituted its first Sabbath School, which quickly enrolled 116 students.

Rabbi Leon Harrison immediately succeeded Rabbi Sonneschein when the latter resigned in 1890. During the subsequent years, membership grew rapidly. By 1894, Temple Israel boasted the largest Confirmation class in the city. In 1902, as a result of the synagogue's financial stability, it invited members of the community to join as associate members, paying whatever they could afford. Nevertheless, the Jewish population began slowly to move away from the Temple's location. As a result, Temple Israel's three hundred members dedicated a new home at Kingshighway and Washington in 1908, adding the Temple Israel house in 1932. Although Sunday Services drew large crowds in the new building, Rabbi Harrison discontinued them. It seems that more non-Jews than Jews were attending, and he felt that his message was not reaching his own congregants.

Membership grew, but probably not as fast as in other St. Louis congregations. Temple Israel's location often worked against the possibility of a more accelerated increase in membership. Following Rabbi Harrison's tragic death in 1928—he was struck by a subway train in New York City—the temple board entered into merger discussions with B'nai El and Shaare Emeth. Both Shaare Emeth and Temple Israel were engaged in a rabbinic search at the same time. Toward the end of 1929, opposition to merger arose. Opponents felt that a combined congregation would be too large for any of the existing synagogue structures and would require the construction of a new building, which would be an excessive financial burden for the congregation. Shortly thereafter, Temple Israel engaged Rabbi Ferdinand Isserman.

As soon as Isserman joined the congregation, he faced the aftereffects of the stock market crash. Yet, Isserman successfully raised the money to enlarge Temple Israel's overcrowded religious school facilities. Sensitive to democratic ideals in the synagogue, the temple dismantled its plan of assigned pews under his guidance and replaced its long-standing policy of minimum dues, allowing members the opportunity to pay what they could afford.

Because of transportation problems due to gasoline rationing in 1942, Isserman persuaded the board by a narrow margin to replace Friday evening services with earlier vesper services and regular Sunday morning services (instead of the lectures that had dominated the pulpit of his predecessors). The board quickly rescinded its decision during Rabbi Isserman's leave of absence to serve the American Red Cross in North Africa the following year.

Following World War II, membership climbed dramatically, growing from five hundred in 1945 to twelve hundred by 1953, with over nine hundred children in the religious school. This required school sessions on Saturday and Sunday, eventually moving into double sessions on Sunday morning. Thus, the congregation sought to move once again to accommodate its growing membership and its move away from the location of the synagogue. Initially land was purchased at Clayton and Warson, but the City Council rejected Temple Israel's request to build there because of the alleged potential for overcrowding. Deciding not to fight City Council, the temple purchased land at Ladue and Spoede Roads. This time, the City Council of Creve Coeur rejected the temple's application to build. Refusing to be rejected a second time, the temple fought for its right to build, all the way to the Missouri Supreme Court. In 1962, Temple Israel dedicated a new synagogue for its nearly fourteen hundred members.

While the congregation's board busied itself with fighting legal battles, other developments occurred. Confirmation was moved to tenth grade (from the ninth) in 1963, and Bar Mitzvah ceremonies were once again permitted in 1963, having been prohibited since 1960.

Rabbi Isserman's poor health forced him to resign his pulpit in 1963. Rabbi

Martin Katzenstein succeeded him, having served since 1961 as associate rabbi. Rabbi Katzenstein resigned in 1967, when the Temple's nearly sixteen hundred members elected Rabbi Alvan Rubin to lead them. Throughout his tenure, the congregation kept building in order to meet the religious needs of its growing membership. Thus, Temple Israel added a chapel (1970) and an auditorium (1971). The congregation developed the Edison Retreat Center in Troy, Missouri, in order to serve the spiritual needs of its congregants (dedicated 1974). In 1978, Temple Israel established Camp Kee Tov.

When Rabbi Rubin retired in 1987, Rabbi Mark Shook succeeded him. In 1994, Temple Israel's membership totaled 1480 family units.

References

Abrams, Z. *The Book of Memories* (St. Louis: 1932).
Losos, Joseph O. *From Leffinwell to Spoede: Highlights in the History of Temple Israel* (St. Louis: n.d.).
Rosenkranz, Samuel. *A Centennial History of Congregation Temple Israel 1886–1986* (Creve Coeur, MO: 1986).
Synagogue Histories File, American Jewish Archives.

CONGREGATION SHAARE EMETH, REFORM. *St. Louis, Missouri.* Calling themselves the St. Louis Temple Association, sixty-three members of Congregation B'nai El formed a new and more liberal Reform congregation in 1867. By 1869, this group had built a synagogue structure at Seventeenth and Pine Streets, naming it Shaare Emeth. The young group elected Rabbi Solomon H. Sonnenschein to lead them. Differences of opinion between the congregation and its rabbi over matters of Reform forced Sonneschein to resign in 1886. Sonneschein—amid a great deal of controversy—had been accused of taking steps to become a Unitarian minister. A group who agreed with the rabbi that the progress of Reform at Shaare Emeth was too slow left the congregation to form Temple Israel, bringing Rabbi Sonnenschein with them.

Rabbi Samuel Sale came to Shaare Emeth the following year. Under his guidance, the congregation grew, requiring a move to larger quarters in 1897 to Lindell and Vandeventer. In the interim, services were held at the Second Baptist Church, whose congregation earlier had met at Shaare Emeth after a fire in its church.

The Junior Congregation formed in 1910 at the congregation is one of the first on record. In 1911, Shaare Emeth extended full voting privileges to women in the congregation. By 1912, membership reached 223 members. The temple invited Rabbi Louis Witt to occupy its pulpit in 1919. In 1927, the congregation was forced to vacate its location because of the city's street-widening project, meeting again at the Second Baptist Church before dedicating its own facility in 1932 at Delmar Boulevard and Trinity Avenue in University City.

Shaare Emeth engaged Rabbi Julius Gordon in 1929. In 1939, Shaare Emeth celebrated its first Bar Mitzvah. By 1944 membership reached nine hundred families, with six hundred children in the religious school. When Rabbi Gordon died in 1954, Rabbi Burton Levinson succeeded him. He served five years, until members elected Rabbi Julius J. Nodel to its pulpit.

While land was purchased on Ladue Road in 1966, the congregation rejected plans to build there for many years. Rabbi Jeffrey Stiffman succeeded Rabbi Nodel in 1971. He had previously served as assistant rabbi and returned to serve as co-rabbi a year before Rabbi Nodel's retirement. Shortly thereafter, the congregation built a religious school and office at Ballas and Ladue (dedicated 1974). Construction continued in the new location with a sanctuary (dedicated 1979).

Under Rabbi Stiffman's leadership, Shaare Emeth initiated a day camp, a special education program for the hearing impaired, and special classes for the learning disabled. In 1994, membership of Shaare Emeth remained at fifteen hundred, a limit determined by the congregation.

References

Abrams, Z. *The Book of Memories* (St. Louis: 1932).
Synagogue Histories File, American Jewish Archives.

SHAARE ZEDEK SYNAGOGUE, CONSERVATIVE. *St. Louis, Missouri.* Twenty-six men signed the original Articles of Incorporation to found Shaare Zedek as an Orthodox synagogue in 1905. Services began in a rented hall on Vandeventer and Finney Avenues, before the young congregation rented a private house on Evans Avenue. With a membership of fifty in 1907, Shaare Zedek moved to a larger private residence on Cook Avenue, converting it for use as a synagogue. In 1912, members built a new facility on Page and West End (expanded with a school wing and an auditorium in 1928).

During the years 1911–1916, members conducted unsuccessful merger discussions with B'nai Amoona. Rabbi Bernard Abramowitz served the congregation from 1914 to 1922, followed by Rabbi Louis Lebendeger (1922–1929). Between the years 1929 and 1935, members of the congregation led worship. Members invited Rabbi Ephraim Epstein to lead them in 1935. He served until his death.

Recognizing the westward shift of the St. Louis Jewish population, Shaare Zedek moved to a large residence on Delmar in 1943, holding services there until 1951. The following year, the congregation purchased land at Hanley and Amherst in University City, where it quickly built classrooms and a chapel. In 1955, Shaare Zedek's 550 families added a sanctuary and auditorium. The congregation added a religious school wing, offices, a library, and a social hall in 1962.

When Epstein died in 1971, members elected Rabbi Arnold Asher as senior rabbi, he having served as associate since 1967. He worked to promote interfaith relations and social justice in his rabbinate. When he died suddenly in 1978, Rabbi Zalman M. Stein joined Shaare Zedek. Stein emigrated to Israel in 1983. During his tenure, Shaare Zedek affiliated with the United Synagogue of America, the national organization of Conservative synagogues, now called the United Synagogue of Conservative Judaism.

Rabbi Kenneth Greene came to Shaare Zedek in 1983. He focused his attention on education and the pastoral care of his congregants. Although the St. Louis Jewish community continued to move westward, Shaare Zedek decided to remain in University City. Its seven hundred families renovated the facilities in 1989. The congregation implemented a parallel minyan in an egalitarian worship format in 1988. When the assistant rabbi, Dov Bard, left the congregation in 1993, the congregation disbanded this alternative worship program and returned to a position that did not count women in its minyan. In 1994, Shaare Zedek's membership stood at 530 family units.

References

Abrams, Z. *The Book of Memories* (St. Louis: 1932).
Synagogue Histories File, American Jewish Archives.

UNITED HEBREW/ACHDUT ISRAEL, REFORM. *St. Louis, Missouri.* Founders established Achdut Israel (United Hebrew Congregation), the first Jewish congregation west of the Mississippi, as an Orthodox congregation in 1837 (legally incorporated in 1841). Members held their first services on the High Holidays on the upper floors of Max's Grocery and Restaurant at Second and Spruce. Residents referred to the congregation as the "old Polish congregation" because they held services according to Polish custom. In its early years, the congregation did not maintain continuity in its lay governance. In 1844 alone, four men served as president at United Hebrew. This change in leadership made growth difficult for the congregation.

In 1848, United Hebrew purchased the four-year-old Baptist Church at Fifth and Green Streets (now Lucas) for use as a synagogue. The following year, a group of women in the congregation founded the Hebrew Ladies' Benevolent Association "to relieve suffering among those of our own sex and persuasion who stand in need of help." During the cholera epidemic of that year in St. Louis, three of the members of the group, including its president, died from cholera, a direct result of their charitable work.

When Rabbi Isaac M. Wise visited the city in 1850, he encouraged the three congregations (United Hebrew, B'nai B'rith, and Imanu-El) to merge. The former congregations merged to form B'nai El and invited United Hebrew to join—and then withdrew the offer.

United Hebrew elected Henry Kuttner to lead it in 1857. Kuttner's initial tenure was short. He left to serve neighboring B'nai El, but returned in 1870 to serve United Hebrew until 1878. In the interim, Henry Vidaver served the congregation. During his tenure with the congregation, United Hebrew built its first synagogue on Sixth Street between Locust and St. Charles (1859). In the new facility, the congregation instituted moderate reforms by permitting, in 1860, the cantor to use a mixed quartet, including non-Jewish singers. Rabbi Henry J. Messing (1878–1911) succeeded Kuttner. During the first year of his association with United Hebrew, Rabbi Messing persuaded its leadership to join the Union of American Hebrew Congregations, the national organization of Reform synagogues. He also established a religious school for the congregation and instituted Confirmation, which to a large extent replaced Bar Mitzvah in the congregation.

In 1881, the congregation modified its form of worship, the same year it moved into a new synagogue—fitted with family pews—at Twenty-first and Olive. Though congregants permitted Rabbi Messing to offer some of the shorter prayers in English, they still insisted that sermons remain in German on alternating weeks. Toward the end of the century, President Samuel Marx attempted to abolish the custom of covering heads during worship. A small group countered him. The group proposed that the congregation discontinue its reforms and return to Orthodoxy.

As the population moved westward, the congregation chose to follow. Thus, in 1903, United Hebrew moved to a converted church at Kingshighway and Enright and added a community building, Harbuger Hall. In this new building, the congregation ruled (1913) that the rabbi could read from the Torah bareheaded, the same year the congregation adopted the *Union Prayer Book,* the prayer book of the Reform movement.

Rabbi Samuel Thurman led the congregation from 1914 to 1958, succeeding Rabbi Goodman Lessing's brief tenure. During Thurman's long association, the congregation moved once again to South Skinker (1927). Members added the Samuel Thurman Educational Building in 1957.

Rabbi Jerome Grollman led the congregation from 1958 to 1990, having served as assistant rabbi from 1948 to 1958. Shortly after his arrival, he instituted a high school program in the Religious School. He restored daily services, offered Bar/Bat Mitzvah, and reintroduced Torah honors and the pre–High Holiday penitential prayers of Selichot.

United Hebrew dedicated its new facility on Conway in West St. Louis County in 1989, the year before Rabbi Grollman's retirement. When Rabbi Grollman retired in 1990, Rabbi Howard Kaplansky, who previously served as assistant rabbi and had returned in 1985, succeeded him. The old building (built in 1925 on the western edge of Forest Park) became the Missouri History Society's library and research center, opened to the public in 1992. In 1994, United Hebrew Temple's membership roster listed over fifteen hundred family units.

References

Abrams, Z. *The Book of Memories* (St. Louis: 1932).

Ehrlich, Walter. "Origins of the Jewish Community of St. Louis." *American Jewish History* 77, no. 4 (June 1988): 507–29.

Makovsky, Donald Irving. "Origin and Early History of the United Hebrew Congregation of St. Louis, 1841–1859, the First Jewish Congregation in St. Louis." (M.A. thesis, Washington University, 1958).

Priwer, Jane. *The United Hebrew Congregation, St. Louis, Missouri, 1837–1963* (St. Louis: 1963).

Synagogue Histories File, American Jewish Archives.

YOUNG ISRAEL OF ST. LOUIS, ORTHODOX. *St. Louis, Missouri.* Young Israel of St. Louis was founded in 1936 as an Orthodox synagogue affiliated with the National Council of Young Israel. The group originally met in private homes and then met in the Romanian Shul, beginning in 1937. Beginning in 1945, the Young Israel met in space provided by another Orthodox congregation, Bes Midrash Hagadol. During the years 1945–1959, the congregation met in a variety of locations for short periods of time before moving to a house on Olive Street in 1959. In 1963, the congregation moved to its first permanent facility on Groby Road. In 1967, a splinter group formed another congregation, arguing that Young Israel had become "too religious." Some years later, another group separated from Young Israel to form Agudas Israel, complaining that Young Israel was "not religious enough" (1980). Young Israel renovated its facility in 1985. Nine years later, the Young Israel of St. Louis moved to Delmar Boulevard.

Following the brief tenure of rabbis in the early 1950s, Rabbi Yakov (Gerald) Jacobs (1955–1960) served the congregation. Rabbi Yitzhak Abramson (1963–1964) succeeded him, before Rabbi Abraham Pelberg (1964–1967) joined the congregation. Rabbi Simkah Krauss (1970–1980) served Young Israel before members elected Jeffrey Bienenfeld (1980–   ) as their religious leader. Rabbis Krauss and Bienenfeld both emphasized learning and achieved greater consistency in observances among their congregants. In 1995, membership stood at 130 family units.

Reference

Synagogue Histories File, American Jewish Archives.

N

NEBRASKA

TEMPLE ISRAEL, REFORM. *Omaha, Nebraska.* Julius and Max Meyer, two local merchants, made sporadic attempts to start a congregation beginning in 1866. By 1869, they successfully attracted a nucleus of eleven men to meet to establish a congregation. They founded Temple Israel two years later. This group immediately purchased cemetery property. In addition, they sought property to build a synagogue and engaged in the process of finding rabbinic leadership. That first year, Alexander Rosenspitz served them and confirmed the first confirmands of the congregation's short-lived Sunday School.

While Temple Israel continued to hold regular worship services, it witnessed a long succession of itinerant religious leaders during its early years. By 1884, with fifty members, Temple Israel dedicated Nebraska's first permanent synagogue at Twenty-third and Harney Streets. With the new building came decisions regarding ritual practices. Men and women sat together in the Harney Street Temple. Services included a choir and an organist and the decision that members may "have hats off during services—except such as may have conscientious scruples on the subject."

Membership reached 120 by the end of N. I. Benson's (1885–1889) term as religious leader of Temple Israel, the same time the congregation joined the Union of American Hebrew Congregations, the national organization of Reform synagogues. As a result, Rabbi William Rosenau became the first graduate of the Reform movement's Hebrew Union College to occupy Temple Israel's pulpit. As soon as he arrived, Rosenau refused the board's request that he wear a head covering and tallith while leading worship services. When Rosenau resigned in 1890, Rabbi Leo Franklin came to Omaha to succeed him. Franklin encouraged the adoption of the *Union Prayer Book,* the uniform prayer book of the Reform movement, by Temple Israel shortly after his arrival in Omaha.

Rabbi Abram Simon followed Franklin in 1898. Simon directed his attention to the Sunday School, particularly because the significant enrollment of nonmember children—whom the temple felt obligated to educate—placed a financial drain on the synagogue.

Dr. Frederick Cohn succeeded Rabbi Simon in 1904. During his tenure, Temple Israel moved to Park Avenue (1908). In the new building, the congregation abolished the practice of selling pews (1913). During World War I, the synagogue became the symbol of the Jewish community's patriotism, with an American flag draped over the ark and a special flag with gold stars for each young man serving in the Armed Forces. In 1937, Temple Israel celebrated its first Bar Mitzvah since the 1880s.

Rabbi David Wice joined the congregation shortly before Rabbi Cohn's retirement in 1934. When he left in 1940, Rabbi Arthur J. Lelyveld succeeded him in the pulpit. Under his leadership, Temple Israel grew to three hundred families. He officiated at the temple's first Bat Mitzvah in 1943. The following year, following the trend of other Reform congregations, Temple Israel raised Confirmation from ninth to tenth grade.

Rabbi Lou H. Silberman succeeded Rabbi Lelyveld in 1944. The following year, members officially changed the name of their congregation from the Congregation of Israel to the Congregation of Temple Israel. At the same time, the board recognized the extensive repairs needed for the building and the shift of its membership westward in Omaha.

In 1951, Temple Israel purchased a lot on Cass Avenue, the year before Rabbi Sidney Brooks came to the congregation. Rabbi Brooks upgraded the Religious School and revitalized the youth group program. In 1954, Temple Israel moved into its new facilities. The synagogue added a religious school wing in 1962 and a chapel three years later. Rabbi Sidney Brooks retired in 1985. Rabbi Stephen Barack (1985–1988) succeeded him before the congregation elected Rabbi Aryeh Azriel (1988–   ) to its pulpit. Membership stood at nearly 775 family units in 1995.

References

Gendler, Carol. "The First Synagogue in Nebraska: The Early History of the Congregation of Israel of Omaha." *Nebraska History* 58, no. 3 (Fall 1977): 323–41.
———. "The Jews of Omaha—The First Sixty Years." *Western States Jewish Historical Quarterly* 5, no. 3 (April 1973): 205–24; 5, no. 4 (July 1973): 288–305.
Somberg, Suzanne Richards, and Silvia Greene Roffman. *Consider the Years, 1871–1971: Congregation of Temple Israel, Omaha, Nebraska* (Omaha: 1971).
Synagogue Histories File, American Jewish Archives.

NEW HAMPSHIRE

TEMPLE ADATH YESHURUN, REFORM. *Manchester, New Hampshire.* The first record of an established synagogue, known as B'nai Jeshurun, on Elm

Street in Manchester and led by a Rabbi Peter Axel dates to 1889. By 1891, the community records listed twenty-one family members of the congregation, primarily immigrants from Lithuania. As the congregation grew, social differences played themselves out in the form of liturgical differences. By 1897, these disputes ended with the Russian immigrant members, primarily from the Ukraine, leaving the congregation to form their own Congregation Anshe Sephard.

A year later, the passage of legislation requiring the registration of religious institutions prompted its seventeen members to incorporate Adath Yeshurun, in 1900. The congregation met for worship on Central Street, then Pine Street. In 1902, the young congregation purchased a small cottage for use on Laurel Street. The growth of Adath Yeshurun prompted its members to construct a new building on Central Street in 1911, complete with an upstairs balcony for girls and women and an adjacent shed for the preparation of poultry for kosher slaughtering.

Though a difficult financial condition had plagued the congregation, as it did the entire Manchester community, members eventually became more prosperous and moved northward from their original concentration in the area of Lake Avenue. As a result, members began to drive their cars to worship. Attitudes toward ritual changed. Thus, congregants demanded a change in the Orthodox ritual from Rabbi Abraham Hefterman, who led the congregation from about 1926. For example, they requested that at least one High Holiday sermon be delivered in English rather than in Yiddish. He refused, and he resigned.

Feeling unsuccessful in the area of Jewish education, both congregations joined together in 1938 to form a religious school that met at the Jewish Community Center (formerly the YM/YWHA).

Following World War II, a visiting rabbi suggested that all should rise to recite the Mourner's Kaddish (prayer for the dead), a practice inconsistent with Orthodox tradition. At about the same time, men and women began to sit together in worship. Slowly, Orthodox customs gave way to Reform innovation. Though the tenure of both rabbis who succeeded Rabbi Hefterman was short, they did succeed in introducing such reforms such as organ music and the adoption of the *Union Prayer Book,* the uniform prayer book of the Reform movement. Yet, the congregation maintained a traditional service as well for several years and never abandoned the wearing of *yarmulkes* (skullcaps) and *tallitot* (prayer shawls).

The members of Adath Yeshurun selected Rabbi Samuel Umen to lead the synagogue in 1954. Anxious for a new synagogue to reflect the changes they anticipated with the coming of a new rabbi, Adath Yeshurun moved to Beech Street across from the Jewish Community Center. While members entered into a discussion concerning the development of a synagogue center, that plan never grew beyond the discussion stage. Percival Goodman designed the new synagogue (dedicated 1959).

In its new home, Adath Yeshurun returned to the former approach of administering its own religious education program. Following a lengthy dispute over the rabbi's officiation at mixed marriages of nonmembers—complicated by growing dissatisfaction with the religious school—the community school was reinstituted in 1970; Rabbi Umen resigned the following year.

Rabbi Arthur Starr immediately succeeded Rabbi Umen. Following the trend of the Reform movement of the time, Rabbi Starr introduced more Hebrew into worship, encouraged congregational participation, instituted aliyahs, and engaged a cantor. By 1976, with few ritual practices separating Adath Yeshurun from Temple Israel, congregational leaders made another attempt at merger. Discussions took place over two years, but too many differences were unresolved to pave the way for a merger. Thus, the congregations remain independent with buildings less than a quarter-mile apart. In 1979, fire destroyed most of the building, which necessitated its extensive rebuilding and refurbishing. In 1994, Adath Yeshurun listed over 350 membership units.

Reference

Temple Adath Yeshurun's Centennial Anniversary Journal 1891–1991 (Manchester, NH: 1991).

TEMPLE ISRAEL, CONSERVATIVE. *Manchester, New Hampshire.* In 1897, a group of Russian Jews, dissatisfied with the liturgy at Adath Yeshurun, formed their own synagogue, Anshe Sephard. The early congregation worshiped in a variety of locations, until it found a permanent home on Central Street. Feeling unsuccessful in the area of Jewish education, both congregations joined together in 1938 in the formation of a religious school that met at the Jewish Community Center (formerly the YM/YWHA).

In 1958, Rabbi Abraham Hefterman, an Orthodox rabbi trained in Lithuania, left Adath Yeshurun—when it became Reform—to become rabbi at Anshe Sephard. In 1958, the synagogue dedicated its new building at Salmon and Pine Streets, taking the name Temple Israel. In the new sanctuary, members built family pews. That same year, Temple Israel affiliated with the United Synagogue of America (now the United Synagogue of Conservative Judaism), the national organization of Conservative synagogues. The following year, Rabbi Jacob Handler (1959–1964) succeeded Hefterman. He focused his rabbinate on interfaith work in the community. Rabbi Joel Klein (1964–1977) succeeded Handler. As a trained psychologist, he emphasized counseling in his rabbinate. He also advocated an equal role for women in the congregation and counted them for minyan starting in 1972.

With Temple Israel and Adath Yeshurun both in new buildings, the congregations took back individual control of their joint program of religious education, which had been supervised by the Jewish Community Center. By 1970, the burden of operating separate schools was too great, and the community school was reinstituted.

In 1976, with few ritual practices separating Adath Yeshurun from Temple

Israel, congregational leaders made another attemperger; the first attempt failed in 1974. Since negotiators could not resolve such issues as endowment funds and the practice of dietary laws in the kitchen, merger talks failed once again. During this period of time (1977–1979), Temple Israel operated without religious leadership. Rabbi Richard Polirer joined the congregation in 1979. He emphasized education in his rabbinate and established a variety of courses for adults. In 1995, membership exceeded 140 family units.

Reference

Temple Adath Yeshurun's Centennial Anniversary Journal 1891–1991 (Manchester, NH: 1991).

NEW JERSEY

JEWISH EDUCATIONAL CENTER, ORTHODOX. *Elizabeth, New Jersey.* Unlike most other synagogue communities in North America, the Jewish Educational Center (JEC) in Elizabeth is a complex of institutions designed to meet the religious, social, and educational needs of the Orthodox community of Elizabeth. First and foremost, the Jewish Educational Center is an educational institution (founded 1939 by Rabbi Pinchas Teitz; opening its first school in 1941). It consists of the Yeshiva (founded 1940) and Mesivta of Elizabeth (founded 1955), Bruriah High School (founded 1963), and two synagogues (Murray Street and Adath Jeshurun). While two other synagogues are part of the Elizabeth community and led by the community rabbi, they are not part of the Jewish Educational Center corporate complex. Historically, the JEC rabbi served as the rabbi of Elizabeth's (Orthodox) Jewish community, founded in 1881, rather than rabbi of any one particular synagogue. Though the records of the early rabbis are not extant, these individuals served as religious leaders of the community: Rabbi Moshe Leib Bernstein (1881–1911), Rabbi Joseph Konvitz (1911–1919), Rabbi Elozor M. Preil (1919–1933), and Rabbi Pinchas Teitz (1935–1995).

The JEC built its first synagogue in 1947 on Elmora Avenue, where it remains. In 1955, the community built a second synagogue on North Avenue (in the Westminster or North Elizabeth section of the city). This second synagogue, called Adath Israel (originally founded 1925), is named for the synagogue it subsumed.

Holche Yosher Ahavas Achim merged into the JEC in 1966. Local residents had founded Holche Yosher in 1886 and built their first synagogue on Park Street. A dissident group incorporated Ahavas Achim in 1886 and built a synagogue opposite Holche Yosher on Park Street. A fire in 1906 destroyed that synagogue, which members later rebuilt. In 1920 these synagogues merged to form Holche Yosher Ahavas Achim. Another synagogue, Anshe Sfard (founded 1910), merged into the JEC in 1972.

Reference

Silverstein, Norman Mark. "The History and Development of the Jewish Community in Elizabeth, New Jersey." (Senior thesis, Rutgers University, 1979).

CONGREGATION AHAVATH TORAH, ORTHODOX. *Englewood, New Jersey.* Eight Jewish residents of Englewood met at the home of Jacob Reznick in 1895 to form a minyan for the upcoming High Holidays. This group held services in a house on Liberty Road, moving to a rented house on Durie Avenue the following year. Following the second High Holidays, the group moved to Humphrey Street in 1897. Ahavath Torah moved in 1912 to Englewood Avenue, where it remained until 1960. That year, the congregation relocated to Broad Avenue. The congregation affiliated with the Union of Orthodox Jewish Congregations, a national organization of Orthodox synagogues.

Several individuals served the congregation in its early years, and these men led Ahavath Torah in its later years: Benjamin Walfish (1958–1960), Isaac Swift (1960–1984), and Shmuel Goldin (1984–   ). Swift helped to build up the Orthodox Jewish community in Bergen County, where he founded the Yeshiva Day School (Englewood). Goldin established educational programs for women in the synagogue and programs of outreach for community members.

In 1995, membership at Ahavath Torah stood at 540 family units. In addition to regular services, Ahavath Torah holds an auxiliary minyan for overflow from the main sanctuary, a Sephardic minyan for those who prefer a Sephardic mode of worship, and an early morning minyan for those who wish to pray very early in the day.

References

Congregation Ahavath Torah: An Oral History (Englewood, NJ: 1995).
Synagogue Histories File, American Jewish Archives.

TEMPLE EMANU-EL, CONSERVATIVE. *Englewood, New Jersey.* Feeling the need for a congregation that would meet their needs, a group of young Jews met in 1928 for services at Congregation Ahavath Torah under the guidance of Rabbi Max Maccaby. Motivated by Rabbi Stephen S. Wise, this group of twenty-five families decided to incorporate as Temple Emanu-El of Englewood. The new institution met in private homes, with Rabbi Benjamin Schultz serving as part-time rabbi for about a year, until it moved its quarters to the Plaza Theater and then to the Busch Building on West Palisade Avenue.

Rabbi Zvi Anderman became the first full-time rabbi to serve Temple Emanu-El. Rabbi Ephraim Fischoff succeeded him. In 1935, Emanu-El members met with representatives from Temple Ahavath Torah to discuss a possible merger, but members from both congregations abandoned these discussions. That same year, Emanu-El took ownership of property on Tenafly Road and built its first permanent home.

Rabbi Fischoff resigned, and Rabbi Samuel Berman succeeded him. Members expanded the building the following year, the same time Rabbi Berman resigned. Israel R. Margolies, then a senior student at the Jewish Institute of Religion, succeeded Berman.

In 1946, Temple Emanu-El entered into discussions once again with Ahavath Torah and the nascent Jewish Community Center about using nearby property on Tenafly Road to house all three organizations. Though agreement had seemed possible, Congregation Ahavath Torah eventually withdrew from the project. Emanu-El's membership reached three hundred in 1948.

Rabbi Margolies introduced his new *Prayer Book for Sabbath and Festivals,* designed to provide a traditional service with greater explanation for temple members. In 1952, the congregation planned its new facility on Tenafly Road, originally conceived to blend into the Jewish Community Center (dedicated 1957). Rabbi Margolies resigned the same year. The congregation decided to seek placement through the (Conservative) United Synagogue of America. As a result, Rabbi Benjamin H. Tumin joined the congregation.

At about the same time, the congregation assumed the sole responsibility for educating its children, disbanding the Community Hebrew School it had operated since the 1930s. In 1955, Rabbi Tumin left Emanu-El. The following year, the congregation joined the United Synagogue of America, the organization of Conservative synagogues. At the same time, Rabbi Arthur Hertzberg became Temple Emanu-El's new religious leader.

Temple Emanu-El built a new religious school in 1965 just after the destruction of its first synagogue structure on the Tenafly property. In the mid-1970s, the congregation's financial situation deteriorated. At about the same time, women of the congregation demanded equal rights. In 1978, the ritual committee decided to allow a Bat Mitzvah to take place on Saturday with the mother of the Bat Mitzvah joining her husband on the *bima* (platform) for a "family" aliyah. This began the process for granting full equality to women in synagogue life. When Hertzberg retired in 1985, Emanu-El members invited Rabbi Stephen Listfield to lead them. He devotes a great deal of his attention to adult education at the synagogue. In 1994, Temple Emanu-El's membership stood at just under six hundred family units.

Reference

Synagogue Histories File, American Jewish Archives.

AHAVAS ACHIM, ORTHODOX. *Highland Park, New Jersey.* A small group of newly arrived immigrants from Eastern Europe organized Ahavas Achim in New Brunswick in 1889. During its first decade of operation, the congregation met in members' homes or in a variety of temporary locations in downtown New Brunswick. In 1900, Ahavas Achim moved to a small building on Richmond Street, formerly the home of the Salvation Army. In 1911, members enlarged the building; they added a vestry in 1947. Shortly thereafter, the women of Ahavas Achim formed a sisterhood and established a Hebrew school. In 1950, membership peaked at three hundred. In 1961, the congregation constructed a new sanctuary at the same location. Fire destroyed the sanctuary (and most synagogue records) in 1980. Members met for worship first in the vestry room and then in a local high school.

These men served as religious leaders of Ahavas Achim: Israel Marcus (1909–1918), Samuel Baskin (1918–1930), Abraham Shapiro (1931–1933), and Pesach Raymon (1938–1984). In 1986, Rabbi Ronald Schwarzberg joined Ahavas Achim. Under his leadership the congregation of 250 members moved to its present location on South First Avenue in Highland Park (dedicated 1986). Membership in 1995 stood at 270 family units.

Reference

Patt, Ruth Marcus. *The Jewish Scene in New Jersey's Raritan Valley 1698–1948* (New Brunswick, NJ: 1978).

HIGHLAND PARK CONSERVATIVE TEMPLE, CONSERVATIVE. *Highland Park, New Jersey.* In 1926, a small gathering of men concerned about meeting the Jewish educational needs of their families joined together as the Highland Park Hebrew School Association. The school met in a vacant store on North Fourth Avenue. The group grew and met for High Holidays at the local Masonic Temple. In 1930, the association built its own home on North Third Avenue. The congregation engaged Rabbi Isadore Shalom (1930–1937) as its first religious leader. Rabbi Philip Listoken succeeded him (1937–1945). The building slowly became a social and religious center for Jews living in Highland Park.

Under the guidance of Rabbi Sidney Schulman (1945–1949), the congregation built a new structure on South Third Avenue (dedicated 1949) and took the name of Highland Park Conservative Temple and Center. Shortly thereafter, Rabbi Philip Ritholtz (1949–1963) became the religious leader of the temple. Two years after his arrival, the congregation of one hundred members expanded the building to meet the needs of the congregation's growing program of activities and services. For further development, the membership purchased an adjacent lot on Benner Street.

By 1960, membership had reached three hundred families. Thus, the congregation expanded once again, building a religious school and youth center. In 1964, members elected Rabbi Yakov Hilsenrath to the pulpit. He launched an extensive educational program, which included a daily nursery, a high school, a youth program, and an adult studies program. Following Hilsenrath's retirement in 1994, Rabbi Eliot Isaac Malomet joined the congregation. In 1995, membership exceeded 570 family units.

Reference

Kroll, Harry. *Highland Park Conservative Temple and Center Tribute Book* (Highland Park, NJ: 1968).

B'NAI KESHET, MONTCLAIR JEWISH CENTER, RECONSTRUC-TIONIST. *Montclair, New Jersey.* Founders established this congregation in 1978 and immediately affiliated with the Federation of Reconstructionist Congregations and Havurot, the national organization of Reconstructionist synagogues. They met for worship in a building on Valley Road before relocating to two different churches in the area. In 1995, the congregation moved into its first permanent home on South Fullerton Avenue.

These rabbis served the congregation: David Klatzker (1978–1979), Joy Levitt (1980–1985), Marc Hurwitz (1986–1987), and Dan Ehrenkrantz (1988–   ). In 1995, membership exceeded 150 family units.

Reference

Interview, Dan Ehrenkrantz, June 28, 1995.

ANSHE EMETH MEMORIAL TEMPLE, REFORM. *New Brunswick, New Jersey.* Six representatives of the small Jewish community in New Brunswick applied for a charter for a congregation in the name of Anshe Emeth in 1859, although worship services took place in private homes before the formal establishment of a congregation. Once these recent immigrants from Germany had incorporated the congregation, they met for worship on Peace Street. In 1871, the congregation moved to a more permanent location on Neilson Street.

The congregation adopted the first *Union Prayer Book* when it was printed in 1894. Three years later, Anshe Emeth moved to its newly built synagogue on Albany Street. It took Anshe Emeth forty years to secure the services of a full-time rabbi. In 1899, Rabbi Morris W. Waldman became the congregation's first rabbi. The following year, members introduced organ music into their worship.

In 1926, the congregation voted to change the name to Anshe Emeth Memorial Temple in order to honor the Jewish war dead. With only eighty family members, Anshe Emeth Memorial Temple dedicated its new sanctuary on Livingston Avenue between Sanford and Delevan in 1930. The following year, Rabbi Nathaniel Keller joined the congregation, where he served until his death in 1961.

The congregation encountered anti-Semitism on a variety of occasions, and vandals defaced the synagogue with swastikas in 1934. Women on the board representing sisterhood were given the power to vote by 1936. In 1948, Anshe Emeth Memorial Temple engaged a "complete Christian Choir" to assist in worship services, completely ignoring a resolution passed by its own board in 1933 requiring all choir members to be Jewish. In an expression of support of the merger of Hebrew Union College with the Jewish Institute of Religion, the congregation affiliated with its patron, the Union of American Hebrew Congregations, the umbrella organization for Reform synagogues, in 1950.

Anshe Emeth Memorial Temple instituted confirmation in 1954. In 1955, the congregation included 283 members, with 217 children in its religious school.

Thus, it purchased an adjacent building to accommodate its growth. In 1957, membership increased to 350 member families. By 1964, a new religious school building was built. The temple introduced Bat Mitzvah in 1966. With five hundred students in the religious school in 1967, the congregation established a satellite school in East Brunswick. As an alternative some years later, bus transportation brought students to the New Brunswick location.

The neighborhood deteriorated around the synagogue, and inner-city New Brunswick experienced race riots in the late 1960s. Many Jews left the neighborhoods around the temple and moved into the suburbs. Though the congregation considered moving, a long-range planning committee in 1975 advised the synagogue to take a principled stand and not to abandon its location.

Committed to remain in the same location, the congregation expanded in 1978. With six hundred families in 1984, Anshe Emeth established a "caring community" program to reach out to its members in various times of need. As an experiment, the congregation instituted early Friday evening services in 1985 as an alternative to a later Sabbath service. In 1994, membership stood at over seven hundred.

Rabbis who served Anshe Emeth Memorial Temple include Morris Waldman (1899–1903), E. Friedlander (1903–1905), Gustave N. Hausman (1905–1907), H. Veld (1907–1909), ? Solomon (1909–1910), J. Ludwig Stern (1910–1913), Ludwig Roeder (1913–1920), Jacob Goldstein (1921), Hyman Schatz (1921–1925), J. Sarachek (1925–1927), Arthur Maurice Hirschberg (1927–1931), Nathaniel Keller (1931–1961), Jack D. Spiro (1962–1967), Harvey W. Fields (1968–1974), and Bennett Miller (1974–   ).

References

Anshe Emeth Memorial Temple Commemorative Journal, 1859–1985 (New Brunswick, NJ: 1985).

Gertman, Stuart. "A History of Anshe Emeth Memorial Temple of New Brunswick, New Jersey" (Term paper, Hebrew Union College–Jewish Institute of Religion, 1969). Small Collections, American Jewish Archives.

Patt, Ruth Marcus. *The Jewish Scene in New Jersey's Raritan Valley 1698–1948* (New Brunswick, NJ: 1978).

CONGREGATION B'NAI JESHURUN, REFORM. *Newark (later Short Hills), New Jersey.* A group of immigrants from Central Europe came to Newark, New Jersey, and, led by Isaac S. Cohen, incorporated the "Sacred Congregation of B'nai Jeshurun" in 1848, after meeting in Cohen's home for a year. They held their services in Hebrew and German first in an attic of an old building on Arlington Street and then in a former church on Harrison (now Halsey) Street. With only twenty-two members in 1854, this young congregation engaged Isaac Schwarz as its religious leader. Moving from location to location, it erected its first permanent home on Washington Street and Maiden Lane in 1858. When members did not reelect Isaac Schwarz in 1860, a group of dissidents left B'nai Jeshurun to form Oheb Shalom, inviting Isaac Schwarz to become the first religious leader of this new congregation. In 1861, the remaining synagogue members organized the Hebrew Orphan Asylum (eventually becoming the Jewish Child Care Association and then merging with the present-day Jewish Family Service Agency). Schwarz's successor, Sigmund Kaufman, organized the congregation's day school in 1863, teaching German, English, and Hebrew. When Kaufman left in 1865, B'nai Jeshurun members elected David S. Seligman to lead them.

With a membership of ninety-five families in 1867, B'nai Jeshurun built a new temple on Washington and Williams Streets. One year later, Joseph Leucht became the religious leader of the congregation. Reflecting its move toward Reform Judaism, B'nai Jeshurun discontinued the practice of observing the second day of festivals (1871), adopted *Olath Tamid,* the prayer book of Rabbi David Einhorn (1872), and abolished the requirement of a head covering for worship (1882). The congregation became officially Reform in 1881 by joining the Union of American Hebrew Congregations, the national organization of Reform synagogues. Rabbi Leucht began delivering his sermons in English in 1882. One year later, the congregation held Confirmation services in English as well. By 1892, B'nai Jeshurun adopted the *Union Prayer Book,* the uniform prayer book of the Reform movement, and made other changes in ritual, such as rising for the *Shema* prayer and the benediction. Membership reached 155 in 1897.

Rabbi Solomon Foster succeeded Leucht in 1905, having joined the congregation as associate rabbi in 1902. During his tenure, B'nai Jeshurun established a Women's Association (1912) to help raise funds for the congregation to build its new structure on High Street and Waverly Avenue (dedicated 1915). Once in the new building, members founded a brotherhood (1920). Foster established the New Jersey Normal School for Jewish Teachers (1926), which trained Sunday School instructors for Reform congregations. He retired in 1940, and Rabbi David Wice joined the congregation. Rabbi Ely Pilchik succeeded Wice in 1947. At the beginning of Pilchik's tenure, membership reached seven hundred families, with approximately six hundred children in the religious school.

By 1956, the congregation acquired property in South Orange and operated religious school classes there. When B'nai Jeshurun moved to Short Hills on South Orange Avenue in 1968, 850 of its then 1110 member families already resided outside Newark. When Rabbi Pilchik retired in 1981, Rabbi Barry H. Greene, who had joined the congregation in 1959 as assistant, succeeded him. In 1994, the membership of B'nai Jeshurun reached nearly 1050.

References

The Essex Story: A History of the Jewish Community of Essex County, New Jersey (Newark: 1955).

Greene, Barry H. *Our One Hundred Fortieth Year, Tracing the History of Congregation B'nai Jeshurun* (Short Hills, NJ: 1988).

The Jewish Community Blue Book of Newark (Newark: 1925).

Religion Is the Life of Israel (New York: 1929).

Synagogue Histories File, American Jewish Archives.

OHEB SHALOM, CONSERVATIVE. *Newark (later South Orange), New Jersey.* Eighteen immigrants from Bohemia—former members of B'nai Jeshurun (founded 1848), who left when their religious leader Isaac Schwarz was not reelected—organized Oheb Shalom (generally called the Boehmische Gemeinde) in 1860. Isaac Schwarz served as Oheb Shalom's first religious leader. The early congregation met for daily, Sabbath, and holiday worship in a small frame building on Prince Street. This congregation, because of its members' country of origin, came to be known as the Bohemian Shul.

Beginning in 1870, Rabbi Tintner led Oheb Shalom. Under his guidance, members founded the Miriam Frauen Verein (1880), the congregation's women's auxiliary (which became the Miriam Auxiliary after World War I). In a new structure built down the same street (1884), Oheb Shalom introduced family pews and the organ. In addition, the congregation adopted for use a prayer book, prepared by Marcus Jastrow, which included significant liturgical changes. Rabbi Bernard Drachman (1885–1888) addressed his congregants alternately in English and German from the pulpit. During the tenure of his successor, Rabbi Wolf Willner (1888–1890), Oheb Shalom introduced the organ to enhance worship.

What may be seen as a tendency toward ritual reform was continued by Rabbi Bernard Gluck (1890–1906) but kept in check by his successor, Rabbi Charles I. Hoffman (1906–1940). During Hoffman's tenure, Oheb Shalom welcomed many special-interest clubs in the congregation, including the Young People's Hebrew Union, Jewish Working Girls Club, the Lasker Literary Society, the Montefiore Literary Society, the Progressive Literary Society, and the Ladies Patriotic Relief Society. The Miriam Frauen Verein opened a Summer Sewing School for Jewish girls in 1906 because many Jewish girls were attracted to Christian missionary centers because sewing was taught there. Oheb Shalom also became a center for Zionist meetings and activity.

In 1911, Oheb Shalom moved to its new quarters on High Street. In 1913, the congregation helped to form the United Synagogue of America (now the United Synagogue of Conservative Judaism), the national organization of Conservative synagogues, and became a charter member. Following Hoffman's retirement, Rabbi Louis M. Levitsky (1940–1972) joined the congregation. He expanded the congregational program of adult education. In 1958, Oheb Shalom moved from Newark to South Orange on Scotland Road. In 1972, Rabbi Alexander Schapiro (1972–1992) succeeded Levitsky. Under his guidance as a human rights activist, Oheb Shalom entered into a collaborative venture with the local Jewish community to develop a senior center. In addition, the congregation opened its doors to programs serving Jews and non-Jews in recovery from alcoholism, chemical dependency, and other compulsive behaviors. During Schapiro's tenure, the Oheb Shalom religious school merged with the B'nai Israel school in Elizabeth and the Beth El program in South Orange (1982). The following year, Congregation Beth Torah of Orange merged into the congregation. Following Rabbi Schapiro's death in 1992, Rabbi Lawrence Troster became the religious leader of Oheb Shalom (1993–   ). Oheb Shalom maintains a wide-ranging program of activities and services, including the Mickey Freid Nursery School, the Academy for Jewish Studies (for children), and the Dr. Louis Levitsky Institute of Jewish Studies (a diversified program of adult education). In 1995, membership at Oheb Shalom exceeded 630 family units.

References

The Jewish Community Blue Book of Newark (Newark: 1925).

Kussy, Nathan, and Sarah Kussy. *Highlights in the History of Congregation Oheb Shalom, Newark, New Jersey* (Newark: 1950).

Synagogue Histories Collection, The Joseph and Miriam Ratner Center for the Study of Conservative Judaism.

Synagogue Histories File, American Jewish Archives.

ADAS ISRAEL SYNAGOGUE CENTER, ORTHODOX. *Passaic, New Jersey.* Founders of Chevra Adath Israel, as its founders called the original organization, organized the congregation in 1921, holding their first services the following year in a storefront on Monroe Street. In 1925, congregants built their first permanent home at Tulip and Montgomery Streets. Members added additional stories to this one-story building in 1937. The next year, the congregation engaged Leon Katz (1938–1984) as its spiritual leader. Under his direction Adas Israel established its Hebrew School. A private school, operating on Madison Street, merged into the Adas Israel school in 1938.

In 1950 the congregation acquired a house on Van Houten Avenue; thus, members held services in both locations. When this plan proved inadequate, the congregation erected a new synagogue in 1955 on Broadway, while continuing to operate the Tulip Street location until 1967. At the same time, the Hillel Academy Day School (also known as the Passaic Hebrew Institute) relocated to the synagogue's new site (dedicated 1959). When Rabbi Katz retired in 1984, Adas Israel elected Solomon F. Ryback to its pulpit. In 1995, membership neared two hundred family units.

Reference

Personal interview, Solomon F. Ryback, July 31, 1995.

TEMPLE SHAREY TEFILO-ISRAEL, REFORM. *South Orange, New Jersey.*

Temple Sharey Tefilo

Founded in East Orange in 1874 by eleven men—five from one family—members of Sharey Tefilo worshiped in a rented hall on Main Street. By 1880, members pushed for a change in seating women separately from men. In 1895, the congregation moved to its own quarters on Cleveland Street, under the guidance of J. Lubin (1895–1902), its religious leader. These individuals succeeded Lubin: Meyer Gross, Samuel Kaplan (1926–1929), Marius Ranson (1930–1948), Sidney Goldstein (1948–1949), Avraham Soltes (1949–1960), Lester Roubey (1960–1966), and Charles Annes (1966–1982). In 1912, the women of the congregation organized an auxiliary. The congregation affiliated with the Union of American Hebrew Congregations, the national organization of Reform synagogues in 1921. The congregation erected a building on Prospect Street (1927). Twenty years later, it purchased an estate in East Orange on South Harrison Street as a "Temple Annex for religious school meetings" and as a "new social home" (1947). These functions moved to the main building, where members eventually built a religious school building (1962).

Temple Israel

About twenty families living in Maplewood and South Orange formed Temple Israel. Members conducted services and religious education classes in private homes. By the following year, membership had increased to over one hundred families. That same year, the congregation moved into the Kip-Riker mansion on Montrose Avenue and Scotland Road in South Orange. Rabbi Marius Ranson became the congregation's religious leader. Rabbi Herbert Weiner (1948–1982) succeeded him. With cramped facilities, members built a wing in 1954. In 1967, members built a third building to expand the temple complex.

Temple Sharey Tefilo-Israel

A shift in demographics forced the inevitable merger of Sharey Tefilo with Temple Israel in 1982. Rabbi Bruce Block (1982–1985) guided the transition, with the merged congregation occupying the building that previously had housed only Temple Israel. In 1985, Rabbi Harvey Goldman succeeded Rabbi Block. Under his direction, the congregation grew and initiated a preschool and parenting program. The older members of the congregation formed their own Renaissance Group in 1992. In 1995, Temple Sharey Tefilo-Israel included a membership of over 725 family units.

Reference

Religion Is the Life of Israel (New York: 1929).

CONGREGATION B'NAI YESHURUN, ORTHODOX. *Teaneck, New Jersey.* With the guidance of Yeshiva University, three Teaneck couples initiated an organizational meeting in 1958 for B'nai Yeshurun, the first Orthodox congregation in Teaneck. Meeting in the basement of one of its founders, the congregation reached fifteen families by the end of the year. By that time, the group decided to engage Rabbi Label Dulitz as its part-time rabbi. Shortly thereafter, B'nai Yeshurun acquired its first home, an old house on the corner of West Englewood Avenue and Jefferson Street.

Rabbi Macy Gordon succeeded Rabbi Dulitz in 1961. As a result of constant growth, members eventually tore down the house and rebuilt on the same site in 1971, with approximately seventy member families. There the congregation pioneered certain patterns in contemporary Orthodoxy: Honors are not auctioned or sold; funds are not solicited during worship; and donations are not publicly announced. These rabbis succeeded Gordon: Aryeh Weil (1985–1994) and Steven Pruznansky (1994–   ). Both religious leaders emphasized education and the performance of mitzvot, as well as outreach to the community.

In 1976, B'nai Yeshurun's membership reached 240 families. It opened a nursery school the following year. At about the same time, a group, feeling that the congregation was overcrowded, left B'nai Yeshurun and formed Rinat Yisrael. In 1995, because of overcrowding, B'nai Yeshurun conducts five daily minyans. In 1996, the congregation will dedicate its new building adjacent to the current synagogue to accommodate the membership of over five hundred family units.

References

Appelbaum, Joy Zacharia. *The History of the Jews of Teaneck* (Teaneck, NJ: 1976).
Synagogue Histories File, American Jewish Archives.

MONMOUTH REFORM, REFORM. *Tinton Falls, New Jersey.* During the winter months of 1958–1959, discussions took place concerning the need for a Reform congregation in the Tinton Falls area. Twenty-two families attended an organizational meeting in March 1959, holding their first services the following month. Shortly thereafter, the congregation joined the Union of American Hebrew Congregations, the national organization of Reform synagogues. For eight years, the congregation met in the Shrewsbury Presbyterian Church. Initially served by student rabbis and cantors from Hebrew Union College–Jewish Institute of Religion, Monmouth Reform elected its first ordained rabbi, Richard Steinbrink, two years after its founding (1961).

Steinbrink left in 1966, one year before the congregation, led by Rabbi Edward Ellenbogen, moved into its permanent home in Tinton Falls. Other rabbis followed: Harry Scherer (1970) and Alton Winters (1971–1981). Winters established a variety of adult education programs for the congregation.

In 1977, the congregation, with a membership of 190 families, expanded its facilities by building a wing for its religious school. Ten years later, the synagogue expanded once again, enlarging its sanctuary and social hall to accommodate its 250 member families.

Rabbi Sally Priesand, the first woman ordained a rabbi in America, joined the congregation in 1981. She encouraged the congregation to use more Hebrew in its liturgy, to read the Torah weekly (rather than monthly as had been the case), and to hold worship services on the festivals as they occur (rather than on the closest Sabbath). During her tenure, the congregation took a leadership role in the local community's anti–drunk driving coalition, as well as in Tinton Falls programs for feeding and providing shelter for the homeless. Monmouth

Reform Temple became one of the early members of the Union of American Hebrew Congregations to adopt constitutional policies with regard to the status of non-Jews in the congregation. In 1994, membership stood at 320, with a religious school enrollment of 186. The congregation anticipates the implementation of a building expansion program in the next few years.

References

Pine, Alan S., Jean C. Hershenov, and Aaron H. Lefkowitz. *Peddler to Suburbanite: The History of the Jews of Monmouth County, NJ* (Deal Park, NJ: 1981).
Synagogue History File, American Jewish Archives.

HAR SINAI CONGREGATION, REFORM. *Trenton, New Jersey.* Eleven men formed the Har Sinai Cemetery Association in 1857. These men founded Har Sinai Hebrew Congregation as an outgrowth of the Cemetery Association. Before the congregation's formal incorporation in 1860, founders met for religious services in private homes and then in rented quarters. In its early years, members conducted worship in German and Hebrew.

Leon Kahnweiler, president of Har Sinai, acquired for the congregation in 1866 its first permanent home, formerly a Lutheran chapel on North Montgomery Street. However, it seems that Kahnweiler never deeded the property to Har Sinai. Thus, owners sold the property at public auction in 1872. Left without a home, the congregation drifted until Toretta Kaufman set out to save the Montgomery Street property.

Har Sinai left Montgomery Street in 1903 and moved to Front and Stockton, where it erected its second house of worship the following year. Shortly thereafter, Har Sinai engaged Nathan Stern as its first Reform rabbi. English replaced German during worship. In 1922, the synagogue joined the Union of American Hebrew Congregations, the national organization of Reform synagogues. Rabbi Abraham Holtzberg joined Har Sinai in 1924.

Har Sinai dedicated its present structure on Bellevue Avenue in 1930. When Rabbi Holtzberg died in 1951, Rabbi Joshua O. Haberman came to Trenton to succeed him. He left in 1969, and Rabbi Bernard Perlmuter succeeded him. During his tenure, the congregation contemplated moving beyond West Trenton but the cost of the plan became prohibitive. In 1982, Har Sinai welcomed Rabbi David Gelfand to its pulpit. Rabbi David Straus succeeded him. In 1995, membership stood at 465.

References

128th Anniversary Service, Har Sinai Temple (Trenton, NJ: 1985).
Synagogue Histories File, American Jewish Archives.

NEW MEXICO

CONGREGATION ALBERT, REFORM. *Albuquerque, New Mexico.* Before the Territory of New Mexico was acquired by the United States as a result of the Mexican-American War (1846–1847), Jews were prohibited from entering it. Once the railroad reached Albuquerque, the city and its small Jewish community grew rapidly. Despite a great deal of activity, there was no permanent place for worship. In 1897, a group of "Hebrew citizens" met to form a congregation. Founders auctioned off the privilege of naming the congregation to the Grunsfeld family, who chose to honor the pioneer merchant Albert Grunsfeld, who had died in 1893.

Dr. William H. Greenburg came to serve Temple Albert as its rabbi in 1898. He guided the congregation as it prepared to move into its first permanent home at Seventh and Gold. Rabbi Pizer Jacobs succeeded Rabbi Greenburg in 1900, shortly before dedicating Temple Albert's new synagogue. The secretary of the congregation, Alphonse Fleischer, played a significant role in these early years, beginning with the establishment of religious school classes. Rabbi Jacobs left in 1902, and Rabbi Jacob H. Kaplan took over the religious leadership of the Temple. In 1905, Temple Albert organized a choir to sing during worship. When Jacobs left in 1907, members elected Rabbi Edward Chapman to occupy its pulpit. Under his guidance, Temple Albert's children organized the Temple Aid Society, for the purpose of charity and establishing a library.

Dr. Mendel Silber succeeded Rabbi Chapman in 1910. Then came Rabbi Moise Bergman (1914–1922). All of these early rabbis were active in bringing the Jewish and non-Jewish communities in contact with one another. In particular, Rabbi Silber led the members in organized relief for victims of World War I, as well as for the relief and rebuilding of Jewish communities in Palestine and help during the Spanish influenza epidemic of 1918.

Rabbi Raphael Goldenstein came to Temple Albert in 1923 to succeed Rabbi Silber. During his short tenure, the synagogue joined the Union of American Hebrew Congregations, the national organization of Reform synagogues; transformed the Ladies Aid Society into a Temple Sisterhood; and enlarged and reorganized the choir and Sunday School. Other rabbis followed: Dr. J. F. Schwab (1924), Dr. David Solomon Nathan (1925–1928), Herbert I. Bloom (1929–1931), and A. L. Krohn (1932–1938).

During the Depression, Temple Albert simply tried to keep itself afloat, encouraging nonmembers and members (even those in arrears) to attend worship services and programs. Discussions took place about whether to affiliate with a local Orthodox group to meet the financial pressures of the time. With sixty-four members and eleven Sunday School children in 1934, the congregation voted not to reduce dues and to try to continue as an institution.

Like many of his predecessors, Rabbi Krohn became actively involved in community concerns. When Krohn went to Washington on behalf of hard-hit farmers in the Middle Rio Grande Conservancy District, the board only marginally voted to retain his services. As a result, Rabbi Krohn decided to resign. Rabbi Solomon Starrels succeeded him in 1938.

While membership reached eighty-seven in 1944, World War II dampened the desire of members to participate in congregational activities and worship.

When Rabbi Starrels resigned in 1948, Rabbi David Shor began his long tenure with Temple Albert and its membership of 125 families. A growth in membership necessitated a move to larger facilities. Thus, Temple Albert moved to Lead Avenue, between Oak and Mulberry 1951. Two years later, the membership of Temple Albert added a religious school wing to its new building. By 1958, membership grew to 250 families. Thus, more classrooms were added to the already enlarged structure.

When Rabbi Shor retired in 1978, Rabbi Paul Citrin joined Temple Albert. He encouraged the work of the Temple's Social Action Committee to respond to the needs of the community. In addition, Rabbi Citrin emphasized congregational support for Israel. During his tenure, the congregation initiated the Temple Albert Summer Academy day camp and the Parenting Support Group for parents of infants and toddlers. In 1980, Temple Albert sponsored the immigration of a brother and sister from Vietnam to Albuquerque, and in 1982 the congregation moved into new facilities at Natalie and Louisiana, NE. By 1994 membership reached nearly six hundred family units.

References

"First Synagogue at Albuquerque." *Western States Jewish Historical Quarterly* 11, no. 1 (October 1978): 46–48.
Rothenberg, Gunther. *Congregation Albert, 1897–1972* (Albuquerque: 1972).
A Time for Dedication: Temple Albert (Albuquerque: 1984).

NEW YORK

TEMPLE BETH EMETH, REFORM. *Albany, New York.* Founders organized the congregation, North America's fourth-oldest Reform synagogue, under the name Beth El in 1838. The following year, these founders dedicated their first house of worship on Bassett Street. Two years later, congregants purchased a church building on Herkimer Street, which they converted into a synagogue (dedicated 1842). The secession of eight members in 1841 to form Beth El-Jacob undoubtedly stimulated this move. Rabbi Isaac Mayer Wise, the organizer of Reform Judaism in America, came to Beth El in 1846. He introduced several changes at Beth El that were not universally well received. He insisted on decorum during worship. He introduced a mixed choir that sang both English and German hymns. Wise also shortened certain prayers and eliminated others.

As a result of an altercation between Wise and temple leadership during Rosh Hashanah 1850, the congregation splintered into two groups. The group loyal to Wise withdrew from Beth El and founded Congregation Anshe Emeth, meeting for the first time for worship on Yom Kippur at Madison Avenue and Pearl Street, then at Green and Hamilton. By the following year, this new group purchased a church building at South Pearl and Herkimer and converted it for use as a synagogue. Anshe Emeth members instituted family pews in their synagogue, apparently the first congregation in North America to do so. Wise served this new synagogue until he left for Cincinnati in 1854 when Rabbi Elkan Cohn succeeded him, serving for six years. While maintaining a two-day observance of Rosh Hashanah, he discontinued the practice of observing the second day of other holidays. Rabbi Martin Mayer served Anshe Emeth briefly before Dr. Max Schlesinger succeeded him in 1864.

Beth El continued its separate existence in its new home at Ferry and Franlin (dedicated 1864) until 1885 when, unable to secure the services of a religious leader, it merged with Anshe Emeth. Merger discussions began as early as 1875. As families held dual memberships and Beth El adopted the reforms that once separated them, a merger became possible. Dr. Schlesinger led this new congregation, now called Beth Emeth. In 1889, the enlarged group moved to a new location at Lancaster, Swan, and Jay Streets. Dr. Martin Meyer succeeded Schlesinger, serving from 1903 to 1906. His successor, Samuel Goldenson, came to Albany in 1907. Goldenson served until 1918, when Eli Mayer succeeded him. Rabbi Marius Ranson served from 1921 to 1929, when Rabbi Bernard Bamberger came to lead the congregation. During his tenure, Beth Emeth underwent a difficult time of economic distress and social upheaval.

Rabbi Samuel Wolk succeeded Bamberger in 1945. During his term of office, Beth Emeth moved to Academy Road where Percival Goodman designed a new home for the congregation (dedicated in 1957, a short time after Rabbi Wolk's death). Rabbi Alvin Roth succeeded Wolk, having come to Albany to serve as assistant the previous year. As temple membership grew rapidly, so did the need for a new building. Thus, expansion took place in 1959. By 1962, Beth Emeth's membership stood at over one thousand family units and continued to grow.

In an unusual relationship, Rabbis Bernard Bloom and Martin Silverman served as co-rabbis from 1972 to 1984. When Bloom left Beth Emeth, Silverman remained as senior rabbi. Rabbi Scott Shpeen became senior rabbi in 1992, having joined the congregation in 1985 as assistant.

References

Congregation Beth Emeth, 1838–1938 (Albany, NY: 1938).
Congregation Beth Emeth of Albany, New York: Its History and Ideals (Albany, NY: 1957).
Synagogue Histories File, American Jewish Archives.

HEBREW INSTITUTE OF RIVERDALE, ORTHODOX. *Bronx, New York.* Orthodox residents of the University Heights community in the Bronx founded the Hebrew Institute of University Heights in 1918. It met in rented facilities for ten years before developing its permanent home on University Avenue (1928). In 1968, the congregation rented a private home on Andrews Avenue to accommodate additional worshipers. These rabbis served the congregation: Simon G. Kramer (1938–1963) and Maurice Lamm (1963–1970). In his rabbinate, Kramer emphasized the building of post-Holocaust European Jewry, support for the State of Israel, and the education of children through the development of a day-school movement. When Lamm came to the congregation, the West Bronx neighborhood was already changing. Thus, he focused on programs that he believed would help stabilize the congregation in the area. These included adult education, the men's club and sisterhood, and the development of the Akiba Hebrew Academy. Toward the end of his tenure, he devoted his energies to the relocation of the synagogue. Following the sale of the University Heights building in 1968, members still held services in that locale until approximately 1975, when few members were left to warrant the effort.

Following a decline in the University Heights neighborhood, thirty-five former member families of the Hebrew Institute, who relocated to Riverdale, established the Hebrew Institute of Riverdale in 1971. The fifty members of the new Hebrew Institute met at the Whitehall on Henry Hudson Parkway. Rabbi Avraham (Avi) Weiss became the religious leader of the congregation in 1973. Weiss concentrated his efforts on education and outreach, and he developed an international reputation in the area of activism, especially on behalf of Soviet Jewry and Israel. Weiss developed an adult education program (the Alan Wasserman Midrasha) and a supplementary school program (the Jewish Youth Encounter Program). He also developed programs for women, helping to define the role of Orthodox women in prayer. In addition, he concentrated his efforts on the physically and mentally challenged, as well as elderly shut-ins in the Bronx.

In 1980, the Hebrew Institute built its own permanent facility on the Henry Hudson Parkway in Riverdale and converted an adjacent private home. Though there is a *mechitza* (partition separating men and women during worship), men and women have equal access to the *bima* (raised platform in the front of the sanctuary). There is an emphasis on equality of participation within an Orthodox context. Thus, there are no seats for rabbis or officers on the *bima* itself. Women hold monthly separate worship services in the social hall, and beginner's services are held in the adjacent building. Many people take advantage of the variety of programs at the Hebrew Institute, and the congregation listed over 650 membership units in 1996.

Reference

Personal interview, David Mann, July 5, 1996.

RIVERDALE TEMPLE, REFORM. *Bronx, New York.* Sixty-seven local residents founded the Riverdale Temple as a "liberal congregation" in 1947. Rabbi Charles Shulman became the synagogue's first religious leader. Shortly after the organization of the congregation, members started a religious school and established a sisterhood. Shulman introduced the wearing of a tallith and a head covering during worship, as well as two days of holiday observance. At the same time, he instituted a professional choir of non-Jews. In its early years, the congregation met in a variety of temporary locations. In 1954, Riverdale Temple dedicated its home at 246th Street and Independence Avenue in the Bronx.

Following Shulman's death in 1968, the congregation elected Rabbi Morris Kertzer, a popular author and graduate of the Conservative Jewish Theological Seminary, to its pulpit. Six years later, Burt Siegel, a Reform rabbi who had served as assistant to Kertzer, succeeded him. He focused on teaching in his rabbinate.

In 1979, the congregation elected Stephen Franklin, also a Reform rabbi, to the pulpit. Under his direction, Riverdale Temple instituted a policy of tuition-free education in its Religious and Hebrew Schools. Franklin worked to improve the aesthetic of worship through the expansion of choral music and the use of the organ during worship. In addition, the congregation developed a nursery school and summer day camp. Riverdale Temple affiliated with the Union of American Hebrew Congregations, the national body of Reform synagogues (1947–1979, then again in 1988). In 1994, the membership of Riverdale Temple exceeded 735 family units.

Reference

Synagogue Histories File, American Jewish Archives.

TREMONT TEMPLE/SCARSDALE SYNAGOGUE, REFORM. *Bronx (later Scarsdale), New York.* Fourteen women met in the Bronx in 1906 to form the Tremont Sisterhood, primarily to establish a Jewish school for children in the neighborhood. Shortly after the school's founding, these women recognized that the school needed a synagogue to nurture Jewish youth into adulthood. Thus, joined by a group of men in the community, they decided to organize a Reform congregation (the Tremont Temple Society), with the help of Rabbi Rudolph Grossman. During these early days, the congregation met at the New Masonic Temple on Washington Avenue. Rabbi Clifton Harby Levy joined Tremont Temple as its first religious leader in 1906. Shortly after he joined the congregation, Tremont Temple introduced Confirmation (1908).

When the congregation obtained its charter in 1909, it originally sought the name Kol-Hoamim (For all the people). Members abandoned that name in favor of Tremont Temple Shaare Elohim, Congregation Gates of Mercy, stipulating that women would not be considered eligible for membership. In 1916, Tremont Temple adopted the *Union Prayer Book,* the prayer book of the Reform movement. Rabbi Levy resigned in 1919, and Rabbi Maurius Ranson succeeded him.

The Temple's membership built its first home on the Grand Concourse and Boulevard between Tremont Avenue and 180th Street (dedicated 1910), building a sanctuary in 1920. Following Rabbi Ranson's one-year tenure, several rabbis succeeded him for similarly short periods of time—often leaving over controversies about ritual matters and matters of freedom of the pulpit—before the election of Rabbi Irving F. Reichert in 1923, the year after the temple joined the Union of American Hebrew Congregations, the national body of Reform congregations. Prior to Rabbi Reichert's engagement with the congregation, local Sinai Temple unsuccessfully approached Tremont Temple to amalgamate the two synagogues. Reichert served until 1930 when Rabbi L. Elliot Grafman joined Tremont Temple. Again Sinai came to Tremont Temple for a possible merger. With the temple suffering financial hardship, Grafman left in 1934, when Rabbi Jerome Rosenbloom came to serve the congregation.

By 1943, membership dwindled to eighty-six families. Two years later, Rabbi Albert S. Goldstein succeeded Rabbi Rosenbloom. Tremont Temple engaged Rabbi Maurice J. Bloom in 1955. Membership increased to 380 by 1956. Bloom served until the early 1960s, when Rabbi Abraham Krantz succeeded him, serving until 1975. During the last years of his tenure, the Temple struggled to survive in the Bronx and even created a branch (Temple Beth El) at Co-Op City.

Founders established Scarsdale Synagogue in 1961, with Rabbi David Greenberg (1961–1980) as its religious leader. Members held services at the local Congregational church. Scarsdale Synagogue joined the Union of American Hebrew Congregations in 1963. Four years later, the women of the congregation formed a sisterhood. In 1969, the congregation built classrooms, offices, and a social hall on Ogden Road in Scarsdale. In 1976, Scarsdale Synagogue merged with Tremont Temple. The merged congregation built a new sanctuary on Ogden Road in 1977, funded by the sale of Tremont Temple's Grand Concourse building.

Members elected Rabbi Stephen A. Klein to the pulpit of the merged congregation in 1981. Under his direction, members actively participated in a Helping Hands Committee and in social action projects, such as a program to feed the homeless and hungry. Klein moved the congregation to celebrate holidays on their actual days rather than on the closest Sunday, which had been Greenberg's practice. In 1995, membership stood at four hundred family units.

References

Religion Is the Life of Israel (New York: 1929).
Rubinstein, Peter. "A History of the First Thirty Years of the Existence of Tremont Temple of the Bronx" (Term paper, Hebrew Union College–Jewish Institute of Religion, 1967).
Synagogue Histories File, American Jewish Archives.

CONGREGATION BAITH ISRAEL ANSHEI EMES (KANE STREET SYNAGOGUE), CONSERVATIVE. *Brooklyn, New York.* In 1854, twelve Bavarian and Dutch Jews joined together to form the nucleus of Congregation Baith Israel in Brooklyn. This group formally organized the congregation in 1856. In the early years, members met at various homes for worship before establishing a temporary place of worship on Atlantic Street (now Avenue). In 1862, with a membership of thirty-five, congregants built a synagogue on Boerum Place and State Street. Thus, this facility became known as the Boerum Schule. There Baith Israel started a Sunday School. In the new location, members made several failed attempts at ritual reform. As a result, several discontented members left to form Beth Elohim, a Reform congregation. Nevertheless, the membership did institute these reforms at Baith Israel: abolition of the greater part of the *piyyutim* (liturgical poems) and *duchenen* (priestly blessing) and the establishment of family pews. Baith Israel held its first confirmation for girls in 1873, and in 1904 the congregation installed a pipe organ and established a mixed choir.

In the latter year, membership dwindled to thirty. The congregation acquired a church and adjacent school building at Harrison Street (now Kane Street) and Tompkins Place, which it converted for use as a synagogue (dedicated 1905). That same year, the synagogue called Rabbi Israel Goldfarb to its pulpit. Shortly after his arrival, he established a Talmud Torah. During his early tenure, the congregation's membership and program of activity expanded.

In 1908, Talmud Torah Anshei Emes of Degraw Street merged into Baith Israel to form Baith Israel Anshei Emes. That same year, the women of the merged congregation formed a sisterhood. Three years later, the members renovated the synagogue. In 1913, the synagogue became a founding member of the United Synagogue of America (now the United Synagogue of Conservative Judaism), the national organization of Conservative synagogues. In 1924, a fire nearly destroyed the upper floor of the school building, but the damage was repaired. In 1953, members renovated the synagogue once again.

In 1960, Rabbi Goldfarb retired. Several rabbis succeeded him on a part-time basis. One of these rabbis, Raymond Scheindlin (1979–1982), started a choir program and founded the DeRossi Singers, singing music of the composer Salomone DeRossi. In 1971, members formed a Young Couples Club. The following year, members established a nursery school and a *prozdor* (high school). That same year, the congregation elected its first woman to the board of trustees. In 1975, Baith Israel counted women in the minyan and gave them Torah honors.

In 1982, Jonathan Ginsburg became the congregation's first full-time rabbi since Goldfarb's retirement. He established an Adult Education Institute, raised the educational standards of the religious education programs for children, and developed programs for young singles. Rabbi Jonathan Ginsburg left the congregation in 1987; Geoffrey Goldberg (1987–1988) succeeded him. Rabbi Debra Cantor joined the congregation as its religious leader in 1988. In 1995, membership neared two hundred family units.

Reference

Synagogue Histories Collection, The Joseph and Miriam Ratner Center for the Study of Conservative Judaism.

CONGREGATION BETH ELOHIM, REFORM. *Brooklyn, New York.* In the midst of Civil War strife, a group of forty-one people met in downtown Brooklyn in 1861 to form Beth Elohim. George Brandenstein served as the first religious leader. The congregation met for worship at Granada Hall on Myrtle Avenue. Brandenstein led worship in German and Hebrew. Shortly after these first services, the congregation moved into a former church on Pearl Street, near Sands (dedicated 1862). In this location, the women of the congregation organized themselves into the Ladies' Society Benos Zion, focusing primarily on charitable activities. When membership reached over eighty in 1882, Beth Elohim sought another location to house its growing congregation. Thus, Beth Elohim's members moved to another former church on State Street, near Hoyt (dedicated 1885), under the leadership of Dr. Samuel Sparger, who succeeded Brandenstein in the pulpit.

In the new location, members installed an organ and introduced a choir for worship. English slowly replaced German during worship. The congregation opened its religious school to all children in the community, regardless of their synagogue affiliation. In 1991, Dr. George Taubenhaus succeeded Dr. Sparger as religious leader of Beth Elohim. Under his direction, the congregation eliminated the observance of the second day of holidays. He left the congregation in 1901.

Rabbi Alexander Lyons succeeded Taubenhaus in the pulpit (1902–1939). During his tenure, women formed the Women's Auxiliary (later to be called Sisterhood). Lyons tried to bring Judaism's message to non-Jews in the community. In 1909, members consecrated Beth Elohim's current home at Eighth Avenue and Garfield Place. Twenty years later, on the opposite corner, members dedicated the six-story Temple House, used for all congregational activities. Shortly thereafter, the Depression took its toll on the financial resources of the congregation. As a result, membership dropped significantly.

Rabbi Isaac Landman joined the congregation to assist Lyons in 1931. When Lyons died in 1939, Landman became the sole rabbi in the congregation, serving until 1946. Landman focused his attention on Jewish scholarship, and later he became editor of the *Universal Jewish Encyclopedia*. In his first year at Beth Elohim, he started an Adult Academy Program with courses and speakers.

Like Landman, Rabbi Eugene Sack came to Beth Elohim as an assistant. When Landman died a few months after Sack's arrival in 1946, Sack continued to serve the congregation. Soon after he arrived, the bank threatened foreclosure on the temple, anticipating the sale of the buildings to the local Catholic diocese.

Following the successful renegotiation of finances, Beth Elohim entered a phase of growth. The congregation upgraded its religious education program. The congregation granted women full membership privileges. In 1953, membership exceeded seven hundred families, with a religious school population of over 550 children. Sack put into place an extensive array of programs and activities in the congregation.

Sacks retired in 1978 just as Brooklyn experienced a renaissance. Rabbi Gerald Weider succeeded him as religious leader of Beth Elohim. Under his direction, the synagogue expanded its programs for youth and fulfilled its original vision of making Beth Elohim a synagogue center, in the vision of Mordecai Kaplan. In 1990, the congregation completely repaired and restored the synagogue and Temple Center. During Weider's tenure, Beth Elohim opened an after-school center (1978), early childhood center (1978), and day camp (1979). In 1994, membership of Beth Elohim exceeded 485 family units. In 1995, the congregation anticipated opening a day school.

References

The 130th Anniversary Celebration, Congregation Beth Elohim (Brooklyn, NY: 1992).
Religion Is the Life of Israel (New York: 1929).
Synagogue Histories File, American Jewish Archives.

BROOKLYN JEWISH CENTER, CONSERVATIVE. *Brooklyn, New York.* In 1919, Louis Cohen—along with Moses Ginsberg and Samuel Rottenberg— organized the Brooklyn Jewish Center, the second New York City congregation to function as both synagogue and center (under the influence of Rabbi Mordecai Kaplan, founder of the Reconstructionist movement). Together these men purchased land on Eastern Parkway, between Brooklyn and New York Avenues. Rather than depending on donations, as for most building projects, they financed the center through floating a bond issue. With temporary offices nearby on Eastern Parkway, membership quickly rose to one hundred. As soon as founders built a basement, the center held High Holiday services. In the same unfinished structure, they established a school. In 1920, Rabbi Israel H. Leventhal became the founding rabbi of the Brooklyn Jewish Center. Shortly thereafter, membership rose to two hundred. As the building grew closer to completion, the center implemented more activities, including an extensive program of adult education. Even Columbia University established an extension center in the new facility. This model facility sought to serve the religious, cultural, recreational, and social needs of the local Jewish community.

By 1922, the Brooklyn Jewish Center listed five hundred members, representing a variety of religious affiliations. As a result, members faced many ritual decisions. Seating arrangements in the new synagogue posed the first obstacle. In a search for a new approach to tradition, members reserved center-aisle seating for men and women who wanted to sit together during worship. Likewise, they arranged outside sections for separate seating of men and women.

The congregation in its early years faced severe financial challenges that hampered the completion of the building (dedicated 1922). It sold pews to raise funds, initially refusing, however, to place memorial plaques anywhere in the building. Later, financial necessity forced the modification of this practice.

In the early years of the Brooklyn Jewish Center, members implemented a highly successful weekly public forum lecture that featured prominent speakers of national reknown. These auditorium lectures drew large crowds. This forced the second major ritual controversy in the congregation over whether to require the wearing of hats should the lectures be moved to the sanctuary. As a compromise, program planners held the lectures in the sanctuary only when the lecturer consented to wear a hat during the presentation.

The Brooklyn Jewish Center quickly became the focal point for a great deal of Brooklyn Jewish activity. Organizations held meetings and banquets there. By the end of 1923, membership exceeded one thousand. In 1927, the Center engaged playwright Moss Hart as its social director. To meet the needs of its members, the center issued a periodical, which developed in 1933 to a weekly twenty-four-page magazine called the *Brooklyn Jewish Center Review,* edited by Louis J. Gribetz. That same year, Albert Einstein dedicated a library at the center for Nazi-banned books. During World War II, as the center again faced severe financial difficulties, its members launched a committee on Civilian War Activities, which mobilized the community for a total war effort. Like many similar congregations, the Brooklyn Jewish Center reached its membership peak in the 1960s. On a typical Sabbath morning, 250 people worshiped in its sanctuary. The decline of substantial numbers of young children led to the close of its afternoon religious school. The construction of municipal housing projects in the area brought a sudden influx of children into the public schools. In response, young parents left the area surrounding the synagogue.

Rabbi Abraham Bloch succeeded Rabbi Leventhal in 1980, when the latter religious leader retired from the active rabbinate. Because of financial circumstances, the congregation—while still worshiping in its building—sold its facility to Ohole Torah, a Lubavitch elementary school. As a result, it confined its activities to Sabbath and holiday services, as well as a modest program of weekend activities. In 1994, the congregation attracted only twenty-five people regularly to Sabbath morning services.

References

Jubilee Book of the Brooklyn Jewish Center (Brooklyn: 1946).
Synagogue Histories Collection, The Joseph and Miriam Ratner Center for the Study of
    Conservative Judaism.
Synagogue Histories File, American Jewish Archives.

UNION TEMPLE, REFORM. *Brooklyn, New York.* In 1851, a group of Alsatian and German immigrants founded an Orthodox synagogue in Brooklyn under the name Kahal Kadosh Beth Elohim. The group rented quarters on North Second Street before purchasing a former church on South First Street in 1860. At this location, Beth Elohim also operated a day school for its children. In 1876, this group built a new home on Keap Street, thereby acquiring the name "the Keap Street Temple." The congregation used this building until its merger with Temple Israel in 1921.

Synagogue founders established Temple Israel in 1869 as a Reform congregation. It worshiped first in the YMCA building at Fulton Avenue and Galatin Place, before converting a former church on the south side of Greene Avenue in 1872. Raphael Lewin served Temple Israel as its first religious leader. Temple Israel remained in this location until 1891, when it consecrated a new building at Bedford and Lafayette Avenues. It built a school building in 1901. Among the many religious leaders who served Temple Israel, these individuals led the congregation: Rabbi Leon Harrison (1886–1891), Alexander H. Geismar (1892–1898), Leon M. Nelson (1898–1904), Rabbi Judah L. Magnes (1904–1906), Martin A. Meyer (1906–1908), and Nathan Krass (1908–1917). During Harrison's tenure, membership increased. He established a Ladies Aid Society in 1886. Magnes concentrated his efforts on education.

Beth Elohim adopted certain reforms during its early history. During the ministry of Rabbi Isaac Schwab (1876–1878), Beth Elohim introduced *Minhag America,* the prayer book of Isaac Mayer Wise, the founder of American Reform Judaism. When Beth Elohim merged with Temple Israel to become Union Temple in 1921, the combined institution continued on the path of Reform Judaism. This newly amalgamated synagogue built an eleven-story Temple House on Eastern Parkway (dedicated 1926). This self-contained building, not unusual for synagogue architecture of its period, eventually included a gymnasium, a roof garden, a banquet hall, and a ballroom in addition to a sanctuary, classrooms, and meeting space. The Depression undermined plans for a separate sanctuary. Thus, in 1942, the congregation changed its auditorium (designed originally as theater and concert hall) into a sanctuary.

Union Temple invited Rabbi Sidney S. Tedesche to its pulpit in 1929. He succeeded Rabbi Simon Cohen (1907–1929) and Rabbi Louis Gross (1917–1921), who had served Beth Elohim and Israel before the merger. During World War II, Union Temple opened its doors to service personnel while transforming itself into a Red Cross workshop, blood bank station, and emergency disaster center.

In 1955, Rabbi Tedesche retired, and Rabbi Alfred L. Friedman succeeded him. The following year, membership peaked at 872 families. By 1963, suburbanization ill-affected the membership, reducing its rolls to 676. Following the services of an interim rabbi in 1965, Rabbi A. Stanley Dreyfus joined the congregation and served until 1979. These rabbis succeeded Dreyfus: Charles D. Mintz (1979–1981), Jay J. Sangerman (1981–1983), Neal I. Borovitz (1983–1988), Selig Salkowitz (1988–1992), and Linda Henry Goodman (1992–   ). Union Temple's program of activity includes a preschool and a religious school, as well as a program of Adult Jewish Studies. In 1994, membership of Union Temple stood at 230.

References

Religion Is the Life of Israel (New York: 1929).
Synagogue Histories File, American Jewish Archives.

TEMPLE BETH EL, CONSERVATIVE. *Buffalo, New York.* Twelve men met together in 1847 in the Western Hotel (Pearl Street and the Terrace) to found the first Jewish congregation in Buffalo, only twelve years after the first Jew settled in the city. This congregation, chartered as Synagogue Beth El, began its religious activity in the home of Abraham Jacobs on Beak Street before moving into the Hoyt Building on Main Street. Abraham Ansel (1848–?)

served the congregation as its first religious leader. In 1848, members moved the locus of activity to the Armory on Main and Eagle Streets; and in 1850, Beth El dedicated its first synagogue building on Pearl Street.

Noted philanthropist Judah Touro bequeathed funds to Beth El on his death in 1854 that significantly bolstered the finances of the congregation. By the following year, membership reached over sixty. Fire from a local hotel severely damaged the synagogue building in 1865, but the congregation did not move to Elm Street until 1874. In 1881, Beth El members abolished the practice of auctioning Torah honors and then distributing tickets for them.

At the end of the nineteenth century, Beth El members faced their first ritual challenge when they voted to allow men and women to sit together during worship. Beth El moved to Richmond Avenue in 1911, two years after the Beth El Women's Society came into being. Beth El affiliated with the United Synagogue of America (now the United Synagogue of Conservative Judaism), the national organization of conservative synagogues, at its founding in 1913. Between 1913 and 1919, membership grew from 68 to 250, thus placing the financial foundation of the temple on a sound basis.

Following nearly eight years of discussion, Beth El installed an organ in the temple in 1930. In 1944, members expanded the synagogue to include an enlarged auditorium, additional classrooms, an enlarged kitchen, and a recreation room. That same year, girls won the right to celebrate a Bat Mitzvah in the congregation. Beth El moved to Eggert Road at Sheridan Drive in suburban Tonawanda in 1982.

Following Ansel's tenure, numerous men served the congregation as religious leaders for brief periods. These men enjoyed longer tenures: H. Lowenthal (1860–1862), Israel Warrensky (1862–1872), Philip Bernstein (1872–1878), Bernard Cohn (1878–1882; 1889–1895), David Wittenberg (1895–1899), L. Ettinger (1900–1906), Arthur Ginzler (1906–1910), Jacob Landau (1911–1913), Max Drob (1913–1919), M. Menachem Eichler (1919–1927), Israel Efros (1928–1934), Reuben J. Magil (1935–1940), H. Elihu Rickel (1940–?), Gershon Rosenstock (?–1951), Milton Feierstein (1951–1971), Herman Horowitz (1971–1976), and Samuel Porath (1976–1989). In 1989, Robert Eisen became the religious leader of the congregation and emphasized adult education in his rabbinate. In 1995, membership at Beth El exceeded 575 family units.

References

Adler, Selig, and Thomas Connolly. *From Ararat to Suburbia: The History of the Jewish Community of Buffalo* (Philadelphia: 1960).
Synagogue Histories File, American Jewish Archives.
Temple Beth El's First Century (Buffalo, NY: 1947).

BETH ZION TEMPLE, REFORM. *Buffalo, New York.* In 1850, eleven men, dissatisfied with the Polish rite at Beth El, formed Beth Zion, using a German liturgy. It met in several temporary locations until it disbanded about the year

1863. At just about the same time, twenty-two men gathered at the Lower Kremlin Hall on Main Street to organize a new Beth Zion, the first Reform congregation in Buffalo. Within days, twenty-four additional people joined their efforts. Members invited Dr. Isaac N. Cohen to serve them as their first religious leader. Toward the end of 1864, this growing group purchased a former church on Niagara Street (dedicated 1865). Even in this new institution, reforms did not come easily. In 1868, the Ritual Committee was instructed to include the wearing of hats as a requirement for worship. Nevertheless, Beth Zion became a charter member of the Union of American Hebrew Congregations, the national body of Reform synagogues, when it was founded in 1873. That same year, members abolished the use of German in the temple school. By 1878, the struggle over head coverings surfaced again. This resulted in the decision to allow members to choose whether or not they wished to cover their heads during worship.

Under the direction of Rabbi Samson Falk, Beth Zion established its place in the community. Rabbi Israel Aaron succeeded him in 1887. During his tenure, Beth Zion held services in a variety of locations before moving to Allen and North Streets in 1890, to a new, exotic Byzantine structure designed by Edward A. Kent. When Rabbi Aaron died in 1912, Rabbi Louis J. Kopald assumed the pulpit (1913). Two years later, members expanded the new building by adding classrooms, a gymnasium, and a small auditorium. By this time, membership had increased to 270.

Illness forced the retirement of Rabbi Kopald in 1922. His assistant, Rabbi Joseph L. Fink, was elected to succeed him in 1926. Three years later, Beth Zion expanded its facilities once again, adding additional classrooms and office space. Like his predecessor, Rabbi Fink retired because of illness. Rabbi Martin Goldberg, who had served the congregation as associate, assumed the responsibilities of leading Beth Zion, succeeding him in 1959.

In 1961, a fire completely destroyed Beth Zion. In addition to a variety of temporary locations, the congregation met in the suburban branch of Beth Zion built in 1958 to serve the religious education needs of the synagogue's children. Members waited until 1967 before dedicating their new house of worship. In 1972, a splinter group of Temple Beth Zion joined some unaffiliated members of the Buffalo Jewish community to form Congregation Havurah, a group seeking greater participation in worship and ritual. Rabbi Ronne Friedman became the congregation's religious leader in 1994. The membership of Beth Zion in 1995 exceeded 1250 family units.

References

Adler, Selig, and Thomas Connolly. *From Ararat to Suburbia: The History of the Jewish Community of Buffalo* (Philadelphia: 1960).
Fiftieth Anniversary (Buffalo, NY: 1915).
Synagogue Histories File, American Jewish Archives.

TEMPLE BETH-EL, REFORM. *Great Neck, New York.* In 1928, four men, commuting on a train to New York City, conceived of the idea to organize a religious school and High Holiday services in Great Neck in order to lay "the foundation for a permanent Temple." With the assistance of prayer books and a Torah from Central Synagogue, eighty-six family units attended the first service at the local Community Church. Shortly thereafter, the new congregation installed Rabbi David Goodis as rabbi of the congregation. The group held Sunday School classes at Kensington School.

Following Rabbi Goodis's untimely death in 1930, Rabbi Jacob Philip Rudin came to serve Beth-El. Rudin worked hard at bringing the Jewish community and the non-Jewish community together, especially through the vehicle of choir music. While the congregation sought to serve Jews of all affiliations, the Temple was decidedly Reform from its inception. Initially, Beth-El held Bar Mitzvahs. In 1932 Rabbi Rudin determined that the ceremony interfered with Confirmation. (Later, in 1951, Rudin partially made up for this decision by celebrating the Bar Mitzvah of eight adult men.) In 1932, with a membership of 135 family units, Beth-El built its own house of worship on Old Mill Road. The congregation concentrated its efforts on adult education by establishing an Adult School of Jewish Studies. Years later it became an extension program of Hebrew Union College–Jewish Institute of Religion, New York. In 1940, several individuals in the congregation, with the encouragement of congregational leaders, formed Temple Israel, a Conservative congregation.

In 1946, the ceremony of Bar Mitzvah returned to Beth-El. The following year, the synagogue joined the Union of American Hebrew Congregations, the national body of Reform congregations. While Rudin served in the Navy, Rabbi Abram M. Granison led the congregation (1941–1944). From the beginning of statehood, Rudin led the congregation in its ardent support of Israel.

Following World War II, the suburbs grew and so did Beth-El's membership: to seven hundred in 1950. Thus, Beth-El added a variety of programs for its young people. To accommodate its school enrollment of over six hundred, Beth-El expanded its facilities in 1950. In the late 1950s, with an overflowing membership, a group of Beth-El members formed another Reform institution, Temple Emanuel.

In 1970, Beth-El expanded once again. Having come in 1958 as assistant rabbi, Rabbi Jerome Davidson became senior rabbi at Beth-El in 1971, when Rudin retired. Davidson drew the congregation into controversies over the Vietnam War, the civil rights struggle and the plight of Soviet Jews. He also focused his energies on the youth of Beth-El. In 1974, a group of women celebrated what the congregation called *Ayshet Mitzvah* (Bat Mitzvah for a woman). That same year, Beth-El introduced the *Gates of Prayer* prayer book. Cantor Barbara Ostfeld Horowitz, the first woman invested as cantor, served Beth-El from 1976 to 1988. In 1994, membership of Beth-El exceeded 1640.

References

Deckoff, Harold, ed. *Temple Beth-El of Great Neck Dedication Book* (Great Neck, NY: 1950).

Fiftieth Anniversary, Temple Beth El, Great Neck, New York (Great Neck, NY: 1978).
Synagogue Histories File, American Jewish Archives.
Temple Beth-El of Great Neck (Great Neck, NY: 1988).

YOUNG ISRAEL OF NEW ROCHELLE, ORTHODOX. *New Rochelle, New York.* Following the growth of the Orthodox Jewish community in New Rochelle, a small number of families joined together in 1968 to form Young Israel of New Rochelle. This young congregation immediately affiliated with the National Council of Young Israel, the national organization of Young Israel synagogues. The group met for worship on Coligni Avenue (1968–1972) before moving in 1972 to North Avenue. Members elected Rabbi Stanley Wechsler (1968–1980) as the congregation's religious leader before inviting Rabbi Reuven Fink (1981–   ) to lead them. Whereas Rabbi Wechsler had worked to organize this developing congregation, Rabbi Fink stressed education for youth and adults in his tenure. In 1995, membership of the Young Israel of New Rochelle exceeded two hundred family units.

Reference

Personal interview, Reuven Fink, July 26, 1995.

ANSCHE CHESED, CONSERVATIVE. *New York, New York.* In 1828, a group of German, Dutch, and Polish Jews seceded from B'nai Jeshurun to form Ansche Chesed. The congregation began its worship in rented quarters on Grand Street before it moved in 1836 to a group of rooms at Center and White Streets above the New York Dispensary. Leo Merzbacher became the first religious leader of the congregation in 1843. He served simultaneously at Rodeph Sholom. Max Lilienthal succeeded Merzbacher in 1845 as rabbi of the United German community including Ansche Chesed, Rodeph Sholom, and Shaarey Hashamayim.

In the 1860s the congregation moved to Norfolk Street. In this location, members introduced family pews and a pipe organ. In 1873, Ansche Chesed built a new synagogue at Sixty-third Street and Lexington Avenue. A year later, the congregation merged with Adas Jeshurun to become Temple Beth-El. This new congregation merged with Congregation Emanu-El.

However, in 1876, a group calling itself Chebra Ansche Chesed—perhaps dissatisfied with the merger—formed on the East Side. Following the movement of the Jewish community to Harlem, the group relocated in 1893 and incorporated two years later as Congregation Ansche Chesed. In 1908, the new Ansche Chesed and its seventy members dedicated a Harlem synagogue on 114th Street and Seventh Avenue. Nearly a decade later, Ansche Chesed joined the United Synagogue of America (now the United Synagogue of Conservative Judaism), the national organization of Conservative synagogues.

Following the move of congregational members to the Upper West Side, under the direction of Rabbi Jacob Kohn (1911–1931), the congregation built a new synagogue at One-hundredth Street and West End Avenue (dedicated 1928). Following the Depression, Kohn left as a result of the congregation's inability to pay his salary. Thus, student rabbis served the congregation. In the early decades of the synagogue in this new location, renowned Cantor Adolph Katchko led worship services. The congregation also became home to Beit Hayeled, a progressive Jewish school.

Rabbi Joseph Zeitlin followed Kohn. His ardent Zionism drew sharp criticism from members and eventually led to his dismissal. Yet he succeeded in developing a West Side Community Center at Ansche Chesed. These rabbis followed Zeitlin: Manuel Saltzman (1952–1958), Morton Wallach (1962–1964), Joseph Sternstein (1964–1970), and Henry Glazer (1970–1981).

In the 1960s and 1970s, as the neighborhoods surrounding Ansche Chesed changed, membership in the congregation shrank dramatically. In 1979, with the impetus from Rabbi Wolfe Kelman, executive director of the (Conservative) Rabbinical Assembly, Ansche Chesed members invited young Jewish groups from the West Side to join the congregation as a means of preventing it from disappearing completely. In 1980 Rachel Cowan joined Ansche Chesed as part-time program coordinator. Along with her husband, writer Paul Cowan, she helped revitalize the synagogue by introducing a variety of programs into the congregation, including a Hanukkah arts festival. At the same time, different semiautonomous minyans began worshiping in separate spaces in the building. In addition, the Havurah School, an independent institution, took up residence at Ansche Chesed, as did the West Side Jewish Community School. Those who created *The Jewish Catalogue* and made it central to their Jewish lives repopulated the synagogue. These members rebuilt the synagogue and took on the responsibility of its function without the benefit of rabbinic leadership. Michael Strassfeld, the founding director of the National Havurah Committee and coauthor of *The Jewish Catalogue,* became Ansche Chesed's executive director. He later became its rabbi. In 1994, Ansche Chesed's membership totaled over 450 family units.

References

Ansche Chesed, 160 Years, Just the Beginning (New York: 1989).
Gurock, Jeffrey. *When Harlem Was Jewish, 1870–1930* (New York: 1979).
Synagogue Histories Collection, The Joseph and Miriam Ratner Center for the Study of Conservative Judaism.
Synagogue Histories File, American Jewish Archives.

B'NAI JESHURUN, CONSERVATIVE. *New York, New York.* Growing out of a dissatisfaction with the Sephardic customs at Shearith Israel, a group of twenty-eight Ashkenazi Jews formed B'nai Jeshurun in 1825. The group modeled its ritual on the Great Synagogue of London, looking to Chief Rabbi Solomon Hirschell of that city for guidance. One-and-a-half years later (1927), charter members dedicated their first synagogue on Elm Street. A variety of individuals, including Israel Baer Kursheedt, helped direct the course of the institution in its early years, and B'nai Jeshurun elected Samuel Isaacs as its religious leader in 1839. When the membership outgrew this facility (150 members), it built a new house of worship on Greene Street in 1850.

In 1944, before the move to Greene Street, the synagogue prevented a group of B'nai Jeshurun members, dissatisfied over an election of officers of the congregation, from entering the synagogue one Saturday morning to celebrate a Bar Mitzvah. The group that closed the synagogue, a minority of B'nai Jeshurun's members, left the congregation to organize Shaaray Tefila in a small downtown room in 1844. Samuel M. Isaacs, rabbi of B'nai Jeshurun, joined the new synagogue as its religious leader. At about the same time, B'nai Jeshurun eliminated the practice of selling Torah honors, opting instead for a rotation system.

Relations between Shearith Israel and B'nai Jeshurun always remained cordial. When B'nai Jeshurun inaugurated its ambitious Educational Institute in 1854, a large of group of members of Shearith Israel helped to sponsor the educational program. In the new Greene Street location, Morris J. Raphall, a defender of Orthodoxy and a controversial figure in the proslavery movement during the Civil War, served as B'nai Jeshurun's religious leader.

In 1865, members moved to a new synagogue on Thirty-fourth Street. Its membership included some of the most prominent of New York City's Jewish community. In the new location, the congregation placed the reading desk in the upper end of the synagogue rather than in the center aisle. Other changes followed, including the introduction of confirmation (1869) and an organ and choir (1877). When Raphall died in 1868, Henry Vidaver succeeded him, serving until 1874. Henry Jacobs succeeded Vidaver and remained until his death in 1893. Jacobs focused a large part of his rabbinate on the children of the congregation. During this period, B'nai Jeshurun played an active role in the establishment of the Board of Delegates of American Israelites (1859) and the Jewish Theological Seminary (1886). The congregation also chose to join the Union of American Hebrew Congregations, the national organization of Reform synagogues, when it merged with the Board of Delegates in 1878. It discontinued this affiliation in 1884. It joined in founding the United Synagogue of America (now United Synagogue of Conservative Judaism), the organization of Conservative synagogues, in 1913.

Members dedicated a fourth house of worship in 1885 on Madison at Sixty-fifth Street. The following year, the new structure survived a fire, which destroyed many congregational records. In 1889, B'nai Jeshurun published its own prayer book for use on the Sabbath and holidays. It contained several slight changes, including the elimination of less-important liturgical poems and the introduction of a few English prayers. During the rabbinate of Stephen S. Wise (1893–1900), B'nai Jeshurun actively built up its religious education program for children and organized a sisterhood (1894). Following Wise's resignation, Joseph Mayer Asher (1900–1907) served the congregation. He built up the level of Hebrew instruction at the synagogue. Benjamin Tintner (1908–1911) succeeded Asher one year after his departure. He exerted an effort to organize the young people of the congregation. During his tenure, the congregation introduced English into its liturgy, especially during the *Musaf* (additional) service for the Sabbath and holidays. Following Tintner's resignation, Judah L. Magnes (1911–1912) led the congregation. Magnes gained a reputation as chairman of New York's Kehillah, an experimental attempt to mold New York into one Jewish community. He later became the founding president of Hebrew University of Jerusalem. Magnes worked to counter a trend toward Reform in the congregation. He eliminated the organ and choir. Magnes also reworked the dues system so that even Jews of modest means could affiliate. Joel Blau (1913–1917) came to B'nai Jeshurun when Magnes left.

In 1917, B'nai Jeshurun dedicated a new home on Eighty-eighth Street, near West End Avenue for its less than one hundred members. The following year, Rabbi Israel Goldstein joined the congregation. He focused his attention on the civil and religious distress brought on by World War I and the upbuilding of Palestine, as well as the need for Jewish education. Goldstein introduced a late Friday evening Sabbath service (1918), as well as *Yizkor* (memorial) services on the last days of major holidays. He also reintroduced several parts of the worship service previously eliminated during the period of liturgical reform in the congregation. By 1919, membership exceeded two hundred.

B'nai Jeshurun members erected a community center in 1928, which provided a locus for an extensive program of religious, cultural, and social activities. In 1934, membership exceeded one thousand families, with a religious school of 325 children. Goldstein's Institute of Adult Jewish Studies attracted large numbers to regular classes. William Berkowitz joined the congregation in 1951 as associate rabbi and succeeded Goldstein in 1960. While B'nai Jeshurun remained a strong community fixture in the 1950s, with nearly sixty community organizations holding meetings and programs at the synagogue, by the 1980s, the congregation's membership dwindled as the neighborhood changed around it.

With the support of Rabbi Wolfe Kelman of the Rabbinical Assembly, the national organization of Conservative rabbis, Rabbi Marshall Meyer joined the congregation in 1985; at the time, the congregation neared dissolution, with only eighty members. Meyer felt that he could revive the synagogue, which he served until his death in 1993. He successfully revitalized the congregation. Under his direction, B'nai Jeshurun instituted an educational program for Christians and Moslems, established a homeless shelter, and served meals to AIDS patients. In addition, Meyer stressed the need for Jewish literacy in the congregation and introduced a variety of educational programs to help congregants reach that goal. On a typical Sabbath evening in 1995, over one thousand worshipers joined in prayer. Rabbi Roland Matalon, who served as assistant to Meyer, succeeded Meyer at his death. In 1995, membership at B'nai Jeshurun stood at fifteen hundred.

References

Davis, Moshe. "The Synagogue in American Judaism: A Study of Congregation B'nai Jeshurun, New York City." In Harry Schneiderman, ed., *Two Generations in*

Perspective: Notable Events and Trends 1896–1959 (New York: 1957), pp. 210–35.

Goldstein, Israel. *A Century of Judaism in New York* (New York: 1930).

Grinstein, Hyman. *The Rise of the Jewish Community of New York 1654–1860* (Philadelphia: 1945).

140th Anniversary, Congregation B'nai Jeshurun, New York City, 1825–1966 (New York: 1966).

125th Anniversary, Congregation B'nai Jeshurun, New York City, 1825–1950 (New York: 1950).

Synagogue Histories Collection, The Joseph and Miriam Ratner Center for the Study of Conservative Judaism.

Synagogue Histories File, American Jewish Archives.

BROTHERHOOD SYNAGOGUE, CONSERVATIVE. *New York, New York.* In 1954, a group of twenty-three men and women met with Rabbi J. Irving Block to form the Brotherhood Synagogue (Congregation Beth Achim). Shortly thereafter, the young congregation moved to West Thirteenth Street in Greenwich Village, where it shared a sanctuary with a Presbyterian congregation as part of its vision of community brotherhood. From its inception, the congregation had an open-door policy: no fixed pews, no reserved seats, no tickets for the High Holidays. In addition, the congregation focused its energies on outreach to the State of Israel, the struggle of Jews in foreign countries, and collecting food for the hungry and clothes for the poor.

The congregation moved in 1975 into a landmark building in Gramercy Park, originally a Friends Meeting House, erected in 1859 and closed since 1958. In this new location, the congregation has established programs for handicapped children and a coffeehouse for young people. It was among the first congregations to open its doors to the homeless of New York City (1982). It has assisted the African-American community, as well. Since 1986, the synagogue has participated in a unique program supervising a seminary student intern from the (Episcopal) General Theological Seminary. When Rabbi Block retired in 1994, Rabbi Daniel Adler succeeded him. Membership stood at seven hundred family units in 1994.

Reference

Synagogue Histories File, American Jewish Archives.

CENTRAL SYNAGOGUE, REFORM. *New York, New York.* In 1839, a group of German Jews, members of B'nai Jeshurun, founded a new congregation, Shaar Hashomayim. This group met for worship in a little hall in a building on Attorney Street. In 1845, Rabbi Max Lilienthal began his service at Shaar Hashomayim. As a circuit rabbi of sorts, he simultaneously led two other congregations (Anshe Chesed and Rodeph Sholom) as well. Though his attempts at maintaining decorum during worship met with great opposition, Lilienthal did successfully institute Confirmation during his first year. Shortly after Lilienthal's arrival, members purchased a former Protestant church at the corner of Fourth

Street and Avenue C. When congregants forced Lilienthal to resign over a trivial matter, Emanu-El approached Shaar Hashomayim—as well as the other German congregations—to merge. Only Shaar Hashomayim seriously considered the offer, but its members feared Emanu-El's proclivity for Reform Judaism.

In 1846, a group of eighteen Bohemian Jewish immigrants joined together to form a Bohemian Culture Society (Boemische Verein), meeting for worship as Ahawath Chesed. They gathered for services on Ludlow Street in a place called "Coblenzer's Hotel." After the group moved to other locations during its early history (Ridge Street and then Columbia Street), in 1864 Ahawath Chesed members moved into a former church on Fourth Avenue and Avenue C. The following year, this young synagogue invited Dr. Adolph Huebsch to become its religious leader. He introduced moderate reforms into the congregation, focusing a great deal of his attention on the education of youth. In 1872, the congregation's 140 families dedicated the synagogue's current house of worship at the corner of Lexington and Fifty-fifth Street. Six years later, Ahawath Chesed joined the Union of American Hebrew Congregations, the national body of Reform synagogues.

Upon Huebsch's death in 1885, Dr. George Alexander Kohut became the new rabbi of the synagogue. He championed a more Conservative position in Jewish life. As a scholar, he produced a Talmudic lexicon, funded by the congregation. Rabbi David Davidson succeeded Kohut in 1894, remaining with the congregation until 1900. He too emphasized education in his rabbinate, establishing the David Davidson Institute College and the Society for the Aid of Jewish Prisoners. During his tenure, Ahawath Chesed and Shaar Hashomayim merged to form one congregation, utilizing the synagogue structure built by the former congregation (1898).

Rabbi Isaac Moses succeeded Davidson in 1901, retiring in 1918. Moses' manuscript became the basis for the Reform movement's *Union Prayer Book.* During Moses' tenure, the congregation considered moving to the Upper West Side, where many congregants had already moved. However, sentiment for the building motivated the congregants to retain the old building. When Dr. Nathan Krass succeeded Moses (1918), the congregation underwent a significant change. During Krass' tenure, the synagogue changed its name from Ahawath Chesed–Shaar Hashomayim to Central Synagogue. Krass preached in English instead of German.

When Krass left the congregation, Central Synagogue underwent one of the most difficult periods in its history. As part of an attempted merger with the Free Synagogue in 1922, Dr. Stephen S. Wise led both congregations. This attempt at amalgamation lasted only two years.

Jonah B. Wise came to Central in 1926. He revitalized the congregation. Wise introduced the revised *Union Prayer Book,* the uniform prayer book of the Reform movement, and eliminated the practice of wearing hats during worship. He also founded the Message of Israel in 1934, a weekly radio broadcast from the sanctuary of Central Synagogue, helping to develop a relationship between

Christians and Jews, an emphasis of his rabbinate at Central. In 1926, Central Synagogue—and its six hundred members—purchased the former YMCA building on East Sixty-second Street for use as its Community House, where its religious school and offices were maintained. In 1939, German Jewish families formed Congregation Habonim in this community house before separating into its own congregation. The sanctuary of the congregation was dedicated as a landmark in 1958.

Rabbi David Seligson succeeded Wise in 1959, having served as an assistant since 1945. Under his guidance Central Synagogue members constructed a new Community House building at East Fifty-fifth to house the expanding activities of the congregation (1968).

Rabbi Sheldon Zimmerman succeeded Seligson in 1972, having served as assistant since 1970. He emphasized adult education at Central Synagogue and established a College of Jewish Studies. Under his direction, Central Synagogue became the first synagogue to reach out to Jewish alcoholics and drug addicts. In 1980, Central Synagogue absorbed Mt. Neboh Congregation, formerly of Washington Heights (founded 1912). Rabbi Zimmerman served until 1985.

Central Synagogue elected Rabbi Stanley Davids to its pulpit in 1987. Concerned about Israel, he directed much of his attention to her survival. Rabbi Peter Rubinstein succeeded Davids in 1991. In 1994, membership of Central Synagogue reached 1250 family units.

References

Central Synagogue, 140 Years (New York: 1979).
Guide to the Archives, Central Synagogue (New York: 1994).
Religion Is the Life of Israel (New York: 1929).
Schwarz, Herbert. *Your Temple, A Unique Story of Devotion, Faith and Service* (New York: 1958).
Synagogue Histories File, American Jewish Archives.

CONGREGATION EMANU-EL OF THE CITY OF NEW YORK, RE-FORM. *New York, New York.* Congregation Emanu-El is one of the largest synagogues in the world. Among religious sanctuaries in New York City, it is second in size only to the Cathedral of St. John the Divine and St. Patrick's Cathedral. Founded in 1845, the congregation can be traced to the *Cultus Verein,* established in 1844. Thirty-three immigrants from Germany established Emanu-El, but they did not import their reforms from Europe.

The new congregation rented its first quarters in a private dwelling at the corner of Grand and Clinton Streets (in what was later called the Lower East Side). Members invited Rabbi Leo Merzbacher to become Emanu-El's first rabbi, having been part of the *Verein.* Three years after its founding, the congregation moved to a former church building on Chrystie Street. By 1854, Emanu-El moved again. This move to Twelfth Street reflected a gradual increase in financial prosperity. In this new structure, the congregation introduced family pews to its members. Only fourteen years later, the congregation built a major edifice at Fifth Avenue and Forty-third Street.

According to Hyman Grinstein, members slowly instituted changes from traditional practice between 1845 and 1864. However, at the first meeting of the congregation, members eliminated the auctioning of Torah honors. Afterwards, members quickly made changes that made the atmosphere for worship more American: weekly sermons, removing hats for worship, reduction in the amount of Hebrew used during prayer, introduction of Sunday services, and the abolition of the Bar Mitzvah. Members used a hymn book beginning in 1848. The following year, Emanu-El introduced organ music to the congregation. In 1854, the temple discontinued the observance of the second day of festivals.

Between the years 1848 and 1854, Emanu-El operated a Jewish elementary day school, one of the first such schools in New York City. After the day school closed, the synagogue introduced supplementary education for its children.

When Merzbacher died in 1856, Samuel Adler succeeded him. As one of the conveners of a rabbinical conference in Philadelphia in 1869, he set forth a philosophy that reflected the working philosophy of Emanu-El. Adler rejected supernatural revelation and the eternal validity of Mosaic law. He advocated the role of the Jewish masses in changing rituals to fit contemporary needs. Adler also supported the inclusion of women in ritual and education. As Adler was unwilling or unable to address the congregation in English, members invited R. J. De Cordova, a popular speaker and writer, to speak to the congregation from the pulpit twice a month. This arrangement worked until 1864. Eventually members asked Dr. James Gutheim, an articulate English speaker, to assist Rabbi Adler. This plan satisfied the need for English to be preached from the pulpit until Gutheim resigned in 1872. Members finally resolved the problem of English when they elected Gustav Gottheil to the pulpit in 1873. He remained until 1899. Rabbi Gottheil led the congregation in the area of Christian-Jewish relations, liturgical change, and social service activities. He founded the Emanu-El Sisterhood for Personal Service in 1889.

The debate over Sunday services occupied the congregation for nearly two decades toward the end of the nineteenth century. Eventually the congregation introduced Sunday "lectures." These lasted until 1945. In 1895, Emanu-El adopted the *Union Prayer Book,* the prayer book of the Reform movement.

Following Gottheil's retirement, the congregation invited Rabbi Stephen S. Wise to its pulpit. When Louis Marshall, Emanu-El's president, refused to allow Wise freedom of the pulpit, he declined the offer. An exchange of letters that followed became a controversy that quickly moved into the pages of the Anglo-Jewish press. The search for Gottheil's successor, beginning in 1899, ended when Rabbi Judah L. Magnes came to lead the temple in 1906. In the interim, Rabbi Joseph Silverman, who had been serving as assistant to Gottheil, had continued to minister to the congregation.

Magnes, an ardent Zionist, preached about Zionism from the Emanu-El pulpit.

His growing dissatisfaction with Emanu-El's interpretation of Reform Judaism led to his eventual resignation in 1911.

Beginning in 1915, Rabbi Silverman introduced a brief service of prayer each weekday at noon. In addition, he advocated opening the sanctuary for meditation throughout the day. According to Rabbi Ronald Sobel, little liturgical change followed for the next twenty-five years. Unlike most Reform congregations, Emanu-El resisted a pro-Zionist position, which usually accompanied the affiliation of immigrant Jews from Eastern Europe whose membership Emanu-El discouraged. The congregation reached out to help Americanize these new immigrants but refused to adjust ideology in order to make them feel more comfortable.

Rabbi Hyman Enelow joined Rabbi Joseph Silverman as co-rabbi in 1912. He focused his rabbinate on the children and young people of the congregation, including the development of the Junior Society. Enelow was a scholar and author and gained particular renown as a Hebraist.

Beginning in 1923 and throughout its ten-year existence, Emanu-El housed the Hebrew Union College (still in Cincinnati) School for Teachers. When neither Hebrew Union College nor the Union of American Hebrew Congregations, the national organization of Reform synagogues, could bear the financial burden of the school, Emanu-El supported it for several years on its own.

In 1923, Dr. Nathan Krauss joined Rabbi Hyman Enelow as co-rabbi, replacing the retiring Rabbi Joseph Silverman. An eloquent preacher, Krauss drew crowds to the congregation, competing with Stephen S. Wise preaching at Carnegie Hall. Krauss suffered an incapacitating illness in 1932 and retired two years later.

Members formed Emanu-El's Men Club in 1920, but it did not become active until the merger of Emanu-El with Beth El in 1928. With Beth El's five hundred families, Emanu-El could easily build its new structure at Fifth Avenue and Sixty-fifth Street (dedicated in 1930). As a result of the merger with Beth El, Rabbi Samuel Schulman, Beth El's rabbi, joined the rabbinic staff of Emanu-El. While the name of the merged congregation stayed Emanu-El, the new structure included a Beth El chapel.

Financial problems following the Depression hit the congregation hard. Between 1930 and 1945, Emanu-El lost one-third of its members. Following Krauss' retirement, Rabbi Nathan Perilman joined the congregation to assist Rabbis Schulman and Enelow. Dr. Samuel H. Goldenson joined the rabbinical staff in 1934, following the retirement of Drs. Krauss, Enelow, and Schulman. Goldenson continued the antinationalist and antiritual stance of his predecessors. He was also an advocate of social action and sought to introduce the revised *Union Prayer Book* with its emphasis on the prophetic ideals into the congregation. Goldenson retired in 1948. Rabbi Julius Mark succeeded him and during his tenure, Mark emphasized Zionism. As an apparent result, Emanu-El saw tremendous growth. Dr. Nathan Perilman returned to Emanu-El in 1968 to succeed Mark and remained as senior rabbi for nearly six years. He focused his energies on the education of children and adults. Rabbi Ronald Sobel joined the congregation in 1962, becoming senior rabbi in 1974. Under Rabbi Sobel's leadership, Emanu-El reached out to the homeless and hungry by sponsoring a men's shelter, a program to feed the hungry, and a meals-on-wheels program. In addition, the congregation has intensified its efforts in adult education and fostering relationships with the non-Jewish community. In 1994, membership stood at over three thousand family units.

Temple Beth El

Organized in 1874, Congregation Temple Beth El was an amalgamation of Anshe Chesed (founded in 1828) and Adas Jeshurun (founded in 1866). As an Orthodox congregation, Anshe Chesed's members first worshiped on White Street, moving to Green Street in 1835. Five years later, the congregation built a synagogue on Henry Street. In 1850, Anshe Chesed on Norfolk Street erected the largest synagogue in New York. Growing in prosperity, the congregation moved to Sixty-third and Lexington in 1871.

Influenced by the Reform movement in Germany, these German-Jewish founders incorporated Adas Jeshurun in 1866 and sought to create a similar Reform institution in their new land. They first worshiped in rented rooms in Everett Hall, then erected their own building on West Thirty-ninth Street later the same year. Members elected Dr. David Einhorn as their first rabbi. A leader in the Reform movement, he opposed slavery from the pulpit. Beth El and Adas Jeshurun merged under his leadership.

Rabbi Kaufmann Kohler succeeded Dr. Einhorn at Beth El in 1879. Kohler introduced the English sermon. Ten years later, he introduced English prayers to the congregation. The congregation adopted the *Union Prayer Book* in 1893. During Kohler's tenure, the congregation experimented with Sunday services at his initiation. Then he introduced the late Friday evening service.

Beth El moved to Fifth Avenue and Seventy-sixth Street in 1891. Dr. Samuel Schulman joined the congregation in 1898 and became senior rabbi in 1903. Schulman reintroduced Sunday services the year after he arrived in New York. Following the merger of the congregation with Emanu-El, its memory was perpetuated through the Beth El Chapel.

References

Brinner, William H. and Moses Rischin, eds. *Like All the Nations? The Life and Legacy of Judah L. Magnes* (Albany, NY: 1987).

Grossman, Cissy. *A Temple Treasury: The Judaica Collection of Congregation Emanu-El of the City of New York* (New York: 1989).

Moral and Spiritual Foundations: Addresses for the Celebration of the Hundredth Anniversary Celebration of Congregation Emanu-El of the City of New York (New York: 1945).

Religion Is the Life of Israel (New York: 1929).

Selected Works of Hyman Enelow, 4 vols. (Kingsport, TN: 1935).

Shapiro, Robert. *A Reform Rabbi in the Progressive Era: The Early Career of Stephen S. Wise* (New York: 1988).

Sobel, Ronald. "A History of New York's Temple Emanu-El: The Second Half Century" (Ph.D. dissertation, New York University, 1980).

Synagogue Histories File, American Jewish Archives.

When Yesterday Becomes Tomorrow: 125th Anniversary Celebration of Congregation Emanu-El of the City of New York, 1845–1970 (New York: 1971).

FIFTH AVENUE SYNAGOGUE, ORTHODOX. *New York, New York.* When a group of members of Congregation Zichron Ephraim grew dissatisfied with the choice of that congregation to allow men and women to sit together in worship, they founded Fifth Avenue Synagogue (Hebrew name: Kehillat Ateret Zvi). Imanuel Jakobovits (1959–1967) guided the early congregation as founding rabbi. He offered a weekly Talmud class, organized a junior youth group, and instituted the normal panoply of synagogue activities. In addition, he focused his attention on issues regarding the division of church and state. Next, Rabbi Emanuel Rackman served the Fifth Avenue Synagogue (1967–1977), emphasizing Israel and community in his rabbinate.

Rabbi Nisson Elchanah Shulman (1977–1985) succeeded Rackman. He continued study and worship as the focus of the synagogue program. Rabbi Sol Roth came to the congregation in 1986. His academic interests are highlighted in his approach to the rabbinate at Fifth Avenue Synagogue. Under his direction, the congregation added a preschool and a Young People's program. In 1994, the congregation listed three hundred families as its membership.

Reference

Personal interviews.

CONGREGATION HABONIM, REFORM. *New York, New York.* Refugees from Germany founded Congregation Habonim ("builders") in 1939, a year to the day after Kristallnacht. Rabbi Hugo Hahn led these founders from Essen, Germany, where his own synagogue was ransacked and burned to the ground. Central Synagogue brought him from Europe as its "assistant rabbi" in order to save him and his family. Instead of building a community *landsmanschaft,* the founders of Habonim sought to create a central community synagogue for German refugees. Throughout its history, well-known European rabbis, immigrants to the United States, spoke from the Habonim pulpit.

Founding members held their first services at Central Synagogue. There they reestablished the Frankfurter Lehrhaus. The congregation had a liberal religious outlook, but in its early years it used an Orthodox prayer book for weekday and Sabbath services and a Conservative prayer book for holidays. Habonim also implemented a program of religious education for member children, initially using German as the language of instruction. As the congregation grew, it held additional classes in Washington Heights and Queens. The synagogue also conducted regular services in Queens for members who lived there. By 1940, as membership exceeded available space at Central Synagogue, Habonim held High Holiday services in Town Hall. The following year, members started a camp for their children in the Catskills (1941). In 1944, Habonim joined the Union of American Hebrew Congregations, the national organization of Reform synagogues. Habonim left Central Synagogue completely in 1945 and occupied rented facilities.

In 1958, Habonim dedicated its permanent home on West Sixty-sixth Street near Central Park. In 1960, the congregation purchased a house in Rego Park, for services and classes, which it eventually transferred to Selfhelp, an organization designed to assist elderly Nazi victims. At about the same time, the youth group of the congregation established Camp Shalom, a summer program for disadvantaged youths in the neighborhood.

Rabbi Bernard Cohn, the son-in-law of the founding rabbi, led the congregation from 1962 to 1990 before Rabbi Jay Rosenbaum succeeded him. Under Cohn's direction, the congregation granted women equal rights in 1975, a rather late change for a Reform congregation. Cohn also placed a strong emphasis on education for members and their children. While other congregations expanded, this congregation has seen its membership units of nine hundred, at its peak, plummet to fewer than five hundred in 1995.

References

Congregation Habonim, Fortieth Anniversary Journal (New York: 1979).
Synagogue Histories File, American Jewish Archives.

HEBREW TABERNACLE, REFORM. *New York, New York.* In 1905, German-Jewish founders met to form the Hebrew Tabernacle Association in Harlem. Shortly thereafter, they formed a Sunday School, the primary reason for the establishment of the association, at Riverside Hall on Seventh Avenue. By the end of the first year, the school boasted of a student population of over 150. Association organizers incorporated the Hebrew Tabernacle as a religious institution in 1906, meeting on West 130th Street. While members covered their heads and wore prayer shawls, Hebrew Tabernacle introduced the mixed choir and organ into worship. Parts of the ritual were offered in English, as well.

Two years later, amid city opposition, Hebrew Tabernacle acquired the building next to the synagogue, dedicating the combined and expanded structure in 1910. Financial difficulties forced the temple to sublet its facilities shortly after the renovations were completed. Nevertheless, by 1911, the school population exceeded three hundred, rising to five hundred only one year later. In the following years, enrollment declined, until a new wave of immigration increased enrollment in the late 1930s and 1940s. Yet, adults did not follow their children (registered in religious school) by joining the synagogue as members.

During World War I, fearful of dual-loyalty accusations, some members felt that the predominantly German membership of the congregation could become an embarassment. A demand that "all Germans" in the congregation withdraw was issued but never acted upon.

As African Americans moved into the area of Harlem around the synagogue—and as the entire community experienced general immigrant relocation—the Jewish community began its move outside of the area. School
enrollment dropped to 170. Hebrew Tabernacle joined the exodus from the
neighborhood to West 161st Street in Washington Heights (dedicated 1927). At
about the same time, Rabbi Lissman retired.

Dr. I. Mortimer Bloom succeeded Lissman in the pulpit. Against the wishes
of the board, Lissman wanted to remain in an active role with the congregation.
As a result, he established a new congregation, Riverside Synagogue, to serve
the area of Broadway, between 105th and 120th Streets, the location to which
he had wanted to move Hebrew Tabernacle in the first place.

In its new location, Hebrew Tabernacle grew once again. In 1921, 407 children enrolled in its school. In its new surroundings, members dedicated themselves to charitable works in the community and to building up the land of
Palestine. By the beginning of the next decade, Hebrew Tabernacle affiliated
with the Union of American Hebrew Congregations, the national body of Reform synagogues. Hebrew Tabernacle retained an Orthodox tradition with, for
example, a daily Orthodox minyan meeting as late as the 1950s and 1960s.
Rabbi Bloom emphasized decorum in worship. Among other innovations,
Bloom advocated that Confirmation take place on the Sunday before Shavuot
rather than on the holiday itself.

The Depression ill-affected the strides Hebrew Tabernacle was making in its
new location. By 1931, its building was foreclosed. Shortly thereafter, the congregation reorganized under the new name, the Hebrew Tabernacle of Washington Heights. This new group purchased the synagogue building once again.
In this new capacity, the congregation cosponsored many activities with the
Community Council of Washington Heights.

Rabbi Bloom resigned in 1933, at the request of the board. The board rejected
his plan to focus the limited resources of the congregation on its girls. Bloom
believed that as a result of his influence, the girls' families (following marriage)
would affiliate with the congregation and thereby increase temple membership.
In 1934, Rabbi Naphtali Frishberg succeeded Bloom. When he left after four
years, Hebrew Tabernacle engaged Rabbi Ahron Opher. Opher introduced the
Reform Sabbath prayer book, but used the Conservative prayer book for the
High Holidays.

Following Kristallnacht in Germany in 1938, Hebrew Tabernacle became
home to many German refugees. During World War II, members actively assisted these immigrants and reached out to refugees and American soldiers in
Europe. In 1946, Jacob Polish became the synagogue's rabbi. Polish centered
his rabbinate around Zionism. Rabbi Robert Lehman succeeded Polish in 1956.

In the early 1950s, members began to move away from Washington Heights,
forcing the temple to confront the same issues it had faced when moving from
Harlem. Yet, it was financially unable to build a new home for itself. In the
1960s, Hebrew Tabernacle opened a branch school in an apartment at 218th

Street and Seaman Avenue in Inwood. By 1973, the Hebrew Tabernacle was ready to buy a former church at 185th and Fort Washington Avenue (dedicated 1974). Apparently, sometime during the late 1970s, members from local Temple Beth Am–the People's Temple and the Temple of the Covenant joined the Hebrew Tabernacle, without the benefit of a formal merger. Subsequently, Beth Am reorganized and became an independent institution once again.

While the 1990s has seen some gentrification in the area, enrollment in the school of Hebrew Tabernacle is low and membership is declining because of the aging of its membership. Thus, the congregation focuses on reaching out to the elderly in the neighborhood and the new group of younger people moving into the area. In 1994, membership of the Hebrew Tabernacle was 145.

References

Ehrlich, Evelyn. *A History of the Hebrew Tabernacle Congregation of Washington Heights* (New York: 1985).
Gurock, Jeffrey. *When Harlem Was Jewish, 1870–1930* (New York: 1979).

TEMPLE ISRAEL, REFORM. *New York, New York.* Founders of Hand in Hand (Yod be-Yod) Congregation established their first home at East 215th Street in Harlem. Charter members quickly established a school for its forty-five children, calling it the Gates of Learning. In 1874, the synagogue membership moved to larger quarters on 124th Street, leasing a former church on 116th Street in 1876 (purchased 1880). Maurice Harris, still a student, became rabbi of the congregation in 1882 (officially installed 1884). In 1887, the congregation acquired a former church building on 125th Street and Fifth Avenue (dedicated 1888). At about the same time, the congregation changed its name to the Temple Israel of Harlem.

In 1907, Temple Israel dedicated its new synagogue on 120th Street and Lenox Avenue. In 1909, the congregation joined the Union of American Hebrew Congregations, the national organization of Reform synagogues. At about the same time, members began to move from Harlem to Manhattan's Upper West Side. In 1914, Temple Israel absorbed a small congregation, Shaaray Borocho. Temple Israel sold its building in 1920 before moving to its current location on West Ninety-first Street (dedicated 1922). Recognizing its location, it took the name Temple Israel of New York (1924). Just before moving into the new building, the congregation gave women of the congregation full equality in congregational life. In the new location, Temple Israel grew considerably, exceeding 950 members in 1929. There, Harris continued his emphasis on Jewish education for adults and children. Despite the Depression, the congregation maintained a lively activity program in its Community Center. At the same time, it supported a Sabbath School on Saturday mornings for underprivileged children at the Neighborhood House of Federation Settlement on East 106th Street.

Rabbi William Franklin Rosenblum succeeded Harris, who died in 1930. During World War II, the congregation participated actively in the War Finance

Program. In 1966, Temple Israel moved to East Seventy-fifth Street. When Rosenblum retired (1963), Rabbi Martin Zion succeeded him. In 1991, Rabbi Judith Lewis, who had served Temple Israel as Director of Education since 1985, succeeded Zion in the pulpit. In 1995, membership in Temple Israel exceeded four hundred family units.

References

Gurock, Jeffrey, *When Harlem Was Jewish, 1870–1930* (New York: 1979).
98th Anniversary of Temple Israel of the City of New York (New York: 1968).
100th Anniversary of Temple Israel of the City of New York (New York: 1970).
Religion Is the Life of Israel (New York: 1929).
Synagogue Histories File, American Jewish Archives.

THE JEWISH CENTER, ORTHODOX. *New York, New York.* In 1912, Rabbi Mordecai M. Kaplan, who later founded the Reconstructionist movement, became interested in reformulating the synagogue in order to provide a social context for young Jews. He began to hold services in his home. He laid the cornerstone for the Jewish Center on West Eighty-sixth Street in 1917. The following year, Kaplan himself became rabbi of the Jewish Center. As an alternative to the traditional synagogue, Kaplan wanted to develop an institution that would serve all of the educational, social, and religious needs of the Jewish community. The resultant four-story building included an auditorium for movies, a synagogue library, a women's gallery, a gymnasium, a swimming pool, a steam bath, classrooms, a club room, and a dining room (dedicated 1918). Two years later, after a struggle over Orthodoxy with the membership, Kaplan resigned in order to found the Society for the Advancement of Judaism. Thirty-five members left the Jewish Center and joined Kaplan in the founding of the Society for the Advancement of Judaism. After the controversy that had developed during Kaplan's leadership over his non-Orthodox theology, the leaders of the congregation arranged for an act to be passed by the State Legislature of New York to ensure that the synagogue would remain Orthodox.

Dr. Leo Jung succeeded Kaplan and served until his death in 1987. At the Jewish Center and through a wide array of community activities, Jung successfully established a modern orthodoxy in North America, one that joined Torah and *Derekh Eretz* (Torah-true Judaism and modern thought). As a prolific writer and scholar, he lectured a great deal at the Jewish Center and in the community, bringing together the culture of western civilization with Orthodox Judaism. Unlike many of his colleagues, Jung preached in English, not Yiddish. He encouraged congregational singing and stressed synagogue decorum. In 1928, he founded the Jewish Center Day School. This school functioned until the mid-1930s, when Jung turned it into a Hebrew and Sunday School. Jung led the Jewish Center in the celebration of American holidays. He also encouraged the participation of women in traditional roles in the synagogue.

Dr. Norman Lamm, who later became president of Yeshiva University, served first as associate rabbi, then as rabbi from 1958–1976. While Lamm never officially succeeded Jung, he continued Jung's tradition of Torah and *Derekh Eretz.* Rabbi Isaac Bernstein served the congregation from 1977 to 1981. Dr. Jacob J. Schacter joined The Jewish Center in 1981. He particularly developed a program of outreach for singles and increased membership in the congregation. In 1995, the congregation listed 440 membership units.

References

Goldsmith, Emanuel, et al. *The American Judaism of Mordecai M. Kaplan* (New York: 1990).
Joselit, Jenna Weissman. *New York's Jewish Jews: The Orthodox Community in the Interwar Years* (Bloomington, IN: 1990).
Jung, Leo. *The Path of a Pioneer: The Autobiography of Leo Jung* (New York: 1980).
Kasten, Menahem M., Norman Lamm, and Leonard Rosenfeld, eds. *The Leo Jung Jubilee Volume* (New York: 1962).
Lamm, Norman. *Torah Umadda: The Encounter of Religious Learning and Worldly Knowledge in Jewish Tradition* (Northvale, NJ: 1989).
Libowitz, Richard. *Mordecai M. Kaplan and the Development of Reconstructionism* (New York: 1983).
Schacter, Jacob J. *Reverence, Righteousness and Rahamanut: Essays in Memory of Rabbi Dr. Leo Jung* (Northvale, NJ: 1992). See especially Marc Lee Raphael, "Rabbi Leo Jung and the Americanization of Orthodox Judaism," pp. 21–92.
Scult, Mel. *Judaism Faces the Twentieth Century: A Biography of Mordecai Kaplan* (Detroit: 1994).

KAHAL ADATH JESHURUN EIM ANSHE LUBTZ, ELDRIDGE STREET SYNAGOGUE, ORTHODOX. *New York, New York.* Among the earliest Russian immigrants in New York City to found a synagogue, these charter members established a congregation in 1852. It first met in an attic on Bayard Street, and Abraham Ash served as the congregation's first religious leader. With an increase in membership, the congregation moved to Elm and Canal Streets later that same year. The following year, continued growth forced another move, to a former courthouse on Pearl and Centre Streets. In this location, the founding group officially adopted the name Congregation Beth Hamedrash. Following a disagreement over the hiring of a particular ritual slaughterer, some dissidents left Beth Hamedrash to form the Beth Hamedrash Livne Yisroel Yelide Polen (House of Study of the Children of Israel Born in Poland) under the religious leadership of Judah Middleman, the former congregation's matzah baker. This new congregation met at Walker and Baxter Streets before settling on Bayard Street. In 1899, this group merged with a group of newcomers from Kalwarie (a town on the border of Poland and Lithuania), forming the Sons of Israel Kalwarie. The merged congregation built its own synagogue on Pike Street in 1903. Ten years later, the congregation founded the Young Israel movement.

The Beth Hamedrash congregation of fifty-six members moved to a former church building on Allen Street (1856). In this new location, the synagogue became a pioneer in the training of Jewish professionals (such as ritual slaugh-terers) to serve the American Jewish community. Two years later, the congre-gation officially incorporated as Beth Hamedrash of the city of New York. A disagreement between Ash and the president, Joshua Rothstein, led to the for-mation of another synagogue, Beth Hamedrash Hagadol. This new congregation, led by Ash, consisted of a large majority of former Beth Hamedrash members. The new congregation located itself at Grand and Forsyth Streets, then to Lud-low and Hester. In 1885, Beth Hamedrash Hagadol moved to a former church on Norfolk Street.

The split left the original Beth Hamedrash in dire financial straits, forcing it to merge with Congregation Holche Josher Wizaner (Those Who Walk in Right-eousness), together to form K'hal Adath Jeshurun (ca. 1884–1886, taking the name officially in 1890). In 1872, the merged congregation engaged Isaac Gellis to serve as religious leader. After the merger, the former Beth Hamedrash va-cated the Allen Street property (following a successful suit against the Manhat-tan Railway Company), and the newly amalgamated congregation moved to a new building on Eldridge Street (dedicated 1887). Following the dedication, leaders brought Phineas Minkowsky and his choir from Odessa to guide the congregation in worship (1892). At about the same time, Chevra Knesses Yisroel Anshe Russiya merged into K'hal Adath Jeshurun (1890).

Although historian Jeffrey Gurock has argued that education was never a priority of the congregation and contributed to its demise, the congregation did institute a Hebrew School for its members (beginning in 1901). In 1909, the congregation merged with another group: Chevra Aron David Uzvi Nochim Anshe Lubtz (Congregation Aaron David and Harris Nathan of the People of the Town of Lubtz). This congregation, founded in 1889, had been worshiping on Allen Street, down the street from K'hal Adath Jeshurun's former synagogue. Prior to the merger, Chebra Ahron David Anshei Luptz had merged with Con-gregation Agudath Achim Bnai Zvi Nachim Anshe Lubtz (1908). At the time of the consolidation, K'hal Adath Jeshurun included 135 members, and the other synagogue listed 123 on its membership rolls. At the time of the merger, the new institution took the name Kahal Adath Yeshurun am Anshe Lutz.

In 1909, following the move of some of the synagogue members uptown to Harlem, former congregants formed a "branch" under the same name (with variant spelling), Khal Adath Jeshorum. This new congregation claimed that the merger of the former congregation had been illegal and fought it unsuccessfully.

Rabbis Moshe Mordecai Rivkind and Binyamin Meir Levy led the congre-gation in the early years of the twentieth century, when membership peaked at approximately eight hundred. It deteriorated rapidly after 1930—the last time its sanctuary was regularly used—probably the result of migration from the neighborhood. In 1989, the congregation began the process of restoration under the auspices of the Eldridge Street Project (formed in 1986). This effort placed the Eldridge Street Synagogue on the State and National Register of Historic Places (1980). In 1994, the membership stood at forty units.

References

American History Workshop, Eldridge Street Project.
Gurock, Jeffrey. ''A Stage in the Emergence of the Americanized Synagogue among East
    European Jews: 1890–1910.'' *Journal of American Ethnic History* 9, no. 2
    (Spring 1990): 7–25.
Synagogue Histories File, American Jewish Archives.

KEHILATH JESHURUN, ORTHODOX. *New York, New York.* Founders established this congregation as Anshe Jeshurun in 1872. Rabbi Jacob David Wil-
lowski, the Slutska Rav (also known as the Ridbaz), served as the first religious
leader. In 1902, members of Kehilath Jeshurun laid the cornerstone for their
new building on East Eighty-fifth Street between Park and Lexington Avenues.
This building included a massive sanctuary, a choir loft, and a chapel. In 1904,
Kehilath Jeshurun members invited Rabbi Mordecai Kaplan to become their first
English-speaking religious leader. Yet, two years later, they also invited Rabbi
Moses Z. Margolies (also known as the Ramaz) to become the senior ''rav'' to
Kaplan's junior position as ''minister.'' Eventually, a right-wing contingent in
the congregation—assisted by rabbis of the Agudath ha-Rabbanim, the Orthodox
rabbinical union—forced Kaplan to resign because of his radical interpretations
of Judaism (which later formed the basis for Reconstructionist Judaism). Rabbis
Herbert Goldstein and Elias Solomon succeeded Kaplan. However, they too
remained only a short time, because of the difficulty of the structure of relationships between the Ramaz and his colleagues.

In 1921, Kehilath Jeshurun rapidly began losing members who moved to the
Upper West Side. Rabbi Joseph Lookstein, who joined as assistant to Margolies
in 1923 and succeeded Lookstein upon his death in 1936, helped rebuild membership. With the support of Margolies, Lookstein introduced a new sense of
decorum into worship, which included announcing page numbers and an explanation of certain prayers within the context of worship as well as unison and
responsive readings.

Lookstein maintained records and reflections on all aspects of synagogue life,
which he used to teach rabbinical students at the Rabbi Isaac Elchanan Theological Seminary (RIETS), the Orthodox rabbinical seminary housed at Yeshiva
University. While members considered his sermons a highlight of the worship
experience, according to historian Jenna Weissman Joselit, Lookstein seldom
preached fiery sermons. Instead, he gently persuaded his congregants to observe
the practices and principles of Orthodox Judaism. Lookstein successfully transformed a nearly moribund institution into a social center for the Orthodox Jewish
community, developing strong personal relationships with congregants. He participated actively in the Synagogue Council, the New York Board of Rabbis,
and the chaplaincy program of the Jewish Welfare Board, something Orthodox
rabbis previously eschewed.

In 1937, to honor the memory of his grandfather-in-law, Lookstein established
the Ramaz Day School (nine hundred students in 1995). By 1947, membership

reached 250 families and 650 seatholders at Kehilath Jeshurun, the largest number up to that time. Joseph Lookstein served until his death in 1978, when his son Rabbi Haskel Lookstein succeeded him.

Rabbi Haskel Lookstein instituted beginner's services for people with little connection to Judaism or limited knowledge of Jewish worship and ritual. In 1995, membership stood at nine hundred families.

References

Interview with Robert Liefert, July 11, 1995.

Joselit, Jenna Weissman. *New York's Jewish Jews, The Orthodox Community in the Interwar Years* (Bloomington, IN: 1990).

Lookstein, Joseph. *Two Psalms of Praise* (New York: 1973).

LINCOLN SQUARE SYNAGOGUE, ORTHODOX. *New York, New York.* Lincoln Square Synagogue began in 1963 by offering High Holiday services in a hotel on West End Avenue and Seventy-fourth Street. The following year, the young congregation claimed an apartment on West End Avenue as its first permanent home. Members dedicated the synagogue's present house of worship on Amsterdam Avenue in 1970. In 1986, the congregation acquired an adjacent bank building.

Lincoln Square Synagogue grew under the charismatic leadership of its first rabbi, Shlomo Riskin (1964–1983). He transformed the synagogue into a center of prayer and study and reached out to the previously nonobservant in the growing Lincoln Center neighborhood. In 1968, Lincoln Square Synagogue initiated its Joseph Shapiro Institute of Jewish Studies, established under the leadership of Rabbi Ephraim Buchwald. This program offered a wide range of educational opportunities. In 1975, Rabbi Buchwald introduced the ''Beginner's Minyan'' for newcomers to Orthodox worship.

Rabbi Saul Berman (1984–1990) succeeded Riskin. He expanded the educational offerings of the congregation and implemented a Lehrhaus program for those with advanced text skills. Under Berman's direction, social action also became a primary concern of the congregation.

Rabbi Simcha Weinberg succeeded Berman in 1991. By 1994, membership had grown to two thousand adults, with over five hundred children in youth groups, more than one thousand adult education students (weekly) and approximately eleven hundred worshipers at five different minyans every Shabbat morning.

Reference

Synagogue Histories File, American Jewish Archives.

METROPOLITAN SYNAGOGUE, REFORM. *New York, New York.* Founded in 1959, Metropolitan Synagogue invited Judah Cahn to serve as its founding rabbi. The congregation emphasized music in the synagogue with an active choir and music program. Since its founding, the congregation has continued to feature premieres of music and other forms of art each year. In 1959, Metropolitan Synagogue met at Community Church at East Thirty-fifth Street, where it continues to share facilities. In 1960, the congregation established its Covenant Club, in place of the more familiar sisterhood and brotherhood. In place of sermons, Rabbi Cahn often invited major figures to enter into a dialogue with him on the pulpit.

Following Cahn's retirement in 1982, Rabbi Joel Goor succeeded him. Under his direction, the congregation expanded its program of adult Jewish studies and introduced a variety of Jewish cultural programs to the members. Goor also introduced a Hebrew Home Study program as an alternative to Sunday School for children. In 1994, membership in the congregation was 240 membership units.

Reference

Synagogue Histories File, American Jewish Archives.

OHAB ZEDEK, ORTHODOX. *New York, New York.* As a fire at Ohab Zedek in the early 1990s destroyed many of its records, the precise documentation of its history is difficult. A group of Hungarian Jews founded the First Hungarian Congregation Ohab Zedek in 1873 on Manhattan's Lower East Side, in a frame building on Avenue B and Houston Street. Shortly thereafter, as membership increased, the congregation moved to the New York Assembly Rooms (Third Street and Avenue C) and then Beethoven Hall. As the congregation's service of the benevolent needs of its members seemed to overwhelm its religious services, synagogue leaders separated these emphases one from the other.

In 1881, Congregation Ohab Zedek dedicated its own building on Columbia Street. Several years later, Ohab Zedek joined with Congregation Shomrei Hadath to establish a Talmud Torah. Just before members purchased the former Rodeph Sholom synagogue on Norfolk Street (1886), Congregation Shomrei Hadath merged with Ohab Zedek. In 1891, Ohab Zedek acquired the building next to the synagogue and installed a *mikvah* (ritual bath), the same year Rabbi Philip Klein joined Ohab Zedek as its religious leader. As an active leader in community affairs, Klein led the War Relief Drive in New York (1914). Klein was also a vigorous supporter of Orthodox Judaism in New York and became national president of Agudat Israel, a right-wing Orthodox body.

In 1894 the congregation acquired a building on Rivington Street, to which it moved its Talmud Torah. As members of the synagogue community moved uptown into Harlem, the congregation planned a new synagogue for 116th Street (dedicated 1906). The Ohab Zedek Sisterhood formed in 1909; and in 1912, Ohab Zedek invited Cantor Joseph (Yosselle) Rosenblatt from Hamburg to join the synagogue as its cantor. Six years later, Ohab Zedek absorbed Congregation Shearith Bnai Israel into its membership. In 1923, the congregation merged with Congregation Pincus Elijah, founded by Pincus Elihu Stern.

As the Jewish community moved out of Harlem to the west side of Central

Park, the congregation felt a need for a congregational presence there. Thus, Ohab Zedek dedicated a new house of worship on Ninety-fifth Street in 1926, shortly before the death of Rabbi Philip Klein. Rabbi Isaiah Levy, who had assisted Rabbi Klein since 1924, succeeded him. He died in 1931, and Rabbi Moses Sherman succeeded him.

Ohab Zedek established the Beth Hillel Hebrew Institute in a new Talmud Torah building adjacent to the Ninety-fifth Street building in 1939. Rabbi Jacob Hoffman joined the congregation as its religious leader in 1938.

When Rabbi Theodore Adams came to the congregation to succeed Hoffman at his retirement in 1953, Ohab Zedek was in a state of decline. With a membership down to less than 350, Ohab Zedek had lost its membership to congregations elsewhere in New York City and the suburbs. By 1965, as a result of Adams' efforts, membership grew to five hundred. During his tenure, the congregation established the Beth Hillel Foundation School adjacent to the synagogue. This helped to attract some young members to the congregation. Yet the congregation still felt the impact of the deterioration of the local neighborhood.

Ohab Zedek elected Rabbi Raphael Marcus to its pulpit in 1975 to succeed Adams. After the five-year tenure of Marcus, Rabbi Avraham Marmorstein joined the congregation (1980–1987). In 1988, Rabbi Allen Schwartz came to Ohab Zedek. Between 1989 and 1994, membership grew from 140 family units to over 520, with Sabbath worship attendance rising from about one hundred to over five hundred. Under Rabbi Schwartz's leadership, the synagogue developed an extensive program of educational, outreach, social, community, and religious services. In 1994, membership exceeded five hundred family units.

References

Lyford, Joseph P. *The Airtight Cage: A Study of New York's West Side* (New York: 1966).
Synagogue Histories File, American Jewish Archives.

PARK AVENUE SYNAGOGUE, CONSERVATIVE. *New York, New York.*
A group of German-speaking Jews in Manhattan founded a synagogue in 1882, calling it Temple Gates of Hope, Sha'are Tikvah. When this group converted a church on Eighty-sixth Street for use as a synagogue, the institution came to be known as the Eighty-Sixth Street Temple. About twelve years after the congregation's founding, it joined together with Congregation Agudat Yesharim, whose name became the Hebrew name of the congregation. As it sought to meet the needs of its members, the congregation did not grow rapidly. Up until 1919, membership reached only fifty. A nearby synagogue, the Seventy-Second Street Temple, was itself the product of a merger of Beth Israel and Bikkur Cholim, both Lower East Side congregations. In 1920, this amalgamated congregation joined with the Eight-Sixth Street Temple, Agudat Yesharim.

In 1923, the congregation officially changed its name to the Park Avenue Synagogue. In 1927, this congregation dedicated its new sanctuary on Eighty-

Seventh Street (also close to Park Avenue). The following year, Park Avenue Synagogue merged with Atereth Israel, a group of Alsatian Jews who had been worshiping on East Eighty-second Street.

Rabbi Milton Steinberg joined Park Avenue's 240 members in 1933. During his tenure, the congregation affiliated with the Conservative movement. Steinberg died in 1950. During his short life, he had developed a national reputation as an excellent teacher and writer. His assistant, Rabbi Simon Novack, assumed the leadership of the congregation following Steinberg's death. The congregation erected a school wing and community house in his memory (dedicated 1954). Rabbi Judah Nadich joined the synagogue in 1957. Nadich introduced the Conservative prayer book to the congregation and discarded some of the past reforms.

In 1980, Park Avenue Synagogue members dedicated a new building to serve the growing membership and to honor the memory of the children murdered in the Holocaust. By 1984, membership reached over eleven hundred families. When Rabbi Nadich retired in 1987, Rabbi David Lincoln succeeded him. He guided the congregation toward more traditional observance and advanced the rights of women in the congregation. Though the congregation has been affiliated with the United Synagogue of America, the national organization of Conservative synagogues, it last rejoined in 1987. In 1994, membership stood at nearly fifteen hundred.

References

Religion Is the Life of Israel (New York: 1929).
Synagogue Histories File, American Jewish Archives.

RODEPH SHOLOM CONGREGATION, REFORM. *New York, New York.* In 1842, a group of approximately eighty people met in a room on Hudson Street to form a congregation under the name Rodeph Sholom. The following year, members consecrated its synagogue on Attorney Street. The following year, members founded the Bikkur Cholim Society, long associated with Rodeph Sholom. As part of the arrangement with two other congregations (Emanu-El and Beth El), Rabbi Leo Merzbacher became Rodeph Sholom's religious leader. He remained under 1844, leaving the congregation over a dispute regarding whether married women should wear wigs to cover their heads.

Rabbi Max Lilienthal succeeded Merzbacher in 1845. During his tenure, Rodeph Sholom shared responsibility for the Union Day School. In 1849, members established the Chebra Ahavath Noshim Society and the Achyoth Zion. During the years 1850–1855, Rodeph Sholom had no rabbinic leadership. In 1853, the congregation of 189 members moved to Clinton Street, where it built a new home.

Henry A. Henry served the congregation as religious leader from 1855 to 1858. Under his leadership, the congregation actively participated in affairs confronting the fledgling American Jewish community, such as relief for the epidemic in New Orleans in 1858–1859 and the Mortara case, about the same time. When Henry left Rodeph Sholom in 1859, B. L. Kronreuther came to lead the congregation. During the years 1863–1868, Rodeph Sholom once again found itself without religious leadership. Yet it participated in the effort to form an "association of United Hebrew Congregations" and cooperated in the work of the Hebrew Free School Association of New York.

Rabbi Aaron Hahn served Rodeph Sholom from 1868 to 1874. He introduced a choir and organ as well as family pews at the rededication of the synagogue, where it altered its worship service (1875). Following a presentation by Rabbi Aaron Wise during the dedication of the new building, members invited Wise to lead them. He remained with Rodeph Sholom until his death in 1896. During his tenure, the congregation participated in the establishment of the Board of Delegates of American Israelites (1878).

In 1887, fire nearly completely destroyed the temple building. Members rebuilt the structure and worshiped there for two more years before moving into the former Temple Beth-El building at the corner of Lexington Avenue and Sixty-third Street. In 1891, the women of the congregation established the Rodeph Sholom Sisterhood.

Dr. Rudolph Grossman succeeded Wise in 1897. He introduced the revised edition of the *Union Prayer Book*. Three years later, he established a junior sisterhood. The following year, the congregation joined the Union of American Hebrew Congregations, the national organization of Reform synagogues.

Rodeph Sholom members supported refugees from the persecution of the Black Hundreds of Russia in 1905 and the San Francisco earthquake victims of the following year. In 1927, the Women's Association merged with the Sisterhood in order to focus the welfare, social, and cultural efforts of Rodeph Sholom's women. Following Grossman's death in 1927, Rabbi Mitchell Salem Fischer served as interim rabbi (1928–1930). In 1929, Rodeph Sholom and its 750 members moved to Eighty-third Street, near Central Park West.

Rabbi Louis I. Newman joined the congregation in 1930 to serve as its religious leader. He introduced Sunday Morning Community Services (discontinued 1949). In 1958, Rodeph Sholom founded a nursery school. In 1965, the temple purchased four brownstone houses adjacent to the temple, facing Eighty-fourth Street. Five years later, beginning with nursery and kindergarten, Rodeph Sholom became the first Reform congregation to sponsor its own day school, which it housed in these buildings. In 1972, the temple established a full day-school program through sixth grade. In 1976, Rodeph Sholom initiated its first Bar and Bar Mitzvah program for adults. The following year, the day school moved into its new building adjoining the temple structure.

Rabbi Gunther Hirschberg became senior rabbi of the congregation in 1972, having previously served as cantor and associate rabbi. Under his leadership, Rodeph Sholom established a Community Concerns Committee to function as the outreach and social action arm of the congregation. Hirschberg died in 1989. Rabbi Robert Levine succeeded Hirschberg in 1991. In 1994, membership at Rodeph Sholom exceeded 950 family units.

References

Religion Is the Life of Israel (New York: 1929).
Synagogue Histories File, American Jewish Archives.

TEMPLE SHAARAY TEFILA, REFORM. *New York, New York.* A group of fifty B'nai Jeshurun members, dissatisfied over an election of officers of the congregation, were prohibited from entering the synagogue one Saturday morning for a Bar Mitzvah. Realizing that they were in the minority, those who had closed the synagogue and thereby prohibited this group from entering organized Shaaray Tefila in a small downtown room in 1845 (officially chartered in 1848). Samuel M. Isaacs, rabbi of B'nai Jeshurun, joined the group of Jews primarily from Holland and England as its religious leader. Two years later, this new congregation consecrated its synagogue edifice on Wooster Street, a central location for the Jewish community at the time.

This new congregation, like its predecessor, followed Orthodox Jewish practice. Shaaray Tefila was a member of the Board of Delegates of American Israelites, which was formed in 1859 to protect the interest of Jews in America and abroad. By 1862, membership reached two hundred; with the neighborhood changing around the congregation, Shaaray Tefila decided to move. Thus, it leased property in 1863 on Thirty-fourth Street, between Sixth and Seventh Avenues, the same property its owners leased to B'nai Jeshurun. While merger talks ensued as a result, they did not come to fruition. Instead, Shaaray Tefila leased the Armory Building at Thirty-Sixth Street and Broadway, where it remained from 1864 to 1869.

In this new building, the congregation initiated its first religious school, registering 140 children (1865). Two years later, the congregation took an interest in the educational work of Isaac Leeser and his Maimonides College and established a scholarship there. By the end of the decade, members readied themselves to move once again, into a new synagogue which they built at Forty-fourth and Sixth. As part of this preparation, members made slight changes in ritual. The ritual committee asked mourners to remain in their seats instead of coming forward to recite the Mourner's Kaddish prayer. The committee asked the congregation to pray silently and follow the Reader. While someone read the Torah, no one could enter or leave the sanctuary. English became the language of recitation for the prayer for the government. The rabbi was asked to deliver a sermon on every Sabbath and holiday. Liturgical poems called *piyyutim* were abbreviated. In general, the ritual committee called for more decorum during worship. The congregation adopted all of these suggestions.

Nevertheless, the structure of the Forty-fourth Street Synagogue reflected the Orthodox practice with separate seating for men and women. In order to reduce

the synagogue's debt, a direct result of the new building, Shaaray Tefila consolidated with the Beth-El congregation in 1871. Beth-El, organized in 1853,
had reached a membership of fifty-six, nearly all of whom joined Shaaray Tefila.

Toward the end of Samuel Isaacs' career (1873), the congregation engaged
Rabbi Frederick de Sola Mendes to assist him. When Isaacs retired in 1877, de
Sola Mendes succeeded him. Prior to his retirement, Shaaray Tefila continued
to reform its ritual by reducing the amount of chanting and shortening the service
through the elimination of much liturgical poetry (*piyyutim*). Once Isaacs retired,
worship reform came more quickly. These reforms included the near elimination
of all chanting and *piyyutim* and the reading of the prophetic portion (Haftarah)
in English. In addition, de Sola Mendes shortened the additional or *Musaf* service and permitted Bar Mitzvah boys to offer an English prayer toward the end
of the worship service. By 1880, members pressed for the introduction of an
organ, mixed seating, and a mixed choir. Additional reforms subsequently followed. The congregation asked Rabbi de Sola Mendes to read the majority of
the service in English and to read (instead of chant) the Torah. However, the
congregation was yet unwilling to make similar changes in holiday ritual. Yet,
Shaaray Tefila introduced Confirmation in 1881.

When the Jewish Theological Seminary was founded in 1886, the congregation wholeheartedly supported the endeavor. At the same time, Shaaray Tefila
continued to consider ritual reforms such as the amount of Torah to be read on
each Sabbath and the number of Torah honors given to people.

In 1889, Dr. Mendes founded the Shaaray Tefila Sisterhood of Personal Service and the Shaaray Tefila Journal. At the same time, the congregation knew
it had to move again. In 1893, the congregation acquired property at Eighty-
second Street near Amsterdam Avenue. Although members succeeded in selling
their building, the move did not take place until the following year. Thus, Shaaray Tefila worshiped in Carnegie Hall and established a religious school at the
Hotel Endicott. In preparation for occupying their new home, members made
more sweeping changes in the ritual. The wearing of the prayer shawl became
optional, and the service was shortened. Shortly thereafter, the congregation
joined the Union of American Hebrew Congregations, the national organization
of Reform congregations (1902).

With its new location on the West Side of Manhattan, people referred to
Shaaray Tefila as the West End Synagogue. The congregation introduced late
Friday evening services and adopted the *Union Prayer Book,* the uniform prayer
book of the Reform movement. After 1900, membership rose steadily from 240
in 1901 to five hundred by 1916. Thus, the congregation invited Rabbi Nathan
Stern to assist Rabbi de Sola Mendes (1915), officially succeeding him in 1920.

Rabbi Hyman Judah Schactel joined Shaaray Tefila as its assistant rabbi in
1931, even as the congregation still felt the severe effects of the Depression. In
1937, arson fire ravaged the synagogue, but, by the end of the year, members
had rebuilt most of the damaged structure. Schachtel was known for his anti-
Zionist stance in the congregation. When Rabbi Schachtel left the congregation

in 1943, Rabbi Bernard Bamberger succeeded him. As a scholar, Bamberger emphasized education in his rabbinate. During his tenure, the congregation moved to East Seventy-ninth Street and Second Avenue (1958). Bamberger served until 1971. Philip Schecter succeeded him briefly in 1971, after which time the congregation elected Harvey Tattlebaum, who had served as an assistant in 1962–1965, to its pulpit. Tattlebaum, an ardent Zionist, guided the congregation in the area of education and social action. In 1995, membership exceeded thirteen hundred family units.

References

Cohen, Simon, *Shaaray Tefila: The History of Its Hundred Years* (New York: 1945).
Grinstein, Hyman. *The Rise of the Jewish Community of New York 1654–1860* (Philadelphia: 1945).
Religion Is the Life of Israel (New York: 1929).
Synagogue Histories File, American Jewish Archives.

SHEARITH ISRAEL (SPANISH AND PORTUGUESE SYNAGOGUE), ORTHODOX. *New York, New York.* The history of Shearith Israel begins with the arrival of twenty-three Jews in 1654 in New Amsterdam. However, we can only date worship services there to 1695. Historian Jacob Rader Marcus suggests that Colonial Jews founded the congregation as Shearith Jacob. When a group reorganized the congregation in 1730, they took the name Shearith Israel. The congregation used a private house on Mill Street for worship during the first three decades of the eighteenth century. In 1730, the congregation consecrated a new home elsewhere on Mill Street for the growing Jewish community. Its architecture followed the Sephardic synagogues in London and Amsterdam. The following year, members erected a synagogue center for use by the community. In 1758, the congregation purchased an adjoining building.

In 1776, Gershom Mendes Seixas, the congregation's religious leader, led Shearith Israel congregants from New York to escape British occupation—eventually to return. In 1790, members added a fifth building to the growing structure. The assignment of seating occupied a great deal of discussion during these early years, specifically with regard to how close to the front of the women's gallery unmarried women might be seated. In 1802, Shearith Israel established the Polonies Talmud Torah for the religious education of its children.

By 1818, after the city decided to introduce a gutter into the synagogue yard (1796) and a new water pump into the synagogue (1799), the congregation decided to move. While many congregants preferred a move north to suburban Greenwich Village, the majority chose to stay in the same area and build once again at the same location on Mill Street. In 1825, the Ashkenazic element in the synagogue created its own organization for worship called the Hebra Hinuch Nearim. This group reflected growing dissonance with the Sephardic style of worship and eventually established B'nai Jeshurun.

The move of the Jewish population determined that the facility would serve the congregation only until 1834. Thus, the congregation met in rented quarters for approximately a year, until members built a new synagogue on Crosby Street. In 1852, Shearith Israel members participated in the organization of Mt. Sinai Hospital. The 1850s saw a rapid deterioration of the neighborhood. Thus, congregants moved their synagogue once again, to Nineteenth Street and Fifth Avenue in 1860.

Members helped organize Montefiore Hospital in 1885 and the Jewish Theological Seminary of America in the following year. After a great deal of negotiation, the congregation purchased land on Central Park West and Seventieth Street, where it built its new synagogue in 1897. After that time, Shearith Israel made many improvements to the building, including a major expansion in 1954.

Since the beginning of its congregational life, Shearith Israel's liturgy has reflected Sephardic tradition, while yielding only slightly to the influence of Ashkenazic Jews in the community. Prayer books originated at Shearith Israel serve the entire Union of Sephardic Congregations (established by Rabbi David de Sola Pool at Shearith Israel in 1928 and now known as the World Sephardi Federation).

Throughout its history, Shearith Israel members established numerous organizations that reflected their desire to put teaching into action. These included the Hebra Gemiluth Hasadim (to provide general relief), 1785–1790; Kalfe Sedaka Mattan Basether (charity to be dispensed anonymously), 1798–1816; Hebra Hased Va-amet (burial society), established 1802; Hebrew Relief Society (for poor children), established 1828; New York Hebrew Assistance Society (for the relief of indigent Jews), established 1840; Female Hebrew Benevolent Society, 1820–1870; Association for the Moral and Religious Instruction of Children of the Jewish Faith, 1838–1846; the Ladies Sewing Association, established 1847; the Ladies Army Relief, established 1861; the Ladies Aid Society, 1878–1896; the Envelope Society (a fund-raising endeavor), 1889–1896; and the Sisterhood, established 1896.

Beyond its charitable activities, Shearith Israel, as an institution, took a stand on a variety of issues confronting the Jewish community. These include the Russian Treaty (1832), the Mortara case (1858), the Johnson immigration law (1924), and the British White Paper that restricted immigration to Palestine (1929). While the Damascus blood libel (1840) roused American Jewry to unite, Shearith Israel stood in opposition to such a union, fearful that it might be overcome by the Reform tendencies of some of its constituent members. Nevertheless, Shearith Israel joined with other congregations in order to create a united voice in the Board of Delegates of American Israelites for the growing American Jewish community to respond to specific challenges. However, when the Union of American Hebrew Congregations succeeded the Board of Delegates, Shearith Israel decided not to join the new organization. As an alternative, Shearith Israel and its rabbi helped to establish the Union of Orthodox Jewish Congregations in 1898. And a decade later in 1909, the congregation wholeheartedly joined the New York Kehillah, a short-lived experiment to create a unified Jewish community in New York City. However, when Judah L. Magnes took on a posture of pacifism during World War I, which was perceived to be the position of the Kehillah as well, Shearith Israel withdrew from the body. But the experience encouraged Shearith Israel members to support the Synagogue Council of America and the New York Board of Rabbis.

Beginning in the mid-1850s, following the lead of other New York congregations, Shearith Israel engaged rabbis as well as hazanim. While many religious leaders served the congregation, these rabbis are generally associated with the history of Shearith Israel: Henry Pereira Mendes (1877–1920), David de Sola Pool (1907–1969), and Marc Angel (1969–   ). Mendes became a leading voice for Orthodox Judaism. Rabbi de Sola Pool translated ancient Sephardic liturgy in order to make it more meaningful for the worshiper and strengthen the Sephardic custom of worship. He is best known perhaps as Shearith Israel's historian, collecting information and publishing extensively about the history of the congregation.

Angel has strengthened the position of the Sephardic community in New York through his extensive writing and community activities. He established the Sephardic House at Shearith Israel in 1978. In 1994, membership at Shearith Israel exceeded 625 family units.

References

Angel, Marc D., ed. *Rabbi David de Sola Pool: Selections from Six Decades of Sermons, Addresses and Writings* (New York: 1980).

Grinstein, Hyman. *The Rise of the Jewish Community of New York 1654–1860* (Philadelphia: 1945).

Markovitz, Eugene. "Henry Pereira Mendes: Architect of the Union of Orthodox Jewish Congregations." *American Jewish Historical Quarterly* 55 (1965): 364–84.

Phillips, N. Taylor. "The Congregation Shearith Israel: An Historical Review." *Publications of the American Jewish Historical Society,* no. 6 (1897).

———. "Unwritten History: Reminiscences of N. Taylor Phillips." *American Jewish Archives* 6, no. 2 (June 1954): 77–104.

Pool, David de Sola. *The Crosby Street Synagogue (1834–1860) of the Congregation Shearith Israel* (New York: 1934).

———. *The Mill Street Synagogue (1730–1817) of the Congregation Shearith Israel* (New York: 1930).

Pool, David de Sola, and Tamar de Sola Pool. *An Old Faith in the New World: Portrait of Shearith Israel 1654–1954* (New York: 1955).

Synagogue Histories File, American Jewish Archives.

SOCIETY FOR THE ADVANCEMENT OF JUDAISM, RECONSTRUCTIONIST, CONSERVATIVE. *New York, New York.*

After a struggle over change at the Jewish Center, Mordecai Kaplan founded the Society for the Advancement of Judaism in 1922 "for the sole purpose of emphasizing the ways and means whereby Judaism might become operative once more in the life of our people." Shortly thereafter members elected him rabbi for life. Kaplan emphasized the upbuilding of Palestine, Jewish education as a lifelong endeavor, freedom of thought in the interpretation of tradition, and the reconstruction of the synagogue as a center for Jewish life.

The new group met in a small private house on West Eighty-sixth Street. In the early days even Kaplan himself was not sure whether he wanted to recreate the Jewish Center, establish an ideology for a new movement, or just build a new synagogue. There was little disagreement over ritual in the incipient stages of the new organization, as the key issue became one of identity. Kaplan argued for the name "American Synagogue," before settling on the Society for the Advancement of Judaism (SAJ). In order not to appear like a synagogue, the SAJ opened its facilities to Zionist organizations, which needed a place to meet, as well as to educational organizations. Within a few years of its founding, several chapters of the SAJ evolved (including ones in Scranton, Cleveland, Chicago, Hartford, New Bedford, Manhattan Beach, and Brooklyn). Yet, the SAJ affiliated with the United Synagogue of America (now the United Synagogue of Conservative Judaism), the national organization of Conservative synagogues (1922), as well as the Federation of Reconstructionist Synagogues and Havurot, the national organization of Reconstructionist synagogues (1969).

Kaplan introduced Bat Mitzvah as the first change in ritual in 1922—one for his own daughter. He also slightly altered the prayers asking for the restoration of the sacrificial cult, but members overruled his attempt to introduce mixed seating during worship. He altered many of the traditional forms of blessing, as well as deleting the Kol Nidre chant on the evening of Yom Kippur. In 1923, he initiated the publication of the *SAJ Review,* which contained his philosophy. In 1925, Kaplan separated the society from the synagogue. Thus, the SAJ became the fountainhead for what eventually developed into the Reconstructionist movement. The *SAJ Review* continued publication until the Depression.

The SAJ became more than a synagogue but not a center—"a seven-day synagogue," as Israel Levinthal called it. Kaplan focused on raising funds for Palestine, building a program of adult education, and created an extensive music program. In 1925, he established a board of arbitration, an updated version of a rabbinic court, for arbitrating disputes among community members.

Kaplan officially retired in 1968, but he still preached on the High Holidays. Rabbi Alan Miller, who served previously as his assistant, succeeded him. He initially followed Kaplan's model and then guided the synagogue from a "Freudian perspective," according to Rabbi Edward Feld, who succeeded Miller in 1992. During Miller's tenure, a group broke away from the SAJ to form the West End Synagogue (1984). In 1995, membership stood at two hundred family units.

References

Libowitz, Richard. *Mordecai M. Kaplan and the Development of Reconstructionism* (New York: 1983).

Scult, Mel. *Judaism Faces the Twentieth Century: A Biography of Mordecai Kaplan* (Detroit: 1994).

STEPHEN WISE FREE SYNAGOGUE, REFORM. *New York, New York.* The Free Synagogue is the work of Rabbi Stephen S. Wise, who founded it in 1907. Wise held his first services in the auditorium of the Hudson Theater. From its onset, the Free Synagogue maintained a policy of "no pew-holders" and "no standardized membership dues." The rabbi had "absolute freedom of the pulpit." The Free Synagogue held regular services in Carnegie Hall, beginning in 1910. In 1923, Wise built a synagogue at West Sixty-Eighth Street, which also housed the Jewish Institute of Religion, which Wise founded in 1922. In 1929, eleven hundred families affiliated with the synagogue. When the Free Synagogue constructed a new synagogue building in 1932, the Jewish Institute of Religion became the sole tenant of the former Free Synagogue building.

The synagogue reflected the social activism and ardent Zionism of its rabbi. In addition, under the leadership of its associate rabbi, Sidney Goldstein (1907–1953), the congregation developed an extensive program of social welfare. These rabbis succeeded Wise: Edward Klein (1949–1980), Balfour Brickner (1980–1990), and Ira Youdovin (1990–1994). In 1995, the membership at Stephen Wise Free Synagogue included over 635 family units.

References

Religion Is the Life of Israel (New York: 1929).
Stephen Wise Free Synagogue Archives, New York, New York.

SUTTON PLACE SYNAGOGUE, CONSERVATIVE. *New York, New York.* Before the turn of the century, founders established an Orthodox synagogue (Orach Chayim) to serve residents in the vicinity of Forty-second Street, from First Avenue to the East River (now known as Sutton Place), under the religious leadership of Meyer Freeman. The congregation received its charter in 1901. In its early years, the congregation made its home on First Avenue between East Fiftieth and Fifty-first Street, before moving to a former church on Fifty-first Street. There are no extant records from this early period.

Rabbi David B. Kahane became the congregation's religious leader in 1950. He focused his attention on outreach efforts. Under his guidance, Sutton Place Synagogue affiliated with the United Synagogue of America (now the United Synagogue of Conservative Judaism), the national organization of Conservative synagogues. By the late 1960s, the congregation needed new facilities to accommodate its growing membership. In 1971, Abby Rockefeller purchased a portion of the synagogue property in order to develop Greenacre Park, now adjacent to the synagogue. As a result, the congregation purchased property on East Fifty-first Street and Fifty-second Street. Because it is the closest synagogue to the United Nations, Sutton Place Synagogue reaches out to Jewish personnel there, calling itself the Jewish Center for the United Nations.

In the early 1970s, the congregation moved to the Fifty-second Street building so that a new building could be built on the Fifty-first Street site (dedicated 1975). The current emphases of the congregation are outreach and education.

The synagogue's best-known program is called Jewish Town Hall (established 1981), which features an interview exchange with the Sutton Place Synagogue rabbi and leading dignitaries. Rabbi Richard Thaler joined the congregation in 1993, and Sutton Place listed its membership in 1995 as twelve hundred individuals.

Reference

Personal interviews, 1994 and 1995.

RECONSTRUCTIONIST SYNAGOGUE OF THE NORTH SHORE, RE-CONSTRUCTIONIST. *Plandome, New York.* A group of eight Roslyn residents met in 1957 to discuss the philosophy of Mordecai Kaplan in order to form the basis of a congregation and formed a *havurah* (fellowship group). Using the Reconstructionist prayer book, they met in each other's homes. The incipient congregation founded a Hebrew school for its children in 1959. That same year, the congregation rented space in Manhasset Hall, using that facility until 1961, when it moved into the Onderdonk House (1961–1966) and then the Friends Meeting House (1967–1974). In 1974, the congregation moved into its first permanent home in Roslyn Heights. In 1980, a congregational split occurred, resulting in the formation of a second synagogue. In 1993, the Reconstructionist Synagogue of the North Shore moved to its new building in Plandome on Plandome Road.

Following service by Daniel Merritt, a student rabbi, from 1961 to 1962, these individuals served the congregation as religious leaders: Aaron Weiss (1962–1964), Paul Ritterband (1964–1966), Ira Eisenstein (1967–1977), Dennis Sasso (1974–1977), Jeffrey Schein (1977–1978), Arthur Seltzer (1978–1980), and Emanuel Goldsmith (1980–1981). Members invited Rabbi Lee Friedlander to become their religious leader in 1981; in 1986, they invited his spouse, Rabbi Joy Levitt, to share the pulpit. In 1995, congregational membership neared three hundred family units.

Reference

Newman, Tobie, and Sylvia Landow. *That I May Dwell among Them: A Synagogue History of Nassau County* (Nassau County, NY: 1991).

FOREST HILLS JEWISH CENTER, CONSERVATIVE. *Queens, New York.* Founders established the Forest Hills Jewish Center in 1931, having organized a sisterhood and a Hebrew school the previous year. This group engaged Rabbi Solomon Landman, a graduate of the Reform Hebrew Union College, as its religious leader. However, when the congregation embraced Conservative Judaism in 1934, members invited Rabbi Ben Zion Bokser (1934–1984) to serve as their "founding rabbi." Bokser was a scholar and liturgist who prepared a Sabbath and High Holiday prayer book used throughout the Conservative movement. The first year of Bokser's tenure, the Forest Hills Jewish Center joined the United Synagogue of America (now the United Synagogue of Conservative

Judaism), the national organization of Conservative synagogues. Upon Bokser's death in 1984, Rabbi Gerald Skolnik, who had served as assistant since 1981, succeeded him. In 1985, to honor Bokser, the city changed the name of the street in front of the synagogue to Ben Zion Bokser Square.

Members first met for worship in rented rooms on Kessel Street, before building their own synagogue on Kessel Street (1939) with approximately seventy family members. In 1949, with over four hundred family members, the congregation moved to a new building on Queens Boulevard. However, members retained ownership of the Kessel Street building for educational classes and informal worship (until 1955). At about the same time, the congregation moved into its new building, the Midway Jewish Center merged with the Forest Hills Jewish Center. In 1950, the merged institution organized a preschool. Four years later, members built a youth center. In 1963, the congregation helped found the Solomon Schechter Day School of Queens.

By 1980, membership exceeded eighteen hundred families. Activities expanded greatly to accommodate the large membership. The congregation established a Parent-Child Drop-In Center in 1983. While the congregation slowly allowed women to participate in the rituals of the congregation, first as a group on Simchat Torah in 1953 and at a Saturday morning Bat Mitzvah in 1981, in 1995 the congregation permitted women to participate equally in the ritual of the synagogue and receive Torah honors. Membership of the Forest Hills Jewish Center stood at 950 family units in 1995.

Reference

Synagogue Histories Collection, The Joseph and Miriam Ratner Center for the Study of Conservative Judaism.

BETH EL, CONSERVATIVE. *Rochester, New York.* Following a visit to Buffalo's Temple Beth El, a group of ten Rochester Jews, formerly members of Orthodox B'nai Israel, incorporated Beth El Congregation in 1915. The group initially met in its newly acquired home on Oxford Street. Though members had intended to build a new structure at the Oxford Street location, they instead purchased a former church at Park Avenue and Meigs Street (1917). Student rabbis from the Conservative Jewish Theological Seminary served the congregation before it elected Dr. Joel Blau as its religious leader. Blau introduced moderate reforms in the liturgy to the congregation. In 1919, Rabbi Jacob S. Minkin succeeded Blau.

Under Minkin's guidance, the congregation established a Sisterhood (1919) and Men's Club (1923). He also instituted daily worship services and intensified the Hebrew School curriculum. In 1920, Beth El affiliated with the United Synagogue of America, (now the United Synagogue of Conservative Judaism), the national organization of Conservative synagogues. By 1925, Beth El's membership roster reached two hundred families. Jeremiah Berman (1929–1939) succeeded Rabbi Minkin. In 1950, Beth El members dedicated a school and auditorium building at Winton Road and Hillside Avenue. A fire destroyed this building in 1960, and the congregants rebuilt it. Two years later, the congregation of 1150 families built a synagogue next door on Winton Road. Rabbi Henry Fischer (1939–1946) succeeded Rabbi Minkin. Rabbi Stuart Rosenberg (1946–1956) succeeded Fischer before members elected Rabbi Abraham J. Karp (1956–1972), a scholar of American Jewish history. Karp emphasized religious education for children and adults in the congregation. Rabbi Dov Peretz Elkins (1972–1976), known for his work in interpersonal relations, self-esteem, and group dynamics, served the congregation; members then elected Rabbi Shamai Kanter (1977–   ) to lead them. Under his leadership, the congregation granted ritual equality to women (1994) and counted them in the minyan. In 1995, membership at Beth El exceeded eleven hundred family units.

References

Karp, Abraham J. "Overview: The Synagogue in America—A Historical Typology." In Jack Wertheimer, ed., *The American Synagogue: A Sanctuary Transformed* (Cambridge: 1987).
Rosenberg, Stuart E. *The Jewish Community of Rochester, 1843–1925* (New York: 1954).
Synagogue Histories Collection, the Joseph and Miriam Ratner Center for the Study of Conservative Judaism.
Synagogue Histories File, American Jewish Archives.

B'RITH KODESH TEMPLE, REFORM. *Rochester, New York.* Twelve immigrants—peddlers and merchants—gathered together in a private home on Clinton Street in 1848 to organize a religious society. Previously, the group had held occasional worship services in the same location. Though little is known about its early years, the Rochester city directory of 1855 does list a synagogue on Front Street served by Marcus Tuska as "rabbi." The congregation moved to a church building on St. Paul Street in 1849, remaining there until 1876, when members built a new building on the same street. Services continued there until 1894.

Against strong opposition, the congregation introduced an organ and choir in 1862. Thereafter, Reform took hold of the congregation. When the board initiated family pews seven years later, a small group withdrew and established a separate congregation, later to be known as Aitz Ranon. That same year the congregation established a Sabbath School for its children. The congregation's day school closed when children began attending public schools. Once members elected Rabbi Max Landsberg to the pulpit in 1870, reforms came rapidly. By 1874, B'rith Kodesh gave its members the opportunity to remove their hats. In 1879, the congregation abolished the practice of wearing hats for worship. In 1883, B'rith Kodesh members introduced a new prayer book almost entirely in English. B'rith Kodesh moved into its newly constructed building on Gibbs Street in 1894. Landsberg instituted Sunday lectures there in 1899. He transformed these lectures into worship services in 1911, when the congregation discontinued late Friday services.

When Rabbi Landsberg retired in 1915, Rabbi Horace Wolf succeeded him, having served as assistant since 1909. His passion for social justice and welfare impacted on the program of the congregation. During his early tenure as assistant, fire destroyed the synagogue on Gibbs Street (1909). B'rith Kodesh rebuilt and dedicated the synagogue the following year. In 1922, Wolf insisted on the implementation of an unassigned pew system. As membership and enrollment in the religious school increased, the members built an annex in 1924.

When Rabbi Wolf died in 1927, Rabbi Philip S. Bernstein became the new rabbi, having served briefly as assistant. Unlike his predecessors, Bernstein wanted to move B'rith Kodesh into the mainstream of Jewish life. He took an active role in Zionism and led the return to Friday evening services, traditional observances of the holidays, memorial prayers on Passover, a weekday Hebrew School, and Bar Mitzvah. During Bernstein's service as a chaplain in the Armed Forces during World War II, Rabbi Horace Manacher led the congregation (1942–1945). Following the war, Bernstein returned to Europe to work with displaced Jews.

In 1962, B'rith Kodesh's 1250 members dedicated their new house of worship on Elmwood Avenue. When Rabbi Bernstein retired in 1974, Rabbi Judea Miller succeeded him, having joined the congregation as assistant rabbi the previous year. Under Rabbi Miller's leadership, the congregation took an active role in issues of social justice. Joining together with other synagogues and churches, congregants worked for the welfare of all, especially African Americans and the homeless and hungry. In 1995, Rabbi Miller died. That year, Temple B'rith Kodesh listed its membership at over 1350 family units.

References

McKelvey, Blake. "The Jews of Rochester: A Contribution to Their History during the Nineteenth Century." *American Jewish History* 40 (September 1950): 57–73.
One Hundred Years of Consecration (Rochester: 1948).
Rosenberg, Stuart E. *The Jewish Community of Rochester, 1843–1925* (New York: 1954).
Synagogue Histories File, American Jewish Archives.
Temple B'rith Kodesh 1848–1948 (Rochester: 1949).

CENTRAL SYNAGOGUE OF NASSAU COUNTY, REFORM. *Rockville Centre, New York.* The congregation grew from a group of fifty-eight interested families who met at the Milburn Country Club in 1935. The following year the congregation worshiped for the first time. McIntosh Studio served as the first synagogue, before the congregation moved to the Masonic Hall Lodge on Lincoln Avenue. At the same time, the congregation founded a religious school with thirty children, as well as a women's organization. During its first year of existence, Rabbi Roland B. Gittlesohn served the congregation as its first religious leader (1936).

Central Synagogue held its first Confirmation in 1937. Two years later, the religious school grew to 160 and met at the Wilson School. When Rabbi Gittlesohn returned from army service during World War II (1946), the congregation joined the Union of American Hebrew Congregations, the national organization of Reform synagogues. One year later, Central Synagogue's 277 families dedicated their first permanent house of worship on DeMott Avenue, on property they acquired in 1940.

While Bar Mitzvah (for boys) had been an integral part of the congregation since its founding, the first Bat Mitzvah (for girls) did not take place until 1949, the same year members organized a Men's Club. When membership reached over six hundred families in 1952, the synagogue built a school building on the same property. Rabbi Gittlesohn accepted the pulpit at Temple Israel in Boston in 1953; Rabbi George Lieberman joined the congregation a few months later in 1954. During his first year, membership exceeded eight hundred families. Lieberman instituted an annual Institute for Public School Teachers (1957) and, actively pursuing the cause of interfaith relations, an annual Institute for Christian Sunday School Teachers and Educators (1958).

In 1962, Central Synagogue became the site of the Long Island Extension center of Hebrew Union College–Jewish Institute of Religion. When Rabbi Lieberman retired in 1979, Rabbi Lewis Littman succeeded him in the pulpit. Shortly after he arrived, Rabbi Littman instituted the first adult Bar and Bat Mitzvah service. He also established Selichot Services, penitential prayers prior to Rosh Hashanah.

Rabbi Littman left the congregation in 1982, and Rabbi Paul Joseph succeeded him. Joseph focused his attention on adult education in the synagogue. When he left in 1988, Rabbi Jeffrey Salkin succeeded him. Salkin emphasizes preaching, adult education, and rebuilding the youth program in his rabbinate. In 1994, the congregation's membership stood at slightly over four hundred.

References

Golden Jubilee Journal, Central Synagogue of Nassau County (Rockville Centre, New York: 1986).

Newman, Tobie, and Sylvia Landow. *That I May Dwell among Them: A Synagogue History of Nassau County* (Nassau County, NY: 1991).

Synagogue Histories File, American Jewish Archives.

WESTCHESTER REFORM TEMPLE, REFORM. *Scarsdale, New York.* In 1953, eight families joined together to explore the possibility of forming a Reform synagogue to serve the Scarsdale community. Forty families joined the charter congregation, led by Rabbi Eugene Lipman on a part-time basis. The following year, the congregation grew to 120 families, with one hundred children in its religious school. The temple held its activities in the Buser Building in Hartsdale and invited Rabbi Maurice H. Schatz to lead the congregation (1954).

The following year, Rabbi David Greenberg joined Westchester Reform Temple (WRT). In 1959, members dedicated the new temple building on Mamaroneck Road in Scarsdale. Rabbi Erwin Herman served as interim rabbi in 1961, before Rabbi Jack Stern, Jr., joined the temple the following year. Under his leadership, the congregation grew. It dedicated a new sanctuary in 1970, as well as its Irving Berkelhammer classroom wing. In 1971, the congregation formed an adult choir. By 1976, the religious school enrollment grew to over 620 children.

Stern emphasized social action in his rabbinate. As a result, the congregation received the Abraham J. Heschel Award from the (New York) Federation of Jewish Philanthropies for its outstanding contribution to aged and impoverished Jews. In 1982, the congregation built an outdoor sanctuary. The following year, WRT initiated its parenting center. In 1986, the congregation expanded its religious school to include a nursery school and joined an interfaith coalition to work against hunger and homelessness in Westchester County.

Rabbi Jack Stern, Jr., retired in 1991; Rabbi Richard Jacobs succeeded him. Under his direction, the congregation adopted the *Gates of Prayer* as its prayer book and instituted a caring committee to support congregants in times of crisis. In 1994, membership at Westchester Reform Temple exceeded 925 family units.

References

The First Forty Years, 1953–1993: Westchester Reform Temple (Scarsdale, NY: 1993).
Synagogue Histories File, American Jewish Archives.

YOUNG ISRAEL OF SCARSDALE, ORTHODOX. *Scarsdale, New York.* Founders established Young Israel of Scarsdale in 1968 and elected Rabbi Stanley Raskas to lead the congregation (1968–1970). The synagogue held its services in a private home on Baraud Road. Rabbi Reuven Grodner (1970–1983) succeeded Raskas. During his tenure, Young Israel moved to its present quarters on Weaver Street (1978). At the end of his term with the synagogue, the congregation permitted Bat Mitzvah girls to deliver *divrei Torah* (sermons) from the *bima* (raised platform in front of the sanctuary) as long as a *mechitza* (curtain separating men and women) stood in front of the ark. Previously, girls delivered such messages from the rear of the sanctuary.

Rabbi Jacob Rubenstein joined Young Israel of Scarsdale in 1983. The following year, the congregation discontinued its religious school, as most of the congregation's children attended day schools. In 1994, the congregation built an addition to the synagogue. Membership stood at nearly four hundred family units in 1994.

Reference

Synagogue Histories File, American Jewish Archives.

TEMPLE SOCIETY OF CONCORD/KENESETH SHALOM, REFORM. *Syracuse, New York.* The formation of an organized Jewish community in Syracuse began when twelve German newcomers to Syracuse, primarily peddlers, came together for worship in 1839. This group formed Keneseth Sholom, Society of Concord (incorporated 1842). As the founding group grew, it moved to a private home on Mulberry Street (now State Street). In 1841, the congregation elected Abraham Gunzenhauser as its religious leader. The following year, the small synagogue moved its services once again, to the Townsend block of Water Street.

Joseph Goodman succeeded Gunzenhauser in 1846, about the same time Keneseth Sholom moved to larger quarters. The congregation purchased a private house for synagogue use at the corner of Mulberry and Madison Streets. When Rabbi Isaac Mayer Wise, the organizer of Reform Judaism in North America, dedicated the synagogue, he planted the seeds for change among the minds of the congregants.

These religious leaders succeeded Goodman: Jacob Levi, Bernard Illowy, Herman Birkenthal, Solomon Deutsch, Isaac Cohen, and David Burgenheimer. By 1851, membership grew to eighty families, ready to dedicate its own temple on Mulberry and Harrison Streets. This building program caused ritual controversies to surface when the congregation decided to build separate seating for men and women while placing the readers' desk in the front of the synagogue, facing the congregation.

During the Civil War, the controversies that surfaced during the building of the new synagogue in 1851 surfaced once again. No longer sensing any resistance, the Society of Concord quickly introduced organ music, choir singing, the English translation of Hebrew prayers, and family pews. The Orthodox dissenters, losing control of the congregation in the midst of an election of officers, resigned to form their own congregation, Adath Jeshurun (1864). The remaining Orthodox minority resigned when the congregation introduced the policy of requiring all men to remove their hats during worship.

The Society of Concord unsuccessfully attempted to establish a synagogue school on various occasions. During Rabbi Adolph Guttman's tenure (beginning in 1883), the congregation firmly established such a school. He also introduced Confirmation to the congregation. Guttman preached only in German, until he felt comfortable speaking publicly in English. Guttman also instituted various organizations in the synagogue, such as the Men's Club.

When Herman Leiter died in 1904, he bequeathed funds for the congregation to build a new home for itself. As a result, the Society of Concord dedicated a new synagogue on Madison Street and University Avenue in 1911, the first synagogue to move out of what had been called the Jewish neighborhood—though its members previously had moved. Members referred to this building as the new Temple of Concord. Rabbi Benjamin Friedman assumed leadership of the congregation in 1919.

In 1923, the temple introduced an unassigned pew seating system. Two years later, Adath Jeshurun rejoined the membership of the Temple Society of Concord. About the same time (1928), the temple gave the privilege of sitting on the board of trustees to women in the congregation.

As a result of the congregation's constant growth, the temple built the Hiram and Mabel Weissberg Religious School in 1961, accommodating more than five hundred children in the school. Membership itself stood at nearly seven hundred.

Rabbi Theodore Levy succeeded Friedman in 1969, having joined him as associate in 1962. Levy forthrightly expressed his views on the issues of the day from the pulpit, leading the congregation in an aggressive campaign of community social action. He also brought the Bar and Bat Mitzvah back to the synagogue, something which had been discarded early in its life. Levy also worked to enhance interfaith relations in the community.

In 1979, membership exceeded eight hundred. Rabbi Sheldon Ezring succeeded Levy in 1989. Ezring emphasized family programming, adult education, and family life education in the congregation. In 1994, membership stood at over 750 family units.

References

1839–1964: Our First One Hundred Twenty-five Years: The Temple Society of Concord (Syracuse: 1964).

Rudolph, B. G. *From a Minyan to a Community: A History of the Jews of Syracuse* (Syracuse: 1970).

Society of Concord, One Hundredth Anniversary (Syracuse: 1939).

Synagogue Histories File, American Jewish Archives.

Temple Society of Concord, 150th Anniversary (Syracuse: 1989).

Temple Society of Concord, 140 Years (Syracuse: 1979).

BET AM SHALOM, RECONSTRUCTIONIST. *White Plains, New York.* In 1955, a group gathered in White Plains to study the tenets of Reconstructionism, the philosophy of Rabbi Mordecai M. Kaplan. Shortly thereafter, twenty-five families joined together to form Beth Shalom Synagogue (1956). Kaplan's philosophy included religious naturalism and a rejection of the notion of "chosen people." He also argued in favor of gender equality and Zionism. The elements of his philosophy provided the foundation for the establishment of the congregation. The new synagogue joined the United Synagogue of America, the national organization of Conservative synagogues, and the Federation of Reconstruction Synagogues and Havurot. Members met for worship in a local church. In 1959, members acquired the Clovelly Estate—originally built in 1925—on Soundview Avenue. Its previous owner (Temple Israel) had converted it for use as a synagogue.

In 1965, the congregation split into Bet Ami, a Conservative synagogue, and Beth Shalom, a Reconstructionist synagogue, before reuniting for fiscal reasons in 1968 under the name Bet Am Shalom. Later the reunited congregation discontinued its affiliation with the Conservative movement. In the mid-1980s, the congregation struggled over the issue of whether or not intermarriage ceremonies could take place in the synagogue. Ultimately, the congregation decided against them. Rabbi Lester Bronstein joined the congregation in 1989 as the first full-time religious leader. According to historian Baila Shargel, his leadership—unlike the religious naturalism of Kaplan—encouraged a "relaxed community spirituality." In 1991, Bet Am Shalom expanded its facilities; in 1995, membership of the congregation stood at 250 family units.

References

Bet Am Shalom Synagogue 1956–1981 (White Plains, NY: 1981).
Shargel, Baila, and Harold Drimmer. *The Jews of Westchester: A Social History* (Fleischmanns, NY: 1994).

THE HEBREW INSTITUTE OF WHITE PLAINS, ORTHODOX. *White Plains, New York.* In 1914, a small group separated from Temple Israel Center in order to form its own Orthodox synagogue. The early group held services in a furniture store in the Miles Building on Martine Avenue under the direction of Rabbi Max Hoffman. Later the group rented space at the corner of Main Street and Mamaroneck Avenue. Following the receipt of an official charter for The Hebrew Institute of White Plains (1915), the congregation of slightly more than thirty families built a permanent home for itself at South Lexington and Fisher Avenues (dedicated 1918). Various individuals served as religious leaders in the early years of the congregation.

In 1925, Samuel D. Feldshon became the rabbi of the Hebrew Institute. In 1940, membership reached 120 families. That same year, the congregation merged its religious school with local Temple Israel. This arrangement continued until Temple Israel relocated in 1948. The congregation eliminated the practice of auctioning Torah honors during High Holiday services in 1942. In 1941, the women of the congregation founded a sisterhood. Rabbi Feldshon died in 1949; David Roth became senior rabbi, having previously served as associate rabbi. That same year, the congregation built a new synagogue at Greenridge Avenue and Rutherford Street (dedicated 1950). In 1951, the men of the congregation founded a brotherhood. Following Roth's resignation in 1952, Rabbi Murray Grauer became the religious leader of the congregation. The following year, membership exceeded four hundred families with a religious school enrollment of one hundred students. By 1958, membership approached five hundred families, with a school population of 230.

In 1970, the congregation expanded its facilities with the addition of a school wing and chapel. Later in the 1970s, congregational membership declined to 350. Thus, the Hebrew Institute dropped its plan to expand its facilities beyond the initial expansion in 1970. In 1976, a fire of suspicious origin nearly destroyed the synagogue; as a result, the congregation refurbished its facility. In 1984, The Hebrew Institute installed a Holocaust Memorial. The congregation joined other local organizations in the support of SHORE (Supporting the Homeless Is Our Responsibility). In 1994, membership stood at over 280 family units.

Reference

Synagogue Histories File, American Jewish Archives.

NORTH CAROLINA

TEMPLE BETH EL, REFORM. *Charlotte, North Carolina.* In 1942, Rabbi Elihu Michaelson assumed the pulpit at Temple Israel. His Orthodox influence encouraged the founding of Temple Beth El by eight families two years later in 1944. Initially meeting in private homes, the incipient congregation moved to the Hotel Charlotte. Shortly thereafter, the congregation met upstairs over Dowtin's Foodstore on Morehead Street. Harry Golden, famed humorist and writer, wrote the congregation's first constitution.

When the congregation grew to forty-six families in 1946, Beth El moved to Providence Road (dedicated 1949). As membership increased, members added an educational building and fellowship hall. In 1970, a group that disagreed with Rabbi Gerber left and formed Congregation Beth Shalom. In 1983, membership was 320 families. In 1987, Beth Shalom merged with Beth El.

These rabbis served the congregation: Philip Frankel (1943–1951), Nathan Hershfield (1951–1953), C. Melvin Helfgott (1953–1959), Israel J. Gerber (1959–1972), Bernard M. Zlotowitz (1972–1974), Lawrence I. Jackofsky (1974–1976), Harold I. Krantzler (1976–1986), Robert A. Siegel (1986–1992), Robert Shapiro (1992–1993), and James Bennett (1993–   ).

In 1992, Temple Beth El built a new synagogue facility elsewhere on Providence Road to become part of Shalom Park, a unique experiment in which fifty acres are devoted to the religious, social, educational, and fitness needs of Jewish and non-Jewish members. Its membership in 1994 reached 630.

Reference

L'Dor Va'Dor: Temple Beth El, 50 Years (Charlotte: 1994).

JUDEA REFORM CONGREGATION, REFORM. *Durham, North Carolina.* Thirty-one families founded Judea Reform Congregation in 1961 to serve the religious needs of Reform Jews living in the Durham/Chapel Hill area. Rabbi Efraim Rosenzweig served as the first religious leader. The congregation worshiped in local churches in its early years, and the Judea Reform Congregation dedicated its own house of worship in 1971. Following the dedication, membership increased to one hundred families. Rosenzweig emphasized the need to foster interfaith relations during his rabbinate.

In 1976, when Rabbi Rosenzweig retired, Rabbi Eric Yoffie came to Durham to lead the congregation. Yoffie concentrated on expanding the educational opportunities of the congregation, while adding more tradition to Sabbath and holiday observances.

The congregation dedicated a new sanctuary in 1980, the same year Rabbi John Friedman succeeded Yoffie in the pulpit. During his tenure, Judea's membership and scope of activities grew dramatically, reaching three hundred families in 1986. Friedman used more Hebrew found in the liturgy and reintroduced many rituals once discarded by Reform Judaism, such as Bar/Bat on Saturday morning during the reading of the Torah and Havdalah. He also strengthened the congregation's commitment to Israel and worked in building interfaith relations in the community. In 1994, membership at Judea Reform included 428 family units.

References

Rogoff, Leonard. *Migrations: A Social History of the Durham–Chapel Hill Jewish Community* (Chapel Hill: forthcoming).
Synagogue Histories File, American Jewish Archives.

EMANUEL, REFORM. *Greensboro, North Carolina.* Beginning in 1907, a small group of worshipers met for High Holiday services in Greensboro under the leadership of Mr. and Mrs. Emanuel Sternberger. These founders wanted to provide a context for worship for the six Jewish girls in residence at the local state women's college (later to become the University of North Carolina at Greensboro), and they invited Rabbi G. Mendelsohn to lead them in worship. This formative group held services in a rented second floor of a grocery store on South Elm Street.

Formal records can be traced to 1908, when the founders called themselves the Reformed Hebrew Congregation and purchased a Friends Church on E. Lee Street to be used as a synagogue. Beginning in 1910, the congregation called itself the Greensboro Hebrew Congregation. While there was a passing reference made to the congregation as Temple Emanuel in 1915, congregants did not take on that name officially until a Conservative congregation, Beth David Synagogue, was formed in 1949.

In 1924, the congregation moved to a new location "overlooking Fisher Park." Temple Emanuel expanded in 1949. In 1980, members built a new synagogue across Florence Street while still maintaining and refurbishing the old structures.

Rabbis who served the congregation included Louis Egelson (1910/11?–1914), Friedlaender (1914–1915), Simon Cohen (1916–1917), Montague Cohen (1918–1919), Max Kauffman (1924–1925), Milton Ellis (1925–1931), Frederick Rypins (1931–1959), Joseph Asher (1958–1968), Arnold Task (1968–1989), Richard Harkavy (1989–1994), and Fred Guttman (1995–   ). Task emphasized social action in his rabbinate. Harkavy helped the congregation to develop relationships with other Jewish institutions in the community. In 1995, membership neared 375 family units.

Reference

Synagogue Histories File, American Jewish Archives.

O

OHIO

TEMPLE ISRAEL, REFORM. *Akron, Ohio.* In 1864, a group of twenty of Akron's Jewish community members joined together to form the Akron Hebrew Association. The group rented a room on Howard Street for worship services. The following year, the young congregation formed a school for instruction in Hebrew and German. When the group outgrew its Howard Street location, it moved to larger quarters in the Minor J. Allen building in the heart of the city at South Howard Street. In 1871 a debate ensued regarding the uncovering of heads during worship. The congregation resolved to allow individuals to make the personal decision whether or not to cover the head. However, the congregation did insist that no prayer shawl be worn.

The congregation joined the Union of American Hebrew Congregations, the national body of Reform synagogues, in 1874. Nine years later, the congregation moved to a former church on South High Street. The women of the congregation formed an auxiliary organization in 1901, calling it a sisterhood in 1911. In 1907, when its religious leader Rabbi Isidore Philo resigned, the synagogue—as well as its religious school—closed for several months. In 1911, the membership vacated this building and built its own synagogue on Mirriman Street, naming it Temple Israel, to serve its two hundred member families and their eighty children in religious school.

In 1921, the congregation organized its own Boy Scout Troop. During and following the Depression, the congregation cut back drastically on its services to the community. In 1951, with 450 member families, the congregation expanded its facility to include a chapel, a library, a religious school, and offices.

These men served Temple Israel throughout its history as religious leaders: Aaron Suhler (1871–1878), A. Burkheim (1878–1882), S. M. Fleischman (1882–1897), Isidore E. Philo (1897–1908), Louis D. Gross (1909–1917), Abraham Cronbach (1917–1919), David Alexander (1919–1944), J. Marshall Taxay (1945–1953), Morton M. Applebaum (1953–1979), Mark A. Golub (1979–1983), and David M. Horowitz (1983–   ).

Under Rabbi Horowitz's direction, Temple Israel joined with other congregations in Akron to reach out to the unaffiliated. In addition, the congregation made its facilities available to numerous community groups such as Alcoholics Anonymous and other self-help and support groups. Temple Israel also introduced a free mother's-day-out program. In 1994, membership at the temple exceeded seven hundred family units.

References

Cronbach, Abraham. "Autobiography." *American Jewish Archives* 11, no. 1 (April 1959): 3–81.
Synagogue Histories File, American Jewish Archives.
Yesterday, Today and Tomorrow: Temple Israel 1865–1953 (Akron: 1953).

TEMPLE ISRAEL, REFORM. *Canton, Ohio.* A group of families established the CKBC (probably standing for Chevrah Kaddish Bet Canton) in 1885, calling home a building on South Market Street between Second and Third Streets. Later, the congregation moved one block north to the Isaac Harter Bank Building. As the congregation grew, it needed larger quarters and moved again, to a building on the corner of North Market and Sixth Streets. Aaron Amchol served the early congregation as religious leader. I. E. Philo succeeded him. Then came a string of religious leaders serving short terms.

During Rabbi L. Nusbaum's tenure, the congregation moved to Second and Market North, at about the same time the women organized the Ladies' Aid Society (1892). In 1919, the Canton Hebrew Congregation dedicated its first newly constructed home and became known as the McKinley Avenue Temple. Rabbi Carl Herman (1917–1922) served in this new location, succeeded by Rabbi Charles Latz (1922–1945). In 1938, the men of the congregation established a men's club. Rabbi George Lieberman succeeded Latz in 1945. By this time, congregational membership exceeded two hundred families. Lieberman emphasized Zionism in the congregation, as well as the congregation's responsibility to world Jewry.

With the synagogue renamed Temple Israel, members dedicated their new building in 1952 on Twenty-fifth Street, just after the board installed Rabbi Paul Gorin to succeed Lieberman.

Rabbi Gorin retired in 1981, succeeded by Rabbi Jon Spitzer. Rabbi Spitzer emphasized the need for outreach to the community by serving community members with special needs. In 1994, membership of Temple Israel stood at 411 family units.

Reference

Synagogue Histories File, American Jewish Archives.

ADATH ISRAEL, CONSERVATIVE. *Cincinnati, Ohio.* The congregation considers its date of founding to be 1847. However, Polish Jews founded a synagogue, Gates of Heaven, in 1850 on Vine Street. When Gates of Heaven merged with Reform Bene Israel in 1852, those who disagreed with the merger formed Adath Israel. In its early years, Adath Israel moved from place to place, relocating to Seventh and Walnut in 1860.

As a result of the East European immigration of the 1880s, the synagogue grew. The women of the congregation organized an auxiliary in 1890. Adath Israel moved to its first permanent home on Ninth and Cutter Streets in 1896. When the Jewish population moved up to Avondale, the synagogue followed, dedicating its own building on Rockdale Avenue in 1918, the same year Rabbi Louis Feinberg joined the congregation. Under his leadership, the religious and educational program of the synagogue grew. Adath Israel moved to Lexington and Reading Roads in 1927. In 1933, the men of the congregation formed a Men's Club.

Following Rabbi Feinberg's death in 1949, Rabbi Fishel Goldfeder became senior rabbi, having joined as associate in 1945. In 1953, Adath Israel went into private arbitration over the question of mixed seating in the congregation, which it ultimately installed following the proceedings. The congregation made its initial move to Amberly in 1967 with the building of a new sanctuary when membership reached over nine hundred families. Upon Goldfeder's retirement, Rabbi Sidney Zimelman joined the congregation (1981–1991). In 1990, Adath Israel broke from the city rabbinate's kosher supervision and decided to supervise its own. Rabbi Irvin M. Wise succeeded Zimelman in 1992. Shortly before his arrival, Adath Israel voted equal ritual privileges to women of the congregation. In 1995, membership exceeded 710 family units.

References

Sarna, Jonathan, and Nancy H. Klein. *The Jews of Cincinnati* (Cincinnati: 1989).
Synagogue Histories Collection, The Joseph and Miriam Ratner Center for the Study of Conservative Judaism.
Synagogue Histories File, American Jewish Archives.

CONGREGATION AGUDAS ISRAEL/GOLF MANOR SYNAGOGUE, ORTHODOX. *Cincinnati, Ohio.* Polish immigrants to Cincinnati founded Bnai Jacob on Clinton Street (date unknown), and Rumanian immigrants founded Anshei Sholom (1901) on Clark Street (1922). These two congregations merged to form Agudas Israel Congregation and acquired a former church on Forest Avenue in Avondale in 1932. Agudas Israel affiliated with the Union of Orthodox Jewish Congregations. In 1952, Rabbi David Indich joined the congregation as its religious leader. In 1957, Agudas Israel and its two hundred families moved to Golf Manor on Stover Avenue. Shortly thereafter, members founded numerous affiliates and special interest groups. Membership quickly grew to over 350 families. In 1967, the congregation erected its sanctuary (dedicated

1968). Following Rabbi Indich's retirement in 1989, Rabbi Hanan Balk became spiritual leader of Agudas Israel. In 1994, the congregation listed 250 membership units.

References

Sarna, Jonathan, and Nancy H. Klein. *The Jews of Cincinnati* (Cincinnati: 1989).
Synagogue Histories File, American Jewish Archives.

ISAAC M. WISE TEMPLE/K. K. BENE YESHURUN, REFORM. *Cincinnati, Ohio.* In 1840, a group of dissatisfied members left Bene Israel in order to form a new congregation. This group met in a room of the Workum home on Third Street. In 1842, this group of fifty adopted a constitution and became K. K. Bene Yeshurun (Holy Congregation of the Children of Righteousness). Some members attempted to reunite Bene Israel with Bene Yeshurun in 1845, but this effort failed. In 1848, Bene Yeshurun dedicated its first permanent house of worship, the Lodge Street Synagogue. That same year, the congregation established its Talmud Yelodim Institute, a school for children, which functioned until becoming only a Sunday School in 1868 and was fully dissolved in 1914.

The first eruption in the young synagogue occurred when Rabbi James Gutheim (1847–1849) introduced a choir and revised the order of worship. His resignation followed. After seven years and the tenures of two Orthodox religious leaders (H. A. Henry and A. L. Rosenfeld), the congregation called Rabbi Isaac Mayer Wise, the architect of Reform Judaism in America, to its pulpit (1854). During his first year in religious leadership, Wise directed the choir while he played a violin. He also installed an organ. Shortly after his arrival, the congregation adopted Wise's prayer book, *Minhag America* (1857). He also introduced a memorial service that followed the chanting of the Kol Nidre on Yom Kippur evening. In 1855, members expanded the Lodge Street synagogue. In 1858, the congregation abolished the observance of the second day of holidays, except for Rosh Hashanah, which they did not abolish until fourteen years later. In 1859, the entire congregation passed a resolution requesting all merchant members of the congregation to close their businesses on Saturday. The Lodge Street Synagogue became too small for the congregation's 224 families, but the Civil War disrupted plans for a new temple. In the meantime, Bene Israel and Bene Yeshurun congregations considered building a synagogue that would house a merged institution. Bene Yeshurun dedicated a new synagogue on Plum Street in 1866. The congregation constructed this new building with family pews. Bene Yeshurun adopted the *Union Prayer Book* in 1893 and the second volume for the High Holidays the following year.

Wise established the Union of American Hebrew Congregations, the national body of Reform synagogues, in 1873 and Hebrew Union College, the seminary of the Reform movement, in 1875. Wise died in 1900. Dr. Louis Grossman succeeded Wise, having come to serve as adjunct rabbi in 1898.

In 1903, the congregation built the Isaac M. Wise Center on Reading Road and Whittier to serve as a religious school. The Wise Social Center received its official name in 1915 to reflect the establishment of an auxiliary named in Wise's memory to attract young people to the congregation. The Wise Social Center merged with a similar group from the Rockdale Temple in 1929, and both organizations eventually dissolved and joined the new Jewish Center in 1934. However, the Wise Center maintained its name. In 1906, Grossman instituted children's worship services.

By 1921, the Whittier and Reading Road property became inadequate. Thus, Wise Temple members built a new structure farther north on Reading Road at Crescent (dedicated 1927), calling it the Isaac M. Wise Temple Center. In 1930, the congregation eliminated its system of "fixed dues," allowing individuals to give according to their personal means. In 1931, the Reading Road Temple (a previous consolidation of Ahabath Achim/John Street Temple and Sherith Israel/ Mound Street Temple) merged into Bene Yeshurun, forming a congregation of over nine hundred families, with Reading Road's Rabbi Wohl serving jointly with Rabbi James Heller, who had come as associate to Bene Yeshurun in 1920 and succeeded Grossman shortly thereafter (1921). As active Zionists, both emphasized support for Palestine in the congregation. During the Depression, the city of Cincinnati used the basement of Plum Street Temple as a men's shelter for the homeless.

Plum Street Temple underwent major renovations in 1950 and 1974. In 1975, the National Register of Historic Places added the Plum Street facility to its roster. The building remains in use. Rabbi Heller left Bene Yeshurun in 1950 and in 1953 Rabbi Albert Goldman came to Cincinnati to serve as co-rabbi with Wohl (who retired in 1966). Goldman actively worked toward improving interfaith relations in the community while working for civil rights for all. In 1955, the congregation built a new building next to Wise Center in order to accommodate the growing religious school population.

In 1970, Bene Israel of Hamilton, Ohio, became an affiliate of Bene Yeshurun. The following year, Rabbi Goldman introduced a program of rabbinical internship in the congregation. When the congregation vacated its Avondale facility in 1973, it fully returned to Plum Street before building the Isaac M. Wise Center on Ridge Road in Amberly Village (dedicated 1976).

Goldman retired in 1980; Rabbi Alan D. Fuchs succeeded him the following year. Fuchs concentrated his efforts on outreach to unaffiliated and intermarried Jews and on adult Jewish education. Rabbi Lewis Kamrass succeeded Fuchs in 1989, having previously served as assistant rabbi. During his tenure, the congregation worked to introduce family education programs, as well as activities for young singles. In addition, social action became an important priority of Isaac M. Wise Temple with over one-third of its 1280 families participating in programs such as a "High Holiday Mitzvah Bag" food drive. Isaac M. Wise Temple maintains a day camp and an extensive library. Plans are underway to expand the facilities in 1995 or 1996 to accommodate the growing number of programs.

References

Heller, James. *As Yesterday When It Is Past: A History of the Isaac M. Wise Temple, K.K. B'nai Yeshurun, 1842–1942* (Cincinnati: 1942).

Sarna, Jonathan, and Nancy H. Klein. *The Jews of Cincinnati* (Cincinnati: 1989).

Silverstein, Alan. *Alternatives to Assimilation: The Responses of Reform Judaism to American Culture 1840–1930* (Hanover, NH: 1994).

Synagogue Histories File, American Jewish Archives.

ROCKDALE TEMPLE/BENE ISRAEL, REFORM. *Cincinnati, Ohio.* Jonas Joseph, founder and first president of K. K. Bene Israel, organized the Cincinnati Jewish community in 1824 to form a congregation in the pioneer community. In the early years, it worshiped in a building west of Main between Third and Fourth. In 1828, the congregation moved its worship to Front Street between Main and Sycamore, then in 1830 to Fourth Street between Sycamore and Broadway. Appealing for funds from communities around the country, the congregation dedicated its first house of worship on Broadway in 1836. In 1842, the congregation attempted its own Sunday School, following the model established by Rebecca Gratz in Philadelphia. It failed a short time after opening.

By 1846, membership of Bene Israel reached 150. In order to accommodate this growing community, the congregation built a new synagogue on the same site (dedicated 1852). During the construction, the congregation worshiped with local congregation Shaare Shomayim on Vine Street. Once Bene Israel's building was finished, Shaare Shomayim's members merged with Bene Israel (1852). In 1848, Bene Israel introduced a mixed choir during worship and one English prayer in 1851. In 1855, Bene Israel elected Dr. Max Lilienthal as its first religious leader. He introduced additional reforms that resulted in decorum in worship. Furthermore, he discontinued the practice of selling Torah honors, abolished certain prayers, and refused to participate in Tisha B'av services. Those who rejected his reforms started their own congregation Sheerith Israel. Other reforms included the introduction of the triennial reading of the Torah, the reading of the Haftarah in the vernacular, and the preaching of a sermon in German one week and English the following week. The congregation also introduced an organ, added English and German prayers, and removed expressions from the liturgy such as "release from present bondage."

As congregants began to move west of the synagogue, the board recognized the need to relocate. Thus, members built a new synagogue on Mound Street (dedicated 1869). Membership immediately increased. There they adopted the prayer book of Isaac M. Wise, *Minhag America.* In 1873, Bene Israel participated in the founding of the Union of American Hebrew Congregations, the national body of Reform synagogues. Hebrew Union College, the rabbinical seminary and academic arm of the Reform movement, held its first sessions in the Mound Street classrooms. Two years later, men removed their hats during worship; they abolished the second day of Rosh Hashanah the following year.

Lilienthal died in 1882, but Dr. David Philipson did not succeed him until

1888. He introduced the *Union Prayer Book,* the uniform prayer book of the Reform movement. Following the movement of its congregants to the suburbs, Bene Israel joined with Bene Yeshurun in the operation for a limited time of a joint school for younger children in Walnut Hills. Then the congregation moved the entire synagogue program to Rockdale Avenue (dedicated 1906, expanded 1917). Following the dedication of the new synagogue, Bene Israel introduced the Children's Harvest Service, held in conjunction with the festival of Sukkot. In 1913, the women of the congregation formed the Rockdale Avenue Temple Sisterhood, which helped to maintain branch schools in Norwood and later Price Hill. The congregation also introduced Sunday services (during the winter months only), beginning in 1919.

Rabbi Victor Reichert came to Rockdale Temple in 1926 as assistant rabbi. He succeeded Rabbi Philipson in 1938. By the 1950s, members had moved away from the temple once again. The temple dedicated its new facility on Ridge Road and Cross-County Highway in Amberly in 1969. Rabbi Murray Blackman succeeded Rabbi Reichert in 1962, having served as assistant since 1956. Blackman actively participated in community affairs.

Following Blackman's resignation, Rabbi David Hachen led the congregation for only one year. He saw the congregation through its move to its new facilities in Amberly. Rockdale Temple elected Rabbi Harold Hahn to the pulpit in 1969. He expanded the congregation's activity program and introduced the study of Israel into the religious school's curriculum. During Rabbi Hahn's tenure, the congregation introduced transportation services for those otherwise unable to attend services, as well as RockDial, an FM radio–telephone system that allowed homebound people to phone in for services and programs. Rabbi Hahn died after a long illness in 1979.

Rabbi Howard Simon succeeded Rabbi Hahn in 1981. Under his leadership, the congregation joined in the opening of a joint education program of the Reform congregations, the Cincinnati Reform Jewish High School. Rabbi Mark Goldman succeeded Simon after his resignation in 1986. Goldman introduced instrumental music to holiday worship. Under his guidance, Rockdale Temple opened a Nursery School (1986). In 1994, membership of Rockdale Temple exceeded one thousand family units.

References

The 1994 Rockdale Temple Anniversary Directory (Cincinnati: 1994).
One Hundredth Anniversary, 1824–1924, Rockdale Avenue Temple (Cincinnati: 1924).
Philipson, David. "The Cincinnati Community in 1825." *Publications of the American Jewish Historical Society,* no. 10 (1902): 97–99.
Sarna, Jonathan, and Nancy H. Klein. *The Jews of Cincinnati* (Cincinnati: 1989).
Synagogue Histories File, American Jewish Archives.

ANSHE CHESED/FAIRMOUNT TEMPLE, REFORM. *Cleveland, Ohio.*
The early years of Anshe Chesed reflected the earliest development of the Cleveland Jewish community. Its origins can be traced to a small group of Bavarian

Jews who in 1839 formed the Israelite Congregation. Members held services in private homes until the growth of the congregation warranted larger quarters. Within a year, this fledgling group purchased a house at Water Street and Vineyard Lane (now West Ninth Street and Columbus Road) and converted it into a synagogue. But within a year, intergroup tension, spurred on by newcomers to the community, developed in this small group. The greater part of the membership walked out and formed its own synagogue, Anshe Chesed, renting a room for worship on Prospect Street.

This new Anshe Chesed devoted itself to education and immediately established a day school for its twenty-two children. When a fire destroyed the Israelite Congregation's Water Street building in 1845, the two congregations reunited as the Israelitic Anshe Chesed Society. This renewed institution quickly built a new home for itself on Eagle Street (dedicated 1846). Growing to eighty families in 1850, the congregation engaged its first full-time rabbi, Isidor Kalisch, to be chiefly responsible for Anshe Chesed's educational program. Within a few months, a new feud tore at Anshe Chesed's seams, apparently over Rabbi Kalisch's association with the congregation. His fifty supporters, primarily German latecomers to Cleveland, left Anshe Chesed with Kalisch to form Tifereth Israel. Despite periodic merger proposals, this split could not be healed. Members elected B. L. Fould to succeed Kalisch.

Anshe Chesed grew to one hundred members in 1858 but, apparently because of financial problems, closed its school in the same year Fould left the congregation. Disagreements over ideology probably contributed to the school's closing as Reform Judaism began to take hold in the congregation. Reforms in the service had been made as early as 1852. The congregation eliminated a few prayers, abolished the auctioning of Torah honors, and introduced German sermons. In one incident in 1861, synagogue officials called for police assistance to remove three congregants who refused to follow the newly instituted policy of decorum. While the congregation flirted with Orthodoxy briefly in 1860 with the hiring of an Orthodox religious leader, the congregation decidedly turned Reform when it renovated its synagogue building. The congregation installed an organ and made room for a mixed choir. But these reforms were insufficient for large numbers of members, who saw more rapid progress taking place at neighboring Tifereth Israel. As a result, this group—with founding members among them—joined the competing congregation. Gustavus Cohen, who had led Anshe Chesed, joined Tifereth Israel when his contract with the former congregation expired in 1866.

Cohen stayed with Tifereth Israel for a year before going on to Milwaukee. He returned to Anshe Chesed after only a few months and remained until 1873 with a membership exceeding 150. He instituted English worship services and what is claimed as the first mixed choir in a congregation in this country. Cohen's successor, Rabbi Michael Machol (1876–1906), argued vociferously for only moderate reforms in the observance of traditional holidays and Sabbath. During his tenure, Anshe Chesed moved to Scovill and Henry Streets (1887).

Rabbi Louis Wolsey led Anshe Chesed from 1907 to 1924. During his tenure, activities expanded beyond the worship and education that dominated the early years of temple life. Wolsey discarded the little German that remained in the congregation and introduced the *Union Prayer Book.* In 1912, the congregation became known as the Euclid Avenue Temple in recognition of the large structure it dedicated there that year. By 1916, membership increased to over 710.

By the time Wolsey left the pulpit in 1924, he had turned anti-Zionist. Rabbi Barnett Brickner succeeded him the following year, leading the congregation until 1958. Brickner devoted himself to repairing what he considered to be a rift between Judaism and life, devoting his energies to education. He also restored practices he felt had been inadvertently removed from Reform worship, such as the Kol Nidre prayer on the Day of Atonement and the *yizkor* (memorial services) on the major holidays. He also introduced consecration for children entering religious school. As a great orator, Barnett Brickner gained considerable national stature.

The congregation dedicated its Fairmount Temple at Fairmount and Green Roads in 1957. The following year, Rabbi Arthur Lelyveld joined the congregation. He remained until his retirement in 1988. Under his direction, the congregation grew substantially. As an active Zionist and social activist, Lelyveld programmed activities for the congregation in these two important community arenas. Rabbi David Gelfand succeeded Lelyveld in 1988. Following his predecessor, he too emphasized social action in his rabbinate. In addition, Gelfand expanded the educational program of the congregation for the entire family. In 1994, membership at Fairmount Temple exceeded 2050 family units.

References

Gartner, Lloyd P. *History of the Jews of Cleveland* (Cleveland: 1987).
Peskin, Allan. *This Tempting Freedom: The Early Years of Cleveland Judaism and Anshe Chesed Congregation* (Cleveland: 1973).
Silver, Samuel. *Portrait of a Rabbi: An Affectionate Memoir on the Life of Barnett R. Brickner* (Cleveland: 1959).

THE TEMPLE-TIFERETH ISRAEL, REFORM. *Cleveland, Ohio.* In a split with Anshe Chesed in 1850, the founding forty-seven members of Tifereth Israel brought their rabbi, Isidor Kalisch, with them. The new congregation worshiped in a hall on Seneca Street and held religious school classes in a building on Lake Street (later Lakeside Avenue), before moving to worship in a large hall on Superior Street. Kalisch remained until 1853, leaving as result of the financial strain of the new building on Huron Street (dedicated 1855). Reform gathered speed in the early 1860s with the installation of an organ, the removal of the women's gallery, and the introduction of family pews (1861). The reader faced the congregation during prayer (rather than the Holy Ark) and eliminated many of the prayers from the worship service. Men stopped covering their heads in prayer by the end of the decade, and the rabbi discontinued the practice of wearing vestments. Members no longer read the Torah with cantillations. Tifer-

286   THE TEMPLE-TIFERETH ISRAEL, REFORM

eth Israel eliminated the second day of holidays and no longer called members to the Torah, whose reading cycle the congregation lengthened to three years from the familiar one-year cycle. The synagogue conducted its worship in German and English, as well as Hebrew.

Because Tifereth Israel made more rapid progress than did Anshe Chesed in regard to liturgical reform, a large group of people, including some of Anshe Chesed's founding families, left Anshe Chesed in order to join Tifereth Israel. Thus, for the first time, with a membership of eighty families in 1865, Tifereth Israel truly rivaled its sister congregation in both numbers and community influence. Gustavus Cohen, who previously had led Anshe Chesed, joined Tifereth Israel (and brought thirty-four members with him) when his contract with the former congregation expired in 1866. Nevertheless, he remained with the new congregation for only a year and returned to Anshe Chesed, to be replaced later by Jacob Mayer, an ardent reformer. During his tenure, the congregation affiliated with the Union of American Hebrew Congregations, the national organization of Reform synagogues. In addition, the temple held its first Confirmation (1868). When Mayer resigned amid rumors that he had converted to Christianity, congregants elected Rabbi Aaron Hahn to serve the congregation (1874–1892). Hahn concentrated on intellectual lectures in the congregation and in the community, arguing strongly for Reform Judaism. He particularly voiced opposition to those who persisted in keeping their hats on during worship, pushing for a congregational vote, which required the removal of hats in 1875. Hahn eventually resigned when the congregation felt that his universalist views of religion took precedence over his particularist views of Judaism.

Rabbi Moses J. Gries came next to serve the congregation (1892–1917). During his tenure, activities increased beyond the worship and education that had dominated the early years of temple life. Tifereth Israel expanded, building a large edifice on East Fifty-fifth and Central in 1894, with a membership exceeding eight hundred by 1917. Gries argued for radical changes such as the transfer of the Sabbath to Sunday. Gries created a variety of societies in the congregation in order to meet the needs of his constituency and reach out into the community.

Abba Hillel Silver succeeded Gries in 1917, leading The Temple until 1963. A forceful orator and Zionist, he exercised a great deal of community influence from the pulpit of Tifereth Israel, simply called The Temple by this time. Silver also gained notoriety for his work in organized labor. He also restored many Jewish rituals that had been discarded by those rabbis who preceded him. In 1924, The Temple's more than fourteen hundred families moved to East 105th street and Ansel Road, at University Circle and what is now called Silver Park (dedicated 1959 in Rabbi Silver's memory). Silver also eliminated from the synagogue those recreational activities and secular educational programs that he felt were irrelevant to its mission as a religious institution.

In 1946, Rabbi Abba Hillel Silver joined with Rabbi Barnett Brickner (of Anshe Chesed/Fairmount Temple) to establish Temple Emanu El (with Rabbi

Alan Green as its religious leader). Two years later, a group of anti-Zionist members of the congregation founded the Suburban Temple.

In 1947, members of Tifereth Israel added a War Service (memorial) Alcove to the temple. Three years later, members added The Temple Museum of Religious Art to the large physical plant of the synagogue. In 1958, the congregation expanded its facilities to include a library, offices, and additional classrooms. Following Rabbi Abba Hillel Silver's death in 1963, members elected his son, Rabbi Daniel Jeremy Silver, to the pulpit. The younger Silver had been serving as associate rabbi, then rabbi, since 1956.

In memory of the elder Silver, the congregation founded the Abba Hillel Silver Memorial Archive and Library (1963) and the Abba Hillel Silver chair at Western Reserve (now Case Western Reserve) University (1964). During his tenure, Daniel Silver added an antiquities collection and ritual to the Temple Museum (renovated 1988). Under his direction, Tifereth Israel established a branch in Beachwood (1972). He emphasized scholarship and learning in his rabbinate.

When Rabbi Daniel Silver died in 1989, Rabbi Benjamin Kamin, who had been serving as associate since 1985, succeeded him. Under his direction, the congregation dedicated a new sanctuary in its Beachwood Branch, the East Building (1994). In 1994, membership of the congregation exceeded fifteen hundred family units.

References

Gartner, Lloyd P. *History of the Jews of Cleveland* (Cleveland: 1987).

Peskin, Allan. *This Tempting Freedom: The Early Years of Cleveland Judaism and Anshe Chesed Congregation* (Cleveland: 1973).

Raphael, Marc Lee. *Abba Hillel Silver: A Profile in American Judaism* (New York: 1989).

The Temple, 1850–1950 (Cleveland: 1950).

AGUDAS ACHIM, ORTHODOX. *Columbus, Ohio.* Five Eastern European immigrant men incorporated Agudas Achim in 1889, but evidence seems to suggest to historian Marc Lee Raphael that these men founded the congregation approximately four years earlier. This group dedicated its first synagogue on South Fifth Street in 1896, close to the Central Market Hall location where services were previously held.

By 1907, the fledgling congregation outgrew its quarters and dedicated a new synagogue at Donaldson Street and Washington Avenue. This structure served as the group's synagogal home for more than forty years. Members from Agudas Achim and Tifereth Israel unsuccessfully discussed the possibility of merger several times during the first decade of the latter's existence.

In its early years, a number of non-ordained men served Agudas Achim, holding brief tenures, until Rabbi Isaac Wiernikowsky began his service to Agudas Achim (1908–1911). Rabbi Morris Taxon assumed leadership in Columbus in 1912. He was reportedly the first Orthodox rabbi in North America to preach in English during the High Holidays. When he resigned in 1918, Rabbi Solomon

Neches succeeded him. As an ardent Zionist, Neches focused a great deal of his attention on Zionist activity in the congregation and community.

Rabbi Isaac Werne (né Wiernikowsky) returned to Columbus in 1921, serving a second tenure with Agudas Achim until 1932. He introduced a variety of innovative programs—within a strict Orthodox context—such as a late Friday evening "Open Forum" that featured brief prayers, reading, and singing, as well as a lecture and discussion. He also continued the Zionist activity established by his predecessor, Rabbi Neches.

Amid severe financial difficulty for the congregation—and for the rest of the country—Agudas Achim engaged Rabbi Mordechai Hirschsprung as its rabbi in 1932 to succeed Werne. As a legalist, he concentrated his efforts on helping congregants to follow Jewish law punctiliously, something which often led to controversy within the congregation.

In order to help Agudas Achim face the obstacle of serving congregants who had moved far from the synagogue—as well as a school population that had outgrown its school facility—members leased a building on Bryden Road in 1942. This became the Agudas Achim Educational Institute, the forerunner of the Torah Academy day school.

Rabbi Hirschsprung left Agudas Achim when the synagogue sought a rabbi who could relate to the youth (1948), about the same time unsuccessful merger discussions with Beth Jacob began. Under the guidance of Rabbi Samuel Rubenstein (1949–1982), the congregation dedicated its new synagogue on East Broad Street in 1951. Under Rubenstein's leadership, Agudas Achim members founded Heritage House for the elderly. In 1982, Rabbi Alan Ciner succeeded Rubenstein. Ciner focused his rabbinate on youth and education. In 1995, membership exceeded eight hundred family units.

Reference

Raphael, Marc Lee. *Jews and Judaism in a Midwestern Community: Columbus, Ohio, 1840–1975* (Columbus: 1979).

BETH JACOB, ORTHODOX. *Columbus, Ohio.* A group of eleven Orthodox men founded Beth Jacob in 1898. They sought to worship in the Sephardic (Spanish-Portuguese) ritual rather than the Ashkenazic (German-Polish) mode of worship at neighboring Agudas Achim. A rather poor founding group, Beth Jacob members held their worship services in private homes. However, by 1909, this group of original founders, mostly peddlers, grew to more than one hundred members. As a result, despite the financial burden, Beth Jacob dedicated its house of worship on Donaldson Street in 1909, the same year it founded its Ladies Auxiliary.

Without religious leadership for its first decade of existence, Beth Jacob engaged Simon Holland in 1910 (or 1911). He served for four years. In 1919, Beth Jacob created a Va'ad Hakashrut (community board to supervise Jewish dietary laws). In a partnership with local Congregation Ahavas Sholom, Beth

Jacob engaged Rabbi Ephraim Pelkovitz for a tenure of three years, beginning in 1922. While his primary responsibilities focused on serving the needs of Beth Jacob, he preached on the second day of holidays at the other synagogue.

Rabbi Leopold Greenwald, a historian and international Jewish legal expert, began his service with Beth Jacob in 1925. He lectured widely and developed a reputation in the community for his uncompromising orthodoxy, especially with regard to the dietary laws. As an active Zionist, Greenwald participated in Zionist activities throughout the community. Toward the end of his tenure, the synagogue considered merging with Agudas Achim. The failed attempt to merge prompted the congregation to build a new facility on Bulen Avenue in 1952. Rabbi Greenwald died three years later. Rabbi Solomon Poupko succeeded him (1955–1957).

In 1957, Rabbi David Stavsky joined Beth Jacob as its religious leader. Under his direction, the congregation built a new synagogue on College Avenue (dedicated 1969) with a *mechitza* (partition separating men and women in prayer). The following year, the Columbus Jewish community built a new *mikvah* (ritual bath) at Beth Jacob, under Stavsky's guidance. In 1975, the congregation's membership reached 280. Stavsky developed a variety of popular programs to reach out to congregants of all ages—particularly youth—including the popular "Cola and Shmoos" sessions during Sukkot and "Teenage Sabbath," when teenagers in the congregation take over the entire service. In 1994, membership at Beth Jacob exceeded 320 family units.

References

Raphael, Marc Lee. *Jews and Judaism in a Midwestern Community: Columbus, Ohio, 1840–1975* (Columbus: 1979).

———. "75 Years of Synagogue Growth: Highlites of Beth Jacob's Past." *Synagogue Journal* (1974).

Stavsky, David. "A Mechitza for Columbus." *Jewish Life* (Winter 1974): 22–27.

TEMPLE ISRAEL/B'NAI ISRAEL, REFORM. *Columbus, Ohio.* In 1868, a majority of members from Orthodox Bene Jeshurun (founded 1851), finding it too difficult to reform worship in their synagogue, decided to form a Reform congregation, B'nai Israel. Two years later, this young institution dedicated its own house of worship at the corner of Friend and Third Streets. As soon as the congregation moved into its new facility, members made numerous changes. They introduced choir music into worship. They adopted *Minhag America* as their prayer book, along with English prayers and hymns instead of Hebrew. They set up family pews as a reflection of their stand on equal rights for women in worship, and they insisted on sermons in English and German. All of these efforts focused their desire to maintain decorum in the service.

By this time, Bene Jeshurun had dissolved. Its members joined B'nai Israel, turning their assets over to their new congregation. B'nai Israel's rabbi, Judah Wechsler, joined the congregation in 1870. Under his guidance, B'nai Israel took additional steps toward Reform Judaism by permitting non-Jews to sing in the choir, eliminating the second day of holiday observance, and permitting men to worship without covering their heads. Wechsler also focused his attention on promoting interfaith activities. In 1873, the same year Wechsler resigned, the congregation joined the Union of American Hebrew Congregations, the national organization of Reform synagogues, as a founding member, thus solidifying its standing as a Reform institution.

Samuel Weil succeeded Wechsler in the pulpit, remaining only three years. His successor, Emanuel Hess, left the following year, amid financial difficulties in the congregation, after he officiated at the wedding of a nonmember without permission. Rabbi Benjamin Aaron Bonnheim succeeded Hess. He remained until 1883. Bonnheim concentrated his rabbinate on the education of the congregation's children. He instituted a confirmation ceremony that included a choral performance and a public examination of the children. Bonnheim left the congregation after a bitter feud with a congregant over his right to perform circumcisions when asked to do so.

Felix W. Jesselson succeeded Bonnheim. During his rabbinate, which lasted until 1890, the congregation finally raised itself out of debt. While he was in the pulpit at B'nai Israel, the board resolved to require congregants to remove their hats for worship. Rabbi Alexander Geismar, the first American-born rabbi to serve B'nai Israel, succeeded Jesselson in 1890 and remained in Columbus only two years. At about the same time, B'nai Israel members established a Hebrew Relief Association, which provided food and lodging for immigrants who stopped in Columbus on their way out west.

Geismar's successor, Maurice Eisenberg, stayed in Columbus for only one year, but controversy marked his tenure, with frequent clashes with congregational leadership. Louis Weiss succeeded Eisenberg in 1893. Weiss improved the Sabbath School, then moved it to Sunday. He directed his energies to interfaith activities in the community. B'nai Israel elected Rabbi David Klein to its pulpit in 1896. While he continued some of the work of his predecessors, his innovations included preaching in German once each on Rosh Hashanah and Yom Kippur and closing the temple during his three-month summer vacation. He also instituted the practice of using secular music during the High Holidays.

The congregation moved in 1904 to a new temple on Bryden Road. When the congregation refused to give Klein a raise in salary as promised, Klein left to start his own short-lived congregation, Beth El. Rabbi Joseph Kornfeld succeeded Klein at B'nai Israel in 1906. He introduced Sunday services for Jews and non-Jews in 1911, although he had argued for their introduction shortly after he arrived in Columbus. During his tenure, the congregation changed its name to Temple Israel. When Kornfeld left Columbus in 1922, Rabbi Jacob Tarshish succeeded him. His lectures and sermons drew large crowds. He left the temple in 1932 when he refused to forego his program of commercial broadcasting.

Rabbi Samuel Gup succeeded Tarshish in 1932. Gup's rabbinate focused on interfaith activities in Columbus. He left in 1946. Rabbi Jerome Folkman succeeded Gup in 1947. During his tenure, the congregation moved to East Broad Street (1959). As a family therapist, Folkman concentrated his rabbinate on working with families in the congregation. While introducing no significant ritual changes, he did place silver ornaments on the Torah, which met with criticism, as did his desire to wear a pulpit tallith. Following Folkman's retirement in 1973, Rabbi Edward D. Kiner led the congregation (1973–1977). Kiner focused his attention on family education and the participation of parents in the religious education of their children. Dissidents who did not support the continuation of Rabbi Kiner's leadership in the congregation left Temple Israel to form Beth Shalom Congregation.

Rabbi Harvey Goldman (1978–1985) succeeded Kiner. Rabbi Bradley Bleefeld led Temple Israel as senior rabbi from 1987 until 1995. He previously had served as assistant rabbi (1975–1977). Bleefeld concentrated on religious education. As a result of his efforts, more students continue their religious education through Confirmation. In addition, he promoted the active participation of congregants in local, regional, and national Jewish activities. Furthermore, Bleefeld led the congregation to house the homeless in synagogue facilities and join in a variety of food distribution programs. In 1995, Temple Israel's membership exceeded 850 families, the same year members elected Rabbi Arthur Nemitoff to Temple Israel's pulpit.

References

Gup, Samuel. *An Outline History of the Congregation Temple Israel* (Columbus: 1946).
Raphael, Marc Lee. *Jews and Judaism in a Midwestern Community: Columbus, Ohio, 1840–1975* (Columbus: 1979).
Synagogue Histories File, American Jewish Archives.

TIFERETH ISRAEL, CONSERVATIVE. *Columbus, Ohio.* Established as the First Hungarian Hebrew Church, a group of Hungarian Jews founded this congregation in 1901. The new congregation met for services in private homes under the religious leadership of Leon Dumb (1902–1904), Morris Einhorn (1904–1908), and Morris Lichtenstein (1909–1910). In 1909, the congregation moved into its own building on South Parsons. Arthur Ginzler (1911–1912) succeeded Liechtenstein. Growing slowly, the group grew to only thirty-three members in 1912, the same year the women of the congregation formed a sisterhood, although the congregation built a new building at the South Parsons location in 1914. Like so many other congregations of its kind, Tifereth Israel engaged a variety of individuals who served various functions, including leading worship, in its early years. By 1915, Tifereth Israel felt financially stable enough to engage ordained clergy, beginning with Rabbi David Shohet, a graduate of the Jewish Theological Seminary, the rabbinical school of the Conservative movement. During his three years with Tifereth Israel, he introduced the nonsectarian observance of American holidays to the congregation. Rabbi Morris Schussheim (1917–1919) succeeded Shohet.

Members from Orthodox Agudas Achim and Tifereth Israel unsuccessfully discussed the possibility of merger several times during the first decade of the latter's existence. Rabbi Jacob Klein (1919–1924; 1926–1927), a strict rationalist, succeeded Schussheim. Under his direction, Tifereth Israel declared itself Conservative (1922), affiliating with the United Synagogue of America, the national organization of Conservative congregations, now called the United Synagogue of Conservative Judaism.

Shortly before moving into a new structure on East Broad Street, Tifereth Israel engaged Rabbi Solomon Rivlin (1927–1930) as its religious leader. He concentrated his work on Zionist activities. When members dedicated the new synagogue home on East Broad Street in 1927, they stressed the need for decorum in prayer. The congregation also rejected separate seating for men and women and eliminated daily worship from the synagogue schedule. This new facility placed a great financial burden on the congregation; even the rabbi resigned to save the synagogue money (1930). At the same time, membership declined drastically. When Rabbi Nathan Zelizer joined Tifereth Israel (1931–1944; 1946–1974), he discovered a membership of under one hundred families. Therefore, he spent a significant portion of his first ten years with the synagogue engaged in an intensive membership drive. His efforts resulted in a rise in affiliation to 168 in 1936. Forty members joined in 1938 alone. By the end of the decade, membership increased to about four hundred families.

In a campaign led by Samuel Melton, the congregation built a new educational center in 1948 to meet the needs of an expanding school population. As an expression of his philanthropy, Melton established the Melton Research Center in Jewish education at the Jewish Theological Seminary in 1959. Among its first activities, the Center sent a staff of four members to Tifereth Israel in order to test new educational theories and publications. Later, Florence Melton funded the Discovery Program, a two-year high school curriculum, sponsored jointly with other synagogues and the Columbus Jewish Federation.

Additional expansion took place in 1960 with a new social hall and chapel. In the early 1970s with membership at eight hundred families (1975), the congregation made a commitment to stay at the Broad Street location. Rabbi David Zisenwine (1974–1976) succeeded Zelizer. During his tenure, the congregation voted to give women the right to be counted as part of the minyan. Rabbi Sheldon Switkin served (1976–1979) before the congregation elected Rabbi Harold Berman in 1979. In 1985, the synagogue expanded further by building a new and larger chapel with atrium (dedicated 1991). In the late 1980s, the congregation initiated a cultural exchange program with the neighboring Islamic Center. In 1994, membership exceeded 1175 family units.

References

Congregation Tifereth Israel, 1901–1991 (Columbus: 1991).
Raphael, Marc Lee. *Jews and Judaism in a Midwestern Community: Columbus, Ohio, 1840–1975* (Columbus: 1979).

TEMPLE ISRAEL, REFORM. *Dayton, Ohio.* Twelve Jewish men gathered in 1850 under the leadership of Joseph Lebensburger to form a Hebrew Society. Each day, these men met for worship in a small room above a shop. Four years later the Hebrew Society incorporated as Kehillah Kodesh B'nai Yeshurun. Shortly thereafter, the group moved to a location between First and Main Streets. In 1863, the congregation dedicated a former church at Fourth and Jefferson Streets as its first permanent home. The congregation opened a religious school in 1869. As a result of the influence of Cincinnati's Rabbi Isaac Mayer Wise, the congregation instituted many reforms in these early years: Wise's own Reform prayer book, *Minhag America* (1861); an organ (1865); the elimination of the prayer shawl (1869); the abandonment of yahrzeit memorial candles in the synagogue (1874); family pews (1875); and a mixed choir (1875). In 1881, English replaced German as the synagogue's language of record. The congregation became a founding member of the Union of American Hebrew Congregations, the national organization of Reform synagogues, in 1873.

Many individuals served as religious leaders in the early years before members elected Rabbi Max Wertheimer, the first American-trained rabbi to serve the congregation, beginning in 1889. Four years later, the temple dedicated its new house of worship at First and Jefferson Streets. When Wertheimer left in 1900, Rabbi David Lefkowitz succeeded him and was active in interfaith community activities. Membership during his tenure remained stable at 150 families. Lefkowitz left in 1920; Rabbi Samuel S. Mayersberg succeeded him. A strong orator, Mayersberg advocated police reform from the pulpit. Membership grew to two hundred before he left in 1927, the same year the congregation moved to a new building at Salem and Emerson Avenues. In this new building, the congregation began to use the name Temple Israel for the first time.

Rabbi Louis Witt came to the congregation in 1927. He concentrated his rabbinate on the development of interfaith understanding in the community. By 1945, membership in the congregation reached five hundred. When Witt retired in 1947, Rabbi Selwyn Ruslander came to lead the congregation. He served during the most active period of growth of the temple. During his tenure, the congregation built a new sanctuary at the Salem and Emerson Street location (1953). He reintroduced the Bar Mitzvah and introduced the Bat Mitzvah. In addition, Ruslander added Hebrew to the Religious School curriculum.

During the 1960s, membership exceeded eleven hundred family units. Ruslander died in 1969; his associates Rabbis Joseph Weizenbaum and Howard Greenstein led the congregation in the interim. Rabbi P. Irving Bloom came to Dayton in 1973. Under his direction, the congregation moved to a new location (1994). In 1995, membership of Temple Israel neared eight hundred family units.

References

Copland, Sidney M. *Temple Israel, 125th Anniversary, 1850–1975* (Dayton: 1975).
Synagogue Histories File, American Jewish Archives.

THE TEMPLE/CONGREGATION SHOMER EMUNIM, REFORM. *Toledo (later Sylvania), Ohio.* In 1870, a short-lived attempt to establish Congregation Shomer Emunim failed. Though seventy Jewish families lived in Toledo at the time, they preferred an Orthodox form of worship. By 1875, thirty families, pledging funds to build a synagogue, organized a Reform congregation. They chose the name Shomer Emunim (Guardian of Faithfulness), a name suggested by Rabbi Isaac Mayer Wise. They also chose Wise's liturgy, *Minhag America,* for their new congregation.

The incipient congregation immediately purchased a former Baptist Church at the corner of Adams and Superior for its first permanent home. Members invited Rabbi Benjamin Eger to become Shomer Emunim's first rabbi that same year. His tenure lasted only five years, when the temple developed financial trouble. Even the temple building had to be moved, to make room for a new Masonic Temple to be built on its former grounds. It took another five years to reestablish the congregation with thirty-six families.

Rabbi Tobias Schanfarber became rabbi to the congregation in 1886, but he served only one year. Rabbi Edward Benjamin Morris Brown succeeded Schanfarber, with an equally short one-year tenure. However, during these two years, the congregation grew strong enough to erect a new sanctuary on Tenth Street between Monroe and Washington. The congregation continued to grow, and it moved in 1907 to a former church building on Scottwood Avenue. In this new location, David Alexander, the congregation's religious leader, served for fourteen years. During his tenure, the women of Shomer Emunim established a women's auxiliary and placed an organ in the synagogue.

In 1917, the temple and its members dedicated the Collingwood Avenue Temple. This building served the needs of the members until 1973. Dr. Joseph Kornfeld succeeded Alexander in 1924, serving his congregants in Toledo for ten years. When he left, Rabbi Leon Feuer became the religious leader of Shomer Emunim. As an active Zionist, Feuer worked with other American Jewish leaders to press for the establishment of the modern Jewish state in Israel.

Feuer retired in 1972, and the congregation elected Rabbi Alan M. Sokobin to its pulpit. The following year, Shomer Emunim dedicated its new facility on Sylvania Avenue in Sylvania to accommodate the large westward movement of the Jewish community. Because of Sokobin's interest in building a cohesive Jewish community, the congregation built its new synagogue adjacent to a Jewish communal complex that houses most of the Jewish communal institutions in the area. In 1991, Rabbi Samuel Weinstein succeeded Rabbi Sokobin. Rabbi Weinstein emphasized adult education and social action in his rabbinate. In 1994, the membership of Congregation Shomer Emunim exceeded 725 family units, with nearly four hundred students in the religious school.

Reference

Synagogue Histories File, American Jewish Archives.

RODEF SHOLOM, REFORM. *Youngstown, Ohio.* In 1867, fifteen charter members founded Rodef Sholom. They rented rooms on the Porter block of West Federal Street to house the congregation. Several religious leaders served before the election of Lippman Liebman to the pulpit in 1868. He modified the worship service. In 1869, the congregation moved to a storefront, where it introduced an organ for worship. The following year, the congregation added a choir.

Rodef Sholom joined in the formation in 1873 of the Union of American Hebrew Congregations, the national body of Reform synagogues. In 1874, Rodef Sholom moved to Federal and Hazel Streets. Henry Block (1886–1887) succeeded Liebman. In 1887, the congregation dedicated its new building at Lincoln Avenue and Holmes Street (Fifth Avenue). Rabbi J. B. Grossman came to Rodef Sholom in 1888. He served until illness forced his retirement in 1912, except for the years between 1893 and 1899, when he led a congregation in Philadelphia. During the interim, M. P. Jacobson (1895–1897) and Emanuel Schreiber (1897–1899) led Rodef Sholom. Activities increased significantly during Grossman's rabbinate, and the congregation and its Sunday School grew considerably.

Rabbi I. E. Philo came to Youngstown in 1913 to lead Rodef Sholom's ninety members. Three years later, the congregation moved to Elm Street and Woodbine Avenue (dedicated 1915). Deeply committed as a social activist, Philo led the congregation to work for peace, social justice, human rights, and racial equality, amid threats from the local Ku Klux Klan. Philo retired in 1942. Rabbi Abraham Feinberg (1942–1946) succeeded him.

Dr. Sidney Berkowitz served the congregation next (1946–1983). During his tenure, the congregation did extensive renovation, with a religious school addition and a new chapel (1954). In 1967, the congregation stood at over seven hundred members. In 1967, Rabbi Berkowitz introduced a short vesper service for Friday evening. When Berkowitz retired, Rabbi David Powers led the congregation (1982–1989). He worked a great deal in fostering relations between Jews and non-Jews in the community.

The congregation elected Rabbi Jonathan M. Brown to the pulpit in 1989. The congregation has been embroiled in various debates over the wearing of head coverings; currently, a head covering may be worn but can be provided only by a Bar/Bat Mitzvah family or wedding party (and not by the congregation). Brown emphasizes education in the congregation. He introduced a program in which the Sabbath is celebrated in the home (and not in the synagogue) and has been active in programs that strive to feed the hungry. Membership in 1994 neared six hundred family units.

References

Congregation Rodef Sholom 1867–1992 (Youngstown, OH: 1992).
Hollander, Lois. "A Seventy-year Saga of Rodef Sholom Congregation." *Youngstown Jewish Times,* October 1, 1937, pp. 5–13.
Synagogue Histories File, American Jewish Archives.

OKLAHOMA

TEMPLE B'NAI ISRAEL, REFORM. *Oklahoma City, Oklahoma.* Moved by an address by Rabbi W. H. Greenberg of Dallas, Texas, twenty-one men established B'nai Israel in 1903. Religious leadership came from student rabbis at Hebrew Union College in Cincinnati. In 1904, members elected Arthur Lewinsohn to its pulpit even before his ordination at Hebrew Union College, but ill health forced his resignation shortly thereafter.

Rabbi Joseph Blatt joined the congregation in 1906 and served until shortly before his death in 1946. During the first year of his tenure, a sisterhood formed as the Jewish Ladies' Aid. In 1915, the group joined the National Federation of Temple Sisterhoods. The congregation had met in a variety of locations in its early years of existence; under Rabbi Blatt's leadership, B'nai Israel dedicated its permanent home at Broadway Circle in 1908. It later built a Temple Center in 1926, three years before the men of the congregation formed a Men's Club.

Rabbi Blatt developed an extensive program of activities for youth and adults with study at its core. Active in civic affairs, Blatt also worked at developing relationships between congregational members and non-Jews in the community. Rabbi Joseph Levenson succeeded Blatt in 1946. He served in the Army chaplaincy in 1950–1951, during which time Rabbi Israel Kaplan led the congregation as interim rabbi. During Levenson's association with the congregation, B'nai Israel established a nursery school (1950). Like his predecessor, Levenson actively developed relationships between Jews and non-Jews in the community.

With property donated by Julius Krouch, B'nai Israel built a new home on Pennsylvania Avenue between Forty-eight and Forty-ninth Streets (dedicated 1955). In the new location, the congregation introduced Bat Mitzvah with a greater emphasis on Hebrew language-acquisition skills. When Levenson retired in 1976, Rabbi David Packman succeeded him. In 1994, membership of Temple B'nai Israel stood at over 380 members.

References

50th Anniversary, Temple B'nai Israel (Oklahoma City, OK: 1953).
Shevitz, Amy Hill. "Notes toward a History of the Oklahoma City Jewish Community."
    Western States Jewish History (forthcoming).
Synagogue Histories File, American Jewish Archives.

EMANUEL SYNAGOGUE, CONSERVATIVE. *Oklahoma City, Oklahoma.* Four Eastern European immigrant founders incorporated Congregation Immanuel (legally changed to Emanuel Synagogue in 1949) in 1904 as an Orthodox synagogue. This small congregation first met on the second floor of a building on West Grand owned by the Herskowitz family, founding members of Emanuel. Some suggest the congregation chose the name Emanuel to honor Emanuel Herskowitz.

In 1917, Emanuel moved to a newly erected building at Reno and Dewey Streets. In 1932, members added an educational wing to this modest brick building. During its early years, it struggled to maintain itself as an Orthodox congregation. In 1938, the board of the synagogue proposed holding two concurrent services for the High Holidays, one exclusively in Hebrew and one with a mixture of Hebrew and English.

In anticipation of a move to a new location, the congregation affiliated with the United Synagogue of America (now the United Synagogue of Conservative Judaism), the national organization of Conservative congregations (1946). Ritual changes and the introduction of mixed seating culminated in this formal affiliation. In 1949, following a move of most congregants away from the center of Oklahoma City, the synagogue's location, Emanuel moved to a building on Forty-seventh Street between Western and Francis Avenues. In this new location, under the religious guidance of Israel Chodos, membership grew from 280 in 1949 to 340 in 1952. Among his other community activities, Chodos regularly appeared in a regular local television program called "Your Bible." At his insistence, Emanuel introduced late Friday evening services.

In 1960, Emanuel permitted women to sit on its board of directors. Amid a great deal of debate, the congregation gave women Torah honors in 1978 and counted women in the minyan beginning in 1991. In 1982, Emanuel merged its religious school and youth group with Reform B'nai Israel.

Under the guidance of Rabbi Charles Shalman, Emanuel developed a Solomon Schechter Day School from preschool through grade six in 1985. Two years later, he successfully built a *mikvah* (ritual bath) adjacent to the synagogue.

These men served Emanuel as religious leaders: Jacob Keilin (1921–1925), Meyer Cohen (1925–1929), M. Labkovsky (1929–1930), Milton Rosen (1930–1938), Melvin Goodman (1938–1946), Aaron Decter (1946–1947), Israel Chodos (1947–1955), Aaron Tofield (1955–1957), Oscar Fleischaker (1957–1959), Marvin Tomsky (1959–1969), David Novak (1969–1972), Leonard Lifshen (1972–1978), David Maharam (1978–1982), A. Charles Shalman (1982–1993), Daniel Shevitz (1993–   ). In 1995, Emanuel listed 210 membership units on its roster.

References

Emanuel, 1904–1984, 80 Years of Faith (Oklahoma City: 1984).
Shevitz, Amy Hill. "Notes toward a History of the Oklahoma City Jewish Community." *Western States Jewish History* (forthcoming).

TEMPLE ISRAEL, REFORM. *Tulsa, Oklahoma.* Founders of Temple Israel organized the congregation in 1914. Abraham Feldman (1914–1915), then a student at Hebrew Union College in Cincinnati, served the synagogue before members elected Rabbi Jacob B. Menkes as their religious leader (1917–1919). Temple Israel met in a variety of temporary locations in its early years. In 1919, the congregation dedicated its first house of worship, at Fourteenth and Cheyenne Streets, and Rabbi Charles B. Latz (1919–1924) joined Temple Israel the same year.

Rabbi Latz organized study classes for the sisterhood (organized 1919) and brotherhood (organized 1920) of the congregation. These rabbis succeeded Latz: Samuel S. Kaplan (1924–1927), Jacob B. Krohngold (1927–1929), Benjamin Kelsen (1929), Hyman A. Iola (1929–1935), Abraham Shusterman (1935–1941), Ely Pilchik (1941–1947), Randall M. Falk (1945–1946), Morton C. Fierman (1947–1951), Norbert Rosenthal (1951–1976), and Charles Sherman (1976–   ).

In 1932, Temple Israel members dedicated a new home on South Rockford. That same year, members formed a choir. During Rabbi Shusterman's tenure with Temple Israel, the congregation introduced Bar Mitzvah and Friday night Torah reading. Rabbi Falk concentrated his energies on the religious school. Rabbi Rosenthal focused his efforts on a variety of holiday celebrations and educational programs. In addition, during his tenure, Temple Israel celebrated its first Bat Mitzvah and engaged its first full-time cantor.

Rabbi Charles Sherman emphasized education in his rabbinate as well as outreach programs for intermarried couples and Jews by Choice. He advocated social justice and religious action, as well as fuller participation in the Reform movement and community at large. In 1995, membership of Temple Israel neared five hundred family units.

References

Falk, Randall. "A History of the Jews of Oklahoma with Special Emphasis on the Tulsa Jewish Community" (Rabbinical thesis, Hebrew Union College, 1946).
Synagogue Histories File, American Jewish Archives.
Temple Israel Dedication 1955 (Tulsa: 1955).
Temple Israel Family Album (Tulsa: 1984).
Temple Israel Memorial Volume (Tulsa: 1943).

OREGON

BETH ISRAEL, REFORM. *Portland, Oregon.* Nineteen charter members founded Beth Israel in 1958 as a traditional congregation, but its nature quickly changed as the Reform element became active in congregational affairs. Members met in Burke's Hall for worship. In 1861, Beth Israel dedicated its synagogue on the corner of Fifth and Oak. Members established a day school at Sixth and Oak (1862), closing it when the Portland public school system developed. In 1863, the congregation elected Julius Eckman to its pulpit to serve its thirty member families. Isaac Schwab (1867–1872) succeeded him. By 1866, the congregation had become split between Orthodox and Reform elements, which led to the Orthodox group leaving to form Ahavai Sholom. Moses May served the congregation from 1872 to 1880. Within a year of his arrival, amid stormy protest, May persuaded the congregation to adopt Isaac Mayer Wise's prayer book, *Minhag America.* During his tenure, Beth Israel joined the Union of American Hebrew Congregations, the national organization of Reform synagogues (1879). May left because the congregation sought a more moderate reform; the conflict ended in the drawing of the rabbi's pistol on a leading member of the congregation, who had physically attacked him.

Alex Rosenspitz succeeded May (1881–1883) before Rabbi Jacob Bloch (1883–1900) joined the congregation. Under Bloch's guidance, Beth Israel grew rapidly. During Bloch's tenure, Beth Israel constructed a new synagogue on Main Street (dedicated 1889). Rabbi Stephen S. Wise (1900–1906) succeeded Bloch. There he championed a free pulpit and frequently exchanged pulpits with local Christian clergy. Wise introduced voluntary contributions for dues and established worship services for children. When he left to form the Free Synagogue of New York City, members invited Rabbi Jonah B. Wise to occupy the pulpit. Jonah Wise led the congregation to become actively involved in civic affairs and concentrated his efforts on the education of children. In addition, he helped new immigrants in the community.

In 1914, Beth Israel dedicated its new building at Twelfth and Main Streets. A fire destroyed the building in 1923. Members met for worship at the First Presbyterian Church while building a new structure. Rabbis Max J. Merritt (1926–1927) and then Frederick Braun (1927–1928) succeeded Wise for short interludes. In 1928, the congregation moved to Nineteenth, Flanders, and Glisan Streets, the same year Rabbi Henry J. Berkowitz (1928–1949), an author of children's books, joined the congregation. Yet, the Depression and the wars placed a heavy financial burden on the congregation. Berkowitz introduced music and drama to enhance communal worship. He also established a "Quiet Hour of Music" for all faiths each Sunday afternoon and focused a great deal of energy on the education of children in the congregation. Under his direction, the men of the congregation established a men's club (1928).

Following the death of Berkowitz in 1949, Rabbi Julius Nodel (1950–1959), an ardent Zionist, served the congregation, which reached a membership of 750 families the last year of Nodel's tenure. Beth Israel erected a Memorial Temple House in 1949 and established a Berkowitz Memorial Museum there in 1952. Nodel focused on choir music and religious education, establishing a series of special interest and activity clubs for children. He fought against Christian missionary work. Beth Israel built a Religious School annex in 1957. Following the retirement of Rabbi Nodel in 1959, members of Beth Israel elected Rabbi Emanuel Rose (1960–   ) to succeed Nodel.

In 1993, the congregation added an additional building, which included a chapel, a social hall, and offices; the members also added an additional wing to the religious school. In 1995, the membership of Beth Israel exceeded 960 family units.

References

"News from the Portland Jewish Community in 1885." *Western States Jewish Historical Quarterly* 9, no. 3 (April 1977): 235–37.

Nodel, Julius. *The Ties Between: A Century of Judaism on America's Last Frontier* (Portland: 1959).

Stern, Norton B., and William M. Kramer. "Mayer May, Pioneer Portland Rabbi." *Western States Jewish Historical Quarterly* 21, no. 2 (January 1989): 103–13.
Synagogue Histories File, American Jewish Archives.
Wechsler, Judah. "Portland Jewry Seen by a Minnesota Rabbi in 1884." *Western States Jewish Historical Quarterly* 15, no. 1 (October 1982): 22–24.

NEVEH SHALOM, CONSERVATIVE. *Portland, Oregon.* A group of members of Beth Israel, dissatisfied over reforms, especially when the congregation adopted Isaac M. Wise's prayer book, *Minhag America,* founded Ahavai Sholom in 1869. That same year, Julius Eckman became Ahavai Sholom's first religious leader. Prior to incorporation, the young congregation held services at a location at Front and Madison before moving to Stark Street between First and Second. Following Eckman's election to the pulpit, members of Ahavai Sholom purchased a lot on Sixth and Oak, where it built a synagogue (dedicated 1869). Under Eckman's direction, the congregation established a school for its children. Eckman left Ahavai Sholom in 1873. Little is known about the religious leaders who immediately followed him.

Robert Abrahamson joined Ahavai Sholom in 1886, having served briefly as cantor in 1880 and as religious leader from 1882 to 1884. Abraham W. Edelman served in the interim. When Abrahamson returned in 1886, he served for thirty-five years. Following the conclusion of his second tenure, membership dwindled to thirty-five.

In 1895, members from Neveh Zedek (founded 1900) and Ahavai Sholom merged for financial reasons. This consolidation proved unsuccessful, and the two synagogues separated in 1897. Congregation Neveh Zedek Talmud Torah resulted from the merger in 1902 of the two Russian congregations Neveh Zedek and Talmud Torah (founded 1893). Nehemiah Mosessoh, the first religious leader of Talmud Torah, served the merged congregation. He remained only one year, as did his successor, Adolph Abbey. As a result, half of the congregation left to join Shaarie Torah (founded 1902).

In 1906, Ahavai Sholom moved to Park and Clay Streets. In 1911, Neveh Zedek Talmud Torah also moved to a new house of worship. Immediately after the erection of its new building, Rabbi Wolf Willner came to Ahavai Sholom. He remained only one year. In 1917, the congregation's finances permitted the engagement of a successor to Willner. Membership stood at only eighty-five members. The congregation engaged Arthur Montaz, who remained only a short time. As the influenza epidemic of 1917–1918 hit the congregation hard, it was in no position to hire a rabbi. In the interim, the congregation attempted to modify its ritual by introducing prayer books with English and by eliminating the sale of Torah honors. In 1921, Rabbi Nahum Kreuger joined Ahavai Sholom as its religious leader (1921–1925). At his encouragement, Ahavai Sholom joined the United Synagogue of America (now the United Synagogue of Conservative Judaism), the national organization of Conservative congregations, in 1921.

In 1923, Ahavai Sholom suffered damage from a fire set by an arsonist. As a result, members chose once again not to merge with Neveh Zedek. Instead, even with a membership decline, they rebuilt on the same location (rededicated 1924). Each tenure of most of the rabbis who served the congregation after the fire lasted little more than a year. Only Herbert Parzen stayed longer (1928–1932). Both Neveh Zedek and Ahavai Sholom became active in Zionist circles. At Neveh Zedek, members formed a Kadima Society for high school students. At Ahavai Sholom, the Rashi Club provided the context for Zionist discussion. Rabbi Mayer Rubin led Neveh Zedek from 1928 to 1935. For the most part, however, this congregation also experienced a rapid turnover in rabbinical leadership. Membership decline reversed upon the arrival of Rabbi Edward T. Sandrow at Ahavai Sholom in 1933. Yet, he too proposed a merger between the two congregations. Rabbi Philip Kleinman, who had accepted an earlier offer at Ahavai Sholom (1921) but never served, led Neveh Zedek from 1937 to 1956. Kleinman introduced a variety of programs for younger members, including junior services, programs for newly married couples, and a Jewish Boy Scout Troop.

Beginning in 1937, Rabbi Charles Sydney led Ahavai Sholom through the tragedy it, like most congregations, felt during and after World War II. During his fourteen-year tenure, he stabilized the congregation. Membership grew from 200 to 350 families between 1940 and 1950. In 1952, Ahavai Sholom built a new synagogue on Thirteenth Street, just after Rabbi Sydney resigned his position. Rabbi Ralph Weissberger succeeded him briefly. Rabbi Joshua Stampfer (1953–1993) succeeded Weissberger. Rabbi Jack Segel served Neveh Zedek from 1958 to 1961.

Though several attempts at merger were made earlier, the congregations of Neveh Zedek and Ahavai Sholom had to wait until 1961 for a successful merger to form Congregation Neveh Shalom under Rabbi Stampfer's direction. Ahavai Sholom lost its building to freeway construction. Neveh Zedek's membership had dwindled to 170 at the time of the merger. Stampfer established a nursery school, as well as a series of speakers. He emphasized education in his rabbinate, inside and outside the congregation. After the synagogue's roof collapsed, the merged congregation met temporarily in the Neveh Sholom building before moving to a new location on Peaceful Lane, off Dosch Road (dedicated 1964).

In 1973, the congregation gave women full participation in ritual. When Stampfer retired in 1993, Rabbi Daniel Isaak succeeded him. In 1994, membership exceeded 960 family units.

References

Lowenstein, Steven. *The Jews of Oregon 1850–1950* (Portland: 1987).
Miranda, Gary. *Following a River: Portland's Congregation Neveh Shalom, 1869–1989* (Portland: 1989).
"News from the Portland Jewish Community in 1885." *Western States Jewish Historical Quarterly* 9, no. 3 (April 1977): 235–37.

Stampfer, Joshua. *Pioneer Rabbi of the West: The Life and Times of Julius Eckman* (Portland: 1988).
Toll, William. *The Making of an Ethnic Middle Class: Portland Jewry over Four Generations* (Albany: 1982).

P

PENNSYLVANIA

KENESETH ISRAEL, REFORM. *Allentown, Pennsylvania.* In 1893, a small group of people, primarily German immigrants, gathered in the Hunsicker Building on Hamilton Street to form a Reform congregation. As a result of this first meeting, these founders established a religious school. In 1903, the group purchased a lot on North Sixth Street between Chew and Gordon Streets. Shortly thereafter, the congregation filed a charter of incorporation for Keneseth Israel. Three years later, Keneseth Israel sold the lot on North Sixth and built a synagogue on South Thirteenth Street (dedicated 1906).

Immediately after moving into their first home, congregants formed a Ladies' Auxiliary (later sisterhood). These women paid for the newly instituted choir and organ, as well as the newly founded Free School for Religion (housed at the Sheridan School at Second and Liberty Streets). During World War I, membership expanded to sixty family units.

In 1932, the congregation acquired an activities building on North Fourteenth Street for its growing membership (eighty-seven in 1937). By 1952, members sought to build a new building to accommodate the growing activity program of the congregation of nearly two hundred families. Thus, Keneseth Israel erected a new facility at Leh and Chew Streets (1953). In 1962, the membership purchased a property at North Twenty-third Street for use as a religious school. Three years later, membership exceeded 370 family units.

In the 1980s, the congregation expanded its activities to include a variety of programs of personal assistance to those in need, as well as outreach to the unaffiliated and intermarried. In 1994, membership stood at five hundred family units.

These religious leaders served Keneseth Israel: Phineas Israeli (1902–1903), Morris Mandel (1903–1909), Joseph Leiser (1909–1913), Theodore Joseph

(1913–1916), Joseph Tarshish (1916–1919), Ira E. Sanders (1919–1924), Harry N. Caplan (1924–1943), Baruch Braunstein (1943–1950), Louis M. Youngerman (1950–1960), Rayfield D. Helman (1960–1961), Stephen A. Schafer (1961–1971), Donald R. Berlin (1971–1976), Arthur Z. Steinberg (1976–1977), Herbert N. Brockman (1977–1986), Michael N. Stevens (1986–1987), and Martin P. Beifield, Jr. (1987–   ).

Reference

Synagogue Histories File, American Jewish Archives.

CONGREGATION SHAARAI SHOMAYIM, REFORM. *Lancaster, Pennsylvania.* In 1855, twenty-one Jews gathered under the leadership of Jacob Herzog to form a Congregation Shaarai Shomayim (officially chartered in 1856). He owned the Torah and provided the congregation with its first place of worship, serving as Shaarai Shomayim's first president. In 1857, a group opposed Herzog's leadership and formed its own board, with Leon Baum as president. This opposition resolved itself with the death of Herzog six months later.

In 1866, with only fifteen members, the congregation worshiped on the upper floor of a store located on Penn Square. Services took place in a variety of additional locations that year before members purchased property on Orange Street and built a synagogue there (dedicated 1867). Under the influence of Rabbi Benjamin Szold, who participated in the dedication, the congregation adopted the prayer book that he had edited and introduced several changes: the discontinuation of the wearing of a prayer shawl, except by the reader or when taking the Torah from the ark; the introduction of family pews; and the installation of an organ.

In 1883, the congregation engaged its first ordained rabbi, Morris Ungerleider. Three years later, following a great deal of debate, the synagogue's board passed a resolution allowing members to remove their head coverings during worship should they choose to do so. Under Ungerleider's influence, Shaarai Shomayim passed a resolution formally adopting Reform Judaism in 1888, just months before he left the service of the congregation.

Rabbi Solomon Schaumberg assumed the pulpit in 1889; Rabbi J. Schweitzer succeeded him the following year, likewise serving a limited tenure of approximately one year. In 1892, Rabbi Clifton Harby Levy arrived in Lancaster to lead the congregation. Levy's tenure was limited to two years, but he greatly influenced the congregation. He insisted on decorum during worship services. Under his direction, the congregation eliminated the observance of the second day of holidays and abolished the practice of covering one's head during prayer. Prior to his resignation, Shaarai Shomayim joined the Union of American Hebrew Congregations, the national organization of Reform synagogues.

Rabbi Isidore Rosenthal succeeded Rabbi Levy in 1894. He stayed with the synagogue for twenty-seven years. The year following his arrival, Shaarai Shomayim's seventy members sold the Orange Street Temple, preparing to move to a new location at North Duke and James Street. On the day of its intended dedication in 1896, a gas explosion ripped through the structure. Six months later, members dedicated a repaired temple.

When attendance declined at congregational worship, Rabbi Rosenthal introduced Sunday services (1917). He resigned in 1919, but continued to serve the congregation until 1921. That year, Rabbi Maurice Youngerman came to Lancaster to lead the temple. Because he wanted to concentrate his efforts on the religous school, he persuaded the board to discontinue Sunday services. With registration open to all Jewish children in Lancaster County, school registration reached 115 in 1922.

Dr. Nathanial Cantor succeeded Rabbi Youngerman in 1923 and served only two years. During his brief tenure, he terminated Saturday services and opened a branch school in Columbia, which operated only a few years. Rabbi Raphael Goldstein came next to the congregation in 1925. Goldstein quickly reinstituted Saturday services and asked that only mourners stand for the Memorial prayer of Kaddish (a practice that Reform Judaism had changed).

Rabbi Daniel Davis succeeded Rabbi Goldstein in 1927. Davis sought to bring order to what he perceived as disorder in the structure of the service and congregation. He introduced an ''open forum'' for discussion following his sermons and founded the Brotherhood (1927) and youth groups. In addition, he reintroduced a variety of rituals that a previous generation and its rabbi had abandoned, including the wearing of the prayer shawl and the celebration of the Bar Mitzvah. Arguing for a division between church and state, the congregation took a political stand in 1946 against the local school district's policy of ''release time'' for religious instruction.

Rabbi Daniel Davis left in 1947, and Rabbi Lester Roubey succeeded him. As a religious liberal, Rabbi Roubey rejected many of the traditional rituals that Rabbi Davis had returned to Shaarai Shomayim. Though he remained until 1953, it was not without controversy. He led the board, for example, in a resolution in 1949 to remove the flag of Israel, which had become a permanent part of the pulpit.

Following Rabbi Roubey's departure from Lancaster in 1953, Rabbi William Sanderson joined the congregation. He served only two years. The following year, members elected Rabbi Samson Shain to lead them. During the early months of his tenure, the congregation purchased the property adjacent to the temple in order to erect a religious school building. Rabbi Shain died in 1976; Rabbi Stanley Funston succeeded him, but left in 1979.

Rabbi David Sofian assumed the pulpit in 1980. He improved and expanded the program of religious instruction in the synagogue. Sofian worked to change the ritual pattern in the congregation, which led among other things, to a reconstruction of the pulpit in order to accommodate more participants in worship services. Following Rabbi Sofian's resignation in 1993, members elected Rabbi Jack Paskoff to the pulpit of Shaarai Shomayim. Membership stood at 245 in 1994.

References

Brener, David. *The Jews of Lancaster, Pennsylvania: A Story with Two Beginnings* (Lancaster, PA: 1979).

―――. *Lancaster's Gates of Heaven: Portals to the Past* (Lancaster, PA: 1976).

Synagogue Histories File, American Jewish Archives.

ADATH JESHURUN, CONSERVATIVE. *Philadelphia (later Elkins Park), Pennsylvania.* Wolf Ettinger and Moses Blumenthal fueled the founding of Adath Jeshurun in 1858, seeking to establish a community institution for the Jewish education of their children. These founders established Adath Jeshurun as an Orthodox synagogue "dedicated to God and Torah for the use of themselves, their children of the community and this city of Brotherly Love." The group met for worship in Union Hall at Third and Brown Streets from 1858 to 1865 before establishing a synagogue on the corner of New Market and Noble Streets (1865–1875). In the New Market location, the congregation's first cantor, Moses Cohen, introduced choir music into congregational worship (1873). In 1875, Adath Jeshurun purchased Rodeph Shalom's former home on Juliana Street and relocated there. In that location, members installed an organ (1876) and introduced late Friday evening services (1883). As the congregation continued to grow—as did Philadelphia's Jewish community—Adath Jeshurun needed a larger home. In 1886, Adath Jeshurun dedicated its new synagogue at Seventh Street and Columbia Avenue. By 1896, German had been abolished as the language for the congregation's liturgy and English took its place. In 1901, Adath Jeshurun's members established a school for unaffiliated children in the Strawberry Mansion section of North Philadelphia. In 1911, Adath Jeshurun moved to North Broad Street, a year after members rejected a proposed merger with Rodeph Shalom. In consideration of this decision, in 1913, Adath Jeshurun became a founding member of the United Synagogue of America (now the United Synagogue of Conservative Judaism), the national organization of Conservative synagogues. In the aftermath of World War II and the Jewish community's move north in the city, the congregation decided to relocate its activities. Adath Jeshurun built several branches to accommodate congregational needs. The congregation established a nursery school in Melrose Park at Old York Road and Ansley Avenue (1949–1958)—where it also administered a midweek Hebrew school—and a suburban branch in Elkins Park on Ashbourne Road (1959–1964). In 1958, the congregation purchased land at Ashbourne and Old York in order to initiate a multiphase building program. Six years later, the congregation relocated to Elkins Park on Old York Road (1964). In this new location, Adath Jeshurun gave its women full ritual equality in the congregation (1973).

These men served the congregation as religious leaders: Samuel B. Briedenbach (1858–1861), S. Nathans (1866–1868), Elias Eppstein (1868–1888), Henry Iliowizi (1888–1901), Bernard C. Ehrenreich (1901–1906), Jacob H. Landau (1906–1910), Max D. Klein (1910–1960), Yaakov G. Rosenberg (1960–1978),

Seymour Rosenbloom (1978–). Charles Davidson, a leading synagogue composer, serves as cantor.

Under the rabbinates of Eppstein, Iliowizi, Ehrenreich, and Landau, the congregation slowly moved from its Orthodox moorings toward Conservative Judaism, with an emphasis on programming for the youth of the congregation. Klein devoted himself to religious education and the upbuilding of Palestine (later Israel). Klein also developed a prayer book for the congregation called *Seder Avodah* (adopted 1960, revised by Rosenberg 1987). Rosenberg emphasized the observance of ritual and mitzvoth, as well as social action. He advocated equal religious rights for women of the congregation. Rosenbloom also emphasized adult education and more participation of congregants in the ritual and governance of the congregation. In 1995, Adath Jeshurun's membership exceeded one thousand family units.

Reference

Maslin, Simeon. *One God, Sixteen Houses* (Philadelphia: 1990).

BETH SHOLOM, CONSERVATIVE. *Philadelphia (later Elkins Park), Pennsylvania.* Founders established this congregation in 1917. In recognition of the World War I Armistice, charter members adopted the name Beth Sholom (meaning "House of Peace"). However, many founders originally wanted to name the synagogue "Logan Congregation Ahavas Israel." In 1919, Beth Sholom affiliated with the United Synagogue of America (now United Synagogue of Conservative Judaism), the national organization of Conservative synagogues. Beginning in 1920, Rabbi Mortimer Cohen served Beth Sholom as its founding rabbi. By the time the congregation built its first permanent home at Broad and Courtland (dedicated 1922), membership exceeded three hundred.

In 1926, Cohen introduced late night services on Fridays and later Beth Sholom installed an organ in its sanctuary (1935). In 1939, the congregation developed a high school program. The congregation followed the move of its congregants to Elkins Park and relocated at Foxcroft and Old York Road. In its new location, Beth Sholom's one thousand member families built a school and community center (dedicated 1952), with a swimming pool, before Frank Lloyd Wright designed the sanctuary itself (dedicated 1959), asking that it be renamed the "American Synagogue."

Rabbi Aaron Landes succeeded Cohen in 1964, shortly after the congregation introduced daily services. The following year, the American Institute of Architects designated the sanctuary as a National Landmark. In 1967, members added a new school wing to the building to accommodate the growth of the religious program. In 1974, congregants founded the Forman Day School. That same year, Beth Sholom significantly expanded its program of adult education. Three years later, the board of trustees passed a resolution to allow women "upon request" to receive Torah honors, except on the High Holidays.

In 1978, the congregation won a battle with the Rabbinical Assembly over its desire to have live music on the Sabbath. That same year, the West Oaklane Jewish Community Center merged with Beth Sholom, bringing its 150 families into the Beth Sholom membership. In 1984, Beth Sholom established a Hebrew Free Loan Society. In the late 1980s, the local Solomon Schechter Day School merged with the Forman Hebrew Day School to become the Forman Center of the Solomon Schechter Hebrew Day School and moved to the Mandell Educational Campus (of the Federation of Jewish Agencies) in Melrose Park.

References

Beth Sholom Archives, Philadelphia, Pennsylvania.
Cohen, Mortimer J. *Beth Sholom Synagogue* (Philadelphia: 1959).
Synagogue Histories Collection, The Joseph and Miriam Ratner Center for the Study of Conservative Judaism.

BETH ZION–BETH ISRAEL, CONSERVATIVE. *Philadelphia, Pennsylvania.*

Beth Israel

German and Polish immigrants founded Beth Israel in 1840. These founders met for worship at a small site on Adelphia Court and dedicated their first home in 1849. From the beginning, Beth Israel's program included a strong emphasis on synagogue music. In 1908, the growing congregation built a Moorish Temple in Strawberry Mansion near East Fairmount Park. It remained in that location until 1957, before securing temporary quarters at Greenbrier Country Club in Wynnefield Heights. Beth Israel closed its doors in 1963 as a result of demographic changes in the area.

Beth Zion

With a nucleus of eighty members, founders established this urban synagogue in 1946. Rabbi Benjamin H. Tumin (1947–1948) became the congregation's first religious leader. Rabbi Yaacov Rosenberg (1948–1955) succeeded him. In 1954, Beth Zion members consecrated a former Gothic church on Eighteenth and Spruce Streets off Rittenhouse Square as its home. The following year, members elected Rabbi Reuben Magil to its pulpit.

Beth Zion–Beth Israel

Beth Zion merged with Beth Israel in 1964 and moved into the Beth Zion synagogue building. The Daughters of Beth Israel and the Women's Club of Beth Zion merged to become one sisterhood organization. The men's clubs of the two synagogues combined as well. Rabbi Magil became the religious leader of the combined congregation. In this merged congregation, liturgical music retained the prominence it had previously enjoyed in Beth Israel. In 1984, the Nezner Congregation in Queens Village (founded in 1889 by Eastern European Jews) merged into Beth Zion–Beth Israel.

Beth Zion–Beth Israel extended full religious rights to women. It maintained the only full Jewish library in center-city Philadelphia. Beth Zion-Beth Israel claims to be the first congregation to plan specifically for the hearing-impaired and the first to hold a public seder. Its Purim ball grew into the Federation of Jewish Philanthropies in Philadelphia. As an urban congregation, its social action program included a literacy program and feeding program for the homeless in the area. In 1995, membership stood at 550 members.

References

Synagogue Histories Collection, The Joseph and Miriam Ratner Center for the Study of Conservative Judaism.
Synagogue Histories File, American Jewish Archives.
Temple Beth Zion–Beth Israel Collection, Philadelphia Jewish Archives Center, Balch Institute for Ethnic Studies, Philadelphia, Pennsylvania.

HAR ZION, CONSERVATIVE. *Philadelphia, Pennsylvania.* The founding group of Har Zion moved to the Wynnefield area in the 1920s. Feeling the need for a neighborhood house of worship, a small group established the congregation in 1923. Founders held their first services in a private home before moving to the Wynnefield Club. Har Zion members built their first home in 1924. At the same time, the women of the congregation formed a sisterhood. In 1926, the congregation developed an annex that it acquired from a neighboring church. Two years later, the membership built a school building. Rabbi Simon Greenberg led the congregation from 1925 to 1946 before leaving to become vice chancellor of the Jewish Theological Seminary of America. Under Greenberg's guidance, the congregation became a model of the synagogue-center with a wide array of activities.

Rabbi David Goldstein (1947–1969) succeeded Greenberg. Under his direction, Har Zion developed a program that permitted the enrollment of children in religious school regardless of whether their parents were members. In addition, the congregation established a Hebrew high school and junior college (A. M. Ellis Midrasha) that permitted the student to transfer to Gratz College with full credits.

In 1952, Har Zion built a community center and established a day camp. In 1956, members of the congregation founded a Solomon Schechter Day School, which met at Har Zion until 1976. It also housed the Akiba Lower School until 1976, as well. Membership reached sixteen hundred in 1965, with over five hundred children involved in United Synagogue Youth programs.

Rabbi Gerald Wolpe became the religious leader of the congregation in 1969. When he arrived, the congregation operated its main synagogue in Wynnefield and a satellite facility in Radnor. This satellite began as a day-camp site, but a group of local congregants developed the site into a full religious, social, and educational program. Under Wolpe's direction, both sites merged into the Penn Valley site on Hagys Ford Road in 1976. Shortly thereafter, Wolpe advocated an equal role for women in religious ritual in the synagogue. He concentrated his efforts on education. Thus, Har Zion's religious school became the first Conservative afternoon school to receive accreditation from the United Synagogue of America, Commission on Jewish Education. Nearly five hundred children attend the Har Zion preschool. Additionally, he introduced a variety of innovative educational programs, including the Kirschner Family Program, which examines the changing family structure within the Jewish community; the Leviettes Conference, which focuses on many aspects of Conservative Judaism as it confronts the twenty-first century; and the Fishman Institute, which concentrates on adult education. Under Wolpe's guidance at Har Zion, there are a variety of special interest groups, which include twelve-step programs for those in recovery from drug and alcohol addiction, older adult groups, a kosher cooking program for elderly shut-ins, spirituality groups, diet support groups, and birthing and tot educational programs. In 1995, membership stood at fifteen hundred family units.

References

Har Zion Temple, 1924–1949 (Philadelphia: 1949).
Simon Greenberg Collection, The Joseph and Miriam Ratner Center for the Study of Conservative Judaism.
Souvenir Book, Har Zion Temple (Philadelphia: 1933).
Synagogue Histories Collection, The Joseph and Miriam Ratner Center for the Study of Conservative Judaism.
Synagogue Histories File, American Jewish Archives.

KENESETH ISRAEL, REFORM. *Philadelphia (later Elkins Park), Pennsylvania.* Initially Orthodox in observance, Keneseth Israel was founded by a group of German Jewish immigrants in 1847, and German was named the official language of congregational worship and business. By 1855, Keneseth Israel adopted Reform Judaism. The congregation began its history on North Second Street but, like other congregations, moved a variety of times during its history: to New Market and Noble Streets (1853); Sixth and Brown Streets (1863); North Broad Street (1892); and York Road and Township Line, Elkins Park (1957). Congregational growth and a need for larger facilities prompted each move.

Dr. David Einhorn, one of the founders of Reform Judaism, came to serve Keneseth Israel in 1861, having literally escaped from his former pulpit in Baltimore, because of his outspoken opposition to slavery. Dr. Samuel Hirsch, another outspoken reformer, succeeded Einhorn in 1866. As one of the primary architects of the 1885 Pittsburgh Platform, which articulated the principles of Reform Judaism, Hirsch moved the congregation in the direction of the radical positions reflected in the platform during his twenty-year tenure.

During Rabbi Joseph Krauskopf's association with Keneseth Israel, beginning in 1887, members made the transition to English. Krauskopf prepared his own prayer book and established a format for worship that included Friday evenings and Sunday mornings.

Dr. William H. Fineshriber succeeded Krauskopf in 1924. He reinstituted many of the ceremonies like Bar Mitzvah and Saturday morning Torah readings that his predecessors had discarded. In addition, he introduced the *Union Prayer Book,* the Reform movement's prayer book, for adoption by the congregation. Under his leadership, the congregation reflected his anti-Zionism.

Keneseth Israel elected Rabbi Bertram Korn, a native son of the congregation, to its pulpit in 1949. He made Friday evening services the central focus for worship and concentrated on a program of religious education, growing in the midst of the post–World War II baby boom.

Shortly after Rabbi Korn's death in 1980, Rabbi Simeon Maslin became senior rabbi of the temple. In his own words, he "attempts to maintain the traditional Jewish tension between the universalistic and the particular, stressing at the same time the responsibility of the Jewish community for the welfare of all people and the need to assure Jewish survival through the practice of *mitzvot*— Jewish rituals—and the study of Torah.'' Under his leadership, the congregation is greatly involved in community service, particularly in the area of feeding the hungry and providing shelter for the homeless.

In 1982, Temple Judea merged into Keneseth Israel. Its legacy can be found in the Judea Museum located in the Keneseth Israel lobby. Judea was originally established in 1930 by congregants of Keneseth Israel who moved northward and wanted a branch Sunday School in North Philadelphia to meet their needs. Rabbi Meir Lasker served this congregation for over thirty-five years. In 1994, membership at Keneseth Israel stood at 1756 family units.

References

Korn, Bertram. "Our Keneseth Israel Heritage" (Philadelphia: 1955).

Maslin, Simeon. *One God, Sixteen Houses* (Philadelphia: 1990).

110th Anniversary, Reform Congregation Keneseth Israel 1847–1957 (Philadelphia: 1957).

Reform Congregation Keneseth Israel: Its First 100 Years 1847–1947 (Philadelphia: 1950).

Reform Congregation Keneseth Israel Marks 125 Years Serving Its Members and the Total Community 1847–1972 (Philadelphia: 1972).

Silverstein, Alan. *Alternatives to Assimilation: The Responses of Reform Judaism to American Culture 1840–1930* (Hanover, NH: 1994).

Synagogue Histories File, American Jewish Archives.

Yearbooks. Reform Congregation Keneseth Israel.

MIKVE ISRAEL, ORTHODOX. *Philadelphia, Pennsylvania.* According to historians Edwin Wolf and Maxwell Whiteman, Mikve Israel grew out of a loose association of Jews who banded together for worship in the mid-1740s. Its formal life as a congregation began gradually, perhaps most notably with the acquisition of a borrowed Torah scroll in 1761 and worship services in a private home on Sterling Alley. While Kahal Kadosh Mikve Israel, the official name of the congregation, did not obtain its charter until 1773, founders had officially opened a synagogue on Cherry Alley (now Street) two years before.

Hazzan Gershon Mendes Seixas arrived from New York in 1780 and, with the help of a group of men, reorganized the congregation in 1782, following the model of New York's Congregation Shearith Israel. Shortly thereafter, the group purchased an old bakehouse and lot on Third and Cherry and built a new facility. Even with the opposition of the local Reformed German Church, which did not want a synagogue in the neighborhood, members built this new synagogue with seating around the periphery of the sanctuary in the Sephardic style. When Seixas returned to New York's Shearith Israel in 1784, the *adjunta* (board) invited his replacement in New York, Hazzan Jacob Raphael Cohen, to replace him in Philadelphia. Cohen remained until his death in 1811. During the early years of Cohen's tenure, financial strains plagued the congregation. At the same time, members actively participated in the struggle for civil rights for Jews in Pennsylvania and throughout the United States. Emanuel Nunes Carvahlo succeeded Cohen in 1814–1817, and Abraham Israel Keys served the congregation from 1824 to 1828.

In 1825, the congregation built a new structure on the same site at Third and Cherry, which it occupied until 1859. Four years after Mikve Israel built its new home, Isaac Leeser came to the congregation as religious leader (1829). As the leading Jewish leader of the period and editor of *The Occident,* Leeser promoted the development of a unified American Jewish community. He stressed Jewish education on all levels, joining with Rebecca Gratz in the promotion of the Sunday School, as well as the creation of a day school sponsored by the congregation (1830). He wrote school books for the children, prayer books for his congregation, and prepared the first English translation of the Bible. Leeser wanted to create a model for Jewish religious leadership that resembled the ministry of local Protestant clergy. Thus, he preached regularly from the pulpit. Leeser also encouraged the congregation to become involved in overseas Jewish community concerns such as the Damascus Affair (1840). Leeser left Mikve Israel in 1850 following the controversy stirred by the distribution of an anonymous pamphlet entitled *A Review of the Late Controversies between the Rev. Isaac Leeser and the Congregation Mikveh Israel.*

Rabbi Sabato Morais succeeded him (1851–1897). During his tenure with the congregation, Morais helped to found the Jewish Theological Seminary of America, the rabbinical seminary of the Conservative movement. As such, he became a leader of the movement and a chief proponent of historical Judaism. In 1860, Mikve Israel moved to a site on North Seventh Street, following the pattern of Jewish migration of its congregants.

In 1893, the congregation became vested in a trust established by Hyman Gratz "for the establishment and support of a college for the education of Jews residing in the city and country of Philadelphia" and, in 1895, founded Gratz College. The congregation's religious school became an educational laboratory for students at the college.

Rabbi Leon Elmaleh succeeded Morais in 1898, followed by Julius Greenstone (1901–1902) and Isaac C. Edrehi (1927–1928). In 1909, the congregation moved to Broad and York Streets. Rabbi Abraham A. Neuman (1927–1943) succeeded Edrehi. David A. Jessurun Cardozo (1943–1949) succeeded him before Emanuel L. Lipschutz assumed the pulpit in 1951. Alan D. Corre served from 1955 to 1963. In 1963, Rabbi Ezekiel N. Musleah became the spiritual leader of Mikve Israel. In 1976, Mikveh Israel moved to Independence Mall, sharing a building with the National Museum of American Jewish History, only three blocks away from the Cherry Street site of its original building. It continues to hold services, using the Sephardic mode of worship, in place since the beginning of the congregation. In the new site, these religious leaders led Mikveh Israel: Joshua Toledano (1980–1988), Allan Lazeroff (1989–1990), and Albert E. Gabbai (1990–   ). In 1995, membership of Mikve Israel numbered 250 family units.

References

Dedication of the New Synagogue of the Congregation Mikve Israel at Broad and York Streets (Philadelphia: 1909).

Morais, Sabato. "Mickve Israel Congregation of Philadelphia." *Publications of the American Jewish Historical Society,* no. 1 (1892): 13–24.

Sussman, Lance. *Isaac Leeser and the Making of American Judaism* (Detroit: 1995).

———. *The Life and Career of Isaac Leeser (1806–1868): A Study of American Judaism in Its Formative Period* (Ph.D. dissertation, Hebrew Union College–Jewish Institute of Religion, Cincinnati, 1987).

Synagogue Histories File, American Jewish Archives.

Wolf, Edwin II and Maxwell Whiteman. *The History of the Jews of Philadelphia from Colonial Times to the Age of Jackson* (Philadelphia: 1975).

Yarrish, Herbert. "Beginnings of the Mickve Israel Congregation" (Rabbinic thesis, Hebrew Union College, 1949).

CONGREGATION RODEPH SHALOM, REFORM. *Philadelphia, Pennsylvania.* In the mid-1790s a group of newcomers, unhappy with the Sephardic mode of worship at Mikve Israel, established an institution better suited to their religious needs. Like most others of its kind, the German Hebrew Society—the self-declared name of this group—began as an Orthodox congregation. Organized in 1795, it appears that the congregation built a *mikvah* (ritual bath) by the following year. In 1802, founders dedicated their new synagogue organization and named it Rodeph Shalom. While freedom of choice motivated the founding of Rodeph Shalom, finances forced officials to prohibit members from belonging to another minyan. In 1811, the membership roster counted only twenty-one synagogue seatholders. The following year, Rodeph Shalom received its charter from the Pennsylvania Supreme Court.

In 1819, Rodeph Shalom engaged its first religious leader, Jacob Lippman. After Lippman left the congregation in 1833, several readers led the worship. Though some of the early records that document the early places of worship are not extant, it seems that members held services at the beginning of the nineteenth century in a building on Margaretta Street below Second. In 1820,

Rodeph Shalom moved to Bread (now Moravian) Street. The following year, the congregation moved to Church Alley between Second and Third. In 1830, Rodeph Shalom changed its place of worship to Pear Alley (now Chancellor Street). Ten years later, the congregation moved to Vine and then to Cherry above Fifth. In 1847, the congregation purchased the Kenild Church located on Juliana Street; this became the first permanent building used by the congregation.

Rodeph Shalom elected Dr. Bernard Illoway to its pulpit in 1853. Dr. H. Vidaver succeeded him in 1859. In 1866, members invited Dr. Marcus Jastrow to occupy the pulpit at Rodeph Shalom. While he eschewed Reform Judaism, he advocated the installation of an organ in the new synagogue, approved the abridgement of the Torah readings, and favored the abolition of selling Torah honors—later abolishing them entirely. He introduced German and later English prayers. In addition, because he believed so much in the family, he introduced family pews, as well. Rodeph Shalom affiliated with the Union of American Hebrew Congregations (UAHC), the national organization of Reform Synagogues upon its inception in 1873. However, as congregational members of the UAHC began instituting major changes in synagogue ritual and practice, Rodeph Shalom withdrew its support from the incipient organization.

The synagogue moved to Broad and Mt. Vernon Streets in 1870, under a Penn grant. In 1879, the congregation joined the UAHC once again. However, Rodeph Shalom supported the Jewish Theological Seminary Association, the Conservative rabbinical seminary, beginning in 1888.

Upon Dr. Jastrow's retirement in 1892, Rodeph Shalom members invited Henry Berkowitz, a member of Hebrew Union College's first graduating class, to lead them as rabbi. Berkowitz firmly set the path toward Reform Judaism for the congregation. He urged the adoption of the *Union Prayer Book,* the uniform prayer book of the Reform movement. During his tenure, Keneseth Israel joined Rodeph Shalom in a variety of projects and programs, including joint worship services, Sunday School, and joint efforts on behalf of Reform Judaism. In 1908, the congregation received a gift in the form of a building located on Jefferson and Broad Street, which it renamed the Benjamin F. Teller Memorial Schoolhouse.

In 1913, Rodeph Shalom unsuccessfully introduced a voluntary dues system. It took years however before the congregation implemented a system of free seating. As a reflection of the women's suffrage movement, the women of Rodeph Shalom formed a sisterhood in 1913. By 1918, this organization included nearly six hundred women.

Harry Ettelson succeeded Berkowitz in 1921, having served as associate rabbi at Rodeph Shalom since 1919. Ettelson paid particular attention to the religious school during his early tenure with the congregation. Struggling with the poor attendance—particularly of men—for worship services on Saturday morning, he introduced early evening Friday services with great success. Rabbi Louis Wolsey succeeded Ettelson in 1925. Wolsey took firm control of the congregation and its religious school. In 1928, at Wolsey's insistence, members built a Byzantine structure on the same site at Broad and Mt. Vernon Streets.

In 1942, Louis Wolsey joined other anti-Zionists in forming the American Council for Judaism. He resigned three years later and called for the dissolution of the group. Recognizing the negative impact of Wolsey's anti-Zionist/Zionist position on the congregation, Rabbi David H. Wice, who succeeded Wolsey in 1947, asked the congregation not to allow itself to become a battleground over the Zionist question. Any controversy over Zionism faded the following year with the establishment of the modern state of Israel. Wice inherited a congregation still reeling from the effects of the Depression and devastated by World War II. Thus, he sought to bring a "sense of concord," as congregational historian Anndee Hochman called it, back to the congregation.

As congregants moved out of Philadelphia into the suburbs, Rodeph Shalom joined other congregations in sponsoring neighborhood religious school classes as early as 1941. In addition, Rodeph Shalom held once-monthly worship services at suburban St. Paul's Church on York Road and eventually leased the Curtis Arboretum for the same purpose. In 1958, Rodeph Shalom consecrated a suburban center in Elkins Park, which it originally sought to develop as a joint venture with Keneseth Israel. Thus, Wice diversified congregational activities within the context of two buildings nine miles apart.

In 1971, the congregation introduced a "Service of Affirmation" for girls at Rodeph Shalom. Three years later, members expanded the suburban center. At about the same time, Rodeph Shalom instituted a Synagogue Council for Community Service. By 1979, the congregation removed all distinctions with regard to ritual between boys and girls and instituted Saturday morning Bat Mitzvah.

With over eighteen hundred families in 1981, Richard Steinbrink succeeded Wice after the latter's retirement. Steinbrink previously served as associate rabbi. Under his direction, programs on social action, as well as those specifically designed for youth, increased at the congregation. Yet, at the same time, membership shrank from the postwar highs. In 1987, Steinbrink resigned. That same year, the congregation refurbished its Broad Street lobby for the Leon J. and Julia S. Obermeyer collection of Judaica.

The following year, Rodeph Shalom elected Alan Fuchs to its pulpit as senior rabbi. Under his leadership, Rodeph Shalom boosted its young adult membership and expanded its religious school programs. He oversaw the total refurbishment of both congregational facilities. In 1994, membership stood at 1630.

References

Berkowitz, Henry. "Notes on the History of the Earliest German Jewish Congregation in America." *Publications of the American Jewish Historical Society,* no. 9 (1901): 123–27.

Davis, Edward. *The History of Rodeph Shalom Congregation, Philadelphia 1802–1926* (Philadelphia: 1926).

Hochman, Anndee. *Rodeph Shalom: Two Centuries of Seeking Peace* (Philadelphia: [forthcoming]).

Rodeph Shalom Collection, Philadelphia Jewish Archives Center, Balch Institute for Ethnic Studies, Philadelphia, Pennsylvania.

Rosenbaum, Jeanette W. "Hebrew German Society Rodeph Shalom in the City and

County of Philadelphia (1800–1950).'' *American Jewish Historical Quarterly* 41, no. 1 (September 1951): 83–93.

Wolf, Edwin II and Maxwell Whiteman. *The History of the Jews of Philadelphia from Colonial Times to the Age of Jackson* (Philadelphia: 1975).

RODEF SHALOM CONGREGATION, REFORM. *Pittsburgh, Pennsylvania.* A small group of members of Shaare Shamayim, the first synagogue in Pittsburgh, withdrew over the decision not to rehire its religious leader, William Armhold. Taking Armhold with them, they formed Rodef Shalom in 1856. In 1859, the congregation took up residence in a hall on St. Clair Street, but Pittsburgh's incipient Jewish community could not support two synagogues. Thus, when Rodef Shalom decided to erect its own synagogue in 1860, its members successfully invited the members of Shaare Shamayim to merge and form one congregation. The new congregation built its synagogue on Hancock (later Eighth) Street (dedicated 1862).

Rodef Shalom remained Orthodox until Isaac Mayer Wise, the organizer of American Reform Judaism, visited Pittsburgh and recommended certain changes to the congregation, beginning with the introduction of Wise's own prayer book, *Minhag America.* Following a vote to accept Wise's reforms, the dissenters left Rodef Shalom to form Tree of Life Congregation. Changes came swiftly. Members shortened the worship service. They eliminated the songs that opened the Torah service. The service leader faced the congregation (rather than the holy ark). Men and women sat together, and an organ was installed.

Louis Naumberg succeeded Armhold in 1865. He quickly made changes. Under his direction, Rodef Shalom removed the women's gallery from the sanctuary and installed family pews on the main floor. Naumberg focused a great deal of his attention on the children of the congregation and their religious education. In 1868, Rodef Shalom discontinued its English studies courses, satisfied that public education was no longer an arm of the Protestant church. However, the synagogue did retain German studies, along with Hebrew and religious education.

Dissatisfied with the exclusive use of German for preaching by the religious leaders of Rodef Shalom, members sought to elect a rabbi who could preach in English and German. Thus, members engaged Dr. Lippman Mayer as their religious leader in 1870. At his suggestion, the congregation adopted David Einhorn's more radical prayer book, *Olath Tamid.* Yet dissatisfaction remained; it erupted when a small group left and founded Congregation Emanuel in 1874 to fully embrace American Judaism unencumbered by any German. This experiment lasted about two years before its seventeen members rejoined Rodef Shalom.

While unsuccessful, the secession did force the membership of Rodef Shalom to Americanize as quickly as possible. This was particularly true during the presidency of Emanuel Wertheimer (1871–1886). With the assistance of Isaac Mayer Wise, he persuaded the congregation in 1873 to dispense with the wearing of hats during worship and to join the Union of American Hebrew Congregations, the national organization of Reform synagogues.

Rodef Shalom withstood the residential changes of Pittsburgh's neighborhoods in the late nineteenth century. When Mayer retired in 1901, Rodef Shalom's 150 families elected Rabbi J. Leonard Levy to succeed him. He preached only in English and attracted people to join the new temple built on Eighth Street (dedicated 1901). Rodef Shalom's women established a sisterhood the following year. Now overcrowded with over 350 members, Rodef Shalom moved to Fifth Avenue near Shadyside in 1907 (dedicated in 1917 because of financial difficulties). Levy prepared his own prayer book for use at the Sunday services held by the congregation.

Following Levy's death, Rabbi Samuel Goldenson came to lead the congregation of over one thousand families in 1917. Shortly after he arrived, Goldenson introduced the *Union Prayer Book,* the prayer book of the Reform movement. Unlike nearly all other Reform congregations, Rodef Shalom still uses the revised *Union Prayer Book* instead of the *Gates of Prayer.*

Goldenson encouraged the congregation to abolish the system of private ownership of pews in favor of unassigned pews. This change helped to pave the way for the development of a more democratic framework for synagogue membership, part of Goldenson's effort to increase membership.

Rabbi Solomon Freehof succeeded Goldenson in 1934. Under his leadership, Rodef Shalom continued to grow. During his tenure, Rodef Shalom added buildings to the religious school to accommodate such growth (1938, 1956). Freehof used the pulpit to display a high level of learning and scholarship. His Sunday lectures drew hundreds each week, and his midweek book reviews drew large crowds as well. As an expert in Jewish law, Freehof gained an international reputation for his work in Reform responsa literature. Among his other writings, he published numerous books on the subject on behalf of the Reform movement.

When Freehof retired in 1966, Rabbi Walter Jacob succeeded him, having originally joined Rodef Shalom as assistant rabbi. Jacob continued Freehof's emphasis on Jewish law and scholarship in the congregation and for the Reform movement. Like his predecessor, Jacob published a wide variety of books on many Jewish subjects, including Jewish law. Jacob introduced late Friday evening Sabbath worship, as well as Bar/Bat Mitzvah to Rodef Shalom. Membership in 1994 at Rodef Shalom exceeded sixteen hundred.

References

Aaron, Marcus L. *One Hundred Twenty Years, Rodef Shalom Congregation, Pittsburgh, Pennsylvania* (Pittsburgh: 1976).
Feldman, Jacob. *The Jewish Experience in Western Pennsylvania* (Pittsburgh: 1986).
Synagogue Histories File, American Jewish Archives.

TREE OF LIFE, CONSERVATIVE. *Pittsburgh, Pennsylvania.* When the membership of Rodef Shalom voted to adopt certain reforms, at the suggestion of Isaac Mayer Wise, sixteen dissenters, led by Gustavus Grafner, left the congregation to form Etz Hayyim, Tree of Life, in 1864. In 1876, Tree of Life held its first Confirmation for boys and girls. The new congregation first met for worship in Grafner's home and then moved to a variety of temporary locations. In 1883, Tree of Life relocated to a former church at Fourth Avenue and Ross Street, about the same time it shortened the familiar Orthodox worship service. In 1886 Tree of Life joined the Jewish Theological Seminary Association, founded to support the training of rabbis for the Conservative movement.

In 1890, a resolution in support of the installation of family pews failed. It passed three years later. In 1898, the congregation elected Rabbi Michael Fried, a graduate of the seminary, to its pulpit. Fried quickly implemented a variety of programs and activities in the synagogue. He encouraged the women of Tree of Life to form a sisterhood shortly thereafter. He also introduced English prayers for the first time in the history of the congregation (1906). When he resigned the same year because of ill health, Rabbi Rudolph Coffee, an active Zionist, joined the congregation. Tree of Life moved to Craft Avenue in Oakland in 1906. In the new location, members established late Friday evening Sabbath services (1909). Rabbi Morris Mazure (1915–1922) succeeded Rabbi Coffee. During his association with Tree of Life, the synagogue affiliated with the United Synagogue of America (now the United Synagogue of Conservative Judaism), the national organization of Conservative synagogues (1916).

Rabbi Herman Halperin succeeded Mazure in 1922 and served Tree of Life for forty-five years. Under his direction, members actively supported the upbuilding of Palestine. He argued for the right of women to sit on the board of trustees (1923) and introduced children's worship services (1932). In 1952, Tree of Life left Oakland, moving into its new home at Shady and Wilkins Avenues in the Squirrel Hill section of Pittsburgh one year later. In 1962, Tree of Life extended the right to Torah honors to women, but waited until 1965 before counting them in a minyan. Solomon Kaplan succeeded Halperin in 1968. Following Kaplan's death in 1982, members elected Alvin Berkun (1983–   ) to the pulpit. In 1995, membership of Tree of Life stood at 850 family units.

References

Feldman, Jacob. *The Jewish Experience in Western Pennsylvania* (Pittsburgh: 1986).
Synagogue Histories File, American Jewish Archives.
Three Score and Ten (Pittsburgh: 1934).

B'NAI B'RITH, REFORM. *Wilkes-Barre (later Kingston), Pennsylvania.* In 1845, thirty individuals established Congregation B'nai B'rith (chartered 1857). In 1849, the new synagogue dedicated its home on South Washington Street, the first synagogue in northeastern Pennsylvania. Moses Strasser served the congregation as its first religious leader. Members used an Orthodox liturgy until 1860, when they adopted David Einhorn's Reform prayer book, *Olath Tamid,* after a visit to the community by Einhorn. In 1881, B'nai B'rith dedicated an additional building at the Washington Street location. In 1897, B'nai B'rith adopted the *Union Prayer Book,* the uniform prayer book of the Reform movement.

When B'nai B'rith decided to conduct Sunday services in the temple, members asked Rabbi David Stern to prepare a prayer book for that purpose (ca. 1882). During the rabbinate of Israel Joseph (1891–1895), the synagogue instituted late Friday evening Sabbath services and joined the Union of American Hebrew Congregations, the national association of Reform synagogues. Members introduced a system of free pews in 1919. In 1922, a group resigned from B'nai B'rith to form a local Conservative synagogue, Temple Israel. Membership in 1936 reached 110 members.

In 1960, Temple B'nai B'rith moved to Wyoming Avenue in Kingston and dedicated a new synagogue there, using furnishings from the former sanctuary in the new synagogue chapel. In 1972, Hurricane Agnes severely damaged the synagogue, as it did much of the Wyoming Valley. As the community began to rebuild, B'nai B'rith served as a base for volunteers assisting local flood victims. In 1974, following much refurbishing, the congregation rededicated its temple. Temple B'nai B'rith initiated a housing project for the elderly in 1984. In 1995, membership of Temple B'nai B'rith exceeded 275 family units.

Religious leaders who served B'nai B'rith included Isaac Strouse (1851–1853), Herman Rubin (1853–1882), Rabbi David Stern (1882–1885), Dr. Victor Rundbaken (1885–1891), Rabbi Israel Joseph (1891–1895), Dr. Marcus Salzman (1896–1931), Rabbi Samuel Wolk (1929–1945), Rabbi Newton J. Friedman (1945–1953), Rabbi Myron Weingarten (1954–1955), Rabbi Albert Friedlander (1956–1961), Rabbi Earl Starr (1961–1969), Rabbi Arnold Shevlin (1970–1992), and Michael Joseph (1992–   ).

References

A Century with Wilkes-Barre (Wilkes-Barre, PA: 1945).
Eightieth Anniversary, Temple B'nai B'rith (Wilkes-Barre, PA: 1929).
Greenwald, Mazie. *History of Temple B'nai B'rith* (Wilkes-Barre, PA: 1989).
Seventy-Fifth Anniversary Celebration (Wilkes-Barre, PA: 1924).
Synagogue Histories File, American Jewish Archives.

R

RHODE ISLAND

TOURO/JESHUAT ISRAEL, ORTHODOX. *Newport, Rhode Island.* In the spirit of Roger Williams and religious equality, Jewish settlers came to Newport and founded a synagogue in 1658. In 1677, the ''Jews and their Nation Society or Friends'' purchased land to be used for a cemetery (preserved in a poem by Henry Wadsworth Longfellow), located at the beginning of Bellevue Avenue and known as ''Jews Street'' in the years prior to the Revolutionary War. Toward the end of the seventeenth century, the Jewish population increased with immigrants from Curacao. In the eighteenth century, important Jewish families fled to Newport, among them the Lopez family. Upon immigration, as others, they threw off their Marrano mask and soon planned the erection of a synagogue.

Designed by Peter Harrison, Touro Synagogue is the oldest synagogue building in the United States (dedicated 1763). The congregation chose Isaac Touro (father of Judah Touro, who later willed funds to support the Jewish community and synagogue of Newport) to serve as its leader and officiate at the dedication ceremony. The sanctuary's structure follows the standards of a Sephardic synagogue, with seats arranged along the north and south walls in order to keep clear the space between the reading desk in the center and the ark at the east end of the structure. One striking feature of the synagogue is its underground passage, which starts beneath the reading desk and goes toward the street. While it might have been built for storage, local tradition holds that it was a hiding place and unfinished channel of escape for people who even in a new free world could not throw off the sense of terror and persecution they had experienced in their past. The synagogue has shared its past with the United States in a variety of ways. In 1780, for example, the General Assembly of the State of Rhode Island held its first meeting in the synagogue building after the British evacuated

Newport. These meetings continued there until 1784. And in 1781, during a visit by George Washington, the city chose the synagogue as the site for a town meeting. As a result of this visit, the well-known exchange of letters between the congregation and Washington took place. The state supreme court also held sessions at the Touro Synagogue sporadically in the early years of the state.

Newport's prosperity dwindled quickly following the American Revolution, and families headed to other communities. By 1791, the Jewish community virtually disappeared from Newport. The synagogue had no rabbi, reader, or ritual slaughterer and essentially closed. The few remaining Jews in the community transferred the congregation's Torah scrolls to Congregation Shearith Israel in New York. When Moses Lopez left Newport in 1822, as the last survivor of the Jewish community, the synagogue was indeed closed, except for funerals for former members who wished to be buried in Newport.

In 1850, residents reopened the synagogue for infrequent worship services. By 1883, after a modest growth in the Jewish population, Touro began to hold regular Sabbath services once again. In 1883, the Newport corporation gave Abraham Pereira Mendes the keys to the synagogue. He reconsecrated the synagogue, but he spent winters elsewhere when he could not attract a minyan on a regular basis during those months.

When Mendes died in 1893, the community reorganized under the name Jeshuat Israel, directed by the watchful eye of Congregation Shearith Israel in New York City, which had the right to take possession of the building. Shearith Israel elected David Baruch as successor to Pereira Mendes. Baruch died in 1899.

Membership reached 125 families in 1926, with over one hundred children in its religious school. At this time, the congregation purchased the old Sheffield house and moved it to a plot of land across from the synagogue to serve its growing needs as a Jewish community center. These rabbis served Touro Synagogue during this period: Saul Baily (1926) and Alter Abelson (1927).

Rabbi Morris A. Gutstein led the congregation for ten years (1933–1943). Rabbi Jules Lipschitz (1944–1948) succeeded him. During his tenure, Touro Synagogue received designation as a national historic site in 1946, as a result of the support of Shearith Israel of New York and Society of Friends of Touro Synagogue, organized in 1948.

Rabbi Theodore Lewis (1949–1987) succeded Lipschitz. During his tenure, the congregation undertook a major renovation project (initiated in 1954, completed in 1961, rededicated in 1963). In 1963, congregation membership stood at 130 families. By 1982, this number had grown to 350. Following Lewis' retirement, Rabbi Chaim Shapiro joined Touro Synagogue as religious leader (1988). Under his direction, the congregation maintained its small religious school and adult education program. Yet, it maintains an active tour program (forty thousand visitors annually) with the support of two affiliated support groups: the Society of Friends of Touro Synagogue and the Touro Heritage Trust Fund. In 1994, membership at Touro Synagogue had declined to 130 family units. Although the Jewish population in Newport continues to decrease, Touro initiated a renovation program (1994), which included the enlargement of the community center of the congregation.

References

Chyet, Stanley. "A Synagogue in Newport." *American Jewish Archives* (April 1964): 41–50.

Fiftieth Anniversary of the Reconsecration of the Synagogue of Congregation Jeshuat Israel (Newport, RI: 1933).

Gutstein, Morris A. *To Bigotry No Sanction: A Jewish Shrine in America, 1658–1958* (New York: 1958).

Lewis, Theodore. "Touro Synagogue—Newport, R.I. 1763–1963." *Bulletin of the Newport Historical Society*, no. 111 (July 1963): 3–20.

Pool, David de Sola. "The Touro Synagogue: Aspects of the Missing Half-Century of its History (1850–1900)." *American Jewish Historical Quarterly* 38, part 1 (September 1948): 57–76.

Synagogue Histories File, American Jewish Archives.

Touro Synagogue of Congregation Jeshuat Israel (Newport, RI: 1977).

TEMPLE BETH-EL/SONS OF ISRAEL AND DAVID, REFORM. *Providence, Rhode Island.* A small group of men met in 1854 to form a new congregation, taking the name Bnai Israel (Sons of Israel). During most of its early years, the congregation met for worship on Weybosset Street and cooperated with the Board of Delegates of American Israelites, established by Isaac Leeser as a representative body of American Judaism.

In 1870, for an unspecified reason, a group of Providence's Jews met to form a new congregation: Sons of David. During its brief three-year history, Sons of David met on Canal Street. Between the years 1873 and 1875, Bnai Israel met in the Music Hall building on Westminster Street. These rival congregations merged in 1874 under the name Congregation of the Sons of Israel and David.

The newly merged congregation moved into new quarters on South Main Street in 1876. The following year, the congregation established a Committee for the Promotion of the Interest of the Congregation, which sought to sponsor a national Jewish convention in Providence. According to one account, the group formed to establish a new congregation, for Reform Judaism, under the name Shaari Shalom or Gates of Peace. Members of the Sons of David and Israel worked out a compromise to absorb this new group into the former congregation and adopt its Reform ideology. Dissenters later formed their own new congregation, called Sons of Abraham (1880), or left to join Sons of Zion, another Orthodox congregation that had been established in Providence in 1875.

The newly constituted congregation met in the Pine Street German Church at the corner of Page and Pine Streets and elected Jacob Voorsanger to its pulpit. The congregation instituted a variety of reforms such as late Friday evening worship, organ music, and a mixed choir, while retaining the dietary laws and the practice of covering one's head during worship. English became the language of prayer, and women sat on the main floor of the sanctuary for worship rather than in the balcony.

Marx Moses succeeded Jacob Voorsanger, who was forced to leave the congregation when he established standards in religious education, much to the dismay of one of the congregation's leaders. Morris Rotenberg followed shortly thereafter. This pattern of short-term tenures of its religious leaders dominated the early history of the congregation.

The congregation moved once again to rented quarters in 1882, to Weybosset Street. It remained there for five years until purchasing a former estate on Friendship Street. Members built a new synagogue in this location in 1890. Rabbi David Blaustein served the congregation in this new location from 1892 to 1898.

By 1896, congregants won the right to choose to worship without hats. The following year, the members adopted the *Union Prayer Book* for use in the congregation. Rabbi Gustav Hausmann served the congregation from 1901 to 1905.

In 1905, a fire caused damage to the synagogue, presumably destroying records from 1854 to 1876. Rabbi Henry Englander came to lead the congregation the same year. At his urging the Sons of Israel and David adopted the *Union Prayer Book II,* specifically designed for the High Holidays, shortly after his arrival in Providence.

The Friendship Street neighborhood deteriorated, and the synagogue felt compelled to move. After selling the building to the Swedish Church, the congregation rented Outlet Hall on Weybosset and Edy Streets. Rabbi Englander resigned in 1910 to join the faculty of Hebrew Union College, and Rabbi Nathan Stern succeeded him in the pulpit. The following year, the congregation dedicated its new synagogue on Broad and Glenham Streets and designated it as Temple Beth-El.

Rabbi Stern left Providence in 1915, and Rabbi Sidney Tedesche served the congregation for the next two years. Rabbi Simon Cohen succeeded him and remained only until 1918. Rabbi Samuel Gup succeeded these men and remained at Beth-El until 1932. Gup immediately attended to the reorganization of the Sunday School program, encouraging the board to allow the children of non-members to attend. In 1921, the congregation instituted, for the first time, the policy of unassigned seating for the High Holidays. Shortly thereafter, the board extended this policy to Sabbath services, as well. About the same time, the board extended limited rights of membership to women of the congregation. The congregation discontinued Saturday services in 1922 unless attendance warranted it and also experimented for a short time with Sunday services.

Following Rabbi Gup's retirement, the congregation invited Rabbi William G. Braude to the pulpit. Because of his long tenure with the congregation, his is the name most associated with the congregation. Rabbi Braude directed a great deal of his attention to education. Among his many early actions, Braude moved Confirmation to the morning of Shavuot from the closest Sunday, which had been the congregation's practice. He also established a standard of requirements for Confirmation that met with some resistance on the part of the membership and their children. He persuaded the congregation to engage a full-time director of education, making Beth-El one of the first midsize congregations to do so. Through Braude's efforts, Beth-El built one of the most substantial synagogue libraries in the country.

By 1940, membership reached 275 families. In 1943, the congregation celebrated its first Bat Mitzvah. Following the death of synagogue member John Jacob Rosenfeld, whose estate included a sizable portion set aside "for the express purpose of erecting a building which will advance the educational purposes of said Congregation of the Sons of Israel and David, and serve as a lecture room, Sabbath School and similar purpose," the congregation used these funds—and those left by Alphonse Lederer—in the building of its Orchard Avenue Synagogue (dedicated 1954).

In 1960, following a long period of time without a cantor, the congregation engaged Cantor Harold Dworkin. This controversial decision to hire a cantor represented a change in the direction of liturgy and worship in the congregation. By this time, membership had reached over nine hundred families, with a religious school enrollment of nearly seven hundred.

During the 1960s, Irving J. Fain, who later gained notoriety in the Reform movement for his initiatives in social action, led the congregation in a variety of social action projects, particularly in the area of civil rights. At about the same time, Rabbi Braude reintroduced the practice of covering one's head during worship (1965) and later the wearing of a prayer shawl.

Rabbi Leslie Y. Gutterman succeeded Rabbi Braude at Beth-El in 1974, joining the congregation as assistant rabbi in 1970. The congregation adopted the *Gates of Prayer* as its prayer book in 1977. In 1994, membership exceeded 1150 family units.

References

Adelman, David C. "Congregation of the Sons of Israel and David (Temple Beth El), The Early Years." *Rhode Island Jewish Historical Notes* 3, no. 4 (August 1962): 195–261.

———. "Early Days of Providence Jewish Community." *Rhode Island Jewish Historical Notes* 3, no. 3 (December 1960): 148–60.

Goldowsky, Seebert. *A Century and a Quarter of Spiritual Leadership: The Story of the Congregation of the Sons of Israel and David (Temple Beth-El), Providence, Rhode Island* (Providence, RI: 1989).

Goodwin, George. "The Design of a Modern Synagogue: Percival Goodman's Beth-El in Providence, Rhode Island." *American Jewish Archives* 45, no. 1 (Spring/Summer 1993): 31–72.

TEMPLE EMANU-EL, CONSERVATIVE. *Providence, Rhode Island.* Under the guidance of the United Synagogue of America (now the United Synagogue of Conservative Judaism), a group of fifteen people founded a Conservative congregation in Providence in 1924 as an east-side alternative synagogue to the

Orthodox and Reform congregations already present in the city. This congregation, Emanu-El, immediately developed a program of education and a religious school for its children. The following year, Emanu-El's Sisterhood came into existence and took on the responsibility of supporting youth programs and adult education. The men of the congregation followed and, in 1928, established a Men's Club.

The incipient congregation met in rented facilities, but it purchased land for a synagogue on Morris Avenue and Sessions Street shortly after its founding. Israel Goldman—while still a student at the Jewish Theological Seminary of America—became Emanu-El's first religious leader (1924–1948). Under his guidance, membership grew and activities increased. Emanu-El dedicated its first in a series of buildings in 1927, beginning with the sanctuary. In 1928, Emanu-El held its first Confirmation. The following year, Rabbi Goldman inaugurated an Institute for Jewish Studies for Adults in the congregation, as well as a Bar Mitzvah Brotherhood and Junior Congregation program. By the end of 1929, membership neared three hundred members, as did the number of students in the religious school. The congregation focused its activities on daily worship as well as on holiday and Sabbath services. In 1935, Emanu-El extended the rite of Bat Mitzvah to girls in the congregation. The synagogue installed an organ for worship, after much debate, in 1937.

Rabbi Eli A. Bohnen (1948–1974) succeeded Goldman. In order to accommodate the growth of religious school enrollment to nearly six hundred and a synagogue membership that neared eight hundred in the early 1950s, Emanu-El dedicated a school building in 1953 and a meeting house in 1959 on adjoining lots on Taft Avenue. In 1955, the synagogue established its own museum. By 1960, membership exceeded eleven hundred, and thirteen hundred by 1967. At about the same time, religious school enrollment began to decline.

The congregation gave women equal rights in worship in the late 1970s. Rabbi Joel Zaiman (1974–1980) succeeded Bohnen, having served as assistant and then associate rabbi since 1962. Once he became senior rabbi of Emanu-El, Zaiman focused his attention on adult education in the congregation. Rabbi Wayne Franklin succeeded Zaiman in 1981. In 1995, membership exceeded 975 member family units.

References

Goldman, Israel M. "The Early History of Temple Emanu-El." *Rhode Island Jewish Historical Notes* 4, no. 1 (May 1963): 3–46.
Temple Emanu-El, The First Fifty Years (Providence: 1974).

S

SOUTH CAROLINA

B'RITH SHOLOM BETH ISRAEL CONGREGATION, ORTHODOX.
Charleston, South Carolina. Members of Kahal Kadosh Beth Elohim who
sought to retain a traditional service when Beth Elohim became decidedly Reform established B'rith Sholom, an Orthodox congregation, in 1854. Members
of this new congregation acquired a building on St. Philip Street, which they
converted for use as a synagogue. In 1874, B'rith Sholom built a new synagogue
and enlarged it in 1929. B'rith Sholom joined the Union of Orthodox Jewish
Congregations of America at its founding in 1898.

In 1911, dissension in the congregation led to the organization of Beth Israel
Congregation. Within days, members purchased a private dwelling on St. Philip
Street for use as a synagogue. Rabbi Solomon D. Goldfarb joined the congregation as religious leader in 1946 and remained only one year. In 1947, the
congregation dedicated a new building on Rutledge Avenue. The following year,
Rabbi Gilbert Klaperman came to the congregation. He remained until 1950,
when Rabbi Joseph Rothstein succeeded him.

Rabbi Nachum Eliezer Rabinovitch became the religious leader of the congregation in 1954. The following year, B'rith Sholom and Beth Israel merged
to form B'rith Sholom Beth Israel Congregation. The merged synagogue occupied the Rutledge Avenue building, formerly home only to Beth Israel. One
year later, under the guidance of Rabinovitch, the congregation founded the
Charleston Hebrew Institute Day School. The school, now known as the Addlestone Hebrew Academy, built a new building in 1957 on synagogue grounds
and subsequently enlarged its facility as the school population increased. During
the tenure of Rabinovitch, which concluded in 1963, the congregation built a
ritual bath to serve the Orthodox community.

When Rabinovitch left the community, the congregation elected Rabbi Hersh

M. Galinsky to the pulpit. During his tenure, the congregation opened a branch (now called the West Ashley Minyan House) in the South Windermere neighborhood for Sabbath and holiday worship. David J. Radinsky succeeded Galinsky in 1970. In 1981, the synagogue added two new kitchens and a social hall to its physical plant. Under Radinsky's direction, the congregation moved the Addlestone Hebrew Academy to a new building adjacent to the local Jewish Community Center (1988). In 1995, the school enrolled its largest student body, a total of 180.

Reference

Synagogue Histories File, American Jewish Archives.

KAHAL KADOSH BETH ELOHIM, REFORM. *Charleston, South Carolina.* Founded in 1749 as the first congregation to practice Judaism in the United States, Beth Elohim still worships in the synagogue that its members dedicated in 1841. This example of Greek Revival architecture is the second oldest synagogue building in the country and the oldest in continuous use. The temple is located on Hasell Street, where in 1838 a disastrous fire destroyed a previous synagogue that members had dedicated in 1794. In the interim, the congregation worshiped in the Hebrew Orphan Society Hall on Broad Street.

For the most part, the newer building followed the arrangement of the destroyed synagogue, with a gallery for women around the interior except for the east wall. On the rear gallery sat an organ, which led to a great deal of controversy in the early days of the congregation. In 1825, the board refused to hear a petition on behalf of some of the members to read select prayers in English, provide a weekly discourse in the vernacular, and require greater dignity and decorum; this forced the group to leave the congregation to form the Reformed Society of Israelites (1825–1833). The introduction of the organ caused the traditionalists to leave the congregation and form their own synagogue Shearith Israel (1841). This new congregation built a synagogue on the north side of Wentworth Street between Meeting and Anson Streets, growing in strength until the Civil War. The reformers gained the support of the cantor at Beth Elohim, Gustavus Poznanski.

The Civil War caused considerable property damage to both synagogues. It rendered Shearith Israel virtually useless, and many of Beth Elohim's ritual objects, including those sent to Columbia, South Carolina, for safekeeping during the war, were lost. In 1866, the congregations merged, selling the Wentworth location to the local Catholic Diocese. As Hasell Street had become a busy thoroughfare, a congregational committee advised the membership that the facility should be moved to another site. Rejecting this proposal, the members determined to repair the damage done to the synagogue building. They did not replace the organ, however, in accordance with the merger agreement. In 1871, the climate of the congregation changed, and members replaced the organ without any controversy.

In 1879, members reconfigured the interior of the synagogue to allow for the installation of family pews. They also moved the reading table from the center of the sanctuary and relocated it in front of the ark. An earthquake struck Charleston in 1886, and the synagogue suffered damage once again. As a result, congregational leadership repaired the building and expanded it slightly. In addition to some other modest changes, Beth Elohim removed the side galleries and enlarged the organ loft. Members rededicated the synagogue in 1887. In 1920, to attract more worshipers, Beth Elohim introduced late Friday evening services. At the time, membership in the congregation neared 130 families.

These religious leaders served Beth Elohim: Moses Cohen (1750–1762), Isaac da Costa (1762–1764), Abraham Alexander (1764–1784), Abraham Azuby (1785–1805), Jacob Suares (1807–1811), Emanuel N. Carvahlo (1811–1814), Hartwig Cohen (1818–1823), Solomon Peixotto (1823–1835), Gustavus Poznanski (1836–1850), Julius Eckman (1850–1851), Maurice Mayer (1852–1859), Abraham Harris (1860–1865), M. H. Myers (1866–1868), J. H. M. Chumaceiro (1868–1874), Falk Vidaver (1875), David Levy (1875–1893), Samuel Lewis (1893), Barnett A. Elzas (1894–1910), Isaac E. Marcuson (1910–1915), Jacob S. Raisin (1915–1944), Leonard Kasle (1944–1945), Sidney Unger (1945–1946), Bertram Klausner (1946–1947), Alan Tarshish (1947–1961), Burton Padoll (1961–1967), Edward Cohn (1968–1976), William A. Rosenthall (1976–1992), and Anthony D. Holz (1992–   ).

Rabbi Jacob Raisin introduced the Bar Mitzvah to the congregation and advocated the equal participation of women in ritual. Burton Padoll spoke out for civil rights for blacks in a hostile environment. William Rosenthall moved the congregation into community relationships with other synagogues. Under Rabbi Anthony Holz's direction, the congregation continued its emphasis on adult education, social justice, and black-Jewish dialogue, as well as expanding in the area of outreach to mixed married families in the community. Because of its historic importance (designated as a landmark synagogue building in 1980), the synagogue attracts ten thousand visitors annually. In 1995, membership exceeded 325 family units.

References

Breibart, Solomon. "The Synagogues of Kahal Kadosh Beth Elohim." *South Carolina Historical Magazine* 80, no. 3 (July 1979): 215–35.
———. "Two Jewish Congregations in Charleston, SC before 1791: A New Conclusion." *American Jewish History* 69, no. 3 (March 1980): 360–63.
The Congregation Beth Elohim of Charleston, S.C. 1750–1883 (Charleston, SC: 1884).
Elzas, Barnett. *The Jews of South Carolina from the Earliest Times to the Present Day* (Philadelphia: 1905).
Reznikoff, Charles, and Uriah Z. Engelman. *The Jews of Charleston* (Philadelphia: 1950).
Synagogue Histories File, American Jewish Archives.

TREE OF LIFE CONGREGATION, REFORM. *Columbia, South Carolina.* In 1896, a group of Columbia's Jews, led by the Trager and Visanska families, joined together to from the Tree of Life society in order to erect a house of worship. The young congregation held services in a private home and a local firehouse. In 1905, Tree of Life Congregation dedicated its own sanctuary on Lady Street, the first in Columbia since General Sherman destroyed the city's original synagogue in 1865.

The congregation organized as a self-proclaimed "liberal orthodox" group, attempting to meet the needs of Reform and Orthodox factions in the community. These factions disagreed over issues such as whether men should cover their heads during worship or whether or not the new synagogue should install an organ for worship. Eventually the traditional element withdrew and formed its own House of Peace synagogue.

While lay leaders led worship in the congregation's early history, rabbis from neighboring communities assisted as well. In addition, beginning in 1908, students from the Hebrew Union College rabbinical seminary in Cincinnati travelled to lead occasional services. In 1914, with a membership of only fourteen individuals, Tree of Life engaged Harry Merfeld as its first religious leader. Four years later, the congregation organized an outreach effort to the soldiers stationed at nearby Camp Jackson by joining with the Jewish Welfare Board in transforming a hall on Main Street into a club for Jewish soldiers. Merfeld left Columbia in 1916. Following World War I, the Jewish Welfare Board sold the synagogue several facilities it had equipped in the community. Tree of Life moved these buildings and converted them for use as a school and community center.

As the congregation experienced severe financial difficulties following Merfeld's resignation, it did not engage a permanent rabbi for many years. Yet, the religious school grew and the congregation built a new community center and religious school in 1933. Four years later, Tree of Life joined the Union of American Hebrew Congregations, the national organization of Reform synagogues. In 1939, Rabbi Jeffrey Ballon joined Tree of Life as its religious leader. He focused his immediate attention on the development of a Hebrew program for adults and children. Later he also took over the activities for the Hillel Foundation at the University of South Carolina in Sumter. Ballon also urged the congregation to participate in Zionist activities, especially following World War II.

In 1945, membership reached fifty-two. Rabbi Ballon resigned in 1948, and Rabbi Paul Liner succeeded him the following year. He concentrated much of his efforts on interfaith work in the community. Liner left in 1951, in the midst of a congregational building project. Rabbi David Samuel Gruber immediately succeeded Liner. Gruber also became the chaplain at Camp Jackson. Shortly after his arrival in Columbia, Tree of Life dedicated its new temple structure at Woodrow and Heyward Streets (1952). Gruber focused his early attention on education of children and adults in the congregation, as well as continuing the interfaith efforts of his predecessors.

In 1968, Rabbi James L. Apple succeeded Gruber. He left two years later to join the Navy chaplaincy, and Tree of Life invited Rabbi Michael Oppenheimer to the congregation (1971). Rabbi Howard Kosovske served from 1975 to 1986. Under the religious guidance of Rabbi Sanford Marcus (1986–), membership at Tree of Life neared 275 family units in 1995.

References

Fischer, Susan Eleanor. *The Tree of Life Temple* (Columbia, SC: 1971).
Hennig, Helen Kohn. *The Tree of Life: 1896–1946* (Columbia, SC: 1946).

T

TENNESSEE

MIZPAH TEMPLE, REFORM. *Chattanooga, Tennessee.* A group of twenty-one young men met in 1866 and formed a society that they chartered as the Chebra Gamilas Chaced, a name changed the following year to the Hebrew Benevolent Association. Services were conducted in the home of Jacob Bach who served as rabbi, cantor, and ritual slaughterer. Soon after the forming of the association, this group of men purchased land for a cemetery. In 1869, Rabbi E. K. Fischer moved his family to Chattanooga and offered his services to the young congregation free of charge. Activities were moved to Concordia Hall in the center of the city's social and civic life. Unfortunately, because of failing health, Fischer was not able to serve the congregation for very long.

Julius Ochs moved to Chattanooga in 1878 and volunteered his services as a layman to lead the Hebrew Benevolent Association. In 1882, the congregation purchased property and built a synagogue on Walnut Street. Isaac Mayer Wise spoke at the dedication and suggested that the congregation change its name to Mitzpah Congregation, which it did in 1888. Though several futile attempts were made to improve the property on Walnut Street, it was not until 1894 that the facility was actually improved.

The first ordained rabbi to serve Mitzpah Congregation, Moses J. Gries, came to Chattanooga in 1889. When he resigned in 1892, Bloch once again led the congregation. In 1896, Harry Wise, Sr., son of Isaac M. Wise and president of the congregation, was asked to lead the congregation until 1901, when Rabbi Louis Weiss was engaged.

Although the congregation was not yet affiliated with the Union of American Hebrew Congregations, it adopted the revised edition of the *Union Prayer Book* in 1899, replacing Isaac M. Wise's *Minhag America.* When Weiss left Mitzpah in 1901, Leo Mannheimer was elected to the pulpit. Under his leadership, the synagogue affiliated with the Union of American Hebrew Congregations, the national organization of Reform synagogues. By this time, the membership of the temple numbered only fifty-four families. Yet, it felt crowded and decided to build a new facility at Oak and Lindsay Streets. With this new building, dedicated in 1904, the spelling of the name of the congregation was changed to Mizpah.

Illness forced Mannheimer to retire, and Rabbi Jonah B. Wise became the spiritual leader at Mizpah Congregation. When he left in 1906, following a six-month interim engagement of Rabbi Theodore F. Joseph, Julian Miller joined the temple as its rabbi. The membership had grown to one hundred families by this time, but the financial trouble that had plagued the congregation since its founding continued to challenge it. Miller left in 1919, to be succeeded by Rabbi Abraham Holzberg, who remained until 1924.

After World War I, membership grew to 154 families and larger facilities were required. Rabbi Samuel R. Shillman led the congregation when Adolph S. Ochs, by now owner of the *New York Times,* donated the funds to purchase a new structure on McCallie Avenue in honor of Ochs' father. In 1928, this new synagogue building was dedicated. Ochs financially supported Mizpah Congregation until the end of his life. Shillman resigned in 1930 and was succeeded by Rabbi Benjamin M. Parker. He stayed only a year, when Rabbi Abraham Feinstein was elected to the pulpit.

Membership grew to 203 families during World War II. Yet, because of a polio epidemic, the congregation was not permitted to hold High Holiday services at the temple. Instead, the services were broadcast to the members over the radio.

Women had been active in the congregation since its founding, and "wives of members" were given the right to vote at congregational meetings in 1954. Because of the dilapidated condition of the building, the Temple Center was razed in 1959 and rebuilt the following year. Feinstein retired in 1966 and was succeeded by Rabbi Lloyd R. Goldman. Then in 1983, Rabbi Kenneth Kanter was engaged by the congregation. During Kanter's tenure, the congregation grew from two hundred to three hundred family units. Kanter left in 1992 and was succeeded in early 1993 by Rabbi Joseph P. Klein.

Reference

Synagogue Histories File, American Jewish Archives.

HESKA AMUNA, CONSERVATIVE. *Knoxville, Tennessee.* Heska Amuna grew out of the Knoxville Hebrew Benevolent Association (organized 1864). In 1890, ten men joined Rabbi A. Michaelof to form Heska Amuna as an Orthodox congregation, chartered in 1891. Shortly thereafter, Rabbi Tagress succeeded Michaelof. After a few years meeting in a variety of locations, the congregation acquired a large house at the corner of Vine Avenue and Temperance Street, which it converted into a synagogue and parsonage. In 1895, Rabbi Isaac Winick took over the religious leadership of Heska Amuna, serving until his death in 1926. Members enlarged the Temperance Street facility in 1902. In 1910, the women of the congregation formed a Daughters of Israel Aid Society. This later developed into a Ladies' Auxiliary (1929). The men waited until 1945 to form a Brotherhood, but the organization dissolved in 1952.

The congregation grew, and in 1920 the synagogue moved to a new facility on West Fifth Avenue. This converted facility seated 350 people and included a religious and Hebrew School. Following Winick's death, members elected Rabbi A. J. Robinson to the pulpit. In 1930, Heska Amuna joined the Union of Orthodox Jewish Congregations of America.

In 1950, recognizing the inadequacy of space available for use in the Fifth Avenue building, the congregation transferred the Hebrew and Sunday Schools to the Jewish Community Center on Vine Avenue, which it joined with the local Reform Temple Beth El. In 1957, Heska Amuna embarked on a new building program. At the same time, the majority of Heska Amuna's members voted to affiliate with the United Synagogue of America (now the United Synagogue of Conservative Judaism), the national organization of Conservative Synagogues. Members dedicated the building on Kingston Pike in 1960. In this new facility, the religious and Hebrew education programs returned to independent operation at Heska Amuna.

Rabbi Max Zucker arrived to assume religious leadership in 1962. He organized the first mixed choir in the synagogue. Rabbi Noah Golinkin (1920–1977) succeeded Zucker. Golinkin focused on education in the congregation. Rabbi Mark Greenspan moved to Knoxville in 1980; he served until 1986. Under his direction, the congregation established daily worship services. Rabbi Yehoshua Kahan succeeded Greenspan (1986–1988). In 1988, the congregation afforded equal rights to women in the congregation with regard to Torah honors and being counted in a minyan. Rabbi Arthur Weiner arrived in 1989. Under his guidance, Heska Amuna became totally smoke-free (1990). In 1995, membership exceeded 260 family units.

Reference

Heska Amuna Synagogue, 100 Year Centennial (Knoxville, TN: 1990).

CONGREGATION ANSHEI SPHARD–BETH EL EMETH, ORTHODOX.

Memphis, Tennessee. This congregation was formed by the merger of two smaller congregations: Anshei Sphard and Beth El Emeth. In 1854, the state of Tennessee issued a charter to the B'nai Israel Congregation in Memphis. Four years later, this young congregation engaged Jacob J. Peres, an Orthodox rabbi. Caught between the Reform and Orthodox factions in the congregation, Peres resigned. Joining with a group of disgruntled members of B'nai Israel, Peres helped to establish a new synagogue in 1861, the Beth El Emeth Congregation. Receiving its charter the following year, Beth El Emeth met on Jefferson Street near Front Street.

In 1870, the congregation dedicated its new facilities. Peres continued his volunteer services to the congregation as he established a career as a business-man and lawyer. Joel Alexander became the congregation's rabbi. He remained with Beth El Emeth until 1872, when Rabbi Ferdinand Leopold Sarner was engaged to lead the congregation, America's first rabbinic army chaplain.

When Sarner died in 1878, and Peres died the following year, the congregation was without any strong leadership. As a result, B'nai Israel and Beth El Emeth merged and, using the funds and property of Beth El Emeth, the newly merged congregation purchased property on Poplar Street and in 1884 erected a new facility there. The merger was not effective; the membership remained constant at 125 member families. Those who did not embrace the merger or Reform Judaism joined with a group of Orthodox Jews who had been worshiping in rented quarters since the first split with B'nai Israel. By 1916, B'nai Israel had outgrown its facility and moved to Poplar and Montgomery. This gave the fledgling Orthodox congregation, which had been worshiping in rented space at Cochrane Hall, the opportunity to purchase the former B'nai Israel building. It soon became known as the "Poplar Street Shul" and functioned as such until 1957 for the disenfranchised members of Beth El Emeth, who retained their original congregational name. During these years four rabbis served the congregation: E. T. Siegel, Alfred Fruchter, Phillip Goldman, and Arthur Levin.

In the 1950s it became evident that if Beth El Emeth chose to remain in its downtown location, it would not survive. Thus, it undertook a building program that moved the congregation eight miles east of its location. But its membership did not increase after the move. They had gambled on the Jewish community moving, but had moved in the wrong direction. The leadership of the congregation considered affiliation with the Conservative movement, but a substantial number of members opposed an ideological change—and the number of members continued to dwindle.

Anshei Sphard had been established by a charter in 1904 and purchased a building on Maiden Lane (later called Market Street). In 1925 this converted wooden house was demolished, and a brick synagogue was built on the same site. Slowly the Jewish community moved out of the Pinch neighborhood, as the area around the synagogue was called, and the membership of Anshei Sphard outgrew its facility. About the same time, the congregation engaged Elijah Stampfer as rabbi and Nathan Greenblatt as cantor. Finally, the Anshei Sphard Congregation built and dedicated a new facility at North Parkway and Bellevue in 1948; this was followed in 1955 by the construction of its Nat Buring Educational Building to house the Sunday School established when it moved to the new location. Rabbi Morton Baum was serving the congregation at the time.

Although the facility served the congregation well for twenty-two years, the cost to maintain the facility was increasing. The Jewish community kept moving east of the city. This put severe financial strain on the dwindling membership of Anshei Sphard. Beth El Emeth was under similar financial stress with a declining membership. Thus, merger talks began between the two institutions.

By 1966, during the tenure of Rabbi Arthur Levin, who had been engaged in 1961, a merger agreement was concluded. After the merger, land was purchased in East Memphis at Rich and East Yates Road for a new building. In 1970 a new facility was dedicated to house the merged congregation. Shortly thereafter, the new synagogue engaged A. Mark Levin as its rabbi. In 1993, the congregation had 380 membership units.

Reference

Synagogue Histories File, American Jewish Archives.

TEMPLE ISRAEL, REFORM. *Memphis, Tennessee.* By 1853, Jews in Memphis "regularly organized" for the purpose of worship. The thirty-six-member B'nai Israel Congregation, Children of Israel, received its charter in 1854. Though stimulated by a financial bequest from philanthropist Judah Touro, the congregation felt unable to build a synagogue. Instead, it worshiped in a variety of rented halls from 1853 to 1857 before leasing the Merchants and Farmers Bank Building at Main and Exchange Streets in 1858. Two years later, B'nai Israel members purchased the property.

Jacob J. Peres came to Memphis in 1858 to serve the congregation as its first religious leader. He established a Hebrew School for the synagogue. Caught in the conflict between members who wanted an Orthodox congregation and those who sought to reform B'nai Israel's ritual, Peres left in 1860. Simon Tuska succeeded Peres. Under his guidance, the congregation introduced many reforms including the elimination of most liturgical poems in the liturgy. He introduced a choir and Confirmation in 1863, as well as Isaac Mayer Wise's *Minhag America* prayer book. Tuska also installed family pews and introduced late Friday evening worship with English discourses and patriotic worship services for Thanksgiving and National Fast Day. In 1864, with some eighty-three members, B'nai Israel opened a Hebrew Educational Institute. Immediately, the school achieved an enrollment of one hundred.

Following Tuska's death at the age of thirty-five, Rabbi Max Samfield served the congregation for forty-four years. In 1875, the congregation resolved to require all men to remove their hats during worship. In 1882, B'nai Israel acquired the property of neighboring Beth El Emeth Congregation on Second Street. Nevertheless, B'nai Israel membership remained steady at about 125.

That same year, the congregation purchased property for a new synagogue on Poplar between Second and Third (dedicated 1884). Within one year, the congregation added forty-five new members to its roster. By 1905, membership reached 262. In 1916, B'nai Israel dedicated a new Temple at Poplar and Montgomery, just after Samfield's death.

Rabbi William Fineshriber succeeded Rabbi Samfield, having come to serve the congregation as associate rabbi in 1911. Before he left in 1924, membership reached 450 families. Rabbi Harry W. Ettleson came next to lead the congregation. During his period of service, members erected a religious school building

(1950). Rabbi James A. Wax came to the temple as assistant rabbi in 1946 before assuming the pulpit as senior rabbi in 1954. He served until 1978. During Wax's tenure, Temple Israel purchased property on White Station Road (1964). Yet, the congregation decided not to build there. Instead, Temple Israel erected a new facility on East Massey Road (1976). In 1978, Temple Israel elected to its pulpit Rabbi Harry Danziger, who had served the congregation since 1964 as assistant. In 1995, Temple Israel's membership exceeded seventeen hundred family units.

Reference

Synagogue Histories File, American Jewish Archives.

THE TEMPLE/CONGREGATION OHABAI SHOLOM, REFORM. *Nashville, Tennessee.* In the 1840s, a group of local residents met for services in a private home. By 1851, the group grew large enough to establish a benevolent society and to purchase a property for the purpose of establishing a cemetery. This group evolved into a congregation that, in 1854, took the name Kahl Kodesh Mogen David. In 1852, Alexander Iser arrived to serve the group as its religious leader. Emanuel Marcusson succeeded him in 1857 at the same time the congregation occupied rented quarters on North Market Street (Twelfth Avenue), where it added a ritual bath. Jonas Heilbron, the religious leader from 1859 to 1861, established the synagogue's first program of religious education for children. Just prior to Heilbron's departure, a splinter group left the synagogue and formed Kahl Kodesh Ohavai Emes (1860). In 1867, these congregations merged, on the condition that the new synagogue obtain a new name and new charter. Thus developed Kahl Kodesh Ohabai Sholom (1868).

In 1876, the new synagogue dedicated a home on Vine Street and joined the Union of American Hebrew Congregations, the national organization of Reform synagogues. After nearly eighty years in this location, Ohabai Sholom moved to Harding Road, where it became known as The Temple (1954).

These men served Ohabai Sholom as religious leaders: J. Kantrovich (1868), David Burgheim (1868–1869), Isidor Kalisch (1872–1875), Alexander Rosenspitz (1876–1878), Julius S. Goldhammer (1879–1886), Isaac Moses (1887–1888), Isidore Lewinthal (1888–1922), Richard M. Stern (1923–1926), Julius Mark (1926–1948), Sylvan Schwartzman (1948–1950), William E. Silverman (1950–1960), Randall M. Falk (1960–1986), and Stephen Fuchs (1986–   ).

At a time when many congregants supported the anti-Zionist position of the American Council for Judaism, Julius Mark's fervent Zionism did not win him great support at the Temple. Under the direction of Sylvan Schwartzman (who later became a professor of Jewish Education at Hebrew Union College in Cincinnati), the congregation placed a great deal of energy in expanding the religious school. Under Falk's guidance, the congregation slowly introduced a few ritual changes, including the permission of head coverings (1960) and the use of a wedding canopy (1960). He also instituted the weekly reading of Torah on

Friday evening (usually reserved for Saturday morning), a practice of many Reform congregations. His insistence on a cantor brought with it a great deal of discontent in the congregation. In 1972, Ohabai Sholom adopted *Gates of Prayer,* the uniform prayer book of the Reform movement. Under the direction of Rabbi Fuchs, the congregation expanded its activities considerably to include alternative worship services and holiday celebrations, as well as a plethora of programs in adult education. The membership of The Temple stood at over 930 family units in 1995.

References

Silverman, William B. *The History of the Vine Street Temple, 1851–1954* (Nashville, TN: 1954).
Synagogue Histories File, American Jewish Archives.
The Temple/Congregation Ohabai Sholom Archives.
The Temple/Congregation Ohabai Sholom Collection, Jewish Federation of Nashville and Middle Tennessee Archives.

WEST END SYNAGOGUE, CONSERVATIVE. *Nashville, Tennessee.* Beginning in the 1850s, a group that eventually became the Khal Kodesh Adath Israel (Congregation Assembly of Israel) began worshiping in private homes. But in 1874 they decided that the time had come to develop a formal institution. Holding services in rented facilities at Old Douglas Hall, the group of twenty was granted a charter by the State of Tennessee in 1876. Its first order of business was to purchase land for a cemetery. In 1880, the group moved to 118 North College Street (now Third Avenue North), where it met until 1883. For the next three years, it met in a building on Cedar Street (now Charlotte Avenue). In 1886, the congregation renewed its charter and changed its quarters once again, this time to a private home, which it remodelled, on North Market Street (now Second Avenue, North). In 1892, synagogue members prepared to move once again; but as they were financially unable to do so, the West End Synagogue remained until 1901, on Market Street, where the facility was expanded. During the congregation's residence on North Market Street, members engaged their first ordained religious leader, Rabbi Julius Loeb in 1897. He was succeeded by M. Leiberman (1899–1901).

As the congregation contemplated moving once again, it decided to construct a facility with family pews. While occupying the Gay Street Synagogue, as it came to be known, membership increased to 250 by 1930. After an unsuccessful attempt to move to Ellston and Twenty-third Avenue in 1945, recognizing the need to erect a modern synagogue with suitable accommodations for a religious school in a location close to the expanding Jewish community, the congregation moved to West End Avenue two years later. Henceforth, the name of the Khal Kodesh Adath Israel became the West End Synagogue. The following year it affiliated with the United Synagogue of America, the national organization of Conservative synagogues. Rabbi Morris Frank was elected to the pulpit in 1946; his untimely death several months later led to the election of Rabbi Arthur

Hertzberg, who remained with the West End Synagogue until 1957. Rabbi Ronald Roth has been serving the congregation since 1985. In 1993, membership stood at over five hundred family units.

References

Synagogue Histories File, American Jewish Archives.
West End Synagogue 1874–1974 (Nashville, TN: 1974).

TEXAS

CONGREGATION EMANU-EL, REFORM. *Dallas, Texas.* Eleven Jewish men living in Dallas, Texas, in the year 1872 formed a group called the Hebrew Benevolent Association to help the sick, bury the dead, and hold worship services. It took three years of holding High Holiday services in rented quarters before thirty-two families formed Congregation Emanu-El in 1875. As this group saw itself as Reform, it adopted *Minhag America* as its prayer book and asked Isaac Mayer Wise to recommend its first rabbi. Members elected Aaron Suhler to serve (1875–1879).

Emanu-El erected its first temple building in downtown Dallas on Commerce and Field Streets in 1876. In addition to a Sunday School, the congregation sponsored a nonsectarian day school, which operated from 1874 to 1888, in which from sixty to seventy children enrolled. This school ceased operation when the city of Dallas initiated a public school system in 1886. Shortly thereafter, George Alexander Kohut (1887–1889) joined the congregation as its religious leader.

At the turn of the century, Emanu-El outgrew its facilities and built a new, larger structure at South Ervay and St. Louis Streets (dedicated 1899). William Greenberg led Temple Emanu-El in this new location (1901–1919). Emanu-El joined the Union of American Hebrew Congregations, the national organization of Reform synagogues, in 1904. Under Greenberg's leadership, Emanu-El instituted the first citywide interfaith Thanksgiving service (1907). In the new sanctuary building came a change in policy, eventually adopted in 1916, that included free seating.

Dr. David Lefkowitz came to Dallas as Emanu-El's rabbi in 1920. During his tenure, he organized a sisterhood (1921) out of the former ladies guild and a brotherhood (1923). Lefkowitz stood firm against the KKK, whose members marched strong in the thousands to the Texas State Fair for Klan Day. Lefkowitz remained until his retirement in 1949, when members elected Rabbi Levi A. Olan to the pulpit. In 1957, with a membership of over one thousand families, Emanu-El built a new temple at Hillcrest and Northwest Highway. Under the guidance of Rabbi Olan, temple members actively participated in community social action projects, including the founding of the Rhoads Terrace Preschool Project for disadvantaged children in South Dallas.

In honor of Olan's sixtieth birthday, supporters initiated the Levi A. Olan Rare Book Collection at the Perkins School of Theology Bridwell Library, which also houses the Sadie and David Lefkowitz Collection of Judaica. Following Olan's retirement in 1970, Emanu-El elected to its pulpit Rabbi Gerald Klein, who had served as associate since 1952. Klein focused his attention on pastoral needs of the congregation. Rabbi Sheldon Zimmerman joined the synagogue as senior rabbi in 1985. Under his leadership, the congregation expanded its program of education for all ages. The temple's Social Action Committee formed the East Dallas Health Coalition, a nonprofit medical clinic serving Southeast Asian refugees and other disadvantaged residents of East Dallas. In addition, Temple Emanu-El joined North Dallas Shared Ministries, which provides emergency assistance to people who live in the northeast area of Dallas County. Furthermore, the congregation helped to found the Dallas Jewish Coalition for the Homeless, which sponsors the Vogel Alcove temporary housing shelter. In 1994, membership of the congregation exceeded twenty-six hundred family units.

References

"Dallas Jewry Engages Their First Rabbi: Congregation Emanu-El in 1875." *Western States Jewish Historical Quarterly* 8, no. 3 (April 1976): 222–23.
"First Synagogue in Dallas, Texas—1876." *Western States Jewish Historical Quarterly* 10, no. 2 (January 1978): 136–37.
"Religious Life in Dallas a Century Ago." *Western States Jewish Historical Quarterly* 20, no. 2 (January 1988): 117–21.
Synagogue Histories File, American Jewish Archives.

CONGREGATION SHAARE TEFILLA, ORTHODOX. *Dallas, Texas.* Founders established Shaare Tefilla in 1986 in order to serve the needs of the Orthodox community of Dallas. At its inception, the congregation affiliated with the Union of Orthodox Jewish Congregations, the national organization of Orthodox synagogues. The congregation established its home on Churchill Way under the guidance of Rabbi Howard Wolk (1986–   ). In 1995, membership stood at 160 family units.

Reference

Personal interview, Howard Wolk, July 13, 1995.

TEMPLE MT. SINAI, REFORM. *El Paso, Texas.* Though the Jewish settlement of El Paso dates to a period of time preceding the Civil War, the first Jewish organization in town, the Mt. Sinai Association, began in 1887. The first official roster listed thirty-two names. As in other communities, the need to purchase cemetery land prompted its organization. Residents founded the El Paso Hebrew Sunday School in 1890. By 1897, the Mt. Sinai organization grew to fifty-three. During these years, the community gathered for worship for the

High Holidays when students from Hebrew Union College in Cincinnati led services.

For reasons of health, Dr. Oscar J. Cohen came to El Paso in 1898 from Mobile, Alabama, where he previously served as rabbi of the synagogue. Realizing that his presence could provide a catalyst for the fledgling Jewish community, members of the now formally organized Temple Mt. Sinai elected him as their religious leader. The group chose Chopin Hall on Myrtle Avenue as a temporary place of worship. This young congregation erected its first permanent home in 1899 on the corner of Oregon and Idaho Streets (now Yandell Boulevard).

Cohen resigned in rabbinate in 1900; Rabbi Martin Zielonka succeeded him in the pulpit. Through his urging, the synagogue joined the Union of American Hebrew Congregations, the national organization of Reform synagogues—but not until "the financial condition of the congregation warrant it" (1902). By 1916, the membership outgrew its home and prepared to move to Montana and Oregon Streets, where the congregation purchased property. With the old building sold and the new one not yet built, the congregation went homeless until the end of 1916.

Between 1928 and 1938, El Paso's population decreased significantly. Economic depression severely hit the community. Following Zielonka's death in 1938, Mt. Sinai engaged Rabbi Wendell Phillips. His spirited Zionism and a sense of urgency to rescue relatives in Europe gave the congregation a new outlook. In addition, he steered the congregation toward the adoption of ritual that Zielonka had eschewed. This trend continued with the election to the pulpit of Rabbi Floyd Fierman in 1949. He introduced the Bar Mitzvah ceremony— and later Bat Mitzvah—and a full Hebrew system into the religious school program. In addition, he instituted regular Saturday morning services, services on the first and last days of Sukkot and Passover, and Yizkor memorial services.

In 1950 the synagogue purchased land where Kern Plaza now stands. While Temple Mt. Sinai intended to build on this property, the congregation sold this parcel of property when it purchased land on North Stanton Street. In 1962, the congregation built a new synagogue there.

Following Fierman's retirement in 1979, Edward L. Cohn led the temple for one year, having come to El Paso to serve as associate rabbi in 1976. Temple Mt. Sinai elected Rabbi Kenneth Weiss to its pulpit in 1980. In 1995, membership stood at over 460 family units.

Reference

Synagogue Histories File, American Jewish Archives.

AHAVATH SHOLOM, CONSERVATIVE. *Ft. Worth, Texas.* In 1892, Jewish residents of Ft. Worth held their first meeting at the home of William Goldstein at Fifth and Calhoun Streets to establish an Orthodox synagogue. Thus, they resolved to form Congregation Ahavath Sholom. In 1895 this young congregation of thirty-one families built its first house of worship at the corner of Jarvis and Hemphill Streets. As the city grew, so did the congregation. As a result, Ahavath Sholom literally moved its wooden synagogue in 1901 to a new site on Taylor Street, where it remained for five years. Membership increased to one hundred.

In 1906, Ahavath Sholom dedicated a new home with school, sanctuary, and social hall on the Taylor Street property. In 1914, Ahavath Sholom built a Hebrew Institute two lots away from its building. This new structure housed offices, classrooms, meeting rooms, and an auditorium. Later, the congregation added a gymnasium to the facility. The women of the congregation—formed into a Ladies Auxiliary in 1915—supported the endeavors of this religious school. The men waited until 1944 to organize into a Men's Club.

Congregational membership continued to grow. In 1952, Ahavath Sholom members dedicated their new house of worship on the corner of Eighth Avenue and Myrtle Streets. In 1960, Ahavath Sholom dedicated new educational facilities. In 1966, the congregation celebrated its first Bat Mitzvah. By 1973, membership exceeded 450 families, growing to over five hundred the following year. This growth in membership resulted in the development of a wide range of educational and social programs including a series of "Young Married" activities, family Sabbath dinners, and youth breakfasts. In order to accommodate the growth of the membership, Ahavath Sholom moved once again. This time, the congregation moved to Hulen and Briarhaven Streets, where it dedicated its new synagogue in 1980. The following year, the congregation permitted the celebration of Bat Mitzvah to take place on Sabbath morning. In 1986, Ahavath Sholom dedicated its Isadore Garsek Patriotic Gardens in memory of its former rabbi, who died the previous year. In 1991, the congregation voted to change the ritual of the congregation to reflect Conservative Judaism.

These men served the congregation as religious leaders: Charles Blumenthal (1908–1912), Abraham E. Abramowitz (1922), Begis (1922), Philip Graubart (1929–?), Isadore Garsek (1946–1979), Alexander Graubart (1979–1981), and Jack Izakson (1981–1991). Rabbi Sidney Zimelman joined the congregation in 1991. Under his direction, the congregation gave full equal ritual rights to women and joined the United Synagogue of Conservative Judaism, the national organization of Conservative synagogues (1992).

References

Congregation Ahavath Sholom, 1980 (Ft. Worth, TX: 1980).
Congregation Ahavath Sholom, 100th Anniversary, 1892–1992 (Ft. Worth, TX: 1992).
Congregation Ahavath Sholom, Seventy-Fifth Anniversary, 1892–1967 (Ft. Worth, TX: 1967).
Synagogue Histories File, American Jewish Archives.

BETH EL, REFORM. *Ft. Worth, Texas.* The beginning of Beth El can be traced to the efforts of Henry Gersbacher, who encouraged thirty charter members in 1902 to join with him in the establishment of a Reform congregation in

Ft. Worth. The group elected Sam Levy as president of this infant organization. The local section of the National Council of Jewish Women (NCJW) was important to this organization's early success. Among other things, NCJW paid for Beth El's first religious leader to come to Ft. Worth to lead High Holiday services. After only a few months, disagreements threatened the stability of congregational life. This led to the resignation of Beth El's first religious leader, a man named Philo. Without a religious leader, the congregation held worship services infrequently. Thus, Beth El turned to the Hebrew Union College rabbinical seminary for student rabbis.

In 1904, the congregation engaged Rabbi Joseph Jasin. He conducted worship services in rented rooms until funds could be secured to purchase a permanent home at Fifth and Taylor Streets (1907). During Jasin's tenure, membership increased to sixty families. Jasin left the community the same year the congregation built its new temple. Rabbi George Zepin succeeded him. Zepin, a staff member of the Union of American Hebrew Congregations, the national organization of Reform synagogues, came to Ft. Worth for two years to guide Beth El. He left the synagogue in the hands of Rabbi G. George Fox.

During Fox's tenure with the congregation, women of the congregation formed a sisterhood (1913). With a membership of 120 families, Beth El outgrew its facility and built a new synagogue structure (1919) at Broadway and Galveston, where the current temple stands.

Rabbi Harry Merfield came to the temple in 1922, when Fox returned to Chicago. Rabbi Samuel D. Doskin succeeded him. Doskin served the congregation from the end of the Depression through the years of the war. Finally, following years of severe financial difficulty as a result of the Depression, the congregation stood debt-free. Then in 1946, fire destroyed the entire facility except for its outer shell. Beth El's 298 families built the present synagogue within those outer walls (rededicated 1949). Rabbi Milton Rosenbaum came to the congregation a year later.

Rabbi Robert J. Schur came to the temple in 1956. While emphasizing the pastoral side of the rabbinate, Schur worked a great deal in the community. During his tenure, Schur initiated *Selichot* services (penitential prayers prior to Rosh Hashanah), an afternoon service for Yom Kippur, and led the congregation to the adoption of *Gates of Prayer* and *Gates of Repentance,* uniform prayer books for the Reform movement. While not initially in favor of the practice of Bat Mitzvah, he allowed the congregation to introduce it nonetheless.

Rabbi Ralph Mecklenburger, having served as associate since 1984, succeeded Schur when he retired in 1986. Under Mecklenburger's direction, Beth El added more Hebrew to its worship and chanting of the weekly Torah and Haftarah readings. He has focused a great deal of attention on adult education and on widening the role of the synagogue in the greater Ft. Worth community. In 1995, membership at Beth El exceeded 440 family units.

Reference

Synagogue Histories File, American Jewish Archives.

B'NAI ISRAEL, REFORM. *Galveston, Texas.* The earliest record of Jewish worship in Galveston dates back to 1856, when Jewish residents prayed in the home of Isadore Dyer (Twenty-fourth Street and Avenue I) in a room set aside for that purpose. Some years later, the group that sponsored the service also established classes for the religious instruction of children. The first extant record of B'nai Israel (1868) describes the congregation's resolve to build a synagogue (dedicated 1870). At about the same time, members invited Alexander Rosenspitz to serve the congregation as acting religious leader and Hebrew School teacher. He served until 1871.

Shortly after Rosenspitz resigned, Abraham Blum became the congregation's leader. During his fourteen-year tenure, membership increased. At his suggestion, the congregation consulted Rabbi Isaac Mayer Wise over the issue of whether men in the congregation should be permitted to worship with their heads uncovered. Following a slight majority decision to permit such worship, B'nai Israel became a charter member of the Union of American Hebrew Congregations, the national organization of Reform synagogues (1875). Rabbi Joseph Silverman succeeded Blum in 1885. He too increased the membership of B'nai Israel. Rabbi Henry Cohen, whose name is associated with B'nai Israel more than that of any other rabbi during its history, came to Galveston in 1888.

In 1890, a terrible hurricane wreaked havoc on Galveston. While many members lost their homes and their lives, the Temple building in downtown Galveston—unlike most other area buildings—remained standing. Led by Rabbi Cohen, congregants assisted the city and their neighbors to restore order to the community. He became nationally known for the role he played following the disastrous hurricane. In an attempt to reach more congregants, Cohen unsuccessfully experimented with a Sunday evening service in 1904. Cohen also played a key role in the Galveston movement of 1907–1914, assisting over ten thousand Jewish immigrants to find new lives in the Midwest and Southwest. In 1915, another devastating hurricane hit the city. This time, it severely damaged B'nai Israel. Members added a community house to the building in 1928.

In 1950, Rabbi Leo Stillpass succeeded Cohen. Two years later, B'nai Israel moved to Thirtieth and O Streets, where it remains. When Stillpass resigned in 1956, Rabbi A. Stanley Dreyfus succeeded him (1956–1965). Other rabbis followed: Robert Blinder (1965–1969), Samuel Stahl (1969–1976), Jimmy Kessler (1976–1981), Alan Greenebaum (1981–1985), Martin Levy (1985–1989), and Jimmy Kessler (1989–).

In 1988, B'nai Israel began making skullcaps available to members and formally permitted Bar/Bat Mitzvahs to both cover their heads and wear prayer shawls. In 1992, B'nai Israel initiated an unsuccessful discussion concerning a merger with the local Conservative synagogue, Beth Jacob. Membership in 1994 at B'nai Israel stood at 130.

References

Dreyfus, A. Stanley, ed. *Henry Cohen: Messenger of the Lord* (New York: 1963).

Kessler, James Lee. *B.O.I.: A History of Congregation B'nai Israel, Galveston, Texas* (D.H.L. dissertation, Hebrew Union College–Jewish Institute of Religion, Los Angeles, 1988).

Kramer, William M., and Reva Clar. "Rabbi Abraham Blum: From Alsace to New York by Way of Texas and California." *Western States Jewish Historical Quarterly* 12, no. 1 (October 1979): 73–88.

Synagogue Histories File, American Jewish Archives.

CONGREGATION BETH ISRAEL, REFORM. *Houston, Texas.* Though records from the incipient years of Beth Israel are not extant, its beginning can be traced to 1854, ten years after the Jews of Houston had established their first Jewish cemetery. The congregation had twenty-two members in 1859, the year the "Hebrew Congregation of the City of Houston" received its charter from the Legislature of the State of Texas. Formal incorporation as "Hebrew Congregation Beth Israel" took place in 1873.

Like other synagogues of the period, Beth Israel worshiped in a variety of settings during its early history. With only twenty-two members, the congregation made its first home in a small room on Austin Street between Texas and Prairie. As the town's population grew, so did membership at Beth Israel, forcing the temple to move to a frame building one block southwest on LaBranch. While the congregation was established as an orthodox institution, minute books that are available reflect the struggle over Reform—the direction in which Beth Israel continually moved—that members confronted early on. There were those who chose to worship without head coverings and to smoke on the Sabbath (which is prohibited by traditional Jewish law). The controversy over head coverings continued for a number of years. Holidays were observed for one day (according to the Reform calendar), but the synagogue was open for two days for Rosh Hashanah (according to the traditional calendar) for those who chose to come to the synagogue on the second day. Given the mathematical exactitude of fixing the calendar, the Reform movement rejected the necessity of celebrating a holiday for two days. In 1861, the board unsuccessfully attempted to enforce a ruling that required members to keep their businesses closed on the Sabbath. Although a move to introduce Isaac Mayer Wise's moderately liberal *Minhag America* as the congregational prayer book failed in 1867, the prayer book was adopted the following year with little opposition. An organ was installed in 1868. However, Beth Israel's major concerns focused on maintaining a cemetery and looking out for the poor in their midst. Eventually, a parallel organization, the Hebrew Charitable Society, was established solely for this purpose.

In 1860, Zacharias Emmich came to Houston as Beth Israel's religious leader.

He was actively involved in encouraging the congregation's rapid movement toward Reform Judaism. In 1867, a Sabbath School and secular school was established. The teaching of secular subjects was discontinued two years later. In 1874, the Franklin Avenue Temple was completed and Beth Israel moved into its new home. The membership gathered in this facility until 1908. During this period, the synagogue moved fully away from Orthodoxy and established itself as a Reform institution. In 1874, Beth Israel members voted to join the Union of American Hebrew Congregations, one year after this national organization of Reform congregations was organized. By 1887, a schism developed regarding ritual—the argument over head coverings acting as an impetus—which resulted in the establishment of an Orthodox synagogue in Houston, Adath Jeshurun, the same year Beth Israel was forced to close down its religious school for six months because of financial difficulties.

Three years passed following the synagogue's move to the Franklin Avenue location before a rabbi, J. D. Meyer, was engaged. He remained until 1877 when Beth Israel was no longer able to pay his salary. Rabbi Jacob Voorsanger, who went on to fame in San Francisco, came to Houston to serve the synagogue in 1879 and remained until 1886. Reflective of the congregation's indecision over ritual matters, specifically regarding the adoption of the *Union Prayer Book* (the uniform prayer book of the Reform movement), among other things, this rabbi too remained only a short time. In 1898, Rabbi Abraham Lazarus was engaged by the temple, and the *Union Prayer Book* replaced *Minhag America*. Unfortunately, Lazarus died after serving one year in the pulpit. He was replaced by Rabbi Henry Barnstein (later, Barnston). For the first time in its history, in the advertisement for a rabbi, the temple declared that it was Reform and that it utilized the *Union Prayer Book.*

By 1908, the membership of Beth Israel, having outgrown its former facility on Franklin Avenue, built a new Romanesque structure on Lamar and Crawford Street. It remained there until 1925. Ritual matters were relatively calm during the period the congregation occupied this building, although the practice of assigned pews was abolished. The congregation faced the challenge of rapid growth, and membership rose to 261, with 150 children in the religious school. Beth Israel rejoined the Union of American Hebrew Congregations, having resigned for financial reasons.

By 1943, with 807 members, Beth Israel was swept into what came to be known as the ''Basic Principles'' controversy, which led to the second major schism in the congregation's history. This struggle over control in the congregation was fought on the battleground of Zionism. The clash came in the trail of the decision concerning who should succeed Barnston in the pulpit and what that successor would represent, with specific regard to the historical anti-Zionist position of the congregation. After perhaps the most turbulent meeting in the congregation's history, which resulted in Rabbi Hyman Judah Schachtel's election to succeed Barnston, a committee prepared a set of basic principles that were to guide the congregation and its members upon application for membership. These were considered to be a restatement of the principles established at the Philadelphia Conference (1869) and the Pittsburgh Platform (1885), including a rejection of the Columbus Platform (1937) and its Jewish nationalism. While there was an attempt to disassociate the election of the rabbi and the issue of Zionism, it was clear that this was the battle over which the war of rabbinic election was fought. The struggle over Jewish nationalism did not leave the congregation unscarred. Rabbi Robert Kahn, serving as assistant rabbi and on leave as an Army chaplain, resigned his position with the Temple. He was asked to lead Temple Emanu-El of Houston, which emerged out of this controversy over these basic principles and Zionism. Hoping to prevent further division in the congregation, President Leopold Meyer asked the temple's Policy Formulation Committee under the chairmanship of I. Friedlander to prepare a restatement of these principles, which was adopted by the board shortly thereafter. With the eventual establishment of the modern state of Israel, these basic principles were formally discarded in the 1960s, but it cannot be said that the controversy was simply assigned to the past. The air of resentment over this clash still lingers in the congregation.

With the post–World War II trend toward suburbanization, Houston's Jewish residents left the inner city. Following the move of its congregants, the congregation dedicated a new building in 1967 on its current site on North Braeswood. This facility has been enhanced numerous times with the addition of facilities to house the Irvin M. Shlenker Day School, the first Reform Jewish Day School in Houston. Rabbi Samuel Egal Karff was elected to serve the congregation in 1975 and remains as the senior rabbi. Under his tutelage, the congregation has grown to become a large, diverse institution, with over eighteen hundred membership units.

References

The Beth Israel Story: A Celebration (Houston, TX: 1979).
Cohen, Anne Nathan. *The Centenary History, Congregation Beth Israel of Houston, Texas, 1854–1954* (Houston, TX: 1954).
Greenstein, Howard R. *Turning Point: Zionism and Reform Judaism* (Chico, CA: 1981).
Maas, Elaine H. *The Jews of Houston: An Ethnographic Study* (New York: 1989).
Synagogue Histories File, American Jewish Archives.

BETH YESHURUN, CONSERVATIVE. *Houston, Texas.* The beginning of Beth Yeshurun dates back to 1887, when a small group attempted to conduct traditional services according to an East European ritual. Insufficient numbers and the lack of a consistent place for meeting prevented this group's aspirations for a permanent congregation from coming to fruition. The informal association of Jews through *landsmanschaften* further subdivided the group. After four years of struggling to organize a traditional Jewish community, a group held a meeting at an unknown location in Houston in 1891 to incorporate formally the two groups (Galician and Russian) into Adath Yeshurun, an Orthodox congregation. The election of officers waited until the following year, when the group elected

P. S. Nussbaum as its president. In the early years, congregants served as cantor. Then Bojarsky and Yasgur served the congregation as religious leaders, as did Rabbi Simon Glazier. By the middle of the 1890s, J. Hurwitz (1897–1906) and Max Epstein, both of whom had moved to Houston, began serving the congregation in rabbinic capacities.

As the group grew in number, worship in private homes gave way to rented facilities. In 1895, the congregation purchased its first home, a former church building, on the corner of Preston and Hamilton. Storms damaged the building in 1900. Although the congregation made repairs, the building proved to be too small for the growing congregation, whose membership was swelled by new European arrivals and those who had left Galveston after the storm that hit that city in 1900. Thus, Adath Yeshurun constructed a new building on the same site in 1904. The following year the Houston Belt and Terminal Company purchased the building, forcing the congregation to meet in temporary quarters once again. The congregation made various attempts to establish a Hebrew School, and when H. B. Lieberman became teacher and cantor, the congregation finally established one (1906). One year later, Dr. Wolf Willner, an active Zionist, began his period of rabbinic service to the congregation. Willner regulated kosher dietary laws in the congregation, introduced early Friday evening and Saturday afternoon worship, improved the religious school, developed youth activities, and encouraged congregational participation in communal affairs.

In 1908, Adath Yeshurun dedicated a new facility at Jackson and Walker. Three years later, members built a new building on an adjacent lot. With the progress came disagreement over a variety of matters. As a result, a small group joined Dr. Willner in an attempt to develop an independent congregation, sponsoring services first as the B'nai Israel Hebrew School, then calling itself the Zion Society, and finally becoming Beth Shalom Congregation. After a few years, this renegade group rejoined the ranks of Adath Yeshurun. While cantors served the congregation during this interim period, between the years 1914 and 1916 I. Smilowitz served as rabbi. Willner left Adath Yeshurun in 1923.

Rabbi David Stern succeeded Willner but remained only one year. Rabbi I. Segal served for four years. Then came Dr. Abraham I. Schechter (1927–1933). In 1925, Adath Yeshurun added a school building. For a short time, Rabbi A. Lobel served the congregation until Rabbi Sanders Tofield occupied the pulpit, beginning in 1934. As a result of World War II, Congregation Beth El joined Adath Yeshurun for its religious school, meeting in members' homes for the duration of the conflict. In 1945, as a result of financial difficulties, Beth El (originally founded in 1934 as a Conservative congregation) joined with Adath Yeshurun (the congregation it had originally broken away from) to form a new synagogue, Beth Yeshurun. This new congregation built a synagogue on Southmore Street.

Rabbi Aaron Blumenthal served until William Malev became rabbi in 1948, serving until 1973. In 1963 the congregation moved to Beechnut Street. In 1994 membership at Beth Yeshurun exceeded two thousand family members, with nearly one thousand students in its religious school and day school. Rabbi Jack Segal has served since 1973 and had been assistant prior to that (since 1965). Under his direction, the congregation granted full ritual equality to women in the congregation.

References

The Golden Book of Adath Yeshurun (Houston, TX: 1941).
Maas, Elaine H. *The Jews of Houston: An Ethnographic Study* (New York: 1989).
Synagogue Histories File, American Jewish Archives.

CONGREGATION EMANU EL, REFORM. *Houston, Texas.* Born out of a dispute within the context of Congregation Beth Israel, Congregation Emanu El was organized by dissidents in 1944. Members of Congregation Beth Israel, founded in 1854, decided to adopt a set of principles in 1943. For full membership in the congregation, Emanu El required its members to affirm these principles in writing. (The congregation rescinded this practice in 1967.) Though all of these principles are important, the second principle, which was at the root of the dispute, is of particular interest. It read:

We are Jews by virtue of our acceptance of Judaism. We consider ourselves no longer a nation. We are a religious community and neither pray for, nor anticipate a return to Palestine nor a restoration of any of the laws concerning the Jewish state. We stand unequivocally for the separation of Church and State. Our religion is Judaism. Our nation is the United States of America. Our nationality is American. Our flag is the Stars and Stripes. Our race is Caucasian. With regard to the Jewish settlement in Palestine, we consider it our sacred privilege to promote the spiritual, cultural, and social welfare of our co-religionists there.

While some will argue that the presence of Zionist ideology caused the disagreement, a large group of Beth Israel members deemed it unthinkable to sign any credo as a condition of acceptance into any form of Judaism. This sense of freedom of belief and thought fueled the formation of Emanu El. This is demonstrated in the preamble to its constitution: "The membership of Congregation Emanu El resolves its members shall not be limited in their freedom of thought and speech, and that its pulpit shall be free to preach on behalf of truth and righteousness in the democratic spirit, and after the pattern of the prophets of Israel."

With early meetings and worship taking place at the Central Presbyterian Church, 190 people formed the nucleus of the new congregation. This group invited Robert I. Kahn to lead them as its rabbi. Membership doubled the first year. The congregation purchased property in 1945, but wartime restrictions on building prevented the immediate construction of a temple facility. In 1949, the congregation dedicated its home on Sunset Boulevard. Additional classrooms were added throughout the years. Since its founding, Emanu El has emphasized adult education and interfaith relations. In 1976, the congregation added the Freda Poler chapel and the Robert I. Kahn Gallery. In 1978, Roy Walter succeeded the retiring Rabbi Kahn. By this time, the congregation numbered fifteen hundred family units. The congregation built a chapel at its cemetery in 1983. By 1994, membership units exceeded two thousand.

References

Maas, Elaine H. *The Jews of Houston: An Ethnographic Study* (New York: 1989).
Synagogue Histories File, American Jewish Archives.

TEMPLE BETH EL, REFORM. *San Antonio, Texas.* Established in 1874, the original membership of Temple Beth El numbered forty-four. One year later, the congregation joined the Union of American Hebrew Congregations (national organization of Reform synagogues) and adopted a form of ritual set forth "in the Ceremonies of *Minhag America,*" which meant for the members worship without covered heads. There is no record to indicate where worship services were held during the incipient years of synagogue formation. Members dedicated a permanent building in late 1875 at the corner of Jefferson and Travis. Following the opening of the synagogue, Beth El sold its pews to members. The congregation received inquiries from rabbis who wished to serve the congregation, but the board chose not to act on any of the inquiries, utilizing lay leaders instead to lead worship. Eventually, in early 1876, it chose to discontinue Friday worship and to meet only for the holidays until a rabbi was installed. In 1877, E. B. Jacobs was given a short-term contract to serve as religious leader of the congregation. When his six-month contract was not extended, apparently because of the precarious financial status of the congregation, the congregation turned once again to lay leaders to lead Beth El in worship.

In 1879, Isidore Loewenthal was engaged by Temple Beth El. During his tenure, the congregation voted to require children to attend Religious School on Saturday and Sunday mornings. When Lowenthal resigned in 1889, Moses P. Jacobson was elected to the pulpit and remained until 1891. By 1892, the board considered the painful question, "Shall this Congregation continue its organization?" The facilities were badly in need of repair. Growth in temple membership was very slow at this time. As a result, High Holiday seats were sold at a high price. Following a vote to continue the efforts of the congregation, the board invited Rabbi J. Hyman Elkin to serve as Beth El's rabbi. He remained until 1897, although the board communicated to him that his Saturday morning lectures were "distasteful" and asked him to "dispense" with them. As a result, he resigned his position.

Rabbi Samuel Marks succeeded Elkin and remained with Temple Beth El until 1920. During his tenure, membership grew, and he advocated the construction of a larger facility. In 1903, a new synagogue was indeed constructed on the same site as the previous structure. By 1908, the sanctuary was overcrowded, and the board chose to eliminate the old system of pew ownership. Instead, a dues system, originally conceived as a means of "renting pews," was developed.

The financial condition of the temple was still unstable. Membership was at only 145. Dues were raised, which resulted in a net loss through the resignation of members. Thus, the membership voted to sell the temple building in 1917, something that was not realized until 1924. By 1919, membership increased to 223. Rabbi Sidney Tedesche came to the congregation in 1919 as associate rabbi and succeeded Marks the following year when Marks retired. Tedesche proved to be a powerful influence on the growth of the institution. Membership increased. He organized the religious school, organized the sisterhood (originally as a Ladies Auxiliary) and brotherhood, and initiated the move to build a new synagogue. Tedesche resigned in 1923, and Rabbi Ephraim Frisch was selected to lead the temple.

With a membership of 390, a new congregational home, with a sanctuary seating capacity of twelve hundred and expansion to sixteen hundred, was dedicated in 1927 at Belknap and Ashby, where the congregation continues to meet and worship. Between 1930 and 1932, the country's financial crisis burdened Temple Beth El as well. By 1935, the congregation's finances showed improvement. In 1938, Dr. David Jacobson was elected to the position of associate rabbi to assist Rabbi Frisch, who had been given a leave of absence because of ill health. In 1942, Frisch formally retired and Jacobson became the sole rabbi of the congregation. Membership had doubled by 1944. In 1948, the congregation assisted in the formation of a new synagogue in San Antonio. Rabbi Jacobson emphasized social action and interfaith relations during his rabbinate. When he retired in 1976, Rabbi Samuel Stahl succeeded him. Stahl continued Jacobson's concentration on interfaith relations while also focusing on the religious education of children and adults. In 1982, the physical plant underwent extensive renovation when a community building and an auditorium were added. In 1994, membership of Beth El totaled 1160 family units.

References

Kallison, Frances R. "100 Years of Jewry in San Antonio" (Master's thesis, Trinity University, 1977).

Sajowitz, William. "History of Reform Judaism in San Antonio, Texas, 1870–1945" (Rabbinic thesis, Hebrew Union College, 1945).

Synagogue Histories File, American Jewish Archives.

U

UTAH

KOL AMI, CONSERVATIVE, REFORM. *Salt Lake City, Utah.* Fifteen years prior to Utah's statehood, a group of Jews organized themselves in Salt Lake City as B'nai Israel. Its first building, dedicated in 1883 on First West and Third South, sat on property referred to as "Tanner's Lot." In 1891, members built a larger building on Fourth Street, a small replica of the famous Berlin Temple. Disenchanted with B'nai Israel's Reform ideology, a small group of its members joined to form the orthodox Congregation Montefiore in 1899. Montefiore dedicated its synagogue on South Third Street and used it until 1976.

Talks about possible consolidation between members of B'nai Israel and Congregation Montefiore began as early as 1947, but serious discussion did not take place until 1960, when Rabbi E. Louis Cardin of Montefiore died; Rabbi Mordecai Podet of B'nai Israel resigned the following year. In 1969, the institutions' religious schools merged—eventually being housed in B'nai Israel.

The merger of B'nai Israel and Congregation Montefiore did not take place until 1972, and Congregation Kol Ami was created. But the new congregation did not sell the independent facilities before its members built a new building, dedicated in 1976, to house the merged congregation. Rabbi Abner Bergman served B'nai Israel beginning in 1973. Under his direction, B'nai Israel, a Reform congregation, merged with Congregation Montefiore, by then a Conservative congregation, to form Kol Ami (1976). As a result, the merged congregation retained its affiliation with both the Union of American Hebrew Congregations, the national organization of Reform synagogues, and the United Synagogue of America (now the United Synagogue of Conservative Judaism), the national organization of Conservative synagogues. Following the merger, members held morning services according to Conservative liturgical practices and evening services according to the Reform tradition. In addition, the congregation became fully egalitarian and maintained a kosher kitchen. However, Kol Ami retained an infrequently used organ for worship. In 1982, a group of about twenty-five families left the congregation to form Chavurah B'yachad. However, this small Reconstructionist congregation still sends its children to the Kol Ami religious school. These rabbis succeeded Rabbi Bergman: Stanley Greenstein (1981–1982), Eric Silver (1982–1986), and Frederick Wenger (1987–). Wenger emphasized adult education and outreach to the intermarried in the community. Under his direction, the congregation grew from fewer than four hundred families to six hundred family units in 1995. Kol Ami actively helped establish small congregations in Park City, Utah; Ogden, Utah; and Logan, Utah. These congregations send their children to Kol Ami for religious education and share the services of Rabbi Wenger, maintaining a dual membership at Kol Ami and their new, small, local congregations.

References

Rudd, Hynda. "Congregation Kol Ami: Religious Merger in Salt Lake City." *Western States Jewish Historical Quarterly* 10, no. 4 (July 1978): 311–25.
Stern, Norton B. "The Founding of the Jewish Community in Utah." *Western States Jewish Historical Quarterly* 8, no. 1 (October 1975): 65–69.
Synagogue Histories File, American Jewish Archives.

V

VIRGINIA

BETH-EL HEBREW CONGREGATION, REFORM. *Alexandria, Virginia.*
Jews began to move to Alexandria by 1850. Most of the Jews who lived in
Alexandria prior to 1859 belonged to Washington Hebrew Congregation. By
the end of the decade, local Jewish residents felt it was time to form a synagogue
of their own. Thus, Alexandria's Jewish community formed two new congregations simultaneously: Beth-El Hebrew Congregation for Reform Judaism and
an unnamed congregation for those who preferred the Orthodox observance of
Judaism. At the time, the language of prayer (Beth-El preferred German to
Hebrew) was primarily what separated the two congregations. Thus, the following year, the Orthodox group joined Beth-El Hebrew Congregation. Beth-El
remained the only synagogue in Northern Virginia until 1914, when Agudas
Achim (Orthodox, then Conservative) was formed.

Shortly after the formation of the congregation, the Civil War broke out.
Given the allegiance of Virginia to the Confederacy and the close proximity of
Northern Virginia to the Union's capital, Beth-El members found themselves
literally caught in the middle. Many left the city; however, by 1862, the growth
in Alexandria's population gave rise to a need for permanent quarters for Beth-
El where members could also establish a program of religious education for
their children. Thus, the congregation rented rooms at Stewart's Hall at the
corner of Pitt and King Streets, where they remained until 1871.

In 1864, Dr. L. Schlessinger became Beth-El's first spiritual leader. H. Heil-
brown quickly succeeded him. Israel Sanger came next to serve the congregation
until 1867, when members elected Rabbi L. Lowensohn to their pulpit. Lowensohn delivered his sermons in English, while services continued to be conducted in Hebrew and German. In addition, although membership dwindled to

twenty-five families, this small group built a new synagogue home for itself on North Washington Street.

Rabbi Benjamin Aaron Bonnheim succeeded Lowensohn in 1873. As a result of major disagreements during his short and stormy tenure, the congregation split. When Rabbi Bonnheim left Beth-El in 1876, the dissident group rejoined the congregation. A succession of rabbis followed before the appointment of Dr. Hugo Schiff in 1939. During the interim, lay readers conducted services, assisted by student rabbis from Hebrew Union College during the High Holidays. At the same time, Beth-El developed a close relationship with Washington Hebrew Congregation. The religious leaders at Washington Hebrew Congregation (Louis Stern and then Rabbi Abram Simon) officiated at life-cycle events and other important occasions.

Following Rabbi Schiff, C. Melvyn Helfgott and Paul Richman served the congregation before Beth-El elected Rabbi Emmet A. Frank to its pulpit. During Frank's tenure, the congregation split, and forty families organized Temple Rodef Shalom in Falls Church. After fifteen years of service, Rabbi Frank left, and Rabbi Arnold Fink succeeded him (1969). Fink moved the congregation away from English hymns and a professional non-Jewish choir. He introduced more Hebrew into the service and added family services on a regular basis. The program of activity at the congregation is quite extensive with a variety of support groups and educational programs meeting various needs of a growing membership. During Rabbi Fink's tenure, membership grew from 350 to nearly one thousand in 1994.

Reference

Bendheim, Leroy S. "Beth-El History and the Jews of Northern Virginia." In David Altschuler, ed., *The Jews of Washington, D.C.: A Communal History Anthology* (Chappaqua, NY: 1985), pp. 66–7.

BETH EL, CONSERVATIVE. *Norfolk, Virginia.* Beth El was organized on February 27, 1870, by the orthodox dissidents of Ohef Sholom. These leaders of Beth El congregation were predominantly Prussian-Posen Jews, many of whom had been founders of the earlier congregations as well as trustees for the purchase of the community's Hebrew cemetery. The breakaway was partially precipitated by the failure of a cantor, L. Harfeld, to secure the post at Ohef Sholom, and he became Beth El's spiritual leader. For ten years the congregation met in rented quarters at Fenchurch and Cove Streets. In 1880 the synagogue building erected by Ohef Sholom on Cumberland Street was vacated by the Methodist Home Missionary Society and sold at auction to Beth El. The congregation worshiped here until 1921, when it erected a sanctuary at 422 Shirley Avenue, enlarged in the early years of the twentieth century. By 1952 the congregation had grown to the point of requiring a new sixteen-hundred-seat sanctuary, which was erected adjacent to the older one, which was converted to a social hall named for a long-time president, Abraham Myers.

In 1873 Harfeld departed to be replaced by Samuel Mendelsohn, one of three alumni of Isaac Leeser's short-lived Maimonides College in Philadelphia. After three years at Beth El, he left for a more liberal congregation in Wilmington, North Carolina. The succeeding century saw some unique rabbis at Beth El. Among those of more than cursory tenure were the autodidact Daniel E. Levy, a member of the congregation who subsequently, like many of Beth El's German Jews, joined Ohef Sholom as Beth El became more dominated by East European immigrants; Herman Benmosche, a native of Cairo, Egypt, who was educated in Koenigsberg and came to Norfolk from London's Spital Square Synagogue; Edward Benjamin Morris Browne, who claimed to have lived in Isaac M. Wise's Cincinnati home while earning an M.D. and to have received private ordination from Wise in 1869; and Russian-born Louis Goldberg, a Harvard graduate who in 1909 became the first alumnus of the Jewish Theological Seminary to serve Beth El and brought the congregation into the mainstream of Conservative Judaism, encouraging it to become one of twelve founding congregations of the United Synagogue. Alexander Alan Steinbach held the pulpit from 1923 to 1934 and was followed by Paul Reich, who led Beth El for forty years, insisting on the congregation's preeminence over other communal agencies. His retirement coincided with an era of demographic change that diminished the congregation's membership and may have caused the recent turnover of rabbis. The later gentrification of the neighborhood revitalized the congregation under Rabbi Charles Freundlich. These men succeeded Freundlich: Jerome Kestenbaum (1972–1974), David Novak (1978–1981), Barton Leftin (1981–1985), Dov Peretz Elkins (1985–1987), and Donald Sobel (1987–1988). Arthur Ruberg joined the congregation as religious leader in 1988. In 1995, Beth El numbered six hundred family units.

Reference

Stern, Malcolm H. "Some Notes on the History of the Organized Jewish Community of Norfolk, Virginia." *Journal of the Southern Jewish Historical Society* 1, no. 3 (November 1963): 21–24.

OHEF SHOLOM, REFORM. *Norfolk, Virginia.* Jews are traceable in Norfolk to 1787, when Moses Myers, who was to become a prominent merchant, and Revolutionary veteran Philip Moses Russell lived there. By the War of 1812, sons of Benjamin Nones of Philadelphia had settled there with other Jews, and they may have met for worship. The death of Solomon Nones led to the purchase of a cemetery plot in suburban Berkley for the embryonic Jewish community, which failed to grow until the 1840s.

Ohef Sholom congregation traces its origins to the arrival in 1844 of Jacob Umstadter, *shochet* (kosher butcher) and *chazan* (cantor), who seems to have gathered a minyan for worship. For the holidays of 1848 the growing group of German Jews organized congregation *Chevra B'nai Jacov,* known in English as the House of Jacob. By 1850 they had purchased land for a Hebrew cemetery to which graves from Berkley cemetery were transferred. Within three years they had secured a state charter for an elementary school, Hebrew and English Literary Institute, that functioned until public schooling became available. School and services were held in rented facilities.

In 1859 the congregation purchased from Jacob Umstadter a plot on Cumberland Street on which its first synagogue was built. Through the 1850s and 1860s a variety of readers functioned as cantors, ending with Jonas Hecht, former cantor of Anshe Chesed, New York's largest German congregation, who lived out his life in Norfolk.

As the disruptions of the Civil War, ending with the burning of Richmond, compelled the state to recharter all organizations, the Norfolk congregation reorganized under the title Ohef Sholom, leasing the synagogue from the Literary Institute and acquiring the cemetery deed. Revised bylaws led to dissidence as some attempted to push for reforms. In the summer of 1869, Bernhard L. Fould was brought from Erie, Pennsylvania, to become the congregation's first rabbi. Within a year, the more traditional members had broken away to form Beth El. Battles over who had rights to the cemetery led eventually to a Hebrew Cemetery Association with three trustees from each congregation. Overtures to reunite the congregations came to naught, so Ohef Sholom moved forward in the direction of Reform, altering the former women's gallery of the synagogue to accommodate an organ and mixed choir. A cantor and organist were engaged, the former having responsibility for the school, which by 1873 met after public school. Saturday religious classes were moved to Sunday and taught by young women volunteers.

Arguments over which Reform prayer book should be used led to a committee assigned to synthesize those of Wise, Einhorn, and Szold; but the Panic of 1873 had so reduced the budget that no action was taken. Rabbi Fould's ill health forced his retirement in 1877, and English-born Bernard Eberson came from Troy, New York, to be his successor. Growth of the congregation led to an exchange of buildings with the Methodist Home Missionary Society; and by 1878 Ohef Sholom was installed on Church Street, just north of Mariner, where it worshiped for twenty-four years. Congregational growth again compelled a move, and a handsome building was erected at Freemason and Monticello, dedicated in May 1902. In the meantime Rabbi Eberson retired, and the congregation elected its first Hebrew Union College graduate, Simon R. Cohen, who left in 1907 to be replaced by Louis D. Mendoza. A disastrous fire in 1916 gutted the Freemason Street sanctuary, and the congregation erected its present classic Greek temple in residential Ghent at Raleigh Avenue and Stockley Gardens. After thirty-eight years of ecumenical preaching, Mendoza retired, to be succeeded briefly by Bernard Starkoff, who found the congregation's reform too radical. He was followed in 1947 by Malcolm Stern, who brought the congregation toward mainstream Reform Judaism, an acceptance of civil rights for blacks, and a pro-Israel stance. A 1951 remodelling of the facilities was soon outgrown, and in 1965 the building was expanded. Harold Hahn had become the thought-provoking preacher and organizer but left after five years to be replaced by Rabbi Lawrence Forman, who became a leader in the creation of the United Hebrew School for Norfolk's congregations.

From 1865, with the formation of the Ladies Hebrew Benevolent Association, the women rendered valuable service to the congregation, raising funds, supplying and supervising the religious school and, for many years, editing the bulletin. The association became Norfolk's section of the Council of Jewish Women in the first decade of the twentieth century. The emergence of Sisterhood as a separate arm of the congregation added strength to the activities. The 1950s saw the development of a men's club and youth group.

Until the 1950s a social barrier existed between Ohef Sholom and the community's other congregations, but this was dissipated by a sharing of social activities surrounding confirmation. Despite a proliferation of congregations in neighboring Virginia Beach and Portsmouth, Ohef Sholom has grown steadily to a membership of over eight hundred family units.

References

Margolius, Elise Levy. *One Hundred and Twenty-fifth Anniversary, Ohef Sholom Temple, 1844–1969* (Norfolk: 1969).

Stern, Malcolm H. ''Some Notes on the History of the Organized Jewish Community of Norfolk, Virginia.'' *Journal of the Southern Jewish Historical Society* 1, no. 3 (November 1963): 12–21.

BETH AHABAH/BETH SHALOME, REFORM. *Richmond, Virginia.*

Beth Shalome

Organizers adopted a constitution for Kahal Kadosh Beth Shalome in 1789, thus founding the first Jewish congregation in Virginia. Charter members of the congregation lived in a diverse geographical area. Shortly after the congregation's incorporation, members established an Ezrat Orchim Society to help indigent travelers. Beth Shalome's early ritual was in Hebrew with an English translation (based on a Spanish rendering of the original Hebrew). The form and order of worship remained unchanged for much of its early history. In the early days of the congregation, Beth Shalome worshiped in a room on Nineteenth Street between Grace and Franklin. It next moved to quarters on the corner of Main and Nineteenth Street. After the building collapsed, the congregation went without a home for several years. Beth Shalome dedicated its new synagogue on Mayo Street in 1822.

Various religious leaders served Beth Shalome in its early years. Isaac H. Judah served as a co-officiant with Isaac B. Seixas before succeeding him entirely. Seixas left in 1828. Abraham Hyam Cohen led the congregation beginning in 1829. He remained for three years. The pulpit stayed vacant for several years before members elected Jacques Judah Lyons in 1838. Rabbi Julius Eckman, the first ordained religious leader to serve Beth Shalome, arrived in Richmond in 1849. He left in 1851. In 1852, members established the Hebrew Beneficial

Society, providing members with sickness and death benefits. In 1853, M. Robinson served Beth Shalome for only two months. Then brothers Henry Jacobs (1853–1857) and George Jacobs (1857–1869) came to serve Beth Shalome in succession. George Jacobs supported the Confederacy and encouraged Beth Shalome to invest its surplus funds in Confederate bonds. During the burning of Richmond in 1865, the congregation lost its records, which had been housed temporarily in a courthouse.

In 1867, a group of women in the congregation requested changes in the liturgy, including the shortening of the service, the harmonizing of congregational voices, and mixed seating. However, the board (called a *junta*) rejected the request. In 1873, Isaac Pereira Mendes came to Beth Shalome. He remained until 1877. Following his resignation, Beth Shalome leaders approached Beth Ahabah about consolidation. Beth Shalome required four things: Ashkenazic Hebrew with mutually acceptable English hymns; the optional wearing of the tallith; a mixed Jewish choir; and covered heads for worship. When Beth Ahabah countered with a requirement of German or English sermons and questions about a mixed choir, discussions about a possible merger fell apart. Beth Shalome hired Joseph H. M. Chumaciero for the High Holidays and then Frommer Cohn until 1898. Beth Shalome remained in the Mayo Street location until 1891. During the last few years of its existence, Beth Shalome members worshiped at Lee Camp Hall. After losing many members to Beth Ahabah, Beth Shalome became moribund and, following Cohn's resignation, merged into Beth Ahabah in 1898.

Beth Ahabah

As an outgrowth of the social and charitable organization Chebrah Ahabat Israel (Association for the Love of Israel, 1839), founders established Beth Ahabah in 1841. Beth Ahabah met in a rented house called the Seminarium on Marshall Street (consecrated 1841). The congregation's first religious leader, Jacob Gotthold, joined Beth Ahabah at its founding. The congregation opened the first Jewish school in the city, the Richmond German, Hebrew, and English Institute (1846), inviting Maximilian Michelbacher to lead it along with the synagogue. The synagogue used the traditional ritual of the Rodelheim prayer book, familiar to the Hagenbach Jews in the hometowns from which most of the congregation emigrated. When the congregation grew to thirty-six members, it purchased a site on Eleventh Street where it worshiped for over fifty years (dedicated 1848). Michelbacher focused his attention on the education of the children, particularly important before the creation of a public school system.

Membership increased to over eighty by 1851. The school enrollment tripled as well. After Beth Shalome's charitable organization went out of existence, Beth Ahabah's members established a Ladies' Hebrew Beneficial Association. This organization eventually became a social service agency. The Confederacy requisitioned the school during the Civil War.

Following Isaac Mayer Wise's visit, the congregation joined the Union of American Hebrew Congregations, the national organization of Reform synagogues in 1875. Subsequently, Beth Ahabah instituted a variety of reforms, including the elimination of all confessional prayers including Kol Nidre and the *"al chet."* Members promoted decorum during the service and prevented young children from attending. Beth Ahabah also reduced the number of Torah honors and instituted the triennial reading of the Torah. Congregants also suggested other reforms such as the use of choir, organ, and English readings, but these were not introduced at the time. In 1876, the congregation abandoned the traditional prayer book in favor of *Abodat Israel,* edited by Benjamin Szold and Marcus Jastrow.

Beth Ahabah's first ordained rabbi, Dr. Albert Siegfried Bettleheim, served in Richmond from 1869 to 1874, primarily responsible for Beth Ahabah's school. During his tenure, he eliminated the kissing of *tzitzit* (fringes of the prayer shawl), as well as the reading of the haftarah. Following the establishment of a secular school system, Beth Ahabah organized a Sunday School (1872). Dr. Abraham Hoffman succeeded Bettelheim in 1875. At about the same time, a group of thirty members, impatient over the slow progress of reform at Beth Ahabah, resigned and formed Beth Israel. Though Beth Israel lasted only six years and failed after a series of tragic events, the presence of former Beth Israel members who rejoined Beth Ahabah then helped expedite the progress of reform at Beth Ahabah.

When illness forced Hoffman to resign in 1878, members invited Dr. Abraham Harris to serve them. During his tenure, members built a new synagogue on the site of the previous one (dedicated 1880). Harris died suddenly in 1891. Edward N. Calisch succeeded him. He worked at interfaith understanding in the community and led the congregation in its anti-Zionist activities. Shortly after his arrival in Richmond, he recommended the removal of head coverings during prayer and instituted his own prayer book, *A Book of Prayer for Jewish Worship,* in 1893 (supplanted by the *Union Prayer Book,* the uniform Reform prayer book, in 1909). In 1904, Beth Ahabah and its 275 members left its site on Eleventh Street and moved to its present location in the West End. In 1919, the president of Beth Ahabah listed these customs eliminated by the membership: dietary laws, unleavened meals on Passover, the sukkah, traditional observance of the Sabbath, the seven-day period of mourning blessings on Friday evening at the onset of the Sabbath, sanctification over the wine, lighting candles for Hanukkah, and circumcision—and eventually the Sunday Service. Calisch supported the war effort during World War I. In 1923, the men of the congregation organized a Brotherhood (reorganized as the Men's Club in 1929).

In 1930, membership reached over 450 members. During World War II, the congregation took an active role in supporting the local armed forces. Calisch supported the anti-Zionist American Council for Judaism. When Calisch died in 1945, members of Beth Ahabah elected Dr. Ariel Leiser Goldburg to its pulpit.

As a Zionist, he reversed the anti-Zionist position of the congregation. Goldburg also focused his attention on interfaith activities in the congregation and community.

In 1958, Beth Ahabah dedicated a new religious school building. Eleven years later, congregants dedicated newly remodeled buildings on West Franklin Street for use as offices, lounges, a library, and meeting rooms. Members elected Rabbi Saul Rubin to succeed Goldburg in 1970, having previously served as assistant and associate. He resigned the following year, and Rabbi Jack Spiro joined the congregation. He focused his attention on adult education in the congregation and community. In 1977, Beth Ahabah established the Beth Ahabah Museum and Archives Trust (dedicated 1983). In 1994, membership at the congregation reached 720 family units.

References

Berman, Myron. *Richmond's Jewry, 1769–1976* (Charlottesville, VA: 1979).
Rosenbaum, Claire Millhiser. *Universal and Particular Obligations* (Richmond: 1988).

BETH EL, CONSERVATIVE. *Richmond, Virginia.* In 1931, a group of members of the Orthodox Sir Moses Montefiore Congregation joined together to form Beth El as a Conservative congregation. Among other things, the breakaway group desired family seating for worship. This group of one hundred people met at the Amity Club and affiliated with the United Synagogue of America (now the United Synagogue of Conservative Judaism), the national organization of Conservative synagogues. Members met for worship at the Scottish Rite Temple. They immediately organized a choir and a sisterhood. A few months later, the congregation leased space in Columbo Hall on West Broad. Joseph E. Raffaeli, Aaron H. Lefkowitz, and Philip Romanov initially served the congregation in succession; Rabbi Morris Frank became the congregation's first Conservative religious leader. Frank died shortly after World War I and his war service.

Depression hit the congregation hard. While the religious school thrived and membership increased to two hundred, the economy forced the congregation to vacate its property on Broad Street, meeting instead in temporary quarters on Monument Avenue. In the spirit of optimism, members purchased a former church on Grove Avenue in 1938 for use as a synagogue. Two years later, the congregation's three hundred members started to build on the adjacent lot. World War II interrupted the completion of the building.

Rabbi Nathan Kollin served Beth El from 1941 to 1949. During his tenure, the congregation assisted in the renewal of a B'nai B'rith chapter and helped create the local Jewish Community Center. In 1949, the congregation dedicated its new sanctuary. Rabbi Michael Kurz succeeded Kollin for a short time before members elected Jacob Milgrom to the pulpit. Milgrom served from 1951 to 1965. During Milgrom's service with the congregation, Beth El installed an organ. He focused his attention on the educational program of the synagogue for youth and adults. In 1957, Beth El dedicated a new educational building.

As an offshoot of Beth El, B'nai Sholom was established in 1965. Then Dr. Myron Berman joined the congregation. During Berman's tenure, B'nai Sholom and Beth El consolidated (1987). When Berman retired in 1993, Rabbi Gary Creditor succeeded him. In 1994, Beth El's membership exceeded eight hundred family units.

References

Berman, Myron. *Richmond's Jewry, 1769–1976* (Charlottesville, VA: 1979).
Synagogue Histories File, American Jewish Archives.

W

WASHINGTON

TEMPLE DE HIRSCH SINAI, REFORM. *Seattle, Washington.* While High Holiday services in Seattle can be traced back to 1897 in Jefferson Hall, the community did not take any action to formally establish a congregation until 1899. That year, seven men met in Morris Hall to begin the process, which eventually led seventy Jewish families in Seattle to join together in order to organize the city's first Reform congregation, Temple De Hirsch. These founders named the congregation for Baron de Hirsch, a philanthropist well known for his efforts to bring Jews from Europe to North America and establish colonies for their resettlement. Students travelled from Hebrew Union College in Cincinnati to lead High Holiday services during the formative years of the congregation. Temple De Hirsch engaged Rabbi Theodore Joseph as the congregation's first religious leader immediately after its formal establishment. The Religious School, instituted by founding members along with the congregation, enrolled sixty-five students.

In 1901, the temple began to build its first structure at Boylston and Marion. However, after the completion of only the basement, which the congregation used in the interim, De Hirsch halted its plans to build, as it was already clear that the intended building would be too small. As a result, the synagogue built at its present site at Fifteenth and East Union (1908) and built the Temple Center in 1924. In 1926, the congregation purchased land north of this building to Pike Street, but did not build a new sanctuary building until 1960. In 1969, a bomb exploded outside the doors to the sanctuary, doing considerable damage. The following year, the congregation refurbished the entire facility. In 1974, the congregation built a new chapel, the Schoenfeld-Gardner Chapel.

Rabbi Samuel Koch succeeded Rabbi Joseph in 1907 and served until his retirement (1942). Koch helped to form many agencies in the Seattle community.

In the congregation, he focused much of his attention on the education of children through the religious school. Furthermore, he developed a significant library for the temple.

The congregation elected Rabbi Raphael Levine as Koch's successor. He continued the tradition of working with Jews and non-Jews by appearing as the Jewish representative on a weekly interfaith television program throughout most of his career. His vision provided the foundation for Camp Brotherhood, an ecumenical undertaking established in 1968. Levine also joined in the founding of Camp Swig, one of the camps established by the Reform movement. Rabbi Earl Starr succeeded Levine in 1970 and continues to serve the congregation as its senior rabbi. Under his direction, the congregation built a retreat center and a cottage (for the retired Rabbi Levine) at its Camp Brotherhood. In addition, he focuses his attention on the youth of the congregation.

Following a year of discussion, Temple Sinai of Bellevue merged with Temple De Hirsch in 1971 to form Temple De Hirsch Sinai. Sinai's facility in Bellevue became a suburban center for the merged congregation. Temple Sinai had begun as a Sunday School established by De Hirsch for its Eastside families. The congregation itself began in 1961 under the temporary name "Eastside Reform Congregation." In 1964, Rabbi Allen H. Podet was elected to serve Sinai, which dedicated its building five years later. In 1995, Temple De Hirsch Sinai's membership exceeded twelve hundred family units.

References

Droker, Howard. "Ohaveth Sholem: Seattle's First Jewish Congregation." *Western States Jewish Historical Quarterly* 17, no. 1 (October 1984): 26–34.
75th Anniversary Book (Seattle: 1974).
Synagogue Histories File, American Jewish Archives.

WEST VIRGINIA

TEMPLE SHALOM/CONGREGATION L'SHEM SHOMAYIM, RE-FORM. *Wheeling, West Virginia.* Founded in 1849, Temple Shalom/Congregation L'Shem Shomayim is the result of a merger in 1974 between the (Reform) Woodsdale Temple (formerly called the Eoff Street Temple/Congregation L'Shem Shomayim) and the (Conservative) Synagogue of Israel. It has been strengthened by the recent consolidation with members of the Agudas Achim Congregation of Bellaire, Ohio, and three earlier congregations.

Congregation L'Shem Shomayim began in 1849 with a purchase of the Mt. Wood Cemetery by a group of Jews from Wheeling. A year later, a small group of Jews in Bellaire, Ohio, organized the Sons of Israel, eventually becoming a Reform congregation. Forming the nucleus of a congregation, the Wheeling group met for High Holidays only during the years 1849–1856 in a private residence. In 1862, the L'Shem Shomayim group moved its worship to Melodeon Hall. In 1872, the congregation acquired new quarters in the Hub Building at Market and Fourteenth Streets. Five years later, L'Shem Shomayim moved to the Odd Fellow's Temple at Twelfth and Chapline. Steps taken to reform this congregation included the introduction of weekly sermons in English in 1879, followed by the first confirmation ceremony one year later.

By 1890, the Bellaire group splintered into two, with the second group founding Agudas Achim. L'Shem Shomayim's Eoff Street Temple was dedicated in 1892, the same year the congregation joined the Union of American Hebrew Congregations, the national organization of Reform synagogues. The congregation, now officially Reform, introduced the *Union Prayer Book,* the uniform prayer book of the Reform movement, in 1897, the same year Rabbi Harry Levi joined the congregation. He served until 1911.

The Sons of Israel Congregation in Bellaire built a new building in 1911. Two years later, Ohev Shalom, an Orthodox synagogue, was founded in Wheeling. In 1923, Agudas Achim moved from the Odd Fellow's Temple, which it had occupied after L'Shem Shomayim, to a small wooden structure on Union Street, formerly the home of one of its members. Three years later, the Synagogue of Israel was founded in the Woodsdale section of the city. The following year, in 1927, the Synagogue of Israel built its house of worship on Edgington Lane. In 1931, Ohev Shalom moved to a hall on Market Street; nine years later, the congregation disbanded and joined the Synagogue of Israel. In 1950, Agudas Achim constructed a new building on Belmont Street. Three years later the Sons of Israel Congregation (in Bellaire, Ohio) disbanded and sold its property, and its members joined the Eoff Street Temple. In 1957, members of the Eoff Street Temple moved to a new site on Bethany Pike; the new facility became known as the Woodsdale Temple. During the school year 1968–1969, the religious schools of the Woodsdale Temple and the Synagogue of Israel merged, followed by talks of merger between the membership of the two synagogues. The merger took place in 1974 creating Temple Shalom; the merged institution joined the Union of American Hebrew Congregations and remained in the Bethany Pike facility. Rabbi Morton Kaplan came to the community to lead this new congregation, where he remained for two years. In 1986, members of Agudas Achim sold their building and joined Temple Shalom. Appointed in 1976, Rabbi Daniel M. Lowy serves this merged congregation.

References

Shinedling, Abraham I. *West Virginia Jewry: Origins and History 1850–1958,* vol. 3 (Philadelphia: 1963).
Synagogue Histories File, American Jewish Archives.

WISCONSIN

BETH EL, REFORM. *Madison, Wisconsin.* Madison's first white settler arrived in 1837, but it was fourteen years before Samuel Kalauber moved in from

Lake Mills to be joined by his brothers Charles, Isaac, and Sigmund. Prague-born Simon Sekeles, who edited a popular German daily, the *Madison Democrat,* was among other arrivals. He became an important communal figure. With the founding of Congregation Ahavath Achim by seventeen families in 1856, chartered in 1859 as Congregation Shaare Shomayim, Sekeles served as hazan until he left for New York in 1863. In that year a brick synagogue, now preserved at a new site as a historic landmark, was erected.

Many immigrants from Eastern Europe arrived in Madison in the 1890s. These new arrivals formed an assortment of orthodox congregations. By the 1930s, some of their descendants argued for a more liberal form of Judaism. Thus, a small group organized Temple Beth El and joined the Reform movement in 1939. Miwaukee's Rabbi Joseph L. Baron persuaded the young membership to engage a refugee from Hitler, Rabbi Manfred Swarsensky. He arrived in February of 1940 to serve the congregation until his retirement thirty-six years later.

The restrictions of World War II deferred building plans for a decade. Services and religious school classes were conducted in a variety of locales, including church vestry rooms, the tearoom of Baron's department store, and an abandoned orthodox synagogue. From 1943 to 1945, the congregation shared the facilities of the First Unitarian Society. For the next five years, services were held at the Workmen's Circle on North Mills Street, while the religious school used the YWCA, the Women's Building, and Turner Hall. Cultural and social activities were held in homes.

Ground was broken on the eve of Chanukah, December 26, 1948, for a suburban site at 2702-2706 Harbor Drive, facing the University of Wisconsin Arboretum and Lake Wingra. However, construction did not begin until June of 1949, with the cornerstone installed on October 2, the day before Yom Kippur. By Rosh Hashanah of 1950, the $170,000 building was dedicated with appropriate ceremonies. Beth El, at last, had a home.

Under Rabbi Swarsensky's leadership the congregation became an important influence on area affairs. Membership grew and a plethora of programs were offered at the temple, requiring a remodeling and enlargement of the building in 1964, doubling the size of the sanctuary and creating larger social facilities on the lower floor.

By 1966 it became necessary to engage a series of assistant rabbis. *Gates of Prayer: The New Union Prayerbook,* with its expanded use of Hebrew and traditional elements, was introduced in 1976. Rabbi Swarsensky became emeritus but continued to contribute to temple and community life until his death on November 9, 1981. Rabbi Kenneth Roseman was called to the Temple in the fall of 1976 and served until Rabbi Jan Brahms took office on January 1, 1986.

Temple membership passed six hundred family units in 1993 and maintains a full roster of affiliates. The school has grown to necessitate two two-hour sessions each Sunday, plus weekday Hebrew instruction.

References

Postal, Bernard, and Lionel Koppman. *American Jewish Landmarks* (New York: 1984), p. 253ff.
Swarsensky, Manfred. *From Generation to Generation: The Story of the Madison Jewish Community* (Madison: 1955).
Synagogue Histories File, American Jewish Archives.
Temple Beth El, *50th Anniversary, 1939–1989* (Madison: 1989).

BETH EL NER TAMID SYNAGOGUE, CONSERVATIVE. *Milwaukee, Wisconsin.* Founders established Temple Beth El in 1923 as a Conservative congregation. Its first two rabbis received ordination from the Jewish Theological Seminary of America, the seminary of the Conservative movement. Its first rabbi, Eugene Kohn, served from 1923 to 1926. Rabbi Philip Kleinman succeeded him. Kleinman remained with the congregation for ten years, struggling against adverse economic circumstances and religious indifference among congregants. Apparently, interest in creating a Conservative congregation as an alternative to Reform and Orthodoxy had waned.

Rabbi Louis J. Swichkow, ordained from Hebrew Theological College, an Orthodox seminary, succeeded Kleinman. During his tenure, membership at Beth El grew. In an attempt to attract local Orthodox synagogues and merge them into Beth El, Swichkow led a building campaign under the aegis of a newly formed Milwaukee Greater Temple, which he served as executive director. Although this endeavor failed, the temple added the name Ner Tamid to the name Beth El in order to emphasize the fact that the congregation had added new elements to it. In 1951, congregants erected a new building for this new synagogue organization. Beth El Ner Tamid reached its membership peak in the early 1960s, with fourteen hundred students registered in its religious school. Because of demographic changes in the neighborhood surrounding the synagogue, the congregation experienced a rapid decline in its membership to four hundred family units and fourteen religious school students by 1985.

When Rabbi Swichkow retired in 1985, the congregation elected Rabbi Gideon Goldenholz to its pulpit, one year after the congregation moved to West Mequon Road in suburban Mequon. In this location, under the guidance of a new rabbi, the congregation grew to 520 family units, with 140 students in the religious school and 72 children in nursery school in 1994. In 1992, the congregation permitted women to receive Torah honors. Two years later, the Beth El gave women full equality by counting women in the minyan.

Reference

Swichkow, Louis J., and Lloyd P. Gartner. *The History of the Jews of Milwaukee* (Philadelphia: 1963).

CONGREGATION EMANU-EL B'NE JESHURUN, REFORM. *Milwaukee, Wisconsin.* Twelve pioneer Jews gathered for worship on Yom Kippur of 1847 in the home of Isaac Neustadtl. This small group organized a cemetery association. The first burial took place within the year. By May 1, 1850, they had formalized as Imanu-Al Cemetery with its plot of ground "above Fifteenth Street," ultimately paid for by 1854. The tiny community created Congregation Imanu-Al for the High Holidays of 1849, meeting in a room over Nathan Pereles' grocery on Chestnut Street. The population grew; yet, attempts to purchase land for a synagogue dissipated in ethnic strife. The Polish Jews, in January 1854, broke off to form Ahabath Emuno. A year later, the German Jews seceded to create Anshe Emeth. In August of 1856, Isaac M. Wise came from Cincinnati and was invited to address the community's two hundred Jews, now divided into three congregations. In two lectures Wise spoke against conservatism and for unity, with the result that Imanu-Al and Ahabath Emuno merged to become B'ne Jeshurun, which adopted Wise's prayer book, *Minhag America.*

The new congregation, numbering seventy families, elected attorney Nathan Pereles (grandson of the grocer) president. In 1857, they brought Isidor Kalisch from Cincinnati to be Milwaukee's first rabbi. His leadership, introducing such reforms as confirmation and mixed seating, met with sufficient enthusiasm for the congregation to erect its first synagogue on Fourth Street, between State and Prairie (now Highland Avenue), and induced the fifty families of Congregation Anshe Emeth to merge (in 1859). But factionalism was endemic. The failure of B'ne Jeshurun to move or enlarge led to the withdrawal in 1869 of thirty-five members, who formed Congregation Emanu-El, electing Rabbi Edward Browne as its first rabbi. When Emanu-El abandoned the practice of covering the head, it was clear that it had moved fully into the Reform movement. In 1872 the congregation erected a building at Martin and Main (now Broadway and State Streets). Rabbi Moritz Spitz served the congregation from 1872 to 1879, followed by Isaac S. Moses (1879–1887), Sigmund Hecht (1888–1899), and Julius Meyer (1900–1904).

Several rabbis served B'ne Jeshurun briefly between the years 1860 and 1869, after Kalisch was dismissed as a result of financial problems confronting the congregation. In 1869, Rabbi Elias Eppstein was elected to the pulpit; the new rabbi, as well as competition with the "Reformers," led B'ne Jeshurun to build at Tenth and Cedar (now Kilbourn Avenue) a tall Gothic structure. This building was ultimately purchased by the county and removed to make way for the present County Court House. Eppstein served until 1880, followed by Emanuel Gerechter (1880–1892), Victor Caro (1892–1912), and Charles S. Levi (1912–1927). Levi was a graduate of Hebrew Union College and brought B'ne Jeshurun well into American Reform, although until 1904 he was still required to give lectures in German as well as English.

In 1900, a third congregation formed on the South Side under the name Temple Sinai. Never achieving much prominence, its membership rejoined the other congregations when Sinai disbanded in 1915.

Affected by demographic changes in the years immediately following World War I, the Emanu-El congregation bought the Temple's present site and erected a facility at 2419 East Kenwood Boulevard. The new location attracted so many members of B'ne Jeshurun that merger (in 1927) became inevitable, compelling Rabbi Levi to take early retirement. The combined congregation adopted the name Emanu-El B'ne Jeshurun.

Beginning in 1904, when Rabbi Samuel Hirshberg (its first Hebrew Union College alumnus) arrived to lead Emanu-El, the congregation grew and began to exert influence in the wider community. The merger brought the need for an associate rabbi. Joseph L. Baron was elected and remained with Hirshberg until the rabbi retired in 1947, when Baron succeeded, retiring four years later. Sympathetic to Zionism, both rabbis were active in the Milwaukee Zionist Congregation. Though some members supported these efforts, others were active in the Milwaukee American Council for Judaism, an anti-Zionist organization. Joseph Baron was succeeded by Herbert A. Friedman (1951–1955), followed by Dudley Weinberg (1955–1976), whose successor, incumbent Francis Barry Silberg, had been his associate. Weinberg is recalled for his many innovations in education for all age groups and for his strong advocacy of civil rights.

Although the congregation has spawned two flourishing suburban congregations, it remains preeminent with well over thirteen hundred membership units.

References

Swichkow, Louis J., and Lloyd P. Gartner. *The History of the Jews of Milwaukee* (Philadelphia: 1963).
Synagogue Histories Files, American Jewish Archives.

PART II
CANADA

O

ONTARIO

DARCHEI NOAM, RECONSTRUCTIONIST. *Downsview, Ontario.* In 1962, Rabbi Lavy Becker of Congregation Dorshei Emet, the Reconstructionist Synagogue of Montreal, joined with a layperson to call a meeting to organize a Reconstructionist synagogue in Toronto. About twenty-five people joined this effort and met in a study group for twenty years. In 1972, once again as a result of a call from Rabbi Becker, a group gathered formally to found a congregation. This congregation's activities grew from holiday services to monthly services with periodic visits from student rabbis.

In 1981, with fewer than forty member families, the congregation engaged Rabbi Richard Hirsch (1981–1983) as its religious leader and secured rented space in the B'nai B'rith building in Downsview. Within eighteen months, membership doubled. These rabbis succeeded Hirsch: Barry Blum (1984–1986), Deborah Brin (1986–1990), and Lawrence Pinsker (1991–). Darchei Noam is affiliated with the Federation of Reconstructionist Congregations and Havurot, the organization of Reconstructionist synagogues and fellowships in the United States and Canada. Activities in 1995 included a variety of special interest groups and caring community committees, as well as a wide variety of opportunities for adult education. Its membership in 1995 neared three hundred family units.

Reference

Personal letter, Harvey Freeman to Kerry Olitzky, March 27, 1995.

CONGREGATION BETH SHALOM, ORTHODOX. *Ottawa, Ontario.* Founders established Congregation Beth Shalom in 1956, as the merger of two synagogues: Congregation Adath Jeshurun (founded 1892) and Congregation Agudath Achim (founded 1902). The newly amalgamated synagogue immediately affiliated with the Union of Orthodox Jewish Congregations, the national organization of Orthodox synagogues in North America. In 1961, another Orthodox synagogue, Sons of Jacob, merged into the existing amalgamation. Members of Adath Jeshurun, also an Orthodox congregation, worshiped in a small house of worship on Murray Street (dedicated 1895) and then its twenty-five members moved to King Edward Avenue (dedicated 1904, addition dedicated 1921). Congregants of Agudath Achim, also an Orthodox congregation, erected their building only a few blocks away on Rideau Street in 1912 and added to it in 1928. These men served Congregation Adath Jeshurun: Simon Fyne (1912–1920), Max Mintz (1924–1926), Julius Leikin (1927–1928), and Nathan Kollin (1929–1932). These men led Agudath Achim: Rabbi Joseph Berger (1902–1927), Abraham H. Freedman (1931–1936), William Margolis (1937–1938), Oscar Z. Fasman (1940–1946), Emanuel L. Lifschutz (1946–1952), and Simon Eckstein (1952–1956). In 1957, Beth Shalom members built a synagogue on Chapel Street, adjacent to the Jewish community center, whose master plan included both structures. In 1980, the congregation established a branch, Beth Shalom West, on Chartwell Avenue in Nepean.

These men served Beth Shalom as religious leaders: Simon Eckstein (1956–1976), Saul Aranov (1976–1980; 1986–1993), Basil Herring (1980–1986), and Ely Braun (1993–   ). In 1995, Beth Shalom's membership exceeded 550 family units.

Reference

Dedication, Beth Shalom Synagogue, 1957 (Ottawa: 1957).

CONGREGATION MACHZIKEI HADAS, ORTHODOX. *Ottawa, Ontario.* Founders incorporated Machzikei Hadas as an Orthodox congregation in 1909. The members met in a variety of temporary locations until 1927 when the congregation built a facility on Murray Street at King Edward Avenue. In 1974, Machzikei Hadas moved to lower Ottawa to a suburban section in Virginia. Membership grew there from one hundred families in 1974 to five hundred families in 1995. In this location, members launched and maintained a community *eruv* (which extends "private space" and allows things to be carried within it on the Sabbath) and served as base for Clergy for a United Canada.

While numerous part-time rabbis served the congregation in a cooperative arrangement with local congregation B'nai Jacob, Rabbi Stanley Webber (1960–1962) became the first full-time religious leader solely responsible to Machzikei Hadas. He emphasized education in his rabbinate. Under his direction, Machzikei Hadas affiliated with the Union of Orthodox Jewish Congregations, the North American organization of Orthodox synagogues (ca. 1960). Rabbi Abraham Rubin (1962–1967) succeeded Webber. Rabbi Reuven P. Bulka, known for his work bridging psychology and Judaism, joined the congregation as religious leader in 1967. During his tenure, he worked to foster relations between the synagogue and other Jewish community institutions, as well as with non-Jewish organizations. In 1978, Machzikei Hadas celebrated its first Bat Mitzvah; and in 1994, the congregation became the first in the history of the Commonwealth to be granted a Coat of Arms.

Reference

Personal interview with Reuven Bulka, May 26, 1995.

HOLY BLOSSOM TEMPLE, REFORM. *Toronto, Ontario.* Seventeen men organized Holy Blossom Temple in 1856 as an institution to provide the Jewish community with a cemetery and ritually slaughtered meat. While the origin of the name Holy Blossom is not clear, it seems to stem from a reference to apprentice priests as "holy blossoms." Thus, early founders referred to the new congregation as "early blossoms of Jewry," which eventually became "holy blossoms" before members took the name Holy Blossom, Toronto Hebrew Congregation.

Founders built a synagogue in 1875 on Richmond Street. In 1885, the congregation introduced mixed seating. In 1897, shortly after the congregation moved to Bond Street, when the president installed a hand organ in the synagogue, three trustees placed it in the street. These men served Holy Blossom in its early years: Herman Philips (1883–1890) and Rabbi Barnett A. Elzas (1890–1893). Rabbi Abraham Lazarus (1893–1898) advocated late Friday services and left as part of a compromise decision to implement them. David Wittenberg (1899–1900) succeeded Lazarus before Rabbi Solomon Jacobs (1901–1920) joined the congregation. Rabbi Barnett Brickner, a staunch supporter of Reform Judaism served the congregation for five years (1920–1926). Brickner introduced the *Union Prayer Book* (the uniform prayer book of the Reform movement), limited holiday observance to one day, and instituted Sunday morning services.

Rabbi Ferdinand Isserman (1925–1929) succeeded Brickner. He fostered interfaith relations by the first exchange of pulpits in Canada with a Christian minister (1928). Isserman modernized the organization of the Religious School and encouraged the formation of a sisterhood and other groups.

Maurice Eisendrath came to Holy Blossom to serve as religious leader (1929–1943). During his tenure, Holy Blossom affiliated with the Union of American Hebrew Congregations, the national organization of Reform synagogues, the organization he later served as president. Upon Eisendrath's arrival, congregants agreed to the option of removing hats for worship—initially having been startled by his appearance at Rosh Hashanah services without a head covering. In 1938, with a membership of only 250, Holy Blossom left Bond Street and built a new structure on Bathurst.

Rabbi Abraham Feinberg (1943–1956) succeeded Eisendrath. During his leadership, membership tripled. He replaced Sunday morning services with Friday evening worship. He added more Hebrew liturgy, implemented daily services and expanded the role of the cantor. During his tenure, Holy Blossom helped to form Temple Sinai. Feinberg also focused his attention on adult education and advocated race relations by inviting black preachers to speak from the Holy Blossom pulpit. Jacob Eisen succeeded Feinberg.

Rabbi W. Gunther Plaut (1961–1977) promoted extensive programs in education, particularly for youth. Rabbi Harvey Fields (1978–1982) succeeded Plaut; members elected Rabbi Dow Marmur to the Holy Blossom pulpit in 1982. In 1995, the membership of Holy Blossom Temple neared nineteen hundred family units.

References

100th Anniversary Holy Blossom Temple Bulletin (Toronto: 1956).
Synagogue Histories File, American Jewish Archives.

CONGREGATION SHAAREI SHOMAYIM, ORTHODOX. *Toronto, Ontario.* In 1928, under the leadership of Louis Rasky, a group formed a new synagogue under the name Brothers of Jacob/B'nai Jacob (later Beth Israel) Congregation. The new group built a synagogue home on McKay Avenue. The women of the congregation formed a sisterhood in 1932. Following some financial difficulties in the congregation, a dissident group formed a new congregation on Christie Street, calling itself the Hillcrest Congregation (1931). This new organization changed its name to Shaarei Shomayim in 1934, led by Israel Halevi Horowitz (1933–1938). Shaarei Shomayim later settled in new facilities on St. Claire Avenue West (1936). In this new location, members elected David Monson (1939–1943) and then Dr. Judah Washer (1944–1952) as their rabbi. In 1948, membership climbed to four hundred families. Under Dr. Washer's leadership, the synagogue established a nursery and kindergarten in the Talmud Torah building it erected adjacent to the sanctuary (1949).

The men of the congregation established a men's club in 1950. As a result in the growth of membership, Shaarei Shomayim built an adjoining youth center (1955), under the direction of Rabbi Walter S. Wurzburger (1953–1966). He established the Shaarei Shomayim Institute for Adult Studies, accredited by Yeshiva University's Department of Adult Education. In 1955, the synagogue built a youth center on St. Clair Avenue to house its developing programs for youth. In 1966, Shaarei Shomayim moved to a new location on Glencairn Avenue. The following year, Rabbi Emanuel Forman joined Shaarei Shomayim as its religious leader (1967–1971). In the new location, the congregation considered whether to install family pews and use amplification on the Sabbath, forbidden according to Orthodox Judaism. Though the congregation did not install family pews, it did install a specially designed amplification system. The congregation became more observant and discontinued the use of amplification even for the High Holidays. Rabbi Henry Hoschander led the congregation from 1972 to 1991. Under his leadership, B'nai Jacob amalgamated with Shaarei Shomayim (1975), as did the Dovercourt Shul–Mackzikei Bnei Yisroel (1981).

In 1977, membership grew to eight hundred families, reaching 1350 by 1986.

Under the direction of Rabbi Mark Dratch (1992–   ), Shaarei Shomayim emphasized education in its extensive program of activities. In addition to a wide range of courses for adults, Shaarei Shomayim also sponsors an extensive youth program, day care center, and programs for older adults (including games and exercise). In 1994, membership exceeded fourteen hundred family units, with over five hundred attending weekly Sabbath services.

Reference

Synagogue Histories File, American Jewish Archives.

Q

QUEBEC

DORSHEI EMET, RECONSTRUCTIONIST. *Hampstead, Quebec.* Rabbi Lavy Becker founded Congregation Dorshei Emet, the Reconstructionist Synagogue of Montreal, in 1960. It immediately affiliated with the Federation of Reconstructionist Synagogues and Havurot. Seven years later, under his guidance, the congregation built its own building on Cleve Road in Hampstead. In 1976, Rabbi Ron Aigen joined the congregation as its religious leader. In 1985, Dorshei Emet passed a resolution that welcomed the non-Jewish partner of a member Jew as a *ger toshav,* a non-Jewish sojourner. In 1993, the congregation adopted a policy to "welcome gay and lesbian Jews, their Jewish partners and families, as full members of our congregation." In 1994, membership at Dorshei Emet neared 420 households.

Reference

Synagogue Histories File, American Jewish Archives.

TEMPLE EMANU-EL–BETH SHOLOM, REFORM. *Montreal, Quebec.* Alongside two Orthodox congregations in Montreal, a group of nineteen individuals sought to establish a Reform alternative institution, Emanu-El, in 1882. Shortly thereafter, it joined the Union of American Hebrew Congregations, the North American organization of Reform synagogues. For fifty years, Emanu-El remained the only Reform congregation in the province of Quebec. In the initial document of formation, its thirty-six members agreed (among other things) to adopt *Minhag America* as its prayer book and engage an organist and choir, thus clearly distinguishing it from the other synagogues. For the first three years, the group met for worship at Albert Hall, before leasing the former Zion Church on Beaver Hall Hill.

Samuel Marks became Emanu-El's first religious leader (1882–1889). In

1884, members replaced *Minhag America* with a more traditional prayer book prepared by Marcus Jastrow. As a result of increasing membership, Emanu-El moved to larger quarters at Drummond and St. Catherine Streets in 1889, the same year Marks resigned. By 1892, feeling a need for a permanent home, the congregation built its own place of worship on Stanley Street under the guidance of its president, Samuel Davis. Regarding its religious leadership during this building phase, S. Eisenberg (1889–1890) succeeded Marks as religious leader of the congregation before Hartog Veld (1891–1899) joined Emanu-El three years later.

In 1896, Emanu-El adopted the *Union Prayer Book,* the uniform prayer book of the Reform movement, for worship. When Veld left Montreal, E. Friedlander (1899–1901) succeeded him. Rabbi Isaac Landman came next to Emanu-El (1901–1904). Rabbi Joseph Kornfeld served the congregation from 1904 to 1906. Rabbi Nathan Gordon led the congregation for a decade (1906–1916), then remained as a member once he left the rabbinate. In 1911, the congregation moved to Sherbrooke Street, having outgrown its facility on Stanley Street. Here the congregation introduced family pews. In addition, Rabbi Gordon led most of the worship in English. Samuel Schwartz succeeded Gordon in 1916, remaining until 1919. Max Merritt served Emanu-El from 1920 to 1925.

By 1922, members expanded the institution by building a religious school on the adjacent lot. Rabbi Herbert Samuel served only one year, in 1926, dying suddenly in office. The following year, Rabbi Harry Stern, whose name is most associated with Emanu-El, joined the congregation. Under his direction, Emanu-El established a College of Jewish Studies program of adult Jewish education in 1928. He also created the Institute on Judaism for Christian Clergy and Educators, an annual fellowship dinner for Catholics, Protestants, and Jews. He promoted interfaith dialogue in the community, using Emanu-El as a forum for major figures in religion, politics, and the city. Because of his liberal stance toward mixed marriages, Stern became a controversial figure in the pulpit of Emanu-El throughout his tenure. In 1940, the congregation added to its building and created a museum for ceremonial arts in 1953. Emanu-El enlarged its sanctuary in 1957. Following a fire that destroyed the 1911 structure, the congregation rebuilt (dedicated 1959).

Stern established the Institute on Judaism for the Christian Clergy in 1942. In addition, he developed an Institute for Teachers of the Protestant Schools of Montreal. Stern also reestablished Hebrew as a requirement for religious school education. Stern retired in 1972.

In 1982, Emanu-El merged with Temple Beth Sholom (founded as a breakaway in 1953). Beth Sholom's rabbis included: Paul Liner (1954–1961), H. Leonard Poller (1962–1972), Mark Golub (1972–1979), and David Powell (1979–1980). The combined congregation, Temple Emanu-El–Beth Sholom, worships in a synagogue in Westmount, built in 1958 in the same location as Emanu-El's 1911 building. The merged congregation saw a series of rabbis: Bernard Bloomstone (1972–1983), Louis Cashdan (1984), Kenneth Segal

(1984–1987), and Saul Besser (1987–1988). In 1989, synagogue members elected Rabbi Leigh Lerner to lead them. He made headcoverings available for worship (1990), instituted daily services (1991), made prayer shawls available (1994), and instituted a two-day observance for Rosh Hashanah. In 1994, the congregation included eleven hundred family units as members.

References

Synagogue Histories File, American Jewish Archives.
Temple Emanu-El Jubilee Celebration (Montreal: 1932).

CONGREGATION TIFERETH BETH DAVID JERUSALEM, ORTHO-DOX. *Montreal, Quebec.* Congregation Tifereth Beth David Jerusalem grew out of a series of mergers of a group of congregations. Beth Yitzchok joined Beth David in 1955; Kehal Yeshurin joined the new synagogue two years later. Founders established the Jewish Community of Eastern Cote St. Luc and Hampstead in 1958. In 1962, Tifereth Jerusalem joined the group of synagogues. And, finally, in 1965, Beth David joined the amalgamation of congregations to form Tifereth Beth David Jerusalem. This new congregation affiliated with the Union of Orthodox Jewish Congregations.

Beth David

Taking the name Beth David to honor the first president of the congregation, Pinchas ben David Elimelech Pinsier, Roumanian Jews founded the congregation. In 1888, these founders organized a community organization, a Kehilla. Two years later, the group held worship services on Fortification Lane with High Holiday services on Notre Dame Street. In 1890, Beth David rented the former Shearith Israel synagogue building on Cheneville Street, taking ownership in 1894. In 1903, the Ohel Moshe synagogue merged into Beth David. That same year, the women of Beth David established a Ladies Auxiliary. The women's organization established a free school for local children that served over one hundred in the community. Rabbi J. Herschorn joined Beth David as its religious leader in 1926 and later became chief rabbi of Montreal. Rabbi Telcher succeeded him in 1936 and remained until 1965. In 1929, Beth David moved to St. Joseph Boulevard.

Tifereth Jerusalem

Members, primarily Russian immigrants, established this synagogue in 1904 on land donated by Ross Realty Company. As a result, members referred to the synagogue (literally erected by the members in 1911) as the Rossland Synagogue. They also called it "Der Roite Shul" because of its red-brick exterior. It operated a school on Marquette Street and established a Free Loan Assocation. The congregation operated a second building, which it called "Der Veise Shul" because of its white-brick exterior; they also referred to it as Chaverim Kol

Yisrael. Beginning in 1954, as members left for new areas of the city, the congregation alternated holding services in the two buildings.

Beth Yitzchok

Abraham Yitzchok Luterman founded the Beth Yitzchok synagogue in his home in 1904. He named the congregation to honor the memory of the family member after whom he was named. The eleven men who joined Luterman in the establishment of Beth Yitzchok hailed from the Ukraine. When members converted the upstairs of the building into a women's gallery, the Luterman family moved elsewhere. Although the congregation did not have its own religious leader, Beth David's Rabbi Herschorn visited the congregation on a regular basis. The women of the congregation formed a sisterhood in 1940.

Kehal Yeshurin

While the extant records of Kehal Yeshurin are limited in scope, founders established it on Colonial Avenue in 1904 before later moving to Fairmount Avenue. Its members initiated a Free Loan Society and a study group (Chevra Mishnayes). The study group met on the annual anniversary (*yahrzeit*) of the death of any of its members.

The Jewish Community of Eastern Cote St. Luc and Hampstead

The founders of this community sought to establish an Orthodox community in the sparsely populated area of Cote St. Luc and Hampstead in 1959, beginning with services for the High Holidays. The early congregation met in a rented home on Baily Road. Members founded a sisterhood and a Sunday Breakfast Group (which operated as a men's club). In 1960, Rabbi David Hartman joined the community as its first religious leader. He established regular daily services and educational programs for youth and adults. As a result of his door-to-door campaign, he brought two hundred new member families into the congregation during his first year. The congregation built its synagogue on Baily Road in 1965. Rabbi Hartman immigrated to Israel in 1971. Rabbi Eliahu Jacob Steinhorn succeeded him (1971–1972), before Rabbi Joshua H. Shmidman joined in 1974. In 1990, the membership fully renovated and expanded its Baily Road facility; and in 1995, membership stood at nine hundred family units.

Reference

Shimshon Hamerman, *Highlights of Our Living Past, 1886–1965* (Montreal: 1965).

INDEX

Boldface page numbers indicate location of main entries.

About the Author

KERRY M. OLITZKY is Director of the School of Education at Hebrew Union College–Jewish Institute of Religion, New York, where he also directs the Graduate Studies program. He is the author of numerous books and journal articles and has written extensively in the field of American Jewish History, particularly on the history of Reform Judaism. With Lance J. Sussman and Malcolm H. Stern, he published *Reform Judaism in America: A Biographical Dictionary and Sourcebook* (Greenwood Press, 1993). Dr. Olitzky is annual special issue editor on aging and judaism for the *Journal of Psychology and Judaism* and chairs the editorial board of *Compass*, a magazine for teachers.

ISBN 0-313-28856-9

90000>

EAN

9 780313 288562

HARDCOVER BAR CODE